KV-199-989

THE CHILD IN FOCUS

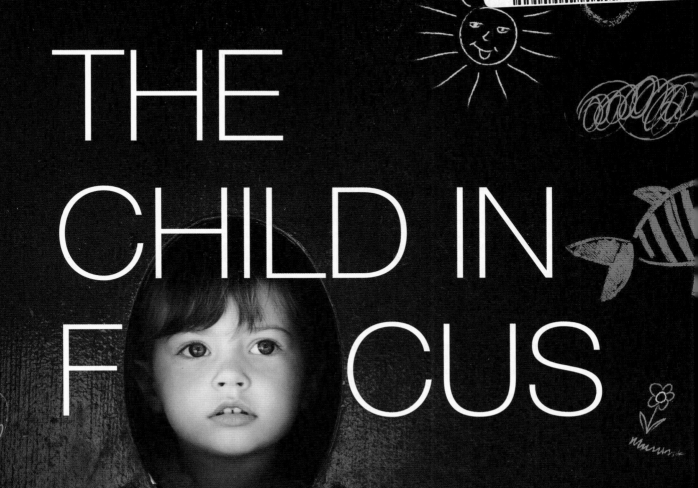

LEARNING AND TEACHING
IN EARLY CHILDHOOD EDUCATION

Estelle Irving and Carol Carter

with Frances Burton | Melissa Colville | Ann Hooper

Mary Hughes | Sue Lancaster | Ginette Pestana

OXFORD
UNIVERSITY PRESS

Oxford University Press is a department of the University of Oxford.

It furthers the University's objective of excellence in research, scholarship, and education by publishing worldwide. Oxford is a registered trademark of Oxford University Press in the UK and in certain other countries.

Published in Australia by
Oxford University Press
253 Normanby Road, South Melbourne, Victoria 3205, Australia

© Estelle Irving and Carol Carter 2018

The moral rights of the authors have been asserted

First published 2018

All rights reserved. No part of this publication may be reproduced, stored in a retrieval system, or transmitted, in any form or by any means, without the prior permission in writing of Oxford University Press, or as expressly permitted by law, by licence, or under terms agreed with the reprographics rights organisation. Enquiries concerning reproduction outside the scope of the above should be sent to the Rights Department, Oxford University Press, at the address above.

You must not circulate this work in any other form and you must impose this same condition on any acquirer.

ISBN 9780190304539

Reproduction and communication for educational purposes

The Australian *Copyright Act 1968* (the Act) allows a maximum of one chapter or 10% of the pages of this work, whichever is the greater, to be reproduced and/or communicated by any educational institution for its educational purposes provided that the educational institution (or the body that administers it) has given a remuneration notice to Copyright Agency Limited (CAL) under the Act.

For details of the CAL licence for educational institutions contact:

Copyright Agency Limited
Level 15, 233 Castlereagh Street
Sydney NSW 2000
Telephone: (02) 9394 7600
Facsimile: (02) 9394 7601
Email: info@copyright.com.au

Edited by Sandra Balonyi
Cover design by OUPANZ
Text design by OUPANZ
Typeset by Newgen KnowledgeWorks Pvt. Ltd., Chennai, India
Proofread by Liz Filleul
Indexed by Mei Yen Chua
Printed in China by Leo Paper Products Ltd

Links to third party websites are provided by Oxford in good faith and for information only.
Oxford disclaims any responsibility for the materials contained in any third party website referenced in this work.

Contents

Extended Contents

PART TWO — EARLY CHILDHOOD LEARNING AND TEACHING

PART THREE — PROFESSIONAL PRACTICE

Introduction

This is a book about early childhood learning and teaching, designed as a textbook for Initial Teacher Education (ITE) programs, but with relevance to students in all early childhood education courses. The age focus is birth to eight, spanning prior-to-school education and into the early years of primary school. Greater attention is given to the prior-to-school setting, but the transition into primary school, primary school teacher practice and adaptation of curriculum and pedagogy for this setting are included.

The idea for this book came from our experiences of teaching pre-service teachers in a Bachelor of Early Childhood Teaching program. The topics we present here reflect the content and perspective of that program and address the national Graduate Teacher Standards described by the Australian Institute of Teaching and School Leadership (AITSL), the Australian Curriculum, and the National Quality Standard (NQS) of the Australian Children's Education and Care Quality Authority (ACECQA).

'A book about early childhood learning and teaching.' How simple that sounds, but in that one simple statement, there are hidden layers of meanings, contested theories, and great variation in curriculum and pedagogical practice.

Beneath the surface of the practice of how and what children are taught is a history of theories, values, beliefs and assumptions. This book examines those theories that have had the greatest impact on current practice in Australian early childhood education. While you will be introduced to these theories and practices, it is important to understand that the variations matter. They are not neutral, descriptive differences with no greater significance than of 'colour' and 'shade'. Different theories translate into different educational practices that include curriculum and pedagogy choices. These are the 'how, what and why we teach' questions that are examined in this book.

You will find yourself drawn to some theorists and want to embrace the practices that derive from their theoretical perspective. How and why this occurs relates to your life experiences, including your family's values and practices and your own formal education. It is important though to not let these experiences close you off from new ideas and practices. The choices you make will have a real impact on the lives of children and their experiences of education. Reflecting on questions about why we do one thing or act in one way and not another is a key practice for early childhood teachers: this practice begins while you are a student. Opportunities to critically reflect are built into this book.

The theoretical framework for this book derives largely from *sociocultural theory*. If we summarise this perspective into one key idea it is that learning is a *social activity* that occurs in specific social and cultural time and place contexts and is mediated through *relationships*. This understanding is the ribbon that is threaded through the book.

The book is also influenced by *post-structuralist theory*, which challenges us to question our assumptions, beliefs and practices and inspires a particular image of the child as an active co-constructor of their own learning.

Both of these perspectives are described in Chapter 3, Theorists and Theoretical Perspectives, and referred to throughout the book.

Two specific sociocultural theorists are given prominence in this book: Urie Bronfenbrenner and Lev Vygostsky. You will encounter these theorists in more detail throughout the chapters, so only a brief outline is provided in this general introduction.

Urie Bronfenbrenner

Bronfenbrenner provides us with the *ecological systems model*. The ecological systems model (or theory) recognises that development occurs in the context of the whole environment. Whether this is at the level of the family, or the wider context of the politics, economy and policies, the environment plays a major role in development.

Bronfenbrenner's child-centred model is the third direct influence on the content and orientation of this book.

You will see other representations of Bronfenbrenner's model and encounter it with variations of its original name—for example, it is also referred to as the socio-ecological systems model—but the principle of interconnected, surrounding environmental systems in which a child develops remains the core idea. The child is always positioned at the centre of Bronfenbrenner's ecological model: the centrality of the child provides the inspiration for 'the child in focus' of this book—focusing on the child and their individual experiences and characteristics, while considering the impact of the surrounding environments. This focus gives the book a wider frame, with consideration of childhood as socially constructed, so that our interest is broader than simply how children learn, and how/what to teach them.

Bronfenbrenner's ecological model recognises that children develop within a system of *interconnected relationships* between the individual, their family and wider society.

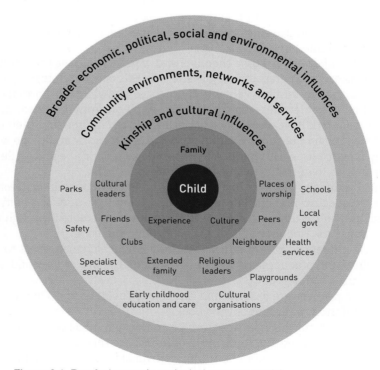

Figure 0.1 Bronfenbrenner's ecological systems model

Adapted from Bronfenbrenner, 1979, in Victorian Early Years Learning and Development Framework, 2016, p.5.

In its original form the model uses specific terms to describe four different 'systems' or contexts, represented in the model as circles that surround the child.

The first system is referred to as the *microsystem*—the small (micro) view of the child and their immediate surroundings. The microsystem is the immediate environmental context of relationships in a child's life, encompassing family and early education and care settings. As the surrounding systems move outward and away from the immediate surroundings and face-to-face relationships of the family context of the microsystem, the next system of peers (friends) and neighbourhood is the *exosystem*. Beyond that is the wider system of the *macrosystem*.

A fourth system of particular relevance to early childhood education is referred to as the *mesosystem*. This 'system' involves the relationships or connections between the microsystems (environmental contexts)—that is, between the people and institutions in a child's immediate environment (the first setting). A particularly relevant example of the mesosystem that is examined in detail in the book is the communications and the relationship between a child's parents and the early learning centre or primary school the child attends. The importance of these connections at the mesosystem level is highlighted in this book through the attention given to developing relationships and understanding and working with families in Chapter 13, The Importance of Relationships, and Chapter 14, Working with Families and Communities.

As the systems expand out, the influence on the child becomes less personal and less direct, but Bronfenbrenner's model acknowledges that children's growth and development can also be affected by both direct and indirect influences and experiences, including institutions in which children do not actively participate but that involve people and institutions related to the child. An example of this indirect influence on the child is the parents' workplace. The conditions and expected hours of work, pay, and so on, affect the family and the child. The Global Financial Crisis illustrates how indirect systems can influence child development and learning in the mesosystem example: the financial crisis originated in the USA—far away from an Australian child's microsystem—and beyond the control of parents who may have lost their job as the flow-on effect of the economic crisis caused companies in Australia to contract or collapse. What effects might this sudden change of circumstances have on the family and the child? Perhaps small changes initially: cancelling extra-curricular activities and cutting back on entertainment and leisure activities. If unemployment continued, the effects and the strains on family relationships would increase. Eventually, the family might fracture and have to move … and a cycle of wider impacts could disrupt the child's development and learning.

The child's gender, age, health and temperament also affect the child's learning and development, so the child's own biology may be considered part of the microsystem; recognising this, the model is sometimes called the 'Bio-Ecological Systems Model'.

More recently, a fifth system—the chronosystem—was added to some representations of Bronfenbrenner's model. *Chrono* means 'time', so the chronosystem refers to environmental events and transitions over the life course, as well as changing socio-historical circumstances/events (i.e. time and place affects development).

All of these aspects of Bronfenbrenner's model are considered in this book.

This model underpins the *Early Years Learning Framework (ELYF): Belonging, Being & Becoming* (DEEWR, 2009). You will become very familiar with this framework as the EYLF is a key national document, developed to inform and inspire better practice for everyone working with young children and their families—including professional early childhood teachers. It acknowledges the educational impact (what and how children learn) of all interactions and experiences with young children and the importance of ensuring that in early childhood services, these experiences and interactions support children's learning, development and wellbeing. Recognising this educational impact, the EYLF refers to everyone in this position as 'educators'. In this book, we have chosen to use the word 'teacher' when we refer to professionals with a formal teaching qualification. In the context of the EYLF, teachers are educators, but not all educators are teachers.

The themes of the EYLF—'Belonging, Being & Becoming'—recognise that the child is simultaneously negotiating and developing their identity (belonging), experiencing their childhood (being) and developing (becoming).

EYLF Learning Outcomes

The EYLF describes five explicit *learning outcomes* for children:

1 Children have a strong sense of identity
2 Children are connected with and contribute to their world
3 Children have a strong sense of wellbeing
4 Children are confident and involved learners
5 Children are effective communicators (DEEWR, 2009).

These learning or educational outcomes might surprise you as they are not outcomes of specific knowledge. Instead, they are about the conditions required for learning as a shared, social activity, and they are about the child's overall development, connection with others, engagement in the educational setting and, eventually, their capacity to contribute to society.

Lev Vygotsky

Vygotsky is the second sociocultural theorist whose ideas are at the heart of this book. Vygotsky viewed learning and cognitive development as social and collaborative—that is, built through social interactions. Social interactions require communication and Vygotsky regarded language as a 'cultural tool' and linked the development of language and the development of cognition, or thinking. Language is culturally specific, learnt in the child's culture.

Taking the basic idea of learning as a social activity further, Vygotsky theorised that a child's learning and cognitive development could be extended through 'scaffolding' provided by a person who was more knowledgeable. Scaffolding provides support that allows growth (cognitive development): it is not about doing something for a child, but allowing the child to safely extend their experience and, hence, their learning. 'What the child is able to do in collaboration today he will be able to do independently tomorrow' (Vygotsky, 1987).

In the EYLF, scaffolding is defined as 'the educators' decisions and actions that build on children's existing knowledge and skills to enhance their learning' (DEEWR, 2009, p.14).

Scaffolding occurs in what Vygotsky termed the Zone of Proximal Development (ZPD). In this zone, children are able to perform thinking or problem-solving skills and strategies that they would not be able to achieve on their own.

Vygotsky's theory has many implications for teaching, including that learning and teaching should be meaningful to the child and not separated from what children learn outside the classroom.

References to Vygotsky are included throughout the book.

The lessons we have taken from Bronfenbrenner and Vygotsky about learning being a social activity apply to our relationships with all our pre-service teacher students in Initial Teacher Education courses, including you. We don't expect (or even want) you to simply accept and replicate the content of this book. Instead, we encourage you to engage actively and thoughtfully with the ideas and information—that is, to engage in *reflective practice* with its questions of: 'What am I doing? Why am I doing it? What are the outcomes of what I do? How might I do it differently?'

Where possible, we have referred to the pre-service students we teach and included their responses to the issues we have raised, whether in the classroom or while they were on practicum placements. Where appropriate, we have also included some examples of the pre-service teachers' work, just as we look for opportunities to share our students' work in our classes. In all this, we have tried to replicate some of the opportunities for reflection and discussion we have with our pre-service teacher students. We acknowledge the input of these students from Holmesglen Institute, Melbourne, and thank them for their willingness to share their learning with you. Our intention is to engage with you, too, and to invite you into our reflective 'classroom'. You will 'hear' our individual voices and teaching styles reflected in the different chapters as we have tried to stay as true as possible to our face-to-face teaching style.

As a pre-service teacher, your experiences are parallel to the experiences of children, identified in the themes of the EYLF: while *being* a pre-service teacher, you are in the process of *becoming* a teacher, and, importantly, you *belong* to a community of pre-service teachers.

We hope you will feel part of our learning 'community' of students and share the enthusiasm and commitment we have for early childhood teaching and learning. Being an early childhood teacher is one of the most exciting, challenging and rewarding professions possible.

Bronfenbrenner U (1979),
DEEWR (2009),
VEYLDF(2016),
Vygotsky (1978).

About the Authors

Dr Estelle Irving

Estelle has more than twenty years of academic experience, lecturing and developing courses in early childhood development and education and as an academic sociologist, with specialisations in the sociology of childhood, sociology of health and sociology of work. Until recently, Estelle was Program Leader, Bachelor of Early Childhood Education at Holmesglen Institute. Her current role includes curriculum development and accreditation of tertiary education courses. Estelle has previously been a Senior Research Fellow/Senior Project Manager at the Centre for Community Child Health at Murdoch Children's Research Institute (Royal Children's Hospital, Melbourne), where she was the Managing Editor and principal writer for *Childcare and Children's Health* and writer for policy briefs distributed nationally to government ministers, policy makers and key stakeholders in early childhood education and care services.

Estelle was a member of the Victorian Curriculum and Assessment Authority (VCAA) Learning and Development Advisory group and is an expert advisor for the Raising Children Network: she regularly reviews and develops content for this website.

Dr Carol Carter

Carol recently joined the English Language and Foundation Studies Centre (ELFSC) at the University of Newcastle where her role is Coordinator/Lecturer of the Foundations in Education Course. In her previous role, Carol was a Higher Education Lecturer in Early Childhood Education at Holmesglen Institute. She has extensive experience as a teacher educator at universities in Australia and South Africa. Her PhD examined the role of oral art forms in supporting drama pedagogy and intercultural understanding within teacher education. She has published and presented numerous papers and workshops nationally and internationally. Some of her most recent work involves examining ways in which the arts create dialogical spaces and support cultural identities in early childhood, primary and higher education contexts. Another research interest that she continues to explore is identifying strategies and techniques to support and enhance learning and teaching in diverse higher education contexts.

Frances Burton

Frances is a Higher Education Lecturer in Early Childhood Education at Holmesglen Institute where she teaches Mathematics Learning for the prior-to-school and primary school community. Frances has many years of experience as a primary school teacher and Numeracy Coordinator in the early years program. Frances is currently undertaking a PhD in early mathematics.

Melissa Colville

Melissa is a Higher Education Lecturer in Early Childhood Education at Holmesglen Institute, where her specialisation is in infant and toddler learning, child development and children's play. Melissa has many years of experience as a teacher in early childhood education and care settings. She is currently undertaking research on higher education and diploma staff supporting diploma pathway entry students in their transition from various educational settings into Bachelor of Early Childhood education programs.

Ann Hooper

Ann has a distinguished history as an educator for twenty years, primarily in the independent school sector. She has been Head of Science and Information Technology at Caulfield Grammar School, where she developed online differentiated units of work aimed specifically at highly able students.

In 2001 Ann was appointed as Head of Junior School at Shelford Girls' Grammar, responsible for all elements of running the kindergarten and primary school. From 2008 to 2014, Ann was Deputy Principal and Head of Junior School at Lauriston Girls' School with responsibility for all aspects of the kindergarten and primary school.

Ann has developed and lectured in early childhood education courses, with specialisation in children with exceptional talents, and the professional role of early childhood teachers. She is currently working as Head of Curriculum at Christ Church Grammar School in Melbourne.

Mary Hughes

Mary has more than thirty years of experience in education, both in the primary and tertiary sectors. She is a qualified Reading Recovery teacher and has extensive experience in literacy intervention programs in primary schools. In her role as a school leader, Mary focused on curriculum development, professional learning and literacy leadership. Coaching and mentoring others, particularly beginning teachers, was a key part of Mary's role in schools. Mary is currently completing a Doctorate in Educational Leadership. Her doctoral research examines the role of pedagogical leadership in early childhood education with a strong focus on the role of the Educational Leader. Mary is currently a lecturer at Holmesglen Institute specialising in the areas of Literacy and Leadership.

Sue Lancaster

Sue is currently working in Higher Education as a Lecturer for the Bachelor of Early Childhood Teaching at Holmesglen Institute. Her particular areas of interest include engagement with families and communities, and inclusive strength-based practices for marginalised groups of children; children who present with disabilities and high learning needs; children who are gifted and talented; and children from Aboriginal and Torres Strait Islander backgrounds. Sue is a strong advocate for children's learning, development and wellbeing, committing her skills and energy in supporting and mentoring students through practicum placement to further their understanding of the roles and responsibilities in becoming a professional teacher to enhance their engagement with young children. Sue has worked in various early childhood roles; as a practitioner and leader in kindergartens, family support, long day care, occasional care and early childhood intervention; and as Policy Adviser to Government for young children's access and participation in mainstream services and support for Regional Networks.

Ginette Pestana

Ginette currently teaches at the education faculty of Monash University, specialising in early years science education and creative arts. Ginette is an experienced early childhood teacher and is deeply interested in supporting young children's learning especially through music. She is currently undertaking a PhD with a research focus on early childhood music education.

Guided Tour

Chapter objectives

In this chapter, we will:
- consider what we mean when we refer to child/children
- introduce the variety of ways in which children and childhood have been seen and imagined
- reflect on your image of the child and concept of childhood and how this 'theory within' is *where our teaching begins*
- consider the nature/nurture debate and be introduced to theorists with differing perspectives on how we become the people we are
- introduce the concept of 'reflective practice', which begins with examining our own image of the child.

A list of **Chapter Objectives** and **Key Terms** at the start of the chapter pinpoints important concepts

Key terms

agency
Early Years Learning
    Framework (EYLF)
kindergarten

nature
negative reinforcement
nurture
positive reinforcement

tabula rasa
The United Nations
    Convention on the
    Rights of the Child

What is a child? What do you 'see' when you look at a child?

Perhaps you have never consciously thought about your own image of the child and the question, 'What is a child?' may seem to have an obvious answer: don't we all see the same thing? Surely, a child is just that—a child! Our understanding of *childhood* may also be taken for granted. Many of the Initial Teacher Education students I teach talk about childhood as a precious—even a magical—period of innocence and play with a sense of wonder that needs to be protected. This idealised image is represented so often in popular media that it is easy to assume that this view is 'true' and accepted by everyone, at least as an ideal. However, as this chapter will reveal, there is enormous variation in the ways children and childhood are and have been seen, imagined and understood.

Each chapter opens with **a vignette** to illustrate a theory and kick-start your thinking before you delve into a particular topic.

The **Key terms** are bolded as they appear in the text, and **margin notes** provide definitions to help with your understanding, and with revision.

Nature or nurture?

In this debate, **nature** means what is *in* us—what we are born with—it is *not* about the outdoors or gardens. In the context of scientific understanding of the twenty-first century, we can think of 'nature' as our DNA or genetic code, but thinking of genes and DNA is a relatively new concept. Most of the theorists and philosophers you are about to meet could never have known about DNA and genes: their understanding of 'nature' would have been linked to what were believed to be essential, innate qualities—good and bad, for example— and their ideas reflected religious doctrines.

In everyday language, **nurture** usually refers to the loving, supportive care we give children, but in this long debate, nurture means much more: it encompasses the whole physical, social and cultural environment, including child-rearing practices, relationships, resources and the community in which children are reared. Nurture reflects the time and place context of a child's life; nature, by contrast, is timeless. If the boys who killed James Bulger really were born evil, then the environment they were born into would not have made a difference to their innate character and actions.

If you believe the boys who tortured and killed James Bulger were 'born evil' (as some media headlines claimed), you are likely to be on the side that argues that 'nature' defines or determines who we are. If, by contrast, you side with Tony Blair's assertion that society is to blame, you probably favour 'nurture' arguments and look to the environment as an explanation of character and actions.

nature what is in us—what we are born with.

nurture the whole physical, social and cultural environment in which a child is reared.

Sinking and floating vegetables

Jan, the teacher in a four-year-old pre-school class was reading *Who Sank the Boat?* by Pamela Allen to her class during story time. The children were really engaged with the story and were very surprised at the ending when it only took a little mouse getting on board the boat to sink it.

Case studies showcase real-life education experiences from both students and teachers.

Reflecting on why we act in one way and not another is a key practice for you as a student and as an early childhood teacher. '**Stop and reflect**' sections encourage you to reflect on your own experiences and education. '**Stop and think**' sections consolidate learning by asking you to answer questions based on the text

STOP AND REFLECT

- Is this belief still held?
- How important do you think education is in shaping the person you are?
- When you imagine yourself as a teacher, do you think you will make a difference to making children the people they become?

STOP AND THINK

- Who or what is the 'Author of things'?
- What does Rousseau mean by 'everything degenerates in the hands of man'?
- If we are thinking about educating/rearing children, what follows from this belief?

SUMMARY

- Our image of the child shapes our interactions with children, including our practice as teachers.
- Paraphrasing Malaguzzi, our image of the child and concept of childhood is what drives and shapes our teaching philosophy and practice.
- An important aspect of the teacher's role is reflective practice. We can begin this by reflecting on our own image of the child.

FURTHER REFLECTION

How do you define children/childhood? In what ways do you think children differ from adults? These questions might help you answer this reflection question:

- What activities do you think characterise children?
- Is it useful to describe specific ages and stages in childhood? Explain your answer.
- When does childhood end? Is this satisfactorily defined by age or can we include other criteria?

GROUP DISCUSSION

1 How might the theorists you have been introduced to in this chapter account for the actions of James Bulger's killers?
2 What responsibility does society carry in this? If society is responsible, could this crime have been avoided? How?

Lecturer resources, including an instructor's resource manual and multiple choice questions, are also included.

CLASS EXERCISE

Collect a variety of prospectuses for schools and, paying close attention to the words and images that are used to promote the schools' approaches to education, categorise each in terms of which theorist they are most closely aligned to.

At the end of each chapter, there are a **summary**, **further reflection** questions, **discussion questions** and a **class exercise**.

For lecturers, there are extra resources available: icebreakers, tutorial activities, sample essay topics, short-answer questions, and more. Please go to the OUP website page for this title, and click on Lecturer Resources for more information.

A list of **Further readings**, with commentary, will direct you to additional print and online resources to learn more about key topics covered in the text.

FURTHER READING

Cleverley, J. & Phillips, D.C. (1987) Visions of Childhood: Influential Models from Locke to Spock. St Leonards, NSW: Allen & Unwin.
I highly recommend this fascinating book; it provides examples of images and concepts of childhood and groups them under chapters that include 'On seeing children throughout history', 'The loss of innocence: the Freudian child' and 'The thinking machine'. It provided overall inspiration for this chapter. Many editions are available.

A **Glossary** at the end of the book compiles the key terms and their definitions for easy reference.

developmentalism
Various developmental theories that all involve clear stages linked to maturation.

Developmentally Appropriate Practice (DAP)
A term used by the NAEYC to describe programs grounded in child development theory and research designed to meet the developmental needs of children.

evaluation
Observing, measuring and using evidence for the purpose of judging and ascertaining value.

event samples
Brief narratives written preceding and following a specified behaviour; useful for identifying the causes and possible consequences for certain behaviours and interactions.

Acknowledgments

All the authors thank the anonymous readers of the original book proposal and chapters. Their suggestions and responses were much appreciated.

Many people at Oxford University Press deserve our thanks for their support and guidance, but we would like to give particular thanks to Katie Ridsdale, who first initiated the idea of *The Child in Focus*. We are grateful for Katie's ongoing support, great conversations and her interest in and enthusiasm for the project.

The author and the publisher wish to thank the following copyright holders for reproduction of their material.

123RF, 121, 273 (garden), 333, 334, 488; All ACARA material identified by is material subject to copyright under the Copyright Act 1968 (Cth) and is owned by the Australian Curriculum, Assessment and Reporting Authority 2013. **For all Australian Curriculum material except elaborations**: This is an extract from the Australian Curriculum. **Elaborations:** This may be a modified extract from the Australian Curriculum and may include the work of other authors. **Disclaimer:** ACARA neither endorses nor verifies the accuracy of the information provided and accepts no responsibility for incomplete or inaccurate information. In particular, ACARA does not endorse or verify that: The content descriptions are solely for a particular year and subject; All the content descriptions for that year have been used; and The author's material aligns with the Australian Curriculum content descriptions for the relevant year and subject. You can find the unaltered and most up to date version of this material at http://www.australiancurriculum.edu.au This material is reproduced with the permission of ACARA, 266; Age of Montessori. www.ageofmontessori.org, 166; Bureau of Meteorology, 273 (weather); Creative Commons by Share Alike 4.0 Department of Education Employment and Workplace Relations (DEEWR), 265; Early Childhood Australia, 309 (top); Getty Images/AFP, 159/Eric Audras, 268/Jamie Grill, 179/Tom Martin, 487/Moment, 165, 178/Science Source, 23/Ariel Skelley, 438; Imagefolk/Charles Gullung, 207; Interaction Institute for Social Change/Angus Maguire, 401; Professions Australia, 292; Shutterstock, 104, 115, 157, 158, 183, 211, 213 (all), 227, 238, 242, 262, 266 (top & middle), 267 (far left), 273 (playdough, rainbow, sandpit), 427, 485, cover;

Courtesy of Professor Iram Siraj, 163; © State of Victoria (Department of Education and Training), 377, 378; Stocksy/Amanda Worrall, cover (child); Tasmanian Archive and Heritage Office, 15; From 'Declaration of the Rights of the Child', by United Nations Office of the High Commissioner, Human Rights © 1959 United Nations. Reprinted with the permission of the United Nations, 47; Extract from Young, M, (2015), 'Tuning in to toddlers', *Research in Practice Series*, Vol.22 No.3, Early Childhood Australia;

Every effort has been made to trace the original source of copyright material contained in this book. The publisher will be pleased to hear from copyright holders to rectify any errors or omissions.

PART ONE
FOUNDATIONS

Beginning with an introduction to the scope and theoretical framework of *The Child in Focus*, Part 1 considers foundational questions about how we 'see', imagine and understand children and childhood.

Chapter 1 begins with the question: What is a child? Acknowledging Malaguzzi's assertion that 'Each one of you has inside yourself an image of the child that directs you as you begin to relate to a child' (Malaguzzi, 1993, p.10), the reader is invited to reflect on their own image of the child. Key theorists and philosophers, whose ideas about children and childhood have contributed to current ideas and practices, are introduced and used to illustrate the variety of ways in which children have been seen, and the nature/nurture debate.

The foundations theme continues in Chapter 2, where the concept of childhood as socially constructed is examined. The links between technology, literacy and formal education and their contribution to the emergence of the modern concept of childhood are described, and the proposition that childhood is profoundly changing is examined. An underpinning key teaching and learning point is that teachers can and do have an impact, not just on individual children's lives—what children learn; whether they are inspired to learn more or learn that they are not valued, for example—but on how childhood is perceived, experienced and valued.

Chapter 3 moves to an examination of the key theorists and theoretical perspectives that contribute to early childhood education.

- Chapter 1: What is a Child? Concepts and Images of Childhood
- Chapter 2: Social Construction of Childhood
- Chapter 3: Theorists and Theoretical Perspectives: Early Childhood Development and Learning

What is a Child? Concepts and Images of Childhood

Estelle Irving

Chapter objectives

In this chapter, we will:

- consider what we mean when we refer to child/children
- introduce the variety of ways in which children and childhood have been seen and imagined
- reflect on your image of the child and concept of childhood and how this 'theory within' is *where our teaching begins*
- consider the nature/nurture debate and introduce theorists with differing perspectives on how we become the people we are
- introduce the concept of 'reflective practice', which begins with examining our own image of the child.

Key terms

agency
Early Years Learning
    Framework (EYLF)
kindergarten

nature
negative reinforcement
nurture
positive reinforcement

tabula rasa
The United Nations
    Convention on the
    Rights of the Child

What is a child? What do you 'see' when you look at a child?

Perhaps you have never consciously thought about your own image of the child and the question, 'What is a child?' may seem to have an obvious answer: don't we all see the same thing? Surely, a child is just that—a child! Our understanding of *childhood* may also be taken for granted. Many of the Initial Teacher Education students I teach talk about childhood as a precious—even a magical—period of innocence and play with a sense of wonder that needs to be protected. This idealised image is represented so often in popular media that it is easy to assume that this view is 'true' and accepted by everyone, at least as an ideal. However, as this chapter will reveal, there is enormous variation in the ways children and childhood are and have been seen, imagined and understood.

Here is the view of a pre-service teacher from my class in an Initial Teacher Education course, beautifully expressed in a reflective essay:

> I believe each and every child is born naturally innocent, but also enters the world with a set of predetermined genes inherited from each parent, that contributes to a genetic make-up, 'their inherent nature or disposition', which if nurtured and tended with love, care and respect, becomes the creation of an amazing being, with talents and capabilities beyond imagination.

I also believe caring and nurturing relationships, and bonds made by children in the early years and throughout their lives, if positive and esteem building, can make the difference between a child growing up with confidence and faith in their own abilities, to one who struggles constantly, and moves through life with a sad and jaded perspective.

My concept of childhood is one where children should be allowed to be 'children', where natural independence, talents, and interests are nurtured and channelled in ways that help them reach their full potential. In an ever-changing, fast-paced and competitive world, where social justice is often absent, it seems many children miss out on the beauty and freedom that childhood should offer. (Kim McDonald, Bachelor of Early Childhood Teaching, Year 1 reflection piece).

Introduction

In Australia today, there is no one agreed-upon concept of childhood. Instead, there is a wide and diverse range of views, though most people assume that their view is shared by others. One area where there is consensus is that most early childhood teachers accept and practise within a learning framework that is built upon and actively promotes a particular view of children. This view, articulated in the **Early Years Learning Framework (EYLF)** will be discussed later in the chapter and references to the EYLF are found throughout the book.

Some of the views introduced in this chapter (and the practices they justify) may seem astonishing, absurd or even cruel; others may resonate with your own views and therefore seem 'normal'. Be careful about any assumptions about what is normal. The variety of concepts and images you will be introduced to are evidence that images of the child and concepts of childhood change over time, and new images emerge to challenge or repudiate older images. These changes reflect wider societal changes and concerns.

The ideas, theories and concepts you will be exposed to will challenge you to reflect on the way in which you understand and see children and childhood; your views and understanding of children are likely to change in the course of your studies.

Before we meet the theorists with their diverse concepts and practices, let us take a step back to look at the rationale for beginning with the question, 'What is a child?' In a textbook about early childhood teaching and learning, why do our concepts of childhood and the images we hold of children *matter*?

Here is one view that answers that question:

> There are hundreds of different images of the child. Each one of you has inside yourself an image of the child that directs you as you begin to relate to a child. This theory within you pushes you to behave in certain ways; it orients you as you talk to the child, listen to the child, observe the child. It is very difficult for you to act contrary to this internal image.
>
> (Malaguzzi, 1993, unpaged)

We shall discuss Malaguzzi in more detail later: here we are interested in his assertion that we all have an image of what a child is and that image (or the more developed *concept*) shapes our interactions with—and expectations of—children. Malaguzzi elaborates on this by saying, 'Your image of the child [is] where [your] teaching begins' (1993, p.10). At its most

Early Years Learning Framework (EYLF) a national framework that provides broad direction for practice in early childhood services for educators, teachers and other professionals, volunteers, students and for family and community who work within or attend these services. 'Belonging, Being & Becoming' are the themes of the EYLF.

simple, this means that how we understand any situation involving a child, and what we *do* with or for the child will reflect this image. As a specific example, Malaguzzi says '… if your image is that boys and girls are very different from one another, you will behave differently in your interactions with them' (1993, p.10). This understanding—that our ideas, whether consciously articulated or not, shape our practice—underpins this chapter.

Specifically, our internal image of the child affects:

- our expectations of the child, including what we think they can or cannot do
- the experiences and learning environments we create for children
- how we discipline children (behaviour management)
- the things we give or do not give children
- the things/experiences we believe are either appropriate or inappropriate to children's learning and development.

To illustrate this, consider this vignette.

> Twelve-month-old Jo is transfixed by a mobile that is moving with the breeze coming from an open window. Outside it's cold, but Jo is dressed warmly, tucked into a fluffy sleeping bag and the cot Jo is lying in has padded protectors wrapped around its bars, so the cold air does not directly blow onto Jo. Jo's mother comes into the room to shut the window and put the heating on. This stops the movement of the mobile, and Jo screams in protest. Jo's mother …

STOP AND THINK

- Let us stop there and consider: What does Jo's mother do next?
- What might she be thinking that prompts her to respond in this way?
- What effect might her next actions have on Jo?

Here is an alternative to the scenario:

> Twelve-month-old Jo is transfixed by a mobile that is moving with the breeze coming from an open window. Outside it's cold, but Jo is used to cool air, and enjoys seeing the play of light and shadow, and the movement of the curtains, even if the draught sometimes blows directly onto the cot. Jo's mother comes into the room and stands between the cot and the open window. This stops the movement of the mobile, and Jo screams in protest. Jo's mother …

What is the difference here? First of all, the scenarios have been created to highlight some changing beliefs about what children *need*, what they *should have* and what we can *expect* of young children. Jo is an infant: do babies need to be kept in climate-controlled environments, or does the experience of varying temperatures build strength and resilience? What about safety concerns with padded cot bars? When you answered the question of what happened next, did you anticipate that Jo's mother comforted Jo, or alternatively told Jo off (i.e. disciplined her) for screaming, or did you imagine that she opened/moved away from the

ESTELLE IRVING

window and (following Jo's evident interest) shared in Jo's delight in the movement of the mobile?

The start and finish of both scenarios are the same, but the in-between details vary significantly: these details provide clues to the *image of the child* that informs Jo's mother's actions and response.

The next example is much more confronting for two reasons: first, it is real, not created; second, the details are deeply challenging to ideas about what children are capable of and what characteristics define a child.

The case concerns a two-year-old boy, James Bulger, who was kidnapped from outside a shop in the UK in 1993. CCTV images showed the unfolding events as the little boy, in the short time while his mother's attention was distracted, was approached by his kidnappers, held by the hand and led away. The image of the innocent little boy, who trusted strangers enough to be led away without a fuss, was hard to bear, but the real shock was to see the kidnappers. They were themselves children: two boys, both aged ten.

Little James was subsequently tortured by the boys, and finally, horribly, they killed him.

Rather than focusing on the horrific details of this crime, I invite you to consider the two boys in this case. There is no doubt that their actions were cruel in their impact and devoid of compassion or empathy, but how can we make sense of this crime?

Here are some questions that emerged in public responses to the crime:

- What could have motivated the boys?
- Could this crime have been avoided?
- Who or what is to blame? Is society to blame? Is the violence-saturated media to blame? Is it poor parenting or something in the boys' natures?
- If the boys' natures were the root cause, were they born evil or were they born innocent and then corrupted by society?
- If the latter is the case, does that make the boys themselves a type of victim? Were they let down (or corrupted) by a system that allowed them access to violent video games, and a society where they were not challenged as they led a crying, injured child on a day when they should have been in school?
- Or, perhaps the boys were simply playing a game, the consequences of which they could not have predicted or understood. If that is the case, were the boys unable to differentiate between what is real and what is imagination? Is that one of the ways in which we understand the difference between a child and an adult?

You may have noticed that I keep referring to the boys as *children*, and legally there is no doubting they were indeed children. According to British and Australian law, childhood ends when we turn eighteen and until then, children do not have the same status as adults and they are neither tried nor sentenced as adults. Referring to the boys as children implies that they were not capable of fully understanding or being responsible for their actions, but at ten, is that a reasonable assumption to make? Even referring to them as 'murderers' is contentious and reflects an assumption that the killing was premeditated: murder is not accidental, so if it was accidental or without premeditation, then it cannot have been murder. Are ten-year-old children capable of the required premeditation?

The media speculated on all of these questions, and the public response was, understandably, shock—but it was also divided. Tony Blair, the then British Shadow Home Secretary (and later, Prime Minister), cast blame on society and pronounced that 'We hear of crimes so horrific they provoke anger and disbelief in equal proportions … These are the ugly manifestations of a society that is becoming unworthy of that name'. Reflecting public sentiment of blame and frustration, the Prime Minister of the time, John Major, proclaimed that 'society needs to condemn a little more, and understand a little less'.

This is a distressing case and it raises very difficult questions that may challenge your ideas about how we understand and define children and childhood. Because the boys were legally children and therefore (like all children) entitled to privacy and protections, we will never fully know the answer to the question of motivation for these particular boys. Nor will we be able to 'test' our beliefs about the boys' characters, but our responses to the case and, in particular, the answers we give to the questions about cause and blame are very important. They go to the heart of the issues raised by Malaguzzi's 'image of the child' and highlight our core beliefs about children.

Two recurring questions, raised by the James Bulger case, are 'What makes us who we are?' and 'Can we be born evil, or is evil the result of our environment?' These questions tap into a long debate, which is summarised as 'nature or/versus nurture'.

Nature or nurture?

In this debate, **nature** means what is *in* us—what we are born with—it is *not* about the outdoors or gardens. In the context of scientific understanding of the twenty-first century, we can think of 'nature' as our DNA or genetic code, but thinking of genes and DNA is a relatively new concept. Most of the theorists and philosophers you are about to meet could never have known about DNA and genes: their understanding of 'nature' would have been linked to what were believed to be essential, innate qualities—good and bad, for example— and their ideas reflected religious doctrines.

In everyday language, **nurture** usually refers to the loving, supportive care we give children, but in this long debate, nurture means much more: it encompasses the whole physical, social and cultural environment, including child-rearing practices, relationships, resources and the community in which children are reared. Nurture reflects the time and place context of a child's life; nature, by contrast, is timeless. If the boys who killed James Bulger really were born evil, then the environment they were born into would not have made a difference to their innate character and actions.

If you believe the boys who tortured and killed James Bulger were 'born evil' (as some media headlines claimed), you are likely to be on the side that argues that 'nature' defines or determines who we are. If, by contrast, you side with Tony Blair's assertion that society is to blame, you probably favour 'nurture' arguments and look to the environment as an explanation of character and actions.

nature what is in us—what we are born with.

nurture the whole physical, social and cultural environment in which a child is reared.

The theorists: differing concepts of childhood

The following accounts of selected theorists and philosophers demonstrate the variety of ways in which children and childhood have been 'seen'—that is, how these little beings have been imagined or conceptualised. Some theorists clearly favour a 'nature' view of human beings, while others argue strongly that nurture (the environment) creates who we are. A third group reflects current thinking that both nature and nurture are important and it is

ESTELLE IRVING

the interaction between our genes and our environment that properly answers the 'nature/ nurture' debate. This more complex understanding, which recognises the importance and dynamic quality of the interaction between genes/DNA and the environment, reflects current scientific thinking.

The theorists have been chosen for two reasons:

1 to illustrate the variety of images of children/childhood
2 because each is still relevant to our current ideas about, and images of, children.

I like to imagine these philosophers and theorists standing behind us, challenging and encouraging us to see children through their own eyes, despairing when we ignore their messages. Each passionately believed they were right, and each, in their own way, wanted the best outcome for children—but even those outcomes are imagined differently.

The shadows cast by these theorists are long, but not necessarily visible until we seriously and consciously reflect on our own ideas and how these developed. We can choose to step out of those 'shadows'—but only if we are aware that there are alternatives available.

John Locke (1632–1714)

Locke, an English philosopher, is the first of our thinkers. What Locke saw in children was, initially, nothing. According to Locke, the child's mind *at birth* was blank, without ideas or understanding and with no substance. Locke described this as **tabula rasa**, or a blank slate.

tabula rasa the theory that at birth the (human) mind is a blank slate.

> Let us suppose the mind to be … white paper void of all characters, without any ideas. How comes it to be furnished? Whence comes it by that vast store which the busy and boundless fancy of man has painted on it with an almost endless variety? Whence has it all the materials of reason and knowledge?

(Locke, 1959, p.5)

As a philosopher, Locke employed reason and logic to argue for 'nurture' and against a 'nature' position—though he did not use those actual terms. He argued that, if babies are born with innate reason, ideas and knowledge, then this should be apparent from the start of life. Since this is not evident, Locke's question became: Where do the contents of the mind come from? This is what he is referring to in the quote above as the furnishing of the mind 'with an almost endless variety'. Not surprisingly, given that Locke was a philosopher, he was particularly interested in the question of how reason and knowledge develops, and how it does so 'with an almost endless variety'.

For Locke, the clear answer is '… from *Experience*. In that, all our knowledge is founded …'; 'all the materials of reason and knowledge' (Locke, 1959, p.5) are derived from experience and perception. Knowledge is determined by experience, derived initially from the baby's senses, or in Locke's terminology, 'sense perception', which he contrasted with thinking and reasoning.

Locke identified two sources of experience:

1 *sensation*—experience obtained through the senses, e.g. hot and cold, sweetness, hardness
2 *reflection* (referred to as 'internal sensation')—through which we perceive how our own mind works. So reflection leads us to ideas that include thinking about thinking, as well as doubting, reasoning and willing.

While Locke asserted that the *mind* of the baby is like a blank slate, he also observed that there are different talents and interests evident early in life. Locke advised parents to watch their children carefully in order to discover their 'aptitudes' and to nurture their children's own interests rather than force them to participate in activities they dislike or have no interest in. Nurture here means to support and encourage these individual aptitudes.

Of special interest to those involved in early childhood education is Locke's observation that the mind of the child is most susceptible to experience in the period of early childhood. He suggested that 'the little and almost insensible impressions on our tender infancies have very important and lasting consequences'. In this, Locke's understanding is strikingly similar to current thinking about the importance of early experiences and their lasting impact.

According to Locke, the 'associations of ideas' or impressions made when we are young are more significant than those made when we are mature because they are the foundation of the self.

If, as Locke asserts, knowledge is determined by experience (derived from sense perception), early experiences in particular become crucial to who we are and what we become—not just what we learn.

An Essay Concerning Human Understanding (Locke, 1959, p.1) begins with a statement that makes the importance of education clear: 'I think I may say that of all the men we meet with, nine parts of ten are what they are, good or evil, useful or not, by their education. 'Tis that which makes the great difference in mankind'.

In other words, 'Education maketh [makes] the man'.

STOP AND REFLECT

- Is this belief still held?
- How important do you think education is in shaping the person you are?
- When you imagine yourself as a teacher, do you think you will make a difference to making children the people they become?

Educating the mind

Locke's concept of tabula rasa raised questions about how the mind could best be 'furnished' through education. In *Some Thoughts Concerning Education* (1693), Locke explains how to educate the mind (i.e. how to fill in the blank slate) using three distinct methods:

1 the development of a healthy body
2 the formation of a virtuous character
3 the choice of an appropriate academic curriculum.

Early experiences should, according to Locke, help the child's body to become accustomed to weather extremes, and develop what we would now refer to as 'resilience'. Over-protecting the child would render them less able to endure cold, for example.

Locke was particularly concerned with the development of virtue, which he defined as a combination of self-denial and rationality. He believed that education should instil these qualities and the role of education was therefore less about instilling knowledge and more about the development of moral character, including rationality. Much of *Some Thoughts Concerning Education* (1693) is concerned with how to instil virtue in children.

First teach how to learn

Locke argued that parents or teachers must first teach children *how* to learn and enjoy learning. The instructor 'should remember that his business is not so much to teach all that is knowable, as to raise in him a love and esteem of knowledge; and to put him in the right way of knowing and improving himself' (Locke, 1959, p.89).

Parents should create in their children a 'habit' of thinking rationally and children should, Locke argued, be treated as rational beings. Discipline should be founded on esteem and disgrace, rather than on rewards and punishments. This approach reflected Locke's belief that children understand reasoning 'as early as they do language, and … they love to be treated as rational creatures, sooner than is imagined. 'Tis a pride should be cherished in them …' (Locke, 1959, p.81). The habit of rational thinking and the love of learning should be internalised by the child—not externally imposed. Children learn to think and behave rationally through practising rational thought and behaviour, not by being compelled to obey.

Locke's legacy in current thinking

Locke may have developed his ideas 300 years ago, but in some ways, they are remarkably similar to current ideas expressed, for example, in the EYLF. We can discern Locke's presence, or the 'shadow' his ideas still cast, in:

- our understanding of the importance of early experiences and the lasting impact they have on our development and later learning
- the practice of observing children closely, following their interests and supporting their particular aptitudes
- the belief that parents and teachers should inspire in children a love of learning
- a belief in the importance of a holistic education for young children, rather than education that is only focused on the mind
- the belief that children learn best when they are engaged and interested, rather than when they are threatened or lectured to.

Jean-Jacques Rousseau (1712–1778)

Jean-Jacques Rousseau believed that children are innately good. In that aspect, we could assume that Rousseau is an advocate for 'nature' rather than 'nurture'.

The child in nature—free and uncorrupted

Rousseau's view and concept of childhood is complex. This complexity is captured in the quote, 'Man is born free but everywhere he is in chains'. What are the 'chains' Rousseau refers to? The answer for Rousseau is, society.

For Rousseau, the natural moral state of human beings is to be compassionate and kind, but civilisation (or society) has corrupted humanity, making us cruel, selfish and bloodthirsty, and taking us away from our natural state.

In Rousseau's view, society corrupts, but 'Whatever is natural is good' (Rousseau, cited in Cleverley & Phillips, 1987, p.36).

Education should follow nature

Children should learn through and in nature, not through what Rousseau regarded as the arbitrary rules of society:

> Let him early find upon his proud neck the heavy yoke which nature has imposed upon us, the heavy yoke of necessity, under which every finite being must bow.

> Let him find this necessity in things, not in the caprices of man: let the curb be force, not authority.
>
> (Rousseau, cited in Cleverley & Phillips, 1987, p.35)

Rousseau's philosophy of education is concerned with developing children's character and moral sense so they may learn to practise self-mastery and remain virtuous even in the unnatural and imperfect society in which they live.

> Everything is good as it leaves the hands of the Author of things; everything degenerates in the hands of man.
>
> (Rousseau, 1979, p.37)

STOP AND THINK

- Who or what is the 'Author of things'?
- What does Rousseau mean by 'everything degenerates in the hands of man'?
- If we are thinking about educating/rearing children, what follows from this belief?

Émile or, On Education (1762)

To promote his educational philosophy, Rousseau used a novelistic style of fictional writing to describe a system of education that would enable the 'natural man' to survive 'corrupt society' (Rousseau, 1979). The book was titled *Émile or, On Education*. In this book a boy, Émile, and his tutor are used as characters to illustrate how a nature-based education that protected the child from society could be implemented—at least in theory—and Rousseau's goal of the creation of an ideal citizen might be created through this education.

Émile is raised in the countryside, which Rousseau believed to be more natural and therefore a healthier environment than the city. In this environment, the tutor guides Émile through various learning experiences, but nature is the true tutor and the lessons for Émile come from nature.

Early education for Émile and, by extension, for all children '… consists, not in reaching virtue or truth, but in preserving the heart from vice and the spirit from error' (Rousseau, 1979, p.60).

How is the heart preserved from vice and the spirit from corruption, or in Rousseau's word, from 'error'? The answer from Rousseau is to provide early education in nature, away from the corrupting influence of civilisation and society. The lessons from nature will then sustain children when they return to 'society'.

Developmentally appropriate education

Rousseau did not see childhood as a continuous and unified period of life. Instead he identified different stages of childhood and, based on that observation, he advocated for different educational methods in different locations, based on the stage of childhood. We now refer to this as 'developmentally appropriate' (or developmentally differentiated) education.

The first stage identified by Rousseau is to the age of about twelve, when children are guided by their emotions and impulses. It is in this stage that Rousseau believed children should be removed from the corrupting influences of 'society' and reared in nature. During the second stage, from twelve to about sixteen, reason starts to develop. The third stage, from the age of sixteen onwards, is when the child develops into an adult.

ESTELLE IRVING

Rousseau's legacy

Many of Rousseau's ideas and the educational practices he advocated are still evident in current educational philosophy and practice, albeit in a modified form. His legacy includes:

- natural education—learning in nature, with nature as the teacher
- belief in the corrupting influence of society—learning about yourself when removed from society and living in nature
- freedom, not constraint, in education
- child-centred education
- the belief that education should be concerned with development of character and moral sense, not rules and regulations
- learning through *doing* (natural consequences), rather than through *instruction*.

Note: Though I refer to 'the child' as boys and girls, Rousseau's beliefs and educational philosophy only applied to boys.

John Wesley (1703–1791)

John Wesley's image of the child reflected the religious views of a strict and austere eighteenth-century Christian sect that was powerful at that time.

The sinful child

This church believed literally in heaven and the fire and brimstone of hell. Through this lens, what Wesley saw in children was, first and foremost, 'original sin' (inherited from Eve, as described in the Bible). In Wesley's eyes, sin was evident in pride and vanity, as well as stubbornness, greed and cruelty, but most clearly, sin was demonstrated in children's wilfulness.

In order to save children (if possible) from damnation and hell, the solution was, according to Wesley, two-fold: children must be reared in the fear of God and their will must be broken.

> As self-will is the root of all sin and misery, so whatever cherishes this in children insures their after-wretchedness and irreligion; whatever checks and mortifies it promotes their future happiness and piety … Heaven or hell depends on this alone, so that the parent who studies to subdue it in his child works together with God in the renewing and saving a soul. The parent who indulges it, does the devil's work.
>
> Break their wills betimes. Begin this work before they can run alone, before they can speak plain, perhaps before they can speak at all. Whatever pains it costs, break the will if you would not damn the child. Let a child from a year old be taught to fear the rod and to cry softly … Break his will now, and his soul shall live, and he will probably bless you to all eternity.
>
> (Wesley, 1829, p.389)

It is worth taking the time to carefully read the quote above to gain an accurate sense of what Wesley was proposing, particularly the age at which he suggested a parent should break the will of their child.

According to Wesley, self-will is the heart of all sin and misery, so breaking the will of the child is the first task of child-rearing. Children must submit to the will of their parents, who must make the child realise that they are 'more foolish, and more wicked than they can possibly conceive' (Wesley, 1829, p.389). For parents who shared Wesley's religious views, the prospect of 'doing the devil's work' (Wesley, 1829) and condemning their child to hell would have been terrifyingly real. Wesley realised, however, that parents (and particularly mothers) might find it difficult to adhere to the strict principles and practices that he deemed necessary to break the child's will.

In *Thoughts on the Manner of Educating Children* (in Wesley & Emory, 1835), Wesley attacked the Rousseau-like, child-centred approach to education as 'the most empty, silly, injudicious thing' and insisted that religion be instilled from the very first—before nature can take root.

> The bias of nature is set the wrong way; education is designed to set it right by 'mildness' where this is possible, but by 'kind severity' where it is not.
>
> (Wesley & Emory, 1835, p.457)

Indulgence of any sort must be avoided and children must not be allowed to gratify their senses:

> The desire of the eyes must not be fed by pretty playthings, glittering toys, red shoes, necklaces and ruffles. (advice to mothers)
>
> (Wesley & Emory, 1835, p.457)

Strict routines were necessary, with no indulgences whatsoever. Corporal punishment was used liberally, with the belief that:

> If you spare the rod, you spoil the child; if you do not conquer, you ruin him. Break his will now, and his soul shall live, and he will probably bless you to all eternity. (Susannah Wesley, John Wesley's mother)
>
> (Wesley & Emory, 1835, p.173)

As you can probably imagine, in this harsh regime of child-rearing where fear and discipline were the primary methods of control, there was no room for play. Instead, play was regarded as a dangerous indulgence:

> He that plays when he is a child, will play when he is a man.
>
> (proverb, cited by Wesley)

For girls, as for boys, there was no play:

> She that plays as a girl, will play when she is a Woman.
>
> (Wesley & Emory 1835, p.457)

STOP AND THINK

- Does Wesley have a lasting legacy, discernible in current attitudes towards children?
- Do his ideas still resonate in twenty-first century Australia?
- How would his advice to parents to use corporal punishment to compel a child to be obedient be received now?
- Are children over-indulged today?

Friedrich Froebel (1782–1852)

The historical figure who has probably had the most lasting impact on the educational environments we create for young children is Froebel, the creator of the **kindergarten**. The first kindergarten was built in 1832 in Germany, but Froebel's image of the child, drawn from a romantic notion of the garden/nature, had wide appeal that transcended national boundaries. Consequently, kindergartens were established in many countries, including Russia, Japan and the USA.

kindergarten
'children's garden'

ESTELLE IRVING

It is very likely that you attended a kindergarten, though you may have called it kinder or 'kindie'. The word 'kindergarten' means 'children's garden' and this term is the key to understanding Froebel's image of the child. Froebel's kindergarten was both a garden for children to play and learn in, and a garden in which children grew according to their inner potential and nature's plan, which Froebel understood as God's/the creator's plan.

In the era in which Froebel lived, the physical and social environment was being transformed by industrialisation, with the development of factories and the growth of industrial cities. The kindergarten was a place away from the adult world and, in that period of rapid industrialisation and the growth of industrial cities, kindergartens were intended to be places of beauty and cultivated education that would nourish the souls and spirits of young children and infuse them with a love of nature.

'Kindergarteners' (translated as 'child gardeners') tended to the children with loving care, just as gardeners tend to their plants. Both the kindergarteners and actual gardeners base their practice on knowledge (of children, of the seasons, of the conditions in which they will thrive) and both types of gardeners nurture growth and development with an image of what the final, fully developed person/plant should be like. Religion animated Froebel's image.

In applying the garden metaphor quite literally, Froebel perceived children as tender and precious, requiring appropriate environmental conditions, special care and nurture.

> The child grows in nature and, like the tender shoot of a plant, children need the right conditions to ensure they grow according to the laws of Nature/God.
>
> (Lawrence, 2012, p.194)

Growth as an unfolding

Froebel imagined the child's growth as an 'unfolding' through which the essential being (physical and spiritual) emerged. In that sense, just as a seed contains all the potential to grow into a plant, the same applied to children. All the elements of the child were there at birth, ready to unfold, but, just as a plant seed needs water and sun, the child's growth needs the right conditions in order to thrive. According to Froebel, a baby is born with a spiritual essence or life-force that seeks to be 'externalised' (or expressed in growth), through self-activity.

> As a kernel of seed-corn dropped from the plant has life within it which develops of itself, so the child lives and grows in close relationship to the whole of life. The child's life in its awakening is first shown in activity. He is active in expressing his inner life in outward form …
>
> (Lilley, 2010, p.99)

Understanding young children

> The ability of a human being to grow in felicity to his full power and to achieve his destiny depends solely on a proper understanding of him in his childhood. He must be understood not only in his nature but also in his relationships, and treated in ways which are appropriate.
>
> (Lilley, 2010, p.93)

If you did attend kindergarten, the pictures below probably have many similarities to the kindergarten you attended: they illustrate the enduring appeal (educational and aesthetic) of this specially designed and equipped learning environment.

Figure 1.1 Kindergarten, Tasmania, 1911

Source: Google images.

Look closely at the photographs. In Figure 1.1, we can see a home corner, pictures displayed at the children's level, child-sized chairs, tables and miniature brooms for purposeful 'play'. Figure 1.2 shows kindergarten children playing with natural materials—sand, water, etc.—in a sand pit, just as children do in kindergartens and early learning centres today.

The importance of play

> Play is the purest, most spiritual activity of man at this stage [childhood] … It gives … joy, freedom, contentment, inner and outer rest, peace with the world. It holds the source of all that is good … Is not the most beautiful expression of life at this time a playing child? A child wholly absorbed in his play?
>
> (Froebel, 2005, p.55)

Play, in Froebel's educational philosophy, was not 'free', but *purposeful*. Froebel is recognised for his play-based 'curriculum' and 'pedagogy', but it was a particular type of play that was orchestrated in the kindergarten and through which the child developed spiritually and physically (Bruce, 2012). Valuing and promoting play, even if it was purposeful play, contrasted strongly with the traditional view of the times, which associated play with idleness and regarded it as unworthy or worthless, or even dangerous. Wesley is an example of this view. Of course, the notion that adults could play was, for Wesley, anathema. For Froebel, play is the purest expression of children; for Wesley, play is the pathway to hell.

ESTELLE IRVING

Figure 1.2 Children's kindergarten play

Education for young children

Kindergartens were primarily educational institutions, designed for children's whole being (spiritual and educational). They were specifically planned for the needs and nurturing care of young children. The conditions, materials and activities needed, according to Froebel, were songs, stories and specially designed activities with specific objects that were progressively introduced by the kindergarteners to the children as they developed (Bruce, 2012).

Specialised training for kindergarteners

Froebel attributed such importance to the educational role of the kindergarteners that he believed that specialised training was required. Women were, he believed, especially suited to the kindergartener role because they were uniquely positioned to understand the importance of education for young children:

> Women will understand how important it is that the children whom they have borne with so much pain and suffering should from the beginning receive an education such as they intuitively desire for them, an education which will relate to the divine, human and natural aspects of the child's own being. First, then, our enterprise will give a training in the care of children.
>
> Froebel (2005)

Just as early childhood teachers now select specific items or resources and plan experiences and activities that they believe will optimise children's learning and development, Froebel's kindergarteners provided specially designed objects—called 'gifts'—to the children in their care. The first gift was a woollen ball, given to babies to hold and manipulate. The kindergarteners designed activities that they believed facilitated learning and development in children. In the early kindergartens, these activities were called 'occupations'. Children played, but play was purposeful, shaped by both the gifts and the occupations.

Loris Malaguzzi (1920–1994)

Malaguzzi, whose discussion of the importance of making explicit our internal 'image' of the child provides a frame for this chapter, resonates in many ways with our current understanding of young children and the recognition of the environmental context of early childhood learning and development. Malaguzzi is classified as a 'nurture' advocate in that he gives great importance to the environment, but his image of children highlights their inner/innate qualities and potential as well as children's fundamental need for social connection and communication.

The following statement from Malaguzzi can be read as a repudiation of, or direct challenge to, many of the 'images' and assumptions made about children outlined in this chapter. The final sentence of his statement captures the essence of Malaguzzi's image of the child and it is this image that we can see reflected in current policies and teaching practices, discussed later in the chapter:

> Our image of children no longer considers them as isolated and egocentric, does not only see them as engaged in action with objects, does not emphasise only the cognitive aspects, does not belittle feelings of what is not logical and does not consider with ambiguity the role of the reflective domain. Instead our image of the child is rich in potential, strong, powerful, competent and, most of all, connected to adults and children.
>
> (Malaguzzi, in Penn, 1997, p.117)

For Malaguzzi, the child is not an empty vessel or 'blank slate'; nor is Malaguzzi promoting an image of the child as passive, incomplete and 'lacking' or deficient in maturity, development and knowledge. Instead this is a 'rich', strong and positive image. Malaguzzi's image of the child is as a citizen and contributor, the subject of rights, not needs; and born with 'a hundred languages' (UNESCO, 2010).

Reggio Emilia

Like Rousseau, Wesley and Froebel, Malaguzzi's image of the child was the foundation of an educational philosophy that was translated into an educational program. Reggio Emilia is the name of the Italian village where, in the aftermath of the devastations of the Second World War, the citizens collectively invested in and created a unique educational project inspired by Malaguzzi's educational philosophy with its roots in his image of the child.

Malaguzzi's legacy

Reggio Emilia is now used to describe an educational approach based on Malaguzzi's philosophy. This philosophy and the approach it inspired continues to inspire many educationalists today. Reggio Emilia societies, dedicated to continuing Malaguzzi's work, thrive in many countries, including Australia. Below is an excerpt from the 'Reggio Emilia Australia Information Exchange':

> We know that children are born with amazing potential and capacities: curiosity, a drive to understand, the ability to wait, to wonder and to be amazed, the capacity to express themselves in many ways and the desire to form relationships with others and with the physical world.
>
> (www.reggioaustralia.org.au)

ESTELLE IRVING

The stress on the importance of relationships and communication, together with recognition of the environment itself as an active contributor to children's learning and engagement, are distinctive elements of Malaguzzi's enduring influence. You will see these elements highlighted throughout this book; for example Chapter 13 is specifically focused on relationships.

Observing children in the twentieth century

Advances in science in the twentieth century, and the growing belief that science offered a new, more rational pathway to progress, provided new ways of seeing and understanding children. This in turn led to new regimes or ways of managing, teaching and caring for children. We can identify two perspectives that emerged with the rise of science and its image of the child as a subject of scientific study.

1 Psychology, as a branch of science, offered a new perspective inside the *mind* of the child.
2 Science and its application in child-rearing practices and the management of children offered the prospect of the 'perfect' child.

In this era, we can detect a shift in how children were seen and understood. Informing this new perspective was the rise of science. The shift moved attention away from spiritual or religious views that were concerned with souls or spirits, to a new, science-based interest in the physical health of bodies and *minds* (and later to *brains* as super computers). The new scientific lens moved attention away from gardens and nature to the scientific laboratory, where children were clinically tested and their progress was measured and graded according to standardised norms. In the kindergarten, nature is seen as the natural and best environment for children to thrive and be understood. By contrast, the new scientific perspective assumed that children could best be understood if they were examined and experimented on in laboratories, away from the context of their home and family.

Science promised a new, rational (unlike the 'irrational', emotional approach of the past), objective approach to child-rearing. Scientific principles and processes quantifying data derived from scientific observation, testing and measurement were used.

The child in the laboratory

In the early twentieth century, competing discourses of childhood (representing different concepts and ways of seeing children) emerged. The child in the garden is the first metaphor and it remained an important concept—represented in the kindergarten movement—though this was also challenged by, and eventually modified in response to, the new scientific lens and acceptance of scientific principles.

The child in the laboratory is the second metaphor, with the rise of scientifically trained experts measuring, weighing, testing (including IQ) and timing children and proposing scientific principles for child-rearing.

Science: a new, objective approach

In the late nineteenth and early twentieth centuries, concerns were raised about the health of children. In Melbourne's and Sydney's inner-city suburbs, high infant mortality and morbidity (including child malnutrition) rates were particularly worrying.

Federation in Australia in 1901 was regarded as the birth of a new, vibrant nation, peopled with a new 'race'. Children assumed a new status as the carriers of this race. The state had a clear, vested interest in their future, but interest in children was not confined to the state: many organisations focused on children's health, education and wellbeing.

Science promised a new, objective approach to child-rearing with a better, more ordered and healthier future. But to reap the benefits of science involved changes of attitudes and changes to the way children were seen, cared for and educated.

An example of this imperative to change and adopt the new discourse of science was articulated by a leading child psychologist, Susan Isaacs. Speaking from her position as an expert in psychology and child development, Isaacs posed the question, 'What should we do?' (Isaacs, 1929, p.2) Changing beliefs, attitudes and practices, she suggested, are not

> ... simply a change of custom, nor the passing of one tradition in favour of another. It is that mothers and nurses have begun to turn away from mere custom and blind tradition, to science. ... we have now begun to base baby-rearing on proved scientific knowledge ... In the care of the child's mind also, this is beginning to be true.

> (Isaacs, 1929, p.2)

Isaacs' popular book, *The Nursery Years: The Mind of the Child from Birth to Six Years* represented a new interest in the science of the mind through psychology and a new perspective from inside the mind of the child. The most influential person in this new perspective was Freud.

Sigmund Freud (1856–1939)

Interest in and concerns about the psychological wellbeing of children are currently taken for granted. We are familiar with this perspective of looking at behaviours, expressions, moods, affect (emotional expression) and interactions with others as indicators of a child's mind and health. We are also familiar with examining our own behaviour (and the behaviour of others) for unconscious motivations, and with analysing dreams as a type of portal into our otherwise hidden desires, fears and forgotten (repressed) experiences. It is likely that at some stage we might visit a psychologist, counsellor or psychotherapist who encourages us to revisit traumatic events and to use talking as a therapy.

This new perspective originated from Freud, the 'father' of psychoanalysis. When we talk about repression, or ego, or the unconscious, we are using the language of Freud, for whom psychology and psychoanalysis reveal the previously hidden inner life of the mind.

Freud changed the way children were (and are) seen, though in a more confronting and challenging way. He claimed that children are neither 'innocent' nor 'blank sheets', but are, on the contrary, sexual beings from birth. Freud argued (using 'scientific evidence' gained from his observations of children and accounts from his patients) that sexuality did not suddenly emerge at puberty, but developed in a series of stages, from infancy. We need to be clear here: Freud was not claiming that young children were engaging in overtly sexual activity, nor did he condone any sexual interaction between adults and children. We also need to understand that his use of the term 'sexuality' was not straightforward, as this quote clarifies:

> You will perhaps protest that all this is not sexuality. I have been using the word in a far wider sense than that in which you have been accustomed to understand

> it [i.e. linked only to reproduction, which makes it impossible] for you to recognise in its true significance, the easily observable beginnings of the … mental erotic life of children.
>
> (Freud, cited in Cleverley & Phillips, 1987, p.61)

However, Freud was clear that psychology and psychoanalysis reveal the otherwise hidden, inner life: children are neither 'innocent' nor 'blank sheets'—they are sexual beings, from birth. Freud (2001) identified four stages of sexual development in childhood:

1 *the 'oral stage'*—visible in the pleasure of sucking
2 *the 'anal stage'*—children learn to control their bowels and gain some power or control over when and how they will give or withhold their faeces. Freud refers to the 'gift' of faeces (or withholding this 'gift') as a sort of control over parents
3 *the 'phallic stage'*— in which boys discover their penis and girls discover that they lack a penis. Freud attributed 'penis envy' to girls when they discovered this lack
4 *the final stage, from six to puberty*—a period of sexual latency. In this stage, Freud argued, sexual urges are repressed.

The details and extension of Freud's theory (for example, the Oedipus complex) are not important here. What is important is the new understanding of children and the changed perception that arose from the 'discovery' of infantile and child sexuality.

Freud was not an educationalist and his image of the child did not translate into educational practice. However, his image has been and continues to be influential and it has contributed to changes in the way children are 'seen' and cared for and, in particular, to understanding the importance of early experiences on psychological health and wellbeing.

Scientific child-rearing: 'behaviourism'

A different application of scientific methods can be seen in behaviourism. Two theorists associated with this new branch of psychology, with direct implications for children and child-rearing, are John Watson and B.F. Skinner.

John Watson (1878–1958)

Watson epitomises the new scientific approach and lens through which children were seen and understood as subjects of scientific study and amenable to improvement through the application of scientific methods.

Watson believed that applying the principles of scientific methods developed in the natural sciences (such as biology) to the study of children would allow behavioural scientists and psychologists to develop the 'perfect' child. In what now seems an astonishingly optimistic tone, Watson proclaimed:

> Give me a dozen healthy infants, well-formed, and my own specified world to bring them up in and I'll guarantee to take any one at random and train him to become any type of specialist I might select—doctor, lawyer, artist, merchant-chief, and, yes, even beggarman and thief—regardless of his talents, penchants, tendencies, abilities, vocations, and race of his ancestors.
>
> (Watson, 1930, p.104).

How was this amazing feat going to be achieved? For Watson, the key was through controlling or manipulating the environment. Using this method, Watson proposed to control behaviour and, ultimately, to create the type of child the scientist wanted.

Science uses observation and collection of objective data, which is then analysed to form principles and 'rules' that allow scientists to predict what will occur in the future. Watson's conviction that objective rules and principles of behaviour could also be derived from a scientific approach to studying children is evident in his claim that 'psychology as the behaviourist views it is a purely objective experimental branch of natural science. Its theoretical goal is the prediction and control of behaviour' (Watson, 1930, p.5).

According to the behaviourists (including Watson), it is not heredity (nature) but 'nurture'—the environment and the responses it elicits—that create the child. Since families are characteristically subjective (preferring and favouring their own children over others, for example) and parent–child relationships are emotional rather than objective and scientifically precise, it follows for Watson that the best conditions for child-rearing would be in scientific institutions, with scientific practices, rather than in families.

Fortunately, even Watson conceded that this was not a realistic goal, but the advice he offered parents for guiding child-rearing reflects his commitment to science.

Watson's child-rearing advice

> There is a sensible way of treating children. Treat them as though they were young adults. Dress them, bathe them with care and circumspection. Let your behavior always be objective and kindly firm. Never hug and kiss them, never let them sit in your lap. If you must, kiss them once on the forehead when they say goodnight. Shake hands with them in the morning.
>
> (Watson, 1928, p.18)

It is interesting to note that Watson does not refer to boys specifically in his advice, but the emotionally distanced, objective practices he advocated were strongly linked to gender stereotypes in which 'boys don't cry' and being a 'Mummy's boy' was intended as a humiliating taunt.

STOP AND REFLECT

- What is your response to Watson's suggested 'sensible way of treating children'?
- What would this experience be like for a young child?

Watson's child-rearing advice was adopted in many households and it affected real children. It is possible that you might have an older family member—a grandfather or great grandfather, for example—who was reared using this type of objective, unemotional practice in which physical affection and expressions of love were discouraged or even repudiated.

You might like to consider how this has affected this person's sense of self, ability to express emotions and, even possibly, ability to feel that they were loved.

Note: In Chapter 3 the concept of 'attachment' is discussed. It will give you greater insight into the potentially damaging impact of objective 'scientific' child-rearing.

ESTELLE IRVING

Conditioned responses

In 1920 Watson attempted to condition an emotional response (fear) in a nine-month-old child, Albert (referred to in the literature as 'Little Albert'). Watson devised a laboratory experiment whereby every time Albert was shown a furry white object, a loud banging noise was made. On their own, and before the experiment, furry white objects such as a rat, a rabbit and cotton wool did not produce any negative reaction in the baby. Quite quickly though, Little Albert responded with distress at being shown any furry white object. This was a learnt response: Watson's scientific experiment was a success! This 'success' in eliciting a new and predictable response, conditioned by the association of a fluffy white object and a loud banging noise meant that every time Little Albert saw a similar object (i.e. *stimulus*), his response was the *conditioned* response of fear.

For the behaviourists, this study provided 'evidence' that even complex behaviours, including emotions, could be learnt through manipulation of the environment, using stimulus to condition the desired response. In an era where science was widely regarded as holding the promise of a better world, Watson's claims had enormous popular appeal, though some critics raised serious concerns about the possibilities of creating a controlled population. Novelist Aldous Huxley was one vehement critic. Huxley darkly satirised the future where the population was psychologically manipulated through conditioning in his futuristic novel *Brave New World*, published in 1932.

As a scientist, Watson was committed to studying what could be *observed*, so his focus was on observable behaviour: the concept of **agency**, or free will and conscience, would have been foreign or simply irrelevant to his instrumental image of the child as a scientific specimen.

A significant limitation to Watson's 'conditioned child' arose from the laboriousness of conditioning each child's behaviour by manipulating the environment, as demonstrated in the Little Albert 'experiment'. Note that I have put 'experiment' in inverted commas here because I want to draw attention to the ethical issues raised by such an intervention, which traumatised a young child. Such 'experiments' would now be considered unethical and abusive; they would simply not be permitted today.

agency the ability to act independently, to make own free choices and decisions, and to impose these choices on the world.

B.F. Skinner (1904–1990)

Watson's crude (i.e. unrefined) 'classical conditioning' was further refined and developed by B.F. Skinner. If you have studied psychology, you are likely to have heard of 'Skinner's box', in which a contained animal (rat) learnt to press a lever to deliver a pellet of food. Skinner's box demonstrated a more sophisticated refinement of behaviourist principles of 'change the environment, change the response/behaviour'. Skinner (1953) focused on learnt behavioural changes, rather than simple 'conditioned' responses. The rat in the box learnt to adopt behaviour that brought reward (the pellet of food) and to avoid behaviour that brought punishment (an electric shock). This learnt behavioural change is referred to as 'operant conditioning'. It recognised that behaviour can be reinforced. It is affected by its consequences, but the process is not simply trial-and-error learning—positive or negative reinforcement can be used.

Behaviour reinforcement

Behaviour can be changed by giving reinforcement following the desired response.

Behaviour reinforcement can be positive or negative: **positive reinforcement** strengthens behaviour; **negative reinforcement** can also strengthen behaviour through the removal of an unpleasant reinforcer.

Obviously, in current practice we cannot and do not use anything like the electric shock 'punishment' or behavioural deterrent, but the principles of reinforcement (positive and negative) are widely used for behaviour modification. More subtle variations of the carrot (reward—positive reinforcement) and the stick (punishment—negative reinforcement) are used to build desired behaviour in children and to discourage undesired behaviour.

Applying science to infant care/environment

Skinner was a huge enthusiast for the possibilities of science and his vision extended to technological innovation that incorporated scientific principles for child health.

The 'air crib', developed by Skinner for his second child Deborah, was a 'climate controlled environment' for babies (Joyce & Faye, 2010). It is not to be confused with 'Skinner's box', though both creations used the behaviourist principle of controlling 'behaviour' by controlling the environment.

The air crib was intended to be the application of scientific principles for controlling a child's environment to improve the physical health and comfort of the child and to make infant care more routinised and less onerous for parents.

> In that brave new world which science is preparing for the house-wife of the future, the young mother has apparently been forgotten. Almost nothing has been done to ease her lot by simplifying and improving the care of babies ... We asked only one question: Is this practice important for the physical and psychological health of the baby?

> (Skinner, cited in Cleverley & Phillips, 1987, p.125)

Most of my Initial Teacher Education (ITE) students react with horror at the idea of the 'air crib': it seems to them to be science gone mad, and looks like a science experiment that would be better suited to rats than children. This seems to be a common response, and not surprisingly, the air crib was not adopted into widespread child-rearing practices. While we might reject Skinner's air crib, his insistence that this was scientifically sound in keeping young, vulnerable children in a climate-controlled, safe environment, away from the dangers of open fires, animals, stairs and germs—and even with the benefit of allowing freedom of movement, unencumbered by clothing—is accurate. It is interesting to note also, that there is no 'horror' associated with the use of humidicribs for premature babies: these are life-saving.

Again, our image of the child is relevant here.

STOP AND THINK

- What is your response to Skinner's air crib?
- What aspects of development and learning does the air crib prioritise?
- What aspects of development and learning are overlooked?
- What might the effects be on children and their sense of 'belonging', 'becoming' and 'being'?

negative reinforcement strengthening behaviour by removing an unpleasant reinforcer

positive reinforcement reinforcement through reward; used to strengthen behaviour

ESTELLE IRVING

The Early Years Learning Framework (EYLF)

The EYLF is the national framework applicable to the practice of *all* early childhood professionals in Australia. The EYLF is referenced in many chapters in this book, but in this chapter our interest is specifically on the image of the child it conveys.

'Belonging, Being & Becoming' are the themes of the EYLF and they link to the image of the child. Echoing Malaguzzi, in the EYLF children are seen as capable and active learners, with the capacity and right to contribute to their own learning, to 'actively construct their own understandings and contribute to others' learning' and to be involved in decisions about their own learning (DEEWR, 2009, p.9).

> Viewing children as active participants and decision makers opens up possibilities for educators to move beyond pre-conceived expectations about what children can do and learn. This requires educators to respect and work with each child's unique qualities and abilities.
>
> (DEEWR, 2009, p.9)

Importantly, children's learning is seen as 'dynamic, complex and holistic'.

'Being' specifically 'recognises the significance of the here and now in children's lives' and 'Childhood is a time to be, to seek and make meaning of the world' (DEEWR, 2009, p.7). This emphasis is explicitly on how children understand, interact and make sense of the world and their experiences, including their relationships with others. This emphasis on the child's meaning-making and the message that the everyday, lived experiences of children are valuable in themselves is at variance with theorists such as Wesley, for whom childhood was only considered to be preparation for adulthood. Childhood as such had no value, and concepts such as agency and 'being' were not just irrelevant, but dangerous.

The EYLF articulates 'practice principles' to guide educators in their goal of 'ensuring that children in all early childhood education and care settings experience quality teaching and learning' (DEEWR, 2009, p.5). The EYLF takes for granted that all early childhood educators (including teachers) must themselves be 'trained' in the care and education of children, and that this is important work. This echoes Froebel's claim that 'First, then, our enterprise will give a training in the care of children'.

With further echoes from Froebel, the EYLF has a specific emphasis on play-based learning. If we return to an earlier quote from Froebel, this link with the EYLF is now more visible and multilayered: it is not just the importance of play-based learning and the development of an appropriate 'curriculum' that links Froebel across two centuries to the twenty-first century EYLF, it is also the value each gives to relationships: 'He [the child] must be understood not only in his nature but also *in his relationships*, and treated in ways which are appropriate'.

Compare that statement with this from the EYLF: 'Their [children's] earliest development and learning takes place through these relationships, particularly within families ...' (DEEWR, 2009, p.7). These themes of the importance of relationships to early childhood teaching and learning and the specific 'practice principle' of working in partnerships with families are the subjects of Chapters 13 and 14.

Locke's presence is also evident in the EYLF. Specific links back to Locke's view of the child and early childhood education are evident in the shared focus of following the interests of children and encouraging learning that inspires a love of learning. The conviction that early experiences matter, and that they form the foundation of all later learning, is also a legacy we can trace from Locke to the EYLF.

Reflective practice

The question that framed this chapter—'What is a child?'—links to a key practice for current early childhood teachers. This practice is called *reflective practice*. This involves ongoing, active thinking about (or *interrogating*) one's own beliefs, values, assumptions and prejudices, and how these shape what we do, including how we manage, care for and educate children.

To illustrate this, let us return to the first scenario in this chapter, where we left Jo screaming when the movement of the mobile stopped. Behind Jo's mother's actions we can identify four questions that provide a foundation for reflective practice for all teachers, and especially for early childhood teachers:

1 What is she doing?/What did she do? This question becomes the early childhood teacher's reflective practice question: *What am I doing?*
2 Why did she do that? This question becomes: *Why do I do what I do?*
3 What happens next?/What was the outcome? This question becomes: *What are the outcomes of what I do?*
4 How could she have managed this differently? This question becomes: *How could I do it differently (better)? And, if I did this, what might the outcome be?*

Imagine now that you are the *teacher* in a room where Jo is lying in the cot, watching the dancing movements of the mobile. What will you do? Why will you do that? What are the likely outcomes? When you consider these questions, reflect not just on what Jo does next (stops screaming? screams more intensely? shares your delight in the mobile?), but on what Jo might have *learnt* from this interaction and what the *meaning* of this is for her.

The excerpt from the EYLF below extends our understanding of reflective practice, and adds another term commonly used in early childhood literature: 'critical reflection'. You will hear more about both reflective practice and critical reflection in other chapters in this book and, no doubt, in your lectures. While you read this excerpt, think particularly about the second dot point: 'What theories, philosophies and understandings shape and assist my work?' and remember Malaguzzi's point that the 'theory within you pushes you to behave in certain ways; it orients you as you talk to the child, listen to the child, observe the child' (1993, p.9).

> Reflective practice is a form of ongoing learning that involves engaging with questions of philosophy, ethics and practice. Its intention is to gather information and gain insights that support, inform and enrich decision-making about children's learning. As professionals, early childhood educators examine what happens in their settings and reflect on what they might change. Critical reflection involves closely examining all aspects of events and experiences from different perspectives. Educators often frame their reflective practice within a set of overarching questions, developing more specific questions for particular areas of enquiry. Overarching questions to guide reflection include:
>
> • What are my understandings of each child?
> • What theories, philosophies and understandings shape and assist my work?
> • Who is advantaged when I work in this way? Who is disadvantaged?
> • What questions do I have about my work? What am I challenged by? What am I curious about? What am I confronted by?
> • What aspects of my work are not helped by the theories and guidance that I usually draw on to make sense of what I do?

Cont.

ESTELLE IRVING

- Are there other theories or knowledge that could help me to understand better what I have observed or experienced? What are they? How might those theories and that knowledge affect my practice?

(DEEWR, 2009, p.13)

Critical reflection can also be applied to a set of assumptions about children that are part of the Western tradition of early childhood education and care.

Underlying assumptions

- Children are different from adults, and should be treated differently.
- Young children are seen as *important beings* who achieve their full potential through specialised care/education and in specific environments.
- Play is regarded as important to children's learning and development.
- Children should be segregated into age groups for their care and education. Though this is no longer so clearly the case in prior-to-school settings, it is a fundamental principle for school entry.
- Young children are worth investing in.
- Children are not just 'the future', and childhood is not about simply preparing children for an imagined adulthood: the here and now of their lived experiences of childhood matter.

As an exercise in 'reflective practice', consider the points above. You should now be familiar with the idea that these assumptions or beliefs are not universally shared.

This chapter opened with a quote from Loris Malaguzzi. It is appropriate now to return to Malaguzzi, this time to his conclusion about the image of the child he believed we *should* hold:

It's necessary that we believe that the child is very
intelligent, that the child is strong and beautiful
and has very ambitious desires and requests.
This is the image of the child we need to hold.

(Malaguzzi, 1993, p.12)

STOP AND THINK

- What is your response to Malaguzzi's statement?
- Why does Malaguzzi proclaim that seeing children as intelligent, strong and beautiful is necessary? Does this apply to all children, including for example, James Bulger's killers?
- Did Malaguzzi mean this literally and for all children in all circumstances, or is this statement intended as a general principle and the starting premise for our interactions with children?

United Nations Convention on the Rights of the Child (UNCRC) the key document that actively promotes an image of the child as a holder of specific rights in their own right.

Here is a final, explicit statement of a prevailing image of the child: this time the author is directing us towards a *rights-based* concept of children. I hope you will recognise that Rinaldi (the author) is an advocate of the Reggio Emilia approach. Rinaldi is referring to children's rights as a birth right, linked to agency, and to active and valued contributions made by children. Rinaldi is also indirectly referencing the **United Nations Convention on the Rights of the Child** (UNCRC, 1989). The convention is the key document that actively promotes an image of the child as a holder of specific rights in their own right—they are not derived from their parents or other adults. This important document is discussed in detail in Chapter 2. Its implications for your role as a teacher are considered in Chapter 10.

> Our image is of a child who possesses his or her own directions and the desire for knowledge and for life. A competent child!
>
> Competent in relating and interacting with a deep respect for others and accepting of conflict and error. A child who is competent in constructing; in constructing his or herself while constructing the world, and who is in return constructed by the world. Competent in constructing theories to interpret reality and in formulating hypotheses and metaphors as possibilities for understanding reality.
>
> A child who has his/her own values and is adept at building relationships of solidarity. A child who is always open to that which is new and different. A possessor and builder of future, not only because children are the future but because they constantly re-interpret reality and continuously give it new meanings.
>
> Our image is of the child as a possessor and constructor of rights, who demands to be respected and valued for his/her identity, uniqueness and difference.
>
> (Rinaldi, 2013, p.16)

A final note

The theorists and philosophers discussed in this chapter had clear concepts of childhood that were founded in their image of the child. For most of them, these concepts were carried through into educational programs and practices. However, it is important to note that these images and concepts were not necessarily applied to *all* children. Many of the theorists assumed that the children they 'saw' and referred to shared their own characteristics of sex*, race and class. 'Other' children, who did not share these characteristics, were either not seen at all, or were seen differently, with different qualities attributed to them. For example, I have already noted that Rousseau did not apply the same benevolent and inspirational philosophy of education to girls, whom he regarded as inferior and unworthy of education except to fulfil a subservient, domestic role.

STOP AND REFLECT

- When you reflect on your image of the child, what does this child look like?
- Does this child share your own characteristics, so that essentially you are seeing children who are like you?
- Are any children not included in this image and in your concept of childhood?
- As a teacher, you will work with a diversity of children: how will you ensure that your concept includes and respects this diversity?

---

*Gender is a twentieth-century concept, so though we now routinely use this lens, it was the lens of *sex* (male or female) that applied previously, with deeply held convictions about what were believed to be the natural differences between the sexes.

ESTELLE IRVING

SUMMARY

- Our image of the child shapes our interactions with children, including our practice as teachers.
- Paraphrasing Malaguzzi, our image of the child and concept of childhood is what drives and shapes our teaching philosophy and practice.
- An important aspect of the teacher's role is reflective practice. We can begin this by reflecting on our own image of the child.

FURTHER REFLECTION

How do you define children/childhood? In what ways do you think children differ from adults? These questions might help you answer this reflection question:

- What activities do you think characterise children?
- Is it useful to describe specific ages and stages in childhood? Explain your answer.
- When does childhood end? Is this satisfactorily defined by age or can we include other criteria?

GROUP DISCUSSION

1 How might the theorists you have been introduced to in this chapter account for the actions of James Bulger's killers?
2 What responsibility does society carry in this? If society is responsible, could this crime have been avoided? How?
3 Compare Wesley's perspective with how you think Froebel might understand this crime.
4 What 'solution' do you think Locke might suggest? How would this differ from Watson's answer to the vexed question of how such acts can be avoided?
5 Which do you think is more important: what we are born with (nature) or the environment (nurture)?

In small groups, discuss:
1 How do we become the people we are?
2 Is it nature (genes) or nurture (environment, child-rearing and education) that makes us who we are?
3 What is the role of education?
4 Can education change who we are? If so, is this limited to gaining more knowledge and understanding, or can this change be more profound? Reflect on your own experience of education, including what you think you will gain from your current studies.
5 Think back to the teachers you experienced when you were a child. What image of children (or concept of childhood) do you think they had?

CLASS EXERCISE

Collect a variety of prospectuses for schools and, paying close attention to the words and images that are used to promote the schools' approaches to education, categorise each in terms of which theorist they are most closely aligned to.

FURTHER READING

Cleverley, J. & Phillips, D.C. (1987) Visions of Childhood: Influential Models from Locke to Spock. St Leonards, NSW: Allen & Unwin.

I highly recommend this fascinating book; it provides examples of images and concepts of childhood and groups them under chapters that include 'On seeing children throughout history', 'The loss of innocence: the Freudian child' and 'The thinking machine'. It provided overall inspiration for this chapter. Many editions are available.

Malaguzzi, L. (1993) 'Your Image of the Child: Where Teaching Begins'. Seminar presented in Reggio Emilia, Italy, June 1993. www.reggioalliance.org/downloads/malaguzzi:ccie:1994

This is the article that invites us to consider our image of the child as 'where [our] teaching begins'. The article is thought-provoking and considers widely the role of the teacher. I recommend reading it to deepen your thinking about your role as a teacher.

Rinaldi, C. (2013) 'Re-Imagining Childhood', Department of the Premier and Cabinet, Government of South Australia.

This is a really important article that informed early childhood education and care policies in South Australia; it provides an interesting and inspiring overview of the Reggio Emilia approach.

REFERENCES

Bruce, T. (2012) *Early Childhood Practice: Froebel Today*. London: Sage.

Cleverley, J. & Phillips, D.C. (1987) *Visions of Childhood: Influential Models from Locke to Spock*. St Leonards, NSW: Allen & Unwin.

Department of Education, Employment and Workplace Relations (DEEWR) (2009) *Belonging, Being & Becoming: The Early Years Learning Framework for Australia*. ACT, Australia: Commonwealth of Australia.

Freud, S. (2001) *The Standard Edition of the Complete Psychological Works of Sigmund Freud*. London: Vintage, The Hogarth Press and the Institute of Psycho-Analysis.

Froebel, F. (2005) *The Education of Man* (originally published 1887; translated and annotated by W.N. Hailman). New York: Dover Publications, Inc.

Isaacs, S. (1929) *The Nursery Years: The Mind of the Child from Birth to Six Years*. London: Routledge.

Joyce, N. & Faye, C. (2010) 'Skinner Air Crib', *Observer*. APS, September.

Lawrence, E. (2012) *Friedrich Froebel and English Education* (vol. 45). London: Routledge.

Lilley, I. (2010) *Friedrich Froebel: A Selection from His Writings*. Cambridge: Cambridge University Press.

Locke, J. (1693) *Some Thoughts Concerning Education*. London: A and J Churchill.

Locke, J. (1959) *An Essay Concerning Human Understanding* (originally published 1690). London: Dent, Everyman's Library.

Malaguzzi, L. (1993) 'For an Education Based on Relationships' (translated by Lella Gandini), *Young Children*, November, *49*(1): 9–12.

Penn, H. (1997) *Comparing Nurseries: Staff and Children in Italy, Spain and the UK*: Paul Chapman.

Rinaldi, C. (2013) 'Re-Imagining Childhood', Department of the Premier and Cabinet, Government of South Australia.

Rousseau, J.J. (1979) *Émile or On Education* (translated by Allan Bloom). New York: Basic Books.

Skinner, B.F. (1953) *Science and Human Behaviour*. New York: Macmillan.

United Nations (1989) 'Convention on the Rights of the Child' (UNCRC). www.ohchr.org/EN/ProfessionalInterest/Pages/CRC.aspx

United Nations Educational Scientific and Cultural Organisation (2010) 'What Is Your Image of the Child?', *UNESCO Policy Brief on Early Childhood*, *47*, January–March.

Watson, J.B. (1928) *Psychological Care of Infant and Child*. New York: W.W. Norton.

Watson, J.B. (1930) *Behaviourism*. Chicago: University of Chicago Press.

Wesley, J. (1829) *The Works of the Reverend John Wesley: Sometime Fellow of Lincoln College* (3rd edn). Oxford, London: John Mason (eBook).

Wesley, J. & Emory, T. (1835) *The Works of the Late Reverend John Wesley: First American Complete Standard Edition*. New York: J Collard Publishers (eBook).

ESTELLE IRVING

CHAPTER 2

Social Construction of Childhood

Estelle Irving

Chapter objectives

In this chapter, you will:

- reflect on childhood as socially constructed
- consider the question, 'Has childhood always existed?'
- understand the link between childhood, technology and education
- discuss the concept of 'discourse' and engage in 'discourse analysis'
- be introduced to children's rights and the key twentieth-century statements of children's rights that record the changing social category and status of children.

Key terms

agentic child	modernity/modern era	socially constructed
discourse	social category	

> Childhood, we know, is a cultural interpretation and construct. Every society, and every historical period defines its own childhood in determining what is meant by, expected of and dedicated to childhood.
>
> (Rinaldi, 2013, 'Re-imagining childhood', p.17)

Figure 2.1

The boys and girls whom I examined from the Manchester factories very generally exhibited a depressed look, and a pallid complexion; none of the alacrity, activity, and hilarity of early life shone in their countenances [faces] and gestures.

(cited in Cleverley & Phillips, 1987, p.103)

This observation from an English doctor in 1833 could well have been made about the child whose photograph we see in Figure 2.1.

There is none of the joy and sense of wonder most of us associate with childhood: this boy looks blank, bewildered and exhausted by a life of labour and deprivation. His work is exhausting, his life is difficult and his life expectancy is short.

The photograph in Figure 2.2 is even more telling: by their size we can recognise them as children, but they are working in hideous conditions, controlled by the foreman who stands at their backs, overseeing their work.

Figure 2.2

These images of child workers in the industrial era of the early nineteenth century tell a story of exploitation and abuse—and of lost or non-existent childhoods—that is irreconcilable with current views of children as precious, innocent and needing special protection. Children like those shown here were used as labourers in mines and factories, precisely because they were small, compliant, cheap and expendable. Though parents no doubt loved their children, the birth of a child to working-class families meant a new mouth to feed, and, within a short time, by necessity,

ESTELLE IRVING

a source of labour to contribute to the family's finances. Their value was measured in economic terms—what they cost to rear and what they could contribute—not in the emotional terms we emphasise today. These children were regarded, at least by the factory and mine owners, as quite literally replaceable. If a child became sick, injured or otherwise incapable of working, they were discarded, to be replaced by another child. There were no sickness benefits or social support for any workers, let alone for children in this era. Their size—the only feature in the photograph above that makes these little beings recognisable as children—allowed them to fit between machines and their small hands gave them dexterity and fine motor skills for tasks such as weaving. These children were illiterate and, with very few exceptions, left no record of their experience; we can only speculate on what sense they made of their lives.

It is likely that these photographs were taken to be used as evidence of the exploitation of children, as proof that children were being treated as adults or worse, simply as a source of labour indistinguishable from animals. Some testimonials from child workers in this era were also recorded by parliamentary enquiries into child labour, as evidence of their exploitation and abuse. The resulting Commissioners' Reports were presented to the British Parliament. These accounts from children as young as six were published as Parliamentary Papers: they are heartbreakingly bleak. Here, for example, is the record, published in 1842, of the testimony of an eight-year-old girl, Sarah Gooder, who worked thirteen-hour days, mostly in darkness, as a 'trapper' (opening and shutting the air-trap door) in a British coal mine:

> I am a trapper at the Gauber Pit. I have to trap without a light, and I'm scared. I go at four and sometimes half past 3 in the morning and come out at 5 [pm]. I never go to sleep. Sometimes I sing when I've light, but not in the dark: I dare not sing then.
>
> (House of Commons, 1842, p.71)

Evidence of this sort to parliamentary enquiries into child labour, together with campaigning by social reformers, did eventually bring about laws that protected children from extremes of work-based exploitation. Prohibiting young children from working was one side of the legislation that protected them from exploitation of the sort so poignantly described by little Sarah Gooder; the other side was the requirement that children must attend at least basic schooling. The protection of children therefore involved provision of education. In that very direct sense, education was associated with the world of childhood, and it separated children from the 'adult' world of work.

The links between education to the emergence of a modern concept and status of childhood will be revisited later in the chapter.

Introduction

In Chapter 1, a foundational question was posed: 'What is a child?' It was suggested that this questioning is the necessary starting point for an early childhood teacher, as 'your image of the child is where your teaching begins' (Malaguzzi, 1993, unpaged). One of the key points established in Chapter 1 is that what we see when we look at a child is interpreted through a very specific *lens* of time and place and filtered through our culture. What we see, and what we imagine a child to be, in turn shapes our interactions with children, including the care and educational institutions our society provides, the laws and policies that are developed, and how and what we teach.

This chapter extends and broadens this discussion. It introduces the concept of childhood as a **social category** that is **socially constructed** and experienced differently in different time and place contexts. It will be helpful to relate this to Bronfenbrenner's ecological systems model introduced in the introduction of this book. In Bronfenbrenner's model, the child is at the centre, surrounded by complex, dynamic, interconnected environmental 'systems'. The 'chronosystem' that surrounds all the other systems highlights the significance of changing times, including changing childhoods.

Changing childhood

This chapter outlines key factors in the time and place context in which childhood as a distinct social category emerged. It makes links from the history of the emergence of modern childhood, to the changes occurring in contemporary Australian society and considers their impact on how childhood is currently constructed and experienced.

> **STOP AND REFLECT**
>
> - In what ways has childhood changed since you were a child? In your answer, be as wide-ranging as possible and consider:
>   - changes to what you owned and used (i.e. what we refer to as the material conditions of childhood)
>   - changes to what you did (i.e. your activities and how your day was spent) and what children do now
>   - changes to how you played and what you played with
>   - changes to how adults related to children
>   - changes to what was expected of children, including behaviours and what chores you were expected to do
>   - changes to care and education for children when you were a child, compared to the situation for children now.
> - Jot down what you think has brought about these changes.

It would be surprising if the list you produced from the reflective questions did not paint a picture of significant change. Among the many changes, one that often seems to resonate strongly with the pre-service teachers in my classes relates to the limited opportunities many children now have to roam and play outdoors.

It is likely that your 'picture' also looks back to a period of greater freedom for children to roam, play and explore outdoors, away from surveillance and supervision by adults. Chapter 4 examines this theme in detail. It begins with an account of the author's strong memories of playing with her sisters in the outdoors. The absence of adult surveillance allowed space for creating and experiencing a *culture of childhood*, with its own rules, rituals and shared sense of belonging, which specifically did not include adults. The sense of freedom and joy captured in the description of this outdoor play evokes a different time, with physical and social spaces claimed by and for children that would possibly be regarded as dangerous and inappropriate in today's society.

ESTELLE IRVING

socially constructed created in society and changing just as society itself changes.

social category childhood is differentiated as a life stage, separate from other age-based social categories in the lifespan, including the socially recognised category of the adolescent or teenager and adulthood.

But the 'freedom' allowed for children was conditional and only occurred in specific areas; it was not a total freedom to do and act as the child wanted. In your account of changes since you were a child, you might have noted that greater obedience and unquestioned respect for authority was routinely expected from children in the past. Parents (and teachers) were authority figures who, if they deemed it appropriate, physically punished children who were considered to be disobedient or challenging. This practice was widely socially accepted and it was part of my experience of primary schooling; boys were quite routinely 'strapped' and girls were hit with a wooden ruler. So, while children were comparatively 'free' from adult surveillance and supervision when they were outside home and school, this freedom did not extend to social interactions with adults. Adults had authority and children were expected to submit to that authority, without question or challenge.

Technological innovations and electronic devices/tablets are very likely to be high on both your list of the changes and your account of what drives those changes. Keep technological innovations in mind, as they are important in the story of how and why modern childhood developed. We shall return to technological innovations later in the chapter.

Here are some of the responses from my ITE students when they brainstormed the 'Stop and reflect' questions in class. You might like to compare your responses to theirs. The changes they noted included:

- *family:* fewer siblings; less stable families; changing roles, expectations and responsibilities; pressure to buy the latest things for children
- *urbanisation:* fewer opportunities for escaping into the outdoors. This was linked to safety concerns, with children more supervised and not permitted to roam in the outdoor environment
- *media:* wide-ranging changes to how we all live, how we spend our time and how we communicate with others
- *work:* mothers working; blurring the distinction between work and private life/home
- *early childhood education and care provision:* children enter formal services earlier and for longer hours than many of the ITE students had themselves experienced
- *education:* duration has been extended; some students reported that their grandparents left school at fourteen or fifteen (or even younger) to enter the workforce; childhood ended well before the current Australian legal age of adulthood was attained
- *gender roles:* no longer is Mum at home, doing the domestic work (and caring for young children); Dads are more involved with child-rearing
- *technology:* children are more sedentary and are frequently looking at a screen; prevalence and use of electronic devices such as television, the internet and social media
- *financial pressures:* greater costs of child-rearing (e.g. of childcare and education)
- *paid care:* children looked after by non-family members rather than by neighbours or extended family
- *activities:* more structured for children now, and busy schedules of extra-curricula classes.

Another area of change identified by the students that has special relevance to ITE— including early childhood education and care provisions and settings—is the greater accountability (and expectations) of professionals, including teachers, who work with children. Given some of the practices in the past, including the use of corporal punishment in schools, this was noted as a positive gain for children.

We can add to this list of changes:

- *globalisation*: political, social and economic. Though not a new phenomenon, the influence of globalisation is intensifying and profoundly affecting many aspects of how we live, and our sense of connection and community
- *consumerism*: growth of a consumer economy and commodification of many services that were previously provided in families or communities. Childcare is an obvious example of this
- *possessions*: cheap production of toys, clothes and other children's possessions mean that children today almost certainly have more 'things' than previous generations. In addition, children are now targeted by advertising as consumers, and they are more aware of brands.

You have probably already noted that many of these changes are interrelated, underlining the interconnection identified in Bronfenbrenner's ecological systems model, in which personal lives are affected by external, public systems and institutions.

Collectively, these changes have created a new material, social and cultural context for childhood, changing the actual experiences of childhood and the ways in which we *see* and understand children and childhood.

Socially constructed childhood

The account above of child workers in industrial Britain and the sketch of changes that have occurred since your childhood (regardless of your current age) illustrate a central point in this chapter: childhood changes. It is not a fixed and universal experience. Instead, childhood is created in society and, as the 'Stop and reflect' exercise illustrates, it changes just as society itself changes. The term used to describe this is 'social construction'; childhood is a socially constructed social category, with a social status that also changes.

As discussed in Chapter 1, there are a variety of ways in which children are 'seen' and imagined, and this perception is the basis of a concept of childhood. But differences in childhood in different eras and places are more than differences of perception. Childhood is part of a society's structure (how society is organised) and its culture. As a social category, childhood is interpreted, experienced and enacted according to the specific political, social and cultural contexts of time and place.

Children have an *ascribed* status and value that reflects the social category of childhood in a specific time and place context. What this means is that the collective *status* and *value* of children as a group, and childhood as a stage of life, comes from the society and culture; it is not achieved by children individually. This ascribed status is different from the way individual children are valued in their own families. For example, though child workers may have been loved by their own parents in the early industrial era, their value in society was measured by their productivity: their status was that of a commodity that could be bought and sold, just as an object is.

Childhood is not defined or determined by biology; there are general norms and sequences of development and learning, but childhood itself is not pre-programmed in our DNA.

> The biological facts of infancy are but the raw material upon which cultures work to fashion a particular version of 'being a child'... what a child is reflects the particularities of particular sociocultural contexts.
>
> (Jenks, 2005, p.129)

ESTELLE IRVING

All cultures recognise the period of infancy as separate and different from other periods in the human lifespan. Given the complete dependency of babies for meeting their basic survival needs, it would be astonishing if this were not the case (and suicidal for any society that did not provide special protection and provision for infants). However, beyond this recognised period of infancy—which ends between the ages of five and seven, when these 'little beings' can reasonably competently feed and dress themselves, talk/communicate and perform basic work skills (e.g. cleaning, gardening)—childhood means very different things in different cultures and socio-historical contexts.

Childhood as an idea, a social category and a lived experience does not just happen automatically: it develops out of certain conditions, and it changes as these conditions change.

Has childhood always existed?

The variation in the status and value of childhood suggests an important question: Has childhood always existed?

In the 1960s, social historian Philippe Ariès published *Centuries of Childhood: A Social History of Family Life*. Using a range of historical artefacts and evidence that included personal diaries, memoirs, clothing, toys, literature and representations in art of the times, Ariès concluded that there was no evidence of differentiation between children and adults. Children, for example, wore smaller versions of 'adult' clothes; children and adults played the same games, ate the same food and participated in the same work. 'Children' were, according to Ariès, simply smaller versions of adults.

On the basis of this evidence, Ariès made what was at the time regarded as an astonishing claim: he asserted that in medieval France, the social category of childhood/children did not exist. The actual term he used was 'sentiment'. There was, he claimed, no sentiment of childhood in that place and historical period. Without an idea or sentiment of childhood, 'small people' who we would now identify as children, were in that time and place, Ariès claimed, simply seen and treated as 'miniature adults'.

To understand this requires a short account of society at that time. Technology and information exchange is at the heart of this account. First, the society that Ariès studied was a traditional, rural, peasant society. Peasants' lives are ruled by nature and the cycle of seasons and tied to planting and harvesting, so the technology was very simple: a hoe for digging the soil, for example, or a scythe for cutting the hay. In that technologically simple society, a long period of apprenticeship or education was not needed and even young 'children' could participate in the work of the community.

The second key point is that peasants in that period were illiterate; they could not read or write and they had no need for these skills. Information was shared orally and only the aristocracy or church leaders had access to written records and books. In oral societies, children are not separated from adults for their education. Instead, it is only through their interactions with adults that children can acquire oral-based knowledge. Talk, songs, chants, sermons and communally shared stories were the mechanisms through which cultural practices, values, traditions and history were passed on from one generation to the next. Similarly, the physical, work-based skills (including hoeing, harvesting, cooking, weaving) required for a person to contribute productively to the pre-literate peasant society could only be learnt though talking with, observing and working alongside more experienced people—that is, 'doing' rather than abstract learning or theorising. No detailed manual of instruction was needed. Since social interaction is essential for this learning and social participation, the separation of children for their education, as occurs now, would have been counter-productive and absurd.

Peasant society was undifferentiated by age-based divisions because age was largely irrelevant to the everyday lives of the peasants. Participation in the social and work life of the village or hamlet was dependent upon a person's ability to comprehend speech, to talk and to work. It was not dependent upon age, except in the sense that the very young (like the very old) are less physically able than healthy, able-bodied and physically mature people.

By contrast, currently in Australian society, age is one of the most significant criteria for access to resources and services, including of course, to educational institutions (pre-school and school in particular). We are now so focused on fine gradations of age that most children can tell you precisely how old they are. We record birth dates and celebrate birthdays, highlighting the significance of 'milestone' ages, which are tied to social status. Age is one of the first things we teach children, and of course it really is important in many ways. Age (rather than ability) is the single criterion for entry into many of our other social and cultural institutions, including school. Age is, for example, the 'gate-keeper' criterion for driving, voting, drinking alcohol, marriage, age of consent—and, as discussed in Chapter 1, age itself is used to define the socio-legal category of childhood.

In some cultures, children must publicly demonstrate their maturity. For example, in Jewish culture, the bar-mitzvah (for boys) and the bat-mitzvah (for girls) require children to commit to a period of study and display their learning to the community as a ritual rite-of-passage into adulthood. In this case, adulthood status within their community is 'achieved'. For most Australian children, however, adulthood is not 'achieved'—turning eighteen automatically gives them adult status. Regardless of culture or ethnicity though, this is the age at which a person legally ceases to be a child and is defined as an adult, even if they are otherwise in a dependent position of living at home with their parents, and still being educated. What is assumed, however, in assigning adult status at the age of eighteen, is that people of that age will have gained the attributes of an adult and will, therefore, be able to participate in and contribute to society. Literacy is key to this participation, and the twelve or so years of education up to the age of eighteen are assumed to have provided adult-level literacy.

By contrast, in rural, pre-industrial peasant society, adulthood and childhood were seamlessly joined. No peasant child in that context ever proclaimed 'I am two and three-quarters. In two years I will go to school!' as my grand-daughter recently told me. For her, age is the key to going to school; for the peasant child in medieval France, this would have been incomprehensible.

The social category and status of childhood that we recognise now had no place in that society. 'Social category' here means that childhood is differentiated as a life stage, separate from other age-based social categories in the lifespan, including the socially recognised category of the adolescent or teenager (another socially constructed, and relatively recent, phenomenon) and adulthood. None of these categories would have made sense to an illiterate peasant. This does not mean, though, that medieval peasant families did not have affection or love for their offspring. In Ariès's words:

ESTELLE IRVING

> The idea of childhood is not to be confused with affection for children: it corresponds to an awareness of the particular nature of childhood, that particular nature which distinguishes the child from the adult, even the young adult. That is why, as soon as the child could live without the constant solicitude of his mother, his nanny or his cradle-rocker, he belonged to adult society.
>
> (Ariès, 1962, p.128)

Bruegel's painting in Figure 2.3 of peasant life in Europe in the nineteenth century depicts the shared life of peasants, with 'adults' and 'children' wearing the same clothes and engaging in the same activities. As a record of the society, it is a type of evidence of the lack of age-based social categories: people of different relative sizes are playing together—play and work involved everyone. 'Children' observed and were involved in all aspects and activities of human life, births and deaths included.

Emergence of the idea and social category of childhood

Clues to when and how the idea and social category of childhood emerged are scattered throughout the previous discussion: they relate to the interconnection between technological innovation and changes in how information was communicated and retained. Education is the 'hero' in this story of the emergence (or construction) of modern childhood, and literacy was the key to the importance of education. In turn, changes in these factors were intertwined with wide-ranging social changes, including changes to families.

Figure 2.3

> ### STOP AND REFLECT
>
> Re-read the paragraph above that outlines the intertwined factors of technological advancement, literacy and education. Take each factor separately and reflect on how each one relates to changes in childhood.

As Western societies became more technologically advanced, other aspects of society were affected and social relations, work and communications also changed.

In Ariès's thesis, the emergence of childhood is associated with the rise of **modernity** (or the **modern era**), starting from around the sixteenth century in Europe. Modernity is the period of the rise of science and associated technological advancement. One particular technology is associated with this emergence of a modern concept of childhood as separate from adulthood. That technology is the printing press.

Prior to the printing press, books were created by hand, not by machines. They were precious, rare and impossibly expensive for any but the rich and powerful. As we discussed earlier, they were also irrelevant to an illiterate peasant who had no need for the knowledge they contained. The advent of the printing press, attributed to Gutenberg in the mid fifteenth century, led to changes that, over time, changed this.

What the printing press allowed was the *mass production* of books and pamphlets: this in turn significantly reduced the cost of producing written works and, over time, books and pamphlets became affordable and accessible to a wider population. As written communication increased and became more expected, so too did the importance of accessing and exchanging information through reading and writing. The printing press 'created a new symbolic world' (Postman, 1989, p.21) with symbols that had to be coded and decoded. Coding (writing) and decoding (reading) are complex, learnt skills that need to be taught.

Full social participation, including access to the resources and opportunities of society, is now dependent upon a person's literacy. This is precisely why literacy is given so much attention in early childhood education. Acquiring literacy is not biologically driven and part of natural development. On the contrary, it requires instruction and takes time; formal education is needed. Chapter 7 will give you an appreciation of the complexities (and rewards) of teaching and learning literacy, and its importance in contemporary society.

Such education generally requires the separation of the pre-literate child from the literate adult (except, of course, the trained literacy teacher who delivers the curriculum) for a significant period of time. Even with formal education, a child of five or even ten years has not yet achieved the level of literacy required for full social, political and economic participation. Until at least the level of functional literacy is acquired, the child is in a position of dependency on adults who are fully literate. It is not their age as such that is the issue, but their lack of the adult skill of reading and writing.

An increasingly intense and extended period of education is needed to allow development of the specialised skills and knowledge required in current Australian society. These skills and this knowledge are not limited to literacy—as the 'learning and teaching' chapters that follow will illustrate—but literacy is the foundation of access to all these skills and knowledge. Imagine, for example, the difficulty of learning science or mathematics to any level of sophistication if you could not read.

modernity/ modern era the period of the rise of science and associated technological advancement.

ESTELLE IRVING

It is not just school-based learning that requires literacy to access. The illiterate (including illiterate adults) are excluded from full and meaningful participation in society; they have the dependent and immature status of children.

STOP AND THINK

- What is important about the printing press?
- What does the printing press do?
- How does this relate to literacy?
- How does the printing press, linked to literacy, drive changes in education that, over time, lead to changes in childhood as a social category?

STOP AND REFLECT

- Think about your life and the importance of being able to read and write.
- Briefly record all the things you have done in the past 24 hours.
- How many of those things are accessed through literacy?
- What would you be excluded from if you were illiterate?

The printing press, though a particularly important technological innovation, was only one innovation that emerged to transform traditional peasant society. The weaving looms that created employment for many children in factories are another example of a technological innovation that had wider social ramifications, including in this case, the exploitation of child workers.

Technological innovations do not occur in a vacuum; they emerge in periods of wider change and, in turn, they link to wider social changes. The printing press, however, is a particularly significant element in the process that led to modern society and the creation of childhood. Separating children from adults, and positioning pre-literate children as dependent and immature, are aspects of the 'sentiment' of childhood that Ariès referred to.

In simple terms, technology (the printing press) and the need it ultimately created for a prolonged period of academic education delivered by experts, with children removed from family and working life, created the separate social category and status of childhood.

There are strong parallels between the importance of literacy in modern society and computer literacy, which is now increasingly required for full social and cultural participation and access to the resources and opportunities of contemporary Australian society. You might like to return to the 'Stop and reflect' questions above and replace being able to read and write with 'access to and ability to use' electronic communication technologies. How many services now assume that potential customers have access to the internet and iPhones, for example?

A parallel communication and information-exchange revolution, similar to that which occurred because of the printing press, is currently happening with the growing dominance and importance of computer literacy. People who do not know how to purchase items or pay bills online, or download forms or make bookings online, are at risk of being excluded from these social activities and opportunities. But, while these skills will increasingly be required for social, political and cultural access, actual reading and writing remain the foundation skills for accessing information and engaging in communication, regardless of the platform for this.

This has been a broad account of the emergence of childhood as a distinct social category, with an attached social status. As we saw in Chapter 1, there have been many variations in actual concepts of childhood, and different ways in which children have been treated, cared for and educated. The overarching commonality between all the theorists and their images of the child and concepts of childhood is that they all regarded childhood as a distinct *stage of life*, and one that is *categorically different* from adulthood.

Is childhood disappearing?

Ariès's claim (supported by a range of evidence) that childhood did not exist in medieval France has been contested by a number of theorists (see, for example, Heywood, 2010), but its central thesis that a sentiment of childhood comparable to the modern sentiment of childhood did not exist, is not disputed. The evidence Ariès presented clearly demonstrated a different perception of 'children', and more importantly for our discussion here, a lack of distinction between children and adults as social categories.

Ariès's thesis raises another question that has particular relevance today: If childhood is a socially constructed category and status that arises out of specific conditions, is it possible for the reverse to occur and for childhood to disappear?

In the list of changes to childhood at the start of the chapter, technological change was noted as being important. We noted briefly above that electronic communication technologies are increasingly required for social participation, but they are only one of the 'screens' that are now part of everyday life. Children are 'digital natives' for whom these screens and technologies are taken for granted and used with ease.

> From the beginnings of life, children in the twenty-first century typically develop in front of a screen. Once solely television based, these screen media have now evolved to be digital, interactive, pervasive, and increasingly under the control of those who use them.
>
> (Calvert & Wilson, 2010, p.1)

There is little doubt that these devices are changing experiences of childhood—including how children learn and how we teach—and challenging the concept of childhood.

These challenges and changes are important, but I want to focus here on another technology (apart from the printing press) that has transformed childhood: the television.

Television was introduced to Australia in 1956, timed for broadcasting the Olympic Games held in Melbourne in that year. Television is now so much a part of family life and childhood that it may be hard even to imagine a time when it was not a household feature. From its introduction, a range of concerns have been raised about television. Concerns specifically about the impact of television on early childhood development include concerns about the effects of viewing violent and/or sexualised content, promotion of consumerism and lack of physical activity. These concerns led the American Academy of Pediatrics to recommend 'no screen' exposure before the age of two years (Royal Children's Hospital, 2009). As a side note, the guidelines for screen time were modified in 2017. This was not because the paediatricians changed their mind about the effects of television, but because of the pervasiveness of screens in almost all environments, and the range of screens that children interact with now. These 'screens' are ubiquitous and varied, so their impacts need to be considered separately. To apply a 'one size fits all' approach to guidelines for children's viewing of screens is no longer viable.

According to one theorist, though, the real significance of television is far deeper than just as a source of passive, sometimes violent and essentially sedentary entertainment that has the potential to compromise the health and wellbeing of young children. Neil Postman attributes television to what he terms 'the disappearance of childhood'. Postman's argument links to the importance of literacy in the development of a modern childhood. He argues that children's lack of literacy in the pre-television world contributed to the perception of children as innocent and needing protection from the adult world, and the separation of children (whose lives were shaped by play and education) from the work-centred, adult world. This adult world that children are separated and protected from is, according to Postman, not so much about the pressures of work, but 'secrets and shames' of adult behaviours and failures.

> The absence of literacy, the absence of the idea of education, the absence of the idea of shame—these are the reasons why the idea of childhood did not exist in the medieval world.
>
> (Postman, 1989, p.17)

It is important to understand that Postman is referring to the *idea* of childhood; his claim is that children 'have been expelled from the garden of childhood' (Postman, 1989, p.97) through their exposure to adult secrets and shames that were hidden from them when print was the medium of communication and information exchange. If you have ever spelt out or written down instead of speaking a word that you did not want children who were present to understand (divorce, sex or death, for example) you will have an idea of what Postman is referring to here. 'Not since the Middle Ages [medieval era] have children known so much about adult life as now' (Postman, 1989, p.97). How do children learn about the 'adult world' and all its failings and shameful secrets? The answer is, through television.

The argument put forward by Postman is two-fold:

1 He refers to television as an open-access medium or, more strongly, a 'total disclosure medium' (1989, p.81). Accessing television does not require any special instruction or education—unlike writing, which requires the ability to decode symbols in order to access information. Toddlers are perfectly capable of turning televisions on, and once on, of watching and processing the images and sounds. Once the television is on, children are exposed to every aspect of 'adult' life, including violence, sex, natural disasters and wars. In a society where information was accessed either orally or through print, children could be protected from such knowledge.

Of course children view television differently from adults, but so too do adults watch, interpret and respond to television shows and scripts differently. No two people will 'see' television in exactly the same way.

> In a literate world, to be an adult implies having access to cultural secrets codified in unnatural symbols. In a literate world, children become adults [though acquiring literacy]. But in a non-literate world, there is no need to distinguish sharply between the child and the adult, for there are few secrets, and the culture does not need to provide training in how to understand itself.
>
> (Postman, 1989, p.9)

2 Children on television are depicted as essentially 'miniature adults'. They are portrayed as sexualised, knowing, consumers, advisors to adults, and they wear clothes and engage in activities that are virtually indistinguishable from those of adults.

At the same time, according to Postman, adults are depicted on television as a sort of big child:

> Everywhere one looks, it may be seen that the behaviour, language, attitudes and desires—even the physical appearance of adults and children are becoming increasingly indistinguishable.

(Postman, 1989, p.13)

What Postman is describing is a blurring of the social categories of adult and child: he refers to the 'adultified' child and their mirror image, the 'childified' adult (Postman, 1989, p.126). This is, he argues, a reversing of the process Ariès described in the creation or emergence of the modern concept (sentiment) and social category of childhood. Here is how Postman describes the 'childified' adult depicted on television:

> With few exceptions, adults on television do not take their work seriously (if they work at all), they do not nurture children, they have no politics, practice no religion, represent no tradition, have no foresight of serious plans, have no extended conversations and in no circumstances allude to anything that is not familiar to an eight-year-old person.

(Postman, 1989, pp.126–7)

The qualities and characteristics that Postman describes as lacking in representations of adults on television are the qualities and characteristics that he associates with adulthood.

STOP AND THINK

- Do you think Postman is right in this?
- What is your response to Postman's argument?
- In considering this, think about the messages conveyed on television about the adult world. What images of the world do we see on television?
- Are these themes of adult failures and shames?
- Do you agree with Postman that children on television (and in the media generally) are depicted as 'miniature adults'? If so, what does this say about adults?
- What (if any) evidence has Postman not considered in his conclusion that childhood is disappearing?

Postman's book was first published in 1989. This means that though it was published in the same year as the world wide web (www) arrived, Postman would not have been aware of this innovation and he could not have anticipated the developments in electronic/digital communication. Perhaps, though, he would have anticipated that young children would become more familiar with and more adept at using the new technologies than adults are. In some ways, the role of the adult as the knowledgeable 'teacher' and the child as needing instruction has been reversed—at least in families where children assist their parents with using these technologies.

ESTELLE IRVING

Childhood in contemporary Australia

Changes to contemporary childhood have been outlined earlier in the chapter, and you have reflected on these in a 'Stop and reflect' exercise.

Here, we will focus on a particular element of change that has altered children's status and the **discourse** around childhood in contemporary Australian society. The focus is 'children's rights'. Changes in the ways children's rights have been understood and articulated vividly illustrate wider changes to the concept of childhood and to children's status. They also link directly to current priorities in early childhood education and care.

What follows is a particularly important example of these changes to the concept of childhood, the status of children and the link to (or expression in) early childhood education, pedagogy and curriculum.

In a paper prepared for the South Australian Government, 'Re-imagining Childhood', Carla Rinaldi from Reggio Emilia explicitly challenged policy makers, politicians, universities, schools, services and teachers to 're-imagine' childhood. She suggested that this was necessary because, she said, the prevailing image of the child at the time promoted a 'deterministic identification of the child as a weak subject, a person with needs rather than rights' (Rinaldi, 2013, p.15). Rinaldi was determined to replace this 'deficit' model— which focused on what children cannot do, rather than recognising their competencies and strengths—with a new image of the competent child. This image can be seen in the policy and practice recommendations she made in the report. The first recommendation is particularly important as it encapsulates the new image Rinaldi is proposing.

Recommendation 1:

Children are citizens from birth.

1.1 Declare the child as the 'competent child' and a possessor of rights. This declaration should be made as a preamble to legislation on child development.

1.2 Changing the language of relevant legislation to included learning and the nature of learning as beginning at birth.

1.3 Conducting a complete review of existing State policies and practices with the lens of the child as a fully participating citizen from birth.

(Rinaldi, 2013, p.43)

As you become more familiar with the EYLF, you will recognise Rinaldi's 'voice' in the image of the child that is promoted in the EYLF, and in its practice principles. Here is an extract from Rinaldi's paper that relates to the environment of early childhood teaching and learning 'spaces':

The objective is ... to construct and organize spaces that enable children:

- to express their potential, abilities and curiosity;
- to explore and research alone and with others, both peers and adults;
- to perceive themselves as constructors of projects and of the overall educational project carried out in the school;
- to reinforce their identities, autonomy and sense of security;
- to work and communicate with others;
- to know that their identities and privacy are respected.

(Rinaldi, 2013, p.47)

discourse
the ideas and frameworks (or paradigms) that dominate social thinking and discussion and, in so doing, 'silence' or marginalise alternative voices or views.

Rinaldi's recommendations and her plea to policy makers and teachers to 're-imagine the child' have been significant in driving changes to early childhood education and care provision. At the core of Rinaldi's paper is a new articulation of the 'rights' of the child, and the corresponding obligations for adults.

STOP AND THINK

Look carefully at the points Rinaldi identified as the objectives for constructing and organising spaces for children.

Consider each one separately in terms of what it says about children's rights.

Now look back to Rinaldi's recommendations, and, focusing on point 1.1, consider this image of the competent child who has rights and link this to the questions below.

- What does this tell you about how early childhood education should be set up and delivered?
- What are the implications for you as a pre-service teacher?
- What rights do you think a child has or should have?

Children's rights

The concept of children's rights is widely accepted in Australia (and many other countries) in the twenty-first century. The quotes below express some of the excitement of early childhood professionals' responses to the key document that articulates children's rights: the United Nations Convention on the Rights of the Child (1989), to which Australia became a signatory nation (i.e. agreeing to uphold the 54 Articles of the Convention) in 1990.

> We are all talking about the new sociology of childhood and how it positions children as full members of society. We are learning to think of children as having rights 'in the now', and not to think of ourselves as being responsible for making decisions on their behalf. Despite this, we still struggle with discourses that position the early years as a time to 'prepare' the future adult and citizen.
>
> (Sims, 2007, p.ii)

> Children share meaning and power with adults (teachers and family members), have their voices heard and acted on, develop agency through having the opportunity to take initiative and play responsible roles, and have their strengths and interests respected. Such a model encourages children to be active citizens, to take control over their own activities, and to be purposeful members of their communities.
>
> (Smith, 2007, p.4)

Though it is now nearly thirty years since the Convention was created, it remains the most significant expression of children's rights. Behind the Convention is a history that began (indirectly) with the legal protections of children in the mid-to-late nineteenth century. These early 'rights' concerned protection of children from extremes of exploitation in workplaces, including specifying the minimum age at which children could be employed and the maximum hours of work per day that older children could be engaged in. The other side of these 'rights' was the provision of compulsory education. These 'rights' were, by current standards, very limited and they perpetuated an image of the child as dependent and vulnerable. In the context of the early industrial era, this was a reasonable view of children.

ESTELLE IRVING

In the twentieth century, an extended idea of children's rights took root, and over time, flourished. In Australia, the birth of the nation through federation of the states and territories in 1901 highlighted the idea that children were future citizens and should be invested in and provided for appropriately. Scientific discoveries at the time suggested that providing for children's health and welfare could have not only lasting positive effects on their wellbeing but also flow-on benefits for the nation. There were also those who believed that, given the 'correct' type of education, children were the best option for ensuring the development of a 'brotherhood of man' and ensuring lasting world peace.

These dual concerns—the need to protect children and to provide for or invest in them for the good of humanity—are reflected in the first international, universally applicable statement of children's rights: the League of Nations Geneva Declaration of the Rights of the Child, adopted in 1924.

Geneva Declaration of the Rights of the Child (1924)

The League of Nations (later to become the United Nations) adopted the Geneva Declaration of the Rights of the Child (1924) on 26 September 1924.

The preamble reads:

> By the present Declaration of the Rights of the Child, commonly known as 'Declaration of Geneva,' men and women of all nations, recognizing that mankind owes to the Child the best that it has to give, declare and accept it as their duty that, beyond and above all considerations of race, nationality or creed:
>
> 1 The child must be given the means requisite for its normal development, both materially and spiritually;
> 2 The child that is hungry must be fed; the child that is sick must be nursed; the child that is backward must be helped; the delinquent child must be reclaimed; and the orphan and the waif must be sheltered and succored;
> 3 The child must be the first to receive relief in times of distress;
> 4 The child must be put in a position to earn a livelihood, and must be protected against every form of exploitation;
> 5 The child must be brought up in the consciousness that its talents must be devoted to the service of fellow men.

As the wording of the 1924 declaration suggests, its developers were concerned with *protecting* and *providing* for children; this reflected its time and place origins in the aftermath of the First World War and the concerns the war raised about the plight of many children whose lives were disrupted by war. The reference in the preamble to 'men and women of all nations' and the duty that 'mankind owes to the Child … beyond and above all considerations of race, nationality or creed' is a direct response to the devastation of the First World War and the creation of the League of Nations as a mechanism to unite countries and safeguard against future conflict.

The Geneva Declaration was very much a product of the political, social and economic times in which it was drafted. The 'rights' it stipulated were limited, but it was, at the time, a significant declaration and it provided a new way of thinking about children as having rights that were separate from their families, and different from general human rights.

United Nations Declaration of the Rights of the Child (1959)

The Geneva Declaration was the predecessor to the United Nations Declaration of the Rights of the Child (1959), which was adopted by the General Assembly on 20 November 1959. The 1959 declaration significantly expands the range and number of 'rights', but like its predecessor, it also expresses rights as protections and provisions based on the recognition of children as vulnerable and requiring special protections.

Here is the preamble to the 1959 declaration and the principles that specifically concern education.

Preamble

Whereas the child, by reason of his physical and mental immaturity, needs special safeguards and care, including appropriate legal protection, before as well as after birth,

Whereas the need for such special safeguards has been stated in the Geneva Declaration of the Rights of the Child of 1924, and recognized in the Universal Declaration of Human Rights and in the statutes of specialized agencies and international organizations concerned with the welfare of children,

Whereas mankind owes to the child the best it has to give,

Now therefore, The General Assembly

Proclaims this Declaration of the Rights of the Child to the end that he may have a happy childhood and enjoy for his own good and for the good of society the rights and freedoms herein set forth, and calls upon parents, upon men and women as individuals, and upon voluntary organizations, local authorities and national Governments to recognize these rights and strive for their observance by legislative and other measures progressively taken in accordance with the following principles:

Principle 5

The child who is physically, mentally or socially handicapped shall be given the special treatment, education and care required by his particular condition.

Principle 6

The child, for the full and harmonious development of his personality, needs love and understanding. He shall, wherever possible, grow up in the care and under the responsibility of his parents, and, in any case, in an atmosphere of affection and of moral and material security; a child of tender years shall not, save in exceptional circumstances, be separated from his mother. Society and the public authorities shall have the duty to extend particular care to children without a family and to those without adequate means of support. Payment of State and other assistance towards the maintenance of children of large families is desirable.

Principle 7

The child is entitled to receive education, which shall be free and compulsory, at least in the elementary stages. He shall be given an education which will promote his general culture and enable him, on a basis of equal opportunity, to develop his abilities, his individual judgement, and his sense of moral and social responsibility, and to become a useful member of society.

The best interests of the child shall be the guiding principle of those responsible for his education and guidance; that responsibility lies in the first place with his parents.

ESTELLE IRVING

The child shall have full opportunity for play and recreation, which should be directed to the same purposes as education; society and the public authorities shall endeavour to promote the enjoyment of this right.

Principle 10

The child shall be protected from practices which may foster racial, religious and any other form of discrimination. He shall be brought up in a spirit of understanding, tolerance, friendship among peoples, peace and universal brotherhood, and in full consciousness that his energy and talents should be devoted to the service of his fellow men.

(United Nations Office of the High Commissioner, 1959)

STOP AND THINK

Compare the 1959 declaration with the 1924 Geneva declaration.

- How have the rights been expanded in the 1959 declaration?
- What remains the same?
- The preamble 'Proclaims this Declaration of the Rights of the Child to the end that he may have a happy childhood …' Do you consider this to be a priority? Can this be considered a 'right'?
- What rights do you think any and every child is entitled to? Why?

United Nations Convention on the Rights of the Child (1989)

One of the most recent policy initiatives in Australia to incorporate an explicit emphasis on children's rights is the development of the Early Years Learning Framework (EYLF), which now guides the provision of early childhood education. The EYLF document, titled Belonging, Being and Becoming, highlights the central role of children's rights in the provision of quality teaching and learning in the early years (birth to 5 years): Early childhood educators guided by the Framework will reinforce in their daily practice the principles laid out in the United Nations Convention on the Rights of the Child (the Convention). The Convention states that all children have the right to an education that lays a foundation for the rest of their lives, maximises their ability, and respects their family, cultural and other identities and languages. The Convention also recognises children's right to play and be active participants in all matters affecting their lives.

(Thomas, 2011, p.5)

In a similar vein, Australia's National Framework for Protecting Australia's Children 2009–2020 signals the fundamentally important role that the UNCRC plays in guiding services and outcomes aimed at reducing child abuse and neglect and promoting the safety and wellbeing of children: Children have a right to be safe, valued and cared for. As a signatory to the United Nations Convention on the Rights of the Child, Australia has a responsibility to protect children, provide the services necessary for them to develop and achieve positive outcomes, and enable them to participate in the wider community.

(Thomas, 2011, p.12)

The policy document then goes on to outline the principles underpinning the National Framework, explicitly highlighting their resonance with the UNCRC.

(Thomas, 2011, p.12)

The United Nations Convention on the Rights of the Child (UNCRC) (1989) is important in a number of ways.

First, as a signatory nation to the Convention, Australia is bound to uphold its 54 'Articles' (or Principles). The Convention underpins many of the professional standards and practices of early childhood education, and, as Thomas's quotes indicate, its principles and view of the child directly inform the EYLF. Both documents refer to a competent, engaged and **agentic** child—a child with agency.

> **agentic child** a child with agency

Second, it significantly expands the range of rights and adds another dimension to the existing concept of children's rights being about protection and provision. This new dimension refers to the child's right for *participation*: the right to 'participate fully in family, cultural and social life'. This involves the 'right' to be *heard*, to have a *voice* and to contribute to decision making about issues that concern the child. Specific articles that articulate this new concept of the child's voice and children's right to participate and the right to be heard, include:

Article 12

State parties shall assure the child who is capable of forming his or her own views, the right to express those views freely in all matters affecting the child, the views of the child being given weight in accordance with the age and maturity of the child.

Article 13.1

The child shall have the right to freedom of expression; this right shall include freedom to seek, receive and impart information and ideas of all kinds, regardless of frontiers, either orally or in print, in the form of art, or through any other media of the child's choice.

STOP AND REFLECT

Find and read the full UNCRC and reflect on the differences between it and the two previous declarations on the rights of the child.

Note: A child-friendly version of the Convention is available specifically so that children can read and understand their rights and not rely on adults to interpret it on their behalf. Looking back over the three iterations of declarations of children's rights, many changes are apparent. These changes reflect wider changes in Australian society in the course of the half a century that divides them.

These changes in childhood also affect how people talk about, engage with and act towards children, both individually and in the institutions that are created for the management, care and education of children. The term that describes these interconnected elements of how we 'see', talk about and educate children is 'discourse'.

ESTELLE IRVING

Discourse

The term 'discourse' is widely (but by no means exclusively) used in the literature of early childhood education, particularly in post-modern theory and analysis. You may have already noticed it in the quote from Sims in the section 'Children's rights' (above) in relation to her excitement at what she refers to as the 'new sociology of childhood' and the changes to how professionals were thinking and talking about new understandings of children's rights and status.

'Discourse' literally means written or spoken discussion of a topic, but its more complex current use refers to the ideas and frameworks (or paradigms) that dominate social thinking and discussion and, in so doing, 'silence' or marginalise alternative voices or views. Recognising this means understanding that discourse relates to *power*—for example, whose 'voice' has authority, and how does this authority privilege the people and institutions of the dominant discourse? If you re-read the quote from Sims, it may provide a different insight into the point she makes when she refers to the 'struggle with discourses that position the early years as a time to "prepare" the future adult and citizen' (Sims, 2007).

The second quote in the section 'Children's rights' also illustrates the connection between knowledge, agency and power described in discourse: 'Children share meaning and power with adults ... have their voices heard and acted on, develop agency ...' (Smith, 2007, p.4).

This concept of discourse was developed by French social theorist Michel Foucault in the early 1970s. Foucault refers to discourse as 'practices that systematically form the objects of which they speak' (Foucault, 1972, p.49). These 'practices' refer to the production, organisation, communication or reproduction of *knowledge*. The 'speaking' Foucault refers to might be literally speech (talk, lectures, sermons), but it can also be writing or broadcasting, and it can be personal, political, academic, professional or media-based. 'Form[ing] the objects of which they speak' means that discourse is more than the way we talk or write about things, because the way we talk about things (the language we use) becomes the way we think about things—it becomes its own reality and authority. Knowledge is not separable from language and words—they are inextricably connected. In some ways, discourse creates our social worlds, and our 'reality'. Knowledge has value, but only if it is within an accepted discourse.

Power and power relations are central to Foucault's concept of discourse. Foucault challenges the notion that there are objective 'truths' and suggests instead that power relations better help us understand how organisations, institutions and professional bodies (and the authoritative individuals in those institutions) gain power and privileges at the expense of alternative views. Examples of professions and institutions that promote particular discourses are the medical profession, the media, policy makers and educationalists.

The language, thinking, practices and institutions of the legal profession provide an example of a powerful discourse in contemporary Australia. Most people in Australia do not have specific legal training, but the language and thinking of this discourse has been incorporated into everyday thinking and it provides a framework for the ways in which we talk and think about our own area of professional specialisation. The discussion above about children's rights illustrates this. The concept of 'rights' is articulated in language that comes from legal discourse. Parents' rights in relation to the education of their children (and in relation to the state) are expressed in legal terms. Teachers also think and talk about their profession in terms that are shaped by legal discourse. Children, parents and teachers all have the right to legal protection and can use the legal system to ensure these rights are upheld in practice. If (hypothetically) a teacher were to hit a child, that child (through their parents) could take legal action against the teacher and, possibly, the school. How would they do this? Almost certainly, the first action taken by the parents would be to seek legal advice. On their own, the parents would not be able to negotiate the legal system—even the language would be difficult for a person without legal training to comprehend. Providing this advice requires the legal professional to refer to legislation and engage directly with the legal system (e.g. the court system). Knowing the language, the process, the 'rules' of the system gives legal professionals power and status that derive from and reinforce the power of legal discourse. We accept the authority, knowledge and language of legal discourse, and incorporate it (at least to some extent) into our own world view and everyday practices.

As this example illustrates, legal discourse has moved beyond the legal profession and has been accepted into other political and social realms, and even into our own personal lives; it is one of the powerful discourses that shape our society and culture.

It is, however, not the only discourse that has this effect; there are other competing discourses that we can identify, including medical discourse/s and, as is increasingly evident in the world, religious discourse/s.

Discourse analysis involves analysis of 'texts'. These texts quite literally include books, but texts extend to much more than just print-based texts. All forms of speech and language— the words we use and the ways in which we put together those words, are regarded as texts for analysis on what they reveal about the link between knowledge and power relations and their institutional presence. Other cultural artefacts are also used in discourse analysis. For example, the use of weighing scales in baby health centres tells us about the incorporation of science discourse into the practices of health professionals, who have been trained to use scientific tools to assess the development of babies. Taking this example further, the design of the baby health centre did not just happen: it was designed to express a set of beliefs and a body of knowledge about babies' needs and how the health professional responds to these needs (e.g. there is likely to be a consultation/practice room). Discourse analysis would examine the architecture and design features of the centre to gain a deeper understanding of the knowledge that has been built into the centre.

Competing discourses

Foucault's concept of discourse emphasises the link between knowledge and power, with the dominant discourse/s holding and exercising power, as we saw in the examples above. However, discourses are always subject to challenge by competing discourses.

In the early twentieth century we saw competing discourses of childhood, representing different concepts and ways of seeing, managing, caring for and educating children:

- 'The child in the garden' remained an important concept represented in the kindergarten movement. Viewed as a tender plant requiring the loving tending of a kindergartener— child gardener—it is the metaphor used in the first discourse. Kindergarteners and a group of experts in the language and practices of the kindergarten articulated this discourse using words and images that were carried into the design and architecture of the kindergartens, and the curriculum of the institutions where the kindergarteners were trained.

- 'The child in the laboratory' is the metaphor for the second discourse, with scientifically trained experts measuring, weighing, testing (including IQ) and timing children, and proposing scientific principles for child-rearing. Applying scientific, rational principles to child-rearing and management was contrasted against the 'irrational', emotion-based, traditional understanding of children. Scientists articulated a discourse of science that was carried into wider thinking and practices, including the school curriculum and, as discussed in Chapter 1, scientific child-rearing manuals and practices.

Many of the practices we currently use in early childhood education and care are articulated and understood in the context of a discourse of science. These are sometimes challenged by a discourse that derives from the earlier kindergarten discourse. For example, testing and measuring children (scientific discourse) may be criticised by the kindergarten type of discourse as only providing a very limited understanding of the child. This alternative discourse is likely to argue for consideration of the 'whole' child, including their spiritual wellbeing, which cannot be measured by science, so there is a real difference in practice that follows from the two discourses.

STOP AND THINK

As an exercise in 'discourse analysis', and keeping in mind that discourse is linked to knowledge and power, think about the *symbols, images* and *words* that are used in these two discourses (kindergarten and science). You may need to refer back to the discussion in Chapter 1 for more details of these discourses.

- What do they imply about how children should be cared for and educated?
- Who is presented as the holder of *truths* about children?
- How have these discourses been brought into and become part of our culture and society (i.e. how are they embedded in social and cultural practices and institutions—e.g. through formal education)?
- What follows in terms of the creation (and funding) of the associated institutions?
- Whose voice is 'privileged' in each discourse? (i.e. who is listened to and given power, authority and status from what they say)?
- Whose voice is silenced?
- Who benefits, and who is disadvantaged?

Reflective practice

What relevance does this have to teaching? A key learning and teaching point from this chapter is that teachers can and do have an impact, not just on individual children's lives, but on how childhood is perceived, experienced and valued. How we talk about children, the environment we create and the learning opportunities we provide for children can be understood as representing a particular discourse of childhood.

In the course of your studies, you will become very familiar with the concept of 'reflective practice' and its importance in the professional practice of early childhood teaching.

Chapter 1 emphasised the foundational importance of reflecting on your own image of the child; now you should understand the importance of reflecting more widely on discourses of childhood, and asking the questions of who (or what) holds the power in the dominant discourse, and who benefits or loses in this. These are key questions for early childhood education.

SUMMARY

- Philippe Ariès claimed that in Medieval France childhood did not exist as a social category that is differentiated from adulthood.
- The importance of education is highlighted in the processes that surround the social construction of childhood. Teachers have agency in this: they (*you*) can be agents of positive change in how childhood is understood, constructed and experienced.
- Childhood is socially constructed, not biologically determined.
- The printing press was a driver of wide social changes that included the creation of modern childhood.
- Literacy is required to enable full social participation and is important in defining adult status.
- Neil Postman asserted that childhood is disappearing because television is an open-access medium that prevents adults from keeping adult secrets and shames. This led to questions about how new technologies are transforming current childhood.
- Michel Foucault's concept of discourse emphasises the link between knowledge and power, with the dominant discourse/s holding and exercising power.
- Understanding childhood as *socially constructed,* in specific 'time and place' contexts and articulated by powerful discourses, means that it is subject to change and, importantly, it can be changed. Discourses are not static and immovable; they can and should be contested. In relation to 'rights', they change over time as new ideas and language emerge to challenge prevailing discourses.

FURTHER REFLECTION

Talk with your grandparents, or people at least two generations older than you, and ask what childhood was like for them.

- At what age did childhood end for them? What marked this change?
- What role did they have in their family when they were children?
- What behaviour was expected of them?
- How were children valued?
- What changes have they observed since they were children?
- What is their view on these changes?

GROUP DISCUSSION

1 Choose a specific day and time slot to conduct a *content analysis* of the themes and images portrayed on television.
2 Does the content you have documented support Postman's claim that television reveals adult failings, shames and secrets?

ESTELLE IRVING

3 If television is a window to the world for children, what picture of the world does it portray?

4 What impact do you think this has on the developing child?

5 How does Foucault's concept of *discourse* help us to understand children's rights as described in the 1924 Geneva Declaration of the Rights of the Child, compared to the words and expressions used in the 1989 United Nations Convention on the Rights of the Child?

6 The medical profession and its world view/language/power/authority/institutions provides us with another example of a dominant and powerful discourse. Discuss the concept of medical discourse in relation to the 'medicalisation' of childhood. *Note:* 'Medicalisation' refers to a 'process where a wider range of everyday human problems is brought into the medical sphere. This means that behaviours, activities, or conditions are given medical meaning, and are medically defined. It also means that medical practices are developed or implemented to control the now medically defined problem. Unusual behaviours or those outside the 'norm' become subjected to medicine, and treatments are developed for them' (Dew & Kirkman, 2002, p.98).

CLASS EXERCISES

1 Collect a wide variety of cultural artefacts (e.g. children's books; advertisements directed at children, or representing children; children's clothing; children's toys, smartphone games; apps) that represent evidence of current views and status of children or childhood.

2 Examine and document these artefacts and analyse them as cultural 'texts'.

FURTHER READING

Postman, N. (1989) The Disappearance of Childhood. New York: Vintage Books.

I highly recommend you read the original text of this thought-provoking and challenging reference. The details of changing childhood and 'evidence' Postman considers are relevant to today's media-saturated environment.

Royal Children's Hospital (2009) 'Policy Brief No. 16, 2009: Television and Early Childhood Development', Melbourne: Murdoch Children's Research Institute and the Centre for Community Child Health.

This policy brief summarises the research evidence that addresses concerns about the impact of television on children's health, development and wellbeing.

Thomas, N. (2011) 'Children's Rights: Policy into Practice', Centre for Children and Young People: Background Briefing Series, no. 4. Lismore, NSW: Southern Cross University.

This paper documents the history of children's rights, and links this to practice issues and considerations that include the EYLF, which explicitly 'highlights the central role of children's rights in the provision of quality teaching and learning in the early years'.

REFERENCES

Ariès, P. (1962) *Centuries of Childhood: A History of Family Life*. London: Jonathan Cape.

Calvert, S.L. & Wilson, B.J. (eds) (2010) *The Handbook of Children, Media and Development*. Malden, MA: John Wiley & Sons.

Cleverley, J. & Phillips, D.C. (1987) 'On Seeing Children Throughout History', in *Visions of Childhood: Influential Models from Locke to Spock*. St Leonards, NSW: Allen & Unwin, Chapter 1.

Dew, K. & Kirkman, A. (2002) *Sociology of Health in New Zealand*. Auckland, NZ: Oxford University Press.

Foucault, M. (1972) *The Archaeology of Knowledge* (translated by A.M.S. Smith). London: Tavistock.

Heywood, C. (2010) 'Centuries of Childhood: An Anniversary', *Journal of the History of Childhood and Youth*, *3*(3), Fall.

House of Commons (1842) 'Report from Commissioners, Children's Employment', Parliamentary Papers. Great Britain: Harvard College Library.

Jenks, C. (ed.) (2005) *Childhood: Critical Concepts in Sociology.* New York: Routledge.

League of Nations (1924) 'Geneva Declaration of the Rights of the Child'. www.un-documents.net/gdrc1924.htm

Malaguzzi, L. (1993) 'Your Image of the Child: Where Teaching Begins', Seminar Presented in Reggio Emilia, Italy, June 1993. Accessed: www.reggioalliance.org/downloads/malaguzzi:ccie:1994.

Postman, N. (1989) *The Disappearance of Childhood.* New York: Vintage Books.

Rinaldi, C. (2013) 'Re-Imagining Childhood', Department of the Premier and Cabinet, Government of South Australia.

Royal Children's Hospital (2009) 'Policy Brief No. 16, 2009: Television and Early Childhood Development'. Melbourne: Murdoch Children's Research Institute and the Centre for Community Child Health.

Sims, M. (2007) 'Editorial', *Australian Journal of Early Childhood* (AJEC), *32*(3), September.

Smith, A.B. (2007) 'Children's Rights and Early Childhood Education', *Australian Journal of Early Childhood* (AJEC), *32*(3), September: 1–8.

Thomas, N. (2011) 'Children's Rights: Policy into Practice', *Centre for Children and Young People: Background Briefing Series*, no. 4. Lismore, NSW: Southern Cross University.

United Nations Convention on the Rights of the Child (1989) (UNCRC). www.humanrights.gov.au/convention-rights-child

United Nations Office of the High Commissioner, Human Rights, 'Declaration of the Rights of the Child', adopted by the General Assembly on 20 November 1959. www.cirp.org/library/ethics/UN-declaration/

ESTELLE IRVING

Theorists and Theoretical Perspectives: Early Childhood Development and Learning

Carol Carter

Chapter objectives

In this chapter, we will:
- reflect on your understanding of theories and theoretical perspectives
- examine theories and theoretical perspectives that have influenced the practice of early childhood education
- consider the theories of particular theorists as they apply to early childhood education
- recognise the significance of different theoretical perspectives for early childhood education
- consider your personal perspectives in relation to different theories of education.

Key terms

accommodation	equilibrium	schema/schemata
assimilation	funds of knowledge	self-efficacy
attachment	identity	self-regulation
belonging	internal working model	spiral curriculum
concrete	maturation	transmission approach
constructivism	operations	Zone of Proximal
developmentalism	primary caregiving	Development (ZPD)
ethology	scaffolding	

> The only real difference between many personal theories and formal theories is that formal theories have been dressed up and know which fork to use.
>
> (Taylor, 2006, p.20)

A theory is a logical collection of structured ideas and principles that explain practices, actions or phenomena. In developing your arguments and writing assignments you will need to carefully consider appropriate theories and theoretical perspectives to develop, support, inform and extend your arguments. Some of the differences between our own personal ideas and the structured ideas of a 'formal' theory are contained within Taylor's (2006) statement.

Think about the ideas of 'dressing up' and the use of 'forks' contained in this description of Carol's clothing habits.

Carol hates dressing up with a passion. If she had her way she would only wear casual clothes that are comfortable and familiar. Yet on occasions where she needs to present herself to others and look her best, such as for a job interview, she will dress up and think carefully about what to wear. Her family feared that she would arrive at her wedding dressed in casual jeans and a T-shirt—but this didn't happen. Despite her own personal ideas, she took note of societal, cultural and family norms and conventions and arrived in a formal wedding gown. Carol also knows that context plays a strong role in what she wears and there are certain special occasions where she may dress up differently, such as for work, a wedding, a funeral or a fancy-dress party. What Carol hates even more than dressing up is the work that goes into finding the suitable outfit to dress up in. The dubious joy of trying on numerous new clothes before finding the right fit. Not to mention the careful consideration that it takes to select clothing items and accessories that go together and contribute to the final product! She finds it incomprehensible that some of her friends will spend hours and hours looking for just the right colour, design, material and so on that they genuinely desire for their outfits. Carol does usually have the knowledge, education and experience to 'know which fork to use' at a 'formal' dinner party. If she was going to a dinner party where forks were used differently or, in fact, forks were not used at all, requiring a different knowledge base, she would need to do some research to know what to do.

So, what does this have to do with 'formal' theories? The aspects and connotations which come into mind when considering the notion of 'dressing up' and 'knowing which fork to use' have been explored in the description of Carol's clothing habits and can be linked to theories, including theories of education. As we explore this further, I will be referring to different theorists who will be discussed in more detail, later in the chapter. It is not necessary during this initial discussion to understand their theories, but rather to think about what constitutes a 'formal' theory.

Aspects of dressing up involving careful presentation, 'looking the best' and being special as opposed to casual are linked to important notions of quality in formalised theories. Ideas of contextualisation and the impact of culture and society in 'dressing up' raises issues of framing theories and how theories are used in context. For example, Lambert and Clyde (2000, p.26) argued that there has been a great deal of misinterpretation of Vygotsky's theoretical perspectives and that 'Vygotsky, who we praise as a great "contextualist" has ironically, been studied *out of context*'. Lambert and Clyde (2000) believe that the re-interpreting and re-contextualising of Vygotskian theory within contemporary frames by those who follow a 'Vygotskian tradition' is what has positively influenced theories within early childhood education. There is a tendency to transport theories of education willy-nilly across countries and cultures that will not work without more careful consideration of contexts.

The trying on, working for refinement and suitability and selecting, combining and coordination that is involved in 'dressing up' are all important considerations in theories of education. Finding the 'right fit' and 'finding what is genuinely desired' links to the crucial nature of researching and reflecting on theories, as well as going back to the original source. The misrepresentation of theoretical perspectives, spoken about earlier, is frequently connected to not reading or paying attention to the original source of the theory. Knowledge of which 'fork to use' is linked to using different knowledges, experiences, research and education to find and interpret appropriate theories of early childhood education.

CAROL CARTER

Introduction

'Different theories about early childhood inform approaches to children's learning and development. Early childhood educators draw upon a range of perspectives in their work which may include: developmental theories ...; sociocultural theories ...; socio-behaviourist theories ...; critical theories ...; and post-structuralist theories' (DEEWR, 2009, p.11). In this chapter, we will discuss these and other theoretical perspectives under the headings:

- developmentalism
- constructivism
- socio-behaviourist theory
- interactionism and humanism
- critical theory
- post-modernism/post-structuralism.

This chapter builds on Chapters 1 and 2, to formally introduce major developmental and educational theorists who have had an impact on early childhood learning and teaching. These theorists include Piaget, Montessori, Dewey, Vygotsky, Bruner, Bandura, Bowlby, Rogers, Maslow, Freire and Bourdieu. Other important theorists have not been discussed, or discussed in detail, in this chapter as they have been embedded in specific chapters in this textbook or, like Bronfenbrenner (as outlined in the Introduction), are given predominance throughout this book.

This chapter is not meant to be the only source for your understanding of theories and theorists. At the end of the chapter you will find a 'Further reading' list containing publications that go into more detail concerning the various theories and theorists. The depth and nature of our discussions are dependent on our own philosophies and attitudes towards education.

STOP AND REFLECT

Before you read the rest of this chapter, think about some of the theories and beliefs about early childhood learning and development that you have come across. It will be useful to write your ideas down so you can return to them at the end of the chapter when you reflect on what you have learnt.

You may not think of your ideas as constituting 'theory', but here are some questions that will help you formalise your thinking:

- What are some ideas you have about how children learn and develop?
- Why do you think children learn and develop in the particular ways you have considered?
- What is your understanding of the difference between personal theories and formal theories?
- How will you decide what theoretical perspectives and sources to include in a written assignment?

Table 3.1 summarises the various theoretical perspectives that will be discussed in this chapter. This is just one way of categorising the theorists we have chosen. There is also some overlap between the different theoretical perspectives, as you will see as you read on.

Table 3.1 Theoretical perspectives in children's learning and development

THEORETICAL PERSPECTIVES	DEVELOPMENTALISM	CONSTRUCTIVISM	SOCIO-BEHAVIOURIST THEORIES	INTERACTIONISM AND HUMANISM	CRITICAL THEORIES	POST-MODERNISM/ POSTSTRUCTURALISM
Core focus	Age and stage theories of development linked to maturational milestones	Meaning and knowledge is constructed from experience	Extended from behaviourism with an emphasis on the role of experiences in shaping children's behaviour	People-centred focus where individuals interpret situations and meaning	Critiquing, emancipating and changing through challenging assumptions and biases	Theories that acknowledge different, relative ways of knowing and reject notions of universal, absolute truths
Theorists Those discussed in this chapter are in colour	Piaget Montessori Erickson Kohlberg Steiner	Piaget Bronfenbrenner Dewey Vygotsky Bruner Malaguzzi Rogoff	Bandura Bowlby **Behaviourists** Skinner Watson Thorndike	**Humanists** Rogers Maslow Pestalozzi **Interactionists** Mead Weber Blumer	Freire Giroux Fromm Habermas Horkheimer	Foucault Bourdieu Baudrillard Canella Kriseva Derrida Deleuze **Post-colonialists** Babha and Spivak
Contribution to early childhood	Contribution to developmentally appropriate practice and activities. Beginning of thinking and debate around children's thinking and learning	Recognition of the role and importance of contexts including social, cultural, and historical contexts. Children as co-constructors of their own learning	Understanding of the impact of adult behaviour and modelling on children's behaviour and the importance of building secure attachments	Emphasis on the whole child and child-centred learning and the importance and role of observation within educational environments	Awareness of the need to critique and challenge assumptions about curriculum and children. Consideration of problem-based education	The need to respond to different ways of knowing. This means using and respecting individual ways of knowing and being. Considerations of and extended notion of children as active agents of their own learning

CAROL CARTER

Developmentalism

developmentalism various developmental theories that all involve clear stages linked to maturation.

Developmentalism comprises various developmental theories that all involve clear stages linked to **maturation**. They all embrace the idea that children grow and develop in a predictable, universal way. Examples of developmental theories where behaviour, skills or needs vary at different stages, largely based on chronological ages, include Erikson's stages of personal and social development; Kohlberg's stages of moral development; Piaget's stage theory; Montessori's planes of development; and Steiner's seven year phases. Howard Gardner's theory of multiple intelligences—though it does not include distinct stages and ages where children develop from one stage to the next—may be seen as a part of developmentalism. Gardner expressed an informed view that at any one time a child may be at very different stages—for example, in interpersonal development as opposed to logical–mathematical development.

maturation moving towards optimal physical, emotional, social and cognitive function through achieving specific developmental milestones.

Developmental theories have contributed to developmentally appropriate practice (DAP), which is discussed in more detail in Chapter 4. DAP involves educators measuring and evaluating a child's development against a developmental 'norm' or 'milestone' and then creating goals to meet the child's developmental needs. Developmental theories can and have been challenged (e.g. by Nolan & Kilderry, 2010) 'because of their Western universal construct of the child that acts to marginalise children and families from diverse backgrounds' (Nolan & Raban, 2013, p.8). In this section on developmental theories, we are going to examine Jean Piaget and Maria Montessori as two theorists who have had an impact on how teachers view early childhood learning and the practice of early childhood teaching.

Jean Piaget (1896–1980)

Differences in the way children think and reason fascinated Jean Piaget and led him to closely observe the development of his own children. These observations became the building blocks for his extensive theories on child development. Piaget's theories stand in direct contrast to the behaviourists, who viewed the child as 'tabula rasa' (a blank slate) or a passive recipient (e.g. Locke, discussed in Chapter 1). According to Piaget, as children experience things in the world, they adjust their thinking to fit with the experience. These experiences commence in the physical world and so the idea of the physical activity of the child in development is significant for Piaget's theory (Bee & Boyd, 2007). Piaget believed that:

- all children, regardless of their time or space, would develop in highly similar ways
- children's development progressed through four distinctive stages
- the development of a child occurs through a continuous transformation of thought processes
- at each stage of development, the nature of the thinking is 'qualitatively different' from the other stages
- we are all born with genetically determined mental structures which are required for cognitive development
- these mental structures are subject to the forces of maturation and as we develop the structures become more powerful in dealing with our experiences in the environment (Piaget, 1963).

schema/schemata mental image/s used to organise our experiences to make sense of the world.

Piaget viewed cognitive growth as a process of adaptation, or adjusting to the world through **schema** (one) or **schemata** (many), which are mental images used to organise our experiences to make sense of the world. He theorised that two processes are involved in adaptation: **assimilation**, which is the process of gathering new information from the environment and fitting it into our existing structures or schema (e.g. dog); and **accommodation**, which is the process of alteration when an existing schema does not work and we need to change our existing ideas in order to fit in the new information (e.g. the concept of 'dog' is challenged by seeing an unknown dog).

Piaget used the term **equilibrium** to describe the balance that is attained between assimilation and accommodation as we adapt to new experiences. Equilibrium occurs when a child's schemas can deal with most new information through assimilation. However, an unpleasant state of disequilibrium occurs when new information cannot be fitted into existing schemas (assimilation). Equilibrium is the force that drives the learning process as we do not like to be frustrated and will seek to restore balance by mastering the new challenge (accommodation). Once the new information is acquired, the process of assimilation with the new schema will continue until the next time we need to make an adjustment to it. When children form new schemas they interconnect these to other schemas through a further process called cognitive organisation.

A developmental stage consists of a period of months or years when certain development takes place. Although students in educational settings are usually grouped by chronological age, their development levels may differ significantly, as well as the rate at which individual children pass through each stage. This difference may depend on maturity, experience, culture and the ability of the individual child.

Piaget believed that children develop steadily and gradually throughout the varying stages and that the experiences in one stage form the foundations for movement to the next. He believed that all people pass through each stage before starting the next one and that no one skips any stage. This implies older children, and even adults, who have not passed through later stages process information in ways that are characteristic of young children at the same developmental stage (Eggen & Kauchak, 2010).

Piaget's developmental stages

The stages described by Piaget are:

- *sensorimotor stage* (birth to two years). This is when children experience the world and gain knowledge through their senses and motor movements. They gain a progressive acquisition of object permanence—knowing that an object exists even when it's hidden
- *preoperational stage* (two to seven years). During this stage children display the following:
  - increased language use including generalisations and symbols
  - lack of rational thought—e.g. showing cats to a dog
  - inability to reverse operations
  - limited understanding of concepts such as the conservation of liquid (i.e. that liquid stays the same in quantity). For example, when liquid is poured into a different container, although the container may look different, the amount of liquid is the same
- *concrete operational stage* (seven to eleven years). During this time, children gain a better understanding of mental **operations**. They begin thinking logically about **concrete** events, but have difficulty understanding abstract or hypothetical concepts:
  - they can consider two or three dimensions simultaneously (e.g. the liquid issue is understood)
  - seriation and classification are logical operations

assimilation
the process of gathering new information from the environment and fitting it into our existing structures or schema.

accommodation
the process of alteration when an existing schema does not work.

equilibrium the balance that is attained between assimilation and accommodation as we adapt to new experiences.

operations
ways of doing something—or procedures, or actions—that are carried out in a particular order or manner.

concrete
something tangible and physical; the opposite of abstract.

CAROL CARTER

- *formal operational stage* (eleven and over). By this stage children can form hypotheses and test them.

Criticisms of Piaget's theories are that they are too prescriptive, highly culturally specific and that they focus too strongly on age-related and isolated stages. The ages at which children go through stages vary a great deal. How they vary will depend on experience, including culture. Also, the lines between different stages may be blurred and children may be within different stages at the same time for different functions and operations. For example, children may be able to form abstract hypotheses and test them through language—e.g. 'all flowers have the same number of petals', or 'if you drop something it will fall to the ground' (formal operational stage)—but may not be able to understand that there are the same number of objects in two rows where the objects are more spread out in one row and so the row looks longer (preoperational stage).

Piaget is also believed to have underestimated children's abilities. For example, Margaret Donaldson (1978) redesigned Piaget's test and tasks, making them more child friendly, setting them in familiar contexts and using familiar adults to introduce what was required in ways that children understood. She found that children understood concrete operational, logical thinking far earlier than Piaget claimed. Piaget's belief that children are strongly egocentric has also been disputed. Egocentric is when the self is at the centre. Egocentric people are not able to distinguish between themselves and others and between their own and others' perspectives.

Piaget's contribution to education—particularly early childhood education—is by opening the door to the area of child development and psychology that led to subsequent diverse theories. He contributed to the notions of active, hands-on learning; discovery learning; and considerations of children's needs, interests and cognition.

Maria Montessori (1870–1952)

Maria Montessori can also be viewed as part of the progressive education movement. She qualified as a medical doctor in Italy in 1896 and was highly involved in social reform, including women's rights and advocating for children. Over several years Montessori developed and expanded her unique Montessori approach, based on her belief that children should be engaged in environments where materials and activities are designed to support their natural development and their capacity to educate themselves (O'Donnell, 1996, pp. 1–4). The core to the Montessori method of education is the belief that children have an innate ability to teach themselves and that education is about finding 'the gold instead of the grain lurking hidden within the inner child' (O'Donnell, 1996, p.iv).

The Montessori 'director' (teacher), or 'subtle off-stage organiser' (O'Donnell, 1996, p.4) is a guide, or observer, who connects the child to a carefully prepared environment and monitors each child's self-development and individual needs within different stages of human development—or the four 'planes of development'. In the first plane (birth to six) the child has an 'absorbent mind', absorbing all aspects of environment, language and culture. In the second plane (six to twelve) the child uses a 'reasoning mind' to explore the world with abstract thought and imagination. The third plane (twelve to eighteen) is characterised by a 'humanistic mind'. The last plane of development (eighteen to twenty-four) sees the adult exploring the world with a 'specialist mind' (O'Donnell, 2014, pp.36–45). Montessori believed that if education followed the natural development of the child, this would have a broader impact in the creation of a cooperative, democratic and harmonious society.

In a multi-aged Montessori classroom, or prepared environment, the Montessori director/directress and assistant carefully design, order and sequence the classroom, practical learning materials and activities to meet children's physical and psychological needs at different stages of development. Independence, individual interests, children working at their own pace free of timetable constraints, personalisation of learning and children learning from each other within a mixed age range are strongly emphasised. Children are able to choose activities and materials from within a range that is considered suitable for their developmental needs.

Montessori materials are designed for children to learn through their senses. In addition to 'instructional materials', such as lacing frames or rods of various sizes, child-size furniture and household items, such as brooms, jugs, dishes and plates are also part of a Montessori classroom (O'Donnell, 1996). Activities are self-corrective, allowing for children to become aware of mistakes and to understand that mistakes are an important part of learning (O'Donnell, 2014, p.53). While Montessori embraced the use of the imagination, she believed that the basis for the imagination was reality and that 'the fancy which exaggerates and invents coarsely does not put the child on the right road' (Montessori, 1917, cited in O'Donnell, 1996, p.11).

> … during the last century, many Montessori principles and materials have been integrated into mainstream early childhood education … while several … remain unique to Montessori education.
>
> (O'Donnell, 2014, p.168)

The building up of close relationships between family and educational setting, the importance of observation, children's agency and respect for children, and moving away from a 'one size fits all' towards an emergent approach to learning can be viewed as Montessori methods and ideas that have had an impact on the look and feel of early childhood contexts.

Montessori approaches have been critiqued on the one hand for not placing boundaries on children's learning and giving them the freedom to choose to participate or not to participate and, on the other hand, having materials and activities that are too structured. There are also concerns around the privileging and early introduction of academic skills at the expense of creativity. While these concerns may be valid, they are frequently linked to a misinterpretation of Montessori methods. The success of particular approaches to early childhood also depends significantly on individual teachers and their interpretation and teaching abilities.

STOP AND THINK

- Why do you think aspects of Piaget's theory are no longer popular or considered appropriate in early childhood education?
- Are there aspects that you think are still relevant? If so, which ones and why?
- How have Montessori's ideas and theories impacted on early childhood education?
- What are some of her ideas that we see in early childhood education today?
- What do you think about her beliefs concerning the imagination and lack of emphasis on fantasy?
- Think about an aspect of your development that may differ from your parents' or grandparents' when they were your age. How might contexts explain this difference?

CAROL CARTER

Constructivism

constructivism
a theory of
knowledge that
argues that people
construct bodies
of meaning and
knowledge out of
experience.

In this part of the chapter, we will first discuss **constructivism** and the different aspects of constructivism and then specifically focus on three socio-constructivist theorists who strongly inform the discussion on constructivism, namely Dewey, Vygotsky and Bruner. John Dewey is often cited as the philosophical founder of this approach. Piaget (1968) is an example of a cognitive constructivist, while Vygotsky (1978) and Bruner (1990) are examples of social constructivists. We have discussed Piaget under developmentalism even though he is considered a cognitive constructivist as well.

Constructivism is a theory of knowledge that argues that people construct bodies of meaning and knowledge out of experience (von Glasersfeld, 1991). Constructivism is a theory about learning, not specifically about a method of teaching. Constructivist principles can be implemented through several different approaches to learning and teaching.

Social constructivism influenced by Vygotsky (1978) suggests that knowledge is constructed in a social context and emphasises the importance of 'co-constructing' meaning and contextual understanding from within socially framed activities. Social constructivism, or sociocultural approaches to learning, recognise children as 'directors' of their own learning and value the role of the educator in guiding, enriching and extending what children are able to know and do (Connor, 2011, p.1).

Vygotsky (1978, p. 89) states that learning by people 'presupposes a specific social nature' and the learners' development 'into the intellectual life of those around them'. So, in social or sociocultural constructivism, as opposed to individual cognition proposed by constructivists following a Piagetian interpretation of constructivism, the construction of meaning is embedded in social and cultural contexts and requires social interaction. Learning is not only influenced by, but grounded in culture: '… understandings are constructed in culturally formed settings' (Mercer & Fisher, 1997, pp.112–17).

To give an example that is relevant to me and my own history and cultural context, the South African isiXhosa phrase *Umntu ngumntu ngabantu* is not well understood within Western contexts even when it is translated ('I am a person because of other people'), since it is not seen to be significantly part of Western-oriented thought, which tends to promote the idea of the development of the individual by individual efforts. However, it seems likely that Vygotsky would have understood it very well, as he introduced the notion of learning through the mediation of other people and the role of culture as a context in which the learning takes place.

Learning and teaching, particularly in early childhood contexts, is informed by sociocultural constructivism. I consider multiple theories and strategies in my construction of what may be effective in supporting learning and teaching. This means that although I firmly believe in constructivism and am resolutely disposed towards constructivist methods, I endorse the view that proficient teaching is not based on individual theories or single theoretical perspectives (Richardson, 2003). Indeed, constructivism itself is not a specific, or particular, way of teaching.

The core of constructivism, which has influenced my learning and teaching, is based on three principles: active construction of knowledge; meaning-making through the process of organising one's experiences (von Glasersfeld, 1987, p.7); and the view that knowledge is socially, historically and culturally constructed. This view does not ignore the inner cognitive constructed knowledge of individuals, but rather stresses that knowledge is situated in a human context.

A quotation by Bruner (1986, p.127) echoes some of my sentiments in relation to constructivism and learning:

> ... most learning in most settings is a communal activity, a sharing of the culture ... in a community of those who share [a] sense of belonging to a culture. It is this that leads me to emphasise ... the importance of negotiating and sharing—in a world of joint culture ...

Phillips (1995, p.5) points out that there is a large body of literature on constructivism in education that is ever increasing. Constructivism has been viewed as a learning theory for a 'number of decades' and focuses on creating understanding from interaction between what learners know and 'ideas and knowledge with which they come into contact' (Richardson, 2003, pp.1623–4). Richardson states that there has only been interest in constructivism as a teaching theory in recent years.

Early childhood educators make use of 'sociocultural theories [socio-constructivism] that emphasise the central role that families and cultural groups play in children's learning and the importance of respectful relationships and provide insight into social and cultural contexts of learning and development' (DEEWR, 2009, p.11).

There are numerous and differing views, perceptions and forms of constructivism. However, von Glasersfeld (1991) believes that active participation in learning, or learning by doing, is an aspect that is common to all who consider themselves constructivists. Learning and teaching methods and approaches that have developed from constructivism tend to favour a 'hands-on' approach based on direct experience and experimentation.

The ideas of Phillips (1995) are helpful in selecting and reflecting on learning and teaching approaches. I have found the graphic representation adapted from Light and Cox (2001, p.18) useful in representing Phillips's ideas and explaining the differences among constructions of knowledge, as illustrated in Figure 3.1.

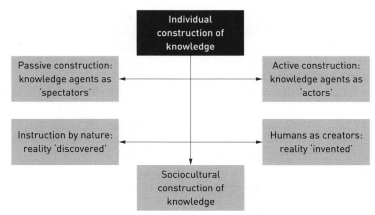

Figure 3.1

Light and Cox's three dimensions of constructivism

Phillips believes that many 'sects' of constructivism can be placed somewhere along these 'dimensions or axes' (1995, p.5). In the horizontal dimension there is continuum of reality. On one side of the continuum, knowledge is discovered in a somewhat passive way. On the opposite side of the continuum, knowledge is relative and actively invented. Phillips believes this to be the most vital and complex dimension of constructivism. Though he believes that constructivist theory can embrace both natural discovery and meaning-making, or human invention, those constructivists who are completely at the 'discovery' end of the axis are 'only minimally constructivist, or not constructivist at all' (1995, p.7). As many constructivist theories consider discovery as a crucial part of learning, the focus of 'instruction by nature' is that there is a pre-existing body of knowledge out there to be naturally discovered rather than constructed by human beings as the creators.

The vertical dimension (Figure 3.1) examines knowledge construction. It indicates knowledge that is individually constructed through 'internal cognitive processes' (Light & Cox, 2001, p.18) to publicly constructed knowledge. Phillips (1995, p.8) believes this dimension can be labelled as 'individual psychology versus public discipline'.

The third dimension in Figure 3.1 reflects the extent to which knowledge is an active or passive process. This refers to the extent of human involvement in the construction of knowledge—whether learning and knowing requires active engagement or merely being a spectator (Light & Cox, 2001, pp.18–19). Phillips (1995, p.10) states that constructing knowledge is an active process where the activity can 'either be physical or mental'. Given Phillips's argument, I interpret the 'passive' side of the continuum as being physically passive.

Some studies support an active constructivist approach to learning. This includes Bainbridge and Macy's (2008, p.65) study 'around pre-service teachers' perceptions of preparedness for literacy', in which they found constructivism worked well but that the use of the **transmission approach** 'led to feelings of frustration'. A transmission approach is a teacher-centred approach, in contrast to a constructivist approach, and is when teaching is the act of transmitting (or feeding) knowledge from the teacher's mouth to the students' heads. Other research (e.g. Mayer) found that teaching approaches based on constructivism are not all effective or suitable for all learners. Mayer believes that this lack of effectiveness is sometimes due to teachers misunderstanding constructivism and equating 'active learning with active teaching', which he sees as a 'constructivist teaching fallacy' (2004, p.15). He points out that constructivism is misused in the promotion of the exclusive use of discovery-based teaching strategies.

Sociocultural constructivism, which informs quality learning and teaching, is based on communal construction, active participation and human creation of knowledge. In the past I have over-emphasised active discovery learning and neglected the notion that constructivism may incorporate being cognitively or mentally active rather than exclusively physically active within learning processes (Mayer, 2004).

transmission approach
a teacher-centred approach whereby teaching is the act of transmitting (or feeding) knowledge from the teacher's mouth to the students' heads.

John Dewey (1859–1952)

John Dewey was part of an American progressive education reform movement in the late nineteenth century. He made an enormous impact on educational thinking in the twentieth century. The progressive education movement was informed by the works of people, some of whom you have been introduced to previously, including Jean-Jacques Rousseau, Johann Pestalozzi and Friedrich Froebel. Dewey believed that education should be embedded in hands-on experiences and should connect to the home and societal values, everyday life and individual interests as well as promoting new interests and experiences. In relation to school education, Dewey (1897) stated:

> The teacher is not in the school to impose certain ideas or to form certain habits in the child, but is there as a member of the community to select the influences which shall affect the child and to assist him in properly responding to these influences (p.78).

The teacher is, therefore, viewed as a facilitator and a guide, with learning being student-centred rather than teacher-driven. Dewey, and other progressive educationists, viewed education as a reinterpretation and reconstruction of lived experiences, with a focus on the child as the centre of education, and where children are engaged and invested in what they are taught.

It is clear from the title and content of our book that these are views that we, the authors of this book, endorse and share. Dewey's philosophy of education was directly in opposition to transmission, rote learning and teaching passive recipients of knowledge and he viewed the use of children's natural curiosity, inquiry, testing and questioning as key to education. He believed that education played a vital role in democracy and that democracy defined culture and contributed to the development of society. Dewey stated that, 'democracy has to be born anew every generation, and education is its midwife' (1915, originally published 1899, p.15). He believed that educational environments should be places to gain knowledge, where activities are important to the learner now and where they are learning to learn. This is in contrast to education that places an emphasis on preparing children for the future. Instead, Dewey asserted that schools should 'be a miniature community, an embryonic society' (1915, p.15). He believed that education should provide children with a foundation that would enable them to use their minds as a powerful tool for societal and personal change.

According to Dewey, teacher reflection (what we now refer to as critical reflection) is vital and children's interests need to be controlled, extended and encouraged by teachers with specific purposes and goals in mind. The learning outcomes described in the Early Years Learning Framework (EYLF) (DEEWR, 2009) take up this idea of specific purposes and goals identified by the teacher.

While both Dewey and Montessori saw the need for children to be active learners, the distinction lies in control, teacher input and guidance, as opposed to potentially more freedom and child direction as in Montessori's philosophy.

Lev Vygotsky (1896–1934)

Vygotsky believed that children are inherently social beings and that learning occurs by means of active knowledge construction through social interaction and participation in sociocultural activities within different contexts and environments. Vygotsky placed a strong emphasis on social interactions and viewed them as being crucial for development from the beginning of a child's life. He saw development as being embedded in the cultural context of children's everyday lives and linked to the way children interact with others.

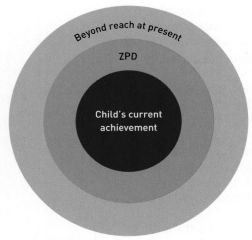

Figure 3.2 Vygotsky's Zone of Proximal Development

Vygotsky believed language exists between an infant and a mother before a child can even talk. In sociocultural construction, he saw thought and speech as being interlinked and language ultimately directing thinking.

> Children not only speak about what they are doing; their speech and action are part of one and the same complex psychological function, directed towards the solution of the problem at hand … Children solve practical tasks with the help of their speech, as well as their eyes and hands.
>
> (Vygotsky, 1978, pp.25–6)

A part of children's knowledge construction is children's participation in what Vygotsky termed 'private speech', which consists of children talking out loud as they complete a task. For example, 'that piece goes there … no, it doesn't fit …' Unlike Piaget's notion of egocentric speech, Vygotsky argued that private speech, using language—which he believed to be the most powerful cultural learning tool—was an adaptive tool that assisted children to learn new skills. While speech is said to become gradually more internalised, I do know some adults, myself included, who talk to themselves on a regular basis!

Zone of Proximal Development (ZPD) the distance between what children can do on their own and what they can do with assistance or guidance.

Vygotsky developed the theory of **Zone of Proximal Development (ZPD)**, which can be defined as the distance between what children can do on their own and what they can do with assistance or guidance (see Figure 3.2). According to Vygotsky, the ZPD 'defines those functions that have not yet mastered but in the process of maturation, functions that will mature tomorrow but are currently in embryonic state' (Vygotsky, 1978, p.38). As interactions are internalised the child moves from an 'intermental' (between child and adult's minds) to an 'intramental' (within the child's mind) level (Vygotsky, as cited in White et al., 2005, p.15).

Sociocultural theory stresses the interaction between people and the sociocultural historical domain in which they live. Vygotsky was interested not only in how adults and peers influence individual learning, but also how cultural beliefs and attitudes affect instruction and learning. Learning is itself culturally shaped and value-laden. In Chapter 4 you will read more about the theories and importance of play. Vygotsky believed play was a central part of the creation of the ZPD: 'In play a child is always above his average age, above his daily behaviour; in play it is as though he were a head taller than himself' (Vygotsky, 1967, p.16).

Jerome Bruner (1915–2016)

During Bruner's 100 years of life we can see many phases and changes of emphasis in his work. Bruner developed a constructivist model of development in which children are actively engaged in 'meaning making' through their interactions with people and the environment. He referred to constructing meaning and the processing of information as a way of understanding development and recognised that meaning-making is derived from an active search for meaning within particular cultural contexts. Bruner (1996) believed that culture 'shapes the mind' and that it is only through cultural participation that the mind reaches its full potential.

Bruner saw education as highly complex and needing to match 'a culture to the needs of its members and their ways of knowing to the needs of the culture' (Bruner, 1996, p.42). He believed education played a minor role in 'how a culture inducts the young into its canonical ways ... may even be at odds with a culture's other ways of inducting the young into the requirements of communal living ... [and education] only makes sense when considered in the broader context of what the society intends to accomplish through its educational investment in the young. How one conceives of education, we have finally come to recognize, is a function of how one conceives of culture and its aims, professed and otherwise' (Bruner, 1996, pp.ix–x). For Bruner, 'When we enter human life, it is as if we walk on stage into a play whose enactment is already in progress—a play whose somewhat open plot determines what parts we may play ...' (1990, p.34).

Bruner believed in carefully structured and guided learning through a process he called 'scaffolding'. The **scaffolding** analogy is concerned with what is erected while a building is being constructed or restored. The scaffold that the adult puts up allows the child to take carefully structured and supported steps in learning and constructing meaning and, once the child manages without help, the scaffold is removed, just as when a building has been completed. So, for Bruner, as for Vygotsky, the role of a *more experienced other* in the learning process was fundamental.

> **scaffolding**
> is guiding the learner to take carefully structured and supported steps in learning and construction of meaning.

Bruner's work (1960) suggests that any learning content or subject matter can be made understandable and accessible to children as long as the instruction is organised, scaffolded appropriately and 'studied through materials that the child can handle himself' (p.43). This is in sharp contrast to the beliefs of stage theorists such as Piaget. Bruner viewed children as active problem-solvers and problem-finders who learn analytically and intuitively through discovery (Olson, 2007). He believed that it was a waste of time postponing the teaching of important areas because they are felt to be too difficult for children. His 'hypothesis that any subject can be taught effectively in some intellectually honest form to any child at any stage of development' underpins the notion of the **spiral curriculum** (Bruner, 1960, p.33). The spiral curriculum is about beginning with basic ideas and then repeatedly revisiting and building upon them at certain intervals until the student has grasped subject or skill areas at a more sophisticated level each time and 'converting the most powerful ways of knowing that is within the grasp of a young learner' (Bruner, 1971, p.18).

> **spiral curriculum**
> beginning with basic ideas and then repeatedly revisiting and building upon them at certain intervals until the student has grasped subject or skill areas at a more sophisticated level each time.

Bruner identified three modes of representation: enactive representation (action-based); iconic representation (image-based); and symbolic representation (language-based). Rather than neatly defined stages, the modes of representation are integrated and only loosely sequential as they 'translate' into each other. For example, in the learning of mathematics we may begin with manipulating counters, or blocks (action-based), move to drawing to represent numbers (image-based) and then use symbols and language to talk about addition, subtraction and so on. So, enactive is where children begin to develop understanding through actively manipulating objects, frequently through play. Iconic is where children become able to make mental images of something and no longer need to have the physical object, thing or experience in front of them. Rather, children may rely on memory. Symbolic mode is using symbols, abstract ideas and symbolic systems to evaluate, make judgments and think critically about the world (Olson, 2007).

Bruner's later work focused on the role of narrative (or the making of stories) in meaning-making, negotiating and understanding human experience and action. The narrative was seen by Bruner to be 'one of the most ubiquitous and powerful discourses' in human communication and identity-forming (1990, p.77). He saw narrative as a means of reasoning, as a form of language and (drawing from Vygotsky) as a cultural tool.

Some ideas that are linked to Bruner's work are:

- constructing interesting, challenging exercises that incite curiosity and create a motivation to learn
- activating problem solving by modelling trial and error, curiosity and enthusiasm
- facilitating the student's reflection and thinking processes by providing aids and dialogues
- helping children to see relationships and patterns
- leading children to develop concepts and make sense of operations
- assisting children to discover principles for themselves.

funds of knowledge sociocultural resources and sources of constructed knowledge and skills that develop through time and are specific to communities, families or individuals.

Many contemporary writings, theories and ideas are embedded in, and consistent with, a sociocultural approach, including the concept of **funds of knowledge**, which 'is based on a single premise: People are competent, they have knowledge, and their life experiences have given them that knowledge' (Gonzalez, 2005). 'Funds of knowledge' is further defined by researchers Luis Moll, Cathy Amanti, Deborah Neff and Norma Gonzalez as 'to refer to the historically accumulated and culturally developed bodies of knowledge and skills essential for household or individual functioning and wellbeing' (1992, p.133).

When teachers take on roles as co-learners, they can come to know their students and the families of their students in new and distinct ways. With this new knowledge, they can begin to see that the households of their students contain rich cultural and cognitive resources and that these resources can and should be used in their classroom in order to provide culturally responsive and meaningful lessons that tap into students' prior knowledge. Information that teachers learn about their students in this process is considered the students' funds of knowledge.

STOP AND THINK

- How would you briefly define sociocultural constructivism?
- Why do you think Vygotskian theories have become important in recent years in early childhood education?
- How would you describe Vygotsky's Zone of Proximal Development in your own words and using an example?
- What do you think of Bruner's statement that learning is a 'communal activity … the sharing of the culture' and how do you think this takes place in early childhood contexts?
- Do you agree with Bruner's notion of a spiral curriculum? Why or why not?
- Dewey has traditionally been seen to have had an impact on schooling. How do you think his ideas may have impacted on early childhood education?
- What are three things you have learnt about the theories of Dewey, Vygotsky and Bruner?

Socio-behaviourist theory

'Socio-behaviourist theorists focus on the role of experiences in shaping children's behaviour' (DEEWR, 2009, p.11). The work of Bandura and Bowlby are examples of socio-behaviourist theoretical perspectives even though, as is explained later on in this chapter, Bowlby is not an educationalist.

Albert Bandura (1925–)

Although Bandura's theories have their roots in behaviourism, it is the cognition and social nature of learning that makes the difference between Bandura and behaviourists such as Skinner. Bandura spoke about observational learning with the core being modelling or imitation of other people's behaviours. Modelling, he said, 'enables people to acquire large integrated patterns of behaviour without having to form them gradually by tedious trial and error' (1977, p.12). He recognised that children acquire favourable and unfavourable behaviours through modelling and that children gradually become more selective in what or who they imitate.

Bandura's four-step model involves the learner:

1 attending to the model (friend, family, models that attract, role models, etc.)
2 remembering what is seen and heard, for later use
3 reproducing the memory of the model's behaviour via imitation
4 receiving reinforcement for accurate imitation.

Based on Bandura's work, educators have come to realise the importance of self-regulated learning and **self-efficacy** in students. **Self-regulation**, as defined by Bandura, involves personal organisation and the attainment of goals through a process of motivating oneself and guiding one's thoughts, behaviours and attitudes. Bandura's work with self-regulation led to his articulation of a systematic process that requires self-observation, judgment and self-response. Self-observation involves assessing one's own thoughts and feelings with a view to goal setting and change. Judgment involves comparing an individual's performance to goals that were set. Self-response is when people may reward or punish themselves for success or failure in meeting their goals. An example of self-response would be rewarding oneself with extra hours of television watching for doing well in an assignment. Self-efficacy is the beliefs and expectations we develop about our own abilities and characteristics resulting in our producing specific performance accomplishments and confidence in our ability to exert self-control (Bandura, 1997).

self-efficacy
the beliefs and expectations we develop about our own abilities and characteristics resulting in our producing specific performance accomplishments and confidence in our ability to exert self-control.

self-regulation
involves personal organisation and the attainment of goals through a process of motivating oneself and guiding one's thoughts, behaviours and attitudes.

John Bowlby (1907–1990)
Melissa Colville

John Bowlby is not an educationalist and is not normally included in a textbook for early childhood education students. However, his work in the mid twentieth century has had a profound and lasting impact on the care, management and education of young children, particularly in early years services and childcare. Bowlby was influenced by Freud and, like Freud, was interested in the impact of early experiences on how children develop a sense of self. If you have heard the term **attachment**, you have heard, indirectly, about Bowlby.

John Bowlby, known as the 'father of attachment theory', is the most important person in the initial development of attachment theory. Bowlby was a British psychoanalyst who studied medicine and psychiatry and worked in a child guidance clinic (Berk, 2013). In a highly influential series of books (1969–1990), based on his own research and clinical experience, Bowlby set out the foundations of attachment theory (Rolfe, 2004). Attachment theory is an ethological theory. **Ethology** emphasises that behaviour is strongly influenced by biology and is linked to evolution. Bowlby believed attachment relationships form due to behaviours that promoted the survival of humans in earlier times. Human infants are

attachment
the emotional bonds that babies develop with their parents and other key caregivers.

ethology
emphasises that behaviour is strongly influenced by biology and is linked to evolution.

born with a set of behaviours that act to keep a caregiver close and signal the infant's needs, especially in times of danger or uncertainty. These signalling behaviours include crying, smiling, babbling, calling and gestures such as raising the arms in the presence of the attachment figure (Rolfe, 2004). In turn, adults are pre-programmed to respond to infants— for example, to approach, pick up and comfort crying babies.

Attachments are the emotional bonds that babies develop with their parents and other key caregivers. For most babies it is their mother and father who become their first attachment figures. However, babies can form more than one attachment relationship, known as multiple attachments. Generally, we talk of the child becoming *attached* to the attachment figure, whereas the attachment figure *bonds* with the child (Rolfe, 2004). Some attachments tend to be stronger than others; there is a hierarchy. Parents tend to be the child's primary attachment, while a teacher might be the child's secondary attachment. It is important to clarify that not every relationship is an attachment relationship; in an attachment relationship one person is clearly the protector. There may be elements of 'protection' in peer relationships, but these are generally seen as 'friendships'.

There are four major phases of attachment. During the *pre-attachment* phase (birth to six weeks) babies use in-built behaviours, such as smiling, crying and gazing, to make contact with others. Babies of this age are fairly indiscriminate in terms of who they respond to or are comforted by: an unfamiliar person or Mum or Dad. During the *attachment in the making* phase (six weeks to six-to-eight months) babies begin to respond differently to familiar and unfamiliar people. They soon smile at, seek closeness to and are comforted most easily by their caregivers, who have become their true attachment figures (Rolfe, 2004). During the phase of *clear-cut* attachment (six-to-eight months to eighteen months-to-two years) separations between the baby and attachment figure indicate that babies have a clear-cut attachment to particular special people in their lives such as Mum and Dad. They deliberately behave to keep these special people close by. During this phase babies experience separation anxiety and stranger anxiety. This is a healthy response and does not mean the child is too attached. In the formation of a *reciprocal relationship* (two years and beyond) the toddler begins to develop increasing cognitive competence, helping them to understand their attachment figure will leave and return, and so their separation anxiety lessens. The child may use techniques to keep the attachment figure closer for a longer period of time—for example, by asking the parent to read a story before departing for work.

Mary Ainsworth (1913–1999)

Melissa Colville

Mary Ainsworth (an American–Canadian) was a developmental psychologist who contributed significantly to the development of attachment theory. Her contribution began when she observed infant-mother interactions in Uganda, Africa in 1954 (Bretherton 1992). Upon returning to the USA Ainsworth developed a tool, The Strange Situation, to measure the emotional attachment between babies/young children and their primary attachment figure (usually their mother). The Strange Situation is usually conducted in a laboratory playroom and consists of seven, three-minute episodes. These episodes include a play period, and separations and reunions between the child and attachment figure. The procedure also involves an unfamiliar adult, both with and without the presence of the attachment figure. The interactions between the child and their attachment figure, along with the child's response to separations, reunions and the unfamiliar adult are observed and recorded. This situation is designed to gradually increase the child's attachment-related stress (being separated from their mother) and increase their desire to be close to their mother, therefore intensifying behaviours that indicate the attachment relationship (e.g. approaching the mother, clinging to the mother and crying). Of crucial importance to the assessment is the way children approach the attachment figure after a separation and during the reunion—how children see the attachment figure as a 'safe haven' in their distress. The Strange Situation is considered a valid measure of assessment as it closely resembles the observations made of children's attachment relationships in the home (known as the Attachment Q-sort). The Strange Situation has been used in many thousands of research and clinical studies since then to measure the security of attachment relationships (Rolfe, 2004). As a result of her research, Ainsworth identified three major attachment categories: secure, resistant/ambivalent and avoidant.

Secure attachment is the strong, affectionate bond that children have with people who are special in their lives (Berk, 2013). The securely attached child selectively seeks and approaches the attachment figure, feels pleasure and joy when they interact, and has the expectation of a caring and comforting response in times of upset and stress. The secure child uses the attachment figure as a secure base and safe haven: a secure base from which to explore the environment and a safe haven to return to. Following a separation from the attachment figure the secure child is easily comforted. Securely attached children freely express their emotions, both positive and negative (Rolfe, 2004). Sensitive caregivers are able to read children's signals accurately. Responsive carers are psychologically and physically available to respond appropriately and quickly and consistent carers are generally predictable in the responsiveness shown. We recognise a young child forming a secure attachment to a new teacher in many ways, including when they smile and show pleasure in greeting the teacher, seek to be held by the teacher and snuggle contentedly in their arms, cry or notice when the teacher departs, smile across the room and take things to the teacher, play well and with concentration when the teacher is nearby, and cooperate with the teacher's request or directions. It is a widely held view that secure attachment is the ideal attachment relationship (Howes & Ritchie, 2002; Rolfe, 2004).

Insecure attachments reveal very different patterns of child–adult interactions. Insecure attachment is the inability to be soothed and comforted by others (Cozolino, 2014). The resistant/ambivalent pattern is a result of caregiving experiences that are inconsistent or insensitive. In this attachment relationship, the child is distressed when the attachment figure leaves; however, unlike the securely attached child, they are not soothed when the attachment figure returns and they remain anxious.

In the avoidant pattern, the child experiences indifference or rejection and therefore considers the attachment figure unavailable. These children avoid the attachment figure, unlike a secure attachment where the attachment figure is clearly preferred, and minimise their emotions, including hiding their distress upon separation. The disorganised pattern (identified by Mary Main) is associated with exposure to frightening behaviours, abuse, and/or major disruptions to attachment (Rolfe, 2004). These children can fear the presence of the attachment figure and demonstrate a range of strange and unpredictable behaviours including freezing or rocking.

The child's attachment relationships with a small number of significant attachment figures lead to the development of an '**internal working model**' (Bowlby, 1969). This internal working model is a cognitive framework for how children understand and think about

internal working model a cognitive framework for how children understand and think about themselves, others and the world.

CAROL CARTER

themselves, others and the world. If the internal working model is based on caregiving that is sensitive, responsive and consistent, then the view of the self that develops is positive: I am lovable and the world of people is generally a place that can be trusted and that has my best interests at heart (Rolfe, 2004). However, if the internal working model is based on caregiving that is insensitive, unresponsive, harsh, rejecting, and/or inconsistent, the view of the self that develops reflects this and is less positive: I am less lovable (or at the extreme, unlovable) and the world of people is generally a place that is not to be trusted and that may not have my best interests at heart (Rolfe, 2004). The insecure child's ways of responding to different kinds of caregiving are called 'psychological defences', such as the child being clingy (resistant/ambivalent attachment), or minimising their emotions (avoidant attachment). This is of great importance because these psychological defences can be generalised to other close relationships as they form over time; these defences can become habitual. It is important to understand that early patterns of attachment shape, but do not determine, the child's developmental pathway. The clinical identification and classification of different patterns of attachment requires extensive, specialised training. The focus for early childhood teachers is to promote secure attachments.

Although many factors can influence a children's attachment relationship, including children's temperaments, the most important factor is the type of caregiving children receive. To build a secure attachment, young children need adults who provide sensitive, responsive and consistent care. This means adults are able to read children's signals accurately (*sensitive*), they respond to these signals physically and psychologically (*responsive*) and they do so on a *consistent* basis. Although attachment relationships are found across all cultures (they are universal), they are determined by the culture in which they are formed. Culturally based child-rearing attitudes, behaviours and norms influence parental styles of responding to children's attachment needs.

Attachment relationships are crucial for children's wellbeing and for their emotional and social development. Social and emotional skills are the foundations of all other domains of children's development (Kids Matter Early Childhood, 2014, p.8). The positive outcomes for securely attached children in comparison to their insecurely attached peers are immeasurable (Rolfe, 2004). When children feel safe and secure (securely attached) they spend their time focused on learning and development (Raikes & Edwards, 2009). Secure attachments to teachers therefore optimise children's ability to learn (Cozolino, 2014). Securely attached children have higher scores on self-esteem and popularity with peers, skills for coping with difficult cognitive or social challenges, and reduced behavioural problems such as aggression and anxiety (Talay-Ongan and Ap, 2005). Secure attachment relationships not only ensure children's overall wellbeing, they also optimise learning by enhancing motivation, regulating anxiety, and triggering neuroplasticity, the brain's ability to modify its connections and develop from infancy to adulthood (Cozolino, 2014).

Building secure attachments with children is part of our professional role. In our EYLF, attachment is linked to children's sense of **identity**. In early childhood settings, children develop a sense of **belonging** when they feel accepted, develop attachments and trust those who care for them (DEEWR, 2009). Belonging is an integral part of a child's identity. Our EYLF (DEEWR, 2009) acknowledges babies' first attachments within their families and one of the most important messages from attachment theory is to protect children's primary attachment relationships—to reinforce parents' attachment with their child. The more

identity
the concept of the self and how one is formed from background and life experiences, some aspects of which there is no choice, such as birthplace, and other aspects where there is choice, such as philosophy.

belonging
feeling accepted, developing attachments and trusting those who care for you.

parents are supported, the more likely it is that their relationship with their child will be secure. There are countless ways we can build partnerships and provide support to families. These include welcoming parents' visits; communicating daily with parents about their child; listening to, valuing and respecting parents' values and beliefs; developing shared goals for the child; engaging in shared decision making; and where appropriate, providing families with links to support outside the early childhood setting. If we sense an insecure attachment, we can try to provide a link for the parent and child to reconnect. For example, we could show the parent the child's recent accomplishments in the program. Familiarity helps to create feelings of comfort and security for young children and provides the foundation upon which further learning can be built. Therefore, children will benefit from having positive reminders of home, such as their comfort items or family photos. Teachers should continually reflect on ways to strengthen their relationships with families.

The interactions between children and early childhood teachers play a major role in how attachment will develop. Involved teaching and caregiving, through physical contact such as hugging and holding the baby or young child, and joint attention interactions, where the teacher and child share interest in and/or jointly act upon some object, event or exchange, will help build a secure attachment (Rolfe, 2004).

Harmonious and consistent separations and reunions build security and a sense of trust for children. It is important that children have someone to go *to*, not just someone to leave *from*. **Primary caregiving**, also termed a 'key person approach', enables each child to have a special person to go to and each parent to have a primary contact. In this approach, each child and family are allocated a primary caregiver (teacher) who works towards establishing a secure attachment with the child and a partnership with the child's parents. The primary carer is carefully selected to match the child and becomes an 'expert' on the child (Greenman et al., 2008). Primary carers respond sensitively to individual children, learn each child's unique ways of communicating and know their preferences. Primary carers can be the person responsible for documentation and tracking of the child's learning and development. Primary does not mean 'exclusive'. The child should not become totally dependent on the presence of one person to be able to have a good day (Greenman et al., 2008). Forming an attachment takes time, and continuity of care, where the child remains with the same teacher over several years, will support the development of a secure attachment. This means babies/young children are not moved to a new group—either the entire group moves with the teacher or the teacher modifies the environment to suit the children's changing needs. Attachment security increases as children spend more time with their primary caregiver.

> **primary caregiving** enables each child to have a special person to go to and each parent to have a primary contact.

Attachment theory has inspired vast research since its initial development and this continues to expand. Our task as teachers is to promote children's secure attachments with their parents, and with ourselves. These secure attachments provide children with a solid foundation for learning. In regard to child development theories, you should take an eclectic approach, as no 'one' theory will provide all the answers. Attachment theory, however, provides a strong foundation for children's wellbeing, relationships, learning and development. As Pendry (1998, p. 1) aptly states, 'Although time will tell if attachment theorists are right, their findings provide an excellent framework to motivate parents and other caregivers to provide highly sensitive and responsive care to children throughout the world, if only for the benefit of humankind'.

CAROL CARTER

STOP AND THINK

- Why do you think two children who observe the modelling of aggressive behaviour on television may respond differently to this experience?
- How will your knowledge of attachment theory impact on how you interact with children at the pre-attachment, attachment in the making and clear-cut attachment phases?
- What are some of the ways in which early childhood teachers and environments could support secure attachments?
- What are three things you have learnt about the theories of Bandura and Bowlby?

Interactionism and humanism

Interactionists focus on humans as opposed to systems and, as such, have strong links to humanism. Interactionists argue that all people are individuals: we are different in shape and size but also in the way that we think and interpret situations. We all have different beliefs and experiences, which in turn affect how we interpret situations and the meaning that we attach to our interaction with other people. Interactionism relates to individuals selecting how they wish to behave based on how they see themselves in interaction with others. Symbolic interactionists focus on day-to-day interaction and, in education, observe what happens directly in classrooms. The kinds of observations interactionists focus on is how teacher expectations influence performance, perceptions and attitudes.

Your self-concept is the view that you have of yourself. Interactionists see our self-concept as changeable, unfixed and shaped by our interaction with others. Classroom interactions can have a negative and positive effect on self-concept. Interactionists also study the impact that stereotyping and labelling (categorising) may have on children in relation to their performance and self-concept. Interactionists argue that predictions made by teachers about the future success or failure of their students will tend to occur, termed the self-fulfilling prophecy. Another common feature between interactionism and humanism is the examination of such notions as self-concept and self-esteem.

Humanism, or person-centred theories, focuses on the whole person and assumes the importance and presences of such human attributes as values, dignity and freedom. The main purpose of humanism is the development of self-actualised, independent people. Self-actualisation, or where people achieve their goals and become a 'fully functioning person', is a part of any humanist perspective. Humanist teachers see cognitive (thought) and affective (feeling) domains as equally important. Educational environments where teaching is viewed from a humanist perspective will be enabling, nonthreatening and collaborative where choice, intrinsic, self-motivation and the promotion of self-esteem is evident. We will examine two people in particular, namely Carl Rogers and Abraham Maslow.

Carl Rogers (1902–1987)

Rogers's person-centred theory of personality change was based on a view that 'the individual has within himself [sic] vast resources for self-understanding, for altering his self-concept, his attitudes, and his self-directed behaviour' (Rogers, 1974, p.116). He disputed the deterministic nature of behaviourists, such as Watson, and psychoanalysts, such as Freud, and maintained that how we perceive a situation ourselves motivates our behaviour. 'As no-one else can know how we perceive, we are the best experts of ourselves' (Rogers, 1959, p.223).

The creation of authentic, genuine environments and relationships involving unconditional acceptance and empathy were seen by Rogers as crucial factors in promoting personality change and self-actualisation. Many of the ideas and views contained in Chapter 13 of this book on the importance of relationships, can be seen to have been influenced by a humanist philosophy. Rogers believed in the inherent goodness and creativity of humankind and that destructive behaviour was caused by negative self-concepts or by negative experiences that alter people's value systems. He viewed childhood experiences as having a major influence on self-actualisation.

The 'self' as a concept contributed to our further understanding of the development of personality. To Rogers, the self surfaces during infancy with an awareness of identity and understanding of 'I' or 'me' experiences (Rogers, 1959). Healthy personality development occurs when the *self-concept* (how we see ourselves and the characteristics we apply to ourselves) is congruent with our *ideal self* (who we want to, or wish to be).

Rogers's views on learner-centred education can be summarised in the following way:

- Learning should be self-directed and the teacher should act as a facilitator. 'A person cannot teach another person directly; a person can only facilitate another's learning' (Rogers, 1959). The focus is on the learner. Therefore, the background and experiences of the learner are essential to how and what is learnt. The teacher as a mentor who guides rather than the expert who tells is instrumental to a learner-centred approach.
- Each learner will process what they learn differently depending on what they bring to the classroom. The only form of meaningful evaluation is self-evaluation. 'A person learns significantly only those things that are perceived as being involved in the maintenance of or enhancement of the structure of self' (Rogers, 1951). Therefore, relevance to the student is essential for learning. Experiences become the core, although being open to consider new and varied concepts is also considered vital to learning. Any new information must be relevant and related to existing experience.
- Learning occurs best in a nonthreatening environment. 'The structure and organization of self appears to become more rigid under threats and to relax its boundaries when completely free from threat' (Rogers, 1969). An open, friendly environment in which trust is developed is essential in the classroom. A classroom tone of support helps to alleviate fears and encourages students to explore concepts and beliefs that vary from those they bring to the classroom. 'The educational situation which most effectively promotes significant learning is one in which (a) threat to the self of the learner is reduced to a minimum and (b) differentiated perception of the field is facilitated' (Rogers, 1959).

Abraham Maslow (1908–1970)

Maslow developed a hierarchy of needs that he claimed to be motivators for development. As individuals mature and their low-level needs are met, such as the need for food and water in order to survive, they develop higher order needs such as self-actualisation. Maslow believed that people's motivation changes as they progress upwards towards the hierarchy.

The hierarchy of needs is generally presented in the form of a triangle or pyramid that does not allow for the upward and downward movement and changing of needs depending on circumstances and contexts. A triangular view implies that there is only a movement upwards from one need to another. Figure 3.3 has been amended to show the potential movement. The left diagram shows the five needs that Maslow originally identified and the right one shows a later eight-tier hierarchy of needs.

Criticisms of Maslow's hierarchy of needs includes the lack of consideration that two or more needs may motivate people at the same time, the assumption that many people may not reach self-actualisation and the reducing of people to five or eight needs.

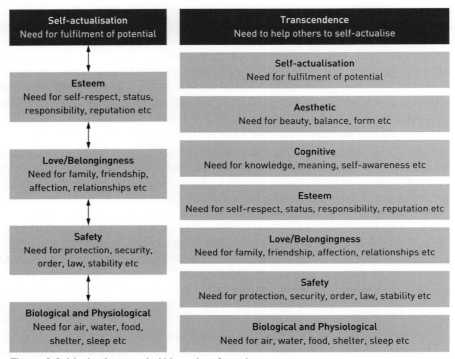

Figure 3.3 Maslow's amended hierarchy of needs

Adapted from White, Hayes and Livesey, 2005, p.236.

STOP AND REFLECT

What image, or self-concept, do you have of yourself in relation to your education?
Has this image changed at different times and/or in different educational spaces?

- How do you think this image was constructed?
- What examples have you seen of labelling and what impact did this labelling have on the person?
- What can we do in our future classrooms to prevent the self-fulfilling prophecy from occurring and promoting positive self-esteems?
- Where would you place yourself in Maslow's hierarchy at the moment?
- What other needs would you identify that people may have that motivate them?
- What needs, or goals, would you still like to achieve?

Critical theory

Critical theory invites early childhood educators to challenge assumptions about curriculum and consider how their decisions may impact on children differently. They are theories that focus on critiquing, emancipating and changing society. Critical theories aim to dig beneath the surface to uncover and challenge assumptions and biases that prevent us from having a clear and informed understanding of how the world works. Critical theorists can also be seen to be critical constructivists.

Interrogating relationships between knowledge, power and authority is central to critical theory (Giroux, 1996, p.30). How knowledge is socially constructed and linked to the intentions and behaviour of those constructing this knowledge is critiqued and questioned. In Giroux's view as a critical theorist, if we are to understand knowledge as constructed then this notion of knowledge has to be linked to ideas and structure of power (1997, p.28). So, critical theorists are particularly interested in power relations and how knowledge is constructed so that some people, and kinds of knowledge, are in privileged positions. They are also interested in how and why certain kinds of knowledge are validated and considered more worthwhile than others (Kincheloe & McLaren, 2008). There are pre-existing patterns that influence power relations in education. For example, my experience has been that where children have a highly authoritarian teacher and they are given power to control their learning, such as in a drama lesson, the pre-existing patterns of power influence what they do, which is frequently to go 'wild' in the drama lesson. Alternatively, even where children have no direct experience of drama processes, but they have a teacher who co-constructs meaning with them, the pre-existing patterns are such that they easily take control within the drama in a way that creates a productive learning environment.

Critical theorists ask such questions as:

- Whose interest does the educational environment represent?
- How can all students be empowered?

Paulo Freire (1921–1997)

There are other important critical theorists, but we are going to focus on Paulo Freire as arguably the one who has had the most impact in terms of our thinking about learning and teaching.

Paulo Freire was a Brazilian educator whose contribution to education included the belief that all education has social and political purposes and that education is about addressing societal problems. He believed that:

- 'education is freedom' and that the process of realising freedom is inseparable from education
- educators have a moral, social and political responsibility to be involved in education for social transformation to create a more just and equitable social world
- education must critically interrogate and challenge inequalities and injustice in order to effect change (MacNaughton & Williams, 2008, pp.313–14).

In his book *Pedagogy of the Oppressed* (1970) Freire argues that societal power structures result in 'oppressed' people. He promoted teachers working for the empowerment of the oppressed by reflecting critically on the social consequences of how and what they teach. The 'oppressed' are invited to explore reform through education. He stated that the oppressors do not perceive their monopoly on having more as a privilege, which 'dehumanizes others and themselves' (Freire, 2000, p.59).

He and other critical and postmodern theorists were concerned with how those who exercise power are able to control and maintain inequalities and injustices that 'dehumanise' and 'silence' others outside this power regime.

Freire advocated for a critical problem-solving approach to education in contrast to a 'banking' approach (comparable to children being viewed as 'empty vessels' needing to be filled with information), leading to empowerment. According to Freire (1970) knowledge is not a substance that can't be transmitted from teacher to learner and can't be deposited like money in a bank.

Freire was particularly interested in transformation through literacy including the importance of dialogue. He believed in critical thinking through the process of dialogue. 'Without dialogue there is no communication, and without communication there can be no true education' (Freire, 2000, p.92). 'Dialogical action', which he wrote about in *Pedagogy of the Oppressed* involved what he called a 'culture circle'. A circle is created in order to provide pedagogical spaces for dialogue in which people can participate and share ideas in an environment of respect and affirmation.

Seven actions of transformation were identified by Freire:

1 *loving*—education is an act of love and courage
2 *transforming*—current organisations are 'instruments of social reproduction'
3 *politicising*—recognising the role of politics in reproducing the 'status quo'
4 *dialoguing*—engaging in critical thinking and dialogue
5 *directing*—teachers must be more than 'facilitators … they must maintain a direction and focus relating to the *process* not the students'
6 *sharing*—doing *with* not *to* the students (a collaborative process)
7 *reflecting*—to support 'liberation and freedom' (Johnstone, 2010, pp.1–10).

Freire's view of *praxis*, cited in MacNaughton and Williams (2008), involves linking teaching actions with critical knowledge of and reflection on these actions, producing a critical evaluation of teaching that informs what is done next. Ideally, in critical approaches to education, curriculum content is developed in collaboration with students (MacNaughton & Williams, 2008, pp.313–15). Praxis involves learning by doing, reflecting on the learning and making links between theory and practice.

Post-modernism/post-structuralism

This perspective involves a deliberate break from the past and a direct challenge to traditional authority and power. It represents a new way of thinking about society, authority, power relations and even language. There are similarities and important agreements between post-modern perspectives and critical theory, particularly in their critique of traditional theories and philosophies. The difference lies in post-modern/post-structuralist rejection of categorisation and the need to draw clear, careful boundaries. The post-modern/post-structuralist theorists we will be discussing in this chapter are Foucault and Bourdieu. We met Foucault in the discussion about discourse in Chapter 2. From Foucault's (1988) perspective, individuals and organisations engage in discourse to endorse, contest or evade relationships linked to existing power–knowledge relationships. What we know about the world always involves a knower and that which is to be known. How the knower constructs the known is what we consider to be our reality.

To understand these new ways of thinking and talking about children and childhood (and therefore our interactions with children), we need to understand what is meant by 'post-modernity' or the post-modern. 'Post' means *after*, so post-modern literally refers to the period after the modern era. 'Modern' here does not mean current society, even though that is how the word is commonly used. Instead, modern society, or modernity, is associated with the rise of science and the belief in progress through science. Industrial society, built upon scientific developments, is modern society. In the modern era, we can identify shared, grand or meta-narratives constructed around a belief in progress and in universal 'truths'.

In Chapter 1 you were introduced to twentieth-century scientific child-rearing, and the belief of the behaviourists that, through objective observation and data collection, 'truths' could be deduced about 'the child'. These objective 'truths' or laws could then lead to accurate and objective rules based on scientific principles for rearing children, just as science had established universal laws about gravity or energy production, for example. Science provided the promise of perfecting children, whether it was through the perfect diet with precise calculation of required nutrients, or through controlling the environment to elicit the perfectly behaved child.

We have moved into a new post-industrial era, where knowledge and services, rather than industrial production, are the basis of our economy. Science is still powerful and in some ways, it still holds the promise of the perfect child—through genetic selection, for example—but it is now more complex and the belief in progress and science that was so powerful in the early twentieth century no longer holds the same promise as it once did, particularly as populations experience unintended effects of science (e.g. global warming).

In our current society, there are no single 'grand narratives' or collective, shared beliefs that we all subscribe to. Society is subject to global influences and forces that are dynamic, shifting and contested, making the future seem far less predictable and stable. In this post-modern era, the certainties of the past are now contested, or simply don't exist.

There is no one 'way of life', no single, shared religion, for example, and no unchallenged voice of authority that provides order and coherence. Instead, there are multiple, differentiated views and individual belief systems, represented in many different 'voices'. These apply to our personal lives, where we are likely to construct our own ideas of what a family is, for example, as well as to challenges to traditional authority institutions. In Chapter 14 you will read that there is currently no consensus about how we define a family. This contrasts with the strong consensus and acceptance of the norm of the nuclear family in mid–twentieth century Australia.

Ideas about children have also changed significantly. Here is a statement from a child developmental expert from the 1960s:

> The mind of the four year old is very different from an adult's mind. Her perception is very literal. Her frame of reference is patchy and insecure. She is struggling to make sense of her experiences. She does not have a very long concentration span, seldom able to follow a narrative thread, she does not relate what is happening to what has happened, does not understand cause and effect in a story. Most four year olds are fairly limited and literal in their vocabulary

(Early Childhood Unit, ABC, 1979, cited in Harrison, 2011, p.37).

CAROL CARTER

STOP AND THINK

- How would you characterise the view of the child represented in these statements?
- How do you imagine the educator who holds this view sees herself in relation to the child?
- What would her role be?

The expert's description of the child would have been accepted without question in the mid twentieth century: it represented an accepted 'truth', derived from objective observation about the child. We now characterise this as a *deficit* image of the child because the child is represented in terms of what she *cannot* do; what she is lacking, rather than in positive terms of what she *can* do. The child is compared to the adult, and is, in this comparison, seen as incomplete. This view shapes a particular way of relating to children, and a pedagogy that is focused on the expert redressing the deficit—through instruction—so that the child is given the knowledge and skills she 'lacks'. The child has no 'voice' in this: education is given to the child, with the assumption that the expert knows best.

The notion of 'truth' and knowledge are key issues of interest for post-modern/post-structuralist theorists who focus on the ways in which these concepts (or constructs) are tied to power and authority. Here is a statement that directly challenges the taken-for-granted belief in a single truth, or even a shared, single reality and highlights the issues of power and authority:

> A truth is authoritative. Its authority lies in its claim to be a statement about a phenomenon that is factual, and therefore, correct. For instance, a developmental truth about a child is a statement about how a child develops that is factual and therefore correct. Western social sciences (including developmental psychology) build truths incrementally through rational scientific investigation ...
>
> (MacNaughton, 2005, p.18)

Note in this statement that MacNaughton is challenging the notion of a 'truth' and the scientific method that was used to deduce 'factual' and 'correct' developmental norms and rules. As a post-structuralist, MacNaughton is concerned with 'challenging beliefs about knowledge and truth that have dominated Western thinking, ... the possibility of objective truth about the social world; and the possibility of establishing a single, universally applicable truth about social phenomena' (2005, pp.16–17). Specifically, one of MacNaughton's objectives in the book is to 'explore(s) how truths about children are linked to culturally biased norms about how children should be' (p.15)—and to challenge or disrupt this bias.

The connection between MacNaughton's claims about 'developmental truths' and the statement about the mind of the four-year-old is made clearer in MacNaughton's next statement:

> Developmental truths express authoritative discourses (systematised ways of speaking, seeing, thinking, feeling and acting) about children and childhood. Within these discourses, the child is but an immature and irrational adult whose progress (development) towards adulthood and towards mature, rational adult behaviour follows predictable, pre-given pathways ... By identifying and monitoring these pathways it is possible to identify which children are developing normally and which are developing abnormally.
>
> (MacNaughton, 2005, p.19)

In post-modern/post-structuralist theory:

- knowledge and power are central concepts
- there is no 'one reality', instead realities are plural, relative and *contested*
- identity is understood to be plural (i.e. identities), not singular and fixed; and identities are both relative and subjective
- emphasis is given to difference rather than similarity or consensus
- context and contest are central concepts, as the following quote makes clear:

> From a postmodern perspective there is no such thing as 'the child' or 'childhood', an essential being state waiting to be discovered, defined and realised. Instead there are many childhoods, each constructed by our understandings of what childhood and what children are and should be.

> (Dahlberg et. al., 1999, cited in Harrison, 2011, p.37)

Post-modern/post-structuralist theory has influenced current perspectives and practices in early childhood education. There is a strong emphasis now on children as capable and active participants in their own learning—as co-constructing their own learning, knowledge and identity.

Agency refers to the capacity and will to act. In post-modernism the agentic child (the child as agent and who has agency) is conceptualised as an active co-constructor of knowledge, culture and identify. Children are not viewed as passive recipients of adult knowledge or social norms. Children's identities are seen as 'complex, multiple, and situated within historical, cultural and social contexts' (Pacini-Ketchabaw & Pence, 2011, p.4). Meaning-making discourse allows 'alternative pedagogies to emerge—pedagogies that allow children and educators to co-construct knowledge and resist dominant understandings that have become normalised' (p.5).

Pierre Bourdieu (1930–2002)

Pierre Bourdieu's work was mainly concerned with power and culture in society, specifically how power operates within and across generations. Bourdieu viewed power as culturally and symbolically created. He believed that people have different social and cultural capital that they bring to the 'game of life' (O'Connor, 2011). He extended the idea of economic capital—the financial resources of individuals or groups—to include social and cultural capital. Social capital are all the resources that an individual or a group has, such as strong social networks or recognition in communities and societies. Social capital is made up of the circles of people who you know. Cultural capital consists of the assets of a person (education, intellect, style of speech and dress, behavioural knowledge and skills—i.e. what you know). The value of cultural capital within a particular context or field determines a person's position within that context or field. People may experience power dynamics very differently depending on the field they are in, their habitus (or personal traits, tendencies and socialised norms that direct our behaviour). Bourdieu argued that criteria for success should not be, but are frequently, particularly capital dependent. We should be aware of the forms of cultural and social capital that are valued within educational environments. He believed that if teachers do not take cultural capital into account they are likely to view 'academic success or failure as an effect of natural aptitudes' rather than understanding that they are linked to the kinds of cultural capital that we bring to an educational environment, which, for some, may be more closely linked to the capital favoured in the environment than for others (Bourdieu

CAROL CARTER

et al., 1994, p.47). I once remember seeing various young children's answers when asked what their name was. Their responses were 'James', 'Lucy', and so on. The teacher did not accept these answers. Eventually, one child—who clearly knew the 'rules of the game'—replied, 'My name is Ashley', using a full sentence. This answer was accepted by the teacher.

SUMMARY

- Various theories and theoretical perspectives have influenced the practice of early childhood education. These are crucial in our understanding of education generally and early childhood education in particular.
- Theories can be personal or formal.
- Theorists can be categorised according to their theoretical perspectives, which include developmentalism, constructivism; socio-behaviourist theories; interactionism and humanism; critical theories and post-modernism/post-structuralism.
- Piaget identified four stages and Montessori four 'planes' of development. Vygotsky spoke about the Zone of Proximal Development (ZPD) and Bruner spoke about scaffolding, which both require the support of a more expert other. Bandura and Bowlby both examined patterns of social behaviour, one in terms of modelling and imitation and the other in terms of attachment.
- Concepts such as self-concept, labelling, self-esteem and self-actualisation can be examined through an interactionist and humanist lens.
- Carl Rogers demonstrated a person-centred, humanist perspective. Maslow originally presented a five-tier and later an eight-tier hierarchy of needs.
- Critical theories, with Freire as an important example, and post-modernism/post-structuralism, while distinct, have much in common, in particular their critique of traditional theories and their focus on power and ways of knowing.
- While we may favour particular theories, and theories have been more or less popular at particular times, it is important to think critically about the theories; take an eclectic view (which takes into account diverse perspectives); and make use of the valuable and useful aspects of the theorists' work and perspectives.

FURTHER REFLECTIONS

How does understanding theories and theoretical perspectives contribute to quality early childhood education?

In answering the reflection question, here are some questions that might help:

- What do you consider to be quality education?
- What are the theories that currently inform early childhood education?
- How do they impact on early childhood frameworks and practices today?

GROUP DISCUSSION

1 What does empowerment mean for early childhood practitioner practice?
2 What relevance do critical theory and post-modernist/post-structuralist theory have to early childhood learning and teaching?
3 Which theories or theoretical perspectives appeal to you the most and why do you think this is?
4 Are the theories selected for this chapter largely teacher-centred or student-centred or both? Why?

CLASS EXERCISES

1 In pairs, select a theorist mentioned in this chapter to research further. Prepare questions and answers and present your information to the class as if you were the theorist (Partner A) and a television interviewer (Partner B). Alternatively, research the theorist further and then get the class to ask you and your partner questions as if you were that theorist. Reflect afterwards in terms of the reliability or validity of your responses.

2 In groups, based on some of the theoretical perspectives in this chapter, come up with a plan of action to assist the students listed below. Explain how different theories support your plan.
   - Angela is often late for class.
   - Liam procrastinates doing his work.
   - Tristin is very shy and doesn't have any friends to play with at recess.
   - Jo does not complete any tasks.

FURTHER READING

Nolan, A. & Raban, B. (2013) Theories into Practice: Understanding and Rethinking our Work with Young Children. Albert Park, Australia: Teaching Solutions.
   This book takes us on a clear, carefully structured journey through the theoretical frameworks applicable to working with young children. It begins with an informative chapter on theories and perspectives. It then has an entire chapter devoted to each of the theoretical perspectives highlighted in Chapter 1. The text ends with practical applications, examinations and understandings. It provides more in-depth information concerning theories discussed in this chapter.

Waller, T., Whitmarsh, J. & Clarke, K. (eds) (2011) Making Sense of Theory and Practice in Early Childhood: The Power of Ideas. Berkshire, UK: McGraw-Hill.
   This book demonstrates the power of ideas and the impact of intertwining theory and practice. Each chapter links early childhood practice and research of the respective authors to seminal theorists including Bourdieu, Vygotsky, Bruner, Freire and Foucault. The intention of the book is to move 'beyond traditional theories of early childhood' and to challenge readers to new ways of thinking.

REFERENCES

Bainbridge, J. & Macy, L. (2008) 'Voices: Student Teachers Link Teacher Education to Perceptions of Preparedness for Literacy Teaching', *Teacher Education Quarterly*, 35(2): 65–83.

Bandura, A. (1977) *Social Learning Theory*. Englewood Cliffs, NJ: Prentice Hall.

Bandura, A. (1997) *Self-efficacy: The Exercise of Control*. New York: Freeman.

Bee, H. & Boyd, D. (2007) *The Developing Child* (11th edn). USA: Pearson/Allyn & Bacon.

Berk, L.E. (2013) *Child Development*. (9th edn). Boston: Pearson Education, Inc.

Bourdieu, P., Passeron, J-C. & de Saint Martin, M. (1994) *Academic Discourse: Linguistic Misunderstanding and Professorial Power*. Stanford: Stanford University Press.

Bowlby, J. (1969) *Attachment and Loss: Attachment* (vol. 1) (1st edn). USA: Basic Books.

Bretherton, I. (1992) 'The Origins of Attachment Theory: John Bowlby and Mary Ainsworth', *Developmental Psychology*, 28(5):759–795.

Bruner, J. (1960) *The Process of Education*. Cambridge: Harvard University Press.

Bruner, J. (1971) *The Relevance of Education*. New York: Norton.

Bruner, J. (1986) *Actual Minds, Possible Worlds*. Cambridge: Harvard University Press.

Bruner, J. (1990) *Acts of Meaning.* Cambridge: Harvard University Press.

Bruner, J. (1996) *Acts of Meaning.* Cambridge: Harvard University Press.

Connor, J. (2011) *EYLF Professional Learning Program: Intentional Teaching.* Australia: Early Childhood Australia.

Cozolino, L. (2014) *The Neuroscience of Human Relations: Attachment and the Developing Social Brain* (2nd edn). New York: W.W. Norton Company.

Department of Education, Employment and Workplace Relations (DEEWR) (2009) *Belonging, Being & Becoming: The Early Years Learning Framework for Australia.* ACT, Australia: Commonwealth of Australia.

Dewey, J. (1897) 'My Pedagogic Creed', *School Journal, 54*(3): 77–80.

Dewey, J. (1915) *School and Society* (originally published in 1899). Chicago: The University of Chicago Press.

Donaldson, M. (1978) *Children's Minds.* London: Fontana Press.

Eggen, P. & Kauchak, D. (2010) *Educational Psychology: Windows on Classrooms* (8th edn). USA: Pearson Education.

Foucault, M. (1988) *Technologies of the Self* (edited by Martin Guzman and Hutton). Massachusetts: University of Massachusetts Press.

Freire, P. (1970) *Pedagogy of the Oppressed.* New York: Herder & Herder.

Freire, P. (2000) *Pedagogy of Freedom: Ethics, Democracy and Civic Courage.* USA: Rowman & Littlefield Publishers.

Giroux, H. (1996) *Living Dangerously.* New York: Peter Lang Publishing.

Giroux, H. (1997) *Pedagogy and the Politics of Hope.* Boulder: Westview.

Gonzalez, N. (2005) 'Beyond Culture: The Hybridity of Funds of Knowledge', in N. Gonzales, L. Moll & C. Amanti (eds), *Funds of Knowledge: Theorizing Practices in Household Communities and Classrooms.* Mahwah, NJ: Lawrence Erlbaum Associates.

Greenman, J., Stonehouse, A. & Schweikert, G. (2008) *Prime Times: A Handbook for Excellence in Infant and Toddler Programs.* Australia: Redleaf Press.

Harrison, C. (2011) 'Choices and Changes in Early Childhood Education in Australia, *AJEC, 36*(1): 37.

Howes, L. & Ritchie, S. (2002) *A Matter of Trust: Connecting Teacher and Learners in the Early Childhood Classroom.* New York: Teachers College Press.

Johnstone, A. (2010) *Reading Freire in Context.* Chicago: Haymarket Press.

Kids Matter Early Childhood (2014) *Early Childhood Mental Health: An Introduction.* Commonwealth of Australia. www.kidsmatter.edu.au/sites/default/files/public/KidsMatter-Early-Childhood-mental-health-an-introduction-web.pdf

Kincheloe, J. & McLaren, P. (2008) 'Rethinking Critical Theory and Qualitative Research', in N. Denzin & Y. Lincoln (eds), *The Landscape of Qualitative Research* (3rd edn). Los Angeles: SAGE.

Lambert E.B. & Clyde, M. (2000) *Re-thinking Early Childhood Theory and Practice.* Australia: Social Science Press.

Light, G. & Cox, R. (2001) 'Assessing: Student Assessment', in *Learning and Teaching in Higher Education: The Reflective Practitioner.* London: Paul Chapman Publishing.

MacNaughton, G. (2005) *Doing Foucault in Early Childhood Studies: Applying Poststructuralist Ideas.* London and New York: Routledge.

MacNaughton, G. & Williams G. (2008) *Teaching Young Children: Choices in Theory and Practice.* UK: McGraw-Hill Publication.

Mayer, R. (2004) 'Should There Be a Three-Strikes Rule Against Pure Discovery Learning? The Case for Guided Methods of Instruction.' *American Psychologist, 59*: 14–19.

Mercer, N. & Fisher, E. (1997) 'Scaffolding through Talk', in R. Wegerif & P. Scrimshaw (eds), *Computers and Talk in the Primary Classroom.* Clevedon: Multilingual Matters.

Moll, L., Amanti, C., Neff, D. & Gonzales, N. (1992) 'Funds of Knowledge for Teaching: Using a Qualitative Approach to Connect Homes and Classrooms', *Theory into Practice.* http://uwyosocialliteracies.pbworks.com/f/MollFunds.pdf

Nolan, A. & Kilderry, A. (2010) 'Postdevelopmentalism and Professional Learning: Implications for Understanding the Relationship between Play and Pedagogy', in L. Brooker & S. Edwards (eds), *Engaging Play*. London: Open University Press, pp.108–22.

Nolan, A. & Raban, B. (2013) *Theories into Practice: Understanding and Rethinking our Work with Young Children*. Albert Park, Vic.: Teaching Solutions.

O'Connor, J. (2011) 'Applying Bourdieu's Cultural and Social Capital and Habitus to Early Years Research', in T. Waller, J. Whitmarsh & K. Clarke (eds), *Making Sense of Theory and Practice in Early Childhood: The Power of Ideas*. Berkshire, UK: McGraw-Hill.

O'Donnell, D. (1996) *Montessori Education in Australia and New Zealand*. Strafford Heights, Queensland: O'Donnell.

O'Donnell, M. (2014) *Maria Montessori*. Sydney: Bloomsbury Publishing.

Olson, D. (2007) *Jerome Bruner: The Cognitive Revolutionary in Educational Theory*. Sydney: Bloomsbury Publishing.

Pacini-Ketchabaw, V. & Pence, A. (2011) 'The Postmodern Curriculum', *AJEC, 36*(1): 5–15.

Papp, L.M., Pendry, P., Simon, C.D. & Adam, E.K. (2013) 'Spouses' Cortisol Associations and Moderators: Testing Physiological Synchrony and Connectedness in Everyday Life', *Family Process, 52*(2): 284–98.

Pendry, P. (1998) 'Ethological attachment theory: a great idea in personality?' *Personality Papers*. http://www.personalityresearch.org/papers/pendry_10.html.

Phillips, D. (1995) 'The Good, the Bad and the Ugly: The Many Faces of Constructivism', *Educational Researcher, 24*(7): 5–12.

Piaget, J. (1963) (translated by Flavell) *The Development Psychology of Jean Piaget*. New York: Van Nostrand.

Piaget, J. (1968) *The Construction of Reality in the Child*. London: Routledge.

Raikes, H.H. & C.P. Edwards (2009) *Extending the Dance in Infant and Toddler Caregiving: Enhancing Attachment and Relationships*. Washington, DC: NAEYC.

Richardson, V. (2003) 'Constructivist Pedagogy', *Teachers College Record, 105*(9): 1623–40.

Rogers, C. (1951) *Client-centered Therapy*. Boston: Houghton Mifflin.

Rogers, C. (1959) 'A Theory of Therapy, Personality and Interpersonal Relationships As Developed in the Client-centered Framework', in (ed.) S. Koch, *Psychology: A Study of a Science* (vol. 3). New York: McGraw Hill.

Rogers, C. (1969) *Freedom to Learn: A View of What Education Might Become* (1st edn). Columbus, Ohio: Charles Merill.

Rogers, C. (1974) 'In Retrospect: Forty-six Years', *American Psychologist, 29*(2): 115–23.

Rolfe, S. (2004) *Attachment Theory. Rethinking Attachment for Early Childhood Practice: Promoting Security, Autonomy and Resilience in Young Children*. Crows Nest, NSW: Allen & Unwin, pp.19–38.

Talay-Ongan, A. & Ap, E. (2005) *Child Development and Teaching Young Children*. South Melbourne: Cengage Learning Australia.

Taylor, J. (2006) 'From Practice to Theory: Reflections on a Journey from Practice to Academia', *Adult Learning, 17*(1): 19–23.

von Glasersfeld, E. (1987) *Construction of Knowledge: Contributions to Conceptual Symantics*. California: Intersystems Publications.

von Glasersfeld, E. (1991) *Radical Constructivism in Mathematics Education*. Dordrecht: Kluwer.

Vygotsky, L.S. (1967) 'Play and Its Role in the Mental Development of the Child', *Soviet Psychology, 5*(3): 6–18.

Vygotsky, L.S. (1978) *Mind in Society: The Development of Higher Psychological Processes*. Cambridge, Massachusetts: Harvard University Press.

White, F., Hayes, B. & Livesey, D. (2005) *Developmental Psychology: From Infancy to Adulthood*. Frenchs Forest, NSW: Pearson Education Australia.

PART TWO

EARLY CHILDHOOD LEARNING AND TEACHING

Chapters 4 and 5 provide an overview of the pedagogical approaches and curriculum views and models that form and shape learning and teaching in early childhood contexts. The focus then shifts to specific subjects, or disciplines, and includes the practicalities of why, what and how learning and teaching occurs within specific subject areas in prior-to-school and school settings.

In these chapters, theory and practical examples are interlinked to provide the reader with an informed understanding of each discrete subject. Theories and approaches that are an important part of all learning and teaching that takes place in early childhood are discussed in detail.

Examples of different learning styles and 'voices' are also provided in Part 2, as well as authentic samples of pre-service teachers' work. You will see a strong commitment to early childhood teaching practices linked to the Early Years Learning Framework (EYLF) and the Australian Curriculum. This approach reflects our understanding that:

> The principles of early childhood pedagogy underpin practice. Educators draw
> on a rich repertoire of pedagogical practices to promote children's learning.
>
> (DEEWR, 2009, p.14)

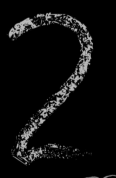

- Chapter 4: Play and Play-based Learning
- Chapter 5: Curriculum and Pedagogy
- Chapter 6: Mathematics
- Chapter 7: Language, Literacy and Children's Literature
- Chapter 8: The Arts in Early Childhood
- Chapter 9: Science

Play and Play-based Learning

Melissa Colville

Chapter objectives

In this chapter, we will:

- reflect on your play experiences
- introduce theory and research supporting the value of play in early childhood
- examine historical and contemporary theories of play and curriculum approaches
- explore various types of play and stages of play for children of different age groups
- discover current trends in children's play experiences, including social and cultural factors
- consider pedagogy and the role of teachers in facilitating children's play, including the transition to more formal learning and teaching in the primary years
- reflect on partnerships between educators and families in promoting play-based learning and development.

Key terms

Developmentally Appropriate
    Practice (DAP)
games with rules

play-based learning
play-based curriculum
practice play

symbolic play
theories of play

> Play is the highest expression of human development in childhood,
> for it alone is the free expression of what is in a child's soul.
>
> Friedrich Froebel

I grew up in the suburbs of Canberra. I was raised in a family of five, the eldest of three girls. My younger sisters were often my playmates, as well as children living in my street or school friends who lived in my suburb. In most of my memories of play I am playing with girls. Boys may have been in the vicinity, but generally, the play was separate. Interestingly, I only now wonder how this may have changed the way I played, and perhaps more importantly, what I learnt about gendered relationships. How did you play? Did you play with both girls and boys? Were they your brothers/sisters? Friends? Neighbours? Relatives?

Under the age of eight, most of my play took place in our front or back yard. We loved to jump and do somersaults on the trampoline, play with our dogs, ride our bikes, and play on the tyre swing. We loved to play hopscotch, roller skate and play cricket (using a tennis ball). We'd run and throw ourselves down the watery slip and slide, and swing around on the clothes line (Mum didn't like that much). One of my favourite play experiences was playing in the cubby house. My sisters and friends and I would role play for hours and hours in the cubby. We created roles for ourselves and imagined we were grown up. We had many sleepovers in the cubby and we liked (and didn't like) to imagine what scary things could be outside.

Most of my childhood play memories take place outside. We liked playing in the dirt, mixing it with water to make mud, and poking the spit-fires with a stick. Have you seen a spit-fire insect? I found them absolutely grotesque! As well as playing in our back yard, we also played in the neighbours' back yard, on the street or in 'the pines'. 'The pines' was a huge forest with playground equipment a ten-minute walk from home. We spent hours exploring the natural environment. I played in the pines with my friends (no adults) from around the age of ten. I don't recall many rules about where I played and what I did, mainly that when I left our street my parents had to know where I was and when I would be back. I had to be home by 5 pm (before dark) and if my friends and I moved from one place to another, such as another friend's house, I had to call my parents and let them know.

My main memories of indoor games were building cubbies with the lounge suite and playing Atari (the old version of PlayStation for those of you who are not familiar with it), but all of my happiest memories are outside. These are all wonderful play memories for me, and yes, I also have some not-so-pleasant memories—mainly arguments with friends—but let's not dwell on those.

When I played I felt happy. I felt both independent and interdependent. I felt free and in control, and I felt powerful.

Introduction

play-based learning 'a context for learning through which children organise and make sense of their social worlds, as they engage actively with people, objects and representations'. (DEEWR, 2009)

This chapter is about children's play and **play-based learning**. The chapter begins by asking you to reflect on your own childhood experiences of play and how those experiences have shaped your views and beliefs about play. There is extensive theory and research supporting the value of play in early childhood. Our early childhood curriculum framework, the Early Years Learning Framework (EYLF) (birth to five years), which guides teachers in developing quality education programs, supports play-based learning for young children. The support for play in school settings, however, is more contentious. Play may not be supported in schools unless it is recreational play, occurring outside the classroom, in what may be considered 'non-learning' time. The word 'play' will, no doubt, bring up a personal image for you that reflects your own unique understanding, knowledge and past experiences. Some of us relish our memories of play as a child (like me), while others might have unpleasant memories. Whatever our personal image, I am hopeful that you will see the important benefits of play for young children, including children in the school setting. Like many others, I believe play belongs at the centre of the early childhood curriculum. Play offers children rich opportunities to make sense of their world as they interact with others and their environment, expanding children's thinking and enhancing their desire to know and learn more (DEEWR, 2009). Children's play changes as they grow and develop, and as this chapter will show, children's play experiences are determined by many factors, including their social and cultural context.

This chapter will highlight historical and contemporary theories of play, along with curriculum approaches and pedagogical practices to facilitate children's play. Play is recognised by the United Nations in the Convention on the Rights of the Child (UNCRC) in addition to, and separate from, a child's right to leisure. This convention recognises the right of the child to rest and leisure, and to *engage in play* and recreational activities. However, play as a means for children's learning is at risk. Although play is supported in our curriculum documents, play in practice is under attack (Hunter & Sonter, 2012). One example is that children have fewer opportunities to play because of the pressure placed on teachers to reduce play-based learning in the curriculum and replace it with academic learning (Ebbeck & Waniganawake, 2010). This, along with other issues in play, will be discussed in this chapter.

What is play?

Play is universal in the sense that all children engage in play regardless of culture. Play is intrinsically motivating (motivation to play comes from within the child, rather than the adult) and powerful for all children in all cultures (Ebbeck & Waniganawake, 2010). However, play is not universal in the way it is defined, understood, supported or valued across cultures (Dockett & Fleer, 1999; Vandermass-Peleer, 2002, cited in Ebbeck & Waniganawake, 2010). Wood (2013) describes play as child-chosen; child-invented; pretend but done as if the activity were real; play focuses on the doing (process not product); it is done by children not adults; requires active involvement and is fun. While there is no agreed definition of play, research has identified some common characteristics: play is *symbolic*; pretend play is where objects assume new meanings and purposes (e.g. a block becomes a telephone). Play is *meaningful*, as children's play reflects what they already know and can do. Play is *active*: it involves physical and/or mental activity. Play is *pleasurable*: children engage in play because they find some sense of fulfilment in their play. Play is *voluntary*: children choose to be involved; they are intrinsically motivated. Play is *rule governed*: all play is governed by some rules, such as the amount of time for play, the equipment that can be used in play or, when children control their play, such as the roles that they will play. Play is *episodic*: play episodes have a beginning, middle and end (Fleer, in Pramling-Samuelsson & Fleer 2009; Wood 2013). Can you see these characteristics in children's play? Although a human activity, play is most often associated with children and with childhood, and has traditionally been viewed in comparison to work. Have you ever heard the saying 'Play is children's work' or 'Play is the work of the child'? What does this mean to you? There is a lot of 'work' involved in children's play. Nell and Drew (2013) view the mastery of play as the most important developmental task for young children. They believe play offers children a natural means to investigate the world and build meaningful knowledge through firsthand experience.

The EYLF: 'Belonging, being & becoming' (DEEWR, 2009, p. 6) defines play-based learning as 'a context for learning through which children organise and make sense of their social worlds, as they engage actively with people, objects and representations'. This definition recognises the important position of children as active players who are capable of initiating and leading their play experiences (Ebbeck & Waniganawake, 2010). Play-based learning is learning through discovery and exploration; at times, this learning may be facilitated through interactions with others, both adults and other children. A **play-based curriculum** is a planned intervention by a skilled educator who is concerned with promoting educational goals that are aimed at realising a child's potential

play-based curriculum
a planned intervention by a skilled educator who is concerned with promoting educational goals that are aimed at realising a child's potential.

MELISSA COLVILLE

(Ebbeck & Waniganawake, 2010). Among other areas of learning, a play-based curriculum includes explicit planned teaching of literacy, numeracy and science. A play-based curriculum also includes teacher intention or direction, produces outcomes and meets standards. In the early years context (birth to five years), an example of this is the five learning outcomes in the EYLF:

- children have a strong sense of identity,
- children are connected with and contribute to their world,
- children have a strong sense of wellbeing,
- children are confident and involved learners
- children are effective communicators.

STOP AND REFLECT

- What do you think about when you hear the word 'play'?
- Why do children play?
- Do only children play?
- I'd like you to think about your play as a child: At what age do your earliest memories of play begin? Can you recall where you played? Did your play involve nature? Who was with you when you played? Did you play alone? Did you have an imaginary friend? What did you play with? What kinds of technologies did you use? What did you play? Was it an organised game or did you make up the rules as you went along? Did you engage in risky play? Were you unsupervised? What rules did adults impose on your play? What did you play at school? How did you feel when you played? What do you notice about your choices, activities and preferences? How did your play reflect the area, background, culture and language of your family?
- Have you seen children today play in the same way? Would you let your children play the same things in the same way you did? Why or why not? What has changed?

Most of us can remember playing. The strength of our memories tells us something about play—it is an incredibly powerful experience for those involved (Dockett & Fleer, 1999). Fleer (2013) notes that memories of childhood are often about fantasy or social play. Is this true for you? Let's now look at the value of these, and other types of play, for children's wellbeing, learning and development.

Play as a learning tool

Early childhood education is underpinned by a strong tradition that regards play as essential for children's learning and development. More than 100 years ago, Friedrich Froebel recognised the importance of play as a young child's way of learning. As you read in Chapter 1, Froebel established his own school, termed 'kindergarten', or the 'children's garden', in Germany in 1837. This kindergarten was grounded in 'play and activity'. Froebel's writings urged parents and teachers to play with children because, through play, they create a genuine bond that promotes mutual respect. Froebel believed that by working together with children, teachers become more open to learning from children and can discover how and what to teach (Nell & Drew, 2013). As discussed in Chapter 1, Froebel valued a certain type of play: it was purposeful, rather than spontaneous and 'free'. Psychologists, theorists and educators such as Rousseau, Dewey, Piaget, Montessori, Froebel, Steiner and Vygotsky (most of whom you were introduced to in Chapter 3) have also advocated for children to learn through play.

STOP AND THINK

Froebel stated that 'play is the highest expression of human development in childhood, for it alone is the free expression of what is in a child's soul'.

- Why do you think play is so important for human development?
- Do you have a story of seeing a child's soul (or individual life-spirit) while they play?

The link between play and children's learning and development is well supported through research-based evidence (Ebbeck & Waniganayake, 2010). Learning through play is one of the eight practices of the EYLF. This framework draws on international evidence and forms the foundation for ensuring that children in all early childhood education and care settings in Australia experience quality learning and teaching. Two theories identifying the relationship between play and cognitive development are described by Piaget and Vygotsky. These two, though quite different theories, dominate early childhood education.

Piaget's theory of cognitive development placed action and self-directed problem-solving at the heart of children's learning and development: by acting in and on the environment learners discover how to control tools and materials, and understand the consequences of their actions. Piaget's image of the child as a scientist is based on children's abilities to work actively to construct knowledge and understanding, through discovery, active learning, experience and social interaction (Wood, 2013). Piaget saw play as an indicator of children's cognitive development (what the child has already learnt) and described three types of play that take place within three different stages of cognitive development: functional play, symbolic play (pretend play) and **games with rules**. According to Riddall-Leech and Raban (2011), Piaget advocated for open-ended learning experiences that encourage children to play and explore uninterrupted for long periods of time.

Vyogtsky believed that the influence of play on development cannot be overstated; play is the most important factor in children's development (Nell & Drew, 2013). In contrast to Piagetian theory, Vygotsky believed that play has the potential to *lead* development, rather than *reflect* development that has already occurred (Dockett & Fleer, 1999). Play is seen to facilitate children's cognitive development; children learn new things through play. Play enables children to function above their current intellectual level and extend their cognitive skills (Vygotsky, 1978, cited in Ebbeck & Waniganayake, 2010). Play creates and provides support at the highest levels of the Zone of Proximal Development (ZPD) where children's learning is assisted by more knowledgeable others (adults, including teachers, or peers) and by the availability of cultural tools (Broadhead et al., 2010). Teachers play an important role in expanding children's knowledge and skills by planning play experiences within children's ZPD; experiences that are not too easy or too difficult to master, but challenging and achievable, building on the child's current knowledge and skills.

games with rules games such as board games, card games and sport, or playground games such as hopscotch and tag, involving two or more players.

MELISSA COLVILLE

theories of
play theories
that uncover
perceptions of
how and why
children play.

Developmentally
Appropriate
Practice (DAP)
a term used by
the NAEYC to
describe programs
grounded in child
development
theory and
research designed
to meet the
developmental
needs of children.

Observations of children's play support both Piagetian and Vygotskian **theories of play**. Whether children are practising what they have learnt (Piaget) or are constructing new knowledge (Vygotsky), it is clear play has a valuable role in early childhood education.

With the endorsement of **Developmentally Appropriate Practices (DAP)** by the National Association for the Education of Young Children (NAEYC) (Copple & Bredekamp, 2009), play received formal professional recognition as a core component and educational tool in early childhood practice (Wiltz & Fein, cited in Fromberg & Bergen, 2015). DAP is a term used by the National Association for the Education of Young Children (NAEYC) to describe programs grounded in child development theory and research designed to meet the developmental needs of children (Copple & Bredekamp, 2009, cited in Van Hoorn et al. 2015). Although not without its critics, DAP has received widespread approval from the early childhood sector. In Australia, play is high on current educational agendas in policy, research and practice. Play also provides the basis of a number of curriculum approaches including the Reggio Emilia approach, Emergent curriculum, Steiner/Waldorf, Montessori and the Walker Learning Approach.

Theory and research support the value of play as a powerful learning tool for children's outcomes. Play supports children's physical (motor skills and spatial awareness), cognitive, language and literacy, and social and emotional development. Development in one of these domains affects the others. This perspective, that development is interconnected, is often called the whole child approach (Nell & Drew, 2013). Ample research shows that play is critical to children's development of symbolic thought, language and literacy, logical–mathematical thinking and problem-solving (Van Hoorn et al., 2015).

Much research has focused on the significance of dramatic and socio-dramatic play as a means for children's learning. Dramatic and socio-dramatic play involves dynamic learning experiences that integrate many areas of learning across the curriculum. Children play with materials, games, possibilities, knowledge, language, concepts and meanings, ideas and emotions, stories, roles, relationships, identities and rules (Wood, 2013).

There is also ample evidence that play promotes children's imagination and creativity. This is an important and sometimes overlooked component of the curriculum (Van Hoorn et al., 2015). Through play children can make satisfying achievements of which they are proud (Barr & Truelove, in Moyles, 2015), developing their sense of wellbeing. These many benefits of play demonstrate the importance of a play-based curriculum for children's learning.

Positive relationships are essential in early childhood education and play is a great relationship builder. Play is important for children to form meaningful relationships with peers, adults and significant others in their lives (Vygotsky, 1978; Bronfenbrenner, 1979; Mendoza & Katz, 2008, cited in Fromberg & Bergen, 2015; Ebbeck & Waniganayake, 2010). These relationships provide a context to support children's learning, development and wellbeing. Through play children are constructing an identity, both individual and social and extending their communication skills (Ebbeck & Waniganayake, 2010). Through play children practise their verbal and nonverbal communication skills by negotiating roles, trying to gain access to ongoing play and appreciating the feelings of others (Spodek & Saracho, 1998, cited in Isenberg & Jalongo, 2014). Play experiences can also teach children to wait for their turn, share materials and experiences, and experience and respond to others' points of view and feelings by working positively through conflicts about space, materials or rules (Isenberg & Jalongo, 2014).

Play is important for children's relationships with the environment and the benefits of play in the outdoor environment cannot be underestimated. Interacting with natural environments allows children to explore, discover and learn with all their senses. Regular outdoor experiences in natural spaces have many benefits for children, including the development of physical skills such as physical coordination, an increase in creative and imaginative skills, strengthening of social relationships, fostering of children's intellectual development, a decrease in childhood obesity, and growth in confidence and self-esteem (Durant & Raban, 2011). Children who have trouble concentrating benefit from playing outdoors, in part because of the space, fresh air and freedom. Children who spend time playing outdoors have better attention spans and classroom performance. Outdoor play also improves children's nature literacy and local understanding (Shepard, 2015) and understanding of the plants and animals that live in our outdoor spaces. Outdoor learning spaces offer a range of possibilities that are not available indoors, including opportunities for more physical, active play. Play spaces in natural environments invite open-ended interactions, spontaneity, risk-taking, and connection with and appreciation of the natural environment (DEEWR, 2009). Outdoor play provides children with increased physical activity, healthy development and overall wellbeing.

Alternate to a play-based curriculum are academic, didactic programs, where the teacher directs children's learning. Teachers following this approach lead children in a highly structured way, through direct instruction, with little or no play. There is limited choice and control for children in these programs. Unfortunately, there is a pressure on teachers to start formal education/academic learning earlier, particularly in the year prior to school. However, this approach does not reflect what scientists understand about how young children learn. Didactic instruction in the early years may actually harm young children's intellectual, social and emotional development. According to Walker (2012) it is a myth that didactic teaching produces greater academic skills and outcomes. Some research indicates that early instruction in reading and other areas may help some students, but these boosts appear to be only temporary (Kohn, 2015). Other research has found that early didactic instruction might actually worsen academic performance (Kohn, 2015).

Gray (2015) reviews research that reveals a number of negative effects of academic pre-schools and kindergartens. A large-scale German study compared children from direct-instruction kindergartens to children in play-based kindergartens. By Grade 4, children from the direct instruction kindergartens were less advanced in reading and mathematics and less well-adjusted socially and emotionally. In a large-scale study in the USA children from play-based pre-schools in Grade 4 were performing better and getting significantly higher school grades than children from academic pre-schools. A play-based curriculum where young children are provided with concrete, hands-on materials and resources to construct meaning, understanding and skills, alongside the intentional instruction and scaffolding of teachers, is crucial (Walker, 2012).

Note: The terms 'kindergarten' and 'pre-school' are used differently depending on the Australian state.

MELISSA COLVILLE

STOP AND REFLECT

- What are your own beliefs and values about the value of play as a learning tool in early childhood?
- Why do you hold these beliefs and values?
- How have your early childhood experiences shaped your views about play?

Historical and contemporary theories of play

Theories of play, first developed during the eighteenth century, uncover perceptions of how and why children play. There are many theoretical explanations of play. Fleer (2013) describes four broad theories of play: classical, grand, developmental and post-developmental. Classical theories of play were popular during the nineteenth century and although they are no longer used, aspects of them can be found in contemporary theories of play. Classical theories include Spencer's surplus energy theory, Lazarus's relaxation and recreation theories of play (1883), Groos's practice theory of play and Hall's recapitulation theory of play (Fleer, 2013). Some of the key theories of child development proposed by major thinkers are known as grand theories. These provide play as part of their theory.

The theories I will focus on in this chapter are:

- *grand theories*, including Erikson's psycho-social theory (1950) and Piaget's theory of play (1962)
- *developmental theories*, including Parten's six stages of social play (1932) and Smilansky's four stages of social play (1968)

- *post-developmental theories*, including Fleer's conceptual play (2010); Goncu and Gaskin's play as a form of cultural expression (2011); and Vygotsky's imaginary situation (2005)
- *contemporary critical and feminist post-structural views of play*.

There are many other theories of play that may be important in our thinking about play. However, the theories I have chosen to focus on in greater depth are those that have been informed by earlier notions of play, and may be more useful for you as future teachers in today's society. At the end of the chapter I will provide further reading for theories of play I have chosen not to include in this discussion.

Grand theories

Grand theories of development include psychoanalytic theory and often refer to stages of development. Grand theories offer historical as well as contemporary value.

Erikson's psycho-social theory (1950)

Erik Erikson drew on Freud's psycho-sexual theory, concentrating on the conflicts between parents and their children (Fleer, 2013). Erikson discussed the importance of children's play for their emotional development (Erikson, 1977). 'Psycho' and 'social' refer to the child's inner psychological state (their mind) being connected to the social context (their relationships). Through make-believe play, children learn about their social world and develop new social skills; play promotes children's social competence. Erikson described eight major stages of psycho-social development that build on previous stages. The first four, which relate to early childhood, are:

- *trust versus mistrust* (birth–eighteen months)
- *autonomy versus shame and doubt* (eighteen months–three years)
- *initiative versus guilt* (three–five years)
- *industry versus inferiority* (six–twelve years) (Van Hoorn et al., 2015).

A crisis occurs at each stage that the child must overcome and each stage builds upon the successful completion of earlier stages. The challenges of stages not successfully completed may be expected to reappear as problems in the future. However, mastery of a stage is not required to advance to the next stage. The outcome of one stage is not permanent and can be modified by later experiences. Erikson emphasised the role of play at each childhood stage of development (Van Hoorn et al., 2015). For example, play is central to the industry-versus-inferiority stage as it provides children with the opportunity to explore their interpersonal skills through initiating activities. Erikson's psychosocial theory is highly and widely regarded. As with any concept there are critics, but in general Erikson's theory is considered fundamentally significant.

Play therapy emerged due to Freud's and Erikson's work. In play children remodel perceptions of their past and the present and explore possible future experiences. Teachers who value Erikson's theory are concerned with supporting children's emotional and social wellbeing. I value Erikson's theory as it combines so well with Bowlby's attachment theory. Relationships, particularly relationships built through social play, provide the foundation for children's learning and development.

MELISSA COLVILLE

Piaget's theory of play (1962)

As discussed in Chapter 3, Jean Piaget described four stages of development: the *sensorimotor stage* (birth–two years), *preoperational* (or symbolic) *stage* (two–seven years), *concrete operational stage* (seven–twelve years) and *formal operations stage* (twelve and up) (Fleer, 2013). The first three stages, relating to children birth to seven, will be discussed in relation to types of play. In the sensorimotor stage, the child is involved in **practice play**, where they repeat an action over and over, such as putting objects inside a container, tipping them out and putting them in the container again. In the preoperational stage of play, the child is able to engage in **symbolic play** and can imagine something that is not present. This could be demonstrated through symbolic action—for example the child pretending to be the mother or the family dog. The concrete operational stage includes play involving games with rules, such as board games, card games, sport or playground games such as hopscotch and tag, involving two or more players (Fleer, 2013). The child constructs knowledge through the process of assimilation and accommodation to reach a stage of balance, or equilibrium, between what is known and what is experienced. Mental structures either change to take account of new data (accommodate) or incorporate the new information within existing structures (assimilate) (Dockett & Fleer, 1999). Piaget's theory can be helpful for our teaching practices in numerous ways: we should provide a wide range of concrete materials and visual aids, and allow children many opportunities for hands-on experiences to build their skills. Our focus should be on the child's thinking and understanding rather than the 'product' of their play, such as something that they have built.

practice play
where children repeat an action over and over, such as putting objects inside a container, tipping them out and putting them in the container again.

symbolic play
where children are able to imagine something that is not present.

Developmental theories

Developmental theories of play draw upon child development theories that use maturation as a point of progression in play. Maturation is the process by which we change, grow and develop: we 'mature'. Maturation determines the sequence of development. These theories usually identify specific stages of play through which children progress. These theories can be used as a guideline for how children develop, and should be used in conjunction with post-developmental theories for a more accurate picture of child development.

Parten's six stages of social play (1932)

Mildred Parten observed and recorded children's play, uncovering the changes in children's play as they developed. Parten described six distinct stages of play that generally, but not always, corresponded to children's ages:

1 *unoccupied play*—where the child is in the vicinity, but does not seek to enter the play (birth–two years)
2 *onlooker play*—where the child observes others play and has little direct involvement (common to toddlers between two and three years)
3 *solitary play*—where the child plays alone, and shows little awareness of, and has no interaction with, others (two-and-a-half–three-and-a-half years)
4 *parallel play*—where the child plays independently alongside, with little or no interaction with others (two-and-half–three-and-a-half years)
5 *associate play*—where the child is involved in the same play experience as others, with similar equipment doing similar things, communicating but with no defined plan or goals (common around three to four years)

6 *cooperative play*—where the child works with others towards a shared goal or plan, cooperating through communication and negotiation (four–six years) (Fleer, 2013).

Dockett and Fleer (1999) identify that it is the contexts in which play occurs that will affect children's play, such as the familiarity of the playmates, who the child is interacting with, the familiarity of the play equipment, the nature of the play and the individual preferences of the child. Social play fosters children's wellbeing and development. Teachers should therefore plan their environment to support children's positive social play with others.

Smilansky's four stages of social play (1968)

Sara Smilansky described four stages of children's social play:

1 *Functional/practice play*—occurs in the first two years of life and involves the repeated use of objects or actions such as bouncing a ball. In practice play infants explore objects using their body (sucking and touching) and progress towards other, more sophisticated, skills such as throwing.

2 *Constructive play*—begins around two years of age when children start to manipulate materials to create or assemble a structure, such as building a castle. These structures may not be representational initially (e.g. representing a castle) but are the child's attempts to produce an effect with the materials they are using.

3 *Dramatic play*—usually occurs from around two or three years of age, and involves children imitating the world around them. This leads to cooperative dramatic play around themes the children agree upon.

4 *Games with rules*—involves children, usually around school age (six years), understanding and following the rules of a game. Games with rules include board games, card games and sports games. Smilansky's investigations of play have been extensive and have contributed much to research and practice (Dockett & Fleer, 1999).

The main criticism of developmental theories of play is the belief that children follow particular stages of play which are universal for all cultures and in all time periods (Fleer, 2013). Children from different cultures have been shown to play very differently from the stages of play that developmental theories tend to suggest all children go through (Fleer, 2013; Rogoff 1990). However, this theory can be useful as a guideline for understanding the development of children's play and the types of play experiences teachers can provide.

Post-developmental theories

Post-developmental theories of play differ from developmental theories of play as they support the view that play complexity builds in relation to the specific types of play activity children experience rather than their age. Play complexity is explained through social and/or psychological means.

Fleer's conceptual play (2010)

This theory focuses on the relationships between play, learning and development. The theory relates to Schousboe's spheres of play (Fleer, 2013, pp.114–15). When play is a leading activity in the community and valued by the community, it acts as a source of development for the child. Conceptual play involves creating an individual or a shared imaginary situation. Fleer details an example where the children have created an imaginary situation (see Fleer, 2013,

MELISSA COLVILLE

p.116—'Going on a bear hunt'). In conceptual play, children use metacommunicative language (e.g. 'swish, swash') to make clear their imaginary actions, they continually move in and out of the imaginary situation (e.g. correcting each other's storylines), there is a doubleness of emotions (e.g. children feel happy to be playing and also frightened when they imagine the father bear growling), the meaning of objects is changed (e.g. a child uses a stick as a torch) and children take on rules and roles (e.g. singing the song 'going on a bear hunt'). Importantly, the play pedagogy for the teacher includes creating imaginary situations for groups of children, expanding children's verbal and non-verbal repertoire and giving children materials to deepen play (Fleer, 2013). This pedagogy will support children to engage in more complex imaginary and social play.

Goncu and Gaskin's play as a form of cultural expression (2011)

This theory of play argues that play should be viewed as a form of cultural expression (Fleer, 2013). Children enact their social and cultural world through a range of expressions that are specific to the cultural communities in which they live. Play varies across cultures because of people's responsibilities rather than abilities (Fleer, 2013). Fleer asks an interesting question in relation to this theory: Do families across generations value play in the same way, and do family play practices change over time? The role of the teacher is to find out what meaning children make through their play so that we can take a broader view of what play is, and how it is defined and enacted within families and cultures (Fleer, 2013). The way each person will interpret children's play will differ. Therefore, we should work in collaboration with others, colleagues and families, to determine the meaning children make through their play. By considering a range of perspectives, we are more likely to form a balanced and less biased view of children's play. We can also use our understanding of children's 'cultural' play to form stronger partnerships with families and children, and to provide opportunities for children to engage in more complex social play.

Vygotsky's imaginary situation (2005)

A critical feature of Vygotsky's theory of play is that play creates an imaginary situation governed by rules. Play is always considered as social; even when children play alone, they draw on themes, experiences and roles that are social in origin and they use social symbols to achieve this (Dockett & Fleer, 1999). The themes involved in children's play all relate to the society and culture in which children are situated, so children's play would be different in different social and cultural settings. Play moves from being based on unplanned collective action in imaginary situations with no rules, to games with rules where the imaginary situation is less evident (Fleer, 2013). An imaginary situation shared by family members where the children engage in imagination and creativity is detailed by Fleer (2013, p.71). Teachers should therefore provide children with opportunities to engage in complex imaginary play to increase their social and cognitive development.

Critical and feminist post-structural theories

Critical and feminist post-structural theories are perhaps my favourite of all of the theories on children's play because they challenge our ways of thinking. Critical and feminist post-structural theories focus on social justice in play. These theories enable us to question children's play and to achieve social justice through a range of pedagogical practices specific to the discourse of femininity, masculinity and sexuality (Fleer, 2013). This perspective questions 'gendered or stereotypical' approaches to being a boy or a girl, for both children and adults. What does it mean to be a girl? What does it mean to be a boy? Post-structural concepts offer us new ways of seeing gender and sexuality, to ask different kinds of questions (e.g. questions around fairness) and to see other possibilities in what may have become accepted everyday practice (Fleer, 2013). These theories challenge the status quo! This is particularly important in our current society, as we do not want to limit children's play opportunities (e.g. home corner is for girls only), and it is our role as a professional to combat prejudice and inequity (DEEWR, 2009). Have you ever been excluded from play? Have you ever been mistreated during play? The teacher's role in play involves challenging children's perspectives. Teachers can engage children in discussions about what they consider to be fair and unfair play. What is fair play? How can we identify unfair play? What can we do about it? (Grieshaber & McArdle, 2011). Children will then construct their own understandings of fair and unfair play. Initial Teacher Education students can find critical and feminist post-structural views of play challenging to understand and enact, but they are important theories that can be used to question our values and beliefs and perhaps most importantly, our pedagogies.

Reviewing all of the above theories, I, like Fleer (2013) believe developmental and post-developmental theories are most useful to early childhood education today. Traditionally, Australian early childhood learning environments have been heavily influenced by developmental and constructivist learning theories, with Piaget's and Vygotsky's work often dominating the agenda (Berk, 2013). Theory and research in early childhood can inform our understanding about the relationship between play and learning, but at the same time, we create our own knowledge about play, considering the complex contextual variables in our settings. We need to question how our own personal theories, values and beliefs influence our practice, and which aspects of our thinking and practice need to be changed (Wood, 2013). There is no single theory that can explain the role of play in children's learning and development, so we need to take an eclectic view by using a range of theories.

STOP AND THINK

- Which theories do you think explain children's play and how?
- How are these theories and approaches relevant to an early childhood education curriculum?

Types and stages of play

Discovery play, manipulative play, physical/active play, creative play, social play, imaginative/ dramatic play and socio-dramatic play all form part of a child's development. How children will engage in these types of play will develop over time and differ for each child.

Discovery play

Discovery play enables children to learn about the world and how it works. In discovery play, babies and young children explore, experiment, find out and discover for themselves; discovery play is open-ended and child-led. Through discovery play, young children explore

MELISSA COLVILLE

the properties and functions of materials, equipment and objects. Babies explore a treasure basket (a collection of natural and household items), handling items and putting them in their mouths. Toddlers experiment with tools to find out how they work with play dough. Pre-schoolers experiment with sand and water, noticing the physical change. School-aged children use a magnifying glass to view different objects. Natural, household and recycled materials, which should be part of our curriculum, stimulate children to explore and discover. The natural outdoor environment provides the perfect place for discovery play, even for young babies. Babies absorb the sights and sounds of the outdoors and learn about the properties of natural objects through their five senses (sight, sound, touch, smell and taste). Children will manipulate tools and equipment with growing skill as their fine motor, gross motor, hand–eye coordination and cognitive skills develop. Children's understanding of the world and how it works will also increase as they develop in all developmental domains.

Manipulative play

Manipulative play involves the skilful use of the hands and therefore play with objects encourages manipulative play. During manipulative play the hands, eyes and brain are training to coordinate. In manipulate play children manipulate and explore objects, parts and materials such as play dough, LEGO, threading beads, puzzles and construction sets. Changes in children's physical development result in changes in their manipulative play. As children's fine motor skills advance, so too will their manipulation of objects. Babies become

increasingly skilful with their hands as they play with rattles, soft toys and other objects. For example, a baby will begin by grasping a cup with both hands and then learn to pass it from one hand to another. Babies will, later, benefit from learning experiences such as modelling with play dough to practise and develop their manipulative skills. Children's manipulative play will also develop in conjunction with their hand–eye coordination and cognitive skills. If we take block play as an example, babies will reach for blocks, put them in their mouth and drop them, while pre-schoolers and school-aged children will build increasingly intricate constructions with small blocks.

Physical/active play

Physical play encourages children to be active. Physical/active play involves the body and its large muscles, allowing children to find out how their bodies move and work. Children also develop gross and fine motor skills through physical/active play, when they participate in learning experiences such as throwing and climbing. Physical/active play can occur both indoors and outdoors and is very important for children's healthy development. During physical/active play children use their energy, learn new things and socialise with others. Young children's physical play will progress and become more advanced as they develop better movement, balance, strength, agility and coordination skills. To develop these skills, children will need opportunities to practise their skills and may need some instruction—for example, when learning how to catch a ball. Babies' physical play skills develop as they learn to sit, crawl and stand, then becoming toddlers who learn to walk, dance and kick a ball. Pre-schoolers ride bikes, run, throw and catch balls, and engage in rough and tumble play. School-aged children's physical skills are even more complex, and they participate in a variety of sporting games that improve their movement and coordination skills. Electronic media has had a great effect on young children's physical play, making children more sedentary. The importance of young children spending a lot of their time engaged in physical/active play cannot be underestimated.

Creative play

Creative play involves making something new from things we already know. Through creative play, young children design, explore, manipulate, ask questions, try out new ideas, take risks and use their imagination to generate something unique and original. Through creating something new and unique, children are expressing their thoughts and feelings, also known as self-expression. Creative play experiences include visual art and construction, role play, music, and movement and dance. Children should have access to many different tools, props and equipment to engage in creative play, including, but not limited to, books, a range of manipulative materials such as clay or play dough, a range of art materials, blocks, costumes and musical instruments, etc. Children grow progressively more creative, especially with exposure to the creative arts. Babies' interest in art is focused on the sensory exploration of art materials such as paint. Toddlers also enjoy the sensory pleasures of art materials, focusing on the process of creating art rather than the final product. Pre-schoolers' creative play is more complex: their art begins to include recognisable subjects and they engage in role play with others. School-aged children depict subjects more realistically in their art and they also perform, read and write with more complexity.

MELISSA COLVILLE

Social play

Social play takes place when children play together. When children play with others they develop social skills and behaviours. Children learn to be collaborative, to cooperate, to compromise and share, to be sensitive to others' feelings, and to be fair and responsible. Young children will begin to show a preference for certain playmates and spend time playing together. Children can often argue during social play and this teaches them about each other's reactions and feelings. Social play can also teach children anti-social behaviour such as rejecting peers, so teachers need to promote pro-social behaviours. Securely attached children (children who receive sensitive, responsive and consistent care) are more likely to be more sociable and engage in positive interactions. Adults, especially parents, are babies' first playmates. Adults initiate play with babies, who soon participate. Adults play an important role in extending and enhancing children's play, for example, through language modelling. There is, however, wide variation in how parents and other adults play with children. Mothers' and fathers' play differs; mothers' play tends to involve a teaching component and to be more verbal than that of fathers, who tend to engage in more physical play, such as tossing babies into the air and run-and-chase games (Lewis & Lamb, 2003). Parten (1932) describes the stages of children's social play as onlooker, solitary, parallel, associative and cooperative play (as described on page 100 of this chapter). It is important to recognise that children differ widely in these stages and will engage in a range of stages at one time—for example, school children engage in cooperative play but, at times, engage in solitary play.

Imaginative/dramatic play

Imaginative/dramatic play involves role play, the use of materials and props, and pretending/fantasy/make-believe play. In imaginative/dramatic play a child might play in the home corner, wearing an apron and using a pot and wooden spoon, imagining they are a chef in a restaurant. Children may also create props and use these as they engage in their imaginative play. Have you ever seen a child engaging in imaginative play, such as creating a pretend bus by lining up small chairs and pretending to be the bus driver?

Imaginative/dramatic play does not require the child to interact with another child. Dramatic play involving play with others, known as socio-dramatic play, will be addressed later in this chapter. Conventional play rules related to the physical world do not apply in imaginative/dramatic play—for example, a child can imagine they are someone else and may talk to a person who isn't there. Children invent scenarios during imaginative play to make meaning of who they are, where they've come from, how to learn about others and the world they live in, and their place in the world (Rowell, 2010). There is great potential for outside imaginative/dramatic play, and most scenarios can include an element of outside play such as a home corner in the sandpit. Imaginative/dramatic play increases in complexity as children grow and develop. Babies and toddlers engage in role play, which often involves imitating the actions, facial expressions and language of others, including peers and adults. Older children's dramatic play is more complex. Pre-schoolers take on roles such as doctor, parent or teacher. Pre-schoolers may look after a sick baby (doll) in hospital (bed with bedding). The dramatic play of school children shows even greater creativity in the way they use props, costumes, movements and language.

Socio-dramatic play

The difference between dramatic play and socio-dramatic play is children engaging in dramatic play can do so on their own. Socio-dramatic play is interactive and involves verbal interaction between two or more children. The higher level socio-dramatic play also requires cooperation between children (Kitson, cited in Moyles, 2015). When children are engaging in socio-dramatic play they understand how different characters behave and this generally begins around three years of age. In early childhood, we typically see children engaging in socio-dramatic play in areas such as the home corner, office area or hospital area. Socio-dramatic play can also include symbolic play, where a child imagines one object is another—for example, imagining leaves as money in outdoor play. One of my favourite socio-dramatic experiences to observe was a group of pre-schoolers who, after being read the story of Snow White, enacted the story by creating the storyline and the roles they would play. Have you ever watched children engaging in socio-dramatic play? What they are able to do is amazing! I also recall observing a child around the age of five pretending to be a veterinarian in the Keeper Kids playspace at the Melbourne Zoo. The veterinarian terminology (language) she was using with the other children was far beyond her years. Socio-dramatic play develops as children's cognitive skills develop, so we would expect to see even more complex play in school-aged children. It is important for teachers to be aware that socio-dramatic play can also include the enactment of real experiences of an intense personal, social or interpersonal nature, such as being mothers and fathers who are having an argument (Flood and Hardy, 2013). Teachers can join in with children to further facilitate their wellbeing, play and learning (Kitson, cited in Moyles, 2015).

Different types of play

A group of children are playing with blocks. What type of play do you think this is? At any one time a child may be involved in more than one type of play. Block play could incorporate all of the types of play discussed above. We cannot underestimate the teacher's role in facilitating children's play, learning and development. This will be discussed later in this chapter (see 'Pedagogy: facilitating children's play').

STOP AND REFLECT

- What types of play have you observed children engaging in?
- What differences have you noticed in how girls and boys play?
- What have you noticed about children with special needs and disabilities in play?
- How does play differ in the school setting?

MELISSA COLVILLE

Who are we observing?

The nature of play changes over the course of children's development. Not all children develop at the same rate and in the same way. The information below describes children's 'typical development of play'. Due to the variations in children's development, the main focus is on different age groups (babies, toddlers, pre-schoolers and school children), rather than achievements at specific ages.

Babies

Babies engage in object play; they practise, manipulate and explore. Babies learn to grasp objects from around four months and place objects in their mouths. Babies experiment with how their body parts work and most babies can put an object into a container and dump it out. Babies laugh, chuckle and squeal aloud in play. They engage in simple exchanges of vocalisations with adults (social play), responding to games such as 'Peek-a-boo' and 'Round and round the garden'. Babies will also look at, smile at or vocalise to other babies and children. Babies' play is quite similar for boys and girls, despite parents' tendency to socialise their baby into gender stereotypic behaviour from birth (Garner & Bergen, cited in Fromberg & Bergen, 2015).

Toddlers

The mouthing of objects decreases in toddlerhood. Toddlers enjoy play with pop-up toys and interactive books (press button to play music). Toddlers' gross motor skills are growing. They love push and pull toys, climbing equipment and small bikes. Older toddlers manipulate with paint, water play toys, blocks and dolls. Toddlers tend to play on their own contentedly, but they like and feel more secure with a familiar adult nearby. Parallel play is present and toddlers may watch other children play with interest, and on occasion join in. Toddlers begin to put words together and understand a range of adult phrases. Toddlers engage in symbolic, make-believe play, where people, objects and ideas become symbols for something else (e.g. when a child uses a block as a train, making train noises as they push the block over the carpet, or when a child adopts the role of a mother in the home corner by wearing appropriate clothes or adopting a suitable tone of voice).

Pre-schoolers

By around three years of age, play preferences are evident and become more inflexible for boys and girls. Girls tend to prefer play with dolls and household items, dressing up and art experiences, while boys tend to play with transportation toys and blocks and engage in more aggressive, rough-and-tumble play (Garner & Bergen, cited in Fromberg & Bergen, 2015). Pre-schoolers are gaining more confidence in their abilities. They plan and build more constructively and by four or five years of age, they are creating elaborate imaginary play situations that involve complex roles and extended scenarios such as putting dolls to bed, washing clothes and driving cars (Bodrova & Leong, cited in Fromberg & Bergen, 2015). Associative and some cooperative play is evident in pre-schoolers' play.

School children

School children's play is usually with those of the same sex and is well organised. School children engage in cooperative play, including games with rules. Children follow or create rules to reach a shared objective in a game. School children may have difficulties coping with losing. They also enjoy chants and songs. Do you remember chants and songs from when you were in school? Friends are important to school children. Playground experiences for many children are based on interactions with friends, so it can be distressing for children who do not have anyone to play with. Creative play and imaginative arts (drama, visual arts, music and dance) are important for school children's learning and development. Through these learning experiences children are thinking and problem solving.

Children with special needs

Teachers may find that some children with special needs have less experience, confidence or ability when engaging in play experiences (Van Hoorn et al., 2015). However, it is important that teachers do not make assumptions about children's knowledge and skills, and instead carefully observe children with special needs to determine their learning and development. The focus should be on what children can do rather than what they cannot, and to consider where children might progress to. We have high expectations for all children, regardless of their level of development and individual needs.

STOP AND THINK

- What are the main forms of play in early childhood?
- What are the stages of play for different ages?
- How might these stages differ for individual children?

Trends in children's play experiences

Previous generations of children disappeared on their own, or in groups, for hours and hours of uninterrupted play, but the world has changed for our children (Caro, 2012). Adults today are increasingly concerned about children's safety and security and this concern has impacted on the physical and social environments in which children play and learn. Other factors influencing children's play include siblings, peers, teachers and the early educational environment, birth order and the developmental level of the child, including the child's social competence, the child's gender and sexual orientation, family influences (e.g. financial security or insecurity, socioeconomic status), and mixed age play (Oden et al., cited in Fromberg & Bergen, 2015). Children's play is also a reflection of where they live and what they have around them (Dockett & Fleer, 1999). Research across diverse communities has shown variations in children's play partners (peers and adults), and variations in the kinds of play experiences children engage in (Goncu et al., cited in Fleer, 2013). Although play themes may differ across cultures, Ramsey (cited in Fromberg & Bergen, 2015) states that the frequency, structure and type of play may be common across cultural groups. While there are clearly changes in play in different situations and across time, there are also elements that seem to remain constant, at least in some cultural contexts. For example, children now may be less likely to play Cowboys and Indians, but they probably play superhero games of some form. It is remarkable that many themes of children's play are similar to those of our parents or grandparents. Is this true for you? This similarity tells us something about our social context and about what has remained important within that context (Dockett & Fleer, 1999).

MELISSA COLVILLE

STOP AND REFLECT

- How do you think children's play has changed over the past several decades?
- What are the differences between your childhood and that of children in the past?
- What opportunities do today's children have to explore the world?
- Are they able to engage with the natural world?
- Do they have opportunities to take risks?
- Do they have opportunities to run barefoot through grass, jump in puddles, climb trees or spend time quietly on their own for the whole day or parts of a day playing in their backyard, or inside, without adult intervention? (Early Childhood Australia, 2013)

Australian children's access to free space for play is rapidly shrinking. This is even more obvious in urban areas in Australia where most of us live (Play Australia, 2015). In the early childhood setting, play is enhanced when children are provided with sufficient space, particularly for active play. It is also increasingly rare for children to have long, uninterrupted blocks of time to play. The amount of time allocated to play reinforces the value placed upon play by adults. Time is needed for children to become involved in more complex and elaborate play, such as constructing an intricate building. Play periods of at least 30–60 minutes are recommended (Gronlund, 2010; Santer et al., 2007). Parents today are often enrolling their young children in structured activities. The increased participation of children in structured educational and recreational activities (sports, dance classes, etc.) has left little time for participation in open-ended, self-initiated free play. Furthermore, it is increasingly rare for children to play either by themselves or with their friends, without supervision. Elkind (2007b) states that social and cultural factors have reduced opportunities for children to play without parental supervision. The friends that I played with as a child, now adults, do not allow their own children to play unsupervised as we once did, and the child's safety, usually from 'a stranger', is the most common reason. My Initial Teacher Education students, who are parents, say the same. Supervision is an important aspect of the teacher's role, so we cannot allow children to be unsupervised. However, we can offer children more space and time to play.

Children today are less likely to have access to outdoor play spaces in natural environments. For many young children designed environments, such as public parks, school grounds or early childhood play areas are their main opportunities for outdoor play (Play Australia, 2015). Deb Moore, a researcher on this subject, writes about the limited natural experiences in children's lives and their disconnection from nature. There is a trend today towards valuing 'structured indoor play' as a more important learning environment than outdoor spaces. Children's indoor play includes manufactured and plastic equipment, computerised toys and screen time with computers, iPads and phones—and this includes babies! Let's consider screen time. The detrimental effects of too much screen time are well researched and guidelines for children have been recommended—for example, children younger than two years of age should not spend any time watching television or using other electronic media (Australian Government, 2018), other than video-chatting (Raising Children Network, 2017). As teachers, we need to provide children with more opportunities for outdoor play in natural environments, and educate parents about the benefits of outdoor play in natural environments.

STOP AND REFLECT

- What are your beliefs and values about the importance of space for children to play?
- What are your beliefs and values about the importance of uninterrupted blocks of time for play?
- What are your beliefs and values about the importance of outdoor play in the natural environment?
- In what ways are new technologies changing children's play?

In today's society, there is a strong emphasis on children's safety and protection from harm, and opportunities for children to engage in 'risky' play are decreasing. Society in general no longer views risk as an important aspect of learning, and instead, we now have risk-averse adults and playgrounds. As Brussoni and colleagues (2012) aptly state, keeping children safe involves letting them take and manage risks; children need to take different types of risks to develop and learn. Risk is not the same as danger because playing dangerously is likely to cause harm. Risky play can be an exciting experience that provides opportunities for challenge, testing limits, exploring boundaries and learning about the risk of physical injury (Little & Wyver, 2012).

Practitioners and researchers from diverse disciplines are beginning to recognise the negative impact such changes are having for children's optimal growth and development (Little & Wyver, 2012). Not allowing children to play freely and explore their environment has a single benefit (safety at that particular time) outweighed by multiple risks such as compromised development, decreased physical exercise, increased obesity, limited spontaneous play opportunities, lack of road sense in later years, and loss of a sense of place and enjoyment (Little & Wyver, 2012). In an Australian study (Little, 2015; Little & Sweller, 2015), in response to factors limiting opportunities for challenging play, teachers cited regulatory restrictions relating to heights, arrangement of gross motor equipment and having inadequate space. This study emphasises the impact of the teachers' perspective: while the Australian Standards for playground equipment allow a maximum height of 1.5 metres, the majority of centres restricted climbing heights to less than 1 metre. While safety issues need to be addressed, avoiding all risk is not the solution, as doing so limits children's participation in worthwhile experiences that promote their optimal health and development. To develop a child's wellbeing, our EYLF (DEEWR, 2009) framework encourages children to take 'considered risks'. It is our responsibility to provide outdoor play environments where the risks of serious injury are reduced, but creativity, challenge and excitement are maintained (Little & Wyver, 2012).

STOP AND REFLECT

- Do you believe there are benefits of risk-taking? If so, what might they be?
- Would you support children's risk-taking? How?
- How can we balance children's health and safety with giving them genuine opportunities to explore, experiment, predict and take managed risks?

MELISSA COLVILLE

One aspect of children's play that has continued over time is gender stereotyped play. Gender identities—what it is to be a boy or a girl—are a strong feature of children's play and often impact on their choices of play and play mates. Children's pretend play is rich in information about how they understand gender relations; they show others what they think girls and women can and should do, and what they think boys and men can and should do (Nutbrown, 2010). Building on previous studies with similar findings, research evidence by Trawick-Smith and colleagues (2015) found that gender stereotyped toy play is 'pervasive among young children and constitutes a large part of their daily experience' (p.407). Gender stereotyped toys for boys (masculine toys) included a fighter jet, construction toy, monster truck and motorcycle, while gender stereotyped toys for girls (feminine toys) included a tea set, baby doll, pony and fairy wand. These gendered toys and gender roles need to be questioned. Stereotyped roles place limitations on who children can be and who children can become. To add further complexity to this issue, some children identify as the opposite sex (female or male) to which they are born. This makes them a target for rejection and bullying by their peers, as they do not fit the 'normal' gender stereotype. Stereotyped choices for toys and play scenarios are a challenge for teachers. Teachers need to be committed to equity and avoid practices that directly or indirectly contribute to gender inequality, prejudice and discrimination (DET, 2016). Therefore, recommended teaching strategies include examining and discussing social media messages with children, rethinking our classroom arrangements, choosing storybooks with cross-gender play scenarios and encouraging children positively when they do engage in a wider variety of cross-gender toy play (Honig, cited in Fromberg & Bergen, 2015).

STOP AND REFLECT

- What gender biases do you think you may have?
- Are you open to equal and diverse experiences for both girls and boys?
- How and when should you intervene in children's play to promote gender equity? (Tansey, 2009)

A review of Australian news articles on children's play in schools has uncovered a belief that despite the positive impacts of play within the school setting (impacts such as children's academic endeavours and overall educational needs and happiness), play experiences during recess and lunch have become limited and sterile. *The Sydney Morning Herald* reports that Australian school children are missing out on essential play experiences (North, 2012). Running or ball games have been banned due to a *perceived* high risk of injury, and playgrounds lack play stimuli and have become spaces where children often wander around aimlessly. *The Age* reported on staggered play times, banned games and smaller playgrounds (Verberne, 2014). *The Daily Telegraph* reports that Australian children are among the least active in the world and lack important physical milestones such as catching, throwing, sprinting and jumping (Dunlevy, 2016). The value of play and opportunities for children to play in schools varies, and it is our responsibility to advocate for rich play-based experiences in the school setting, including risky play.

Like current trends already discussed, Australian teachers have identified children's current play as being supervised by adults, with manufactured toys and the use of safe equipment where playgrounds are carefully policed. Teachers have also identified children's play as having organised play spaces (e.g. a play room) and playtimes (e.g. play dates organised by the parents), age-appropriate toys and non-messy learning experiences (Fleer, 2013). Perhaps most disturbing, Elkind (2007a) describes a phenomenon he refers to as 'play deprivation', where children do not have the opportunity to play and therefore become play deprived. Play deprivation, particularly during the period between birth and seven years, has been linked to impaired brain development, a lack of social skills, depression and aggression (Hughes, 2003). When I discuss the current trends in children's play with my Initial Teacher Education students, they agree that they are accurate. Of course, as they also point out, there are exceptions to the rule, such as those who advocate for non-gendered play, or riskier play. Initial Teacher Education students (some of whom work in early childhood) have talked about the pressures parents place on teachers, particularly around safety and messy play. One Initial Teacher Education student commented that a mother from her service did not want her child playing in the sandpit (messy play) and the staff followed this mother's request. What are your thoughts on this? We clearly need to educate parents about the issues relating to children's current play experiences and have philosophies and policies that support best practice.

When I reflect on the changes in play for children, less time, less space—e.g. less outdoor play, less risky play, little unsupervised play—I can't help but think how lucky I am. I console myself that today's children do not know what they are missing, but I am concerned about the impact these changes will have for children and for our society. For me, perhaps the greatest cause for concern is that our current generation is not getting enough uninterrupted, child-led play in natural outdoor environments. Children need these types of environments to support their sense of identity, community, wellbeing, learning and communication. We have a responsibility, as a play provider, to deliver high-quality, well-maintained play opportunities and play environments that reflect the needs of the children and their families in our community (Play Australia, 2015). Play will continue to change as our society and culture continue to change, so we need to stay knowledgeable about these and other factors impacting children's play experiences.

STOP AND REFLECT

Based on your own values, beliefs and knowledge, what do you think are the implications for the current trends in children's play?

Pedagogy: facilitating children's play

This discussion on pedagogy and the role of teachers in facilitating children's play focuses on teaching strategies and experiences that support children's wellbeing, development and learning in areas including language, literacy, numeracy and science.

How children are viewed impacts enormously on teaching philosophies and curriculum decision making. Hunter and Sonter (2012, p.1) eloquently state 'the child you see is the child you teach'. If children are viewed as innocent, we may act to protect them. If children are viewed in terms of what skills or knowledge they require, the teacher may focus attention on

MELISSA COLVILLE

filling the gaps or deficit (Hunter and Sonter, 2012). Teachers need to understand their view of the child and how this impacts on their teaching. See Chapter 1 to determine and reflect on your view of the child.

Language, literacy, numeracy and science

In the early childhood classroom literacy, numeracy and science learning can often be incidental learning through play; this means that learning happens as a result of being in playful environments rich in language, literacy, numeracy and science, without the need for direct teacher instruction. However, teachers can have a tremendous impact and influence on shaping children's knowledge, skills and feelings towards literacy, numeracy and science. Our focus on literacy, numeracy and science is often stronger in the year prior to school. However, literacy, numeracy and science learning begins from birth. The interactions we have with babies and toddlers provide the foundation for children's later learning. Literacy, numeracy and science are not isolated domains. When children are engaging in a science experiment, they are learning literacy and mathematical concepts. Teachers should guide children through integrated play-based learning to see the connections between ideas within literacy, numeracy and science, as well as with other topics across the curriculum. Let's look at each topic area—language and literacy; numeracy; and science—to see if you can find a connection.

Language and literacy

For many children literacy development begins in their home environments and reflects family and cultural values. Children's literacy development is affected by the context in which it emerges, and this includes early childhood education (Van Hoorn et al., 2015). Children are able to use a wide variety of literacy skills, concepts and behaviours in their play and show interest in, and knowledge of, the many functions and purposes of print (Wood, 2013). An important starting point for teaching language and literacy is literacy-rich environments where children are encouraged to listen, speak, read, write and view in a variety of ways. Children need many opportunities to play and explore the texts and images in books; draw; write; and begin to recognise familiar words. When everyday rituals such as songs, rhymes, telling stories, listening to stories, looking at pictures, reading books and talking are repeated, children's knowledge and understanding builds (Hunter & Sonter, 2012). These play experiences are crucial for babies and toddlers, as well as older children.

Communication is the foundation of literacy. Fluent language use is the basis of literacy learning (Elliott, cited in Ebbeck & Waniganayake, 2010). Teachers should prioritise children's language development to ensure children know how to communicate successfully (Bradford, in Moyles, 2015). The more children hear language used and play with language, the more they learn about how it works. When the time comes for written literacy this understanding of oral or spoken language is invaluable. Writing needs to occur as part of the social context and play-based curriculum—both writing opportunities for children and modelled writing by the teacher. One recommendation is a reading and writing centre with a wide variety of writing materials. Teachers can play with children and scaffold their awareness of print (top to bottom, front and back, beginning and end, left to right, and the relationships between words and pictures, etc.) and identifying and matching letters and sounds (Elliott, cited in Ebbeck & Waniganayake, 2010). These and other literacy concepts can be taught to children as young as two or three years. Young children know that when we hold a book upside down it can't be read!

Literacy should be taught using a range of models of communication including music, movement, dance, storytelling, visual arts, media and drama (DEEWR, 2009). Socio-dramatic play creates contexts for literacy practices because of the connections between story making and telling, pretence, and imagination (Wood, 2013). Play areas such as a post office, bank, restaurant, and/or hospital support children's literacy learning. The objects and materials in these areas—such as notebooks, posters, pencils, diaries and clipboards—will also support literacy learning. To determine the literacy conventions that children are acquiring, teachers can use story dictation (see 'Observation-based planning' in Chapter 11). This observation method allows us to document and assess, in particular, children's language development and their literacy skills.

Reading Chapter 7 of this book will extend your understanding of language and literacy.

Numeracy

An engaging and encouraging numeracy environment develops children's confidence and ability to understand and use numeracy. Children need to know how to understand and work with numbers and mathematical concepts. Teachers should introduce mathematical concepts, methods and language through a variety of appropriate experiences and research-based teaching strategies (National Council of Teachers of Mathematics, 2013). Materials and resources that allow children to play, problem-solve and explore the world 'mathematically' are key elements in the development of numeracy. Blocks and other construction materials, puzzles, and opportunities for using patterns and sorting—e.g. found materials such as

MELISSA COLVILLE

shells, seeds or leaves—all provide experiences that encourage mathematical thinking and the use of mathematical concepts and language (Touhill, 2013). Other recommended materials and resources include instruments for measuring such as calculators, rulers and scales. The organisation of materials can also promote mathematical learning. For example, blocks can be organised so that the differences in size and shape are clear. Children also need to be able to see numbers in their environment (e.g. in posters, on signs and in books).

Children learn about numeracy through their own actions and their interactions with adults. Babies learn about numeracy as they move their bodies about in space (spatial awareness) and listen to older children and adults counting. Playful songs and rhymes such as 'This little piggy went to market' and 'Five little ducks' introduce babies to counting. Toddlers and young children learn about numeracy when teachers count things, look for shapes, use words about weights and measures, talk about the volume a bucket will hold, estimate distances, and divide up and share out food (Connor, 2011). As toddlers become more physically mobile they also begin to understand spatial relationships and distance; these are key mathematical concepts. Therefore, young children need opportunities to climb over, under and through, as well as to look at the world from different perspectives. This all contributes to their development of spatial awareness. It is important to model mathematical language in our discussions and conversations with children: up/down, outside/inside, in/out, more/less, same/different, before/after, in front of/behind, equal, not as many as, naming different shapes (Hunter & Sonter, 2012). Teachers can also help children recognise patterns, sort and categorise objects, talk about time and the patterns of the day, measure and calculate amounts, arrange objects in space and identify shapes. Teachers should also encourage pre-school and school-aged children to communicate and explain their thinking as they interact with numeracy. This will help teachers understand and assess children's numeracy learning (see the section 'Mathematics' in Chapter 6 for more on this).

Science

Scientific inquiry can help us explain the world around us, such as how electricity works and what causes disease. Scientific knowledge can help us predict what might happen, such as a cyclone hitting the coast. Scientific knowledge can also be used to guide technological development to serve our needs and interests, such as high speed travel (Worth, 2010). For young children, scientific inquiry can uncover how solids can turn into liquids, such as ice turning into water, or what happens when we place different objects into a container full of water: do they sink or do they float? Have you ever heard the saying 'children are natural scientists'? Children's curiosity is a powerful tool for their inquiry learning and play. Children need appropriate guidance to turn their curiosity into scientific learning.

Scientific inquiry involves two key components: evidence and explanation. Teachers provide learning experiences that promote scientific inquiry by encouraging children to explore objects, materials and events; and to raise questions, make careful observations and engage in simple investigations. Teachers also encourage children to describe objects (including shape, size and number); to compare, sort, classify, and order; to identify patterns and relationships; and to develop tentative explanations and ideas. Children are encouraged to work collaboratively with others, and share and discuss ideas and listen to new perspectives (Worth, 2010). Materials offer children opportunities for playful explorations of the physical world (Van Hoorn et al., 2015). Children learn scientific concepts through experimenting with a wide range of sensory materials including paints, clays, collage, bubbles, magnets, mirrors, eye droppers, rulers, tape measures, scales, magnifying glasses, fabrics, construction materials, water play, blocks in different shapes and sizes, soil, sand, water, leaves, rocks, climbing structures, plants, animals, and books about science topics. Creative teachers include free and recycled materials in their curriculum (Van Hoorn et al., 2015). The play areas, such as a post office, bank, restaurant, hospital, that were discussed in the literacy section, can also be effective areas for integration of science and mathematical learning. For example, a restaurant area encourages exploration of concepts such as weight, measurement, estimation, volume and mass. Children need time and space to engage in quality science investigations. Some investigations take place over an extended period of time, such as the growth of plants. Worth (2010) makes an important point that work with materials is fundamental to early childhood education; however, a focus on children's thinking on the science of these experiences is rare. Therefore, it is essential that teachers are comfortable with science and their abilities to teach science to children.

STOP AND REFLECT

- What role should teachers play in children's play?
- What do you want to encourage in children's play and why?
- How do your beliefs and values influence your practice?
- What is your understanding of literacy, numeracy and science?
- How might your personal experiences of literacy, numeracy and science impact upon your teaching?

Teachers can support children's wellbeing, development and learning in language, literacy, numeracy and science through a play-based curriculum. Young children in every setting should experience literacy, numeracy and science through effective, research-based curricula and teaching practices. Our learning environments need to be designed with goals and outcomes in mind, building on each child's strengths and interests to meet their individual needs. Children are observed during play and their progress towards meeting learning outcomes and goals is documented (Elliott, cited in Ebbeck & Waniganayake, 2010). Teachers use a range of strategies to support children's learning including a balance between child-led and teacher-led approaches. Teachers also recognise spontaneous teachable moments as they occur and use them to build on children's learning. To enable us to succeed in this challenging and important work it is important that we have the support of our colleagues, centre/school policies, organisation structures and resources.

Reflective practice, involving thinking, learning and understanding, is vital to providing a high-quality literacy, numeracy and science curriculum for young children. We reflect on our environment, our resources, our observations of children, our interactions with children and the children's progress towards our learning goals. We can find out more through publications, websites, discussion groups and networks, and other professional learning opportunities. Providing children with positive experiences of literacy, numeracy and science from an early age helps them to feel successful, and is an essential factor in building their motivation and persistence. By beginning with play, and utilising its innate appeal to children, we can offer each child the best start in their journey to becoming literate, numerate and to becoming scientific thinkers (Touhill, 2013).

STOP AND THINK

- Did you find a connection between literacy, numeracy and science to prove these areas are not isolated domains?
- How might a teacher foster children's language, literacy and numeracy knowledge and skills, and scientific thinking?
- How might a teacher foster this learning in an integrated way?

Formal learning and teaching: primary years

There is a continuum from play to more structured learning, with structured learning generally being associated with the school setting. The Department of Education and Training (2016) encourages teachers to provide similar environments in the early years of formal schooling to continue children's learning and investigating. However, one of the challenges to this is the range of perspectives about play that exist across different contexts. Play is not always supported in school contexts (Fleer, 2013). Hunkin (2014) carried out a research project investigating pre-school and primary teachers' perspectives of educational discontinuity between prior-to-school settings and primary school settings. As a result of this project, there is a case for the promotion of 'intersetting knowledge'. As described by Bronfenbrenner (1979) and Hunkin (2014), 'intersetting knowledge' requires teachers to be knowledgeable about the 'other setting': for the prior-to-school teachers to be knowledgeable about the primary school setting, and for primary school teachers to be knowledgeable about the prior-to-school setting.

Some researchers suggest that school limits and directs children's play (Cheska, 1987, cited in Dockett & Fleer, 1999). Trawick-Smith (2015, cited in Fromberg & Bergen, 2015) argues that play in school is distinctly time bound: there are designated periods for play, and therefore time constraints that limit children's social interactions. Play takes longer if it is to be socially meaningful and beneficial. Classrooms may also be more teacher directed, and include more teacher involvement. Trawick-Smith also notes that sometimes school teachers intervene and interrupt too often in children's play. Teachers therefore need to consider how they make time and space for play in school and the role they will play. Recommendations for transforming school play by Trawick-Smith include providing open-ended materials, for teachers to avoid intervening in children's play too quickly, for children to choose who they play with, and to lengthen play time at every grade level. Fleer (2013) recommends structures to support play, including a play shelf, play box, play area, rotation through play stations, play as part of the timetable, and a play–learning curriculum always being available. To strengthen our partnerships and the outcomes for children, support for play must be gained by colleagues and families. To support children's wellbeing, development and learning, a more gradual transition from a play-based curriculum to more formal teaching and learning in the primary years is needed.

STOP AND REFLECT

- What is the role of play in the school setting?
- Why do you use play in your classroom?
- How do you organise play in your classroom?
- Do you have rules?
- What about play in the playground?
- Does play happen in all grades? (Dockett & Fleer, 1999)

Promoting play-based learning and development

To promote play-based learning and development, partnerships need to be developed between educators and families. Each member of the partnership will bring their own personality, knowledge, skills, understandings and degree of willingness to be in the partnership. In genuine partnerships, families and teachers:

- value each other's knowledge of the child
- build on the strength of each other's knowledge
- understand each other's attitudes and expectations
- value each other's contributions to and roles in the child's life
- trust each other
- communicate freely and respectfully with each other
- share insights and perspectives about the child
- engage in shared decision-making (DEEWR, 2009).

Each person recognises, respects and values what the other does and says. Partnerships involve teachers and parents working together to benefit the child. Partnerships are essential because learning outcomes are most likely to be achieved when teachers work in partnership with families (DEEWR, 2009).

We can partner with families to promote play-based learning by sharing our knowledge, experience and enthusiasm. Experienced teachers know the promise of play from their study of child development theory and observations of children's learning. We need to explain the reasons for our approach and the carefully planned strategies that our approach involves (Broadhead et al., 2010). Typically, our conversations with parents focus on routine matters, such as how much the child ate or whether they slept or rested (Kennedy, 2012). To promote the importance of learning through play, we need our communication to focus on the child as a *learner*. This means communicating the knowledge and skills the child is learning through our play-based curriculum. We need to take the time to communicate how concepts, skills and academic standards are embedded in our play-based curriculum. For example, 'Jeanette played with the blocks today and through our interactions I observed her learning concepts of size, weight, number and balance'. Our discussion should focus on the child's competencies, strengths, interests and general development, as well as their collaborative ways of learning. We can show enthusiasm for the many cognitive, social, health and well-being benefits of play. Parents are more likely to embrace play-based learning if we help them make connections between their values and goals and what is being offered in the

MELISSA COLVILLE

setting (Hunter & Sonter, 2012). To further strengthen our partnership with families, we can communicate what children can learn at home, sharing information and ideas that support the child's learning at home and in other services, therefore strengthening our home–centre link (DET, 2016). Preparing a clear statement of the value of play for children's learning and development is an essential part of a teacher's toolkit (Fleer, 2013).

It is important we use multiple ways to communicate with families about our play-based curriculum. An obstacle to developing shared understandings with families, particularly with ethnic minority or bilingual parents, may be poor communication (Broadhead et al., 2010). Face-to-face contact is recommended in the first instance. Face-to-face communication is more personal and offers non-verbal as well as verbal cues. Miscommunication is less likely in face-to-face communication. Our communication should focus on meeting the needs of the individual family, such as communication with parents whose first language is different from our own. Written and visual communication is also recommended. Our documentation needs to demonstrate what we know about the link between play and learning in a way that is understood by families. Documentation can then be used as a prompt to discuss the play-based curriculum with families. The Reggio Emilia approach to documentation is highly recommended. Documentation is displayed to provide a record of the learning process, and to make learning highly visible to children and families. The centres of Reggio Emilia document their experiences with children, paying attention to the presentation of the children's thinking, ideas and questions, social interactions and relationships. Documenting children's play and projects through photographs, visual arts and writing makes the links between play and academic learning more evident to families (Van Hoorn et al., 2015). The voices of children and families should be included in this documentation to provide further understanding to all stakeholders. Other ways to communicate children's learning include portfolios, work samples and learning stories. Speaking with families about the kinds of documentation they respond to will be invaluable.

We need to be aware that there may be cultural barriers to valuing play-based learning. According to Broadhead et al. (2010), parents, for a variety of reasons, may be unconvinced that playful learning experiences are as effective as didactic ones in supporting children's acquisition of the knowledge and skills they need to succeed in later stages of schooling, and in life. Some parents' educational experiences may have been entirely formal and this may be one reason why they value didactic teaching. We need to consider what kinds of arguments and messages are likely to be listened to by families and what matters for children in our cultural community. For example, the value of both 'preparation for school' and 'preparation for life' is accepted in most cultures (Broadhead et al., 2010). Society places great emphasis on outcomes; therefore, we need to show children's familiarity with literacy and numeracy, their confidence in handling tools and technologies, and their ability to communicate successfully with adults and children. The visible presence of numbers and letters, books and mathematical resources, computers and educational displays can also be a reassurance for parents that children are 'learning'. Parents can be invited to spend time in our classrooms to see, firsthand, the benefits of our play-based curriculum. Parent libraries with resources relating to the play-based curriculum are also recommended. While issues relating to culture can be challenging, there are numerous ways to build and strengthen our understandings of play with families.

STOP AND REFLECT

- Have you ever encountered a parent who criticised a play-based curriculum? How did you or the teacher respond?
- How would you feel if someone referred to something you had put a lot of effort into as 'play'?

In their book *From Play to Practice: Connecting Teachers' Play to Children's Learning*, Nell and Drew (2013) discuss how to be a play workshop coach and conduct a 'play workshop experience'. This workshop gives parents the opportunity to play, in order to understand play's true value and role in the learning process. The workshop these authors describe is one where adults experience the play process in a safe and accepting environment with hands-on activities, reflection and dialogue, and the investigation of theory and practice.

Partnerships take time to develop—time to get to know parents and understand their goals for their child. We need to look for a range of opportunities to communicate and make connections with parents about how (parents' and teachers') goals are being achieved through play-based curriculum. When we make these connections, we need to show a genuine warmth, interest and affection for each child. A consensus with families

MELISSA COLVILLE

that play promotes children's learning will benefit all stakeholders, especially children. Creating a strong partnership to promote play begins with creating a welcoming and inclusive environment where 'all families are encouraged to participate in and contribute to experiences that enhance the child's learning and development' (DET, 2016, p.9). Communication should be ongoing and should focus on the positive and beneficial outcomes of play and play-based learning.

STOP AND REFLECT

- What have you noticed about cultural diversity in children's play?
- Do you think there are cultural variations in children's choices and approaches to play? What examples can you think of?
- What influences the decisions we (parents, community and educators) make about children and play?
- What are the key messages you want to send to families about learning through play?
- Imagine a discussion with a parent who is concerned that their four-year-old daughter is spending a lot of time playing and not doing the kind of work that will prepare them for school. How would you respond to this parent's concern?

Conclusion

We face many challenges in incorporating play into the early childhood curriculum: challenges in responding to those calling for a more academic curriculum, challenges in the materials and environments we create for play and challenges in trying to understand the play we observe (Dockett & Fleer, 1999). The task of understanding play is even more challenging as we try to make connections between the vast research and knowledge base and the expectations of play in practice (Wood, 2013). My advice is to read widely with an open, yet critical mind. I agree with Kathy Walker: the debate should not be about whether we should use a play-based curriculum in early childhood, but *how*. Let's remember that the stakes in this debate are considerable and the child's learning, development and wellbeing are paramount.

SUMMARY

- Play is developmentally appropriate, children love to play, and theory and research support the value of play for children's learning; yet barriers to play such as the affordance of time and the pressure for teachers to reduce play-based learning still exist.
- Complex play, where high level thinking and learning takes place, needs time to unfold. If teachers are pressured to reduce time for play-based learning they need to be able to articulate the compelling benefits of a play-based curriculum for children's learning and development.
- We should value play for the meaning it has for children. Although children's perspectives on play are diverse, they frequently involve powerful, positive emotions and feelings.

- Play is important for children's sense of identity and wellbeing.
- The value of relationships in early childhood education cannot be underestimated. Forming partnerships with parents and families in promoting play-based learning and development will be of great benefit to the children in our care. Moreover, we need to understand various types of play for different age groups and the current trends in children's play experiences to inform our play pedagogy.
- In the context of early childhood education, play needs to be an integral experience and pedagogical approach for children from birth.

FURTHER REFLECTION

- How would you describe a play-based curriculum?
- How would you describe play-based learning?
- What are the benefits of play-based learning for children?
- How would you describe high-quality play?

GROUP DISCUSSION

1 How does your description of high-quality play compare to others? Are there similarities? Are there differences?
2 How can high-quality play take place effectively?
3 What role does the teacher play in a play-based curriculum?
4 What are the challenges and barriers to play you have experienced?
5 How can we effectively assess a play-based curriculum?
6 What questions do you have about play and play-based learning?
7 What types of play are privileged or valued? Why?

CLASS EXERCISE

In small groups:

- Choose one play area indoors and one play area outdoors (e.g. home corner, block corner, arts table, obstacle course, sandpit).
- What is the potential for learning in each area?
- In what ways might children extend the potential for learning through their own actions (such as combining resources) in this area?
- In what ways can teachers extend children's potential for learning in this area? (Adapted from Wood, 2013, p.74.)

FURTHER READING

Dockett, S. & Fleer, M. (1999) Play and Pedagogy in Early Childhood: Bending the Rules. NSW, Australia: Cengage Learning.

This text builds on the information in this chapter from an Australian perspective. Broad topics include theories of play, new ways to look at play, analysing play and play in action. In particular, I recommend Chapter 6, 'Confronting assumptions about play'. For more information on children and play, see 'Culture and play' (Chapter 7). For more information on differences in pretend play; play and gifted young children; and play and young children with special needs, see 'Individual differences in play' (Chapter 11). For further information on play in the school setting I recommend Chapter 14, 'Play at school'.

MELISSA COLVILLE

Ebbeck, M. & Waniganayake, M. (2010) Play in Early Childhood Education: Learning in Diverse Contexts. Vic., Australia: Oxford University Press.

This Australian edited text provides an introduction to the theories behind play, critical ways of thinking about children's play and the practical implications for children's learning and development. This text is particularly helpful in learning about the play of infants (see Chapters 2 and 3). For indicators of children's developing language and literacy; numeracy; and science skills pp.76–7. To learn about science in a culture that differs from the Western view I recommend Chapter 11, 'Children redefine learning in science through play'.

Fleer, M. (2013) Play in the Early Years. Cambridge, UK: Cambridge University.

This text extends on the information given in this chapter. Of particular value, Fleer includes numerous vignettes and real-world examples of children's play (including infants), to help readers connect theory to practice. Many Initial Teacher Education students have found this text helpful. For further reading on historical and contemporary theories of play, see Chapter 5, 'Theories of play'. For further reading on promoting play-based learning and development, see Chapter 10, 'Being a play activist'.

Fromberg, D.P. & Bergen, D. (2015) Play from Birth to Twelve: Contexts, Perspectives and Meanings (3rd edn). New York: Routledge.

This is an edited text that includes many experts in the field, therefore providing an eclectic view. This text helps us explore a variety of theoretical and practical ideas about many aspects of play, including the teacher's role in supporting children's play. See 'Influences of race, culture, social class, and gender: Diversity and play' by Ramsey (Chapter 28), in particular, 'Implications for practice' on pages 277–8.

Hunter, L. & Sonter, L. (2012) Progressing Play: Practicalities, Intentions and Possibilities in Emerging Co-constructed Curriculum. Warner, Qld, Australia: Consultants at play.

A beautifully presented and easy-to-read text, with photos and examples from practice. Hunter and Sonter include many thoughtful questions and practical teaching strategies to support children's play. This text integrates principles and practices, including the place of play, respectful relationships and partnerships, and inclusive learning environments.

Moyles, J. (2015) The Excellence of Play (4th edn). Maidenhead, UK: McGraw-Hill Education.

This edited text asks the reader many thought-provoking questions, promoting deeper reflection on our values, beliefs, understandings and practices in regard to play and play-based learning. Topics include taking play seriously, gender and play, babies at play, play and literacy learning and play with children from diverse cultures.

Nell, M.L. & Drew, W.F. (2013) From Play to Practice: Connecting Teachers' Play to Children's Learning. Washington, DC: National Association for the education of young children.

Recommended, in particular, for its information on the 'play workshop experience', this text helps readers deepen their understanding of the importance of play and how to promote play-based learning in the early childhood setting. See pages 35–41 and 45–53 for more specific detail about conducting a 'play workshop experience'.

Sheridan, M.D. (1999) Play in Early Childhood: From Birth to Six Years. Oxon, UK: Routledge.

This book provides information on the ages and stages in the development of play and the outlines of some significant play sequences.

Sheridan, M.D. (2011) Play in Early Childhood: From Birth to Six Years (3rd edn). Oxon, UK: Routledge.

This is an easy-to-use text that defines play and the ages and stages in the development of children's play. An overview of some of the typical and significant play sequences for children is given, followed by the role of adults. This text would be particularly useful for Initial Teacher Education students in understanding child development and providing developmentally appropriate play experiences for children, and for Initial Teacher Education students on practicum with children from birth to six years.

Van Hoorn, J., Nourat, P.M., Scales, B. & Alward, K.R. (2015) Play at the Center of Curriculum (6th edn). New Jersey, US: Prentice Hall.

This was one of my key texts as an Initial Teacher Education student. It extends the information in this chapter in many instances and is therefore a highly recommended text. For more information on facilitating children's play using numeracy, I recommend Chapter 7, 'Mathematics in the play-centered curriculum'. For indicators of children's developing language and literacy skills I recommend Chapter 8, 'Language, literacy and play'. I also recommend Chapter 9, 'Science in the play-centered curriculum' to extend your understanding of indicators of children's developing science skills .

Wood, E. (2013) *Play, Learning and the Early Childhood Curriculum* (3rd edn). London, UK: Sage.
This engaging text includes contemporary research on play, international contexts and practical examples, and promotes critical reflection in many topic areas. If you are enthusiastic about the outdoor environment I recommend Chapter 6, 'Play and learning in outdoor environments'.

REFERENCES

Australian Government (2018) *Inactivity and Screen Time*. http://www.health.gov.au/internet/publications/publishing. nsf/Content/gug-indig-hb~inactivity.

Berk, L. (2013) *Child Development* (9th edn). Boston: Pearson.

Bodrova, E. & Leong. D.J. (2007) *Tools of the Mind: The Vygotskian Approach to Early Childhood Education* (2nd edn). New Jersey, US: Pearson.

Broadhead, P., Howard, J. & Wood, E. (2010) *Play and Learning in the Early Years*. London, UK: Sage.

Bronfenbrenner, U. (1979) *The Ecology of Human Development: Experiments by Nature and Design*. Cambridge, MA: Harvard University Press.

Brussoni, M., Olsen, L.L., Pike, I. & Sleet, D.A. (2012) 'Risky Play and Children's Safety: Balancing Priorities for Optimal Child Development', *International Journal of Environmental Research and Public Health*, 9: 3134–48.

Caro, C. (2012) *The Adult Role in Child-led Play: How to Become a Learning Ally*. www.nature-play.co.uk/blog/the-adult-role-in-child-led-play-how-to-become-a-learning-ally

Connor, J. (2011) *Being Numerate*. www.earlychildhoodaustralia.org.au/nqsplp/wp-content/uploads/2012/05/EYLFPLP_E-Newsletter_No22.pdf

Copple, C. & Bredekamp, S. (2009) *Developmentally Appropriate Practice in Early Childhood Programs: Serving Children from Birth through Age 8*. Washington, DC, U.S: National Association for the Education of Young Children.

Department of Education and Training (Victoria) (DET)/Victorian Curriculum and Assessment Authority (VCCA) (2016) *Victorian Early Years Learning and Development Framework: For All Children from Birth to Eight Years*. State of Victoria, Australia: Department of Education and Training.

Department of Education, Employment and Workplace Relations (DEEWR) (2009) *Belonging, Being & Becoming: The Early Years Learning Framework for Australia*. ACT, Australia: Commonwealth of Australia.

Dockett, S. & Fleer, M. (1999) *Play and Pedagogy in Early Childhood: Bending the Rules.* NSW, Australia: Cengage Learning.

Dunlevy, S. (2016) 'Australian Children Can't Run, Throw, Catch or Jump According to a Damning New Report', *The Daily Telegraph*, 16 November.

Durant, S. & Raban, B. (2011) *Outdoor Play: Play in the Early Years*. Albert Park, Vic.: Teaching Solutions.

Early Childhood Australia (2013) *Talking about Practice: Adventurous Play—Developing a Culture of Risky Play*. www.earlychildhoodaustralia.org.au/nqsplp/wp-content/uploads/2013/07/NQS_PLP_E-Newsletter_No58.pdf

Ebbeck, M. & Waniganayake, M. (2010) *Play in Early Childhood Education: Learning in Diverse Contexts.* South Melbourne, Vic.: Oxford University Press.

Elkind, D. (2007a) *The Hurried Child: Growing Up Too Fast Too Soon* (3rd edn). Cambridge, MA: Da Capo Press.

Elkind, D. (2007b) *The Power of Play*: *How Spontaneous, Imaginative Activities Lead to Happier, Healthier Children* (3rd edn). Cambridge, MA: Da Capo Press.

Erikson, E. (1977) *Childhood and Society.* London: Paladin Grafton Books.

Fleer, M. (2013) *Play in the Early Years*. Cambridge, U.K.: Cambridge University.

MELISSA COLVILLE

Flood, C. & Hardy, E. (2013) *Early Childhood Education and Play*. Dublin: Gill & MacMillan.

Fromberg, D.P. & Bergen, D. (2015) *Play from Birth to Twelve: Contexts, Perspectives and Meanings* (3rd edn). New York: Routledge.

Gray, P. (2015) *Early Academic Training Produces Long-Term Harm*. www.psychologytoday.com/blog/freedom-learn/201505/early-academic-training-produces-long-term-harm

Grieshaber, S. & McArdle, F. (2011) *The Trouble with Play*. Maidenhead, UK: Open University Press.

Gronlund, G. (2010) *Developmentally Appropriate Play: Guiding Young Children to a Higher Level*. St Paul, MN: Redleaf Press.

Hughes, B. (2003) *Play Deprivation: Impact, Consequences and the Potential of Playwork*. www.playwales.org.uk/login/uploaded/documents/INFORMATION%20SHEETS/play%20deprivation%20impact%20consequences%20and%20potential%20of%20playwork.pdf

Hunkin, E. (2014) 'We're Offering True Play-Based Learning: Teacher Perspectives on Educational Dis/Continuity in the Early Years', *Australasian Journal of Early Childhood, 39*(2): 30–5.

Hunter, L. & Sonter, L. (2012) *Progressing Play: Practicalities, Intentions and Possibilities in Emerging Co-constructed Curriculum*. Warner, QLD, Australia: Consultants at play.

Isenberg, J.P. & Jalongo, G.M. (2014) *Why Is Play Important? Social and Emotional Development, Physical Development, Creative Development*. www.education.com/reference/article/importance-play--social-emotional/

Kennedy, A. (2012) *Evaluating and Communicating about Children's Learning*. www.earlychildhoodaustralia.org.au/nqsplp/wp-content/uploads/2012/11/NQS_PLP_E-Newsletter_No48.pdf

Kohn, D. (2015) *Let the Kids Learn through Play*. www.nytimes.com/2015/05/17/opinion/sunday/let-the-kids-learn-through-play.html?_r=1

Lewis, C. & Lamb, M.E. (2003) 'Fathers' Influences on Children's Development: The Evidence from Two-Parent Families', *European Journal of Psychology of Education*, *18*, 211–88.

Little, H. (2015) 'Promoting Risk-Taking and Physically Challenging Play in Australian Early Childhood Settings in a Changing Regulatory Environment', *Journal of Early Childhood Research*, doi: 10.1177/1476718X15579743.

Little, H. & Sweller, N. (2015) 'Affordances for Risk-Taking and Physical Activity in Australian Early Childhood Education Settings', *Early Childhood Education Journal, 43*(4): 337–45.

Little, H. & Wyver, S. (2012) 'Outdoor Play: Does Avoiding the Risks Reduce the Benefits?' *Australasian Journal of Early Childhood, 33*(2): 33–40.

Moyles, J. (2015) *The Excellence of Play* (4th edn). Maidenhead, UK: McGraw-Hill Education.

National Council of Teachers of Mathematics (2013) *Mathematics in Early Childhood Learning*. www.nctm.org/Standards-and-Positions/Position-Statements/Mathematics-in-Early-Childhood-Learning/

Nell, M.L. & Drew, W.F. (2013) From Play to Practice: Connecting Teachers' Play to Children's Learning. Washington, DC, U.S.: National Association for the Education of Young Children.

North, S. (2012) 'Play Time Vital for Children', *The Sydney Morning Herald*, 3 September.

Nutbrown, C. (2010) *Frogs and Snails, Sugar and Spice*. www.teachearlyyears.com/images/uploads/article/gender-stereotyping-in-the-early-years.pdf

Parten, M.B. (1932) 'Social Participation among Preschool Children', *Journal of Abnormal and Social Psychology*, *27*(3): 243–69.

Play Australia (2015) *Getting the Balance Right: Our New Guide for Risk Management*. www.playaustralia.org.au/

Pramling-Samuelsson, I. & Fleer, M. (2009) *Play and Learning in Early Childhood Settings: International Perspectives* Vic.: Springer.

Raising Children Network (2017) *Screen Time*. http://raisingchildren.net.au/articles/screen_time.html

Riddall-Leech, S. & Raban, B. (2011) *Discovery Play: Play in the Early Years*. Albert Park, Vic.: Teaching Solutions.

Rogoff, B. (1990) *Apprenticeship in Thinking: Cognitive Development in Social Context*. New York: Oxford University Press.

Rowell, P. (2010) *The World Is a Child's Stage: Dramatic Play and Children's Development*. http://ncac.acecqa.gov.au/educator-resources/pcf-articles/WorldisChildsStageDec2010.pdf

Santer, J., Griffiths, C. & Goodall D. (2007) *Free Play in Early Childhood: A Literature Review*. www.playengland.org.uk/media/120426/free-play-in-early-childhood.pdf

Shepard, E. (2015) *8 Science-backed Reasons for Letting Your Kids Play Outdoors*. www.parent.co/8-science-backed-reasons-for-letting-your-kids-play-outdoors/

Tansey, S. (2009) *Playing Fair: Gender Equity in Childcare*. www.partnersinprevention.org.au/wp-content/uploads/Playing-fair-%E2%80%93-gender-equity-in-child-care.pdf

Touhill, L. (2013) *Play-based Approaches to Literacy and Numeracy*. www.earlychildhoodaustralia.org.au/nqsplp/wp-content/uploads/2013/11/NQS_PLP_E-Newsletter_No66.pdf

Trawick-Smith, J., Wolff, J., Koschel, M. & Vallarelli, J. (2015) 'Effects of Toys on the Play Quality of Preschool Children: Influence of Gender, Ethnicity, and Socioeconomic Status', *Early Childhood Education Journal*, 43, 249–56.

Van Hoorn, J., Nourot, P.M., Scales, B. & Alward, K.R. (2015) *Play at the Center of Curriculum* (6th edn). New Jersey, US: Prentice Hall.

Verberne, M. (2014) 'Schools Cutting into Children's Essential Play', *The Age*, 1 September.

Vygotsky, L. (1978) 'Interaction between Learning and Development', in M. Gauvain & M. Cole (eds) *Readings on the Development of Children*. New York: Scientific American Books, pp. 34–40.

Walker, K. (2012) *Teaching and Learning: What Is Best Practice in Early Years?* http://eyes.org.au/wp-content/uploads/2012/05/KATHY-WALKER-Teaching-and-Learning-in-Early-Years.pdf

Wood, E. (2013) *Play, Learning and the Early Childhood Curriculum* (3rd edn). London, UK: Sage.

Worth, K. (2010) *Science in Early Childhood Classrooms: Content and Process*. http://ecrp.illinois.edu/beyond/seed/worth.html

Curriculum and Pedagogy

Carol Carter

Chapter objectives

In this chapter, we will:
- consider the definitions of curriculum and pedagogy and what they mean to learning and teaching environments
- identify and discuss different interests, beliefs and thinking about curriculum and pedagogy
- examine and analyse curriculum and pedagogical models and approaches in early childhood education.

Key terms

arts-based curriculum model   emergent curriculum   inquiry-based curriculum
content or syllabus view of   ideology   pedagogy
   curriculum   integrated curriculum

> The curriculum is never simply a neutral assemblage of knowledge,
> somehow appearing in the texts and classrooms of a nation.
> It is always part of a selective tradition, someone's selection,
> some group's vision of legitimate knowledge. It is produced out
> of the cultural, political, and economic conflicts, tensions, and
> compromises that organize and disorganize a people.
>
> (Apple, 1993, p.222)

When I think about curriculum and pedagogy I think about how carefully and critically we need to examine what we are going to teach, how we are going to teach and why. It is precisely because education is never neutral and always reflects our own and other stakeholders' agendas, philosophies, beliefs and ideals that we need to constantly be considering, analysing and reviewing what we teach in the light of what will best serve the educational needs of the children in our care. Vygotsky (1997, p. 348) states that education 'is never and was never politically indifferent … it has always adopted a particular social pattern and political line, in accordance with the dominant social class that has guided its interests'.

An extreme example of where a curriculum purposefully perpetuated a particular political agenda was the selection of a Christian Nation curriculum in apartheid South Africa in the mid twentieth century that deliberately promoted dominance and division as it was underpinned by bigoted, racist beliefs such as the following:

> When I have control over native education. I will reform it so that natives will be taught from childhood that equality with Europeans is not for them.
>
> (Verwoerd, 1953, in Christie, 1992, p.12)

> We should not give the Natives any academic education. If we do who is going to do the manual labour in the community?
>
> (Le Roux, 1945, in Christie, 1992, p.12)

The following purpose statement from the current South African curriculum is embedded in a very different set of beliefs and political agenda.

The National Curriculum Statement Grades R–12 serves the purpose of:
equipping learners, irrespective of their socio-economic background, race, gender, physical ability or intellectual ability, with the knowledge, skills and values necessary for self-fulfilment, and meaningful participation in society as citizens of a free country …

(Department of Basic Education, 2017)

When we examine the two statements from the same country (South Africa)—different time (1945 and 2017—72 years apart) and different political era (apartheid and post-apartheid—it is easy to see the lack of neutrality within curriculum statements and that curriculum is always a part of 'someone's selection, some group's vision of legitimate knowledge'.

Introduction

I have lively debates and conversations about the complex nature of curriculum with colleagues around the world who are involved in teacher education. While we disagree about many things, the one aspect that we do agree on is our respect for, and belief in, the quality of contemporary early child curriculum frameworks such as the Early Years Learning Framework for Australia (EYLF) and the New Zealand curriculum policy statement, Te Whāriki. However, even when using these frameworks to drive and support learning and teaching there is still the need to interrogate what, how and why we teach to ensure that this matches particular contexts and learners and that we don't become robot-like teachers who simply implement what others have decided for us as opposed to carefully considering the desired skills, knowledge, values and attitudes for specific groups of learners. As you read through this chapter and respond to the various reflective questions asked, keep thinking critically about the various beliefs, values and agendas that contribute to classroom curriculum and pedagogy and the connections to the different views of childhood discussed in Chapter 1.

This chapter will define curriculum and pedagogy and examine many factors that inform and shape these concepts within education generally, and specifically as they relate to early childhood education. The factors include teachers' perceptions, values and knowledge, global and national reforms, as well as the increasing involvement of government. Curriculum approaches that reflect the different visions of the child and society will also be examined. Knowledge of this information will build understanding of the impact of curriculum decisions on children's learning. The enactment of different curriculum approaches in practice will involve making pedagogical choices that influence teaching and learning. The role of early years programs that include play-based, child-centred, child-directed, child–adult co-constructed and emergent curricula will also be examined.

The term 'curriculum' evokes different meanings and understandings, some of which will be explored in this chapter, particularly within the context of early childhood education. Different definitions abound and according to Portelli (cited in Marsh, 2009, p.4), in one year (1987) more than 120 definitions of the term appeared in professional journals. There are many instances where the term 'curriculum' gets used without being clearly defined or clarified, so it is frequently up to the listener or reader to figure out exactly how it is being used. It is a term people know, but it can be difficult to come up with a definition immediately (Churchill et al., 2016).

CAROL CARTER

Discussing and defining curriculum

The word 'curriculum' comes from the Latin root *cur*, which means to run or dash. The Latin word *currere* means to run a set route or course. What do you think are some of the disadvantages or drawbacks of considering curriculum in this way? A set route or course implies an inflexible and single pathway for all. So, a disadvantage could be that such a curriculum view would not cater for individual needs or focus on the strengths of different learners. The notion of 'running a course' also has connotations of finishing as quickly as possible, the product (the course) being more important than the process and a definite step-by-step pattern that is 'set' beforehand and does not consider different learning contexts or learners. The problem with curriculum that does not cater for different needs is that it assumes that everyone learns in the same way and at the same pace. A cartoon that makes this point is where the curriculum for fish (and various creatures) is tree climbing. Obviously this is problematic - for example, fish would need to move out of their environment, elephants would not be able to perform such a function, monkeys would find the curriculum too easy, and so on.

Viewing curriculum in this way is strongly linked to a **content or syllabus view of curriculum**, where curriculum is seen as what is studied as the subject matter or an object, and where the 'the basic component of the curriculum, the syllabus is designed elsewhere by expert curriculum designers and developers, and given to those for whom it is intended for their use' (Grundy, cited in Churchill, et al., 2016, p.190). A syllabus is *a document detailing the content of a course of study or what content should be covered within a specific time-frame and in what order*. Syllabi may have been carefully considered and planned but are mass-produced and are documents that do not take into account different contexts and needs. I am reminded of a step-by-step record book, used in my first year of teaching a class of five- and six-year-olds, in which I had to tick and record the date and time each time I had taught a part of the required syllabus. I was also encouraged to make sure that children had learnt certain skills in order. For instance, it was suggested that until children could identify which was their left and which was their right hands, we should avoid teaching them certain early reading skills. I remember breathing a sigh of relief that I, who still on occasion experience challenges with left–right orientation, had escaped this and been allowed to learn to read.

One alternative view of curriculum is centred around curriculum as an *action*, or what is termed a pedagogical view, where curriculum is seen as more than a document containing subject matter, but rather as a 'dynamic process which engages all participants, especially teachers and students, in its active construction through their work' (Grundy, cited in Churchill et al., 2016, p.190). There is a strong interconnection and relationship between subject matter, participants (teachers and students) and the educational environment, ambience or milieu, as illustrated here.

content or syllabus view of curriculum where curriculum is seen as what is studied as the subject matter or an object.

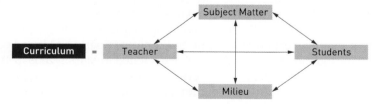

Source: Grundy, 1988, cited in Churchill et al., 2016.

This broader view of curriculum allows for far more flexibility in terms of subject matter and the contextualisation of curriculum to suit the needs of particular groups in educational settings. It also gives participants a sense of ownership over what is being taught and learnt and the type of learning spaces that are established. This view of curriculum joins together and interweaves content (or subject matter) with learning experiences that take place within specific contexts. Curriculum is seen as the lived experience of an educational space, everything that takes place in that space, not just the resources, material, programs and lesson activities and plans. It is also about the teaching and learning relationships, attitudes and feelings that form a part of the learning and teaching experiences (Lunenberg, 2011).

Early childhood curriculum frameworks endorse this view of curriculum with such statements as curriculum being 'All the interactions, experiences, activities, routines and events, planned and unplanned, that occur in an environment designed *to foster children's learning and development*' (DEEWR 2009, p.9, adapted from Te Whāriki). I frequently go into early childhood education settings where my students are engaged in practice-based experiences. While the same curriculum framework document may be used, what is happening in these spaces and how learning and development is supported, are vastly different. Despite being different, they are all examples of a broader view of curriculum than that of simply following a curriculum document.

Curriculum 'as syllabus and subject matter' or, more broadly, 'as action and lived experiences', are just two of many ways in which curriculum can be defined and described. Other ways of defining and classifying curriculum will become apparent when I discuss the ideas and practical aspects of different curriculum approaches. Before we move on to a definition and discussion of pedagogy, I need to draw your attention to views of curriculum that critique the more 'traditional' views discussed here. These critical views highly value elements such as subjectivity, intuition, different ways of knowing, personality and aesthetics. Advocates of these alternative views of curriculum argue that 'curriculum cannot be precisely planned—it evolves as a living organism as opposed to a machine which is precise and orderly' (Lunenberg, 2011, p.5).

'A curriculum may refer to a system, as in a *national curriculum*; an institution, as in a *school curriculum*; or even to an individual school, as in the *school geography curriculum*' (Scott 2008, cited in McLachlan et al., 2013, p.9). There are different categories of curriculum. These include:

- *explicit curriculum*—teaching content or subjects and the specific skills, knowledge and attitudes required for that content or subject. For example, teaching young children a song or dance or teaching children about recycling and sustainability
- *implicit curriculum*—learning from the educational culture that is not directly taught but is part of an educational setting. For example, at the all girls school that I attended we were expected to be polite, well-behaved, respectful, not too boisterous and to act with decorum. These were behaviours that were largely implied, rather than explicitly taught. They may be linked to the hidden curriculum but generally they are part of societal norms and as such are intentionally part of implicit learning
- *hidden curriculum*—is what is learnt but not openly intended (e.g. conformity, good work habits, gender roles and belief systems). It can be both positive and negative and can be

CAROL CARTER

contrary to explicit curriculum. For example, the educational setting may teach anti-bias and social justice but the way in which the setting operates or the people interact may convey a strong opposite message. If children feel disrespected or neglected in school they're learning from that too. But they are not necessarily learning the curriculum that teachers think they are

- *null curriculum*—topics or perspectives that are deliberately excluded from the curriculum. For example, schools with a specific religious orientation may exclude the teaching of theories of evolution
- *extra curriculum or co-curriculum*—programs that supplement or complement the school curriculum such as drama club, athletics, and so on.

Working with children requires us to think very carefully about the clarity of the messages we convey to them, as this real-life vignette illustrates.

One day an exasperated parent came to see me. She was a nurse who worked different shifts at the hospital and generally had time to read with her young six-year-old daughter in the afternoons. However, her daughter, Tanya, who was in my class, flatly refused to read with her and said that I had told them that they should read at night. When I reflected on how this had occurred, I realised that I was indeed in the habit of saying, 'When you read with Mum or Dad tonight …' but had not intended this to be a binding rule! Tanya had also told her mother that I said that she read really well but that she needed to read with more 'sexpression', once again conveying my lack of explicit teaching and clarity and my unintended message.

Another example of an unintended message was one that I learnt from my father. As a young child, I was surrounded by parents and siblings who were very good at sport. I was not. However, I was always willing to participate in different activities. One day, at a special kindergarten day, I participated in a race and ended up, not surprising to my parents, coming last. My gentle father felt immensely sorry for me. He sat me down and carefully explained to me that someone had to come last and that, in fact, because I came last, I made other children feel good about themselves. For years, I saw this as one of my missions in life, and I proudly and sometimes purposefully, let others pass me by.

In some literature, curriculum and pedagogy are written about as if they are indistinguishable, or the same thing. This is particularly unhelpful and makes it almost impossible to reflect on such broad views of curriculum and pedagogy. Pedagogy is frequently seen as the broader, overarching concept under which curriculum and other aspects of education are positioned. My own and others' views are that curriculum and pedagogy are distinct but complementary terms that do overlap at times. *Pedagogy influences the choice of curriculum approach and the practical application of curriculum in educational environments. Curriculum choices impact on pedagogical approaches, strategies and techniques that are used in these educational environments.*

STOP AND REFLECT

- What comes to mind when you think of curriculum?
- What has been your own experience of the way curriculum is viewed?
- How do you define curriculum?
- How have you experienced aspects of the curriculum, such as:
  - hidden curriculum?
  - null curriculum?
  - extra curriculum?
- What is the connection and distinction between a curriculum and a curriculum framework?
- What are some other examples of the different categories of curriculum?
- What do you think are the advantages and disadvantages of seeing curriculum as 'everything that happens in an educational space'?
- How does a teacher's image of the child affect curriculum?

Discussing and defining pedagogy

The term 'pedagogy' originated from ancient Greece and means 'to guide or lead the child' (literally the boy). The pedagogue, in ancient Greece, was a slave who saw to the learning of his master's son (Lucas, 1972). **Pedagogy** is the art of teaching; as such it is 'the underpinning philosophy that drives education: the how and why we educate' (Waters & Angliss, 2005, p.4). Pedagogy is informed by 'scientific' evidence, teaching philosophies and theories and successful teaching experiences. It encompasses knowledge, skills, principles, values, theoretical perspectives, teacher–learner relationships, teaching approaches and learning processes requisite for effective teaching. Discipline-specific pedagogical knowledge includes presenting and depicting subject knowledge in ways that are useful and understandable (Shulman, 1986).

Pedagogy is viewed as an early childhood teacher's *professional practice*, especially those aspects that involve building and nurturing relationships, curriculum decision making, teaching and learning (DEEWR, 2009, p.9). A pedagogical approach consists of a comprehensive set of teaching and learning methods, techniques and strategies that support learning and constitute resources for quality teaching. Pedagogical considerations (Ashman & Elkins, 2009, p.203) include how the teaching is conveyed, what resources and materials are used (overlapping with curriculum) and how learning success is measured in the form of assessment. Aspects of assessment and evaluation are considered in Chapter 12.

The pedagogical approach that is favoured will depend on our view of the child and whether our teaching methods and strategies are based on a more liberal view of pedagogy (where the autonomy and agency of the child is the focus) or a more conservative view that is grounded in the authority of the teacher. If you think back to Chapter 2 and the way in which the child is viewed in today's society, a liberal view of pedagogy will currently predominate in early childhood settings. This is a view of pedagogy that I most certainly favour and subscribe to.

pedagogy is the art of science and teaching.

The quality of pedagogy in early childhood, linked with relationships between teacher and child (discussed in Chapter 13 of this book), is identified as the crucial factor for improving children's outcomes and providing robust, durable foundations for lifelong learning. Teachers need to constantly reflect on, understand and be clear about their pedagogy, what drives their practice and why they work in particular ways. 'Different theories about early childhood inform approaches to children's learning and development. Early childhood educators draw upon a range of perspectives in their work …' (DEEWR, 2009, p.11).

Theories that feature in the EYLF and have been discussed in Chapter 3 impact on teaching and learning in different ways. So, for example, if behaviourist theories impact on pedagogy, we will see rewards, positive re-enforcement and so on being part of the early childhood teachers' practices. Sociocultural theory in practice will see teachers encouraging ways of getting children to share knowledge and experiences and co-construct meaning. The practical application of critical theory could involve shifting power dynamics—for example children being more in control through planning and discussion meetings during group time.

Teachers need to select pedagogical strategies and resources that are relevant to their learners (Duncum, 2002) and this means they need to develop the relevant skills and knowledge. So, for example, those teachers limited to mono-cultural experiences are not equipped for 'teaching in multicultural classrooms' (McFee, 1995, p.190). Within any learning and teaching environment there is a need to provide 'culturally responsive curriculum' (Veblen et al., 2005) and resources that 'reflect the dynamic cultural landscapes in which young people live' (Nicholson, 2000, p.160). Demographic changes in our classroom require us to build up valuable pedagogies that ensure we are taking advantage of individual and cultural differences in learning and meeting diverse educational needs.

Curriculum and pedagogical interests, ideologies and thinking

As Ashman and Elkins (2009) state, curriculum content is not only a reflection of what society values, but also of what it hopes to become. Curriculum is constructed and considered by a variety of stakeholders who have a range of interests and ideals, and represent particular points of view and different goals and purposes that they believe curriculum should be serving. There may be some consensus and overlap with regard to various stakeholders, but curriculum and pedagogical approaches are often contested and the subject of debate and discussion. Various stakeholders include politicians, teachers and principals, students, parents, education 'experts', public servants, industry, business and local communities, and professional organisations. Different beliefs, ideas and biases will impact on stakeholders' views of curriculum and pedagogy. For example, ideas about childhood and parenthood, beliefs about gender, class or race, attitudes towards experts in general or on what qualifies as valued expert opinion or resistance to change ('that's how education was when I was your age and it should remain that way') influence the ways in which stakeholders participate in curriculum and pedagogical debates. Power and status are active factors in the debates, including who is included and who is excluded.

Parents have an interest in the curriculum as an instrument for achievement. They would like to see their children succeeding and generally put their trust in the curriculum for this to happen. Teachers are usually the mediators of curriculum and have to make curriculum and pedagogical decisions on a daily basis. Governments and businesses tend to have interests that are mainly economic.

The *user* of the house will be a better judge than the *builder* (attributed to Aristotle). This means that children or students and their teachers will best be able to judge the curriculum and pedagogical approaches used. Yet frequently the most important stakeholders, namely children, are not consulted with regard to issues of curriculum and pedagogy.

What role, if any, should the child have in curriculum development and evaluation? I believe they should have a significant role. A couple of months ago I observed at a kindergarten, where it was refreshing to see a four-year-old group being asked what they would like to learn about and why, the way in which the children gave serious, thoughtful and careful attention to the question, affirming the beliefs in children as being agents of their own learning and in the contribution that children can and do make to questions about their own learning. It also made me wonder how we could get more teachers to engage children in conversations of this kind, particularly as child-centred curriculum planning is strongly advocated for in early childhood learning and teaching.

Let's examine the major aspects of a curriculum framework in early childhood and the national Australian Curriculum as it applies to the first years of school. As I hope that this text will be used across Australia, and even beyond, I will focus on the EYLF (DEEWR, 2009) and the Australian Curriculum (ACARA, 2017) but trust that you will make this conversation about curriculum more applicable to your own context by examining the EYLF more deeply and also examining curriculum frameworks that apply to you, such as the Victorian Early Years Development Framework (VEYLDF, 2016), and the Victorian Curriculum.

Relationships are a *key focus* in the curriculum frameworks and will be discussed extensively in Chapters 13 and 14. As has already been stated in previous chapters, the EYLF is underpinned by the concepts and visions for learning of 'Belonging, Being and Becoming' (DEEWR, 2009) and has three inter-related elements that are integral to early childhood curriculum and pedagogy. These are: Principles, Practice and Learning Outcomes. In the Australian National Curriculum, Foundation to Year 2 level, knowledge and skills are extended and developed from the EYLF. In the box below, you can see the links with prior-to-school-thinking and practices around the issues of curriculum and pedagogy.

Learning: Foundation to Year 2

Students bring to school a wide range of experiences, abilities, needs and interests. They have a natural curiosity about their world. Their desire to make sense of the world provides a platform to plan and review their learning through interactions with others, experimentation, scaffolding, explicit teaching, practice and play in the classroom and beyond.

The Australian Curriculum builds on the key learning outcomes of the national Early Years Learning Framework.

In Foundation—Year 2, priority in the Australian Curriculum is given to literacy and numeracy development because these are the foundations on which further learning is built. The foundation for the Literacy general capability is built primarily in English; and the foundation for the Numeracy

Cont.

CAROL CARTER

general capability is built primarily in Mathematics. However, both Literacy and Numeracy capabilities are reinforced and strengthened through learning in all areas of the curriculum.

The Foundation—Year 2 English curriculum engages students with listening, reading, viewing, speaking and writing activities for various purposes and contexts. It supports students to create and enjoy a range of literature. It presents explicit strategies for beginning reading and writing, spelling and expanding students' vocabulary. The English curriculum expands students' understanding of the conventions of spoken and written language use at home, at school, socially and in other contexts to promote skills and interest in language and its use and importance.

The Foundation—Year 2 Mathematics curriculum develops a sense of number, order, sequence, pattern and position, using the students' environment. It introduces mathematical symbols and language to communicate and explain mathematical ideas; it presents simple strategies to pose basic mathematical questions and to investigate and solve simple, concrete problems.

The development of movement skills, and social and emotional skills through physical play, and the development of knowledge and skills to help keep students safe, healthy and active are provided for in the Health and Physical Education curriculum. Purposeful exploration in personal and familiar contexts provides an opportunity for students to harness their curiosity about people, places and how their world works, as they develop skills in inquiry and investigation in Science, and Humanities and Social Sciences.

In these early years, the development of sensory, cognitive and affective appreciation of the world is provided through exploratory, analytical and creative practices in The Arts and Technologies curricula, and through the opportunity to learn a language using the Languages curricula.

Resources and support materials for the Australian Curriculum across Foundation—Year 2 are available as PDF documents.

(ACARA, 2017)

STOP AND THINK

- What is the purpose of early childhood education?
- What should the curriculum for young children include?
- How does the curriculum developer cater for the development of the whole child?
- How can early childhood teachers develop a responsive curriculum for young children that has relevance to the context of their family and community?
- Why is there such as strong emphasis on literacy and numeracy skills?
- What are your thoughts and ideas about this strong focus on these skills?

Read through the information in the practice section of the EYLF about holistic approaches, responsiveness to children, Learning through play, Intentional teaching, Learning environments, Cultural competence, Continuity of learning and transitions and Assessment for learning and think about how you could include these practices.

Australian Curriculum (www.australiancurriculum.edu.au/overview/f-2)

- How does the overview of the Learning for Foundation phase interlink with, or differ from, what you know of the EYLF and other curriculum frameworks?

Ideologies

Socially constructed sets of beliefs or worldviews are examples of what sociologists call ideologies. An **ideology** is a collection of conscious and unconscious ideas and attitudes that form a belief system which characterises the thinking, goals and expectations of a group of people. It is 'a broad interlocked set of *ideas and beliefs* about the world held by a group of people that they demonstrate in both behaviour and conversation to various audiences' (Meighan & Harber, 2007, p.212). The following ideologies and different ways of thinking impact on the designing and implementation of curriculum. Curriculum documents are generally blends of ideologies and ways of thinking about curriculum. For more information around these you should consult McLachlan, Fleer and Edwards (2013). Four dominant ideologies inform curriculum: scholar academic; social efficiency; child centred; and social reconstruction.

> **ideology** a collection of conscious and unconscious ideas and attitudes that form a belief system which characterises the thinking, goals and expectations of a group of people.

Scholar academic

Scholar academic embraces the idea that societies and culture have accumulated knowledge over the centuries that has been organised into academic disciplines and constitutes a body of knowledge considered to be what needs to be taught. The child is seen as a 'blank state' needing to be filled with appropriate knowledge. This ideology links to the pre-primary approach where the prior-to-school setting is concerned with getting children ready for content learnt at school and where the curriculum content 'mirrors' primary content. In a centre where scholar academic ideology is visible, the teacher may, for example, show the children a science experiment while the children watch and listen. They are then quizzed on their understandings.

Social efficiency

Social efficiency is where the child is seen as the 'raw material' and the adult is the finished product. The curriculum is viewed as directly and specifically preparing children for the adult world of work through the performance of specific activity and the measurement of objectives. Within a society where social theory predominates, students are evaluated by testing (such as an intelligence test), and educated towards their predicted life role. The teacher is the manager and adjusts the curriculum for particular students. The teacher may be equated with a factory worker, with the children as the machines. If you have not already done so, watch Pink Floyd's 1979 song, 'Another brick in the wall' on YouTube to see strong images that link to this kind of ideological view of education and curriculum.

Child-centred

Children construct their own knowledge and the needs of the child dominate, rather than the needs of teachers, curriculum content, structures or community. This is a strongly supported ideology in early childhood. Such approaches as Montessori and Reggio Emilia are particularly child-centred. Children are active learners who organise and interpret their own reality.

CAROL CARTER

Social reconstruction

Social reconstruction is based on the idea that society is imperfect, or even broken, and has many problems and challenges and that education is the solution to these problems. Within this ideology, education is not just a mechanism to fix an imperfect society but should be used to transform, change and improve society. Education, therefore, is not about maintaining the existing status quo in society, but challenging it. The role of the teacher is empowerment of students to be agents of change. 'Educators need to assume the role of leaders in the struggle for social and economic justice … Educators must connect what they teach and write to the dynamics of public life … and concern for … democracy' (Giroux, cited in McLachlan et al., 2013, pp.13–20).

Teachers' values and thinking about curriculum have an impact on children's learning. Thinking about curriculum over the years has included:

- *scientific curriculum* (early twentieth century), or the application of scientific methods to the study of curriculum
- *intrinsically worthwhile knowledge* (1970s and 1980s), or learning for its own sake rather than from any prescribed list of knowledge and skills
- thinking about curriculum as embedded in *sociocultural contexts* where participants construct meaning; this emerged in the 1960s and 1970s but current influence has been significant and has a strong impact on national curriculum and early learning frameworks
- *critical pedagogy* underpinned by the belief curriculum is designed to give legitimacy to some ideas and suppress others (i.e. it is designed to disrupt and critique conventional forms of understanding)
- *instrumentalism*, a kind of thinking that means a curriculum can be justified in terms of what virtues or experiences are needed for the future (McLachlan et al., 2013).

STOP AND REFLECT

- What do you value?
- How would this impact on your approach to curriculum?
- What kind of environment do you believe children learn in best?
- There have been criticisms and support for national curriculum documents and frameworks. What do you view as some of the positives and negatives of a national curriculum and frameworks?

Twenty-first century education and curriculum reform

Sue Lancaster

Before proceeding to thinking about specific curriculum models and pedagogical approaches that are evident in early childhood teaching and learning, we need to look back, and consider, global and national changes that have had a direct and an indirect impact on curriculum and pedagogy. For this reason, I have included this historically contextualised and highly informative section on change and reform. This section will discuss some of the key factors that have influenced contemporary thinking in terms of education, particularly the importance of developments that require a change in how children in this century will live their life as adults in the future, requiring different skills, knowledge and perspectives, which will all have a direct influence on curriculum and pedagogical considerations.

In the year 2000, *From Neurons to Neighborhoods: The Science of Early Childhood Development* was published under the auspices of the National Research Council Institute of Medicine, Washington, D.C. This comprehensive document raised concerns for children as a result of the 'pluralism of society' and the 'dramatic economic and social change' experienced by people in their everyday lives moving into the twenty-first century. This led to concerns about children's welfare and to the pronouncement that the 'development of children must be viewed as a matter of intense concern for both their parents and for the nation' (National Research Council Institute of Medicine, 2000). In essence, a shared commitment and responsibility for the future of all children was envisaged, underpinned by 'strategic investment', and developed by an interdisciplinary committee.

Thus began the two-and-half years of work by a team of experts from a broad range of disciplines: science, technology, engineering, medicine, behavioural and social sciences, education, and the early childhood and family sector, which supported the project both academically and financially. This was the first time such a broad range of multidisciplinary professional experts had come together with a commitment to develop integrated and comprehensive responses for a better future for young children and their families with goals reported by the committee accordingly:

> The charge to this committee was to blend the knowledge and insights of a broad range of disciplines to generate an integrated science of early childhood development. The charge to society is to blend the scepticism of a scientist, the passion of an advocate, the pragmatism of a policy maker, the creativity of a practitioner, and the devotion of a parent–and to use existing knowledge to ensure both a decent quality of life for all of our children and a productive future for the nation.
>
> (National Research Council Institute of Medicine, 2000)

The spread of globalisation has had an impact on societal change and the movement of people leading to greater opportunity for sharing research, skills and knowledge, and for far-reaching opportunities for trade, political, educational, scientific and economic alliances for future growth and prosperity. The advances in information and communication technology, and the developments in technologies in general, have also influenced globalisation and people's lifestyles. This is particularly noticeable in the way people communicate and, in fact, the way people are expected to communicate. For example, paying bills online has become an expectation including for service organisations within developed nations, with limited support and in some instances additional costs. In the past, the telephone was a device used for business, and for contacting family/friends about important matters or making arrangements on a limited basis. Today the device is likely to be in constant use: sharing your train journey to work, or a photo of what you are eating at a restaurant, or for instant conversation.

Perhaps you have considered and reflected objectively on these changes in technology and mobile devices and how these have changed your communication habits. If this has not been a consideration it would be useful to take time to consider this in view of your

CAROL CARTER

teacher role in the future. There is no doubt that the technologies used today for teaching and learning—including technological curriculum content, pedagogical approaches linked to technology, and tools for assessment and evaluation—will continue to change along with the expectations of the children and young people with whom you engage in your work.

For example, in early childhood environments the impact of globalisation, and information and communication technology enabling families to access instant information about their child's engagement in the education environment may also result in their higher expectations relating to their child's care and education. However, there are also other influences that have brought about changes in educational environments, particularly in the early childhood years prior to school. These include the links between brain research and how children learn, evidence supporting quality professional practices, increasing numbers of children attending childcare (Goodfellow, 2009), and more mothers either returning to or entering the workforce or further study, with governments encouraging workforce participation for all females, regardless of status or other responsibilities.

Australian Government priorities and initiatives

Education had been discussed between state, territory and Commonwealth governments during the previous two decades, resulting in *The Melbourne Declaration on Education Goals for Young Australians*, the basis for the Australian Curriculum for schools and prior-to-school reforms (ECA–ACARA, 2013). In 2006, the Council of Australian Governments (COAG) met to discuss a number of issues with all parties agreeing to work together to develop a National Reform Agenda. This agenda included an agreement that all states and territories would agree to adopt an overarching commitment 'to further raising living standards and improving services by lifting the nation's productivity and workforce participation over the next decade'.

This statement expresses a recognition of the importance of the early years, and a commitment to early childhood, outlined in the COAG Communiqué of February 2006 acknowledging:

- the importance of all children having a good start to life and that opportunities to improve children's life chances, especially for children born into disadvantaged families, exist well before children begin school, and even before birth;
- that high quality and integrated early childhood education and care services, encompassing the period from prenatal up to and including the transition to the first years of school, are critical to increasing the proportion of children entering school with the basic skills for life and learning; and
- a commitment to giving priority to improving early childhood development outcomes, as a part of a collaborative national approach (COAG, 2006).

For those working in early childhood environments this was the beginning of euphoric times with expectations and views from the sector that there was now a recognition of the importance of the early years for young children's learning and development, the recognition of the important role of families for their children's growth and wellbeing and acknowledgment of early childhood teaching as a profession. This would be underpinned by the development of curriculum documents, service policies and practices, based on quality standards and shared outcomes. Alongside this 'excitement' there were also expressions of anxiety and resistance about the level of change—what would it involve, when would there be time to understand and make these changes in an already challenging and busy work environment, and in some cases resentment and disempowerment as teachers felt their existing skills and knowledge were not being valued.

STOP AND REFLECT

- What do you think the potential outcomes of the changes mentioned above relating to education thinking might be in the future, and what might this mean for your practice?
- Think of a time when you have been required to make a change in your workplace or during your education. Write a brief narrative about this change: what was the purpose, what did it involve, how many people were affected, what management strategies for engaging staff were used, what was your role, if any?
- Now think about how you felt about this change.
    1 Was it a calm and easy transition?
    2 Was it a time of confusion?
        - Think about your answers to the above questions; if your answer to Question 1 was 'yes' write down the processes and strategies that made this a calm and easy transition. Were there any areas that could have been improved?
        - Now think and reflect on Question 2; if your answer was 'yes' write down the processes and strategies that made this a time of confusion, and what would have changed your attitude to make this change more palatable.

In the twenty-first century, change will continue to be a factor in all areas of life and lifestyle. Thinking back to the changes noted above, globalisation, technological inventions and research relating to human development and potential are not going to remain static. New technological devices appear at a constant rate, driverless cars are becoming a closer reality not just for demonstration but potentially in the near future for everyday use, and cures for many of our most debilitating health issues are becoming a reality. Young children, adolescents and youth engaged in education environments are exposed to and are learning from the use of sophisticated technology and encouraged to 'wonder' about options, opportunities and ways of learning that have been unavailable in the past. This has evolved by invention, and information and communication technologies setting up a globalised world where education and learning is enriched through access to multiple ideas, theories and practices.

To manage these changes, it is now recognised by governments that education starts in the early years. The EYLF (2009) affirms this statement by recognition of children's learning as a 'core' feature of the planning cycle for children's learning while also recognising that the early years are a time when:

> Children's learning is dynamic, complex and holistic. Physical, social, emotional, personal, spiritual, creative, cognitive and linguistic aspects of learning are all intricately interwoven and interrelated.
>
> (DEEWR, 2009)

The Australian Curriculum also recognises the importance of the early years, including 'children's right to learn through exploration and play' within a 'broad based' learning environment, some aspects of which should be given priority in the Foundation years of school progressing to increasing challenges and specialisation as children move through the school system. This forms a continuum of learning and development through alignment of purpose and principles outlined in the EYLF:

> The Australian Curriculum is aligned with the Early Years Learning Framework and builds on its key learning outcomes, namely: children have a strong sense of identity; children are connected with, and contribute to, their world; children have a strong sense of wellbeing; children are confident and involved learners; and children are effective communicators.
>
> (ECA-ACARA, 2013, p.5)

Both the EYLF and the Australian Curriculum share key purposes for planning for learning, communication about progress, determining what might be impeding progress, identifying children who might need additional support, evaluation of the effectiveness of teaching programs, and reflection on pedagogy that will suit the content and the children involved. The Australian Curriculum also recognises and values the skills and knowledge, and the different backgrounds and expectations, that children bring with them as they commence their move from early years to school environments.

Curriculum models

Now that Sue Lancaster has drawn our attention to global and national aspects of learning and teachers, let us look at different models of curriculum that can be identified. Approaches to curriculum that influence the types of curriculum models we select can be placed along a continuum of aspects such as child-centred versus adult-directed; transmission versus constructivist; mono-cultural versus multicultural; segregated knowledge versus integrated knowledge; predetermined versus emergent; and conforming versus transforming. Approaches to curriculum can be on either side of the continuum or they can be somewhere in between—for example, a curriculum that has both aspects of being child-centred and moments of adult-direction, with explicit and intentional teaching occurring.

There are many different models of curriculum. Following is a discussion of some of these models, namely:

- inquiry-based
- integrated
- emergent
- arts-based
- outcomes-focused.

A unit of work that was designed by one of my Initial Teacher Education students (reproduced with permission from Suppani Sumondis) has been included at the end of the discussion as an example within the inquiry-based model.

Inquiry-based curriculum model

An **inquiry-based curriculum model** can be understood as a process where students are guided to identify questions, gather information, think critically and solve problems related to real-life contexts, by exploring, observing, comparing and investigating (Krogh &

inquiry-based curriculum model is a process where students are guided to identify questions, gather information, think critically and solve real-life problems.

Morehouse, 2014; Nayler, 2014). In an inquiry-based model, different stages are identified to guide students' exploration or investigation. An inquiry-based unit of work incorporates effective questioning to motivate learning and create links between students' prior knowledge and new learning. Students form their own question about the topic and are given time to explore the answers. Teachers work together with the students in extending their ability to develop appropriate, useful and effective questions. An emphasis is placed particularly on developing effective questions, as there is a link between higher order thinking and developing their answers to these questions. Children use their questions as the foundation for effective learning and to develop their own knowledge and understanding, fuelled by what they would like to find out about.

Inquiry-based learning can be used in prior-to-school and school settings and the type or model of inquiry can vary for different ages and subjects. For instance, for children in Years 1 and 2, the multi-stage model that will be discussed using the 'Toys of the past' example is appropriate, whereas for young children a less complex model using four stages may be more helpful. The four stages are:

1 asking questions
2 investigating
3 creating
4 discussing.

Inquiry-based learning promotes an environment that is rich in resources and interactions. Children have opportunities to practise choosing, thinking, negotiating, problem solving and even potentially taking risks. Inquiry-based learning involves children asking questions, investigating, gathering information, considering possibilities, forming conclusions and examining their conclusions.

In the 'Toys of the past' unit of work the inquiry-based sequence of work begins by establishing students' prior knowledge and then scaffolding learning through an intentional process. The learning takes place through the following stages:

- *tuning in.* This establishes prior knowledge through a drawing, to understand children's perception of past, present, timelines and vocabulary. Strategies such as passing the ball, question of the day, discussions and brainstorming are used to capture children's interest and hook them into the investigation
- *finding out.* In Lessons 2 and 3 new information is introduced through shared reading, observing toys and gathering information
- *sorting out.* Lesson 3 incorporates sorting activities in each learning area such as using printed images and iPads to sort toys from past to present, and sorting observation of toys in order to help children make sense of the information they have gathered and gained so far
- *going further.* In Lesson 3 students use Venn diagrams to present their information and practise sequencing of now and then
- *drawing a conclusion.* Lesson 4 draws a conclusion and refocuses on the big idea of past and present through an oral presentation, creating a timeline and self-reflection. This would also help teachers and students know to what extent learning has taken place and could be used for assessment
- *taking action.* Lesson 5 assists students in creating links between their understanding and their experiences in the real world, such as creating an exhibition and inviting parents and students from other classes to view the toys and annotations.

CAROL CARTER

In the primary years of school, there is a strong focus on developing skills, such as 'predicting, hypothesising, generating questions, engaging in dialogue and synthesising findings' (Churchill et al., 2016, p.240). These aspects are to be found within this unit of work.

What do you think are the advantages and disadvantages/limitations of using an inquiry-based model? Here are some, though you may be able to think of many others.

Advantages

Children become active and motivated learners through inquiry. As this approach builds on children's prior knowledge, they can grasp new concepts better and can work from knowing to understanding. All children may not gain the same knowledge but they can discover the knowledge they need and wish to know and can then build on and extend this knowledge. Although an inquiry-based model provides a useful structure it not a linear process as stages can be revisited.

Disadvantages/limitations

The challenges for children who lack self-discipline and the time-consuming nature of the process.

Note: The unit of work that follows is linked to the National Curriculum unit of work, 'Toys of the past'.

Inquiry Unit of Work
Initial Teacher Education Student's work
Toys of the Past (Appendix 1)
History Unit: 1 Year Level: 2 Term: 1 Week: 1
(Lesson was adapted from the Melbourne Museum 2016)

AUSTRALIAN CURRICULUM	
Historical Knowledge and Understanding	The impact of changing technology on people's lives (at home and in the ways they worked, travelled, communicated, and played in the past) (ACHHK046)
Historical Skills	Sequence familiar objects (ACHHS047) Distinguish between the past, present and future (ACHHS048) Pose questions about the past using the sources provided (ACHHS049) Explore a range of sources about the past (ACHHS050) Identify and compare features of objects from the past and present (ACHHS051) Use a range of communication forms (oral, graphic, written, role play) and digital technologies (ACHHS054)
English Reading and Viewing	Know some features of text organisation including page and screen layouts, alphabetical order, and different types of diagrams, for example timelines (ACELA1466)
English Speaking and Listening	Understand that spoken, visual and written forms of language are different modes of communication with different features and their use varies according to the audience, purpose, context and cultural background (ACELA1460) Rehearse and deliver short presentations on familiar and new topics (ACELY1667)

AUSTRALIAN CURRICULUM	
General Capabilities	**Literacy Skills** Comprehending and composing text through spoken, written, visual and multimodal learning **Numeracy Skills** Recognising and using patterns and relationships **Critical and Creative Thinking** Inquiring—identifying, exploring and organising information and ideas **Information Communication Technology Capabilities** Managing and operating ICT Investigating with ICT

Lesson 1

	Tuning in and preparing to find out: What variety of activities would be used to: engage all students in the topic, assess prior knowledge, refine further planning, lead into finding out experiences?	**Assessment/Record keeping**
	Ask children to bring a special toy from home. We are going to be doing something special with them (Include notice to notify parents a week earlier). **Lesson opening/Motivator:** **Individual** Draw a picture of a toy that you got some time ago e.g. when you were a baby, 1 through 8 years old. **Whole class** Pass the ball—share why this toy is important: how old were you, who gave it to you? Do you think they play with toys? Discuss and lead to question of the day. Question of the day: Have toys changed over time? How have they changed? Discuss how we could find out about toys from the past and who we could ask (parents or grandparents). What would we like to know about their toys? Should we interview them? **Small groups** Brainstorm questions to ask parents and grandparents about the toys they play with. **Whole class** Create interview questions: What was their favourite toy, what was it made from, how old were they when they got the toy, who made them, where did they buy them from and what other toys did they have? Send questions home with children for interview. Children will use this interview to present an oral history presentation in a form of show and tell. (Homework during the week).	Portfolio of children's investigation

Lesson 2

	Finding out: experiences to assist students to gather new information about the topic	
Whole-class Introduce concept of continuity and change. Read story using IWB about the past: My Grandmother's Toy Box (download from https://museumvictoria.com. au/education/learning-lab/little-history/my-grandmothers-toy-box/) Discuss and ask questions as the book is read, for example: Marn Grook: Hannah's great-great-great-great-grandfather's toy This is a toy made by an Aboriginal father for his child before British people came to Australia. What do you think it is made of? What might have been put inside the ball for stuffing? What games might the children have played with it? Which toy would you leave for the future? What do you want to add to the toy box and why? How is it similar or different from the toy in the box? Draw a picture of your toy to add to the other toy pictures. (A list of suggestions can be found at https://museumvictoria.com.au/education/ learning-lab/little-history/teacher-guide/my-grandmothers-toy-box-activities /) **Pairs** Observation: Have children explore the toys in the box; have children closely observe each object and question them as to: how does this toy work? What materials is it made from? How is it similar to or different from toys they play with? Encourage writing a sentence for each question.		Anecdotal

Lesson 3

	Sorting out/ Going further: Activities to assist students to process and work with the information and ideas they have gathered about the topic (including exploring values). Present information in appropriate ways.	
Whole class Explain to the children that we are going to continue to explore more about toys from the past. Give specific instructions on how to access resource and explain where this information has come from, i.e. Melbourne Museum. **Individual** Understanding the past: IWB go through the Australia toys images. (Resource link https://museumvictoria.com.au/education/learning-lab/little-history/australian-toys/)		Work Sample Verbal/Anecdotal: do the children understand? Are sorting activities effective?

Allow children to explore images on the iPads

Using the Australian Toys print images for children to explore, manipulate in sorting activities:

- Sort by things they play with and things they don't
- Toys made at home and brought
- Toys played with alone and toys that require friends
- Older and newer toys

Small groups

Venn diagram template—record sets of sorted toys and record similarities in the middle.

Make comparison between two toys from different times.

Make comparison between an old toy and their own.

Share observations

Individual

Practise sequencing with Toys Now and Then interactive. Sorting the toys from oldest to newest. (Access link https://museumvictoria.com.au/education/learning-lab/little-history/toys-now-and-then/)

Lesson 4

	Making a conclusion Activities to 'pull it all together' to assist students to demonstrate what they have learnt and reflect on their learning.	
Oral presentation of parent/grandparent interviews Discussion and feedback What was some vocabulary used e.g. in the past, long ago, before you were born. What were some similarities and differences? **Whole class** Create a timeline: Each child can have an image of a toy. While holding the image ask them to arrange themselves in chronological order, according to the image they have. For each toy discuss what generation of their family might have used it. **Individual** Self: Reflection, inquire, what did you learn about the toys? How do you know they are from the past? How did children play with these toys and how do you play with toys now? What's different?		Anecdotal – Have children grasped the concept? Self-reflection/Portfolio

CAROL CARTER

Lesson 5

	Action Activities to link theory to practice. Children make links to their daily lives.	
Whole class Create an exhibit sorting the images as a display to indicate a time line from present to past using labels such as me, my parents, my grandparent, my great grandparent. Invite other classes to explore exhibit. Invite parents to an exhibit night.		Annotated Exhibition

RECORD OF STRATEGIES USED

Tuning In	Unit	Unit	Unit	Unit	Unit	Unit	Unit
Brainstorming	T1 U1						
Pass the Ball	T1 U1						
Question of the day	T1 U1						
Drawing	T1 U1						
Finding Out	T1 U1						
Share reading	T1 U1						
Observation	T1 U1						
Writing	T1 U1						
Interview	T1 U1						
Electronic picture book	T1 U1						
Sorting Out							
Sorting in order	T1 U1						
Comparing and contrasting	T1 U1						
Venn Diagram	T1 U1						
Going Further							
Practise sequencing with new activity	T1 U1						
Making Conclusion							
Time line	T1 U1						
Oral presentations	T1 U1						
Taking action							
Annotated Exhibition	T1 U1						

Adapted from Murdoch, 2013, p.158.

Integrated curriculum model

An **integrated curriculum model** can be defined as 'the structured organisation of teaching and learning experiences in which significant content, across and within learning areas are selected to develop and extend students' understanding of the world' (Churchill et al., 2016, p.198). An integrated curriculum can be structured from multidisciplinary to interdisciplinary through to transdisciplinary experiences. *Multidisciplinary* involves using ideas, concepts, issues or problems, known as 'big ideas', to connect with a range of subjects. *Interdisciplinary* involves finding overlapping skill and knowledge between subject areas. *Transdisciplinary* focuses on the common skills and knowledge children need. Therefore, an integrated approach to planning a unit of work focuses on the big ideas, findings, skill and knowledge that overlap across subjects and weaving these into the subject areas. It is important in integration that the activities are contributing to knowledge and understanding of the 'big idea' and that they are not questionable, weak, tenuous links. For this reason, not all of the subjects need to be integrated at once.

Looking at landscapes and their features could be an idea for an integrated model. Students explore the big idea such as places and their features in the local environment and are assisted in developing geographical knowledge and skills. Children could begin by examining their natural environment and identifying the difference between natural and man-made features. These ideas are then extended through a recount writing activity. Then they observe and analyse the different types of landscapes and identify distinct features, as well as creating a postcard for a friend. By the end of the unit, they create a report that summarises learning throughout, giving them the opportunity to reflect on geographical features in their own locations.

An integrated curriculum is effective as it reflects a natural way of learning. Murdoch (2013) suggests that 'our brains have a natural capacity for integration'. This approach provides a meaningful connected learning context and therefore the skills, understanding and values are best learnt and assessed within these contexts. Values could also be integrated where students may, for instance, examine the ability to sustain natural environments in the city. This could lead and extend to work on sustainability.

Here are some of the advantages and disadvantages/limitations of using an integrated model.

> **integrated curriculum**
> An integrated curriculum links ideas, skills, content or knowledge across different learning areas.

Advantages

The advantages of an integrated curriculum for students are that it reflects real-life situations; it challenges students to develop their thinking as they work to make connections and understand the big idea. It enables them to have some degree of control over their learning, and they can process and respond to their experience in a range of ways. Overall an integrated curriculum can enrich learning and understanding.

In addition, teachers can manage contents in an overcrowded curriculum. It encourages teachers to work together to structure and meet outcomes across key learning areas.

Disadvantages/limitations

The lack of practical experience in developing an integrated unit of work for an inexperienced teacher could be a disadvantage. If a unit of work is not planned well to meet the needs of individual children, then difficulties may arise. There is also the danger of

CAROL CARTER

ignoring certain discipline-specific skills if integrated models are not interspersed with direct subject teaching.

Emergent curriculum model

An **emergent curriculum model** can be defined as a curriculum that is open-ended, flexible and frequently child-initiated and where children's interests are the primary focus. An emergent curriculum develops with teachers exploring what is interesting, meaningful and relevant to a child. They observe, listen, notice children's inquiries, document what happens and create more questions for children. An emergent curriculum is a positive way to engage children in their own learning and empowers them to make choices about, and take increasing responsibility for, their learning. Although an emergent curriculum, like any other curriculum, involves planning once the initial interests and ideas of the children are explored, retrospective documentation takes place as some activities will be completed by teachers 'thinking on their feet'.

Let us look at some advantages and disadvantages/limitations of the emergent model.

> **emergent curriculum** is open-ended, flexible and includes children's interests as a primary focus.

Advantages

There are many advantages in using an emergent curriculum. Curriculum planning is more purposeful when planning with children, when it responds to their interests and when it involves questions and wonders about their world. This approach enhances opportunities for children's self-expression, oral language and creative abilities, and recognises children as active agents of their own learning. Parents may also have the opportunity to contribute ideas. In addition, teachers build continuity by connecting children's prior knowledge to new learning, leading children to deeper understandings about the topic. Learning is integrated across curricular areas and is based on real-life experiences.

Disadvantages/limitations

The disadvantage of an emergent curriculum is that teachers cannot be fully prepared in terms of resources as the direction of an emergent curriculum can change. However skilled teachers can negotiate with children and come up with solutions for rich learning—for instance, seeing what is available in the community and what parents could offer.

Arts-based curriculum model

An arts-based approach places the arts as a starting point or foundation to plan a curriculum that blends in other learning areas. An **arts-based curriculum model** uses the creative, visual and performing arts as a context to structure and teach other subjects. The arts are used as a medium to organise connections across other learning areas (Churchill et al. 2016, p.200). The arts can be an effective tool for 'making meaning and understanding' (Churchill 2016, et al. p.200). Children come to know about and see the world through 'dialogue, reflection, metaphor and imagination' (Churchill et al. 2016, p.200). Examples of an arts-based approach can be seen in Chapter 8 of this book.

Consider a unit, 'About Me and My Family: Visual arts, Music and Drama', is used as the basis for planning a civics and citizenship, history and geography unit of work. Through visual arts, a drawing is used to inquire about children's families; they share and talk about

> **arts-based curriculum model** uses the creative, visual and performing arts as a context to structure and teach other subjects.

their drawing, gain positive feedback and respond to questions from their peers. This can also reveal children's understanding of different family structures and diversities. Through music, they will learn more about diversities within families. Then they are encouraged to work in pairs to create a piece that expresses their family personality, such as fun, happy or fast paced. Through drama, they are encouraged to create puppets to tell a story; this could be a story that has been told in their family for generations, a holiday or cultural celebration. In English, they will reflect on their planning skills and are supported and encouraged to write a verb that describes their reflective drawings. They will also create a family tree, drawing their grandparents, the members in their family, and include which country their family members are originally from and when they migrated. In geography, collaboratively they will explore the world map, pin the countries of their backgrounds and draw a basic map of Australia.

Advantages

There are many benefits in using an arts-based approach for children's learning and development. Art helps in developing children's cognitive and creative abilities. In art, for a child to present ideas, concepts and experiences involves many thinking skills as they need to plan, organise and make choices about their art work. Art involves problem-solving skills—for instance, how will they draw to communicate their message, how will they organise their family tree and how will they draw a map?

Art also creates important learning dispositions as it involves concentration, patience and persistence to complete a task.

Music and creative expression are important in two ways: they are holistic for a developing child and they help integrate and enrich learning. Cognitively, children explore rhythms, and this skill is transferrable to establish patterning in maths and reading. Physically, children develop their eye–hand co-ordination to play instruments. Socially, children take turns and listen to others' interpretations. Emotionally, they express themselves and, most of all, build their confidence with the arts.

Drama can be used as a driver to extend children's literacy skills. In dramatic play children can reflect, represent and communicate their experiences (Connor, 2011, p.1). Also, as children are exposed to different perspectives, they can respond as an audience and appreciate similarities and differences.

Disadvantages/limitations

A disadvantage of this approach can be the level of confidence teachers have in planning and implementing the Arts.

Outcomes-focused curriculum model

An outcomes-focused curriculum model starts with (and is guided by) desired or intended outcomes that create learning pathways. Measurable learning outcomes are the basis for decisions around learning and demonstrating competencies. It is an approach to planning, delivering and assessing in which first the required results are selected then the skills and knowledge that are needed to achieve those results are identified. This model is organised around what we want children to demonstrate, know and be able to do. It takes into account learning at different paces for individual children. Contemporary curriculum documents focus on outcomes.

Advantages

The advantages of an outcomes-focused model is that teaching and learning is systematic, measurable and there is a clear focus on what children need to know, do and value.

Disadvantages/limitations

The disadvantage is the tendency to reduce knowledge and learning to that which can be measured and standardised and:

> … where learning is reduced to 'acquiring' and where 'evaluating' is reduced to measuring the acquired against some pre-set standardised nor … an over concern for sameness fails to heed the feet of the earth that touches the dancing feet differently for each student.
>
> (Aoki, cited in Neelands, 2001, p.7)

Pedagogical approaches and strategies

Early childhood pedagogical practices are underpinned by qualities such as collaboration and respect and address individual differences among children, including their readiness for different types of learning, their cultural backgrounds, their personalities and their learning preferences. Pedagogical approaches and curriculum content should be age-appropriate, socially and culturally relevant and linked to a strength-based approach to learning and teaching.

You read and learnt a great deal about play-based approaches to learning in Chapter 4. Intentional teaching and active, play-based learning, as two distinct pedagogical approaches, are equally important aspects of adult–child collaboration in an educational environment. Intentional teaching is carefully considered and deliberate. 'We have come to realise that everything we do in our daily interactions with children 'teaches' them something' (Connor, 2011, p. 1).

Intentional teaching is one of the key pedagogical practices in the EYLF (DEEWR, 2009), which underpins young children's learning success.

The EYLF (p.15) explains that intentional teachers:

- actively promote children's learning through worthwhile and challenging experiences and interactions that foster high-level thinking skills
- use strategies such as modelling and demonstrating, open questioning, speculating and explaining
- engage in shared thinking and problem solving to extend children's understanding of ideas and events
- move flexibly in and out of different roles and draw on different strategies as the context changes
- plan opportunities for intentional teaching and knowledge building
- document and monitor children's learning.

Effective pedagogical approaches for the early years are usually intentional in nature and include a combination of direct teaching and the creation of learning environments and experiences that are instructive, resource rich and provide opportunities for discovery and exploration. Intentional teaching and direct teaching are not the same. Direct teaching is where children receive instruction and where knowledge is transmitted from the teacher to the children. It is the direct opposite of a constructivist pedagogical approach (see constructivism in Chapter 3 for further discussion of this).

Effective approaches involve sustained, shared thinking (discussed in Chapter 13), play-based strategies, problem-based learning and active, 'hands-on' experiential learning (James & Pollard, 2011). Active learning involves the learning of concepts and the formulation of ideas through moving, active listening, manipulating, constructing and playing. It has been found that pretend play, using the imagination, promotes cognitive and social development and assists children to regulate their behaviour. Actively joining in children's play, modelling thinking and problem solving and providing challenges and opportunities through such statements as, 'I'm wondering why the water keeps disappearing into the sand' are also effective strategies.

> Have you seen how early childhood teachers use an elaborate conversational style when speaking to young children? This is a deliberate pedagogical strategy for increasing receptive and ultimately language acquisition but it also guides children in making sense of sequential speech patterns and connecting aspects of their experiences.
>
> (Goswami & Bryant 2007)

The *Australian Professional Standards for Teachers* (AITSL, 2011), which aims to improve the quality of teacher and teacher education in Australia has standards that specifically relate to teaching strategies (linked to Professional Knowledge and Professional Practice). These include:

- *Standard 1*—'Know students and how they learn' (e.g. 1.3: 'teaching strategies that are responsive to the learning strengths and needs of students from diverse … backgrounds')
- *Standard 2*—'Know the content and how to teach it' (e.g., 2.1: 'apply … teaching strategies of the teaching area')
- *Standard 3*—'Plan for and implement effective teaching and learning' (e.g. 3.3: 'Include a range of teaching strategies') (AITSL, 2011, pp.8–12).

Specific techniques and strategies informed by the pedagogical approaches can be found in many of the chapters of this book as well as MacNaughton and Williams's 2009 book, *Techniques for Teaching*, which I have recommended for further reading at the end of the chapter. They include techniques such as demonstrating, modelling, describing, facilitating, questioning, problem-posing, brainstorming, providing open-ended materials, grouping, co-constructing, scaffolding, using the Zone of Proximal Development and community building.

Understanding of pedagogical approaches in the early years has increased considerably since the importance of early years learning has been acknowledged and research has been actively pursued in this area. Remember that, while there are no recipes for early childhood teaching and learning, no 'right' curriculum or 'best' pedagogical approaches, we know that what is most required is understanding the children we teach, their levels of development, their strengths and their developmental challenges. This knowledge will guide us towards the pedagogical approaches and strategies that we use within specific early childhood learning and teaching environments.

CAROL CARTER

SUMMARY

- It is worth considering and reflecting on the many beliefs, values and agendas embedded in the discussion on curriculum and pedagogy.
- Among the different ways curriculum can be viewed is the distinction between a syllabus view and a pedagogical view of curriculum.
- Interrelationships exist between curriculum (as dynamic and actively constructed by learners and teachers) and pedagogy (as the art and science of teaching).
- There are different categories of curriculum, including the hidden curriculum, and ideologies and ways of thinking about curriculum.
- Curriculum models include inquiry-based, integrated, emergent, arts-based and outcomes-focused.

FURTHER REFLECTION

What do you need to consider when deciding on pedagogical approaches for different groups of learners?

Here are some questions that might help you answer this reflection question:

- What do you need to know about the learners?
- What do you need to know about the educational context?
- Who should be involved in making those choices and why?

GROUP DISCUSSION

These questions can be used to reflect on curriculum and pedagogy in early childhood. In reflecting on them yourself or contributing to class and group discussions you need to use your own opinions and experiences as well as what you have learnt from reading and engaging with this chapter.

1 What are the differences and similarities between intentional and direct teaching?
2 What would you say to a teacher who believes that an emergent curriculum model did not require any planning?
3 What curriculum model, or combination of models, appeals to you the most, and why?
4 What are the main advantages of the different curriculum models discussed?
5 What are the main disadvantages of the different curriculum models discussed?
6 What do you need to consider when deciding on pedagogical approaches for different groups of learners?

CLASS EXERCISES

1 In small groups, draw an illustration of an *adult-centred classroom* and a *child-centred classroom*; include a teacher and children in each illustration. Present an explanation that supports why it was drawn that way, featuring:
   - classroom layout
   - roles and expectations of teachers and students
   - image of the child
   - pedagogical practices
   - main influencers
   - ideologies
   - theorist/theory-linked.

2 Imagine you have been given the task of creating a new curriculum framework for early childhood.
  – What are the underlying values and principles that would impact on this new curriculum?
  – How would they differ from, or be similar to, the values and principles that underpin the current frameworks?

FURTHER READING

MacNaughton, G. & Williams G. (2009) Techniques for Teaching: Choices in Theory and Practice (3rd edn). Frenchs Forest, NSW: Pearson Education.
  This is an extremely comprehensive and useful guide to teaching techniques that contribute to effective pedagogy. It has information concerning general teaching techniques such as demonstrating, modelling, describing, facilitating, questioning and grouping. Then it also has specialist teaching techniques such as co-constructing, scaffolding and community building.

REFERENCES

Apple, M. (1993) 'The Politics of Official Knowledge: Does a National Curriculum Make Sense?', *Discourse: Studies in the Cultural Politics of Education*, *14*(1): 1–16.

Ashman, A. & Elkins, T. (2009) *Education for Inclusion and Diversity.* Frenchs Forest, NSW: Pearson Education Australia.

Australian Curriculum, Assessment and Reporting Authority (ACARA) (2017) Australian Curriculum. www.australiancurriculum.edu.au/f-10-curriculum/learning-areas/

Australian Government (2008) *The Melbourne Declaration on Educational Goals for Young Children.* http://www.curriculum.edu.au/verve/_resources/National_Declaration_on_the_Education_Goals_for_Young_Australians.pdf

Australian Institute for Teaching and School Leadership (AITSL) (2011) *Australian Professional Standards for Teachers.* www.aitsl.edu.au/.../australian_professional_standard_for_teachers_final.pdf

Christie, P. (1992) *The Right to Learn: The Struggle for Education in South Africa.* Johannesburg: SACHED/Ravan.

Churchill, R., Godinho, S., Johnson, N., Keddie, A., Letts, W., Lowe, K., Mackay, J., McGill, M., Moss, J., Nagel, M., Shaw, K., Ferguson, P., Nicholson, P. & Vick, M. (2016) *Teaching: Making a Difference.* Qld, Australia: John Wiley & Sons.

Connor, J. (2011) *EYLF Professional Learning Program: Intentional Teaching.* Australia: Early Childhood Australia. www.imagineeducation.com.au/files/CHC30113/Intentional_20Teaching_EYLFPLP_E_Newsletter_No2.pdf

Council of Australian Government (COAG) (2006) http://ncp.ncc.gov.au/docs/Council%20of%20Australian %20Governments%20Meeting%20-%2010%20February%202006.pdf

Department of Basic Education (2017) *The National Curriculum Statements Grade R–12* (South Africa). www.education.gov.za/Curriculum/NationalCurriculumStatementsGradesR-12.aspx

Department of Education, Employment and Workplace Relations (DEEWR) (2009) *Belonging, Being & Becoming: The Early Years Learning Framework for Australia.* ACT, Australia: Commonwealth of Australia.

Duncum, P. (2002) 'Clarifying Visual Culture and Art Education', *Art Education*, *55*(3): 6–11.

ECA–ACARA (2013) *Foundations for Learning: Relationships between the Early Years Learning Framework and the Australian Curriculum.* http://foundationinquirylearning.global2.vic.edu.au/files/2013/06/ECA_ACARA_ Foundations_Paper-2cq59mi.pdf

Goodfellow, J. (2009) *EYLF Professional Learning Program: The Early Years Learning Framework—Getting Started.* Australia: Early Childhood Australia. www.earlychildhoodaustralia.org.au/nqsplp/wp content/uploads/2012/05/ RIP0904_EYLFsample.pdf

Goswami, U. & Bryant, P. (2007) 'Children's Cognitive Development and Learning', *Research Survey for the Esme Fairburn Foundation Review*. *UK: University of Cambridge.*

James, M. & Pollard, A. (2011) 'TLRP's Ten Principles for Effective Pedagogy: Rationale, Development, Evidence, Argument and Impact', *Research Papers in Education, 26*(3): 275–328.

Krogh, S. & Morehouse, P. (2014) *The Early Childhood Curriculum: Inquiry Learning Through Integration*. New York: Routledge.

Lucas, C.J. (1972) *Our Western Educational Heritage.* New York: Macmillan.

Lunenberg, F. (2011) 'Expectancy Theory of Motivation: Motivating by Altering Expectations', *International Journal of Management, Business, and Administration, 15*(1).

Marsh, C. (2009) *Key Concepts for Understanding Curriculum* (4th edn). London, UK: Routledge.

McFee, J. (1995) 'Change and the Cultural Dimensions of Art Education', in R. Neperud (ed.) *Context, Content, and Community in Art Education: Beyond Postmodernism.* New York: Teachers College Press, Columbia University.

McLachlan C., Fleer, M. & Edwards, S. (2013) *Early Childhood Curriculum: Planning, Assessment and Implementation* (2nd edn). New York and Melbourne: Cambridge University Press.

Meighan, R. & Harber, C. (2007) *A Sociology of Educating*, UK: Bloomsbury.

Murdoch, K. (2013) *The Power of Inquiry.* Melbourne: Seastar Education.

National Research Council Institute of Medicine (2000) *From Neurons to Neighborhoods: The Science of Early Childhood Development*. Washington, DC: The National Academies Press.

Nayler, J. (2014) *Enacting Australian Curriculum: Making Connections for Quality Learning.* Qld: Queensland Studies Authorities.

Neelands, J. (2001) '11/09—The Space in Our Hearts'. Speech at the 2nd International Theatre/Drama Education conference, Athens: Theatre in education: art form and learning tool.

Nicholson, H. (2000) *Teaching Drama,* New York: Continuum.

Shulman, L. (1986) 'Those Who Understand: Knowledge Growth in Teaching', *Educational Researcher, 15:* 4–14.

Veblen, K., Beynon, C. & Odom, S. (2005) 'Drawing on Diversity in the Arts Education Classroom: Educating Our New Teachers', *International Journal of Education & the Arts, 6*(14): 1–17.

Victorian Early Years Learning and Development Framework (VEYLDF) (2016) Victorian State Government. www.education.vic.gov.au/childhood/providers/edcare/Pages/veyladf.aspx?Redirect=1

Vygotsky, L.S. (1926) *Educational Psychology* (translated by R. Silverman (1997)). Boca Raton: St. Lucie Press.

Waters, M. & Angliss, W. (2005) *Pedagogy in VET: A Background Paper.* Vic.: TAFE Development Centre.

Mathematics

Frances Burton

Chapter objectives

In this chapter, we will:
- learn about the influence of culture and emotion on our mathematical learning, including:
  - the important role of culture in our understanding of mathematics
  - how our feelings influence our views of ourselves as teachers and learners of mathematics
  - the ways in which our cultural beliefs and feelings influence our views of how young children learn mathematics
- discover our role as intentional teachers of mathematics
- explore the need to empower children to use mathematical language and develop the positive dispositions to be confident mathematicians through their experiences with mathematical reasoning, number, geometry, measurement, statistics and probability.

Key terms

attributes	exchange process	perceptual subitising
early understanding of cardinal number	learning story	structure of patterns
	number sense	subitising
conceptual subitising	object permanence	symbols

Our journey begins by relating two small stories involving a two-year-old child. The first is a vignette focused on the child, Alice, and her play experiences with red ice-cream. The second vignette looks at Alice while she and her mother are baking a cake. These vignettes are used as examples to illustrate the ways in which mathematics is part of children's everyday experiences and how we, as early childhood teachers, can build upon these experiences to develop mathematical understanding in young children.

Red ice-cream

Alice and I went on a small adventure, walking, chatting, making our way around the corner on a sunny Sunday afternoon to the local small supermarket to buy a 'red ice-cream'. In the shop, we found the ice-creams in the fridge and, with some assistance, Alice chose which of the ice-creams we would buy, based on the 'red' pictures on the boxes. We then went home with her constant chatter about 'having an ice-cream', and with me reminding her that we had bought 'red ice-creams'.

We also chatted about the 'red' leaves on the bushes she touched and the 'red' car waiting at the 'red' stop sign. We sat in the backyard, eating our 'red ice-creams' and getting ice-cream everywhere! We were having fun and maths was a part of this.

Cake-baking

In this second vignette, Alice is helping her mother make a cake. She is keen to get started so her first job is to carry the various ingredients to the kitchen bench. These include the big tubs of flour and sugar, the small container of butter and, very carefully, with total concentration visible on her face and in her body, Alice carries the eggs, one by one, to the bench; four eggs are needed and only four eggs are left in the fridge. She can't afford to drop one! Soon after, standing up at the bench on her kitchen stepladder, she helps to break each egg, adding them to the mixture, counting with her mum, one, two, three, four, helping to mix them in with a spoon.

Early mathematical concept development and the inclusion of appropriate language are visible in these vignettes through particular concepts such as:

- same and different in terms of the colour red
- early measurement of quantities with the cake-baking
- practising one-to-one correspondence with the eggs.

Children have the opportunity to experience and develop a range of mathematical understandings and language in their prior-to-school years of birth to five. The mathematical concepts and language of the vignettes will be explored later in the section 'Our cultural funds of mathematical knowledge'. Here the initial focus is to emphasise the importance of understanding the child's early mathematical learning in the context of their family culture, including their everyday practices. To extend this, you will be invited to reflect on how this relates to your own past experiences, feelings and confidence with mathematics.

Introduction

Let me begin this section by adding more background to the 'red ice-cream' vignette.

First, close your eyes and imagine the colour red. You may find that your knowledge and emotions about the varied shades of red are attached to objects such as favourite clothes or foods. I can't get past the artistic use of red polka dots by Yayoi Kusama (see opposite).

The colour red may be bright or pale, a fire-engine red or the red of a crimson pencil. As you sort through your varied images of red, you will draw on your own cultural images and experiences. In some cultures, the colour red is associated with strength and danger; in others, red represents celebration, wealth and power, and even the romance of a red rose. Whatever your cultural and personal references are for the colour red, this sorting activity you are doing in your mind's eye is re-living your equivalent of the experiences that the young child Alice is beginning to experience as a two-year-old. It is through these experiences that she will learn her early mathematical skills, concepts and language. She has been building these experiences with mathematics, right from birth.

Alice learns her mathematics through her real experiences in life as well as through her play, though the two are interconnected and Alice does not differentiate between 'life-experience' and 'play'. In the 'Red ice-cream' vignette, Alice is experiencing various reds as she walks to the local shop to buy a 'red ice-cream'.

Source: Yayoi Kusama's installation Kusamatrix at Toru Yamanaka—AFP/Getty Images
(https://au.pinterest.com/margheritaacerb/yayoi-kusama-ascension-of-polka-dots-on-trees/).

Prior to this she was engaged in imaginative shop play. Alice has a little shop in her family room, complete with a range of 'ice-creams', a little counter and a box with some play money in it. There are varied ice-creams including the 'red ice-cream' shaped as a piece of watermelon. Together, we played shops with Alice, asking each person in turn 'Would you like an ice-cream?' We named the particular ice-cream, by colour or flavour or real-life name, for the play symbol. It was given to us and we ate it. This activity led to our shopping expedition to buy a real red ice-cream.

In this vignette, Alice is learning a range of social and language concepts and skills but our focus is on the mathematical language and concepts. The particular mathematical concept that she is learning is the concept of same and different as it relates to colour: Alice learns to recognise varied shades of the colour red and the common 'redness' in varied objects—the concept and language of sameness about red and the concept of difference. The various reds are similar but not identical and at some stage 'red' ends and the colour is pink, orange or mauve—the boundaries of 'redness'. Through her play, Alice explores the look, feel and taste of various red objects. She hears the word 'red' and its variants—light red, dark red, red-blue, red-yellow—and its use in real life—red traffic light, red fire-engine and in this instance, red ice-cream, where red indicates the flavour of the ice-cream. Alice touches some of them, has her attention drawn to others and, of course, she eats one. These experiences in the vignette

FRANCES BURTON

include the red watermelon ice-cream from her home shop play, the red pictures on the box of ice-creams, the red on her ice-cream and the red leaves she sees on her walks.

Alice is also learning about **symbols** (a central mathematical concept) and in this vignette, her learning is directly linked to mathematical learning. This learning occurs through her real-life experiences, seeing stop signs and fire engines, as well as imaginative play with the ice-creams and her ice-cream shop; and also through her exploration of pictures of ice-creams on the box in the shop. The other mathematical concept Alice is learning is the **exchange process** of shopping. She is aware that shopping is about making choices, choosing the object you want in negotiation with the shopkeeper and exchanging something of value equal to your choice.

As a teacher, I know that these mathematical concepts—sorting same and different, reasoning about colour variants, mathematics in everyday life through the use of symbols in the place of real objects, and exchange value and process—are important early mathematical concepts. My role is to scaffold and extend these experiences. This is your role, too.

> **symbols**
> characters used to represent functions and processes, for example +(plus).

> **exchange process**
> exchanging money for goods or items of equal value.

STOP AND THINK

- What is the relevance of this play to Alice's mathematical development? In reflecting on this question, think about the different elements identified in the vignette—i.e. the concept of same and different: symbols, exchange process and value.
- Describe at least one way in which you could further scaffold Alice's mathematical learning for each of these elements.

First of all, children's play with others is the social context where they learn the cultural language, activity and symbols of their family and, later, the broader community. In the vignette, Alice is learning about the social and economic interaction of shopping. She is learning about these in the social context of her family life. This is the microsystem of Bronfenbrenner's ecological systems in action in mathematics.

Children learn mathematics through their experiences, initially within the family context and through play. This is how we define the early learning and experiences of mathematics.

Vygotsky and ZPD in mathematics

Vygotsky (1962) suggests that learning is a *social activity* where the child learns through interaction with significant others. The 'Red ice-cream' vignette is a mathematical example of Vygotsky's concept of the ZPD as Alice extends her understanding of red, of symbols and of the exchange concept while shopping through her experiences with a significant other. It explains the important link between language and thinking when Vygotsky suggests that it is through language that we learn to express the thoughts in our mind. These in turn define for us our thoughts and also allow us to communicate these ideas with others. In this instance, Alice is learning to identify various objects as

MATHEMATICS

belonging or *matching to* the word 'red'. There are variations within the colour and these will broaden her understanding of the colour 'redness' as a concept and when to distinguish it from other colours.

Vygotsky (1967) explains the importance of socio-dramatic or make-believe play to the development of higher mental functions in the young child. Play is the transitional stage between sensorimotor and visual learning to more advanced symbolic thought.

Fleer (2010) discusses Vygotskian thinking when she explains the importance of imaginative play to the child's understanding of symbols. The child learns about symbols as things that stand in place of a real item as she moves between experiences in her everyday world and as she begins to explore her world of imagination. In the first vignette, the red ice-cream in her shop play at home acts as a symbol for a real ice-cream. This includes the pretend shop play, where the purchasing of the red ice-creams demonstrates the exchange element of shopping as well. She then has the opportunity to link her imaginative shop play with a real everyday shopping experience as she shops for red ice-cream and she enjoys the social practices associated with ice-cream eating. The real shopping experience has the potential to broaden her understanding of the meaning of symbols as she can compare the real, or 'everyday', experience with her play experiences as well as the symbols or pictures of red ice-creams on the packets in the shop with her home shop. This provided her with an authentic mathematical experience as she chose the box of ice-creams and handed them to the shopkeeper and observed the exchange of money.

The concepts of difference and same, shopping as an exchange process and understanding of symbols are all important early mathematical concepts enacted in the sociocultural experiences of children's everyday lives.

Our cultural funds of mathematical knowledge

We too bring to our study of mathematics our own cultural views of what teaching and learning of mathematics are and our understanding of the role of a teacher of mathematics to young children. Our own personal experiences in schooling influence how we believe teaching should occur as well as what mathematics we believe children should learn. Often, because they are the most recent experiences, it is our later, more recent and secondary experiences that influence our beliefs about what mathematics is and how we should teach this subject. Our level of mathematical understanding, our confidence and our feelings or emotions towards this subject are influenced by these cultural experiences.

The concept of 'funds of knowledge' (Moll et al., 1992), referred to in Chapter 3, helps us understand our experiences, which together inform our cultural expectations about mathematics.

STOP AND REFLECT

You might find it useful to revisit the concept of funds of knowledge, then relate it directly to teaching mathematics in prior-to-school settings.

FRANCES BURTON

Our feelings about mathematics

Much has been written about the lack of confidence in and negative attitudes towards mathematics held by many early childhood teachers and, for that matter, primary school teachers (Sweeting, 2011, p.iii). Certainly, from my experiences as a tertiary teacher-educator of mathematics, I have anecdotal evidence of worryingly negative attitudes, expressed by students commencing their early childhood teaching course, in statements such as: 'I hate mathematics', 'I'm no good at it', 'I was okay in primary school but in secondary school I got left behind', 'Why can't I use a calculator and formula? Then I can do maths'.

When these students reflect on their experiences, their views are often converted to a statement that 'I want to make maths fun for the children'.

STOP AND REFLECT

- What have your experiences of *learning* mathematics been?
- What model/s of mathematics *teaching* have you experienced?
- How do you think your experiences have shaped your attitude towards teaching mathematics?
- Is it enough for teachers to make mathematics 'fun' for children?

If your experiences and attitudes towards mathematics are similar to those expressed in the statements above, be aware that (unfortunately) you are not alone. There is evidence from research (Sweeting, 2011) that such responses are common among the community of early childhood educators. This is a serious concern: if you 'hate maths', you may pass this anxiety on to the children in your care. The children too will learn to wear the badge 'I hate maths' (see Hachey, 2013, for a research-based discussion of this issue).

One response to negativity in our feelings and a lack of confidence towards mathematics is expressed as 'we need to make mathematics fun for the children!' Much as this represents a positive response to what may have been our own negative feelings from our own personal experiences in learning mathematics, we need to be a bit careful of this response. The focus in the first vignette reflects this view of mathematics as fun. What young two-year-old Alice would remember from the trip to buy an ice-cream may very well be the fun of eating an ice-cream, and the concept of red as a colour was just the topping. Engaging as this experience may be for young Alice, such fun is not the only or major focus in the learning of mathematics for the young child, even when this learning is based in play.

Contrast the little knowledge about *same* and *different* in the colour red lost by young Alice in the fun of eating ice-cream with the deep concentration of young Alice in the second vignette. Here she shows the depth of concentration she requires as she carefully carries the precious eggs, one by one, from the fridge to the counter and cracks them one, two, three, four into the bowl to make the cake. This deep concentration and engagement is indicative of young Alice being stretched into her 'zone of proximal development' (Vygotsky, 1978, p.86). This is the optimal space between what she is confident she knows, both in responsibly carrying the precious eggs and in remembering the number names and applying them correctly with support (scaffolding) from mum. Scaffolding allowed Alice to complete this task, which would otherwise have been beyond her at this stage. There is a place for both of these experiences in the lives of young children, but most importantly we want children to enjoy the challenge that deep learning in mathematics brings: the use of their imagination, creativity and persistence to solve a problem themselves or with the support of their peers.

The teacher's role in children's mathematical learning

The vignettes at the start of the chapter provide anecdotal evidence of young children being able to learn mathematically. I have said that current research indicates children are learning mathematics from birth. Hunting (2013) provides other examples of the early learning of mathematics by children under two. These include a young child pegging items of clothes on a clothes horse, a child pouring water from one container to another in the bath and children eating sultana snacks one by one in a shopping centre (Hunting, 2013). In these examples Hunting is acting as the 'knowledgeable other' (Vygotsky, 1967) as he asks questions about their activities and through this discussion develops their awareness, initial embryonic understandings of mathematical concepts such as one-to-one correspondence (pegging clothes) full, half-full and empty (pouring water) and one-to-one correspondence (eating sultanas).

These examples illustrate the awareness of mathematical events and your role in initiating and developing conversations highlighting mathematical language and concepts. Siraj-Blatchford (2009) provides a series of prompts that you may use to develop or extend a conversation with a toddler or young child. Let me apply some of them to the vignette 'Cake-baking'.

- *Tuning in, show genuine interest*: listen carefully to Alice as she carries the eggs; give her counting and actions of carrying them one by one my full attention (attention on the counting, not on caring that the eggs might be dropped).
- *Respect her decision and choice and invite her to elaborate*: Say things like, 'I am interested in how many eggs you have carried'. Listen to her response.
- *Recap*: 'So you carried [x number] of eggs'.
- *Offer my similar experience as an adult*: 'I like to count the cups full and spoons full when I am cooking'.
- *Clarify ideas*: 'Alice, do you think the eggs will crack when you tap them on the edge of the bowl?'
- *Suggestions*: 'You might try tapping a little harder.'
- *Reminder*: 'Don't forget that when the eggs crack they need to be over the bowl.'
- *Use encouragement to further thinking*: 'You have cracked the eggs carefully. Can you think about how many you have now cracked in the bowl?'
- *Offer an alternative viewpoint*: 'Maybe we could count the shells to check how many.'
- *Speculate*: 'What do you think would happen to the cake if we put [x] eggs in?'
- *Ask open questions*: 'What happens next?' 'How do you …?' 'What do you think?' 'I wonder what …?'
- *Model thinking*: 'I have to think hard before I make cakes. I need to choose a recipe and look in the cupboard to see if I have the ingredients. I might need to shop. I need to check if I have time' (Siraj-Blatchford, 2017).

FRANCES BURTON

These conversations may occur spontaneously and you as the teacher should seize the opportunities they provide to deepen children's mathematical thinking.

Such opportunities should also be *planned* for when you arrange and resource your early childhood learning environment, both inside and outside, and how you plan to create or provoke moments that stimulate children's interests and conversations that are mathematical in focus. Using mathematical language and terms accurately is very important.

Earlier in the chapter I discussed the importance of recognising that, as teachers, we bring our attitudes and feelings towards mathematics: we also bring our knowledge of and skill with the language of mathematics into the lives of young children within the circle of community influences on children. We need to be mindful of this. It is through these sustained conversations that children begin to trial their own use of mathematical language and take their first steps in mathematical reasoning and, with your guidance and support, they may also begin their journey with mark making. We value children's early writing and drawing attempts, including what some adults might think are 'scribbles', because in these moments the child in the act of 'mark making' is attempting to use a symbol in place of a real object or event. These are their first experiences with the creation and use of their own symbols. This may include early expressions of mathematical concepts such as different types of lines, creating more than one mark, creating a circular shape or attempting to write symbols for numbers (Carruthers & Worthington, 2006).

STOP AND REFLECT

- Consider the various activity areas common to many pre-school and long day care centres. These include dress-up areas, block corners, puzzle activities, painting and drawing areas, a library, reading area, construction materials, sand play, small car tracks and jungle gyms.
- Reflect on how you might utilise some or all of these areas to extend children's mathematical language and thinking. Practise a sustained shared conversation about mathematics in one of the activity areas. What might you need to think about?
- Think also of how you might record these moments through anecdotal records or learning stories so the children's mathematical learning is visible to themselves, their families and their communities. Take care to include samples of their mathematical language and, if the opportunity arises, some mathematical mark making.

The evidence is strong that children are learning mathematically in the prior-to-school years. There is research also that indicates that early mathematical learning has later, wider educational benefits for children. Consider this thought-provoking statement by Reid (2016, p.6):

> Several recent longitudinal studies have investigated mathematical development in the transition from preschool to the early years of primary school. For instance, in one study, counting skills and understanding of quantities and the relationships between them in the year before starting primary school predicted children's maths achievement and teacher ratings of competence in maths one year later (Aunio & Niemivirta, 2010). Other studies have demonstrated that, on entry to school, number sense and numeracy knowledge predict maths achievement in later school years
>
> (Aubrey, Godfrey & Dahl, 2006).

> **STOP AND REFLECT**
>
> Do you have evidence of young children's mathematical learning from your experiences in centres or through your own children or those of family or friends? Have you heard mathematical talk? Or, reflecting back, can you now think of missed opportunities?

In addition to Vygotsky, you will have met learning theorists such as Bronfenbrenner and Moll et al. in previous chapters. Let me remind you in essence that the views of these theorists (among others) on the learning of young children underpin this course. These theorists highlight the importance of learning through social interaction, including the role of the significant other (Vygotsky, 1962), the influences of our own experiences, our cultural 'funds of knowledge' according to Moll (1992), or the early 'mesosystem' in the circles of influence of Bronfenbrenner's ecological systems model (1994).

Jean Piaget

Piaget's cognitive theory of learning outlines the child's learning as moving through a series of stages, often associated with age (Ojose, 2008). Piaget identified four stages, three of which are listed below (the fourth stage—formal operational—is not discussed here as it was not seen by Piaget as a stage that young children could reach).

- *sensorimotor stage:* the baby and young child are learning about their world through their senses and eventually recognising that objects exist even if they can't see them. Games such as 'Peek-a-boo' or 'Where am I?' played by parents with their babies strengthen the development of what Piaget refers to as **object permanence**. The baby or young child is learning that the same object may exist whether they can see it or not. A sign that the child has object permanence is the young baby looking at their hand or playing with their feet.

  Children in this stage are learning early number through their parent counting their fingers and toes, other body parts or small numbers of objects. They will also benefit from simple counting rhymes and picture stories shared with them.

- *preoperational stage:* in this second stage, the child has more language and attempts to generalise but often lacks the logic to clearly tie related events together. For example the child can see that 4 and 5 equal 9 but they cannot reverse the problem showing that 9 take away 5 is 4 (Ojose, 2008). The other often-quoted example is the child's lack of understanding of conservation tested through pouring water from one jug to that of a different shape. The child seeing this is unable to recognise that it is the amount of water in the different shaped containers. The child relies on one dimension only, in this instance, it is often height.

  - Practical experiences with volume, shape and number with appropriate questions and explanations will help the child strengthen their mathematical understanding.

....
object permanence when a child can identify that an object exists even when it is out of sight.

FRANCES BURTON

- *concrete operations stage:* at this next stage children now can consider more than one dimension of an object or event. They can use all their senses to understand and test their mathematical understanding. They have language and understanding and through 'hands on' experiences they have deeper understanding of their mathematical concepts. They can order objects according to increasing or decreasing length, mass or volume. The use of 'hands on' activities gives a concrete understanding to abstract concepts. The child is able to make an evaluation as to their solution to a problem and give reasons for their solution.

The usefulness of Piagetian theory is in recognising that all children move through a series of stages. Further benefits from Piagetian theory is acknowledging that the child may be at different stages in varied areas of mathematics and children of similar age may be at different stages.

STOP AND THINK

- What are the main stages of Piaget's theory of learning as applicable to mathematical learning?
- How does Piaget's theory relate to Vygotskian theory?
- Can you tie these theories together to enhance your understanding of how children learn mathematics?
- Can you give some practical experiences to illustrate this?

Maria Montessori

Montessori also explains children's learning as moving through a series of stages or 'sensitive periods'. Figure 6.1 illustrates her view of the early sensitive periods.

Montessori sees these periods as developmental windows of opportunity when children have a special aptitude to learn specific skills or concepts.

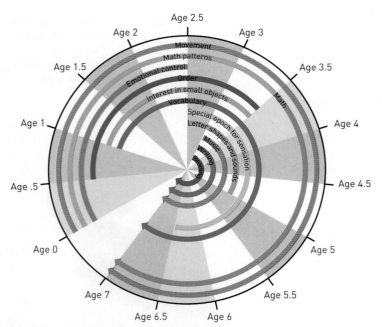

Figure 6.1 Stages of development for early learning from birth to age 7

- *Birth to age six:* the construction of individuality and the absorbent mind. The first stage is where the child learns through their hands and movement. The young child learns through touching, sorting and stacking materials. This is all about giving young babies and children the opportunity to handle a range of objects. They absorb information without conscious effort and will often mimic their parents.
- *The need for order:* from six months young children need some sense of order and, according to Montessori, the lack of order may lead to tantrums.

- *Interest in small objects:* from about the age of one, children enjoy small objects and the handling of these assists children's cognitive understanding of their world.
- *Sensitivity to learning through the senses:* this begins from birth and continues to develop. Supporting the baby and young child to learn through all their senses will enhance the potential. Montessori did not see these 'sensitive stages' as linear but that at times they overlap or co-exist.
- *Six to twelve years old:* acquisition of culture and the cosmic plan. This is the movement from absorbing information to reasoning. The child asks 'why'. The child enjoys collaborating with others and using their imagination.

STOP AND REFLECT

What do you see as important in Montessori's theory of children's 'sensitive periods'? How can you use this knowledge when you are working with babies and young children?

Teaching mathematics through play

I have chosen to describe the two vignettes in detail through the beginning of this chapter as a strategy to amplify—to make highly visible to you through language and images—some of the important issues in the mathematical learning of young children and our own feelings towards mathematics. Zaporozhets (cited in Bodrova & Leong, 1996) brings an image to my mind of an educator with a trumpet amplifying the learning within the ZPD of the child. This is how I want you to see your role in the early mathematical learning of young children. Reflect back on the image of young Alice and her mum cracking the eggs and counting one, two, three, four. This in essence is your role. The difference between this mother–child vignette and your role is the difference between families as first educators of the children and your role as a professional, degree-qualified teacher who will plan for such vignettes to occur using your knowledge of:

- play pedagogy and mathematics
- young children (professionally and personally)
- deep and detailed mathematical subject content (this begins in Montessori's stages of development for early learning but is seen to continue beyond the early learning phase).

Play pedagogy and mathematics

Much has been written about play as the most important process through which children learn, particularly in the prior-to-school context and this is also so for children's early mathematical learning from birth onwards. A detailed discussion of the play pedagogy is provided in Chapter 4. It might be useful for you to re-visit that chapter, this time thinking about how the discussion applies to mathematical learning. Here the discussion is the definition of play relevant to young children's mathematical learning.

The following statement from Vygotsky helps us understand the significance of play to mathematical learning: it also allows us to focus on your role as a teacher in relation to play.

> A child's play is not simply a reproduction of what he has experienced, but a creative reworking of the impressions he has acquired.
>
> (Vygotsky, 2004, p.11, cited in Siraj-Blatchford, 2009, p.10)

FRANCES BURTON

STOP AND THINK

- Can you put Vygotsky's words into your own words, as though you are explaining this to someone who is new to this topic?
- How can teachers support young children's 'creative reworking of the impressions [they have] acquired'?
- Have you observed examples of teachers actively engaged in this work during your practicum experiences? If so, what did they look like in practice?

Here are some suggestions for you to think about when you are organising for mathematics to be visible in your play activities.

- Choose the materials carefully, such as a basket of blocks, and think through the mathematical concepts children might learn through their play (measuring length; exploring how shapes fit together; thinking about the space they take up, or the buildings, towers, houses they might make).
- Ensure children will have time and space to make a long, tall or wide structure. Plan the prompts you might give to provoke their thinking, such as 'tell me about ... what might you do next?' 'Have you thought about ...?'
- Record their play as a process through a **learning story**.
- Make provision for the structure to remain visible for more than one day so children may extend their play.
- Add paper and drawing materials so children might record their structure. Store their drawings so they may revisit them.
- Include their language and examples of any mark-making activity.
- Encourage children to use their own symbols to make their own meaning from this and other mathematical play.

learning story a story about what a child has been observed doing in an early childhood program.

It is important to give children many opportunities through which they can experience and compare the real image with the symbolic image. Encourage children to extend their mathematical play over days and to revisit the images and symbols they have drawn as this gives them the chance and time to make connections to one or more previous experiences and to explain their thinking to others. It gives you time as the 'significant other' to help them draw these connections and extend their thinking into their 'ZPD'. In planning these activities, you need to be aware of the importance of maintaining a balance between child-initiated, teacher-supported and teacher-led activities in mathematics. It is through such extended imaginative 'mature' play, as defined initially by Vygotsky 1967, and further elaborated by his student Elkonin (2000/2005, cited in Leong & Bodrova, 2012) that children—with your support—can become involved in complex imaginative scenarios.

As Elkonin (1978, p.187, cited in Leong & Bodrova, 2012, p.29) puts it:

> A child starts with feeding herself with a spoon; then she uses the spoon to feed everyone; then she uses the spoon to feed her doll; and finally feeds the doll pretending to be the 'mommy' who feeds her daughter (trans. by Bodrova). At this later stage, the play is no longer about the spoon and not even about a specific doll—it is about the relationship between mother and daughter.

The intentional maths teacher

Leong and Bodrova (2012) reiterate the differing stages of imaginative play identified by Elkonin, who suggests that such play supports the pre-school child's development of imaginative and symbolic thought. I am suggesting that such mature imaginative play both includes mathematical concepts within the mature play and also the development of symbolic thought essential to children's understanding of mathematics.

An example of this mature imaginative play is children developing a travel scenario where they explore the complex process of airport travel complete with scanners and exchange of money for tickets. Such mature levels of play used to be a part of child play when children of varying ages developed complex play scenarios over extended periods of play. The older children played many different roles in such play as they initiated the scenario, organised the props, took part in the play, yet clarified the rules and procedures for the younger children. Leong and Bodrova (2012) suggest that this complex of roles may be undertaken by you as the teacher, scriptwriter, actor or props manager: aspects of your role as intentional teacher guiding their play. We will come back to these roles as we look at your role as an intentional teacher of mathematics.

Perry and Dockett (2007) suggest that you need to consider your own dispositions or attitudes towards mathematics through play. What do they mean by this? Sometimes the concept of play is bound into play activities such as children playing with blocks, puzzles, sandpit materials or dress-ups. McLane (2003, p.11, cited in Perry & Dockett, 2007, p.716) expresses a different view when he suggests that 'play is a particular attitude or approach to materials, behaviours, and ideas and not the materials or activities or ideas themselves; play is a special mode of thinking and doing'. In asking you for your disposition or attitude towards play, I am asking you to consider how you view play. Is play the *activities* the child partakes in, or is play in the child's *attitude* and approach to the blocks or sandpit materials and how does this equate with your view of mathematical learning? Children may play with filling and emptying containers in the sandpit. The mathematical play is in their attitude to noticing the containers are full, half full or empty. It is not the activity alone because they may not be exploring a mathematical concept at all. This is quite a contrast to traditional views of how children acquire mathematical knowledge.

There is often an impression that mathematics is the formal acquisition of skills and knowledge, almost the antithesis of play. I hope you are beginning to understand that this is not correct. You have a very important role to play as an *intentional teacher* of mathematics as children learn to explore and build their mathematical concepts expressed through their play.

The first challenge is to define your role as a mathematics teacher in the prior-to-school sector. In the past, early childhood educators tended to leave mathematics out of their planning with the assumption that mathematical learning (and teaching) was beyond the capabilities of young children and was, therefore, the province of school. Young children were simply considered too young for mathematics and it was assumed that it was sufficient to simply let children play. That view has now changed. We understand now that young children are experiencing mathematics in their lives from birth and our role is to give children the language to talk about their experiences, to help them develop their reasoning skills and to make new mathematical concepts visible to them through the experiences we plan and the conversations we hold with them. These are the foundations upon which more

FRANCES BURTON

formal mathematical learning is built. So, while the role of the early childhood teacher is not to formally teach children mathematical concepts such as addition through examples such as 6+4=10, it is to build understanding of the concepts that precede formal mathematical teaching.

Have you thought about your own role in the children's mathematical play? For example:

- do you role play curiosity and playfulness (Bobis, 2010) as parts of problem solving as you creatively explore ideas about how to solve practical problems such as storing mathematical resources?
- do you give children the opportunity to develop mathematical persistence as they make several attempts to cut and tape together enough paper to cover the area of a table for a teddy bears picnic?
- do you create opportunities for mathematical play through the experiences you set for your children?
- do you prepare (and research) the appropriate language to introduce to children as part of your regular planning in mathematics?
- do you take the opportunity, when it occurs, to spontaneously follow children's interests and extend their mathematical language?
- do you use technology such as your iPad or laptop to look up the meanings of mathematical words children are curious about?

Note: I have presented these ideas as questions or prompts for you to consider in your practicum experiences, but I also suggest that you document examples of these both in your own developing teaching practice, and in your notes of what you observe teachers doing. Critical reflection is important here, so remember to document what you tried or observed, its impact, and what and why it could have been done differently.

Intentionally teaching mathematics through play

We have discussed the importance of your role in mathematical play and how through your conversations you may provoke children into thinking more deeply, and you may also give them the mathematical vocabulary to express their thinking and share it with you and their peers and families. Have you considered varied roles you might use as an intentional teacher to assist your children to learn more mathematics through their play? Some of these roles are actor (participant), scriptwriter, producer and props coordinator (Barblett, 2010). You might think of others, but let us explore examples of these roles for you to use to assist children's mathematical learning.

- *Playing shops—actor role:* you may take the customer or shopkeeper role. At varied times you might take on the role of the actor and join in children's imaginative play, so children can be the shopkeeper and you the customer. Together you can scaffold concepts of exchange and learn the mathematical language associated with shopping.
- *Sandpit play—scriptwriter role:* this might mean planning the discussion you might spontaneously or intentionally have with children about their sandpit play. You might practise the questions that encourage children's thinking about the concepts of full, half full, close to empty or counting how many scoops of sand are needed to achieve these levels within the bucket. Alternatively, you might encourage the toddlers and babies to look at their hand, foot or bottom prints in the sand, the space they take or the patterns

made. The pre-school child may build roads and tunnels, learning about use of space and giving directions.

- *Puzzle play—props coordinator role:* here your role is to make sure children have materials, time and space to play in the sandpit or with jigsaws, but it is not your role this time to intervene or stimulate their cognitive thinking in mathematics. You might add a timely additional prop to their play that will take their play further or in a different direction.
- *Daily room preparation—producer role:* have you thought about your role as an intentional mathematics producer when you plan and set up the centre for the daily or weekly experiences of children? How you might orchestrate and manage the daily production of children, mathematical learning experiences and time to ensure that the show runs on time with maximum mathematical learning for all the participants? (Barblett, 2010)

In any one day you need to show all of these skills in your preparation and implementation of mathematical learning opportunities for children.

Young children and mathematics

In relation to your professional knowledge of young children both professionally and personally, we need to explore further the view that all children have the opportunity to have a wide and rich range of experiences. Reflect on your assumptions about young children and mathematics: do you believe some children are born mathematicians? Do you believe boys are inclined to be mathematical and girls better at language? These statements represent some of the assumptions made by teachers that impact on their planning for mathematical experiences for children. It also has consequences in a prior-to-school curriculum focused on following children's interests in prior-to-school settings and their expectations about children and mathematics in the primary school setting.

Would you consider including the home languages of your children in their mathematical learning, and how might you do this? Consider as Moll et al. (1992) ask us to, that children are born into a culture and bring with them cultural experiences that may be quite different from yours into your setting. How do you encourage their home cultural practices in mathematics to become visible in your centre, whether the children are born here with family from overseas or they belong within indigenous communities of Australia? Moll et al. would suggest, as their research exemplifies, that teachers make home visits and learn how other cultures have evolved their own mathematical practices. Such a practice might not be feasible for you as a young teacher and definitely not available to you as a pre-service teacher. What could you do to foster the visibility of the mathematical practices from a child's home? Think about the ways your supervising teacher communicates and builds partnerships with her parent community. How visible is mathematical learning in this partnership? What is the attitude to and image of mathematics that is visible between her and her parent community? Is she pro-active, provoking conversations about mathematics learning, or reactive when answering parental enquiries about mathematical preparation for school readiness? How will you bring mathematics into the relationship between yourself and your community when you teach a group of children?

FRANCES BURTON

Mathematical subject content

Your task is to be accurate in the language and concept development opportunities you use with children through intentional teaching, direct teaching and spontaneous sustained shared conversations. You need also to understand how these early rich understandings will link to the larger and more formal knowledge of mathematics within the school mathematical curriculum.

To support your growth in mathematical content knowledge, I will ask you to revisit and begin to strengthen and demonstrate your own mathematical skills and knowledge at an adult level as well as demonstrate an understanding of what early embryonic concepts look like and sound like in reasoning, number, algebra, geometry, measurement and statistics.

You might find as we now turn to exploring the early conceptual knowledge of mathematics that there are terms that you do not understand. If so, be prepared to use book resources (see Haylock & Manning, 2014) check an online dictionary to find the meanings of terms and create your own mathematical glossary (as well as referring to the one at the end of this book). You are expected to be knowledgeable and demonstrate good self-learning practices as you learn how to be a teacher of mathematics.

We will now begin to look at the concepts involved in the early learning of mathematics. As we do, consider how you might plan, implement and assess children's learning of these mathematical concepts. For examples of assessment in early mathematical learning, see Chapter 12, where I have included some scenarios on assessment in mathematics.

Early concepts in mathematics

All children have the ability to solve mathematical problems, to make sense of the world using mathematics and to communicate their mathematical thinking. (Dunphy et al., 2014, p.8). Children are developing their mathematical reasoning skills through their play and playful conversations. Current research emphasises mathematical knowledge as evolving, and mathematical learning is about finding the relationships (e.g. between numbers, such as 3 is one more than 2 and one less than 4) and explaining them as a way to mathematically explain the child's world. In this instance the child is learning about the relative size of numbers.

As a simple example, our knowledge about the number 2 includes it as one more than 1 and one less than 3. A two-year-old will know that two is their age until their next birthday, when they will become three. They might also know or say that they have two legs and two arms, but not link this knowledge to recognising pair, as in a pair of gloves also means two. They may be able to count to five or ten but not link counting with the concept of number as a quantity. It is in making these links with your support as their teacher that children form rich mathematical concepts and learn to see and explain or think through and give their reasons about the relationships between numbers.

Same and different

Young children begin learning about this concept within their family initially as they recognise their parents and other family members. As the baby becomes a toddler they may have heard how they have the same eyes, hair, smile or fingernails as other family members. Parents may discuss sameness with them, often related to colour, as in our initial vignette.

In our role as teachers we may include picture books such as the Pantone colour book (2012) to discuss colour concepts including the shading within any colour and where the boundaries between red, yellow and orange blur into each other. Other books can be read and discussed with babies and with two–three-year-olds to begin exploring same and different along with early Montessori materials (www.infomontessori.com/sensorial/visual-sense-color-tablets.htm) that extend same and different into concepts of length the child can experience using all of their senses. Through such activities and, later, through the development and exploration of collections, children develop their classifying and reasoning skills. It is through their conversations about same and different and, later, what is and is not a pattern, that children begin to develop their mathematical reasoning skills.

Suggested classifying activities include:

- finding colours, materials, and shapes that share the same attribute. This may be through matching experiences
- recognising and categorising the same category within different categories. If you have visited pre-schools or long day care centres, you are likely to have seen button and animal figurine sorting activities. These are opportunities for children to extend their concept of same and different from colour to shape, size, texture and length. The list is long and it is useful for you to reflect on, add to and share sorting activities you have seen in centres you have visited
- sorting and categorising discrete materials via more than one category (e.g. sorting by colour then by size)
- sorting, classifying and ordering within collections by one or more **attributes**.

The sorting and categorising activities need to be supported by discussion with children about what is the same or different, how they have identified the categories and, with support, encouraging children to create and name their own varied collections.

> **attributes**
> characteristics that define an object or element so that it can be sorted or classified.

Awareness of pattern

These categorising skills can extend to children's early work on the recognition and, later, the creation of patterns. Children should be encouraged to recognise and name their own patterns. They may do this in relation to the clothes they wear, the rhythms they hear in songs, their play with buttons or animal figurines, natural materials, blocks from the block corner, clothes from the dress-up box or patterns in the day. As they recognise similarity within their early patterns, they may notice how they repeat and can contain similar structures, such as 'red green red', or 'blue yellow blue'. Knowledge of similarity within patterns can lead to generalisations about the **structure of patterns** and the beginning of algebraic ideas about the use of symbols. Children require many practical hands-on experiences and thoughtful conversations explaining how they have made the patterns and what they notice about their patterns, before they can generalise. Here, your role as a teacher is to stimulate the activity through the materials you make available to children and the questions you ask that scaffold children's ability to explain their mathematical thinking and self-discovery of pattern.

> **structure of patterns** learning about the ways in which elements are organised and structured to form patterns. The understanding of predictable and integrated elements leads to the ability to generalise.

FRANCES BURTON

You should examine materials and experiences of pattern through your eyes as a teacher of mathematics. Consider how this perspective may focus the questions you ask, such as 'What do you notice about the pattern you have made?' 'Can you see other similar patterns?' 'Can you see or make a different pattern?' 'How are they different?'

These categorising, ordering and patterning skills can also lead to children creating groups with the same number of items within them and then groups with different numbers of items in them. Young children should be encouraged to be creative, imaginative and mathematical in their play. They may be creating a dinosaur-themed park with blocks and figurines, or a horse stable or a greengrocer's shop. In any of these activities as children sort and classify their imaginative groupings, they may notice or you may scaffold their learning and help them question whether they have the same or different numbers of figurines in each group and how would they know. This is the beginning of the child's early understanding of the quantitative or **early understanding of cardinal number**.

> **Early understanding of cardinal number**
> Cardinal number is the quantification concept of number, for example a set of three toys, three balls, three hats, the 'threeness' of the number.

Early number experiences

I want to begin this section on number by asking you to visualise a pie and reflect on the process of how it is made. Just as the richness of the pie is in the complex of different ingredients combined together, so is the richness of children's early learning of number.

Think about a number such as the number 2, which we explored earlier. List all the different facts you might know about this number, share them with a partner and then check your thinking with this list:

- the verbal word two
- the symbol for two
- the name two
- the concept that two has a quantity such as 2 dots, 2 sticks, 2 fingers, 2 hands or 2 legs. This is the cardinal nature of two
- the concept of 2 as one more than 1 and one less than 3
- two as an ordinal number. The child is second in the line (i.e. this is their order as the single digit 2)
- the value or quantitative nature of two will change according to its place in the whole number, for example, 2, 21, 201.

All of these elements come together gradually through children's early number experiences to form their overall understanding of the concept of two. The richness of children's conceptual development, their early **number sense**, will be like the richness of the pie. Both are dependent on the quality of the ingredients and the care in the blending. Early number sense is dependent on the richness and variety of children's experiences and language blended together.

> **number sense**
> being able to understand and work with numbers to perform mental maths operations and use numbers in real-world contexts.

Children learn the names of numbers, some sense of the ordering of the names and later they start to develop ideas about the quantity that number represents. These are all elements of the 'pie' that gradually come together as their knowledge of number—that is, their number sense. This is an evolving concept for all of us as our number sense grows throughout our lives.

Babies learn about number as their parent or educator touches their fingers or toes while repeating traditional rhymes such as 'This little pig went to market'. They learn they have two eyes, two arms, hands, legs and feet and ten fingers and toes. Such learning is in their home languages and within cultural contexts. It is important for educators and teachers to include these rhymes, chants and songs in their everyday practice. The early learning is deepened when they involve touch. The importance of touch, through which babies and very young children's learning experiences link with sensory experience, is discussed in more detail in relation to music, in Chapter 8.

Young children of two or three start to learn about numbers through their daily experiences, including the singing of rhymes and songs such as 'One, two, buckle my shoe' or 'Five little ducks went out one day …' and 'Ten in the bed'. Initially the numbers are 'word chunks' as part of the songs and rhymes (Clements & Sarama, 2009). The numbers have no inherent mathematical meaning. They may be a cultural reference to number but not a conceptual understanding of the concept of '2'. It is only through further experiences where young children begin to count objects or their steps or their fingers that the number words start to develop a separate mathematical meaning. As you read stories to babies or toddlers, such as counting books or books that weave numbers and counting into the story (e.g. 'Goldilocks and the three bears'), they begin to expand their understanding of the number words as separate concepts.

As you develop your own resources of number songs, chants and rhymes, practise singing or saying them and practise the actions that support the number-meanings of the song, chant or rhyme. Children love to join in, and gain satisfaction from engaging in the actions. The actions that the child learns are fun, and they help children remember the rhyme or song, the number order and eventually to distinguish the individual number words.

Toddlers extend their earlier learning about numbers through early physical experiences such as pointing to numbers visible in their environment or counting their steps, claps or ball bounces. They may learn to recognise and say their house number and recognise numbers in their environment. They learn the concept of 'one more' as they seek one more treat or story.

Young toddlers and children learn concepts about the relative size or magnitude of numbers through hearing and later using words such 'one', 'two', 'three', 'more', 'many', and 'a lot'. I am sure many of you will have heard children talk about 'a thousand' as a big number. Children learn these concepts through hearing and seeing numbers in their environment. They will refine their understanding and usage of the word meanings if you create the opportunity to hold a conversation about the meaning of the word using examples such as 'Do you have 1, 2, 3 or more blocks in your trolley? How do you know this?' This gives the child the opportunity to explain their reasoning and for you to add to their understanding. Some terms are comparative—such as 'few', 'many', 'more' and 'a lot'— and children will increase their understanding through much exposure to many practical experiences and intentional discussion.

Not all children have these varied experiences and it is our task as teachers to strengthen and extend their understanding of the language of numbers.

Subitising

Subitising is an important part of mathematics. It refers to 'the ability to recognise small numbers of items automatically without having to engage in conscious counting' (Wynn, 1995, cited in Treacy & Willis, 2003, p.36)

subitising the ability to recognise a number of objects without counting.

FRANCES BURTON

perceptual subitising the instantaneous recognition (usually small numbers under 5).

conceptual subitising makes use of different strategies for identifying the number of items without counting them one by one. For example, breaking six dots into two groups of three.

Through their experiences, young children learn to automatically recognise small groups of the same size and identify them (Treacy & Willis, 2003). This automatic recognition of same small number quantity groups is identified as **perceptual subitising**. Young children of two or three years have a spatial understanding of number (Mulligan et al., 2010). This is evidenced as recognising numbers—for example, the number of fingers, or the dots on a dice or a domino. This informal learning often occurs within the family cultural context and will be in children's home language.

From these early beginnings, children can begin to extend their understanding of number, moving from perceptual subitising to **conceptual subitising** through the experiences we give them. They may see 2 and 3 without counting. We can tie that knowledge together as conceptual subitising of the number 5. The difference between the two forms of subitising (perceptual and conceptual) relates to our task as teachers as we build from children's perceptual knowledge to larger conceptual understandings.

STOP AND THINK

- Could you explain perceptual and conceptual subitising? Have you thought about how you might recognise these skills in young children?
- Can you think of practical activities where you might add to children's understanding of number concepts?

Alongside this early learning about number names and subitising is another element of the 'pie'—that is, counting.

Counting

Below are two perspectives on how children learn to count and then develop their understanding of number quantities. As you read the two perspectives, I want you to consider how they are the same, how they differ and how together you might use both sets of information to better understand current thinking about how young children learn number.

Perspective 1

Perspective 1, the *principles* of counting (Gelman & Gallistel, 1978) may be summarised as:

- *the one-to-one principle*—children understand in their counting that each object has one counting word attached to it. Counting your five fingers and touching each one for each number is evidence of one-to-one correspondence. Giving children the opportunity to set the table for four or give a teddy to each child will help children develop this skill
- *the stable order principle*—there is a set order to the number names. The child who randomly counts 1, 2, 3, 5, 6 is yet to develop this skill
- *the cardinal principle*—the last number said names the group. For example, counting a group of five toys involves counting 1, 2, 3, 4, 5, so the final word—five—applies to the group. There is some suggestion that children may sometimes say the last number name but not recognise that this applies to the group. Experiences in creating and counting

small groups support the development of this skill as does the practice of counting the children in the group

- *the abstraction principle*—children learn that they may count five children, five hats or five giant boots. Though the groups are different, there will still be five objects in each of these groups.
- *the order-irrelevance principle*—children might start at any point in the group of objects and provided they count each item in the group it will make no difference to the total number and name of the group.

STOP AND REFLECT

Reflect on these principles and how they relate to your experiences with young children.

Perspective 2

Perspective 2 identifies *stages* of counting (Clements & Sarama, 2009) in children's mathematical thinking and mastery. The stages are:

- *pre counter*—a random sequence of number names. Children may count 1, 2, 3, 5, 7, 10. Five and 10 are learnt as numbers well before other numbers. Can you think why?
- *chanter*—saying numbers as sound bites. This is where toddlers sing '1, 2, buckle my shoe, 3, 4, knock at the door …'
- *reciter*—saying number names to five and then to ten but knowing only the number sequence. Children may remember to count from one to five from a rhyme, but the words have no quantitative meaning
- *corresponder*—one-to-one correspondence with number names while counting (object counting). For example, children may touch each object in a sequence and say number names in order but don't know that the last number word tells the whole set and they may recount again when you ask *How many?* (whereas the child who can count—the next stage—is one who can say it easily with or without the objects there). They know the last number names the group
- *counter (small numbers)*—counts to 5. Children can implement one-to-one correspondence with the objects they count
- *producer*—children can produce the collection to 5 or 10 but may be unsure once they are past 5 that they have one-to-one correspondence
- *counter 10*—children can make collections up to 10
- *counter and producer*—children can break apart a set of any number up to 10 and still recognise the total.

Children require a breadth of experiences and practice with using the language of counting to develop and strengthen their knowledge of number and counting. Familiarity with number names in their own language will assist their understanding.

STOP AND THINK

You might notice some strong similarities between the two perspectives on how children learn to count. Can you explain the differences?

FRANCES BURTON

Here are some ideas for activities that support children's learning of number and counting.

- The use of dressing up activities in imaginative play, counting games and simple versions of board games will all help children's growing understanding.
- Daily packing up of activities can reinforce one-to-one skills as children count the chairs, books or other objects as they pack them away.
- Children writing their own recipes or creating tally marks will help their understanding of the role of written symbols in number.

Children also learn the beginnings of addition and subtraction as part of their everyday practices as they have 'one more turn' or eat 'another' biscuit. Alternatively, they may learn to take away the missing ninepins as they play bowling games. They share half an apple or some books with their friends, ensuring that they each have the same fair share.

It is through your awareness and planning for activities in number such as these *and* your inclusion of the appropriate language while remembering to record an observation about children's number practices that your understanding of how children are learning number concepts in mathematics develops.

Geometry

The study of geometry involves shape, size, position, direction, and movement and is descriptive of the physical world we live in. Children's spatial sense is their awareness of themselves in relation to the people and objects around them.

(Copley, 2010, p.105)

Consider the following: a child packs the blocks away on the shelves before lunch; the teacher has photos or outlines of the shapes and number symbols on the shelves to support the young child's learning.

What do these simple examples have to do with learning about geometry?

In both examples, children are learning to count and match the number of blocks with the symbols for number, shape, size and spatial relationships as they count, check the image with what is in their hands and fit the number of blocks within a specific area of the shelf.

You might add to their learning with this question: 'Have you put all the large rectangular blocks away on the shelf?' Packing-up activities are an excellent learning opportunity to reinforce and extend the child's understanding of geometry in the form of shape and spatial relationships—how shapes fit in relationship to each other.

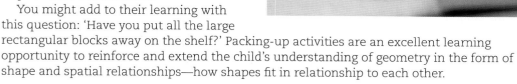

STOP AND REFLECT

How have you seen the block area used when you have visited centres? How has the educator organised the packing away of the blocks? Are there visual aids: symbols that will help the child's understanding of shape and space?

The block corner is a major source of children's early learning about shape and spatial relationships. Have you thought about who uses this space in centres you have visited? How would you ensure all children have time with these experiences?

Other areas and activities where children learn about shape and spatial relationships include:

- *puzzles*—where children need to be able to fit the shape into the space. To do this they may need to rotate or flip the shape

FRANCES BURTON

- *playground climbing equipment*—where children learn how to physically move their body through a range of spaces, adapting their body to meet the demands of the shapes in space
- *bikes, cars and tracks*—where children learn to move their shape in space, learning also to make turns and change direction
- *yoga activities*—where children learn self-awareness of the shapes they can make with their bodies in space
- *treasure-hunt activities*—where children learn to follow map directions and use their directional skills as well as recognising symbols.

Shapes and spatial relationships

Babies learn to recognise shapes in their environment. Initially these shapes are the faces, bodies and movement of their parents or carers. Babies feel shapes using their mouth and then hands and eyes as they develop an awareness of shapes such as small toys and their own bodily self and its relationship to their environment. Babies learn to move and to grasp items. As they learn to roll, crawl, stand, walk, run and dance they develop an awareness of themselves in space. They also develop an awareness of objects in space through actions such as rolling into a couch or table.

Parents, educators and teachers add language to children's movements, naming them as they move in directions (e.g. up, down, forwards, backwards).

Toddlers learn to stack two or three blocks together or to match shapes into some form of shape sorter. During this process, they learn the names of basic shapes such as triangular, rectangular and circular, and movements such as forwards, sideways, backwards and to turn objects to attempt to fit shapes into spaces. As teachers, our task is to name the objects, and draw attention to the relative size of shapes, large or small lids, round or rectangular, and their movement.

We can design small obstacle courses for toddlers so they can experience the movement of their bodies through space and the associated language. The use of treasure baskets (referred to earlier in the chapter) full of varied objects for children to explore builds their sensory awareness of shape and space and, with your help, the beginning language to explain the shapes and sounds they make (Hughes, 2010). Create your own treasure basket from objects found in your kitchen and list the shapes and sounds a toddler might discover.

Pre-school children may learn much about shape and spatial relationships through play in the block corner. They learn the feel and size of varied shapes and how they may join them together to create a tower, road or fencing for their figurines as part of their imaginative play. In all of these varied activities children may learn which blocks will stack on other blocks and which ones won't. They learn persistence as they attempt to build a high tower, but are unaware that they need a solid base to support it so it topples. Encourage children to persist at the task and to look for explanations for why their tower will not stay standing. Allow them to solve their own problem or through the assistance of other children to learn together the importance of a solid base.

To create a road for their cars, children learn direction: turn left and right, go straight or round a bend or curved track. Consider how you might encourage children to add a ramp or bridge to their track and what they will learn about height and speed for their cars in adding this element to their race track. If you provoke children to think about how they could use blocks to create a farm, pony stud or new town, they will need to solve problems of shape and space. It might also create time problems or considerations, as children need time to construct their imaginative environment, play within it and alter it to better meet the needs of their game. Suggest to children that they draw a map or plan of their structures so they might recreate them another day. Add these maps or plans to a share box, so children learn to follow each other's drawings. Ensure that children add their name to their plan. In this way you are creating opportunities for them to explain how their structures were built, using the language of shape and spatial relationships.

Consider how you would plan to regularly include children's learning about shape and spatial relationships in your program. How might you record their skills, interests and language development? What about your own knowledge of shape and space? Are you clear about the difference in names between two-dimensional and three-dimensional shapes (2D and 3D)? How would you explain this to a pre-school child? How would you explain these shapes: a square, a rectangle, a circle and an oval? Be aware of the strength of teaching families of shapes rather than a prototype approach. Reflect on clarifying with young children where you might find two-dimensional faces within three-dimensional shapes. Where would you find these shapes in the kitchen, at home, or the inside or outside area of a centre? Create an opportunity to check your understanding of the names of shapes.

As we end our study of shape and spatial relationships it is useful to see the child's learning links with number as they count the shapes in spaces such as the shelves at packing up time. It also links with measurement as they use blocks to measure the length of a room or the perimeter of a rug.

Measurement

> Young children are inherent measurers and this is reflected strongly in everyday language when they compare, order and match—I can swim right across the pool now; it's too big for me to lift; it won't fit in the box; my hand is bigger than your hand. Personal experiences, such as playing with toys, interactions with other children, conversations with parents, all reinforce children's early development of the concept of attributes that can be measured.
>
> (DEECD, 2009)

Measuring is all about finding out how long, tall, heavy, fast or how much area. We are talking about the various attributes we use in measuring. These attributes include length, height, area, mass, capacity and time. Children have experience informally with measuring from a young age, though most of this is informal and often they are inaccurate in their use of terms. They use 'big' and 'little' when referring to length, size and even age rather than just size. They refer to their little sister; to being bigger than their friend; their hand is smaller than their parent's hand; they have a bigger friend when they mean an older friend.

Before children can learn how to measure they need experiences with the various attributes and to learn the correct language. The language they use with the varied attributes is length (how long or tall something is), capacity (how much something holds), weight (how heavy it is), area (how much space is covered) and time (events take more or less time than each other). These experiences occur through play.

FRANCES BURTON

> Children learn to measure through direct comparisons. They compare two objects and describe one as taller or shorter than the other; holding more or holding less than another; heavier or lighter than another, or covering more or less space than another.
>
> (Miller & Baillargeon, 1990, cited in Clements, 2003)

Children become familiar with some formal measures from their everyday family experiences. They may be familiar with rulers—from older siblings who are at school—or tape measures because the family is measuring the kitchen or garden at home. It is appropriate to let them use these measuring tools, though you can also give them experiences with informal measures such as pop sticks, string, hands or hefting with the body as a balance. It is through these activities that they will gain a broader understanding of the attributes they are learning to measure (Condon & Clyde, 2004).

How do we support measuring experiences?

We can do this by enlisting the children's help with real-life problems. Perhaps we need a new rug for our shared space in a pre-school. The children can work out the length and width of the area to be covered using informal measures such as blocks. We might need to move a cupboard, so children could check the size of the space needed for the cupboard. We can measure the area on the shelves for the blocks so we know there is room for them to be stacked away neatly. Often, measuring experiences involve cooking. This may be measuring the flour and salt in a cup or spoonfuls to make playdough, pizza or pancakes. Children can measure their area by having a friend trace around their body shape on paper. They might measure the heights of their favourite toys by direct comparison or by using an indirect or non-standard uniform unit such as paperclips or popsticks as the measuring tool. In this process they also start to estimate how many popsticks, paperclips or hand spans each favourite toy will be. They can also record their results, strengthening their understanding and use of their own *graphics* (Carruthers & Worthington, 2011).

It is through experiences in the sandpit that children can practise their skills with *volume* and *capacity* as they engage in practical and creative play, perhaps about cooking. Sand itself is a tactile medium with differing qualities as wet or dry. Children can use dry sand to pour into cups, jugs and baking trays and learn from their teacher what full, empty, almost full, over-full, almost half full and just a little bit full mean in comparative terms. Often Initial Teacher Education students working in centres will tell vignettes of how they needed to move the stove to the sandpit to be a part of the imaginative play or they found the children were filling buckets of sand and taking them by bike or car to the stove or other areas of the centre. Informal play with capacity measures occurs as much around the sandpit as in it. Children can use wet sand to mould and sculpt figures such as imaginary animals and measure their height, length and perimeter. On a smaller scale, children can also mould and measure figures using magic sand or playdough.

Time is a more abstract concept for children to learn to measure. Children learn about daytime, night time, today and tomorrow through practical experiences such as how many sleeps until their birthday or how much their bean plants or chickens have grown. Children can record events that are practical and have meaning to their lives on a simple calendar.

The emphasis in all of these early measuring activities of young children should be on informal measuring and appropriate language. Make time to revise your understanding

of the correct terminology for measuring. Create links between your reading and your experiences in centres. Practise the skills of informally estimating and measuring objects: their length, area, weight. Consider how you might measure and record the weather using an informal rain gauge or the temperature by the clothes we wear over different seasons. Measuring should link to children's everyday life as well as their imaginative life.

Statistics and probability

Some people consider statistics and probability as unsuited to young children in prior-to-school settings; however, the beginnings of these concepts should be experienced by young children because they are part of their everyday lives (Knaus, 2013). For example, children hear the language of probability daily in family discussions about the weather, as parents speculate that it might or might not rain; the wind will get worse or maybe not; we might not play outside if it rains.

The language children should hear ranges across the continuum from 'definitely will occur', through increasing doubt about the event, to 'definitely will not occur':

It *definitely will* rain today.

It *is likely* to rain today.

It *might* rain today.

There is a *50/50 chance* it will rain.

It *might not* rain today.

It *is unlikely* to rain today.

It *won't* rain today.

FRANCES BURTON

Any number of similar continuums can be developed with children's active participation, using the continuum of possibilities from possible to impossible for other events. For example: *impossible* might be jumping over the centre roof; *possible* would be jumping from one end of the room to the other. Children enjoy the humour in thinking of impossible events. It challenges them to think of a similar possible event.

STOP AND THINK

Think of and document at least three other examples of activities you could include in your planning for children to learn about statistics and probability that relate directly to their home and everyday experiences.

The beginnings of understanding *chance* or *randomness* can be experienced by children through games such as 'Snakes and ladders' or tossing a coin for 'Heads or tails'. In 'Snakes and ladders' it is the randomness of the roll of the dice that determines whether you go up the ladder or down the snake. In ' Heads or tails' initially children make judgments that, because heads came up this time, it will come up again the next time the coin is tossed. They do not see that each time the coin is tossed they have a fifty-fifty chance of it landing on the side of their choice. Some research has been done with children of mixed ages and the use of spinners. One spinner was evenly distributed over four colours; the other had an uneven distribution of colour. As each spinner was used with the children they eventually realised that the second spinner was unfair, while the first gave them an equally random chance as to what colour would result (Pange, 2002, p.2).

Our role as teachers is to create opportunities for children to experience the randomness (or chance) of events and to make the appropriate language visible.

Children may also be aware of *data gathering*, through surveys completed by their parents. They too can begin to collect and interpret simple data. A good example is the use of the rain gauge to collect information about rain patterns. A rain gauge can be as simple as a container with a popstick left outside and checked on each morning. Children can notice whether there is water in the container and whether it measured on the popstick. The simplest format for graphing this information is to mark the wet line on each stick daily and display them so children can notice the changes and discuss their findings about rain.

Children's interests and consequent questions should lead the collection of statistics. For example, following on from the rain gauge may be questions about whether there would be more or less rain collected if the rain gauge was in different parts of the playground. Data is easily collected by moving the rain gauge to different places or creating more than one gauge.

Children may learn to collect data about the questions that interest them, such as, who has pets, what sort of pet do they have? Other data-collecting examples may include questions about the children's likes and dislikes, or what they are eating for their lunch today—sandwiches or noodles?

The questions need to relate to the real lives of the children and be able to be displayed in a direct comparison of the data. Pocket charts are a simple way to display children's choices. Children might also use blocks or rings on strings to display the data. They need the opportunity to read what the data is saying (i.e. *interpret* the data) and discuss their understandings of the data collected. They may then, with your support, think of other questions they could explore.

Sometimes, as stated earlier in the chapter, as we as the teachers of young children focus in on the mathematical activities or concepts, we overlook the attitudes, awareness and home cultures of the children. I am reiterating my view on the importance of the social and cultural contexts of mathematical learning because I believe it is really important that we, as teachers, remember to include these considerations. Learning mathematics is all about learning a language in a social and cultural context. It is about learning to problem solve, to persist and look for the patterns in the world around us—for children to see the relationships between different aspects of their world as mathematical relationships. Mathematical understandings are not developed in isolation but through children's interaction in their world. This includes their social and emotional interaction in that world. If we give young children a sense of achievement and awareness that they can do mathematics and it is a part of their world and their set of everyday experiences in that world, we will have given them a good foundation in their confidence and in their early mathematical understandings.

SUMMARY

- As an Initial Teacher Education student, your feelings, experiences and beliefs about mathematics can come from your cultural experiences as well as your personal educational experiences with learning mathematics.
- Children learn mathematically both developmentally and through play pedagogy.
- The play pedagogy is central in children's learning of early mathematical language and their understanding of symbols.
- It is important to intentionally teach mathematics and to plan mathematical play, including time and space for 'mature play'.
- It is also important to plan the relevant language to introduce through sustained, shared mathematical thinking together with children and to use a range of prompts to foster children's deep mathematical thinking.
- Children learn mathematics from birth and develop in their mathematical thinking through social interaction with significant others. We also understand that their parents are their first teachers and you as the significant educator have a specific role.
- Children grow in their mathematical knowledge from the wide range of experiences they have and the language they develop that broadens their foundational mathematical concepts.
- Care with planning needs to be taken when considering the mathematical interests of children so that all children have the opportunity to have a wide and rich range of experiences that make links with their home cultures and extend their opportunities, experiences, skills, knowledge, confidence and competence in mathematics.
- Early mathematics learning of young children begins with the mathematical learning of babies and toddlers, including toddlers' and young children's learning about same and different as an example of children's conceptual development and reasoning skills.

FRANCES BURTON

- Children move through a series of stages in their understanding of what a number is, how each number relates to other numbers and the importance for you as a teacher in recognising the various stages children pass through, from rote chanting to a quantitative or Cartesian concept of number.
- Babies learn about the shape of objects in their world through the use of all their senses. Babies and toddlers develop their sense of themselves in space through their early full body movements through the spaces around them. Obstacle courses for toddlers as well as small-world play with shapes extend their experiences. Deliberately and accurately introducing mathematical language into their play is important.
- Pre-school children learn about shapes in space through their outdoor experiences on jungle gyms or through yoga. They learn, too, how to manipulate shapes in the block centre or in their use of puzzles. Packing-up activities—if well-structured by you, their teacher—can add to their understanding of shapes in space.
- Practical measuring activities, such as measuring the space for a new rug, should be included as part of the pre-school program. Sandpit play is important for the early learning of volume and capacity, and children may learn about time informally as they experience their own growth changes as well as measuring those of plants or chickens. Measuring can be a part of children's everyday life, as well as their imaginative play.
- Statistics are a part of the everyday life of children as they work out whether it will rain today. You as their teacher can help them collect the data to inform their choices about the weather or group likes or dislikes. Through this early collection of data children can learn more about interests they share with some of the other children and this can enhance their sense of belonging to the group.
- Mathematical learning for young children needs to be a part of and relevant to their everyday lives. It needs to be visible to them and they should have the confidence to persist in and enjoy their mathematical learning. You, too, as their teacher need to learn to recognise the mathematical learning of babies, toddlers and pre-schoolers and how best you can add to their experiences and language. You have an important role to play in their early mathematical learning.

FURTHER REFLECTION

- Can you describe an early mathematics experience you had? Was it at primary school or secondary school? How did you feel about the experience? If it was a negative experience at that time, can you reframe it now using more positive words?
- What do you believe mathematics is? Is it a set of facts and processes (including some useful tricks) that you learn to use to get the right answer to problems? Is it a set of mathematical understandings about the world through a cultural lens?

GROUP DISCUSSION

1 After reading this chapter on enriching mathematics for young children, reflect on what you have learnt about when young children begin to learn mathematics. Create a shared list of five main points and then order them according to their importance to you.
2 See if you can describe for yourself a young child of two or three learning mathematics. Try to be specific: what might they be doing? What might they be saying? Are they alone or in the company of others? How would this mathematical activity be different if the child was four or five? Share your examples with others. Look for what is common in your examples and how they differ.
3 At the weekend, you visited a major store to seek some computer advice. While there, you noticed a father with his two-year-old daughter. She was playing a mathematical game on his phone. Find

examples of maths apps for young children. Explore them for their mathematical content. What might be their strengths? What concerns, if any, might you have?

4 The children have been comparing and ordering their teddy bears in size. You hear words such as 'my teddy is bigger than/shorter than/a taller bear than yours'. Consider setting up a centre that might help clarify the children's language of length and size.

CLASS ACTIVITIES

1 Consider how you might organise your dress-up corner so that it suits three-year-old children. How might you structure the dress-up play activity so that children learn about same and different? What questions might you be prepared to ask so children will notice sameness or difference?

2 How might you alter the materials in the dress-up centre so they now suit four-year-old pre-school children and allow them to explore the concept of pairs? If a child starts counting '2, 4, 6 …' what would your reaction be? Discuss, as a group, how you might extend this child's mathematical skills through play.

FURTHER READING

Bodrova, E. & Leong, D.J. (1996) Tools of the Mind: The Vygotskian Approach to Early Childhood Education (2nd edn). Englewood Cliffs, N.J: Merrill.
    I recommend that you read (even though it is old now) the chapters on language and post-Vygotskian theorists. This is a really useful explanation of Vygotsky's ZPD in practice and his understanding of children's language. These are essential to your understanding of how children learn mathematics.

Bronfenbrenner, U. (1994) 'Ecological Models of Human Development', in International Encyclopaedia of Education, vol. 3 (2nd edn). Oxford: Elsevier.

Carruthers, E. & Worthington, M. (2006) Children's Mathematics: Making Marks, Making Meaning. (2nd edn). London: Sage Publications.
    Look closely into this book for an understanding of children's early language, development of reasoning and the writing of their own mathematical symbols.

Clements, D. & Sarama, J. (2009) Learning and Teaching Early Maths: The Learning Trajectories Approach. NY: Routledge.
    This book is useful for more information on subitising and children's understanding of number concepts.

Gelman, R. & Gallistel, C.R. (1978) The Child's Understanding of Number. Cambridge, MA: Harvard University Press.
    You really do need to understand the Gelman and Gallistel principles of counting and what this will look like and sound like when you are observing children learning mathemically.

Haylock, D. & Manning, R. (2014) Mathematics Explained for Primary Teachers. London: Sage Publications.
    Refer to this book to reinforce your understandings of the names of shapes.

Hughes A.M. (2010) Developing Play for the Under 3s: The Treasure Basket and Heuristic Play (2nd edn). Oxon, UK: Routledge.
    This is an excellent book to explore for practical ideas on how to develop those early understandings of same and different beginning with suitable experiences for the baby, then toddler, then young child.

Maunz, M.E. (2017) Age of Montessori: Certifying Teachers and Educating Parents. http://ageofmontessori. org/dr-elisabeth-caspari/
    This is a useful website for further ideas on Montessori.

FRANCES BURTON

REFERENCES

Aubrey, C., Godfrey, R. and Dahl, S. (2006) *Early Mathematics and Later Achievement: Further Evidence*. Mathematics Education Research Journal, 18(1), 27–46.

Barblett, L. (2010) 'Play-based Learning' (transcript), *The Early Years Learning Framework Professional Learning Program*. Commonwealth of Australia.

Bobis, J. (2010) 'Playing with Mathematics: Play in Early Childhood as a Context for Mathematical Learning', in L. Sparrow, B. Kissane & C. Hurst (eds), *Shaping the Future of Mathematics Education: Proceedings of the 33rd Annual Conference of the Mathematics Education Research Group of Australasia*. Fremantle: MERGA.

Bodrova, E. & Leong, D.J. (1996) *Tools of the Mind: The Vygotskian Approach to Early Childhood Education* (2nd edn). Englewood Cliffs, N.J: Merrill.

Bronfenbrenner, U. (1994) 'Ecological Models of Human Development', in *International Encyclopaedia of Education*, vol. 3 (2nd edn). Oxford: Elsevier.

Carruthers, E. & Worthington, M. (2006) *Children's Mathematics: Making Marks, Making Meaning.* (2nd edn). London: Sage Publications.

Carruthers, E. & Worthington, M. (2011) *Understanding Children's Mathematical Graphics: Beginnings in Play*. Maidenhead: Open University Press.

Clements, D. (2003) *Learning and Teaching Measurement.* Reston Va: National Council of Teachers of Mathematics.

Clements, D. & Sarama, J. (2009) *Learning and Teaching Early Maths: The Learning Trajectories Approach.* NY: Routledge.

Condon, M. W. F., & Clyde, J. A. (2004) 'Measure for measure: celebrating a young learner at work.' *Young Children.* 59(1), 1–4.

Copley, J. (2010) *The young child and mathematics* (2nd edn). Reston, VA, USA: NAEYC.

Department of Education and Early Childhood Development (DEECD). (2009) 'Measuring Length'. https://www.scribd.com/document/119611641/Read-Me-as-Length.

Department of Education and Early Childhood Development (DEECD) (2009) *Victorian Early Years Learning and Development Framework for All Children from Birth to Eight Years*. Early Childhood Strategy Division, Melbourne: Victorian Government.

Dunphy, E., Dooley, T., Shiel, G., Butler, D., Corcoran, D., Ryan, M. and Traver, J. (2014) *Mathematics in Early Childhood and Primary Education*. National Council for Curriculum and Assessment. Research Report No. 17.

Fleer, M. (2010) Early Learning and Development: Cultural-historical Concepts in Play. Cambridge: Cambridge University Press.

Gelman, R. & Gallistel, C.R. (1978) *The Child's Understanding of Number.* Cambridge, MA: Harvard University Press.

Hachey, A.C. (2013) 'Teachers' Beliefs Count: Teacher Beliefs and Practice in Early Childhood Mathematics Education (ECME)', *Dialog 16*(3): 73–85. file:///C:/Users/user/Downloads/109-552-1-PB.pdf

Haylock, D. & Manning, R. (2014) *Mathematics Explained for Primary Teachers.* London: Sage Publications.

Hughes A.M. (2010) *Developing Play for the Under 3s: The Treasure Basket and Heuristic Play.* (2nd edn). Oxon, UK: Routledge.

Hunting, R. (2013) *What Children Can Teach Adults about Mathematics.* Macleod: Palm Press.

Knaus, M. (2013) *Maths Is All Around You: Developing Mathematical Concepts in the Early Years.* Albert Park: Teaching Solutions.

Leong, D.J. & Bodrova, E. (2012) 'Assessing and Scaffolding: Make-believe Play', *Young Children*, 67(1): 28–34.

Moll, L., Amanti, C., Neff, D. & Gonzales, N. (1992) 'Funds of Knowledge for Teaching: Using a Qualitative Approach to Connect Homes and Classrooms', *Theory into Practice, 31*(2): 132–41.

Mulligan, J., English, L., Mitchelmore, M. & Robertson, G. (2010) 'Implementing a Pattern and Structure Mathematics Awareness Program (PASMAP) in Kindergarten', in *Proceedings of the 33rd Annual Conference of the Mathematics Education Research Group of Australasia.* Fremantle, WA: John Curtin College of the Arts, 3–7 July.

Ojose, B. (2008) 'Applying Piaget's Theory of Cognitive Development to Mathematics Instruction', *The Mathematics Educator, 18*(1): 26–30.

Pange, J. (2002) 'Can We Teach Probabilities to Young Children Using Educational Material from the Internet?' *Journal of Computer Assisted Learning, 15*: 118–28.

Pantone (2012) *Colours* (board book). New York: Abrams Appleseed.

Perry, B. & Dockett, S. (2007) 'Young Children's Access to Powerful Mathematical Ideas', in L.D. English (ed.), *Handbook of International Research in Mathematics Education* (2nd edn). NY: Routledge.

Reid, K. (2016) *Counting On It: Early Numeracy Development and the Preschool Child.* Melbourne: ACER.

Siraj-Blatchford, I. (2009) 'Conceptualising Progression in the Pedagogy of Play and Sustained Shared Thinking in Early Childhood Education: A Vygotskian Perspective', *Educational and Child Psychology, 26*(2): 77–89.

Siraj-Blatchford, I. (2017) 'Sustained Shared Thinking', cited by Sandford Nursery School, 2017. www.sandbank. walsall.sch.uk/core-values/sustained-shared-thinking

Sweeting, K. (2011) 'Early Years Teacher's Attitudes Towards Mathematics'. Thesis submitted for Masters of Education, QUT.

Treacy, K. & Willis, S.G. (2003) *A Model of Early Number Development*, in L. Bragg, C. Campbell, G. Herbert & J. Mousley (eds), 'Mathematics Education Research: Innovation, Networking, Opportunity'. Proceedings of the 26th Annual Conference of the Mathematics Education Research Group of Australasia, vol. 1. Melbourne, Vic.: Deakin University, pp.674–81.

Vygotsky, L. (1962) *Thought and Language.* Cambridge, MA: MIT Press.

Vygotsky, L. (1967) Play and Its Role in the Mental Development of the Child, *Soviet Psychology, 5*: 6–18.

Vygotsky, L. (1978) *Mind in Society: The Development of Higher Psychological Processes.* Cambridge, Mass.: Harvard University Press.

Whiteside, T., (2007) *Level 1 mathematics-They repeat: A mathematics lesson on patterns*. PEEL SEEDS Issue 87 in press, Department of Education. http://www.sofweb.vic.edu.au/blueprint/fs1/prof_learn_res/0.

MATHEMATICS

FRANCES BURTON

Language, Literacy and Children's Literature

Mary Hughes

Chapter objectives

In this chapter we will:
- learn to understand how 'literacy' is defined in our society, economy and culture, and the importance of lifelong learning in the twenty-first century
- examine the important role that oral language plays in children's development and participation in everyday life
- consider the knowledge and understandings that children need in order to begin to read and write and how effective literacy teachers support and extend children's learning
- understand how providing a literacy-rich environment is a key factor in facilitating opportunities for young children to engage in meaningful literacy experiences
- explore the role of literature in developing children's sense of identity, their understanding of the world around them, and the ways it exposes them to other cultures and times in history
- examine the ways children can become 'multiliterate' in early childhood contexts, and how the use of ICT and its applications enables this.

Key terms

alphabetic principle	morphemic knowledge	receptive vocabulary
blending	onset and rime	scaffold
etymological knowledge	phonemes	segmenting
expressive vocabulary	phonemic awareness	visual level of knowledge
intentional teaching	phonological knowledge	vocabulary

Inspiring and empowering children has to be one of the greatest roles we have as teachers.

We can do this through language and literacy, and one of the most effective ways is by reading stories. Recently, I met some of my ex-students at their high-school graduation. Although it had been many years since they were in my Grade 1 class, for most of them the stand-out memory was that of being read to every day. They could still recall some of the books we shared, but they also talked about how they felt while listening to the stories: the excitement, the trepidation, the sense of closeness as they sat together glued to every word. If I was reading just a chapter of a book, there would be groans when it was time to finish or to go home, as they couldn't wait to find out what happened when we continued the story next day.

Over the years in my classroom, reading aloud to children has been a given no matter what age group I am teaching. Older students enjoy having books read to them in serial form, and for some, this might be their main exposure to quality literature. The words they are hearing, the problems to be solved and the meaning of the story are a powerful learning experience. It is a time when they

LITERACY

listen, think and come together. For younger children, there are so many interesting things that happen along the way in picture story books that spark questions and rich conversations. When I read stories aloud, I like to stop, talk and ask questions that help to build a picture in children's heads. Making the most of every gasp, shout, whisper and laugh allows the story to come to life. Not only are children visualising the story, their emotions are working overtime as they think, learn and feel. This 'computer screen' in their heads is far more powerful as a learning tool than any electronic device!

There is strong evidence suggesting that the cognitive benefits of reading aloud to children is staggering, and that those children who are read to every day have a head start at school. Close links have been found between the number of words and vocabulary that children hear and their academic success.

When you read aloud to a child you are engaging their mind, their thoughts and their heart. It all begins with words, language and stories. So make a difference, and 'grow a reader' by engaging with children every day through the stories you share with them. It might be the best memory they have of their time in your classroom.

Introduction

From birth, young children communicate with others in many different ways. In this chapter, we will explore how communication, language and literacy development occurs, and the important role the teacher plays in supporting all children to become readers and writers.

Different theoretical frameworks provide diverse ways of understanding language and development and lead to distinct ways of planning for learning. In this chapter we will draw on the work of several theorists, including Piaget, Vygotsky, Bruner and Rogoff, to help us understand children's early literacy and language development and the importance of connecting learning to their worlds. We will also explore learning to speak, read and write as a developmental process, using the phases of development as benchmarks to plan for future learning. These phases must be used as a guide only, as children of the same age can have very different experiences and abilities.

You already reflected upon your own 'image' of the child in Chapter 1, and now you are invited to consider the image you might have of the 'literate' child. As discussed in Chapter 2, learning to read is a social process, not a biological imperative. We all have to learn how to read and write. So how does this occur? How do young children learn to read and write? And what role does the adult play in the process of becoming literate? There is a large body of evidence suggesting that literacy begins at birth (some even suggest before birth) and that early literacy learning forms the basis of future successful academic achievement. Literacy is crucial to a child's success in life, and must be a shared responsibility of families, communities, early childhood programs and schools.

In this chapter, the importance of oral language as the building blocks for future success in literacy will be explored in detail. Children need to *learn* language, learn *through* language and learn *about* language (Halliday, 2004). They do this best in homes and communities that are speech-rich, so that by the time they begin school most children have acquired the spoken language of their community and are little experts at using this language. You might have noticed that language acquisition blossoms between the ages of two and three.

MARY HUGHES

The concepts, skills and understandings that children need in order to be good readers and writers will be examined in this chapter, along with the role of the teacher in supporting this learning. Discovering what children know and can do is important in planning for new learning. Effective literacy teachers skilfully integrate a range of approaches and resources to meet the diverse learning needs of all children in prior-to-school and school settings.

You will be introduced to the world of children's literature and how it can develop children's sense of identity, their understanding about other people and the world around them, and how quality literature can spark their imaginations. Later in the chapter we will look at how growth over the past decade in communication and information technologies and multi-literacies has had a major impact on how we view language and literacy in the twenty-first century.

Defining literacy

The way we define 'literacy' has changed dramatically over time, and reflects the changes in society, economy and culture. The skills and knowledge needed to participate in society in the 1800s differed from those needed in the 1990s, and an even greater range of literacy is needed as we rapidly progress into the twenty-first century. The increasing use of technology means that the ways we communicate are far more complex than ever before. Attempting to create one basic definition for 'literacy' does not take into account the challenges and complexities that exist and the evolving nature of language and literacy.

The Organization for Economic Co-operation and Development (OECD) (2009) defines literacy as:

> … the ability to understand, use and reflect on written texts in order to achieve one's goals, to develop one's knowledge and potential, and to participate effectively in society. (p.14)

Both the Early Years Learning Framework (EYLF) and the Australian National Curriculum place importance on language and literacy in prior-to-school and school settings. There are, however, key differences that need to be highlighted: prior-to-school settings are guided by learning and development frameworks, while school settings are guided by curriculum documents. The EYLF focuses on the foundations on which early literacy is based, with a specific emphasis on play-based learning. It recognises the importance of communication, language and social and emotional development. The Australian Curriculum, on the other hand, focuses more strongly on Literacy as a subject area with distinct knowledge, skills and dispositions.

The Early Years Learning Framework (EYLF) states that:

> Literacy is the capacity, confidence and disposition to use language in all its forms. Literacy incorporates a range of modes of communication including music, movement, dance, storytelling, visual arts, media and drama, as well as talking, listening, viewing, reading and writing. Contemporary texts include electronic and print-based media. In an increasingly technological world, the ability to critically analyse texts is a key component of literacy. Children benefit from opportunities to explore their world using technologies and to develop confidence in using digital media.
>
> (DEEWR, 2009, p.38)

The Australian Curriculum (2017) goes further, telling us that:

> Students become literate as they develop the knowledge, skills and dispositions to interpret and use language confidently for learning and communicating in and out of school and for participating effectively in society. Literacy involves students in listening to, reading, viewing, speaking, writing and creating oral, print, visual and digital texts, and using and modifying language for different purposes in a range of contexts.

Having a positive and strong start is important in building the foundations that children need in order to become highly literate and powerful learners.

STOP AND THINK

- How do you define 'literacy'?
- What changes have you noticed in the way 'literacy' is viewed in our society?
- Refer to the vignette at the beginning of the chapter. What aspects of literacy are the children experiencing? Why do you think they remember being read to, even years afterwards?

Oral language

> If the person you are talking to doesn't appear to be listening—be patient. It may simply be that he has a small piece of fluff in his ear.
>
> (A.A. Milne, *Winnie-the-Pooh*)

Oral language is a key factor in learning to read and write, and research suggests that children who have developed good control over aspects of oral language experience early success in literacy (Callaghan & Madelaine, 2012). So why is it important that we focus on young children's speaking and listening? This section of the chapter will examine how oral language differs from written language and the implications of this in planning for, and providing opportunities to, enrich children's language. When discussing 'language', we will be referring to oral language; when using the term 'literacy' we will be referring to reading and writing as it is communicated through print and multimedia. The two modes are quite different: oral language relies on the current context—the 'here and now'—while written language is removed from current context in that the writer must provide additional information for the reader.

Speaking and listening can be viewed as the 'building blocks' of literacy, so young children who have lots of opportunities to talk in the early years are off to a great start in life. The diversity of children's backgrounds and the influence of social and cultural contexts shape the way children learn language. Research shows that the ways we interact with children can have a profound influence on how they learn to communicate, as well as building their confidence in speaking to others (DECD, 2013).

So how can we maximise the development of children's language and communication skills in early childhood settings? Play is an ideal context for developing young children's speaking and listening skills. Russian psychologist Lev Vygotsky's theory of cognitive development (as briefly discussed in Chapter 3) posits that information from the external world is internalised through language, and that children's play experiences allow them

LITERACY

to be in constant dialogue with themselves and others. Vygotsky suggested that children's inner speech or 'self talk' helps them to make sense of the world around them, which is essential if they are to develop control over cognition processes such as memory and thought.

> It seems that what is important for a good, natural learning situation is for the child to have a conversation with a person who uses simple language in correct forms and who is flexible enough to change their language to suit the language of the child being spoken to. Playmates do that, but adults do it better and for more of the time.
>
> (Clay, 1998).

One key strategy involves teachers reflecting on how they listen and respond to children on a daily basis. It can be hard to look from a distance at how we talk and interact with children, especially when so much conversation is spontaneous and instant. Being mindful of how our own language behaviours impact upon children's communication and making small changes can have huge benefits for young children's language development. Of course, encouraging and allowing time for children to talk is vital, but we also need to ensure that we are maximising these opportunities for quality interactions.

Giving children plenty of time and space to respond in conversation helps them clarify their thoughts. This 'wait time' allows children to think about what has been said and what they might say in reply. Pauses and hesitations are all part of normal conversation. Being comfortable with silence is also part of the learning experience in communicating with others. Using questions to show genuine interest in what a child has to say takes skill and awareness. We don't want children to feel as though the conversation has become a teaching exercise or an interrogation! Making sure children feel that they are equal partners is important too, with the opportunity to initiate, choose the topic and even close the interaction if they wish. Children learn very early how conversations work, about taking turns, making eye contact and using facial expressions. Sometimes it's difficult not to interrupt or prompt children when they are talking, but listening before speaking usually leads to more high-quality interactions.

Ensuring that opportunities for speaking and listening are purposeful and authentic creates rich language experiences for children (Barrat-Pugh et al., 2005). When experiences are interesting and engaging, rather than contrived or artificial, young children are able to sustain rich conversations both with one another and with adults in the setting. Feeding language into children's play by commenting on what they are interested in, rather than asking questions, is a powerful way of helping them to link language and meaning. Not only do you have a shared focus to talk about, but the conversation is relaxed and non-threatening.

STOP AND THINK

- How can teachers support children's use of home and community language within the early childhood setting?
- Consider the ways teachers can ensure that children have meaningful and authentic opportunities to demonstrate their oral language competencies in the early childhood setting.

Language and speech

Have you ever wondered at the amazing feat young children achieve in mastering the intricacies of the language that is spoken around them? By the time they are around five years old, most children are quite proficient in a language they have only been learning for a few years. So what are some of the contributing factors that enable this to happen? First of all, language is expressed through speech, which is made up of articulation (how speech sounds are made), voice (the production of sound using the vocal chords and breathing) and fluency (the smoothness and natural rhythm of speech). Speech and language do not begin to develop at the same time, as children will first learn to understand the speech of others before they are able to produce speech themselves. Speaking is the expressive form of oral language, and a sound understanding of how language is conveyed to others is required, along with a good grasp of the language. Listening is the receptive form of oral communication and it is necessary for the listener to be able to decode and understand what the speaker has said. Different spoken languages have sounds and sound combinations that are unique to them, and children's speech gradually comes to mirror that used by the family and community to which they belong (Fellowes & Oakley, 2014).

Oral language development

There are many different theories and explanations for children's language acquisition, learning and development. These theories influence our understanding of how children develop into competent language users, and are useful in designing effective learning environments that support children's language development. Over the past century or so, a range of theoretical perspectives has influenced the types of practices that parents and teachers have adopted in nurturing children's early language development. These are:

- behaviourist
- nativist
- maturational
- cognitive developmental
- interactionist
- neurobiological.

Each of these places an emphasis on either nature (biological factors) or nurture (environmental factors) or aspects of both to explain young children's acquisition and development of language (for more information on nature and nurture, see Chapter 1 of this book).

Although there is a common developmental pathway for language learning, children of the same chronological age will develop at their own rate and pace. Phases and milestones are indicators of the typical competencies children might achieve at certain points in their development, but we must also keep in mind the influence of a range of factors other than chronological age.

MARY HUGHES

STOP AND THINK

- What are some of the strengths or advantages of having a set of phases and milestones for children's language development? What are the challenges?
- Think about the nature vs nurture debate in relation to children's language development.

Language diversity

In Australia we have a diverse range of cultures and languages in our society, and this has major implications for early childhood teachers. Respecting and valuing cultural differences and providing opportunities for children to use their first language is important in early childhood settings. So too, is recognising and acknowledging Aboriginal and Torres Strait Islander culture, heritage and language, along with cultures found within the community. Importantly, teachers need an understanding of the 'funds of knowledge' (Moll et al., 1992) or different ways of knowing and doings things that children bring from the home (e.g. making eye contact, asking direct questions).

In addition, support should be provided for children to learn Standard Australian English. To be able to fully participate as a member of society children need to be competent users of the dominant language used by that society.

Components of language

In this section I will present a broad definition of the four main components of spoken language:

- phonology
- syntax
- semantics
- pragmatics.

Phonology

phonemes the smallest parts used to make up whole words.

phonemic awareness the ability to discriminate between different sounds.

The phonological component of language is made up of the many and varied sounds that are used in speaking. **Phonemes** are the smallest parts used to make up whole words, and it is vital that children are able to discriminate between different sounds. The ability to do this starts very early when babies learn to recognise sounds around them, such as the dog barking, the lawnmower and familiar voices. This ability to discriminate is known as **phonemic awareness**. *Intonation* (high and low sounds or 'pitch') and *stress* (emphasis placed on certain syllables) influence how a sentence is communicated and the meaning of it for the listener. Emotional meaning can change depending on the intonation and stress used in a sentence. Children's ability to hear these variations in spoken language is vital to their language and literacy development.

Syntax

Syntax is the grammar or 'rules' of language. Sentences are constructed according to particular rules, and absorbing and internalising these rules and being able to apply them correctly is a prerequisite for communicating effectively. Word order is very important in the

English language. For example, we would say 'Sarah ate her lunch at the table' rather than 'Ate her lunch Sarah at the table'. Most children learn these rules when they are exposed to the structures of spoken language over time. It's very important, therefore, when speaking to young children, to make sure that they hear a variety of ways of constructing sentences through conversations and interactions.

Semantics

Semantics is about the meaning of language, both at a word level as well as sentence construction. In order to comprehend spoken language, an understanding of the meaning of the words used and the relationship between individual words is necessary for precision and clarity. For example, 'The boy sat on the pony' has a different meaning altogether from 'The pony sat on the boy'. How words are used and the way sentences are constructed are fundamental to conveying meaning when communicating with others. Again, it's important when speaking with young children to choose appropriate words and sentence structures that give clear meaning to what is being said.

Pragmatics

The pragmatic component of language involves the practical use of language in a variety of social and cultural contexts. Pragmatics includes taking turns, maintaining the topic, and understanding body language and tone of voice. It also involves an understanding of the practical language used for different social purposes (greetings, making a request) and audience (family, friends, unfamiliar adults). Some children, particularly those with autism spectrum disorder, need to be explicitly taught these skills as they are very often not internalised through everyday interactions.

Scaffolding language

Amy (an educator) is kneeling beside two children at the sand tray. Zoe (2½) is with David (3) and they both love the sand tray. They concentrate really hard as they move large volumes of sand, making noises of mighty machines at work. As Zoe moves off to do something else David looks at Amy and smiles.

Amy [smiling back]: I like what you have done. Can you tell me about it?

David: I am making a quarry.

Amy: It's good that you are making a quarry. I really like it. Tell me how you did it.

David: I got jones [stones] and put the diggers and tacars [tractors] in [pointing to the sand tray].

Amy: So, you got stones first and then put the diggers and tractors in the sand. Why did you want to make a quarry?

David: My daddy wok [work] in quarry.

Amy: I see, so you thought you would make a quarry like the one your daddy works in. Is that right?

David nods his head in agreement.

Amy: You've made a great big quarry here. I'd love to make one like that. So, tell me again David what I do.

MARY HUGHES

David: Here. Make a hole.

He gives Amy a digger and shows her how to move the sand using its front bucket.

Amy: Wow, this is great. I'm moving the sand and making a quarry just like yours.

David and Amy continue with their quarry building and digging, making noises for the machines and discussing their actions.

STOP AND THINK

- Children's language development can be scaffolded in a variety of ways so that new vocabulary and syntax are introduced.
- Discuss how Amy expands on David's language to introduce new words or syntax in the scenario above.
- How does she extend David's comments in order to provide more information?

Speaking and listening: early school years

Can you remember your earliest experiences of speaking and listening at school? Perhaps you recall 'show and tell' sessions where each child was invited to talk to the class about something that interested them. These experiences are valuable in giving children the opportunity to participate in a more formal context of communicating with others. During the early years of school, children's use of language becomes more complex and their understanding of how it is used is more sophisticated. Teachers support and **scaffold** students in using language in challenging ways and for a variety of purposes. There is a focus on extending and enriching **vocabulary** as well as extending children's ability to communicate with different audiences. Halliday's model of the functions of language (1975) supports the development of a repertoire of speaking and listening skills to make meaning within a range of social and cultural contexts (Department of Education (WA), First Steps, 2013). While it is important to provide continuing opportunities for children to engage in speaking and listening, it is also vital that the teacher is involved at all levels.

The model in Figure 7.1 identifies the different purposes for using language so that teachers can provide opportunities for children to develop and use these functions at school. Each function relates to the different ways language is used in different contexts in the community, school and home.

During the early years of school, children's oral language learning and development is more closely linked to curriculum learning areas with a particular emphasis on the English curriculum. This is known as *academic language* and is quite different from *social language*. There is a greater focus on extending children's ability to communicate effectively for a range of purposes, audiences and topics. It is important, however, that teachers plan for explicit skills teaching in the areas of speaking and listening, as well as providing opportunities for children to practise and develop oral language in situations such as role plays, drama and oral reports.

Children's successful progress through the early years of primary school depends heavily upon the support and targeted teaching they receive in the use of language in more complex

scaffold the ongoing support provided to a learner by an expert.

vocabulary the words children must know in order to communicate effectively. In educational terms, it can be described as 'oral vocabulary' or 'reading vocabulary'.

Halliday's Function People communicate to...	Language Sample Speakers learn to...	Literacy Practice in Classrooms
Instrumental Get things done	Identify/explain things, provide information, request assistance	Problem-solving Gathering materials Role playing
Regulatory Influence or regulate the behaviour of others	Set tasks, manage and organise situations, negotiate, persuade	Give instructions Extend interactions Make rules in a game
Personal Express thoughts, opinions and feelings	Express and respond to ideas Agree or disagree Give an opinion	Interact with others Listen to points of view Empathise and encourage
Interactional Get along with others	Initiate and sustain conversations Express agreement and disagreement	Structured play Talking turns in group sessions Rich conversations
Heuristic Seek out knowledge and information	Ask a range of questions Discuss ideas Investigate and hypothesise	Summarise Apply knowledge Answer questions
Informative Convey information to others	Convey information Report information/knowledge Clarify and analyse	Class meetings Create time lines, reports, maps, to demonstrate knowledge
Imaginative Create new worlds, express creative thoughts	Make up and tell stories Play and role-play Perform/recite	Imagine Respond to stories/plays Join in

Figure 7.1

Source: Based on Halliday's 'Functions of Language', adapted from Steely et al., 2017, p.47.

situations. Being familiar with the academic and often more specialised vocabulary required in the school setting enables children to build and extend their language skills in all areas of the curriculum.

In the next section of the chapter, we will examine the foundations of early literacy on which young children can build as they move into the more formal approach of learning to read and write at school. The soundest foundations for early literacy are an active, play-based curriculum, an emphasis on oral learning, and plenty of time for music, movement, song and stories (Palmer et al., 2014).

Understanding reading

Babies enjoy being read to from birth, and there are many benefits to sharing stories with them in a safe and comfortable environment. When they are very young, babies focus on bright colours, faces and patterns and they enjoy the tactile experiences associated with sturdy

MARY HUGHES

cloth and vinyl books. It's not long before they can turn the pages by themselves and point to pictures or objects on a page. As you read earlier in this chapter, listening to the sounds of language exposes babies and children to a rich bank of words that they can draw upon when learning to talk. Babies and children who are read to and talked to frequently in the early years are better placed to learn the skills needed to become proficient readers and writers.

The pathways children follow when learning how to read are as different and diverse as children themselves. Finding out what they already know and their strengths and capabilities allows teachers to plan and adjust their teaching to suit all learners. The EYLF (DEEWR, 2009) states that this learning for very young children should take place in play-based, social settings. It also recommends that **intentional teaching** should be used alongside play-based learning, where teachers 'use strategies such as modelling and demonstrating, open questioning, speculating, explaining, engaging in shared thinking and problem solving to extend children's thinking and learning' (DEEWR, 2009, p.18).

> **intentional teaching** when teachers are explicitly, actively and deliberately engaged in children's learning. Their decisions and teaching strategies are purposefully and thoughtfully considered.

The importance of vocabulary

It is important for young readers (and writers) to have a rich 'vocabulary', or collection of words that they know. This includes **receptive vocabulary** (listening and reading) and **expressive vocabulary** (speaking and writing). Children who have wide receptive and expressive vocabulary will find it easier to comprehend texts compared to those who are limited in the number of words they know. The best way to build on and develop children's vocabulary is, of course, to surround them with rich language and conversation. In the prior-to-school years, teachers can plan appropriate activities and experiences that are supported by lots of talk between adults and children. For children in the early years of school, having a rich vocabulary assists in understanding the meaning of texts when reading, and helps them write accurately using interesting words.

> **receptive vocabulary** the collection of words children can understand and respond to, though they may not be able to say (or write) these words (listening and reading).

> **expressive vocabulary** being able to use vocabulary to put thoughts into words and sentences (speaking and writing).

The importance of topic knowledge

Having a good vocabulary is important in comprehending text, as well as having prior knowledge of the topic being read or discussed. Children who are able to draw on their experience of the world can make connections and have the ability to predict, visualise and find the main idea. In the scenario you read earlier in this chapter, David was able to use his prior knowledge of diggers and tractors to communicate meaningfully with Amy, the educator. He drew on a bank of words (or vocabulary) that he already knew to describe and discuss his play. Amy was therefore able to effectively plan experiences to activate and build on David's prior knowledge of this particular topic or area of learning.

Concepts about print

Having a good knowledge of print concepts is crucial in learning how to read. Knowing where the front page of a book is, where the back is, and which is the right way up are concepts that all children need to be in possession of. Other concepts such as left to right, identifying and matching letters and sounds, and an awareness of the relationship between words and pictures can be taught to children from an early age (Fellowes & Oakley, 2014). Fortunately, it doesn't take very long at all for children to develop this knowledge when teachers model book handling skills and provide hands-on experiences for them. For children who experience written language in other cultures, these concepts about print may be quite strange. The directionality of print is different in Arabic and Hebrew texts, and some Asian cultures write from top to bottom in vertical rows. Teachers who are aware of these cultural differences carefully plan to give children meaningful experiences with books in both their home languages and in English, explicitly focusing on directionality of print.

Recognising single words and letters in print are concepts that can often be difficult for children to grasp. Knowing that words are distinct entities in themselves and that spoken English is not a continuous stream of speech is an important step in developing children's understandings of the written word. Giving them lots of opportunities to play with magnetic letters and identify letters in books builds children's knowledge of how letters work. Of course, having rich conversations while they are doing this not only extends children's knowledge of how print works, but also improves oral language skills.

The concept of punctuation and its role in written text is important if children are to read with meaning. Young children in the early years of school need to recognise and understand full stops, commas, question marks and exclamation marks in the texts they use and read. One of the best ways teachers can help young children's awareness of the concepts about print is to read to them. Every day!

Phonological awareness

Phonological awareness is an important requisite for reading and writing in English, which is an alphabetic language. Children who are easily able to mentally manipulate words, syllables and sounds in spoken language have a head start when it comes to reading and writing. Phonological awareness is a strong predictor of reading success in later years, particularly in the area of decoding (Heath et al., 2006). Most children enter pre-school having learnt much about phonological awareness informally at home. Teachers of young children support this learning by singing songs, chanting rhymes and playing word games that feature intonation, stress and timing—important aspects of phonological awareness. This is why it is vital that teachers of young children sing and use music in their everyday practice. You can read more in Chapter 8 of this book, which talks about the Arts and their importance in young children's lives. As children move towards the early years of school, explicit or intentional teaching of phonological awareness increases through play-based learning.

As already briefly discussed, having the ability to **segment** words into sounds ('making and breaking words') is necessary for children to be able to write and spell—for example, being able to segment the word 'pin' into its three phonemes, *p/i/n*, representing each phoneme heard with the correct letter or grapheme. Being able to form words by **blending** phonemes together for example, *th/r/ee* is a prerequisite for effective writing, spelling and reading. At a slightly more complex level is the ability to segment and blend words using **onset and rime**. The onset of a word is the beginning consonant or consonants, and the rime consists of the part of the word that comes after the onset, always beginning with a vowel—for example, *ch/air; sw/im; th/ank*. The most effective way to support young children's awareness of these is where there is opportunity every day to talk, listen to stories and poems and engage in music and movement.

segmenting the process of breaking words down into segments or discrete units of sound such as vowels or consonants.

blending joining sounds or phonemes together to form words.

onset and rime a form of segmentation of sounds in syllables. A syllable can usually be divided into two parts: the onset, which consists of the initial consonant or consonant blend, and the rime, which consists of the vowel and any final consonants.

LITERACY

MARY HUGHES

As mentioned above, the smallest units of sound are known as phonemes. Developing phonemic awareness is necessary for children to read and write. Once they are aware of the sounds used to produce words, children can use the alphabetic principle to link sounds to letters in the reading process.

It is worth noting here that some authors (particularly international authors) refer to phonological awareness as a generic term for both phonological and phonemic awareness.

The alphabetic principle

alphabetic principle an understanding of the systematic and predictable relationships between written letters and spoken sounds.

Making the connection between the sounds of spoken language and the letters of the alphabet is known as the **alphabetic principle**. Even very young children usually learn to sing the alphabet song off by heart, and this is a good start to learning about the names of the letters. (Just a note that the Australian pronunciation of the letter 'z' is 'zed', not 'zee', which is the way it is pronounced in America. Getting this right is important and saves confusion later on!) Children need to have phonemic awareness and some letter knowledge in order to make the connection between letters and sounds. Many young children make these connections from an early age about the letters and sounds they experience in their environment, for example, the first letter and sound of their name, or the big yellow 'M' for McDonald's. Teachers in the prior-to-school years can provide opportunities for young children to explore letters and sounds by encouraging them to play with plastic and magnetic letters, make letters out of playdough and use paint and interesting materials to make letters. Singing the alphabet song and reading enjoyable books about letters and sounds also supports children's knowledge and development. There is some debate about whether children should know letter names or sounds first, or whether they should be taught together, and the literature is divided on this. Most children are able to learn letter names and sounds together and this knowledge is important in their progression towards reading and writing in the early years of primary school. For children who come from a culture where the language system is logographic (such as Chinese and Japanese) rather than alphabetic, the concept can be difficult to grasp.

Sight words

As children move into the more formal environment of school, their learning will be carefully scaffolded by teachers, who will build on the foundations established in the early years. Knowing some familiar words by sight is a good start. Effective readers are able to read words automatically or 'on the run'. Children build up a bank of sight words by reading them repeatedly over time, and this process differs from child to child. Teaching children high-frequency words (words that appear most frequently, such as *the, look, have, going,* and so on), which they then practise and know 'off by heart', sets them on the path to becoming successful at word recognition. This process is known as 'automaticity' (Munro, 2008). The M100W program engages children in a fun way, with play-based experiences for learning words by sight. Particularly useful for children in the Australian context is the Oxford word list (which is available online), comprising the 307 words most commonly found in children's writing during the first three years of school.

Teaching reading: the four roles of a reader

Effective readers take on four roles when reading: code breaker, meaning maker, text user and text critic (Luke & Freebody, 1999). Code breakers 'crack the code' using their knowledge of sound–letter relationships, high-frequency words and punctuation to decode print. *Phonics* is the name given to teaching letter and sound relationships for both reading and writing. This knowledge enables beginning readers to decode unfamiliar words by sounding and blending the sound–letter patterns. There are a number of *synthetic phonics* programs currently available on the market. These programs present a step-by-step approach, where children learn about the sounds within spoken words and then build up to blending these sounds together to achieve full pronunciation of whole words. Children learn the letter representations for all forty-four sounds of the English language. Once they are able to recognise and say letters and digraphs they learn to blend the sounds to make words. This approach benefits reading and writing as children can put together the sounds in order to read words, and listen for the sounds in words in order to spell them.

On the other hand, an *analytical phonics* approach involves analysis of whole words to detect phonetic or orthographic patterns, then splitting them into smaller parts to help with decoding, breaking words down into their most common components, which are referred to as 'onset' and 'rime'.

The 'meaning-maker' focuses on comprehending the text being read. There are three important aspects of comprehension at work when we read for meaning: *literal* (reading the lines), *inferential* (reading between the lines) and *interpretative* (reading beyond the lines) (Luke & Freebody, 1999). Even for very young children, initiating conversation about a book and connecting it with their prior experiences are helpful strategies in enriching comprehension and understanding.

The 'text user' focuses on the form (or genre) of a text and how it is read. When reading factual books, reading for information is the main purpose; when reading fiction books we focus on the plot and characters. Teachers who draw children's attention to text types by asking questions and prompting discussion about books are helping them to recognise the different ways texts are used.

The 'text critic' explores books, and other forms of text such as movies, advertisements and posters, at a deeper level. As text critics we analyse the author's message, identify any bias or misleading aspects presented and pose questions. With careful scaffolding and support from the teacher, even very young children can talk about these aspects of a text.

Reading procedures

There are five reading procedures outlined below, and each of these is influenced by the Gradual Release of Responsibility Model (Pearson & Gallagher, 1983). This model fits nicely with the construct of 'scaffolding', a term used by Wood, Bruner and Ross (1976) to describe the ongoing support provided to a learner by an expert. The notion of scaffolding is linked to the work of Russian psychologist Lev Vygotsky, who never actually used the term but emphasised the role of the *more knowledgeable other* in bridging the gap from the actual to the potential. Jerome Bruner built on the work of Vygotsky. He used the term 'scaffolding' to describe how teachers and carers jointly construct language with children then gradually withdraw support as children gain mastery over their language (see information about these theorists

MARY HUGHES

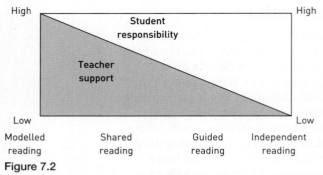

Figure 7.2

Source: 'Gradual Release of Responsibility Model',
Pearson & Gallagher, 1983. Adapted from Anstey & Bull, 2004.

in Chapter 3). Pearson and Gallagher's model, shown in Figure 7.2, is a good illustration of the procedures that teachers use to move children from dependence to independence in mastering reading skills.

It is important for children to observe how a proficient reader makes sense of text, to have the opportunity to practise the strategies with support and guidance from the teacher, and apply what they have learnt independently. It must be emphasised that each procedure will look different in different contexts and classrooms, and teachers will identify when a particular procedure is most appropriate for the teaching and learning needs of children.

Reading aloud

Reading stories aloud to children promotes a love of reading and is a source of pleasure and enjoyment. The introduction to this chapter contained a vignette that described how children remembered, even years later, being read to in the classroom. The feelings that were invoked and the anticipation of what was to come next had stayed with them. Teachers don't always have to have an explicit teaching focus—the purpose can be purely for pleasure. However, valuing reading aloud and modelling effective reading behaviours certainly promotes a positive attitude to reading for young children. The choice of texts can be made by the teacher or the children, and should include a wide range of books and reading material that will allow the listener to make connections, expand their knowledge of the world, challenge their thinking and make an emotional response. At this point, it is worthwhile revisiting the introduction to this chapter and to think about how powerful it is to read aloud to children of all ages.

Modelled reading

The focus of this strategy is on the explicit demonstration of selected reading behaviours such as phrasing and fluency, word identification or comprehension. Children are active listeners, while the teacher 'thinks aloud' at particular places in the text that demonstrate the chosen focus. A 'tuning in' session is used to explain the reading behaviour that will be demonstrated, and a short book introduction orients the children to the text. The teacher pauses at places in the text to 'think aloud' and demonstrate the behaviour. Children have the opportunity to practise the reading behaviour in their independent, small-group and guided-reading sessions.

Shared reading

This strategy provides opportunities for the teacher and students to read together using an enlarged text that all children can see comfortably. This enlarged text might be a big book, or it might be a text that is accessed on the interactive whiteboard. Conversely, it might be another form of text, such as a poster.

Gaining meaning from print and examining the reading process are the main aims during shared reading, and of key importance is building children's confidence in themselves as readers. Of course, enjoyment of the story is important too!

An interesting book introduction will establish children's prior knowledge of the topic, the purpose of the text and its type (e.g. fiction, information). The teacher reads the text with expression, using not only their voice but facial expression as well to convey the meaning of the story. When appropriate, the teacher asks the children to predict, comment or join in. An aspect of the text will be selected for explicit teaching—this might be a specific reading strategy, grammatical structures, vocabulary development, sound and letter knowledge or comprehension skills. Re-reading the text and asking children to join in is a good way to conclude a shared reading session.

Guided reading

This strategy provides an opportunity for children to develop appropriate reading strategies by talking, reading and thinking their way through a text with the help and support of the teacher. A small group of around four to six children are given an individual copy of the text, which is based on their particular reading and developmental needs. The teacher conducts a quick tuning-in session that might activate the children's prior knowledge or extend on it prior to reading. The book is introduced by the teacher and the group discusses the cover, the illustrations, the language patterns used and any difficult words the children might come across. Children then read the text independently while the teacher moves around the group, monitoring and assisting where needed. When all children have worked with the teacher, the group will discuss the book and share their thoughts and opinions.

Independent reading

The focus of this strategy is on the application of previously learnt reading strategies to self-selected texts. Children read silently and are responsible for working through the text, self-monitoring and cross-checking when presented by challenges. It is important that classroom routines and transitions are well established and that a range of appropriate reading material is available for selection. At times, opportunities can be made for children to respond to the text in the form of journal writing, a book report or a think/pair/share activity.

STOP AND THINK

- What sorts of family and community experiences are important for young children before they even begin to learn how to read?
- How does having good phonological awareness help children to be successful in school? Discuss ways you can provide rich experiences for children to improve their phonological awareness.
- Reading aloud to children has many benefits. What can teachers, educators and families do to make reading aloud experiences engaging and meaningful for children?

In summary, most children learn to read quite efficiently during the early years of school. Parents and teachers who provide rich language and literacy experiences from birth to five set children up for success in mastering the reading process during the first three years of schooling.

MARY HUGHES

LITERACY

Understanding writing

Long before they start school, even before they know their letters and sounds, children begin to write. For most children, the experience of early writing or mark-making starts at home with crayons, chalk, markers, paint brushes and even fingers. What we would call 'scribble' is actually the early stages of development in children's writing. In fact, scribbling is to writing what babbling is to speaking. Children need strong encouragement to draw and scribble in ways that are meaningful to them. These experiences provide a firm foundation for children being able to write more easily, effectively and confidently when they go to school.

As young children grow, their hands and fingers become stronger and they develop more control over their writing implements. Soon, they are making circles, oblongs, lines and squares, often randomly on the page, sometimes in rows that resemble written text. If you ask them to read what they have written, they will happily do so, and can often remember what their writing is about days and even weeks later. The links between drawing and writing are discussed further in Chapter 8.

So, how can we encourage young children to experiment with writing? The single most important way to help children prepare for reading and writing is to read stories aloud to them so they learn how print works. This makes their early experiences with written text meaningful, and early writing or mark-making becomes a natural progression in the acquisition of literacy skills.

Drawing attention to everyday writing in the environment, such as signs, labels and instructions, helps children become more aware of print. In pretend play, have a notebook handy for the little doctor or vet to write a script; tickets for a show or ride; menus for the pretend restaurant; and writing implements for the office corner. Many children enjoy writing their name, so providing purposeful opportunities for them to do this using a wide selection of colourful implements and material is important. Using digital technologies that are child-friendly—such as Leap pads, iPads and tablets—is a great way to engage children in early writing experiences that are fun but still provide worthwhile learning experiences. A recent study found that most children draw and write with ease using a tablet, and what matters most for children's learning is the ways teachers use the technology (Couse & Chen, 2014).

Showing enthusiasm for children's efforts and celebrating their achievements boosts confidence and makes young children feel they have your admiration, interest and support. It is important to remember that spelling, correct letter formation and neatness don't really matter at this stage—these skills will come later! Ensuring that early experiences with writing are positive and engaging can set children up for future success as readers and writers.

Learning to write

Learning to write happens gradually, and children need time and practise in order to master the skills, knowledge and strategies they require in order to become successful writers. Turning spoken language into written language is not easy for young children; in fact, it is possibly one of the most challenging tasks we ask of them in the early years of school. Not only do young writers need something to say, but they also need to have good fine motor skills, knowledge of letter–sound relationships and print conventions, as well as being able to read back what they have written. One of the most important skills children need is that of good oral language (Munro, 2008), which is the foundation of writing. Much of their early writing will be their own language structures written down.

In the years prior to school, children will have already gained some knowledge of letters and sounds. They will use these in their early attempts to write as well as making squiggles and marks that they are able to 'read back' as a narrative or story. These narratives or stories will generally have a framework of a beginning, middle and end, and can sometimes begin with 'Once upon a time'. These elements of story structure that children are familiar with are often due to them having been read books by parents, carers and teachers.

Early writing

Children in kindergarten and the first few months of school will generally write stories about familiar things and events, with little awareness of the reader; that is, they will omit background information such as context, time and place. As they develop skills and knowledge about the writing process, an awareness of the reader and a sense of *audience* becomes evident in their writing. Realising that some symbols are letters and some are not is another discovery children make when writing in the English language. They will often use an initial letter to represent a word they are writing, and might then use random letters to complete the word. They also learn that letters can be written in different ways (e.g. 'A', 'a' and '*a*', 'G', 'g' and '*g*'). Directionality (writing left to right) is another principle that children grasp over time, and some children need scaffolding and support with this. Using a small bank of sight words in their writing (such as 'I', 'is' and 'and') is another example of children's transition through this stage. Putting spaces between words is challenging for some, and they will put a full stop between all the words in a sentence (sometimes these 'dots' are bigger than the letters themselves!). Children learn that the use of writing conventions such as spelling, punctuation, capitalisation and grammar helps make their writing clear and easy for the reader to understand. Gradually the notion of spaces between words is grasped by children as they continue to practise their writing skills. Very often, sentences will run on and the writing is that of spoken language, with connecting words such as 'then' and 'and' used to link ideas.

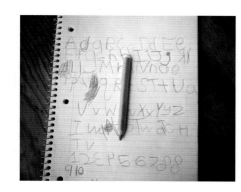

The physical aspect of writing

The physical aspect of writing can be very demanding for some children, especially young writers. They need to have developed a degree of fine motor control, hand–eye coordination and wrist and hand muscle strength. Not only this, but they will also be concentrating hard on letters and sounds, word patterns and print conventions as well as the ideas they have in their heads. No wonder writing can be a tiring task for young children! It is important that writing experiences are geared to children's physical and cognitive development and that these experiences are engaging and enjoyable.

MARY HUGHES

Spelling

I take it you already know

Of tough and bough and cough and dough?

Others may stumble, but not you

On hiccough, thorough, laugh and through?

Well done! And now you wish perhaps

To learn of less familiar traps?

Beware of heard, a dreadful word

That looks like beard and sounds like bird;

And dead: it's said like bed, not bead—

For goodness sake don't call it 'deed'.

Watch out for meat and great and threat.

They rhyme with suite and straight and debt.

(Anonymous)

phonological knowledge the understanding of the relationship between sounds and letters, and the manipulation of these.

This poem is a good example of the intricacies and inconsistencies of the English language. Learning to spell accurately is important when writing, so that the reader can easily decode and understand what is written. Phonological knowledge of words (hearing sounds in spoken language) is usually preceded by orthographic knowledge ('orthography' is the name given to the representation of the sounds of language by written or printed symbols).

Children need to be supported in their early attempts to communicate in writing. Children's use of conventional spelling and writing develops gradually under the careful guidance of teachers who skilfully scaffold their learning. In early childhood settings, children's attempts to write freely using invented spelling and approximations should be encouraged and supported, just as we encourage and support them in other areas of their learning.

visual level of knowledge how words look; concepts about print, letter–sound relationships and spelling patterns in words.

Word knowledge

Spelling and word knowledge include four levels or layers of knowledge: phonological, visual, morphemic and etymological knowledge. **Phonological knowledge** is concerned with the understanding of the relationship between sounds and letters, and the manipulation of these. This includes *segmentation* of words into syllables or units of sound; *onsets and rimes* where the beginning consonant of one syllable word is separated from the rest of the word; and *phonemes*, where the speech sound in words is identified and manipulated, e.g. *c/a/t* as separate sounds.

morphemic knowledge the structures of words and small chunks or parts that help to make a word meaningful.

The **visual level of knowledge** is related to how words look, concepts about print, letter–sound relationships and spelling patterns in words. **Morphemic knowledge** is concerned with the structures of words and small chunks or parts that help to make a word meaningful. Words may have just one morpheme (e.g. desk, jump and swim), or two or more morphemes (e.g. re/new or in/form. Morphemic knowledge also involves an understanding of root words, suffixes and prefixes, and compound words.

etymological knowledge the origins of language and words, or where they have come from.

Etymological knowledge relates to the origins of language and words, or where they have come from. The English language is made up of many words that have been derived from other languages—for example, ballet (French), psychology (Greek), vanilla (Spanish), umbrella (Italian), hamburger (German) and coffee (Arabic).

Learning to spell

In order to be successful spellers and writers, children need to have access to a range of teaching experiences in the school setting where good spelling skills and knowledge are nurtured. Teachers must have a strong grasp of the English spelling system and the ability to implement good teaching practice in order to develop these skills in children. Opportunities should be provided for children to engage in enjoyable and engaging writing tasks where they can apply their developing spelling skills and knowledge. Explicit teaching of the study of words and how they are formed, and a program that builds up knowledge of spelling skills and strategies, are needed in order for children to become competent spellers. Having a variety of books and texts available for children to read so they become familiar with letter–sound patterns and formation of words within texts adds to their exposure of the written word. Shared reading is an excellent strategy that can be used to explore words and spelling patterns. When a classroom environment is print-rich and children are immersed in the written word, there are plenty of opportunities for them to refer to these in their writing (this is known as 'environmental print' and is an important part of any classroom).

Handwriting

Despite the growth of modern technology in communicating the written word, handwriting is still an important skill for young children to master. Being proficient in handwriting benefits children in many ways. Poor or laboured handwriting skills can have a negative effect on children's writing ability as greater mental effort is needed to concentrate and attend to content, detail and organisation of ideas. When handwriting is seen as difficult and time consuming, children can lose motivation and interest, thereby compounding these difficulties. Over time, and with demonstration, modelling and practice, most children can acquire the skills necessary to produce legible and fluent handwriting.

It is important that teachers in the years prior to school provide young children with experiences that will assist in the development of good hand–eye coordination and fine motor skills. This will support and assist their ability to write effectively. For toddlers, this includes plenty of experience in manipulating large and small objects and materials, painting and drawing with a range of implements, threading, pouring, spooning, tracing and grasping. For pre-school children, fine motor skills and developing wrist and hand muscles is important, as well as providing activities to promote hand–eye co-ordination. In the early years of school, these experiences should continue alongside focused handwriting lessons that explicitly teach good handwriting skills. Correct posture, paper position, pencil group and letter formation should be taught explicitly with opportunities for children to practise their handwriting with guidance from the teacher.

Writing procedures

Five writing procedures that children will encounter during the early years of school are outlined below. Just as we discussed in the section above about reading procedures, these are also influenced by Pearson and Gallagher's Gradual Release of Responsibility Model (1983).

1 *Modelled writing* involves the teacher composing a text and 'thinking aloud' while demonstrating the thinking process an effective writer uses when writing. Planning for the

MARY HUGHES

LITERACY

teaching of explicit strategies or processes is an important part of this strategy, and these should be linked to the observed needs of children. Children are not active participants but listen and watch as the teacher composes and 'thinks aloud' the writing process. Children have the opportunity to practise these writing behaviours in their independent, small-group and guided-writing sessions.

2 *Shared writing* involves the teacher and the children collaborating to create a piece of text. During shared writing, the teacher scribes while the children and teacher contribute their ideas in order to compose the text. Shared writing enables children to participate in discussion with others about what should be included in the text and how it should be written. The teacher models how a good writer writes, and draws attention to features of the written text.

3 *Interactive writing* is a collaborative activity in which the teacher and children jointly compose and write a text. They share the decision making about what they will write, as well as the duty of scribe. During the interactive writing process, the teacher serves as facilitator of the discussion and utilises opportunities for specific teaching. Interactive writing is a valuable strategy in that it demonstrates concepts about print, early writing strategies and how words work. It helps children to understand the decoding and encoding process in reading and writing.

4 *Guided writing* is a small-group lesson targeting particular strategies that a group of students most need to practise. The teacher assists children as they attempt to bridge the gap between modelled and demonstrated writing and their own independent writing. Groups should be small and flexible, based on children's current needs, and one or two specific writing strategies are targeted for explicit teaching. As in guided reading, the teacher sits with each child and engages them in a rich conversation about how they will integrate these strategies into their writing during this session. All children are guided and monitored while they write and immediate feedback is given by the teacher.

5 *Independent writing* provides children with the opportunity to practise and apply their knowledge, skills and understandings in construction of their own texts. They might write stories, narratives, use speech balloons, write lists, and so on. It is vital that careful scaffolding of the processes and strategies required to complete the writing task have taken place prior to children working independently. Those children who require a little extra support may need to be part of a small group that constructs a joint text using interactive writing, or the teacher may use elements of guided writing with this group.

Writing is a social and cultural practice that is heavily influenced by context and situation. Children need to be able to access a range of discourses and practices so that they can participate fully in the society in which they live. They also need to have access to, and be familiar with, new and emerging technologies that can assist the writing process.

Literacy-enriched early childhood settings

Providing a literacy-rich environment is a key factor in facilitating opportunities for children to engage in meaningful literacy experiences. But how can we make sure that we give children the proper resources, experiences and opportunities? Play is the perfect vehicle in providing these rich opportunities to build on children's developing literacy skills, along with the important role of the teacher. In this section of the chapter we will consider the use of environmental print; a range of literacy props and tools; providing literacy-focused activity centres and the role of books as an integral part of a literacy-rich environment.

Environmental print

Why is it important to provide a print-rich environment for young children? And how can we represent the linguistic and cultural diversity within early childhood settings? You may think that by immersing children in an environment that is filled with posters, signs, pictures, labels, and so on, they will know what print is and how it works. However, for many young children, print is invisible—in fact, that they don't even notice it. To others it is just one sort of mysterious squiggle among many. Children have to learn that print is significant. They have to recognise that writing is different from pictures, that words and letters are different from numbers (Palmer et al., 2014). Drawing children's attention to the features and functions of print in everyday situations can be done both inside the setting and outdoors. 'Print walks' and role plays involving the use of signs such as *Stop, Exit, Playground, Toilets, Wash Hands* and so on are effective ways to raise children's awareness of print in the environment. Using pictures and symbols to accompany labels and signs provides contextual clues as to the message the print conveys.

Of course, the role of the adult in this process is vital if environmental print is to play an important part in supporting children's literacy development. If the print throughout the setting is *static* it will be hardly noticed by the children. However, if the environmental print is *dynamic* (where teachers purposefully draw attention to it) it can be a powerful tool in helping to develop children's understanding of the written word (Barrat-Pugh et al., 2005). Displaying print in children's home and community languages also helps to establish strong links between the setting and children's diverse cultural and linguistic backgrounds.

A supportive education environment

The walls of Miss K's classroom are brightly decorated with children's artwork. There are tables set up throughout the room, and primary colours appear to dominate. Shelving on the side of the room holds a multitude of games, puzzles and interactive manipulative toys, including blocks, Lego, and coloured shapes that can be arranged in different patterns. An easel with paints is off to one side of the room and newspaper is spread out underneath it to catch the paint drippings. Children are actively involved in doing something throughout the whole room while Miss K is engaged in working with a few children on an art project. Some children are working with puzzles; others are playing with blocks; others are pretending to cook a meal in the 'kitchen'; others are looking at books; and still others are drawing and colouring. One child is at the easel, painting, and two children are at the computer, working with an assistant on a software program about letters and sounds.

MARY HUGHES

After a short while, Miss K calls the children over to a corner. While the children sit on the floor around her, she reads a story out loud to them. They are quiet while the story is being read, and they are all quite enthusiastic to share personal stories that relate to the book afterwards. The children love to tell long stories, some of them not quite relating to the book. Miss K is patient, always encouraging the children to use language to express themselves. When the reading is over, she asks the children to draw a picture about the story and try to write 'words' describing their picture. Miss K has the children share these pictures and 'writing' with the class when they are finished.

The pre-school environment in this scenario comprises various aspects of an engaging and supportive early childhood education setting. Think about how Miss K utilises:

- the physical arrangement of the room
- the materials and resources that are available for the children
- transitions and routines
- the learning and teaching opportunities.

STOP AND THINK

How could you build on this to create a supportive and nurturing learning environment for young children?

Literacy props and tools

A literacy-rich environment will contain a wide range of tools and props that are freely available to children and can be used for a range of purposes. However, it is worthwhile stopping and asking ourselves, 'Are these literacy tools and props appropriate, authentic and relevant for children's play?' To answer this question we need to consider the context in which they will be used and whether they will allow and encourage children's active engagement with them.

Here are some examples of writing and reading tools:

catalogues	written music	charcoal	stamps
alphabet puzzles	photos	crayons	labels
magazines	stories on iPads	markers	tags
maps	'made' books	pens	coloured paper
posters	interactive games	paper	glue sticks
felt board	signs	card	erasers
receipts	felt pens	envelopes	sharpeners
recipes	chalk	notebooks	scissors.
letters	pencils	signs	

An effective literacy-rich environment will have a balance between these writing and reading tools and literacy props that can be used in children's play. There is strong evidence that suggests a relationship exists between 'pretend play' and literacy (Roskos et al., 2010).

Pretend play includes symbolic play, dramatic play and socio-dramatic play (for more information on children's play, see Chapters 4 and 8 of this book).

Some examples of props that can be used in children's pretend play are:

finger puppets	Small World figures	laundry pegs
hand puppets	homewares	fabrics
dolls	dress-ups	natural materials
soft toys	wooden blocks	outdoor equipment.

Literacy learning centres

It is essential that children have the opportunity to access activities and experiences which help them to see themselves as readers, writers, speakers, listeners and viewers. Learning centres can be set up with materials and activities to support children's active, playful and exploratory learning (Fellowes & Oakley, 2014) and should be designed so that children can use them either independently or in cooperation with others. Some of these centres will provide children with the space to engage in writing tasks; some will focus on reading; and still others on using technology for listening or participating in a range of interactive tasks. The learning centres can be placed indoors and outdoors within the setting, allowing children to experience a range of different types of activities.

1 Literacy learning centre: Small world play

2 Literacy learning centre: Cooking activity

3 Listening to recorded stories

4 Literacy games on the iPad

MARY HUGHES

Books

Books are a key resource, not only in creating a literacy-rich environment for young children but also in supporting children's literacy development in many different ways. Storybooks can be used to support reading comprehension, while information (non-fiction) books can provide simple information and pictures about things that interest young children. When adults read books with babies and toddlers, and engage them in conversation, they extend and scaffold the children's vocabulary and pronunciation. Encouraging older children to choose from a wide range of fiction and non-fiction books helps to expand vocabulary and builds on children's knowledge and understanding of a variety of topics.

Books that assist in developing the prerequisites of decoding, such as simple alphabet picture books, can be used with babies through to young children. Also useful are rhyming, poetry and song books that give children the opportunity to learn about the sounds of language. This is important in the development of phonological awareness (there is clear evidence of the links between reading and spelling abilities and phonological awareness in young children).

It is important that books are changed regularly, are enjoyable and interesting, and are appropriate for different developmental levels and abilities. When books are integrated into different play and activity areas in the setting there are greater opportunities for children to engage with them.

Enjoying different genres

This case study, written by a kindergarten teacher, Sarah B., demonstrates the use of non-fiction texts to support children's interest in 'plants we can grow'.

The children really enjoyed the book 'Jack and the Beanstalk' and as a result, they were interested in planting and growing their own beanstalks. To gain more information, I bought in a non-fiction book about planting and growing broad beans with coloured photographs illustrating the stages of growth. The children were fascinated, and keen to plant their own beanstalks outside in the garden. There were many conversations and questions during planting: where was the best spot; what sort of soil should we have; how big will the plant grow; and how should we feed it were among the many issues discussed. They also talked about their experiences of gardening and looking after plants in their own lives.

After planting the broad beans, the children wanted to know more, so I borrowed some books about planting herbs and strawberries. We went on and prepared the garden beds for more planting, with herbs, strawberries, carrots and parsley being among the favoured plants. I ensured that a range of non-fiction texts were available for the children to explore, with colourful, attractive photos of the plants and gardens. These encouraged further conversations relating to growth, plants and looking after the garden. This then led to the children becoming interested in the mini-beasts that lived in and around the garden, so I sourced some books on this topic too. I became aware that placing relevant texts close to the learning experiences I had set up resulted in the children exploring them and becoming engaged.

> **STOP AND THINK**
>
> Teachers who read books to children in early childhood settings give them a wonderful experience and set them up with a lifelong love of reading. This includes books of all genres including storybooks and information books. The children in the scenario above have access to information books about things that interest them in the garden. How can teachers and educators provide opportunities for children to be exposed to a range of books of different genres?

Children's literature

There is no widely held definition of what counts as 'children's literature'. However, it can be broadly defined as 'literature that appeals to the interests, needs and reading preferences of children, and captivates children as its major audience. Children's literature may be fictional, poetic or factual, or a combination of any of these' (Hancock, 2008). Quality literature is important in children's cognitive, social and emotional, and language and literacy development. It plays a role in developing a sense of identity and understanding about the world around them. Children's literature engages children and draws them into a world created by the writer where they are able to respond through their emotions and imagination. They are free to experience other times and places, and different cultures and lifestyles that become real to the reader.

A brief history of children's literature

> Stories are the main way we make sense of things, whether in thinking of our lives as a progression leading somewhere or in telling ourselves what is happening in the world … we make sense of events through possible stories.
>
> (Culler, 1997)

Children's fairytales have evolved over time, and the versions you will read to children today are very different from the ones that were told centuries ago. These tales were part of the oral traditions of communities, and were handed down from generation to generation. One of the earliest collectors and writers of these tales was Charles Perrault (1628–1703), a French writer, who drew on these pre-existing stories and reworked them for his own children. They were widely read and enjoyed by adults as well. *Little Red Riding Hood* was published in 1697, followed by *Sleeping Beauty*, *Puss in Boots* and *Cinderella*. Jacob and Wilhelm Grimm published their versions of popular folk tales with an emphasis on education, and the importance of following advice and instructions. The Brothers Grimm wrote their fairytales at a time in the nineteenth century when cultural assumptions of children were such that they needed to be guided by adults who were responsible for them. Stories needed to provide their young readers with a moral lesson and were very clear in describing the repercussions when the 'rules' were not obeyed!

Most of the books written at this time were quite difficult to read so it is assumed that older children would have shared them with younger siblings. Some examples of these books are *Robinson Crusoe* (Defoe, 1719), *Gulliver's Travels* (Swift, 1726), *The Swiss Family Robinson* (Wyss, 1812) and *A Christmas Carol* (Dickens, 1843).

Another early book that was written to entertain children was *The History of Little Goody Two Shoes* by John Newbery (1765). This book was also moralistic in tone, but did have some entertainment value for young readers (Short et al., 2013).

Lewis Carroll's novel, *Alice's Adventures in Wonderland* was published in 1865 as a book specifically written for children. This book was purely entertaining, and did not contain a moral lesson or instructional purpose. It was hugely popular, and Carroll quickly followed it with two further books, *Through the Looking Glass* and *What Alice Found There.*

Illustrating children's books was unheard of before the mid nineteenth century. Woodcuts were used very occasionally, but it wasn't until 1865 that Sir John Tenniel illustrated Carroll's *Alice in Wonderland* in pen and ink. Shortly after this, English printer Edmund Evans developed a photographic engraving process and engaged talented artists to create colourful illustrations for children's books. These were the forerunner of today's coloured picture story books.

The modern picture story book emerged at the beginning of the twentieth century in Britain, when Beatrix Potter created her 'Peter Rabbit' stories. Her little books were rejected at first. However, she used her own money to publish copies of *The Tale of Peter Rabbit*, which was a huge success.

A London company published the second and subsequent printings of Potter's books, which were characterised by her own clear watercolour illustrations of woodland animals wearing colourful clothes and having adventures in the countryside. Beatrix Potter's unique style of pairing stories with pictures became the model for other authors and illustrators of picture story books that followed.

Modern fairytales

The work of Roald Dahl in the twentieth century fused adventure, magic and fantasy stories with reality to create a new genre in children's literature. He wrote novels for adults before publishing his first story for children, *James and the Giant Peach*, in 1961. Dahl's books fall into four main categories: children's books, picture books, books for younger readers and teenage fiction. Despite being the bestselling author of his time in Britain, he was criticised for violence, sexism and racism in his children's stories. The reading public, however— and especially children—loved his stories, poems and tales, and he is still one of the most enduring authors of our time.

Genres and categories

Children's literature can be easily divided into *genres* or *categories* with similar characteristics (Short et al., 2013). These include traditional stories, fiction, biography, information books and poetry. A variety of *formats* include picture books, easy-to-read books, illustrated books, graphic novels, chapter books, hardcover books, paperback books, series books and eBooks. Selecting the right books for children is important, and careful consideration needs to be given to choosing books that are appropriate to children's age and interests. Young children are generally able to choose books they enjoy, sometimes with a little help and guidance.

If we look back at the introduction to this chapter, the message is clear that children respond with joy and delight to stories and books that spark their imagination and transport them to new and exciting worlds. Teachers who read stories to children foster in them a love of language, words, and the rhyme and rhythm of the language of books. The educational and emotional benefits are lifelong for children of all ages and stages.

Multiliteracies

For many of us, being 'multiliterate' is second nature, and using technology is something we experience on a daily basis in our work and our personal lives. How we communicate with one another in a changing world is far different from how we communicated even a decade ago. Multiliteracies have become increasingly important and this requires new thinking about literacy. During the 1990s, the New London Group coined the phrase 'multiliteracies' to describe an approach to literacy theory and pedagogy that highlights two key aspects of literacy: the proliferation of diverse modes of communication through new communications technologies, and culturally specific literacies required to function in a culturally diverse pluralistic society (New London Group, 1996). For young children, texts are increasingly multimodal and they are being immersed in new technologies from birth. Children are surrounded by images (moving and still) and recognise signs and symbols that help them to make sense of their world. 'They are truly new millennial children and live in a multimodal world where the impact of new technologies is significant and ubiquitous' (Yelland, 2010).

Research by Cohen (2012) into children's use of iPads contended that there are three different types of learning evident during app play:

- tacit learning of the game and how it works
- mastery of explicit learning tasks such as counting and matching
- learning how to transfer the use of skills and content to new games or levels of play.

iPads can be used by teachers to facilitate meaningful teaching and learning experiences with young children as well as to support home–centre communication.

Concerns have been raised regarding the potential developmental harm of exposing young children to screen-based technologies from an early age (Bayhan et al., 2002; Cordes & Miller, 2000). There is also increasing evidence of the effects of 'blue light' from some digital devices, which can be addictive, particularly to adolescents who use devices at night. However, we also need to consider the nuanced and different ways technology has been used to support children's social interactions, collaboration and learning (Jenkins et al., 2006).

Literacy is so much more than just reading and writing. The emergence of new technologies and multiliteracies over the past few years has been rapid. Children are not passive consumers of media; they select and initiate content and activities using a range of technological devices. Concerns have been raised about the potential harm for babies and very young children of screen-based technologies, so a wise and judicious approach is required by teachers and parents in regard to this.

LITERACY

MARY HUGHES

SUMMARY

- Beginning in early infancy, young children communicate with others in many different ways.
- Developmental theory gives us information and guidance on how children develop and learn, while a social constructivist philosophy views learning as a social, collaborative and active process.
- Oral language is a key element in building the foundations for future success, and children learn spoken language in homes and communities that are speech-rich.
- The concepts, skills and understandings children need in order to be good readers and writers are supported by effective literacy teachers who skilfully integrate a range of approaches and resources to meet the diverse learning needs of children in prior-to-school and school settings.
- The role of play is central to the way young children learn. However, the importance of 'intentional teaching' and the role of the teacher are also recognised as being crucial in effective language and literacy learning and development (Fellowes & Oakley, 2014). Teachers who can inspire in children a lifelong love of reading and a passion for books will be remembered by their students even years later.
- Children's literature can develop children's sense of identity, their understanding about other people and the world around them, and the way good books can spark imagination.
- Access to books and texts is no longer limited to paper-based print as the world of multiliteracies and the growth of communication and information technologies offer endless possibilities in influencing language, literacy and literature in the twenty-first century.

FURTHER REFLECTION

- Observe children's language use in a prior-to-school setting. How can you nurture oral language to support children's learning and development?
- What do you need to know about children's home and community languages in order to plan more effectively?
- Can you consider how you might establish literacy-rich environments in an early childhood setting? How would you go about this?

GROUP DISCUSSION

1 Observe a childcare or pre-school setting. What features of a 'print-rich' environment did you see? Compare with others in your group.
2 How does this 'print-rich' environment facilitate the development of foundational reading and writing skills?
3 How might a teacher present a 'balanced approach' to literacy teaching and learning in the classroom? What are the advantages/challenges?
4 Why is it important to know the theories that influence effective literacy teaching and learning?
5 What is the importance of reflection and evaluation in teaching practice? How do you use feedback to improve practice?

CLASS EXERCISES

1 Work in groups to discuss the different types of written texts you should see as part of the environment in childcare, pre-school and school.
2 Compare your group's answers with those of another group. What was different? What was similar?

FURTHER READING

Barratt-Pugh, C., Rivalland, J., Hamer, J. & Adams, P. (2005) Literacy Learning in Australia: Practical Ideas for Early Childhood Educators. Melbourne: Thomson Dunsmore Press.

This book is an introduction to early literacy learning focusing on the literacy needs of children in the first five years. The authors' sociocultural approach emphasises the importance of recognising the everyday events that expose children to and foster literacy learning possibilities.

Fellowes, J. & Oakley, G. (2014) Language, Literacy and Early Childhood Education. Australia: Oxford University Press.

This book builds on the information given in this chapter. It encompasses four main early childhood settings: the family and community, childcare, the pre-school years, and the early years of school. Making explicit links to the Early Years Learning Framework and the Australian Curriculum, this text is based on current research and theoretical perspectives, and includes practical strategies and activities to equip educators with the knowledge and skills they need to effectively support young children's learning of language and literacy. Chapter 22 provides a comprehensive view of the role of literature in children's development and learning. I would highly recommend this text for both pre-service and practising teachers.

Hancock, M. (2008) Celebration of Literature and Response: Children, Books, and Teachers in K–8 Classrooms (3rd edn). US: Pearson.

This engaging text applies reader response theory to children's literature methods to help new and experienced teachers in prior-to-school and school settings. It also includes a CD database of children's literature.

Hill, S. (2012) Developing Early Literacy: Assessment and Teaching. Prahran, Vic.: Eleanor Curtain.

This second edition text includes significant new content with links to the Australian National Curriculum English and the Early Years Learning Framework; evidence-based assessment procedures for improving early language, reading and writing; practical examples of teaching strategies in action in a range of classrooms and settings; further information on oral language and its links to reading and writing; and more information on vocabulary and on the development of comprehension strategies.

Palmer, S., Bayley, R. & Raban, B. (2014) Foundations Early Literacy: A Balanced Approach to Language, Listening and Literacy Skills in the Early Years. Albert Park: Teaching Solutions.

This book places language, listening and literacy within the wider context of children's overall physical and mental growth, recognising the overlap between all areas of early learning and development. Practical advice on helping children to transfer their learning into their own child-initiated activities to build a genuine and solid foundation for early literacy is integral to the book.

Winch, G., Johnston, R., March, P., Ljungdahl, L. & Holliday, M. (2006) Literacy: Reading, Writing and Children's Literature. South Melbourne: OUP.

The fifth edition of this book covers the whole literacy curriculum—reading, writing, speaking, listening and viewing—and illustrates how pre-service teachers can link theory to practice in their classrooms. This edition has a particular focus on children's literature in the early years.

REFERENCES

Adam, H. (2010) 'Children's Literature and The Early Years Learning Framework', *eCULTURE*. Berkeley: Electronic Press.

Allen, K. & Hancock, T. (2008) Reading Comprehension Improvement with Individualised Cognitive Profiles and Metacognition, *Literacy Research and Instruction*, 47:124–39.

Anstey, M. & Bull, G. (2004) *The Literacy Labyrinth.* Frenchs Forest: Pearson Education.

Australian Curriculum, Assessment and Reporting Authority (ACARA) (2017) 'General Capabilities: Literacy'. Australian Curriculum, vol. 8.1. www.australiancurriculum.edu.au

MARY HUGHES

Barratt-Pugh, C. (1998) The Sociocultural Context of Literacy Learning, in C. Barratt-Pugh & Rohl, M. (eds), *Literacy Learning in the Early Years*. Crow's Nest, Australia: Allen & Unwin.

Barratt-Pugh, C., Rivalland, J., Hamer, J. & Adams, P. (2005) *Literacy Learning in Australia: Practical Ideas for Early Childhood Educators*. Melbourne: Thomson Dunsmore Press.

Bayhan, P., Olgun, P. & Yelland, N. (2002) 'A Study of Pre-School Teachers' Thoughts about Computer-Assisted Instruction', *Contemporary Issues in Early Childhood 3*(2): 298–303.

Bodrova, E., & Leong. D.J. (2007) *Tools of the Mind: The Vygotskian Approach to Early Childhood Education* (2nd edn). New Jersey, U.S: Pearson.

Bruner, J. (1990) *Acts of Meaning.* Cambridge, Mass.: Harvard University Press.

Bull, G. & Anstey, M. (2007) 'Exploring Visual Literacy through a Range of Texts', *Practically Primary, 3*.

Burns, M., Griffin, P. & Snow, C. (eds) (1999) *Starting Out Right: A Guide to Promoting Children's Reading Success.* Washington, DC: National Academy Press.

Callaghan, G. & Madelaine, A. (2012) 'Levelling the Playing Field for Kindergarten Entry: Preschool Early Literacy Instruction', *Australasian Journal of Early Childhood, 37*: 13–23.

Carroll, L. (2009) *Alice in Wonderland*. Templar, Dorking UK. [1865]

Clay, M.M. (1991) *Becoming Literate: The Construction of Inner Control.* Auckland: Heinemann.

Clay, M.M. (1998) *By Different Paths to Common Outcomes.* Auckland: Heinemann.

Clay, M.M. (2002) *An Observation Survey of Early Literacy* (2nd edn). Auckland: Heinemann.

Cohen Group (2011) *Young Children, Apps and An iPad*. New York. http://mcgrc.com/publications/publications/

Cohen, S. (2012) 'A 1:1 iPad initiative—Vision to Reality', *Library Media Connection*, 30(6).

Cope, B. & Kalantzis, M. (eds) *Multiliteracies: Literacy Learning and the Design of Social Futures.* South Yarra, Australia: Macmillan.

Cordes, C. & Miller, E. (2000) *Fool's Gold: A Critical Look at Computers in Childhood.* US: Alliance for Childhood.

Couse, L. & Chen, D. (2014) 'A Tablet Computer for Young Children? Exploring Its Viability for Early Childhood Education', *Journal of Research on Technology in Education, 43*(1): 75–96.

Culler, J. (1997) *Literary Theory: A Very Short Introduction.* South Melbourne: Oxford University Press.

Department for Education and Skills (2007) *Letters and Sounds: Principles and Practice of High Quality Phonics.* Primary National Strategy, London.

Department of Education and Childhood Development (DECD) (2013) Great Start, Strong Foundations, Powerful Learners: A Numeracy and Literacy Strategy from Birth to 18. www.decd.sa.gov.au/numeracyandliteracy

Department of Education and Early Childhood Development (DEECD) (2010) iPads for Learning. www.education.vic.gov.au/school/teachers/support/Pages/ipads.aspx

Department of Education and Training (DET) (2006) *Literacy and Numeracy Review: The Final Report.* WA.

Department of Education and Training (Victoria) (DET)/Victorian Curriculum and Assessment Authority (VCCA) (2016) *Victorian Early Years Learning and Development Framework: For All Children from Birth to Eight Years*. State of Victoria, Australia: Department of Education and Training.

Department of Education, Employment and Workplace Relations (DEEWR) (2009) *Belonging, Being & Becoming: The Early Years Learning Framework for Australia.* ACT, Australia: Commonwealth of Australia.

Department of Education, Science and Training (DEST) (2005) Report and Recommendations, National Inquiry into the Teaching of Literacy. (DEST is now Department of Education Employment and Workplace Relations DEEWR). www.DEEWR.gov.au

Department of Education WA (2013) *First Steps. Speaking and Listening Resource Book.* Department of Education WA, Perth. http://det.wa.edu.au/stepsresources/detcms/navigation/first-steps-literacy/

Derewianka, B. (2011) *A New Grammar Companion for Teachers.* Sydney: PETAA.

Fellowes, J. & Oakley, G. (2014) *Language, Literacy and Early Childhood Education*. South Melbourne: Oxford University Press.

Fleer, M. & Raban, B. (2007) *Early Childhood Literacy and Numeracy: Building Good Practice*. Canberra: Department of Education, Science and Training.

Fountas, I. & Pinnell, G. (1998) *Word Matters: Teaching Phonics and Spelling in the Reading/Writing Classroom*. Portsmouth, NH: Heinemann.

Freebody, P. (2007) *Literacy Education in School: Research Perspectives from the Past, for the Future*. Melbourne: ACER.

Freire, P. & Macedo, D. (2001) *Pedagogy of the Oppressed*. Continuum International Publishing Group Ltd. (30th anniversary edn).

Halliday, M. (2004) 'Three Aspects of Children's Language Development: Learning Language, Learning through Language, Learning about Language', in J. Webster (ed.) *The Language of Early Childhood: M.A.K. Halliday* (vol. 4 in *The Collected Works of M.A.K. Halliday*). NY: Continuum.

Hancock, M. (2008) *Celebration of Literature and Response: Children, Books, and Teachers in K–8 Classrooms* (3rd edn). US: Pearson.

Heath, S., Fletcher, J. & Hogben, J. (2006) *Catch Them before They Fall 2003–05: Cost Effective Screening for Children at Risk for Literacy Problems.* Child Study Centre, University of Western Australia and Department of Education and Training Western Australia.

Hill, S. (2012) *Developing Early Literacy: Assessment and Teaching*. Prahran, Vic.: Eleanor Curtain.

Jenkins, H., Clinton, K., Purushotma, R., Robison, A. & Weigel, M. (2006) Confronting the Challenges of Participatory Culture: Media Education for the 21st Century. www.macfound.org/media/article_pdfs/JENKINS_WHITE_PAPER.PDF

Kennedy, A. (2009) 'Let's talk: Having Meaningful Conversations with Children', in NCA Council (ed.), *Putting Children First*. Surry Hills: NCAC.

Louden, W., Rohl, M., Barratt-Pugh, C., Brown, C., Cairney, T., Elderfield, J., House, H., Meiers, M., Rivalland, J. & Rowe, K. (2005). In *Teachers' Hands: Effective Literacy Teaching Practices in the Early Years of Schooling*. Commonwealth of Australia.

Luke, A. & Freebody, P. (1999) 'A Map of Possible Practices: Further Notes on the Four Resources Model', *Practically Primary*, 4(2): 5–8.

Medwell, J. & Wray, D. (2013). Handwriting Automaticity: The Search for Performance Thresholds, *Language and Education, 28*(1): 34–51.

Moll, L., Amanti, C., Niff, D. & Gonzales, N. (1992) 'Funds of Knowledge for Teaching: Using a Qualitative Approach to Connect Homes and Classrooms', *Theory into Practice, 31*(2): 132–41.

Munro, J. (1998) *Assessing and Teaching Phonological Knowledge.* Camberwell, Vic.: ACER.

Munro, J. (2008) *Effective Strategies for Implementing Differentiated Instruction.* Australia: University of Melbourne.

National Inquiry into the Teaching of Literacy (2006) *Teaching Reading: Report and Recommendations.* Barton, ACT: Australian Government Department of Education, Science and Training.

New London Group (1996) 'A Pedagogy of Multiliteracies: Designing Social Futures', *Harvard Education Review*, 66(1).

NICHD Early Child Care Research Network (2005) 'Pathways to Reading: The Role of Oral Language in the Transition to Reading', *Developmental Psychology*, 41(2): 428–42.

Organization for Economic Co-operation and Development (OECD) (2009) *Creating Effective Teaching and Learning Environments: First Results from TALIS*. Paris: OECD.

Palmer, S., Bayley, R. & Raban, B. (2014) *Foundations Early Literacy: A Balanced Approach to Language, Listening and Literacy Skills in the Early Years*. Albert Park: Teaching Solutions.

LITERACY

MARY HUGHES

Pearson, P. & Gallagher, M. (1983) The Gradual Release of Responsibility Model of Instruction, *Contemporary Educational Psychology*, *8*: 112–23.

Reiter, M. (2004). M100W Magic 100 Words. Australia: Magic Words International.

Roskos K., Christie J., Widman S. & Holding A. (2010) 'Three Decades In: Priming for Meta-Analysis in Play-Literacy Research', *Journal of Early Childhood Literacy, 10*(1): 55–96.

Short, K., Lynch-Brown, C. & Tomlinson, C. (2013) *Essentials of Children's Literature* (8th edn). London: Pearson Education.

Steely, A., Flint, K. & Kitson, L. (2017) *Literacy in Australia: Pedagogies for Engagement*. Australia: Wiley (e-book form).

Vygotsky, L. (1978) *Mind in Society: The Development of Higher Psychological Processes.* Cambridge: Harvard University Press.

Winch, G., Johnston, R., March, P., Ljungdahl, L. & Holliday, M. (2014) *Literacy: Reading, Writing and Children's Literature,* (5th edn). South Melbourne: Oxford University Press.

Wood, D., Bruner, J. & Ross, G. (1976) 'The Role of Tutoring in Problem Solving', *Journal of Child Psychology and Psychiatry, 17*: 89–100.

Yelland, N. (2010) 'New Technologies, Playful Experiences, and Multimodal Learning', in I. R. Berson & M.J. Berson (eds). *High Tech Tots: Childhood in a Digital World.* Charlotte, NC: Information Age, pp.5–22.

The Arts in Early Childhood

Carol Carter (with 'Music and Dance' by Ginette Pestana)

Chapter objectives

In this chapter, we will:
- recognise the significance and value of the Arts in early childhood contexts
- consider the important role of the Arts as a means of cultural, emotional, physical and aesthetic expression
- examine key underlying principles of each discrete arts form as modes of expression and communication
- consider the elements and techniques of each arts form for exploring the learning potential and possibilities for young children.

Key terms

aesthetic understanding	holistic education	music
the Arts	media arts	process drama
arts integration	mime	visual art

> Early childhood has been described as a 'golden age of creativity, a time when every child sparkles with artistry'.
>
> (Gardner, 1982)

I only have to think of some of my delight in, and experiences of, young children's Art expressions to agree that it is indeed a time of heightened artistic creativity. Walking into educational spaces where young children's artwork is displayed not only brings a smile to my face, but I am also dazzled by the creativity, uniqueness and beauty that shine through each piece of work. I have witnessed the concentration and confidence of children engaging in Arts-making, untainted by any of the fear, inhibition or hesitation that frequently accompanies engaging adults in Arts work. I observed a three-year-old child covering a plastic bottle with white cotton wool and other white material and unforgivably (and certainly not best teaching practice) asked, 'What are you making?' Unhesitatingly she replied, 'Can't you see it's a snow dinosaur!'—her words and tone indicating her confidence in her artistry and her exasperation with my inability to clearly see what she was creating.

As an inexperienced teacher engaging children around five years old in a drama process, I foolishly gave them an elaborate explanation as to why I 'disappeared' when someone needing their help (myself taking on a role) came into the classroom. The explanation included a statement that 'I could not be seen by adults and so would instantly vanish when an adult came into the room'. So powerful were the children's imaginations, creativity, artistry and belief in the drama process that, when the school principal came into the classroom looking for me, thirty children sat on and around this 'person who needed help' so that she would not be seen and then vanish. Squashed at the bottom of a pile of children, I was faced with a huge dilemma, as I am sure you can imagine. Fortunately, the very wise principal told the children that when I 'returned', they should tell me to come and see her. These, and numerous other experiences, resonate strongly with the notion that early childhood is indeed a 'golden age of creativity'.

Introduction

In this chapter, we begin with an introduction to the Arts consisting of a definition of the Arts and Arts education and a brief examination of the role and significance of the Arts in early childhood teaching and learning. The integrated nature of the Arts and how they can be authentically integrated into other curriculum areas is articulated within the subheading 'Arts integration'. Included in the discussion of the Arts, as a cohesive subject comprising a number of disciplines, is an examination of the benefits of Arts education for social–emotional, physical–cognitive and aesthetic understanding and expression and how the Arts function to support children's symbolic expression, meaning-making and communication. The relationships of identity, intercultural understanding and the Arts, and the uses of artistic media as tools for cultural expression, are also examined. After the examination of Arts integration, each discrete discipline—namely Drama and Storytelling, Visual Art and Media Arts, and Music and Dance—will be addressed as subsections of the chapter. We provide practical, 'hands-on' activities, strategies and techniques for helping children to explore, discover, create and reflect on Arts experiences and to understand the wonders of the process of artistic creation and imagination. The practical experiences are underpinned by philosophies, theoretical perspectives, curriculum and policies that connect the Arts to early childhood learning and development.

the Arts unique, creative forms of visual, verbal, non-verbal and/ or performativity based expression and communication that make use of the senses.

The Arts are unique, creative forms of visual, verbal, non-verbal and/or performativity based expression and communication that make use of the senses. Arts education is learning in, about and through different types of artistic expression. Beyond this and the multimodal nature of the Arts, they are forms that elude definitions because of the fluid, dynamic, flexible nature of the Arts. Despite being actively involved in Arts education and understanding the significance and power of Arts education both as a subject and a teaching and learning tool, I have come to realise, in writing this chapter, how exceptionally challenging and slippery creating one basic definition of the Arts can be.

UNESCO (2006 and 2010) affirms the Arts as crucial to education and as a 'basic universal right for all'. The EYLF emphasises the Arts and the importance of the Arts in early childhood settings. As stated in Chapter 7, the 'modes of communication' associated with emergent literacy in early childhood include music, movement, dance, storytelling, visual arts, media and drama—and making use of the creative arts for expression and meaning-making is an important aspect of Learning Outcome 5 (DEEWR, 2009, pp. 41, 42). Within the Australian National Curriculum (2016), the Arts is acknowledged as a subject area with specific emphasis, in the early years, on creating and making. Curriculum documents delineate the Arts disciplines within this subject area as Drama, Dance, Media Arts, Music and Visual Art.

Both of these documents (the EYLF and the National Curriculum) place importance on the Arts within early childhood educational settings. The distinctions that need to be highlighted here are concerned with the differences in prior-to-school settings—which are guided by *frameworks*—and school settings—which are guided by *curriculum* documents. The Arts focus in the EYLF is as tools of communication and meaning-making in ways that are interwoven into emergent literacy, while curriculum documents focus more strongly on the Arts as a subject area with distinct disciplines. In the EYLF, *movement* is mentioned separately from the other modes of communication, thereby drawing attention specifically to movement with young children. Within national and state curriculum documents movement is embedded into the various performing arts (Dance, Drama and Music) disciplines.

Arts educators have consistently emphasised the collective and individual strengths of Arts disciplines in practice. The Arts are acknowledged as invaluable subject areas as well as powerful tools for transformative education and meaning-making (in Caldwell & Vaughan 2012). As well as supporting children to understand, encode and decode all forms of language, the various Arts forms are themselves languages and symbolic modes of representation that are important for helping children to make meaning. For me, one of the most important aspects of the Arts is that they provide children with different ways of knowing and making sense of their world.

When we ensure that children are given opportunities to explore the Arts, we are contributing to their engaging in forms of communication that are highly likely to impact deeply on how they express themselves and engage with the world (Eisner, 2002). We need to carefully consider the teaching of the Arts and how children are encouraged to participate in order to fulfil this communicative potential. There was, and in some cases continues to be, a pervasive view in early childhood that children should be largely left to explore the Arts on their own and that the Arts is synonymous with children's self-expression. I believe that Arts education has gradually moved away from binary approaches that were *either* very strongly teacher driven *or* were exclusively concerned with providing space for self-expression, to more of a combined, dualistic or multi-focused approach. We will explore some of these approaches in more detail within the discussion of the various Arts disciplines.

Our own experiences of, and attitudes towards, the Arts tend to have a direct impact on how we teach and engage children in the Arts. Where we have experienced positive, enabling Arts activities, we tend to engage children more frequently and effectively in the Arts.

STOP AND REFLECT

- What have been your experiences of engaging in the Arts?
- How have these experiences contributed to how you view the Arts?
- What are your attitudes towards and beliefs about the Arts?
- How will this impact on how you use the Arts in teaching contexts?

THE ARTS

There needs to be a balance between a holistic and an integrated approach to the Arts and the teaching of each discrete Arts discipline. For this reason, I will begin with an example of an integrated approach and a discussion of what I consider to be the most important benefits of the Arts, generally. Thereafter different disciplines—namely Drama and Storytelling; Visual and Media Arts, and Music and Dance—will be addressed as subsections of the chapter. The discussion of the discrete disciplines will include a weaving in of practice and practical examples that are specific to each age group within early childhood education, starting with toddlers and babies, moving to pre-schoolers and ending with the practical applications for school classroom use.

arts integration
when the Arts
are combined,
blended and
taught together
to fuse skills
and knowledge,
as opposed to
teaching each
Arts discipline as
a discrete and
separate form.

Arts integration

When we talk about **arts integration**, we mean that the Arts are combined, blended and taught together to fuse skills and knowledge, as opposed to teaching each Art discipline as a discrete and separate form. The different Arts elements and techniques do overlap and can be taught together, particularly in early childhood. As you read the example from my professional practice entitled 'Grandmother's birthday', think about the ways in which the Arts can be integrated and work together to create rich, authentic learning experiences. This is just one example of numerous ways in which the Arts can be integrated. In the selected example, I make use of a dramatic frame or context to explore and experience different Arts activities. I have explored this particular context with diverse participants, ranging from engaging three-year-old children, to modelling for Initial Teacher Education students.

Grandmother's birthday

Far, far away in a very remote area lives a grandmother, who is the oldest member of our family. Now, because Grandmother is going to turn 100 she needs to have a very special birthday celebration. The children take on roles as various family members as does the teacher, who is a family member designated to organise a surprise birthday party for Grandmother. Children discuss what is needed for the birthday party. Aspects of Visual Art and Media Art are incorporated through the children creating birthday cards, presents and other items.

The media used and the Visual Art elements explored will depend on the pre-school or school context, the age of the children and the outcomes that the teacher is focusing on. The participants could, for example, focus on drawing charcoal self-portraits for Grandmother to hang up on her walls, a PowerPoint for the speech that is going to be made at Grandmother's birthday or using recycled material to create jewellery for grandmother.

The children also engage in Music and Dance through preparing and practising songs and dances that Grandmother would like for her birthday party. For example, the children may work on creating a new and different

birthday song as Grandmother has heard a traditional one so many times in her life and is sick of it, so she needs something new. The context also lends itself to honouring and sharing culturally specific Arts forms that the various 'family' members know. With one group of participants, learning took place around conflict resolution, as family members believed the family was dysfunctional.

The children and the teacher also use mapping and visual images to work out the route they will take to Grandmother's house as she lives far away. Through **mime** and action the children are led through different parts of the journey, singing songs, where appropriate, or listening to music that evokes particular environments that they move through on the way to Grandmother's house. Older participants can take responsibility for setting up the space and leading the class through different parts of the journey. In addition to the Arts, other subject areas can be integrated—for example, language incorporating opposites was part of the journey experience for five year olds; writing about the experience added another experience.

mime using gestures and body movements to portray actions and ideas without the use of speech.

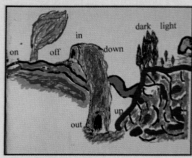

In Grandmother's house, presents are given to the grandmother (teacher) and, once again, there are opportunities for learning about particular Arts elements, such as dynamics, through the Drama context.

For example, Grandmother does not have her hearing aid switched on, so the children are encouraged to sing loudly. Then she suddenly realises that she needs to switch her hearing aid on, so the song is too loud and the children sing softly. Aspects of pitch, tempo and dynamics can be explored within this context. The drama then proceeds in different ways depending on the children's needs and interests and the teaching intentions.

Later in this chapter we will return to the concepts highlighted in the description of 'Grandmother's birthday'.

STOP AND THINK

- What do you see as the strengths, advantages and challenges of Arts Integration being learnt and taught in early childhood?
- How will this impact on how you use the Arts in teaching contexts?
- How could other subjects potentially be integrated within the 'Grandmother's birthday' drama?
- What are some further examples of how the Arts can be integrated?

Benefits of Arts education

The Arts promote and evoke **holistic education** where all aspects of learning are considered and developed, including social, emotional, physical, cognitive and creative domains. The Arts develop collaborative, social and communication skills and are powerful ways of communicating meaning through visual, oral and spatial symbols, including gestures, images and sounds. They enable multimodal expressions and formation of feelings and emotions, personal identity and knowledge-sharing. For example, in the 'Grandmother's birthday' example, children are making use of various symbols and developing social and collaborative skills as they pretend to be family members preparing and negotiating communal experiences. Their responses to the tasks are linked to both the emotional and cognitive domains.

Through the Arts, children's physical development is enhanced as they practise fine and gross motor skills such as cutting and pasting (for making Grandmother's jewellery) practise dance movements (to perform for Grandmother) and use imaginative physical gestures (in climbing the mountains, rowing the boat, etc., to get to Grandmother's house).

holistic education where all aspects of learning are considered and developed, including social, emotional, physical, cognitive and creative domains.

THE ARTS

CAROL CARTER WITH GINETTE PESTANA

When children engage with Arts materials and activities, they make use of problem-solving techniques that depend on Arts-related forms of thinking (Eisner, 2002). This contributes to practice and exposure to higher order thinking skills, creativity, imagination and creative problem-solving skills being a significant benefit of using the Arts with children—for example, deciding on arts media and techniques for Grandmother's birthday, brainstorming what would make a successful surprise party, and reflecting on how to get artwork to the remote area where Grandmother lives.

The value of the Arts also lies in engaging children in aesthetic experiences. **Aesthetic understanding** refers to people's perceptions and affective understanding of what they may consider to be beautiful or pleasing to the senses. The aesthetic experiences should be free of any value judgments, but should relate to what would be considered by different individuals as aesthetically pleasing. It should rather focus on Arts appreciation; engagement with feelings and responses evoked by Arts experiences; and an awareness of dimensions of beauty and the senses. The Arts develop aesthetic sensitivity and our human need for the pleasing and the beautiful. Aesthetic aspects are developed and reflected on in 'Grandmother's birthday'—for example, the encouragement of considerations of what will be needed for the Arts products for grandmother to like them and/or for the family to be proud of them. Grandmother also leads a reflective discussion on the Arts products when she receives them for her birthday and what she considers to be the aesthetic beauty of her different gifts.

The Arts assist children to share and learn about cultures through providing a vehicle to explore, create, represent and reflect on their beliefs and understandings, as well as cultural influences and practices (Roy et al., 2012, pp.15–16). The Arts shape cultural and linguistic symbols, artefacts, traditions and metaphors. In turn the Arts are shaped and re-shaped by cultural and linguistic traditions, symbols and understandings (ACARA, 2011; Roy et al., 2012; Caldwell & Vaughan, 2012). Participants identify, explore and express a multiplicity of diverse viewpoints and perspectives and 'new ways of being' through authentic engagement in collaborative, communal drama [and arts] processes and the negotiation and re-negotiation of different identities (Anderson, 2012; Nicholson, 2005; O'Toole & Dunne, 2015). The Arts have long been identified as having substantial ability 'to open up cross-cultural communication and intercultural understanding' (Donelan, 2009, p.23). The Arts, while able to take on various shapes and forms, is always 'tuned into the social and cultural mores of its times and contexts' (O'Toole et al., 2009, p. 197).

It is due to this cultural dynamic that what is envisaged for the birthday party, how the presents for Grandmother are created and how the physical space has been set up, has not been the same each of the many different times I have used the 'Grandmother's birthday' story. Culturally specific Arts forms and understandings play a major role in this difference of interpretation.

Given the many benefits of Arts education—and the pivotal role that the Arts can play in learning and linking to other learning areas, including literacy—the 'cutting back on Arts education to devote more time to subjects that make children literate [and numerate]' (Gill, cited in Caldwell & Vaughan, 2012) is a grave concern—as is the lack of understanding of the Arts as languages supporting multiliteracies and multimodal forms of expression. In a climate of ever 'narrowing' curriculum and subject hierarchy establishment (McArdle, 2012) as well as the 'devaluing' of the Arts (Russell-Bowie, 2012) it is vital to consider artful learning and teaching strategies within the different areas of the Arts discussed in this chapter.

----

aesthetic understanding people's perceptions and affective understanding of what they may consider to be beautiful or pleasing to the senses.

While teachers and pre-service teachers generally acknowledge the benefits of the Arts, this does not automatically result in practice or ensure the quality and authenticity of Arts experiences (McArdle, 2012; Carter & Hughes, 2016). This is largely due to the attitudes and beliefs teachers develop towards, and about, the Arts.

Drama and storytelling

In this section I begin by broadly defining 'drama' in the many forms it can be used for educational purposes. I then focus particularly on process drama and the use of drama as an educational tool, which I consider the most significant aspect to focus on within prior-to-school and the early years of school setting. The progression of young children from dramatic play to drama and the use of dramatic elements, conventions and techniques will be discussed. Storytelling as an expressive and interactive process for young children is also considered.

Categorisation of drama

Drama is the active engagement of the imagination to project and enact events, situations and roles through improvisation, role play, characterisation and interpretation of texts.

Educational drama, as the name implies, can be used to refer to drama that has an overarching educational purpose or aim (Wagner, 1998, p.5). Historically, there were tensions between process and product and a strong belief in 'Child Drama' (Slade, 1965) driven by a process that was in no way connected to theatre-type drama, which was considered to be the domain of teenagers and adults. However, as process and product are complementary, symbiotic and not binary concepts (Bolton, 1998, p.261), a broad and inclusive definition of what constitutes educational drama is needed to make full use of the potential that drama has for learning and teaching.

Drama for learning and teaching purposes and drama for the purpose of theatre production undeniably have the same roots; they are not mutually exclusive, but are interrelated and should co-exist and work together. For example, theatre practitioners may begin their rehearsals by exploring using drama processes; and process drama work, engaged in with children, may be refined to create a theatre performance. However, drama for learning and teaching and drama for theatre purposes each, according to Bolton (1998), belong to a 'particular *category* of acting behaviour' [emphasis added] dependent on the focus and purpose of the drama activity.

In Figure 8.1 I have attempted to show the interrelatedness of theatre activities and classroom drama but also the difference in focus and purpose. Although product involving theatre activities is an important aspect of Drama that can be focused on with children, the predominant emphasis in the classroom should be on the non-exhibitional, educational process, which includes creative drama and drama in education or process drama (as illustrated in Figure 8.1). Regardless of how classroom drama is viewed, it appears crucial to utilise whatever drama techniques and forms are available that will serve to enrich one's classroom practice and are consonant with one's learning and teaching intentions. So, while the emphasis is not on theatre performance, classroom drama can make use of theatre dimensions and skills. Focus needs to be on both drama as an Arts form and drama as a teaching method, as together they form a valuable and significant part of drama education.

CAROL CARTER WITH GINETTE PESTANA

THE ARTS

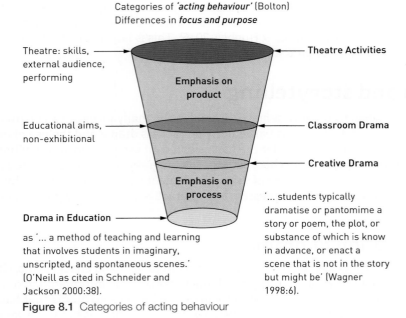

Categories of *'acting behaviour'* (Bolton)
Differences in *focus and purpose*

Theatre: skills, external audience, performing

Theatre Activities

Emphasis on product

Educational aims, non-exhibitional

Classroom Drama

Creative Drama

Emphasis on process

Drama in Education

as '... a method of teaching and learning that involves students in imaginary, unscripted, and spontaneous scenes.' (O'Neill as cited in Schneider and Jackson 2000:38).

'... students typically dramatise or pantomime a story or poem, the plot, or substance of which is know in advance, or enact a scene that is not in the story but might be' (Wagner 1998:6).

Figure 8.1 Categories of acting behaviour

Source: Carter, 2006, p.19.

Dramatic play to classroom drama

Drama has its roots in the spontaneous, imaginative dramatic play of young children in which play is used to practise and recreate the world. Children dramatically model social settings and behaviour they see in it, thereby exploring their world. They express themselves in a safe, fictional environment without risking any negative consequences (Toye & Prendiville, 2000, p.11). It is a blending and unfolding of the child's real and imagined world. While it is important to provide continuing opportunities for young children to engage in dramatic play, the teacher can become increasingly involved at different levels.

Dunn and Stinson (2012, p.120) talk about three requirements for engaging in dramatic play and drama activities for learning in early childhood. The first is 'positive, sensitive and skilled teacher involvement that is informed by a basic understanding of drama elements and structure'. The second is ensuring the drama is driven by children's interests and ideas but not constrained by them. The third is that 'children should be active co-constructors of drama and dramatic play experiences at all stages'.

The effective shift from natural dramatic play to drama, where the teacher finds ways to facilitate and extend learning, is by finding activities and ways into the children's play that are enabling versus intrusive interventions. Becoming involved to extend children's drama experience and encourage problem solving, thereby providing a balance between self-expression and teacher-guided drama, can take place at all early childhood (birth to eight) settings. I have provided some Professional Practice examples on dramatic play here.

Dramatic play

Babies and toddlers

Engage in dramatic play with babies as they explore and observe using their senses and imagination. Exploration can include playing with facial expressions, copying gestures and sounds as we say rhymes, and reading and telling stories to slowly extend their play as objects become something else (e.g. a block becomes a boat, or a carrot becomes a plane). Gentle and unobtrusive ways of engaging toddlers in dramatic play and extending their ideas include 'driving' an imaginary train together.

Pre-school and school children

Playing in the sand could be extended, for example, to a drama centred on hidden treasure or finding ways to sell sand cakes. If, for example, pre-school to Year 2 children are engaged in dramatic play concerning a shop, the teacher could enter the play as a rude, demanding shopper the 'shopkeeper' children have to deal with.

Process drama

As I discussed earlier, the predominant focus within drama in early educational settings is as a method of learning and teaching and as a way of making sense of the world. For this reason the *drama process* is of paramount importance. **Process drama** is a participatory activity where the participants explore a problem, fictional situation, theme, text or idea, often based on a social, moral and ethical dilemma, by working in and out of role. The vehicle for exploration is the artistic medium of unscripted drama (O'Neill, 1995) and there is generally no external audience. Children are free to explore a wide range of roles without having to commit to these roles.

'Drama in education' was the term used by Dorothy Heathcote and Gavin Bolton, who were responsible for the development of the way of working now also described as process drama. The term 'process drama' is closely associated with the work of Cecily O'Neill (1995) and has become widely used among drama teachers in Australia. The strengths of process drama lie in its potential value as a means for exploring, constructing and making meaning. As stated by Wagner (1998, p.8), process drama '… enables participants to look at reality through fantasy to look below the surface of actions to their meaning'. It is used to '… help children become active in understanding themselves and the world, and in creating the future' (Williams, 2002, p.6). In process drama the focus is on participation rather than on rehearsing a performance for an audience. There may be small enactments, but these are more demonstrative in nature, where individuals or small groups share their ideas with others in a dramatic form (e.g. a small group may devise and show their idea to the class via a frozen image or tableau). A real strength of using process drama is that children can have the chance to view the world through the eyes of one or more people and reflect on what they might do if they were those people.

The central purpose of process drama is to bring real-life activities and situations into the classroom in a fictional form. It is about active responses and decision making through exploring topics, issues and problems in make-believe, imagined situations such as Grandmother's birthday party. Process drama relies on the rich resources and experiences of

> **process drama**
> a participatory activity where the participants explore a problem, fictional situation, theme, text or idea, often based on a social, moral and ethical dilemma, by working in and out of role.

THE ARTS

the children themselves. Children are automatically put in the position of directly experiencing something of the world within a safe, non-threatening environment where they are allowed to make mistakes and try things over again and where '… taking on a fictional position provides distance' (Toye & Prendiville, 2000, p.64) that encourages children to explore alternatives.

Process drama takes place in the real world of the classroom and within the fictitious world created by the context. The interrelationship between these two worlds is central to the unique learning and teaching experience that process drama provides. The children's experiences are two-perspectival as they take place on two complementary levels. While experiencing what is happening from the perspective of the role they are taking during the role play, they also view what is happening from their own reality or self—in other words, the learners have access to 'a dual perception of the world' (Bolton, 1992, p.11). 'The boundaries between "self" and "other" meet and merge—the core of our humanity, the essence of compassion, the beginnings of morality, are to be found in our capacity to merge "self" with "other"' (Neelands, 2001, p.45).

Some core dimensions of process drama are:

- context of meaning and pre-texts
- role play
- building belief.

Let's look at each of these in more detail.

Context of meaning and pre-texts

The 'as if' context or *context of meaning* refers to the situation selected and used as the framework within which the learning process takes place and which provides the motivation for the learning process. It is the '… vehicle or context for teaching and learning through the fiction that is established' (Holden, 2003, p.36). For the context to be a context of meaning, the drama situation needs to be one with which children are familiar, one they can relate to, or that they can easily imagine. It is also a context of meaning as from the context, children are supplied with a motivation for exploring particular ideas or carrying out specific tasks. Within a real-life context there would, for example, be a purpose for adding numbers if the context were a shopping mall and the children had a certain amount of money to spend as shoppers. The main context for 'Grandmother's birthday' is (as if we were) at Grandmother's birthday party. Since this process drama is likely to take place over a number of days, a context of meaning on a different day would be (as if we were) on a journey.

The starting point for a process drama is a 'pre-text'. A pre-text is a stimulus for drama that may be a number of sources, including a symbol, story, picture, idea, object, photograph, or image (O'Neill, 1995). For example, if I used a photograph as a pre-text, I might ask the children to speculate on where the photograph was taken, who the people are within it, what they do, what they are called, how they talk, and so on. I would then use the information to locate and start the drama. Pre-texts for 'Grandmother's birthday' that could start the drama could be a story about Grandmother narrated by the teacher, a picture of Grandmother, a large candle as a symbol of a birthday and so on.

Role play

Role play, or taking on a role, is a process whereby participants in the drama 'step into the shoes' of someone else and take on some of the aspects of their lives. It is an effective medium for making children aware that 'people in different times felt, thought, believed and behaved differently from ourselves' (Luff, 2000, p.9). The aim of taking on a role is to give learners different perspectives to engage and learn from within the drama (Toye & Prendiville, 2000, p.63). It is different from characterisation, where the focus is on developing characters whose bearing, movement and gestures belong to them.

Characterisation, as opposed to taking on a role, involves decision making about how to best present a character to an audience through interpretation and observation. Role taking focuses predominantly on how a person thinks, feels and reacts. A person in role is therefore more concerned with attitude and viewpoint than with the outer form of the character. While characterisation will be used for other appropriate forms of drama in the classroom, the predominant focus in process drama is the taking on of a role.

A major distinguishing feature of process drama is the use of the unique teaching strategy of 'teacher-in-role'. The teacher takes on a role in the drama and co-constructs meaning with the students within a fictitious 'as-if' situation. This means that the teacher has a central function, and does not remain peripheral to the action to direct the drama from the sidelines but, rather, shares in the process, takes an active role, and can give direction and guidance from within the drama.

When children take on roles, a safe environment for practising and dealing with life experiences is created. Learners are not afraid to question and make mistakes within their roles. When teachers take on a role in the drama it allows them to step down from their status as the major source of knowledge and increases the channels of communication available in the classroom. For example, the teacher may take on the role of Ziggy the Robot with the children taking responsibility for teaching the robot (see practical examples at the end of this section). The teacher is not restricted to one role within the drama. For instance, in the 'Grandmother's birthday' drama, I initially take on the role of a family member helping to prepare for the birthday. I then take on the role of Grandmother when the actual birthday takes place.

Building belief

This refers to a variety of strategies to enhance the learners' belief in the drama situation. When the context and roles are selected, they are selected in such a way as to build into the situation an experience or a problem that will require children not only to make decisions and think of resolutions, but also to explore how they *feel* about what is happening and what they are doing.

Emotional engagement is a vital feature of process drama that links the thought and feeling domain, places the emotional at the 'heart of teaching and learning' (Norman, 2004, p.16) and encourages multiple perspectives and viewpoints. It broadens and challenges: 'the parameters of what can be seen as legitimate knowledge ... to experience and explore the issues of human concern and intellectual enquiry' (Carroll, 1988, p.21).

Mime is the art of conveying ideas without words. It is a form of non-verbal communication through which body movements, facial expressions and gestures are used to convey emotions, actions, needs and desires. Initial actions (which may be fairly superficial at first) assist young children in particular to build belief in the situation. So, for instance, active engagement in building a park (planting flowers, playground equipment etc.), farming activities (collecting eggs, herding sheep etc.), building a house and so on will lead to commitment to and belief in these places. Going about daily activities in a village, for instance, will lead to greater seriousness and commitment when the village is 'threatened'. Activities such as going on board a ship will make the ship seem more 'real'.

Although the drama context is obviously imaginary, in order to build belief and a feeling of engagement, it is important that everything else within the drama is, and feels, as 'real' as possible. 'Building belief' (making the drama feel more 'real' through a range of techniques), emotional engagement and the authenticity of the experience leads to the learners 'stumbling upon moments of authenticity' and to their being able to 'think from within a dilemma instead of talking about a dilemma' (Heathcote, 1984).

Process drama
Babies and toddlers
Babies and toddlers can be involved in a dramatic experience through the creation of a dramatic space (context of meaning) where they can touch, feel, listen to sounds and observe performance. A wonderful example of this is 'Rain' for babies by Drop Bear Company and Seam (see 'Further reading').

Ziggy the Robot
Mrs Stewart has engaged the Year 2 class in process dramas previously, so she does not need to spend time explaining the rules, how it will work and getting them to understand such aspects as taking on a role. Mrs Stewart tells the children that she is going to take on two different roles in the drama: Professor Star and Ziggy the Robot. She explains that she will be wearing large glasses when she is Professor Star and moving like a robot when she is Ziggy. She also explains that the children will be teachers working in a factory (context of meaning) that creates robots.

Mrs Stewart asks the children to close their eyes: she tells a story of how Ziggy was made (pre-text); talks them through their roles; and paints a picture of where they are as part of the belief building for this drama. At the end of the narration she says, 'When I clap my hands you will be at the robot factory and I will be Professor Star'. She claps her hands and says good morning to the teachers (students in role). As Professor Star, she uses the convention of 'hot-seating' to get the students to ask questions and find out about Professor Star and what they need to teach Ziggy. In this case, Mrs Stewart wants the children to learn about parts of speech so in role as Professor Star she explains that Ziggy cannot speak at all and so needs to learn simple words at this stage. The 'teachers' and Professor Star decide what Ziggy needs to know and create lists of verbs, nouns (etc.) that they want to teach Ziggy. The 'teachers' are divided into groups and each group takes responsibility for teaching Ziggy something different and planning how they are going to teach Ziggy and in what order. Professor Star then leaves the room but can come back at any time if things go wrong with the teaching of Ziggy.

Mrs Stewart, in role as Ziggy, enters the room. She walks around as Ziggy and, as she does not understand any vocabulary at this point, waits for the 'teachers' to help her. Professor Star can come back if nothing happens but in this, and most cases when Ziggy has been introduced to the children, the 'teachers' take responsibility. Ziggy has to be careful that she only learns what is taught to her and does not suddenly start following long instructions and using complex vocabulary. When Ziggy thinks it is time to leave she departs and Professor Star reflects with the 'teachers' on what they have taught Ziggy, what was successful and what they need to consider more carefully next time.

In other lessons Ziggy is taught more complex information such as how to make a sandwich, how to cross the road, about using money and so on.

STOP AND THINK

- What do you understand as the distinction between dramatic play and drama?
- What is your understanding of process drama?
- Looking back at the Grandmother drama, as well as examples such as Ziggy the Robot, what ideas can you think of for engaging children in a process drama using other 'as if' contexts?
- What could you get children to teach Ziggy the Robot? How might this change if the children were three or six years old?

Storytelling

Active storytelling in its simplest form is a term used to describe children enacting a story as it is being told. It is from this that interactive storytelling emerges through the medium of drama (Baldwin & Fleming, 2003, p.50). Storytelling is a human activity that occurs in our everyday lives as a significant communication and meaning-making strategy. The importance of stories and the links between literacy and reading stories to children is widely recognised. Early childhood settings are generally print-rich environments where books are shared. In their homes, children also watch stories on television and listen to audio tapes with accompanying books. What is less evident is where adults tell children stories and encourage children to tell their own stories.

Children need to be engaged in participatory storytelling practices. Both telling a story and listening to effectively told stories without the mediation of pictures and written texts provide a vehicle for children to use their imagination and visualisation. Through storytelling, children are also introduced to, and explore, oral language patterns and vocabulary, supported by movement and non-verbal gestures. It is a collaborative, interactive process that frees the storyteller to directly communicate a personal, narrative interpretation involving a flexible, 'flowing exchange' (Campbell, 2013, p.34) between teller and listeners, unencumbered by sticking strictly to a script.

The storyteller can then guide the process while giving children ownership of the story.

Through oral storytelling, children are 'initiated' into cultural practices. Exploring diverse storytelling practices with young children is a means of enriching children's understanding and appreciation of cultural customs, rituals and routines embedded within cultural identities and traditions. The strength of telling stories in education settings lies in setting up strong intercommunicative relationships, contextualising the stories to suit audience

THE ARTS

needs, using the children as characters in the stories and creating a culture and climate for story sharing. Enticing children into the world of storytelling and providing them with enabling spaces for them to tell you stories is vital. One helpful way of assisting children with storytelling structures and patterns is the convention of the 'forgetful' storyteller. The storytelling begins with, for example, 'Once upon a time there was a … oh no! I can't remember what it was, can anyone help me …?'

Crow and the Waterhole

This is an example of a participatory storytelling session based on the story *Crow and the Waterhole* (Kwaymullina, 2007).

The story is from the Bailgu and Nyamal peoples of the Pilbara region of Western Australia. It is about a crow that constantly sees what she thinks is a much better, braver crow than herself. The crow in the story does all sorts of brave and good things she thinks have been done by the other crow that she sees when she looks into first the waterhole, then the river, then a rock pool and then a rain puddle. Until Kookaburra eventually makes her see that she is, in fact, the brave and wonderful crow that she sees in the water. Selecting stories told by people of a range of cultural backgrounds is one way of extending children's intercultural understanding.

Introduction

Through the start of the story-time session, children can be introduced to and share different cultural practices and traditions where stories may start with, for example, a story-time song, traditional chant (Carter & Sallis, 2016) or some other way in which there is an indication that it is story-time. In addition to identifying and using different cultural practices to start the story and talking about where this particular story comes from, the teacher–storyteller also teaches the children the chants, along with non-verbal gestures and movements that she has created for the different parts of the story, which are as follows.

First

She looks like a crow who could change the world you know
I wish I could be like her
And I am just an ordinary crow
I wish I could be like her

Second

She looks like a crow who is very brave
I wish I could be like her
She looks like a crow who will be ready to save
I wish I could be like her

Third

She looks like a crow that has great faith in others
I wish I could be like her
She treats all like her sister and brothers
I wish I could be like her

Body of the story

Apart from the chants and keeping to the basic storyline, the teacher makes use of her own style, flexibility and audience needs to share the story with the children. During the initial telling of the story the children are encouraged to respond to the chants and to make the appropriate sound effects for the crow, fire, thunderstorm, animals and so on.

I have found that the use of a green and red arrow, which I learnt from reading Brian Way's (1985) work, is extremely effective in indicating when the sound effects are made and when the volume increases and dies down.

In the second telling the children and the teacher work together to continue with the sound effects and also to create movement. The movement is explored with the teacher and all the children participating collectively as opposed to specific children acting and the other children watching. Thereafter, depending on the age or experiences of the children, the storytelling can be extended by the children.

To be most effective, the story should include unanswered questions and/or a sense of the unknown/mystery. This encourages children to try out possible scenarios based on the unresolved or unknown aspects of the narrative. Rather than retelling the narrative in dramatic form, in process drama children are asked to consider other possibilities for the story. For example, the teacher might ask children questions such as, 'What might have happened to the crow in the past that led to the events in the story?' or 'Where might Crow, Kookaburra and the other characters be in six months' time?' Children create their own beginnings or endings to the story. Older children can each be given a section of the story to perform with slight changes (e.g. different characters, locations, time frames and so on). They form a circle around the classroom (performance carousel) and each group performs their piece in order, flowing from one group to the other.

Visual Art and Media Arts

We all have a personal stake in the Arts and in the artworks that are around us. Every one of us is able to take others on a journey of the Arts in our lives. We do not have to see ourselves as 'good at art' in order to engage children in and with art. However, we do need to have an awareness, understanding and appreciation of art and be involved personally in art in some form. You may be thinking at this point that you have no art in your lives. So let me try to convince you that this is not the case. While we may not all have a connection to famous paintings, in addition to having access to art galleries and exhibitions, we all have access to art in our lives. Art is all around us, in nature and in the way we capture special memories in nature. Art is also in the artworks and collections found in our homes.

The aesthetic and utilitarian nature of the Arts is frequently combined, for example, flower arranging, tablecloth painting, creating and laying out of food, clothing, fashion, make-up, room decoration and designing a bedroom—all are examples of aspects of art. People have different perspectives and lenses with which they view art. In giving children opportunities to engage in, and appreciate, artwork, we are moving towards a humanising pedagogy that uses and embraces the oldest forms of sharing and communication.

CAROL CARTER WITH GINETTE PESTANA

STOP AND REFLECT

- What is the role and importance of the Arts in your life?
- How does art touch and inform your life?
- What would you consider to be art?

visual art art forms that are viewed and created for visual perception.

media arts relies on technological aspects and digital materials to creatively communicate stories and explore concepts. Identifying media and technology for a variety of purposes and audiences are important considerations.

Defining Visual Art and Media Arts

Visual art is art forms that are viewed and created for visual perception, so they appeal predominantly to the visual senses and can generally exist in a permanent form. They include visual forms such as painting, drawing, collage, printmaking, sculpture, ceramics, craft, photography, textiles and electronic media, through 'which we communicate to others—we express our feelings, aspirations and dreams, and we attempt to make sense of our ever changing world' (Gibson & Ewing, 2011, p.130). **Media arts** relies on technological aspects and digital materials to creatively communicate stories and explore concepts. Identifying media and technology for a variety of purposes and audiences are important considerations. 'Media artists represent the world using platforms such as television, film, radio, video games, the internet and mobile media' (ACARA, 2011). Communication is at the heart of what has been expressed in terms of both Visual and Media Arts in the above definitions.

Table 8.1 Approaches to visual arts in the early years

PRODUCTIVE	REPRODUCTIVE
Child-centred	Teacher-regulated and unidirectional
Self-expression and creativity	Didactical control and direct imitation
Accessible Art Media	Teacher decides materials/use
Spontaneous, free, 'hands-on', choice	Focus on skills and behaviour
Maturationist and non-interventionist	Routinised and scripted

GUIDED LEARNING	
Teachers as resources	
Blend of unfolding and education	
Free play, careful guiding, inspiration and critical reflection	
Observe, describe, suggest or initiate	

Approaches to visual arts in the early years can be productive, reproductive or through guided learning, as illustrated in Table 8.1 (adapted from Wright, 2003). The approach I most favour is the guided learning approach as it provides the balance between self-expression and teacher-guided activities. That is not to say that the other approaches do not have their place and, particularly in the early years, space needs to be provided for productive self-expression that is not guided by the teacher.

STOP AND THINK

- What do you think are some of the similarities that link visual art and media arts?
- What distinguishes media arts from visual art?
- What distinguishes visual art from performing arts such as drama, dance and music?

Literacy and art

Various stages that children progress through in relation to drawing have been identified by, among others, Lowenfield and Brittain (1987), Derham (1986) and Kellog (1979). Socio-cultural construction of knowledge influences the way children draw, and ages at which children draw in particular ways is dependent on individual children and contexts. The nature of drawings in early childhood is frequently stage specific but not necessarily age specific.

While there are different names for particular forms of drawing, they all display similar orders in which children learn to draw.

LOWENFIELD & BRITTAIN	DERHAM	KELLOG
Disordered scribbling Controlled scribbling	Manipulative stage	Placement stage
Named scribbling	Symbolic scribbling	Shape stage
Early recognisable (pre-schematic)	Recognisable stage	Pictorial stage

All children around the world scribble. At first they are simply exploring, manipulating and beginning to understand the idea of putting marks on paper and may take great delight in watching the colours or lines appear. A child's first experience with a crayon is a sensorimotor experience and an exploration with their hands, eyes and mouth. This exploration may involve banging, throwing, grabbing and mouthing. The first scribbles are simply enjoyable kinaesthetic activities and, given the opportunity, they will draw on their hands or smear paint on their faces. These early scribbles are not initially attempts at communicating or portraying the visual world. The child who is starting to scribble is just beginning to get to know the drawing tools and is interested in its properties rather than what it can do. The random marks on the paper are usually a result of encouragement. Marks are often light coloured in nature and can be a result of banging. Such activities as exploring with making marks with crayon and paper and finger-painting are enjoyable and important for young children.

Gradually, they begin to achieve greater fine-motor coordination, and random scribbles begin to take on definite shapes, and repetitive marks and symbols are drawn. The first marks on paper, which move from random scribbles to more clearly defined shapes and symbols, are children's first form of written communication. Marks gradually become more arranged and significant as children become more proficient and focused on the drawing. Children produce simple shapes including circles, crosses and star-bursts. They start to name their scribbles, which is an important component of the development of literacy. Responses to children's artwork is crucial and should be descriptive and reflective in nature; they should never be judgmental.

The first representational attempt, providing a clear record of children's thought processes, is generally a person with a circle for the head and two vertical lines for legs. Shapes for eyes and arms drawn straight from the circle body are drawn. For most children this occurs at around three years of age and thereafter they continue to search for new concepts, so symbols constantly change and become more complex to include more clearly recognisable representations of objects, and they use their imaginations to name and communicate through the artwork themselves and the stories they tell about their artwork.

It is the interrelationship between drawing, talking and linking visual representations to writing and reading that is crucial to beginning literacy, as was discussed to some extent in Chapter 7. If we are to value art in our and children's lives, and prepare children for multimodal twenty-first century forms of literacy that provide opportunities for multidimensional meaning-making, we need to move away from a hierarchical view. This hierarchical view sees writing as the end point and dominant form of literacy for children. Within this view, drawing is merely seen as a vehicle for assisting children to decode and encode the written word. So, for instance, once children have learnt to put their ideas into written form, they are frequently encouraged to no longer make use of different visual

art forms to make meaning, even though these art forms were previously viewed as being crucial. Mackenzie and Veresov (2013) describe a transition process where drawing as the primary form of communication shifts to an illustrative or supportive role, to eventually no longer being required for communication.

Arts elements

Children need to be assisted to consider, explore and think about, in an enabling as opposed to prescriptive way, various media, such as paint or clay and elements of art including colour, line, shape, space and texture. Some of the 'Further reading' that I have included at the end of the chapter pay attention to these various arts elements and provide interesting practical examples. What I have included here are lesson examples created by Initial Teacher Education students as part of a children's art folio assessment task.

What follows is one out of a potential ten activities where a pre-service teacher drew on the work of various artists as inspiration for the artwork of pre-school children in her assessment task. This is followed by a lesson example from a different pre-service teacher as an example of exploring lines with toddlers.

Wrapped landscapes

Learning Outcome 2: *Children are connected with and contribute to their world*

Learning Outcome 4: *Children are confident and involved learners (DEEWR, 2009, pp.25 & 33)*

This experience helps children to understand the element of space in artworks as well as developing their spatial understanding ability to mentally recreate their physical space. Examining their world from different perspectives contributes to spatial understanding (Yelland et al., 1999, p.14)

Inspiration

- The large-scale instillation of Belgian and French artists Christo and Jeanne-Claude (see http://christojeanneclaude.net/artworks/realized-projects)

Intention

- For children to view their environment from a different perspective and capture their new understandings of their own and artistic space, using a digital camera

Materials

- Large drop sheets of materials, large enough to drape over large objects in the kindergarten environment, and digital cameras

Invitation/process

Using a conversation about the works of Christo and Jeanne-Claude as a provocation, children are invited to change the existing outdoor space, covering up structures and objects to create new perspectives. Educators engage children in conversations around the use of space and about framing a scene to photograph.

CAROL CARTER WITH GINETTE PESTANA

THE ARTS

Reflection

I found that children have a lot of questions about the motivation behind Christo and Jeanne-Claude's works. 'Why did they cover everything in material?' is a common question. I found that when we began to talk about trying the art experience, they had lots of ideas about what and how we could wrap. Though we gave them choices, all the children chose to venture outside with their experience. The photos the children took of their spaces were wonderfully framed! Had

we had access to larger pieces of material some even more thought-provoking pieces would have materialised. The experience did feel limited by the size of the materials and the interference on others' play outside.

Example: Making tracks

This activity is part of an integrated sequence of activities undertaken with toddlers who displayed an interest in trains. It was set up to explore artistic expression and create and reflect on the lines created by toy trains.

Equipment and resources
Paint
Toy trains
Paper smocks

Links to Learning Outcomes (DEECD, 2011)

Learning

4.1.4: Children follow and extend their own interests with enthusiasm, energy and concentration (by following their interest in trains to create artwork)

4.2.5: Children manipulate objects and experiment with cause and effect, trial and error and motion (by experimenting with lines using toy trains)

4.3.1: Children engage with and co-construct learning

Communication

5.1.3: Children use language and representations from play, music and art to share and project meaning

5.3.3: Children use the creative arts, such as drawing and painting, to express ideas and make meaning (children explore with train tracks to explore meaning and use language to talk about line)

Method

Paint pots are filled with paint and toy trains replace the paintbrushes on the paint stand. Children can use the trains to make marks and lines on the paper.

Teaching strategies

Co-construct learning and explore what marks the trains make on paper, use open-ended questioning to engage in the process and promote abstract thinking and apply language to the task, e.g. Tell me about what you're painting; What kind of lines is the train making? What different kinds of lines have you made? Did you drive the train in straight or curly lines? Are they thick or thin? Are they long or short? What do you notice about the marks? What is the difference between the lines made by your train and lines you draw?

Personal reflection on the activity

This experience was enjoyed by the toddlers particularly because it involved a current interest in trains. The activity turned into a messy play experience as hands were dipped into the paint and children continued to explore different ways of making lines and marks on the paper.

Other ideas

Different media for drawing lines and ways of making lines

Direction and appearance

Other artwork exploring lines

Tyre and Roller Printing Work with threads and wool

Glue trails and dribbles line collage

Music and Dance

Ginette Pestana

Walk into any early childhood setting and you are bound to hear someone singing, or music being played and children dancing to it. The use of music and dance is ingrained in early childhood practices and present in early years school settings. Music and dance engage children, provide enjoyment and support their development. To use music and dance successfully in early learning, one must understand the activities purpose and use effective teaching strategies. Almost anyone can sing and dance with children; it is the quality that needs to be addressed.

In this section, best practices of music and dance activities, together with the critical role of the teacher, are discussed. Not only do teachers have to understand the developmental ability of children in music and dance, they also need to recognise and facilitate learning and skill development. They need to see music and dance's potential and explore its possibilities. We will learn the definition of 'active' music-making and how this translates across to different musical activities. Then we will explore the fundamentals of dance and how it manifests in the classroom.

Active music-making

Before the development of modern technology, which enables access to the world's greatest music, most of us were active music-makers: singing, playing instruments and dancing together in our homes or communities. Now, the way we engage with music has become

THE ARTS

CAROL CARTER WITH GINETTE PESTANA

more passive (Niland, 2015a), and the common musical engagements with children are listening or singing along with recorded music. Although there are some benefits to these types of musical engagement, they do not harness the full potential of the contribution of musical engagement towards children's development. Through active music-making, the brain is stimulated, feel-good hormones are released and new skills are learnt. Children's lives are enriched as they learn more about themselves, bond with others and develop cultural awareness (Dinham, 2015).

Active music-making involves interactive, enjoyable musical activities that resonate with children. It provides opportunities for children to perform or try out new skills and gain recognition and confidence in their abilities. It serves as a platform for sharing and receiving positive affirmation from peers, which contributes towards developing interpersonal bonds and solidarity in pursuing shared goals. In the classroom this must start as early as possible. It should be sustained over a long period of time, include group work and performance opportunities, focus on developing an increasing understanding of music elements, and consider children's interests and music genre preferences (Hallam, 2016).

Active music-making with children requires teachers to be familiar with the elements of music so they can musically nurture young children (Greata, 2006). Every musical activity automatically uses different music elements and an informed teacher will help identify and enhance the understanding of these.

Music elements
The key music elements are:

- *duration (beat, rhythm, tempo):* the organisation of sound and silence using beat (regular rhythmic pulse), rhythm (patterns of sound and silence) and tempo (speed of music)
- *pitch (melody, harmony):* the relative highness or lowness of sound. Pitch occurs horizontally (as in a melody) and vertically (as in harmony)
- *dynamics and expression:* the relative volume (loudness) and intensity of sound and the way sound is articulated and interpreted
- *form and structure:* the plan or design of a piece of music described by identifying what is the same and what is different, and the ordering of ideas in the piece
- *timbre (tone colour):* the particular tone, colour or quality that distinguishes a sound or combinations of sounds
- *texture:* the layers of sound in a musical work and the relationship between them.

Adapted from http://www.australiancurriculum.edu.au/the-arts.

Active listening

music is an aural art form that involves the organisation of sound originating from vocals and/or instruments to express ideas or emotions.

Music is an aural art form that involves the organisation of sound originating from vocals and/or instruments to express ideas or emotions and give pleasure to listeners. Since music is an auditory experience, the development of all music skills involves actively listening to music. Active listening is the cornerstone for developing musical ability and serves as a foundation for singing, playing instruments and creating music. It is differentiated from passive listening, where the exposure to music does not elicit a response or a level of engagement. Music played in the background is a classic example of passive listening. By contrast, active listening is a learnt skill that young children need to learn. It involves more than just *hearing* the music. It involves listening with an understanding of the music—appreciating and understanding the music elements and how they combine to form a unique piece of music.

This Chinese character for the word 'listen' with the combination of symbols—eyes, ear, undivided attention and heart—epitomises its meaning. Most of us can hear, but few of us actually really listen. Listening requires one's full attention with a clear focus and intensity. We listen not only with our ears, but with our eyes, mind and heart. Listening to music implies a certain closeness or intimacy with the music that enables us to develop a deeper understanding of it and supports us in developing a relationship with it.

Babies are born ready to listen. In fact, hearing develops in the womb at sixteen weeks. Once born, babies can already differentiate their mother's voice. As they grow, children absorb music and develop a listening vocabulary to help them interpret, and eventually make, music. Active listening needs to be practised over a long period of time due to its complexity. To teach it effectively, one must first understand the components of listening; select appropriate activities to support the skill development; and then use practical techniques to facilitate engagement.

Key practical techniques include providing a conducive environment and using good-quality sound equipment; modelling good listening (i.e. teachers show, through their body language and actions how the music affects them); repetition, where multiple hearings help children absorb the music and scaffold their learning; identifying key aspects of the music; providing a road map for listening and supporting less confident students; and providing key directives of the expectations you have of children while they are listening to the music.

TO LISTEN

Ear — 聽 — You / Eyes / Undivided Attention / Heart

THE ARTS

Auditory Awareness

- *Recognising the presence of sound*

Asking children to be aware of and identify the sounds in the classroom

Auditory Discrimination

- *Distinguishing between sounds*

Listening to a piece of music with contrasting dynamics and asking the children to show the contrast with their body

Auditory Memory and Sequencing

- *Ability to recall a series of sounds in given order*

Play a series of sounds, e.g. sounds of animals and ask the children to remember the sequence

Auditory Imagination

- *Use aural memory to produce new sounds*

Creating a soundscape using voices or instruments to accompany a story

CAROL CARTER WITH GINETTE PESTANA

Active listening

Under threes

Create a night sky with a piece of blue translucent cloth and scattered star shapes on it. Have children lie, sit or stand underneath it. Tell them that this is the night sky and you are going to play some night music for them to listen to. Play appropriate music, such as 'Moonlight Sonata' by Beethoven or 'Clair de Lune' by Debussy—or simply sing 'Twinkle, Twinkle Little Star' and watch children's responses as they listen.

Pre-schoolers and school children

Prepare children by suggesting they close their eyes to listen to a piece of music. Tell them the music they will be listening to tells the story of a boy called Peer going on a journey and having a big adventure. Ask them to listen out for how the music changes. Play 'In the Hall of the Mountain King' from the Peer Gynt suite by Edvard Grieg once (http://www.youtube.com/watch?v=pPLXNmKvLBQ). Ask children what was the same and what was different about the music (repetitive motif; got faster and louder). Listen to the music again and ask children to say 'stop' when they hear something the same or different happening to the music. Confirm what they are hearing. Then ask children what kind of adventure they think the boy was having. After a discussion, tell children that you are going to play the music again, but this time they should show you the adventure Peer is having.

Active listening is an important skill that is sadly often overlooked as a form of music-making in the classroom. All children, regardless of their music ability, should have the opportunity to participate in the experience to create their own understanding and interpretation.

Singing *to*, *with* and *for* children

Singing is the primary form of music-making for children and those caring for or teaching them. Children are born ready to sing. Before the age of one, a young child can match tonal sounds, and recognise and differentiate melodies and rhythms. Singing starts from birth, beginning with cooing, then babbling, experimenting with vocal sounds and inflections, imitation and creating.

Singing presents a challenge to many pre-service teachers. The number of times I have heard in my classes 'I can't sing' is a testimony to their high skill expectations and lack of confidence. It is important to understand, though, that singing is just an action, not a talent. It is a learnt skill and the earlier it is taught, the better. Singing involves the complex use of many small and unobservable muscles, and inappropriate use of them could lead to vocal damage. Good techniques include correct breathing and posture to support the singing voice. Good breathing techniques involve engaging the abdominal and intercostal muscles to help maximise lung capacity to inhale and control exhalation. Good posture involves keeping your torso straight—try to imagine a string pulling you up by the head like a marionette. These techniques should be modelled by the teacher and instilled in children from the start.

Singing in the classroom can be *to*, *with* and *for* children. Each of these words implies a different form of singing and helps us understand the purpose of singing. Singing *to* children is a personal, intimate activity usually conducted on a one-to-one basis or with a small group. Singing *to* a baby or toddler could be in the form of a familiar song to soothe an anxious or upset child or a lullaby to sing them to sleep. With eye contact and undivided attention from the carer, young children respond with interest and focus and build strong attachments. Modelling by singing *to* older children is done in anticipation that they will learn the song. In order to be successful, it is important to choose songs that are simple, within children's vocal range and that have appeal.

Singing *with* children suggests that teacher and children sing together. This is a big sing-song: favourites are requested and everyone joins in. It creates moments of togetherness and a sense of belonging. The use of familiar songs taps into aesthetic enjoyment and shared knowledge, creates an interactive environment and helps develop relationships through social interactions (Niland, 2015b).

Singing *for* children is when a song is performed for children that they enjoy listening to but that is currently beyond their ability. These songs will contribute towards their listening repertoire and enhance their musical neural network (Greata, 2006). They are songs the teacher enjoys singing and will sing with expression. They could be song tales (see 'My Aunt Came Back' at www.youtube.com/watch?v=-lj1zSP7dTw), special songs passed down from family members or from children's cultural backgrounds, or songs that teach musical concepts.

Singing along with recorded music does not have the same value as singing by yourself or with simple accompaniment. Try turning off the CD player and find out if children are actually singing or just mouthing the words. Singing *to*, *with* and *for* children are valuable singing experiences and should be included in any musical experience, from birth to school age.

How to teach a song

There are basically three ways to teach a song: by *rote*, *immersion* or *reading* (Flohr, 2010). Teaching a song by *rote* involves the teacher singing the whole song first, then breaking it down and getting children to echo or sing it back line by line. Lines are then combined gradually. Once children are confident of the melody of each line, the song is put back together. This approach is best done with songs that are short and have clear phrases. This approach is deceptively simple, but it does require the teacher to have a thorough knowledge of the song and the skill to break it down and sing it accurately. This is the cornerstone of the Kodály approach (www.kodaly.org.au/).

The *immersion* approach is quite simple: the song is sung several times and children pick it up gradually. To make the repetition of the song engaging for children, add some variety to it. For example, ask them to sing it louder or softer, faster or slower, using different types of voices, or doing different actions for each variation. Singing games are also very effective. Children might have sung the song twenty times without realising it before it is their turn. Some examples can be found at https://mysongfile.com/songs and www.singinggamesforchildren.com/.

Singing by *reading* notation is a skill that can be learnt but is best taught after listening and singing skills have been developed. This is based on the fundamental belief of 'sound before symbol'. Reading notation is very much like learning to read. We need to hear the sounds first before relating them to abstract symbols.

When using any of these approaches, the teacher must know the song thoroughly to guide and correct children so they are able to sing with confidence, enjoyment and enthusiasm. Making eye contact and using positive facial expressions keeps children engaged and focused. Providing the starting notes helps to guide everyone to start singing at the right

THE ARTS

Table 8.2 Guidelines for appropriate singing activities

APPROXIMATE AGE RANGE	DESIRED SINGING SKILL	SINGING TO	SINGING WITH	SINGING FOR
Under 2s	• Learning how to use their voice • Listening	• Vocal play • Lullabies • Tickles • Wiggles • Peek-a-boo	• Nursery rhymes • Action songs	• Special songs • Cultural songs • Short, simple songs with limited note range and simple rhythms
3–5 years	• Following simple melodic contours and rhythm patterns • Listening	• Short, simple songs with limited note range	• Nursery rhymes • Action songs • Finger plays • Song games • Simple songs	• Special songs • Cultural songs • Simple songs with wider note range and more complex rhythms
5–8 years	• Following more complex melodic contours and rhythm patterns • Listening	• Simple songs with wider note range and more complex rhythms	• Nursery rhymes • Action songs • Song games • Simple and complex songs	• Special songs • Cultural songs • Songs with more complex melody lines and rhythms

pitch. The songs selected should be relevant to young children, tuneful and within children's vocal range. Start with simple melodic lines with fewer notes and progressively get more complex as children's skills increase.

When choosing a song or type of singing activity, also take into consideration the desired singing skill and children's capability. The desired skill provides a focus for the activity. Table 8.2 presents guidelines to help select appropriate singing activities.

Sound exploration and instrument playing

Children are fascinated by sound. They respond to it and they love to make it. Give a child an object and immediately they begin to use their senses to find out what they can do with it. Many of us have seen the look of joy or surprise on a child's face when they discover they have made a sound with an object and that they can make it again.

Music is part of these sounds. It is an aural art form that involves the arrangement of sounds in an organised way to create a unique piece of music. This arrangement combines music elements such as rhythm, pitch, tempo, dynamics, timbre and expression in various ways. Children, through their exploration of sound, begin to develop an understanding of musical concepts as they play loud and soft sounds, high and low sounds and different types of sounds (Greata, 2006).

Sound exploration

Sound exploration is an important first step for young children to take before they can play or further experiment with an object. It is a natural gateway for introducing and nurturing music in young children but, unfortunately, it is often not included in curriculum planning or recognised in practice.

Teachers have an important role in recognising and supporting children's sound exploration. They need to provide appropriate materials in a suitable space, and give children time to explore and support the exploration, which needs to be carefully planned. For example, if the intent is to expose children to different timbres, different types of sound makers will be needed. If the intent is to introduce dynamics, a variety of loud and soft sound makers should be provided.

Care must be taken to select good-quality sound makers that are robust enough to ensure the safety of children. The creation of a permanent sound centre away from quiet activity areas gives children an opportunity to explore sounds for as long as they want to. The teacher should be actively interested in what children are doing and always refer to what they are doing as making *sounds* not *noise*. The teacher should question children, commenting on what they are doing, demonstrating other sounds that can be made and imitating children's actions to affirm them. In other words, they should be attuned to the interests and desires of the children and responsive to encouraging exchanges.

In a beautiful video (at http://inspire-music.org/) a child plays a gathering drum with his father and grandparents, who copy him, thereby affirming the child's actions, and the attuned conversation between the adults and the child support his confidence and well-being. Teachers should also be responsive to spontaneous sound explorations by children. I observed some young children in childcare waiting for their lunch at a table. One child started tapping a steady beat on the table with his hands and the others soon joined in. The teachers immediately responded by telling the children that they were making too much noise and asked them to stop. Can you imagine what could have happened if the teachers had joined in and together they had created a lunchtime rap? It would have been a fantastic opportunity to nurture and support the children's creativity and music interest.

Instrument playing

Instrument playing also starts with exploration. Put an instrument in a child's hand and they naturally want to explore it. Many times I have seen teachers distribute instruments to children and then ask them not to play until they are told to rather than letting them try them out. Given children's natural inquisitiveness and excitement at being given an instrument, telling them to wait is inappropriate and likely to dampen their enthusiasm. Think of the message it sends them.

There are several do's and don'ts to consider when introducing instruments in the classroom:

- Do make sure the instruments are durable, safe and of good sound quality.
- Do ensure children are developmentally able to handle playing the instruments. For example, there is little value in introducing 'boomwhackers' (musical plastic tubes) or a trumpet to very young children as they lack the physical strength and coordination to play them.
- Do provide enough instruments to enable all children to play them during the session.
- Do model how to respect and treat instruments by placing them away gently rather than throwing them into a box.
- Do teach cues to start and stop playing so you have a space to provide instructions or information.
- Do demonstrate how to get the best sound from instruments or the correct way of handling them after children have experimented.
- Don't expect very young children to understand turn-taking and waiting. Try to accommodate this by providing similar instruments for all of them.

CAROL CARTER WITH GINETTE PESTANA

THE ARTS

Percussion instruments are usually the first instruments to be introduced to young children. These instruments are scraped, shaken or struck to produce rhythmic sounds. There are two types of percussion instruments: untuned and tuned. Untuned instruments do not have a set pitch and include body percussion (e.g. clapping, stomping, finger clicking and knee patting); found objects (things you can make a sound with, e.g. saucepan lids); woods (e.g. rhythm sticks); metals (e.g. triangles); skins (e.g. drums); shakers (e.g. maracas); and scrapers (e.g. guiros). Tuned instruments are able to carry a melody line and include pianos, melodic bells, boomwhackers, xylophones, glockenspiels and metallophones.

Instruments can be used in the classroom to guide learning—for example, they can be used to create a loud thunderclap or falling rain to get children actively involved in a story and provide an opportunity to express themselves. When I asked my class of pre-service early childhood teachers to tell me a story about a rainstorm using percussion instruments they used the instruments in various ways to create drama and scenes, tapping into their repertoire of listening experiences for inspiration. I recall one pre-service teacher telling me that she tried this out with the children she teaches and it didn't work. During our discussion to determine why, I discovered that the children were two-year-olds. Understanding children's ability and their ways of learning and knowing plays a huge role in selecting appropriate activities and how to introduce concepts. Much work must be done in the sound exploration stage to develop a bank of listening repertoires before knowledge can be transferred.

Next, children progress to learning how music is organised by using instruments to illustrate different music elements. They can be asked to play the beat or rhythm of a song; play a song softly or loudly or vary the tempo; or play different instruments at different times to understand timbre (see 'Sounds and instruments'). This type of musical play supports children's learning of coordination, ordering and classifying.

Sounds and instruments

Pre-school children

Choose a song or poem that suggests different sounds—for example, 'Rain on the green grass'. First, prepare children by doing different actions to each line; then clap the words and transfer those actions and claps to different instruments.

POEM	SUGGESTED ACTIONS	SUGGESTED INSTRUMENTS TO PLAY THE RHYTHM (WORDS)
Rain on the green grass	Use fingers to portray falling rain	shakers or rainstick
Rain on the trees	Use arms to make the shape of tree branches	triangle
Rain on the house tops	Make a roof shape with your arms above your head and touch fingers together	rhythm sticks or claves
But not on me	Wave arms in a windscreen wiper motion	drums

Variations can be made by changing the dynamics to make loud or soft rain sounds or making the last line a strong statement.

Making and performing music

Richard Gill, the well-known music educator and advocate, said in a TEDx talk (Gill, 2011) that we must get children 'to try to understand that the most important thing about music is to make your own music'. He explained that making music opens children's minds in an extraordinary way and lets them move into a very special world of thinking. It takes them into another realm: one that is natural, one that nurtures their aesthetic sensibilities, one that provides opportunity for creative expression, one that allows for heightened understanding and appreciation, and one that is deeply meaningful and rewarding (Dinham, 2015). It is an experience that every child can be part of, regardless of their abilities and experience.

From a very young age, children make music, either with their voices—humming and singing little tunes—or with any object that can make a sound. This creative skill is lost if the practice of teaching music only includes *reproducing* music. Providing opportunities for making or creating music lies primarily in the hands of the teacher, who needs to recognise its importance and support opportunistic episodes; prepare and equip children with skills; be ready to learn from children; and provide a rich, supportive environment. It is a reciprocal relationship and one that is highly fluid, and the teacher must resist the urge to take over.

A starting point for making music with young children is discovering sound and building a sound repertoire. Children are then provided with opportunities to make sounds, either with their voices, with found objects or with musical instruments. These provide the 'aural palette' from which different sounds can be combined to form an aural picture (McMillan, 1992). Through imitation and experimentation, children then start to spontaneously invent or improvise music. As their skills and abilities develop, they will be ready to finalise their music and document it, and become little composers of music.

There is no right or wrong way to make music: every child's effort is valued and accepted for its own worth. A piano teacher friend of mine shared with me how she was teaching her grandchildren to play the piano. As well as teaching them the technical skills and pieces, she got her grandchildren to make music. She started by asking them to make up a tune. The first version was merely a series of notes. She then asked them to make it interesting by changing the length of the notes—some shorter and others longer. Next she asked them to experiment with the expression (making some notes louder and some softer) and the articulation (short, choppy sounds or smoothly moving from note to note). This resulted in another version of the same notes. She then played the original version and asked them to compare it with the latest version. 'It's a different song; the latest version is so much nicer and more interesting,' they said with pride. This is what makes music, Music. Applying what you know and creating something allows you freedom of expression, ownership and pride in your accomplishment, as well as depth of understanding.

Dance and young children

Children and movement are inseparable. Children respond naturally to music, bopping their heads to the beat or dancing freely. When we use our bodies as an instrument for expression and communication, we are not just moving, we are dancing. Dance is described as an 'inside awareness of movement' (Stinson, 1988, p.3), where the shape the body makes becomes a conscious process. It involves purposeful, intentionally rhythmic, culturally patterned, nonverbal body movements that go beyond the function of moving and hold aesthetic value

THE ARTS

CAROL CARTER WITH GINETTE PESTANA

(Hanna, 1987). Dance is using the body as a vehicle for expression and each movement is a deliberate act. It is deeply satisfying and has been used for centuries as a ritualistic form of social bonding, for cultural identification and for communication purposes. Dance is associated with many benefits, which include psychomotor, cognitive, affective and social benefits. It allows universal access to communicating personal and social expression. Dance has the capacity to engage, inspire and enrich children's learning, supporting embodied thinking, multimodal semiosis, multifocal relating and peer scaffolding (Deans, 2016).

Despite all these benefits, dance is rarely featured as part of the early childhood curriculum. This could partly be due to a lack of understanding of what dance embodies and the mistaken belief that 'creative movement' equals dance. Creative movement involves offering open-ended activities that provide opportunities for participants to respond through movement, with the intention of developing body and spatial awareness. It is exploring movement without being organised to express intent, and is more functional and random in nature (Dinham, 2015). For example, the teacher might play some music and ask children to move like fishes swimming in the sea.

Movement alone cannot be considered as dance, but all dance involves movement. It is the raw material that makes up dance, just as music is made up of sound. Good understanding of movement/dance elements will enable the teacher to build children's capacity for movement ideas and vocabulary and turn them into rich and meaningful dance experiences (Stinson, 1988). Dance consists of different combinations of these elements, and changing any one element changes the dance experience and the inner awareness of the dancer. It communicates an entirely different experience.

Dance elements

Basic dance elements include body, space, time, dynamics and relationships. They answer the questions, What? (body awareness); Where? (space); When? (time); How? (dynamics) and With whom? (relationships).

The body is the vehicle for expression and children must be allowed to discover what their bodies can do. What can they do to move from one spot to another? (e.g. walk, run, jump) What can they do without travelling? (e.g. bend, stretch, melt) What shape can the body make? (e.g. twisted, curled, long) What parts of their body can they move? (e.g. head, fingers, elbows)

Space is where the body moves, and it involves making choices to express or communicate an idea. Children develop understandings of personal space and maintaining that within group spaces. This is a challenging skill for many children as they seem to be attracted to one another and can't help bumping into each other. The body can also move at different levels, such as creeping or crawling on the floor and walking on tiptoes. The body can move in six different directions—forwards, backwards, left and right, and up and down—and it can use different pathways to move, such as straight, curved, zigzag or any combination of these.

Time is the duration, or speed, and rhythm of movement. The duration of movement or stillness could be long or short; the speed could be fast or slow, or getting faster or slower; and the rhythm provides the organisational pattern that gives order to the dance by responding to the beat or rhythm.

How the body moves refers to the quality of movement or the energy expended in movement. Movement can have weight—for example, walking deliberately like an elephant, or creeping like a mouse—or flow that is bound or constrained—such as the controlled or deliberate actions of a robot toy—or a distinct quality, which could be sudden and forceful, like an upward punch, or sustained, like a floating balloon.

Dance involves having different relationships with the dancer's own body parts (e.g. swinging your arms when skipping); with partners or groups involving space (e.g. side by side, facing each other, holding hands, formations); with time (e.g. in unison or after a time delay); and with props, equipment and the environment (e.g. dancing with a scarf or moving around different props on the dance space).

Dance experiences in the classroom

Dance is praxis-based. It involves the application of skills through practice or simply by 'doing'. The range of dance experiences that can be introduced in the classroom is very wide and varies in depth. In the early years, much time is spent understanding and gaining physical mastery of the body and developing movement vocabulary. However, to realise the full potential of dance, one must move away from just providing creative movement opportunities and allow children to make their own dance. Children must learn to be reflective: to examine how they are expressing themselves or what they are communicating. They also need to develop an aesthetic appreciation for dance to deepen their response and understanding of dance contexts and motivations (Dinham, 2015).

Careful planning is required to guide children through a meaningful dance experience. First, the learning outcomes must be carefully chosen to reflect the desired skills and knowledge to be gained by the children. Next, an idea is usually chosen to provide a stimulus for the dance experience. This could be in the form of words, sounds, visuals, kinaesthetic concepts or props. This provides a starting point to interest children and start them thinking about how to translate the stimulus material into movement. The content of a typical dance class involves an introduction, development, culminating dance and closure. The introduction serves as a transition from the previous subject and includes a warm-up and the introduction of the idea.

The development stage frames a series of tasks designed to enable children to learn and create movements through exploring various elements of dance that are linked back to the lesson's outcomes and lead into the culminating dance. This stage of dance draws from previous experiences and provides structure. There should be a beginning, middle and end, and different forms such as narrative, expressing feelings, abstract, and so on. Children should also be allowed the opportunity to perform their dance in whatever format they choose: solo, pairs or groups. The closure is as important as the other parts of the class. It brings a conclusion to the session and provides the teacher with an opportunity to assess children's learning. A cooling down session helps to regulate the body, and the provision of some form of reflection allows for deeper understanding and appreciation. Deans (2016) used reflective storytelling as a means to engage children in critical thinking processes in her dance classes. Asking children to draw their dance experience allowed them to articulate and become conscious of their choices and thinking.

Other aspects that need to be considered in planning dance sessions include the choice of accompaniment, appropriate props or equipment, and safe dance practices and practicabilities. Appropriate accompaniment either in the form of music or sound provides the backdrop for reinforcing concepts. Recorded music is usually a first choice but the voice is also a versatile instrument that can express the different qualities of movement, and a simple drum or tambourine can bring out these expressive qualities. The use of props or

THE ARTS

equipment can support dance experiences. They are not critical to the dance experience but might add some flavour to help initiate, extend, accompany or coax the reluctant dancer. Scarves are my favourite prop as they are so versatile—they can be thrown and caught, waved, swished, used to explore space and connect with others or emphasise movements. Finally, as dance involves movement and a group of children, it is encumbered with practical challenges. The dance space must be adequate and appropriate for the number of children in the class; the class size should be manageable for the teacher to address children's specific needs; and children should be dressed in clothes that allow for freedom of movement while maintaining personal dignity. Establishing rules will encourage sensible, safe and appropriate behaviour.

'Falling Leaves'
Pre-school and early primary
Movement objective
For children to become more aware of the shapes their body can make individually and in groups; and how these shapes can travel and be expressed over different levels.
Lesson structure

TIME	TASK	ACTIVITY
5 mins	Introduction of idea and sharing lesson outcomes	Show children 3–4 different leaves. Pick them up and drop them to see how each leaf moves in the wind. Ask them to describe how they look and move and create a word bank of shapes and actions for the different leaves. Tell them that today's lesson is about these leaves and how we are going to use our bodies to copy the shapes and their movement.
5 mins	Warm-up	Lead a warm-up sequence of isolating body parts and the different shapes you can make with them.
5–10 mins	Developing ideas	Scatter the leaves on the floor. Ask children to walk around the leaves to the beat of a drum. When the drum stops, call out a body part and ask children to use that body part to make the shape of the nearest leaf to them. Repeat several times. Play the drum again and this time ask children to become the leaf that they were last standing next to and move as if the wind was blowing them. When the drum stops, ask them to fall to the ground and create the shape of the leaf on the ground.
10 mins	Culminating dance	In pairs or small groups, ask children to choose a leaf shape. Ask them to create a leaf dance that will tell the story of how they started on the tree and then fell off when blown by the wind and eventually fell to the ground. They will develop this sequence and practise and refine it to perform to the class.
3 mins	Cooling down	Ask the class to lie on the floor and guide them through some gentle stretching.
5–10 mins	Closure	Have a discussion with them about their experience, and provide feedback. Ask children to tell their story or any aspect of it in a drawing. Help record their explanations. This will be used to recall experiences in the next lesson.

In texts and articles that I have read relating to the Arts and young children I have been struck by how frequently the following experience of Howard Ikemoto has been quoted.

> When my daughter was about seven years old, she asked me one day what I did at work. I told her I worked at the college—that my job was to teach people how to draw. She stared back at me, incredulous, and said, 'You mean they forgot?'

It certainly speaks to the attitude and approach of young children that needs to be nurtured during the 'golden age of creativity' spoken about in the quotation that we began with at the start of the chapter. It also speaks to the need to approach the Arts in adulthood, and in our learning and teaching of the Arts, with the same confidence that most of us had about our arts experiences as children.

SUMMARY

- The Arts are closely integrated with early childhood education and they play an important role in cultural, emotional, physical and aesthetic expression.
- Within the Australian National Curriculum, the Arts is acknowledged as a subject area with specific emphasis, in the early years, on creating and making. Curriculum documents (ACARA, 2013) delineate the Arts disciplines within this subject area as Drama, Dance, Media Arts, Music and Visual Arts.
- Broad concepts such as aesthetic understanding and holistic education apply across the Arts.
- Discrete disciplines within the Arts include Drama and Storytelling, Visual Art, Media Arts, Music, and Dance.

FURTHER REFLECTION

How would you create an enabling environment that would encourage children to create and respond to works of art?

These questions might help you answer this reflection question:

- What do you think is an ideal environment that inspires you to be creative and explore the Arts?
- What would an environment look and feel like that would most prevent you from creating and responding to works of art?

DISCUSSION QUESTIONS

Here are some further questions that can be used to reflect on the Arts in early childhood. In reflecting on these questions for yourself or contributing to class and group discussions you need to use your own opinions and experiences as well as what you have learnt from reading and engaging with this chapter.

1 Why do you think the Arts are frequently marginalised or neglected in early childhood?

2 In what ways do you think the Arts contribute to early childhood education?

3 What is the connection between the Arts, meaning-making and literacy?

4 How would you ensure that you make use of the Arts with young children?

5 How would you create an enabling environment that would encourage children to create and respond to works of art?

THE ARTS

6 If you were asked to provide a rationale for engaging children in each Arts form, what would your rationale be for:
– music?
– dance?
– drama?
– storytelling?
– visual arts?
– media arts?

CLASS EXERCISE

I consider it essential to explore and use the Arts to make sense of learning and teaching of them. One way is through the art form of a collage. Create a collage. Share your collage with someone and discuss what you were trying to convey and how. Your collage should be a representation of one or more of these aspects:

- your view of the Arts
- the nature and purpose of the Arts
- the role of the Arts in education
- positive and negative Arts experiences.

FURTHER READING

Anderson, M. & Dunn, J. (eds) (2015) How Drama Activates Learning: Contemporary Research and Practice. New York and London: Bloomsbury.
This book encapsulates a wide variety of drama approaches and contexts. It has three key sections: activating communities, activating learners and activating curriculum. The book caters for novices and experts in the field of drama for learning and teaching.

Cone, T. P., & Cone, S. (2012). Teaching Children Dance (3rd ed.). Champaign, Ill, USA: Human Kinetics, Inc.
This text provides an understanding of the components and benefits of children's dance and in developing skills necessary for enhancing and initiating a dance curriculum. It presents dance as a mode of learning that involves the whole child and uses the body and the senses to collect information, communicate, and demonstrate conceptual understandings. It highlights the fundamentals of program construction and delivery across various teaching situations and includes sample unit plans as guidelines.

Greata, J. (2006). An Introduction to Music in Early Childhood Education. NY: Delmar, Cengage Learning.
This text prepares educators to meet the responsibility of musically nurturing young children. Each chapter has been sequenced to answer the 'Why, What, Who/How and Where', of introducing music in early childhood and explores theroretical underpinnings, current research, developmentally appropriate practices and activities. The text highlights the importance of nurturing children musically at various stages and examines their developmental characteristics and uses them to suggest appropriate activities to sing, move, play and listen to music with young children. In addition, the Lab section after each chapter helps the reader gain an understanding of basic musical elements and terms.

Drama Australia. www.dramaaustralia.org.au
Drama Australia is the peak national body for drama education in Australia. All members of state and territory drama associations have automatic membership to Drama Australia. The website contains a number of useful documents and links for you to access and use. These include a number of important guideline documents such as the Aboriginal and Torres Strait Islander Guidelines for Drama/Theatre Education (2007): www.dramaaustralia.org.au/assets/files/ATSIguidelinesFinalSept07.pdf

The most recently published guideline document is Drama Australia's revised *Equity and Diversity Guidelines* document (2015), which provides advice in relation to drama and diversity: cultural and linguistic; socio-economic status; diversity of ability; gender/gender identities and sexualities. It articulates ways that students can be encouraged to honour and celebrate diversity and explore and express multiple perspectives and identities through drama: www.dramaaustralia.org.au/assets/files/DA_EquityAndDiversity.pdf

O'Toole, J. & Dunn, J. (2015) *Pretending to Learn: Teaching Drama in the Primary and Middle School* (eBook edn). Brisbane, Australia: Drama Web Publisher. https://pretendingtolearn.wordpress.com/

The authors of the award-winning and highly acclaimed *Pretending to Learn: Helping Children Learn through Drama* (2002) have produced a completely revised and updated e-version of the book along with a website. The e-book consists of three sections. 1: information about the basics of drama for beginning drama teachers; 2: information related to such aspects as drama elements, techniques and conventions; and 3: drama units (the two units that are written especially for Foundation to Year 2 are 'The Lighthouse Keeper's Nephew' and 'The Giant Who Threw Tantrums'.

Rain: for Babies and Their Carers, Drop Bear Theatre. http://dropbeartheatre.com/shows/tourable-shows/rain/
This website has information about the 'Rain: for Babies and Their Carers' experience and includes a short video clip of the actual installation. Carers and their babies 'in arms and crawlers' are immersed in a beautiful, mindfully crafted installation space that provides opportunities for connection through sound, touch and performance.

Zachest, K. (2015) *Drama for Early Childhood*. Strawberry Hills, NSW: Currency Press.
This highly practical text focuses specifically on early childhood and has innovative and easy-to-use drama experiences designed for children aged three to eight. There are forty engaging lesson plans with more than 200 activities embedded in these lesson plans.

REFERENCES

Anderson, M. (2012) *Master Class in Drama Education: Transforming Teaching and Leaning.* Sydney: Bloomsbury.

Australian Curriculum Assessment and Reporting Authority (ACARA) (2011) *Shape of the Australian Curriculum: The Arts.* Sydney: ACARA.

Australian Curriculum Assessment and Reporting Authority (ACARA) (2013) *The Arts.* Sydney: ACARA. www.acara.edu.au/curriculum/learning_areas/arts.html

Australian National Curriculum (2016) 'The Arts: Introduction' (vol. 8.1). Sydney: ACARA, www.australiancurriculum.edu.au/the-arts/introduction

Baldwin, P. & Fleming, K. (2003) *Teaching Literacy through Drama.* London: Routledge.

Bolton, G. (1992) *New Perspectives on Classroom Drama.* London, UK: Simon & Schuster.

Bolton, G. (1998) *Acting in Classroom Drama.* Stoke-on-Trent: Trentham Books.

Caldwell, B. & Vaughan, T. (2012) *Transforming Education through the Arts.* New York: Routledge.

Campbell, V. (2013) 'Playing with Storytelling', in R. Ewing (ed.) *Creative Arts in the Lives of Young Children: Play, Imagination and Learning.* Australia: ACER Press.

Carroll, J. (1988) 'Terra Incognita: Mapping *Drama* Talk', *National Association of Drama in Education Journal* (NADIE), March: 13–21.

Carter, C. (2006) 'Some Teachers Will and Some Teachers Won't': Personal and Contextual Constraints in the Use of Classroom Drama. M.Ed Thesis. South Africa: University of Fort Hare.

Carter, C. & Hughes M. (2016) 'Artful Learning and Teaching: Engendering Positive Attitudes and Engaging Reluctant Pre-Service Teachers in the Arts', *The International Journal of Arts Education.* Illinois, USA: Common Ground Publishing, *11*(2), 1–12.

Carter, C. & Sallis, R. (2016) 'Dialogues of Diversity: Examining the Role of Educational Drama Techniques in Affirming Diversity and Supporting Inclusive Educational Practices in Primary School', *NJ: Drama Australia Journal,* *40*(1):78–88.

THE ARTS

Deans, J. (2016) Thinking, Feeling and Relating: Young Children Learning through Dance, *Australasian Journal of Early Childhood, 41*(3): 46–57.

Department of Education, Employment and Workplace Relations (DEEWR) (2009) *Belonging, Being & Becoming: The Early Years Learning Framework for Australia.* ACT, Australia: Commonwealth of Australia.

Derham, F. (1986) Art for the Child under Seven (6th edn). Watson, ACT: Australian Early Childhood Association.

Dinham, J. (2015) *Delivering Authentic Arts Education.* South Melbourne: Cengage Learning.

Donelan, K. (2009) 'Arts, Education as Intercultural and Social Dialogue', in *Education in the Arts: Teaching and Learning in the Contemporary Curriculum.* C. Sinclair, N. Jeanneret & J. O'Toole (eds). Melbourne: Oxford University Press, Chapter 3.

Dunn, J. & Stinson, M. (2012) 'Dramatic Play and Drama in the Early Years: Re-imagining the Approach', in S. Wright (ed.), *Children, Meaning Making and the Arts* (2nd edn). Frenchs Forest, NSW: Pearson Education.

Eisner, E. (2002) *The Arts and the Creative Mind.* New Haven, USA: Yale University Press.

Ewing, R. (2010) *The Arts and Australian Education: Realising Potential.* Victoria: Australian Council for Educational Research.

Flohr, J.W. (2010) *Music in Elementary Education.* Upper Saddle River, NJ: Pearson Education Inc.

Gardner, H. (1982) *Art, Mind and Brain.* New York: Basic Books.

Gibson, R. & Ewing. R. (2011) *Transforming the Curriculum through the Arts*. South Yarra, Vic.: Palgrave Macmillan.

Gill, R. (2011) 'The Value of Music Education'. Sydney: TEDx.

Greata, J. (2006) *An Introduction to Music in Early Childhood Education.* NY, Delmar: Cengage Learning.

Hallam, S. (2016) 'The Impact of Actively Making Music on the Intellect, Social and Personal Development of Children and Young People: A Summary', *Voices: A World Forum for Music Therapy, 16*(2).

Hanna, J.L. (1987) *To Dance is Human: A Theory of Nonverbal Communication.* Chicago: University of Chicago Press.

Heathcote, D. (1984) L. Johnson & C. O'Neill (eds), *Collected Writings on Education and Drama.* London: Hutchinson.

Holden, J. (2003) 'What's This Got to Do with Maths?' *Education Review*, 15(2): 36–42.

Kellog, R. (1979) *Children's Drawings, Children's Minds.* New York: Avon Books.

Kwaymullina, A. (2007) *Crow and the Waterhole.* WA, Australia: Freemantle Press.

Lowenfield, V. & Brittain, W.L. (1987) *Creative and Mental Growth* (8th edn). USA: Macmillan.

Luff, I. (2000) 'I've Been in the Reichstag: Rethinking Roleplay', *Teaching History*, 100(1): 8–17.

Mackenzie, N. & Veresov, N. (2013) 'How Drawing Can Support Writing Acquisition: Text Construction in Early Writing from a Vygotskian Perspective', *Australasian Journal of Early Childhood.* 384: 22–9.

McArdle, F. (2012) 'New Maps of Learning for Quality Art Education: What Pre-Service Teachers Should Learn and Be Able to Do', *The Australian Educational Researcher*, 39: 91–106, doi: 10.1007/s13384–012–0051–2.

McMillan, R. (1992) 'Music Education in Australia', *Victorian Journal of Music Education*, 1: 1–3.

Neelands, J. (2001) '11/09—The Space in Our Hearts', a speech at the 2nd International Theatre/Drama Education Conference, Athens. Theatre in education: art form and learning tool.

Nicholson, H. (2005) *Applied Drama: The Gift of Theatre.* New York: Macmillan.

Niland, A. (2015a) *Music and Children.* Deakin West, ACT: Early Childhood Australia Inc.

Niland, A. (2015b) 'Row, Row, Row Your Boat': Singing, Identity and Belonging in a Nursery', *International Journal of Early Years Education, 23*(1): 4–16.

Norman, R. (2004) *A Dramatic Conception of Curriculum: Artistic, Emancipated and Feminist Possibilities through the Emotional.* University of British Columbia: Department of Language Education.

O'Neill, C. (1995) *Drama Worlds: A Framework for Process.* Portsmouth, NH: Heinemann Drama.

O'Toole, J. & Dunn, J. (2015) *Pretending to Learn: Teaching Drama in the Primary and Middle School* (eBook edn). Brisbane, Australia: Drama Web Publisher.

O'Toole, J., Stinson M. & Moore, T. (2009) *Drama and Curriculum: A Giant at the Door.* USA: Springer.

Roy, D., Baker, W. & Hamilton A. (2012) *Teaching the Arts: Early Childhood and Primary Education*. Melbourne: Cambridge University Press.

Russell-Bowie, D.E. (2012) 'Developing Preservice Primary Teachers' Confidence and Competence in Arts Education using Principles of Authentic Learning', *Australian Journal of Teacher Education*, *37*(1).

Sinclair, C., Jeanneret, N. & O'Toole, J. (eds) (2012) *Education in the Arts: Teaching and Learning in the Contemporary Curriculum*, (2nd edn). Melbourne: Oxford University Press.

Slade P. (1965) *Child Drama* (5th edn). London: University of London Press.

Stinson, S. (1988) *Dance for Young Children: Finding the Magic in Movement.* Reston, VA: The American Alliance for Health, Physical Education, Recreation and Dance.

Toye, N. & Prendiville, F. (2000) *Drama and Traditional Story for the Early Years.* London: Routledge Falmer.

UNESCO (2006) 'Road Map for Arts Education'. The World Conference on Arts Education, Lisborne.

UNESCO (2010) Second World Conference on Arts Education, Seoul.

Wagner, B. (1998) *Educational Drama and Language Arts: What Research Shows.* Portsmouth, NH: Heinemann.

Way, B. (1985) *Development through Drama.* London: Longman.

Williams, G. (2002) 'The Unity of Thought, Feeling and Action', *The Journal for Drama in Education: The National Association for the Teaching of Drama (NATD) Journal*, *18*(1), 35–48.

Wright, S. (2003) *The Arts, Young Children, and Learning.* Boston: Pearson Education.

Yelland N., Butler, D. & Diezmann, C. (1999) *Early Mathematical Explorations.* Needham Heights, Mass: Pearson Publishing Solutions

THE ARTS

CHAPTER 9

Science

Ginette Pestana

Chapter objectives

In this chapter, we will:
- consider how children learn science
- learn about the science curriculum for early childhood
- examine how to support science learning in early childhood
- consider pedagogical approaches for enhancing science learning
- discuss how to assess science learning

Key terms

demonstration

diverse learners

effective questioning

exploration

guided investigation

inclusivity

interactive talk

science literacy

Ronan, who is just under two years old, asked to 'play cars' and 'get set … go!', so we got out the cars and the racing ramp and set it up. He chose a car to put on the ramp and asked me to choose one too. After we placed our chosen cars at the starting gate, he called out 'get set … go!' and released the gate. He watched intently as the cars rolled down the ramp and onto the floor, travelling for quite a distance. He placed more cars on the ramp and repeated the experience until he had run out of cars. As he did this, we had lots of talk about the experience. Was the car too big for the ramp? Did it go quickly? How far did the car go after leaving the ramp? He then collected the cars and repeated the activity, but this time choosing the cars that went smoothly down the ramp.

Ronan just had a lesson in physical science and experienced forces in action. Just as a scientist does, Ronan observed, predicted, experimented, analysed his findings, reported and shared with others.

Introduction

The vignette about Ronan is just one example of science learning and understanding that takes place in early childhood settings. More often than not, though, the teacher working with the child may not regard this as 'science', and the opportunity to develop teaching that extends the experience is lost.

Intentionally teaching science and providing experiences for learning science in early childhood starts with an understanding of what science is. Science, simply put, is the study of the world around us. It involves acquiring knowledge and making sense of our world in a particular way. It raises the question 'I wonder why?' and provides a basis for understanding science and its application to us.

Looking back at the way children were taught science in the past, many of us will have distinct memories of memorising lots of facts, especially chemical element tables. That approach is unlikely to inspire enthusiasm and interest in science, and it fails to engage with the potential learning and teaching possibilities of science. Science teaching is more than transferring a body of knowledge or a compilation of facts, and memorisation is a low-order cognitive skill: it does not require understanding. The main goal of science education is to enable children to be *science literate*—seeing and understanding the world through a science lens. Children learn to make sense of the world through science ideas, and appreciate the science process of gathering and substantiating evidence, and applying science process skills, and attitudes (Rennie, 2005).

Most children are curious about the world around them. It is this awe and wonder that makes them natural scientists. Through careful guidance, teachers in early childhood will be able to extend and support this joy of discovery and lead children to science learning. Understanding how children learn science will enable teachers to use effective pedagogies to deepen children's scientific understanding and help them develop scientific skills and positive dispositions towards science.

How children learn science

Theoretical understandings of learning underpin and provide guidelines for teachers to make practical decisions regarding teaching science. Having a guiding theory provides insights, and opens new perspectives and strategies to deal with challenges (Russell & McGuigan, 2016). There are many learning theories that explain how children learn science and the factors influencing it.

Children 'do' science all the time in their attempt to gain understanding of the world around them. This disposition of curiosity and desire to make sense of the world is evident right from birth, and young children are rightly referred to as 'natural scientists'. Children develop science understanding through their experiences and interactions with others and they try to provide explanations for what they have seen or done (Fleer, 2015). Children develop explanations or their own theories for these phenomena, often putting together different fragments of understanding to create an explanation that makes sense to them, but not necessarily based in science fact (Kelly, 2015). Asking a child how a rainbow got in the sky, for example, might elicit a reply that 'someone painted the sky with the different colours'. In this example, the child who has experience in painting transfers this knowledge to something similar in nature. Drawing on previous experiences to make sense of new ones is a valuable strategy for children, but it can lead to misconceptions. These alternative understandings or misconceptions are often firmly entrenched as they are grounded in the child's own experiences and they are often quite hard to shift. As teachers, it is important to remember that when children enter school, they already possess some principled and sophisticated science ideas and understandings.

The child's active construction of their own understanding and knowledge is deeply rooted in constructivist views of learning and cognitive psychology (Kelly, 2015). Constructivism is based on the belief that learners create meaning through mental formulation and reformulation of concepts that support their search for understanding (Brooks, 2011). These concepts or ideas and understandings, or simply the 'what', form the building blocks of knowledge that allow learners to organise and categorise information which is then applied

SCIENCE

to everyday experiences or as solutions to new problems (Charlesworth & Lind, 2013). Jean Piaget, who was introduced to you in Chapter 3, called these mental structures, or mental representations and operations, 'schemas', and suggested that concept development follows a pathway similar to the stages of cognitive development, which move from the concrete to the abstract (Robson, 2012). The two cognitive processes that help explain this development of scientific thinking are assimilation and accommodation. The children assimilate information by taking in, responding to or internalising experiences. They accommodate the information internally by reconciling the unknown with the known to reach a stage of equilibrium.

Connor and the CD spindle box

Connor (two years) loved playing with cars and was often found lying on the floor watching his cars move on the ground. He found a CD spindle box. He picked it up, looked at it and tried to move it. It didn't move very smoothly. He looked puzzled. Then he lay on the floor and turned the computer disk CD spindle box on its side with the circular face facing him. He started to move it and his face lit up with a big smile. It moved just like his cars.

STOP AND THINK

Children construct ideas or concepts in their mind about things they encounter. These ideas or representations form the basis for making sense of things around them.

- What concept do you think Connor had regarding things that moved?
- Explain how you think he transferred this understanding to the new object, the CD spindle box.

Children, from infancy, construct and use concepts in their everyday activities. Babies soon learn that when things drop from their high chair or pram they always fall downwards, and that you have to use force—push or pull—on a toy to make it move. They learn about the properties of materials and determine that some things are soft and others are hard, and that some things are easier to pick up or see through. They soon learn the difference between living and non-living things—for example, that a doll is not the same as a baby. Children also develop processes that provide the means to apply the new concepts gained, expand current concepts and develop new ones (Charlesworth & Lind, 2013).

As children gain knowledge and experience, their understanding of concepts develops. Vygotsky (1987) believed that concept formation should be considered at two levels: the everyday level and the scientific level. The everyday levels support concepts learnt through direct interactions with the world, such as switching on a light, opening a door or putting on a coat when it's cold. These intuitive understandings of things that surround children in life form the foundation for learning scientific concepts (Vygotsky, 1987). The scientific level involves understanding the scientific concepts behind the phenomena. These scientific concepts, such as forces and temperature that start at a concrete level—must then be abstracted or taken out of specific instances to become conceptual generalisations. The build-up of these concepts happens over a lifetime through experiences with cases, objects and contexts (Russell & McGuigan, 2016). Both the everyday and scientific concept formations are interrelated and when children bring together their understanding of both concepts, it transforms their everyday practice (Fleer, 2015).

Although everyday concepts lay the foundation for scientific concepts, children will not learn the science knowledge behind these actions or develop higher order thinking by themselves. Knowledge, which includes science knowledge, is a human construction and does not exist out there just to be 'discovered' by children. It requires contexts that are culturally embedded and social conditions to bring children's attention to these best-known explanations, which are then passed on from generation to generation (Fleer, 2015). From a social-cultural or cultural-historical theoretical view, concept formation occurs within a community of practice and is enacted through social engagement. This theory focuses attention to a learner's social interactions with an 'expert' other who promotes a learning community where knowledge is constructed together. It is a shared experience and the 'expert' is responsible for presenting science culture and views to the children. Teachers play a pivotal role and must provide a high-quality level of teacher–child interactions to facilitate and develop science understanding (Campbell et al., 2015).

From understanding what children know and can do, a teacher develops a context that takes into consideration the cultural background of the children, rules and regulations, and curriculum expectations to provide an environment that is meaningful for children to develop understanding within a community of learners (Fleer, 2015). Pedagogies that embrace the cultural–historical approach position learning as a social and collective process; have personal and cultural meaning; and see assessment as a collaborative process (Fleer, 2015). The following example demonstrates a learning experience that illustrates the cultural–historical approach in practice.

Sinking and floating vegetables

Jan, the teacher in a four-year-old pre-school class was reading *Who Sank the Boat?* by Pamela Allen to her class during story time. The children were really engaged with the story and were very surprised at the ending when it only took a little mouse getting on board the boat to sink it.

This started a big discussion about 'why things sink and float' and Jan discovered that most children appeared to have the conception that heavy things sink and light things float. Jan decided to extend the children's interest and to challenge this conception. She intended to facilitate the children's understanding of one of the science concepts behind sink and float, which is buoyancy: an upward acting force that a liquid exerts that opposes the weight of the object. Jan set up the water table area with small, light vegetables that sank (like beans) and large, heavy vegetables that floated (pumpkin) for the children to explore. She asked the children questions such as, 'What will happen to the bean or pumpkin when you put it into the water?' 'Why do you think that happened?' Jan set up a class chart where the children could draw the things that sank or floated and she used this as a focus for discussion. Finally, she explained to the children that the water pushes things up and things always go down due to gravity. Things float because the water force is stronger and things sink when their weight force is stronger.

GINETTE PESTANA

SCIENCE

> **STOP AND REFLECT**
>
> In the case study above, the children's original understanding of things sinking and floating was based on their everyday experience of playing with water and objects, such as during water play or playing with bath toys at bath time. The scientific concept of buoyancy would not be understood without the careful intervention of their teacher, 'the expert', and her experience, which provided a shared learning journey in a meaningful context.
>
> - Think back to how you learnt about science concepts. Did someone tell you, or did you find out about them through your own research?
> - When encountering new science concepts that presented a different and contrasting view from what you already knew about it, how did you feel?
> - What did it take to change your mind?
> - How long did it take?

Developing science literacy

Developing and understanding concepts such as buoyancy or forces does not follow a straightforward pathway. It is complicated as children are different: they develop at different rates, learn in different ways and may not be interested in the same things. Teachers cannot assume that the children they teach arrive at the same point of understanding at the same time. These differences pose challenges for the teacher to develop learning experiences that support science concept development for the whole class. When teachers understand how children think, learn and develop concepts, they are placed in a better position to guide children towards deeper scientific understanding (Fleer, 2015).

science literacy
an awareness of currently accepted scientific understanding and how it is presented, as well as questioning and seeking evidence of how and why it shapes our lives.

Science literacy is defined as an awareness of currently accepted scientific understanding and how it is presented, as well as questioning and seeking evidence of how and why it shapes our lives. As teachers of science in the early years, we must aim for deep understanding and conceptual change to facilitate science literacy. We should not be content to just extend interest and imitate experiences or facilitate memorisation of facts. Instead, we should support and assist children to develop higher order thinking skills, such as problem solving and reflection. Teachers need to innovate to gain a deeper understanding of science and how it shapes our lives (Petriwskyj, 2013). For example, instead of just noticing what the weather is, and lamenting about being cooped in on a rainy day, children could be challenged to find out why and when rain happens (water cycle) and how it affects us and animals (supporting ecosystems).

Planning for science experiences begins with the teacher's understanding of how children learn science; then recognises science opportunities in the environment and provides links to science content and curriculum expectations, identifying enabling environments, effective teaching pedagogies and how to assess children's progress.

Early childhood science curriculum

In Australia, prior-to-school early childhood programs are guided by the EYLF (DEEWR, 2009). This framework outlines principles about the educator's beliefs and how to support children's learning; practices that guide the 'doing'; and learning outcomes that relate to skills,

Table 9.1 The five learning outcomes of the EYLF

LEARNING OUTCOME	DESCRIPTOR	EVIDENT WHEN CHILDREN
Children have a strong sense of identity	Children learn to interact in relation to others with care, empathy and respect	develop empathy towards the environment and the part they play with it
Children are connected with and contribute to their world	Children become socially responsible and show respect for the environment	develop an awareness of the impact of human activity on environments and the interdependence of living things
Children have a strong sense of wellbeing	Children take increasing responsibility for their own health and physical wellbeing	use their sensory capabilities and dispositions with increasing integration, skill and purpose to explore and respond to their world
Children are confident and involved learners	Children develop a range of skills and processes such as problem solving, inquiry, experimentation, hypothesising, researching and investigating	make predictions and generalisations about their daily activities, aspects of the natural world and environments
Children are effective communicators	Children interact verbally and non-verbally with others for a range of purposes	interact with others to explore ideas and concepts, clarify and challenge thinking, negotiate and share new understandings

Source: DEEWR, 2009, pp. 20–44.

knowledge and dispositions. The EYLF can be viewed as a foundation that provides many opportunities to develop science literacy, from engaging children in science content, scientific processes and language to developing positive dispositions and attitudes. Science is one of the few subject disciplines identified in the EYLF and the content is spread out either explicitly or implicitly over several of the learning outcomes and their descriptors (Nolan, 2015).

Table 9.1 shows an example from each of the five learning outcomes of the EYLF to illustrate the presence of science learning. The column that gives specific examples of how the learning outcomes are evidenced in science learning is labelled 'Evident when children'. It is through working and playing with science concepts in the early years that the foundations are laid, and understandings can be built upon those foundations (Fleer, 2015). Science experiences also pave the way for developing higher level cognitive skills such as logic and problem solving, which can be applied to other academic areas.

Primary school science curriculum

The science curriculum for the school sector is guided by the Australian Curriculum. The science learning area is structured around a rationale, aims, band level descriptions, information about the organisation of the curriculum, content elaborations, annotated portfolios of student work samples and a glossary (ACARA, 2015b).

Science is viewed as a way of *knowing* and *thinking* and uses reproducible evidence to develop understandings about how the world works. The Australian Curriculum also identifies that science is a 'Human Endeavour' that focuses on the recognition that science is a body of knowledge and understandings and we seek to find answers stemming from our curiosity and interest (National Curriculum Board, 2009).

GINETTE PESTANA

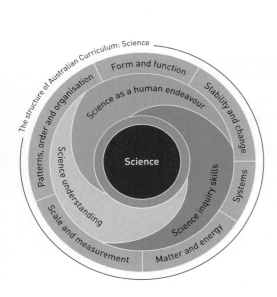

The science curriculum consists of three interrelated strands:

1 *Science Understanding*—related to science concepts and knowledge
2 *Science Inquiry Skills*—skills needed to work scientifically
3 *Science as Human Endeavour*—nature and influence of science.

These three strands aim to develop a student's scientific understanding of the world through understanding, knowledge and skills (ACARA, 2015b).

The science curriculum also identifies 'six key ideas that represent key aspects of a scientific view of the world and bridge knowledge and understanding across the disciplines of science' (ACARA, 2015c).

Under the Australian Curriculum, there are two other areas that have influence over the science curriculum: general capabilities and cross-curricula priorities (ACARA 2015a).

The general capabilities section describes knowledge, skills, behaviours and dispositions that prepare children for the twenty-first century. These complement and share similarities with the EYLF learning outcomes. The cross-curricula priorities include Aboriginal and Torres Strait Islander histories and cultures; Asia and Australia's engagement with Asia; and sustainability. These priorities help prepare children to engage effectively in the global world and contribute to society through social, intellectual and creative pursuits. They also provide contexts for science participation and can be embedded or linked at appropriate times.

Both the EYLF and the Australian Curriculum share similar elements but differ in regards to the emphasis: the EYLF focuses more on the processes and dispositions and the Australian Curriculum identifies key science content that needs to be taught alongside the other streams.

Science content

The core science content areas identified in the Australian Curriculum include Biological science, Earth and space science, Physical science and Chemical science. These content areas should be addressed by teachers in early childhood to provide a foundation for more complex science understanding later. A description of each science content area and some suggestions of what could be covered in the early years are included in Table 9.2.

Table 9.2 Australian Curriculum core science content areas

BIOLOGICAL SCIENCE	EARTH AND SPACE SCIENCE	PHYSICAL SCIENCE	CHEMICAL SCIENCE
Study of life	Study of the earth	Study of the physical world	Study of what things are made up of
Animal (including humans) and plant features, characteristics, growth, needs and habitats	Features and characteristics of the sky (weather, climate and day and night), earth formations and materials	Forces (push and pull), energy (light, sound, magnetism, electricity)	Materials and their properties States of matter and their changes (heating, cooling, rusting)

Each of these content areas provides endless possibilities for developing science activities, and teachers are encouraged to include the range of different content areas rather than favour those areas they are more comfortable with. Biological science is a very popular content area among teachers in early childhood. Most early childhood centres have a 'nature corner', which provides children with opportunities to explore animals or insects in a prepared environment. Very rarely do you see a 'science corner' set up where children explore physical science content such as light and sound sources. Teachers must also be conscious that some of these content areas are rather abstract and careful guidance must be provided to avoid any development of misconceptions.

Unfortunately, many teachers view science teaching as difficult—they lack confidence or do not feel competent in teaching science. The main reasons cited include lack of content knowledge, inadequate training in their pre-service qualification or disengagement with their science learning at school. This deficit is often carried forward into their teaching and becomes a barrier to including science teaching in their class; consequently, it is often avoided.

Rather than focusing on their own perceived 'deficit', teachers should embrace science learning as part of their own learning journey and become co-constructors with the children. The case study 'Birds in their nests' is an example of teacher and child as co-constructors of science.

Birds in their nests

'Spring is here and the birds have been busy building nests,' Cara told the children. A learning area about birds was set up and Cara asked the children to spot any nests being built in the trees in the yard. The children were excited when they spotted one but didn't know what type of bird it was. 'Let's find out,' said Cara, taking out her smartphone and googling Australian birds.

Cara and the children soon found out that it was a blue-faced honey eater. They watched the progress of the nest building and started making nests, birds and eggs in the 'making-corner' using recycled materials. The children discovered the properties of materials for building nests—it had to be strong, flexible and light enough for the birds to carry to their nests. They drew pictures of birds and learnt about the features of the birds and what they were used for.

Cara, who knew very little about birds, embraced this journey of discovery with the children and together they created a stimulating learning experience full of wonder, excitement and science learning.

GINETTE PESTANA

SCIENCE

Science learning in early childhood is not formal and is more about an attitude of mind and a characteristic way of thinking (Russell & McGuigan, 2016). It is about consciously thinking of science and recognising science possibilities or content in what is around us, or in other words, having a 'sciencing' attitude (Tu, 2006). The vignette in the opening of this chapter found Ronan playing with cars on a ramp. It provided an opportunity to introduce the concept of gravitational forces: the cars always went down the ramp. The example about birds and their nests led the way to biological and chemical science for the children when they explored characteristics of birds and properties of nest-building materials. When making cookies, do we just show children how to measure and mix the ingredients? Or do we explain the processes that are happening: the binding of the ingredients, or getting the children to predict what will happen when you add the ingredients together, or questioning why this happens? What a teacher sees and does can either limit or expand children's scientific knowledge. A teacher should be constantly on the alert for those 'teachable' moments and having a 'sciencing' attitude opens the door to more opportunities to learn science.

Water painting

It was a hot day at a childcare centre and the children were playing outside. A teacher started distributing paintbrushes and buckets of water and suggested to the children to paint the ground. The children were involved with the activity for varying time periods. One child noticed that the paintings didn't last long and asked the teacher 'Where did my painting go?' Rather than replying that the water dried up because it was hot, the teacher, alert to the science affordance opportunity, questioned the child: 'Where do you think it went?' This led into a long, sustained conversation and discussion about water evaporation—water changing from a liquid to gas form.

STOP AND REFLECT

- Do you have a 'sciencing' attitude?
- Can you identify the science affordances in the environment around you?
- Have you grasped opportunities to share science understanding with children or were there any missed opportunities to promote science learning and understanding?

Another factor to remember is that science content is constantly evolving: there are new discoveries being announced almost every day. This makes it difficult to keep up or know what science knowledge children need to know in the future. The key thing to remember is that no-one knows or needs to know all the answers because science is what we know at that point in time (Beeley, 2012). Focusing on science content is just a small dent in learning science and should not be the entire focus of learning science. Providing a good grounding in science learning also involves understanding and practising science process skills, developing positive dispositions towards science and understanding how it affects us in everyday life.

Scientific processes and language

Science process or inquiry skills are vital skills that aid scientific inquiry and support other areas of learning. These skills, which start developing from infancy, include asking questions, making observations, experimenting, predicting and communicating. The skills increase in sophistication as children develop to include researching, investigating, classifying, hypothesising and inferring. By equipping children with science process skills, teachers are helping children to develop effective ways to 'find out how to find out' (Petriwskyj, 2013) and be confident in undertaking their own investigations (Campbell & Chealuck, 2015).

Table 9.3 summarises what these skills involve in the early years.

Table 9.3 Science process skills

PROCESS SKILL	DESCRIPTION	EFFECTIVE STRATEGIES FOR EARLY CHILDHOOD TEACHERS TO SUPPORT SKILL
Observing	It is a process where we gather information through our senses. This is fundamental to the scientific thinking process and an important skill for young children to develop. Observing is more than just seeing and involves receiving information about the world. It is a skill that needs to be taught and supported by teachers. It is the first step in gathering information to solve a problem.	• Using interested expressions and providing 'invitations to observe' to make the event the focus of attention and something worth noting • Selecting opportunities that have imminent reactions • Providing time to observe • Using guiding questions
Comparing	Builds upon the process of observation Identifies similarities and differences between events and objects	• Begin by asking children to describe the event or characteristics of the object • Next ask children to compare and discuss the event or objects to determine whether they are the same or different
Classifying	The grouping and sorting of objects into meaningful categories based on an identifiable characteristic	• Providing objects that can be sorted, matched, or grouped in various ways • Ask children for different ways to group objects
Measuring	This is a skill of quantifying observations through standard or non-standard units	• Providing opportunities to measure things in everyday situations • Demonstrating different ways to measure objects
Communicating	The skill of describing a phenomenon through different modes, e.g. oral, written, pictures or graphic It is the means through which scientists share their findings	• Asking children to share with you their discoveries • Providing opportunities to share through different media
Inferring	Categorising observations to try to give them some meaning	• Ask the questions, 'Why?' or 'What do you think caused …?'
Predicting	Making a statement about what you expect to happen in the future based on prior knowledge	• Discuss with children how they could answer the question, 'What do you think will happen when …?'
Experimenting	An experiment is an investigation that has a hypothesis (statement of a relationship that might exist between two variables) and control variables (variables that are defined and are able to control)	• Setting up and implementing a formal learning experience

SCIENCE

GINETTE PESTANA

Using the correct terminology for these processes—for example, classify, infer and investigate—supports the acquisition of scientific language. Teachers need to resist trying to make things simpler or avoiding using this terminology because they are worried it is too sophisticated for children to understand. Scientific language acquisition is highly complex and better success is achieved when learnt in context and used constantly (Dockrell et al., 2007).

Positive dispositions and attitudes

Positive dispositions to science refers to the inherent qualities or characteristics that children have or show towards learning and appreciating science. These characteristics encourage children to respond to learning in a certain way and it is critical that the teacher supports and develops these skills in children. The EYLF highlights nine different dispositions to learning that are also important for science learning: curiosity, cooperation, confidence, creativity, imagination, commitment, persistence, enthusiasm and reflexivity.

Children are curious in nature and teachers can support this by acknowledging their desire to learn or know about something and not dampening any interest in wanting to find out. Teachers' intervention needs to be enthusiastic, relevant, inviting and supportive of children's need to discover. When children ask, 'Why?', 'How can?' or 'What if?', they need to know that teachers will answer with 'I'm not sure, let's find out' or 'Let's try', rather than brushing them aside. Teachers should also learn to know when to jump in or be quiet to allow children to focus on the experience. Children need time to explore and make sense of the world themselves instead of teachers telling them how we see the world (Beeley, 2012). Teachers can also support children by 'wondering aloud' ('I wonder what/how/if …') and providing scientific vocabulary to give them the words they can use to express what they see (Aitken et al., 2012).

Learning science often takes place in social settings and involves children working together towards a common goal. Developing skills such as cooperation are fundamental to working well together. Children will be actively engaged in their own learning when they listen to each other, share work and celebrate achievements. For example, working together to make an outdoor cubby in the yard can support and encourage the disposition of cooperation.

Children feel confident when their abilities, thoughts and ideas are acknowledged, encouraged and supported. The use of a 'Wonder Wall', where children's questions about the science topic being discussed are recorded and acknowledged, provides a visual testimony of all the children's contributions.

Science is all about working things out and children need creative skills and good imaginations to come up with new solutions or novel answers to their science wonderings and investigations. Teachers can encourage children to find and try out different answers to science questions such as why the brick house didn't get blown away in the 'Three little pigs' story. Children can explore building houses with different materials to test out which houses are stronger than others.

Commitment and persistence are valued skills in science learning as children need to learn to value the time and energy taken to deepen their science understanding and learning. Providing engaging science experiences that are stimulating and supporting their interest with open-ended questions provide incentives for children to commit to and persist towards achieving their science goal (e.g. planting a vegetable patch and harvesting the produce at the end).

Children are naturally enthusiastic and feel supported and encouraged when teachers are interested in what they do and get excited with the discoveries and ideas they have. Teachers should notice and support little achievements such as finding the right combination of sand and water to make the perfect sandcastle!

Reflexivity is demonstrated when children review and consolidate their science understandings through discussions and taking evidence. For example, talking about what was in a photo will provide an opportunity for children to express their understanding and reinforce their learning.

Science in everyday life

Science is all around us and it is important for children to recognise the human element of science and the role science plays in everyone's lives. Science knowledge is constructed from explanations made by people that are evidence based and can be changed as new knowledge emerges. A recent article from the ABC announced that researchers revealed that the T-rex was 'not strong enough' for running locomotion. The use of an engineering technique called multibody dynamic analysis, coupled with machine learning, enabled researchers to produce an accurate simulation of the T-rex gait to discover that it could only walk at 18 kmh, which is less than half the speed of the fastest man. This new information changed the previous assumption of the T-rex outrunning its prey and now challenges scientists to consider how it actually caught its prey (ABC, 2017). Science is never static and is always changing as new ways to discover things are being used. It is through science that people develop understanding and explanations of the natural world.

Becoming aware of how science knowledge and applications affect the lives of people sensitises children to the world around them and will enable them to make informed personal and societal decisions in the future. Being science literate raises the awareness of the role and status of scientific knowledge and helps to develop an appreciation for its history and development and the people behind them. Science will become relevant and authentic to children if it is contextualised as a science of human endeavour that is situated in a day-to-day world. Teachers can play an active role in supporting this position by creating learning environments that act as a living example of the interrelatedness of humanity, learning, society and science and providing opportunities that characterise and live science as a way of knowing and acting. These meaningful experiences allow children to connect science learning with everyday life and strengthen their sense of connectedness with the world around them (Smith & Fitzgerald, 2013). Table 9.4 provides examples of how children of different age groups can be introduced to becoming science-literate individuals.

Teachers with a strong understanding of science—or the Nature of Science (NOS)—are more likely to have a positive attitude towards supporting children's scientific learning. By modelling ways of finding out about science, increasing their own knowledge base through cooperative learning and using constructive teaching strategies, teachers can distance themselves from the fear of not knowing enough science content to focus on doing and living science (Edwards & Loveridge, 2011).

GINETTE PESTANA

SCIENCE

Table 9.4 Introducing children to science literacy

AGE GROUP	SCIENCE AS A HUMAN ENDEAVOUR CONCEPT (ACARA 2015)	EXAMPLE
Infants and toddlers	Objects and the world around us can be explored using our senses: hearing, smell, touch, sight and taste	Providing children with a range of everyday materials that can produce sound when hit, scraped or shaken
Pre-schoolers	People use science in their daily lives, including when caring for their environment and living things	Looking after the class pet (e.g. feeding); cleaning their home
Early primary	People use science in their daily lives, identifying the ways humans manage and protect resources (e.g. reducing waste and conserving water)	Bring a 'Nude Food (without excess packaging)' lunchbox to school

---

STOP AND REFLECT

As you prepare yourself to teach science in early childhood, reflect on these questions:

- Do I see science possibilities in the children's everyday experiences?
- Do I provide a learning environment that supports science inquiry?
- Am I confident in my scientific knowledge and understanding?
- Will this become a barrier that stops me from teaching science?
- Do I use scientific language to enhance children's vocabulary?
- How can I support children's understanding of science?

Science learning in early childhood

Science learning in an early childhood setting can happen anywhere and anytime. Children have a natural interest in the world around them, including the classroom. They are curious about phenomena that they have seen and use their senses to observe and play with different objects or situations to gain more understanding and information (Campbell & Jobling, 2010). More often than not, it is the adult's limitations rather than the competencies of the children that restrict the development of scientific thinking—for example, thinking that a particular activity is beyond the understanding of children and avoiding a topic such as water evaporation. What is key is the creation of the right conditions for engaging in science (Fleer, 2015).

Walk into any early childhood centre classroom and you will probably find static displays and interest centres with a particular science focus—for example, 'the nature table'. These experiences could be used to satisfy curiosity where children could follow their own pathways of discovery in science; or children could be guided through an experience by a more enlightened adult who could highlight the science and build it into a quality scientific interaction; or they could simply be lost opportunities where children do not engage in the science experience in a practical way, such as watching an experiment, thus limiting the science learning (Blake & Howitt, 2012).

While these science experiences are planned, science learning can also take place through less formal and incidental opportunities. Tu (2006) highlights this in her research investigating pre-school science environments. She uses Neuman's (1972) use of the word 'sciencing', which describes science-related activities for young children, and his categorisation of sciencing into *formal sciencing, informal sciencing* and *incidental sciencing* to analyse the availability of science materials, equipment and activities in the pre-school classroom. This type of categorisation was also used for research into science affordances in the classroom by Fleer, Gomes and March (2014). They found the presence of these types of science opportunities and also found new categories where teachers created opportunities for using science purposefully, such as being part of a constant area within the classroom, building science into the infrastructure of the centre and using science in everyday life at the centre (see Table 9.5).

Table 9.5 Categorisation of science-related activities

TYPE OF SCIENCE-RELATED ACTIVITY	DEFINITION	EXAMPLE
Formal sciencing	Science activities for the children are deliberately planned and organised by the teacher	Making playdough
Informal sciencing	Learning space is provided within the classroom to promote scientific interaction and exploration	Lightboxes for colour mixing
Incidental sciencing	An occurrence within the class environment invites science learning interactions between the teacher and the children	A rainbow
Science within the constant traditional areas of the pre-school	Recognising that science supports what children do	A sand and water table
Building a science infrastructure into the centre	Including science as part of the curriculum	Planting a garden
Using science in everyday life in the centre	Making science real and meaningful in everyday activities	Using weather websites to determine activities for the day

GINETTE PESTANA

The environment is full of rich science opportunities for young children. These science affordances can only be made possible if teachers play an active role in identifying and supporting science learning in the classroom. Rather than being a limiter, the teacher should recognise the science possibilities or develop a 'sciencing' attitude to enable these science learning opportunities. Teachers should take up the challenge to follow children's interests by joining them on this pathway to new discoveries and igniting their sense of wonder. Making science a part of everyday life creates meaning and relevance for children and empowers them to be science literate. Working and living scientifically helps them to nurture and sustain their curiosity and imagination; work cooperatively; and develop life skills of confidence, commitment, enthusiasm, persistence, communication and being reflective.

So how can this be achieved? Early childhood teachers already support children's learning through meaningful connections and the provision of relevant contexts. This pedagogical strength should be recognised and extended into the area of science rather than treating science as a static body of knowledge to be passed on. With the understanding of theoretical underpinnings behind how children develop science understanding and concept formation, we recognise that children construct their own understanding through play and active engagement with science. Children's learning is enhanced through social interaction and the educator has a pivotal role (Campbell & Chealuck, 2015). Over the years, this knowledge has led to the development of several different teaching approaches and strategies to support both the formal and informal learning of science.

Pedagogical approaches to science learning

The constructivist theory highlights an important fact that children build on their learning from previous experiences and understandings. This prior knowledge is the starting point and it is important that teachers understand this before they can enhance learning. The use of effective questioning can solicit answers that inform the teacher. The simple use of Who? What? What if? If? When? How? Where? and Why? linked to a science idea can promote sustained conversations, investigations, deep thinking, focus and insights into what a child knows (Campbell & Chealuck, 2015). It is important to remember to give children time to answer and to accept whatever answer they give. In the early years children's brains are quite 'fresh' and they do take time to process things. It is not surprising that this can sometimes take days!

Other effective ways of finding out what children know include using other forms of expression such as drawing, moving or dancing, role play and puppets. These multimodal forms linked with a particular science phenomenon not only engage children but allow them to represent and communicate their thoughts. The process of translating thought into a different vehicle also promotes the higher level cognitive skills of reasoning, deep thinking and learning. Consider asking children to dance a thunderstorm: they might dance like the raindrops or become the lightning bolt or simply lie on the floor like a puddle. For all these different forms, it is important to get children to reflect on what they did in order to gain deeper insights into their thoughts.

Teachers can also use provocations or representation, such as a picture, artefact or book, as a starting point to guide children's thinking and probe their understanding. Using dialogic reading or interactive reading with a story such as *The Tiny Seed* by Eric Carle prompts children to start thinking of how a plant grows and what it needs to live, and can promote a lively discussion that reveals their understandings.

After determining children's prior knowledge, the teacher can consider providing experiences and best approaches that link to children's previous schemas or mental representation to create more complex and sophisticated learning (Campbell & Chealuck, 2015). The approaches that provide more formal introduction to science or intentional teaching would be the transmission approach, guided discovery and the inquiry approach.

The transmission approach

The transmission approach, or direct instruction, is teacher focused and emphasises the transfer of knowledge from the teacher to the child. Often stereotyped as being rather *didactic* in delivery without considering the child's input, the transmission approach can be very effective in the hands of a creative teacher. It serves as a useful and simple means of transferring information to a large group of people in a carefully structured, controlled and consistent manner. It is often used to teach topics where large bodies of information need to be transferred and where hands-on and direct experiences with materials are not possible. The transmission approach also provides children with a shared base of knowledge when introducing a new topic and provides explanations to help children understand. To be effective, the information transferred must be carefully selected and sequenced, delivered in easily understood language and include interesting strategies to engage children (Fleer, 2015). In the example below, a teacher explains the concept of a seed growing.

Growing seeds

A three-year-old pre-school class had prepared a Mother's Day gift. They planted seeds in a cup to thank their mums for nurturing them and helping them to grow. The teacher called them together and showed them a cup with some small plants growing from it.

Teacher: Look what I've got here. What's happened?

Sam: It's green.

Anne: Something's grown.

Teacher: Yes, something has grown, hasn't it? Do you remember the seeds we planted? And what we did after that?

Parveen: Yes, I planted lots and lots.

John: I put water on it.

Sam: I put mine outside.

Teacher: Well, the seeds were actually little plants that hadn't grown yet. When we planted them and watered them, the little seeds took in the water and grew fatter and fatter. Then, the skin on the seed popped open and a little root started to grow and pushed down into the soil. Then a shoot came up and reached towards the sun, which is what we see. That's the green part you can see. Soon the plant will get bigger and taller if we take care of it by watering it and putting it in the sun. Look, I've got a picture that shows you what happened to the seed.

GINETTE PESTANA

SCIENCE

The guided discovery approach

exploration
active, hands-
on searching
and discovering
of information,
resources or
spaces.

The guided discovery approach is one that extends from children's play **exploration**. Without support, children are limited to what they can learn, which could result in a missed opportunity for enhancing their science understanding and knowledge. Guided discovery can change an informal learning situation into a rich learning experience. An attuned teacher provides resources for children to explore and plays a key role in highlighting the science when facilitating or scaffolding their learning. It is important that a teacher learns when to step into children's play or exploration. It requires keen observation from the teacher to identify the teachable moment when they can enter into the children's world to extend the learning. By asking and listening rather than telling, a teacher draws on children's enthusiasm to convey a sense of interest and curiosity. Once invited in, a teacher can model asking questions, stimulate discussions and share or co-construct knowledge to facilitate children's science learning, which is what happened in the example 'Pet corner'.

Pet corner

Following a visit from Anna and her dog Charlie from the Responsible Pet Ownership Program, Sue, a kindergarten teacher, set up a 'pet corner', where she placed some toy animals and various pet accessories. Peta and Danush were playing with the toy dogs, making them eat and drink out of the dishes provided. They soon decided to take them for a walk around the classroom. They stopped and introduced their dogs to Sue.

'Look Sue, my dog's name is Charlie just like Anna's,' said Peta. Danush joined in and told Sue, 'Mine's called Baby because he's very little'. Sue told them that the dogs looked very happy as they must have had an exciting walk. The children told Sue where they had gone and then declared that the dogs were hungry.

'I wonder what dogs eat?' Sue asked them. 'They must eat grass like sheep.'

'No, no! They don't eat grass,' shouted the children.

'Maybe some insects, like a frog or a lizard?' Sue offered.

'No, don't be silly. They eat dog food,' replied Danush.

'I wonder what's in the dog food?' Sue asked them. The children didn't know so Sue suggested that they look at the cans of dog food that were on display at the pet corner. After reading the ingredients together, the children found out that dogs eat different kinds of meat.

'Oh, just like lions and tigers!' said Peta.

'Yes, meat-eaters are also called carnivores,' said Sue.

The inquiry approach

The inquiry approach is regarded as the best approach to teaching science (Hacking, 2014). It has been developed from research that views learning as being constructed and is said to effectively reflect the reality of how scientists work (Fleer, 2015). This approach acknowledges that children have legitimate questions that they want to find the answers to. These questions lead the exploration or investigation and the teacher provides the resources and guides the exploration (Campbell & Chealuck, 2015). It is a carefully thought through approach that can turn children's natural curiosity into scientific learning. It is responsive, flexible and open-ended and moves with children's ideas and questions when they emerge (Touhill, 2012). It offers an opportunity for autonomy, deeper participation, relevance and engagement. This approach exists in various forms with varying degrees of involvement from the teacher and the children. In the early years, this approach is mainly supported by the teacher, and is more relevant for direct exploration of phenomena and materials drawn from the environment in which the children live. For example, it would be difficult for children to have hands-on experience with 'dinosaurs' or 'planets'. Worth and Grollman (2003) use a simple inquiry learning cycle (Figure 9.1) to demonstrate how it works and state that this approach closely resembles how scientists work and how children learn. It also provides the opportunity for children to develop science process skills either explicitly or implicitly.

The cycle begins from an extended period of engagement where children notice, wonder, explore or ask questions about a phenomenon. This can emerge from the children or be teacher initiated. The teacher could facilitate this by helping the children to be more aware of what's happening around them and encouraging questioning. Once a question is raised, the teacher supports this by recognising the science possibility and probes further to determine children's understanding and to identify a question that might be investigated further. This leads to a process where more focused and deeper explorations

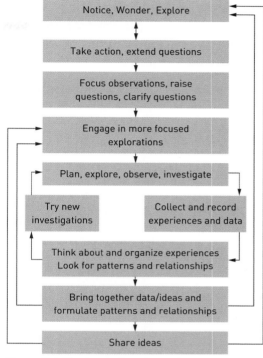

Figure 9.1 The inquiry learning cycle

Source: Hubert Dyasi, CCNY; Karen Worth, Education Development Center Inc.

are made that could include predicting, planning, collecting and recording data. This active, hands-on approach allows children to use their senses to explore and discover. Children also develop science process skills when they bring their ideas together by thinking about them, explaining them and organising these experiences by looking for patterns and relationships. This information is then documented and recorded and shared with the community. The structure is not rigid and from any point, new questions or ideas may emerge that might lead to repeating the process (Worth & Grollman, 2003). The example 'A rainbow over the road' shows how the approach can work in an early childhood setting.

A rainbow over the road

STEPS	EXAMPLE
Notice, wonder, explore	After the rain had stopped, the children went outside. They noticed part of a rainbow across the road next to their kindergarten. Look! There's a rainbow
Take action, extend questions	Let's take a picture of it. When does a rainbow usually appear? Does it appear in the same place?

GINETTE PESTANA

SCIENCE

STEPS	EXAMPLE
Focus observations, raise questions, clarify questions	I wonder what makes a rainbow? Can you touch a rainbow? I wonder what it feels like? Have you seen a rainbow inside the classroom?
Engage in more focused exploration	Look at the photo. Can you see the different colours? What shape is it? Let's find out where a rainbow comes from
Plan, explore, observe, investigate	Rainbows happen after the rain and when the sun starts shining. The sun shines through the tiny raindrops and the light breaks up (refracts) into the rainbow colours Let's see if we can make some rainbows inside the classroom using torches and prisms and sun catchers
Collect and record experiences and data	Record the different ways and positions of the prism that form rainbows by taking pictures and recording children's stories
Think about and organise experiences Look for patterns and relationships	Review pictures and stories with the children and ask them to look for patterns or similar occurrences
Bring together data/ideas and formulate patterns and relationships	Organise the picture and stories into patterns, like the brightest rainbows, or the biggest rainbows Make a class book
Share ideas	Place the book on a library shelf and ask children to read it to their friends to share what they've learnt

Teachers are instrumental in the success of implementing an inquiry approach. They support children when they see themselves as co-learners and work with children to extend their learning. They provide children with the time, space and resources that facilitate deep engagement in investigating their questions and encourage curiosity and wonder (Touhill, 2012).

STOP AND REFLECT

Think about the different pedagogical approaches to enhancing science learning. Which of the approaches have you been using or have you seen being used in the classroom?

- How did you feel about the approach?
- Were the children learning science?
- What was the role of the teacher?
- Now that you've learnt more about different approaches, would you choose a different approach and why?

All these different approaches require different emphases of teacher facilitation and teachers need to develop some key skills and strategies to enhance children's learning.

Enhancing science learning

The key to effective science learning and teaching is the discourse or pattern of **interactive talk** during science experiences and involves the teacher and the child taking on different roles, such as being the 'expert' or 'discussion leader' or 'questioner' (Scott 1998, as cited in Campbell et al., 2015). As the expert, the teacher often explains science concepts at the start or end of a lesson. Teachers could recap the children's previous learning or focus on important aspects of the science idea. Science concepts could be simplified or broken down into smaller manageable parts to communicate them at the child's level and related to a familiar event.

Through introductory discussions, teachers can excite and interest children in the learning experience and children will have an opportunity to reveal their understanding and raise questions about what they want to find out. In small group discussions, children will have opportunities to express their thoughts and views, and listen to others. These discussions allow them to debate conflicting views, adjust their thinking, and share and comment on findings. Children will become active members of the learning community. Group discussions are an ideal opportunity for teachers to introduce and model accurate science vocabulary to children. Used in context and often, these new words can be easily absorbed. It is also important to remember that children should be given time to collect their thoughts to provide thoughtful answers and not to close off the discussion too early before they get a chance. This should also be supported with non-threatening environments to encourage successful interchanges.

The skill of developing **effective questioning** is the most powerful, desired and difficult skill for teachers to acquire. Teachers need to use a wide range of questions to prompt thoughtful responses from children and use both open-ended and closed questions to help guide children at different points of their science learning process. Open-ended questions are useful for generating several different answers and closed questions are useful for directing attention or recalling something. Table 9.6 shows examples of different types of questions and how they can be used in the science classroom.

Teachers also need to learn to teach students how to ask questions that are helpful, useful and that offer potential for investigation. Teachers can role model how to ask questions and support students to develop their own questions in a supportive and accepting environment where questions are welcomed. Questioning is a learnt skill that improves with practice and experience.

In science learning, teachers often plan hands-on investigations to deepen children's understanding. The two most often used investigations in the early childhood classroom are explorations and **guided investigations** and teachers need to be able to facilitate these. Explorations or unguided play experiences are relatively unstructured activities where children are given an opportunity to 'mess about' with selected resources set up by the teacher or with what children have found themselves in the environment. This type of activity provides opportunities for children to get a concrete experience with a phenomenon through observing, handling and experiencing through their senses. Explorations also help to engage learners, stimulate curiosity and promote asking questions. When exploring alongside others, observations, suggestions and actions get shared. For example, the properties of different types of paper can be explored on a light box to see if the light can shine through clearly (transparent); somewhat clearly (translucent) or not at all (opaque).

interactive talk a collaborative exchange and dynamic flow of ideas where participants are active, build on each other's ideas and can have an effect on one another.

effective questioning when a range of responses are accepted, anticipated and built on. Effective questioning engages children and leads them on a journey of discovery and information.

guided investigation the action of children systematically inquiring and investigating through a process of teacher scaffolding.

SCIENCE

GINETTE PESTANA

Table 9.6 Questions for the science classroom

PURPOSE	EXAMPLE
Instigate discovery	How could you find out about …? Why do you think worms prefer dark, damp places?
Elicit children's ideas	Can you tell me more about what you are doing? Why do you think the fairy lights in the garden light up?
Make connections between new and existing knowledge	Now that you've seen the water painted on the concrete yard dry up, how is it like the clothes on the line drying up?
Elicit predictions	What do you think will happen if we leave the ice-cream tub on the counter?
Probe for understanding	What do you mean by …? Why do you think the ice-cream melted when we left it out on the counter?
Promote reasoning	Why do you think the ice-cream in the freezer is hard and the ice-cream left out on the counter is soft?
Serve as a catalyst	What are the other ways you can …? What would you change to make your car go faster down the ramp?
Focus on key science ideas and process skills	Can you see the end of the tuning fork moving, after we struck it? What do you see …?
Encouraging creative thinking and reflection	Can you tell me a bit more about …? This looks familiar. Does it remind you of something?
Directing and recalling	Do the beans we planted look the same as yesterday?

Surface tension explained

It was lunch-time in the four-year-old pre-school class. Noah was the helper for the day and his job was to pour the water from the jug into the children's cups. He was pouring very carefully to make sure he didn't spill any water. For the last cup, he became distracted, poured water to the brim and then stopped to look at it. He noticed that the water had gone beyond the rim of the cup and didn't overflow. He called to his teacher, Jan, and asked her what was happening.

Noah: Look, it's full but the water didn't spill. Why did it do that?

Jan: Let's have a look. I see what you mean. The water level is higher than the rim of the cup and it didn't spill.

Noah: Yeah, why did it do that?

Jan: Let's take a closer look. Can you tell me what shape the top of the water is making?

Noah: It looks round.

Jan: Yes, it is curved and not straight. When you poured the water into the cup to the top, at first the top of the water was straight and level with the rim of the cup. Then when you poured more water, it became higher than the top but it still didn't spill.

Noah: I was very careful not to spill.

Jan: What's happening here is that the top of the water is forming a kind of skin and when you pour more water, it stretches until it cannot hold it any longer, then it spills over.

STOP AND THINK

- What type of question did the teacher, Jan, use?
- What roles did Jan play in helping Noah understand the science concept of surface tension?
- How did Jan support Noah's learning?

Children need long, sustained periods of time to think about what they have seen or experienced, to repeat these experiences again or to solve any problems encountered. A key point to remember in explorations is that they should be 'hands-on' for the children and as much as possible to be 'hands-off' for the teacher. Unsolicited help should not be given in an attempt to 'save' time. Instead, the teacher plays a consultant role by listening to children's descriptions of the exploration, asking pertinent questions and highlighting key findings to support children's experiential learning (Harlan & Rivkin, 2008).

Guided investigations are more formal than explorations and are often based on answering a question either posed by a teacher or in response to a child's query. Often, investigations are set up to find out why things happen or how things work. The teacher first identifies where the child is at in their understanding of the phenomenon and what they are capable of achieving by themselves. Then the teacher plans simple activities, experiments or demonstrations to expand the child's understanding and to broaden experiences. Children go through a sequence of steps, which might involve observing, measuring, recording, manipulating, discussing and interpreting. This type of investigation provides a structured experience of the phenomenon, which supports children in developing explanations for it. For example, children might follow directions to test how to make a car go faster and further when moving down a ramp by adjusting the height of the ramp and recording their findings by drawing or writing in a table, with the teacher's help. To ensure the success of this type of investigation, teachers need to learn how to provide clear and simple instructions on how to carry out a procedure or to do something and use indirect instructions through scaffolding, and encouraging problem solving or inquiry.

Teachers use **demonstrations** to show children a science phenomenon or experiment that may be too dangerous or difficult, or uses too many resources, limiting its availability for children to have hands-on experience. It is also used to show children how to conduct an experiment or explain the steps to be taken. This strategy requires the teacher to carefully plan the sequence of the demonstration to engage children every step of the way. This is important as children are expected to sit, listen and watch the demonstration. If there is no participation or engagement, getting children to sit still is virtually impossible. When demonstrating, teachers must ensure that all children can see what is happening; keep the demonstration short and snappy; involve children with practical tasks during the demonstration; and, if possible, reinforce the main points of the activity with a planned activity or with a recording of what happened (Sharp et al., 2014). For example, if children wanted to find out what type of material is most effective for making a coat to keep Teddy warm in winter, the teacher may pour hot water into glass bottles and wrap different materials around them. They may then place a thermometer inside each bottle and assign different groups of children to watch each bottle and record the temperature after specific time periods.

The physical environment is equally as important as the teacher and the program in helping children learn science. When planning for science activities in the classroom,

demonstration
a practical exhibition and explanation of how scientific phenomena or experiments work or are performed.

SCIENCE

a teacher must consider classroom organisation and management in regard to space, classroom layout and the choice of materials. Children must be provided with space to move from one activity to another and the classroom layout needs to be flexible to accommodate the setting up of different types of activities. The types of materials provided should be relevant to the science learning, and provide opportunities for exploration, extending interest and challenge (Campbell et al., 2015).

Other considerations

Safety is the responsibility of teachers teaching science to children. They must ensure that children are safe at all times during learning experiences. Children must be made aware of what they are doing and the risks involved to their safety and to that of others. Food allergies and cultural considerations must be taken into consideration in planning any sort of science activity. The use of safety equipment such as safety glasses and proper handling of materials must be enforced at all times.

Other factors to consider include the promotion of **inclusivity** and catering to **diverse learners** in the classroom. Teachers should recognise the uniqueness of each individual child, embrace their differences, value all contributions and consider different strategies to include them. All children should be provided with the opportunity to participate and succeed in science activities at their own knowledge and comfort levels. Teachers must balance interactions between all groups, build confidence and self-esteem, value all children's contributions, challenge non-inclusive assumptions and behaviour, and provide accessible materials and equitable distribution of resources.

It is also important to recognise cultural understanding and sensitivity, in particular to the Indigenous perspectives and knowledge systems in Australia, as different cultures view science differently (Campbell et al., 2015). For example, Aboriginal people have a perspective of science that is tied closely with understanding the land. Their understanding of weather and the seasons in Australia makes more sense than imposing the Western perspective of the four seasons on a country that clearly has more variations. (See the Bureau of Meteorology website for Indigenous Weather Knowledge at www.bom.gov.au/iwk/?ref=ftr for more information.)

Teachers must also consider how to integrate science into other curriculum areas to make efficient use of learning time in a crowded curriculum. In the early years, a holistic approach to learning is strongly advocated. Children do not differentiate between different aspects of learning and teachers should not perpetuate a silo effect. Science can easily be linked to maths, literacy, technology and the arts.

Teachers should also develop digital technology skills and incorporate them into their pedagogy to support children's learning. With the advent of smartphones and iPads/tablets, digital technology has entered the early childhood classroom. Children are very familiar with teachers taking photos of their work and achievements, and could likely have the knowhow to do it themselves. This facilitates both the documentation and communication process of learning. In addition, new apps are being created as we speak to create a 'wow' factor. Imagine positioning an iPad over a picture to see the inside of a beating human heart! These apps provide opportunities to start the wondering process and the urge to find out.

inclusivity the act of including children who might otherwise be excluded or marginalised.

diverse learners includes learners from racially, ethnically, culturally and linguistically diverse families, learners with diverse abilities and needs and learners of different socioeconomic status.

Assessing science learning

Recording and documenting children's understanding of science offers authentic and realistic input to planning and implementing science experiences. Before starting an experience, teachers should make a diagnostic assessment to find out children's prior knowledge and understanding. Finding out what children know during the experience through formative assessment enables teachers to tailor the experience to meet the children's requirements and, using summative assessment, sums up children's understanding at a point of time to inform a future judgment. All these forms of assessment are valuable and the form they take should be considered during the planning stage. It would be impossible to go back and gather information after the event has passed.

Assessment in early childhood is mainly done through observation of children or through other forms that make learning visible, such as photographs to capture the wonder experienced or what the children consider valuable, or to show progress or achievements. The teacher could also document conversations, narratives and discussions through learning stories or anecdotal records and mind-maps. Documentation such as work samples (e.g. drawings or posters) created by children could also provide insights into understanding them. Teachers must be mindful to collect evidence of both the product and the process, as well as the context where the learning has occurred, to provide more authentic and relevant assessment. Links to curriculum and planned goals must also be made to determine whether objectives have been met.

Final reflection

Science education in the early years (prior-to-school and primary school) should nurture children's innate curiosity for understanding the world around them and their thirst for knowledge, to lead them into having a lifelong interest in science learning. Teachers have a pivotal role in helping children develop scientific conceptual understanding by extending their knowledge of everyday experiences into scientific understanding. Teachers need to adopt a 'sciencing' attitude to recognise the science affordances found everywhere. Coupled with a positive disposition towards science, teachers will enable rich experiences that will support science learning and understanding in early childhood.

SCIENCE

SUMMARY

- Children learn science through forming conceptual understandings of phenomena in the world that surrounds them. This not only happens alone but through a social process, and experts and cultural environments play a big role in the development of science learning, understanding and helping children become more science literate.
- Supporting science learning in early childhood begins with us, the teachers, in the way we view science either in awe and wonder or with nervous trepidation, and how we recognise science affordances around us and use them to enhance children's understanding of science.

GINETTE PESTANA

- Different pedagogical approaches—such as transmission, guided discovery and inquiry—open possibilities to select best ways to teach children science.
- Teachers are urged to carefully select and use appropriate teaching strategies such as interactive talking, supporting discussions and effective questioning to ensure success in implementing science activities with young children.
- Teachers must also be prepared to effectively organise and conduct explorations and guided investigations, conduct demonstrations, organise the classroom space and choose appropriate materials to facilitate effective science learning in the classroom.
- Other issues, such as safety in the classroom—including all children being culturally sensitive—integrating science into other curricula and the use of ICT digital technology must also be considered.
- Assessing children's understanding of science must be carried out at every stage of their learning to ensure science understanding is being learnt correctly.

FURTHER REFLECTION

- Why do you think it is important to support children's understanding of science?
- How will you support children's understanding of science?
- Do you have a 'sciencing' attitude? Are you able to recognise the science affordances (opportunities) in the environment?

GROUP DISCUSSION

1 Consider the different pedagogical approaches introduced in this chapter. What are the advantages and possible disadvantages of using each approach to teach children about living things?
2 How will you know if a child has gained scientific understanding? Discuss ways of finding this out.

CLASS EXERCISE

Using the information from 'Enhancing science learning', in small groups, devise a simple science experience, then take turns to role-play teacher and child interactions, using the skills described (e.g. effective questioning).

Reflect on what you have learnt about teaching science using these techniques.

FURTHER READING

Campbell, C., Jobling, W. & Howitt, C. (eds) (2015) Science in Early Childhood (2nd edn). Port Melbourne: Cambridge University Press

This textbook provides a comprehensive overview of science education in the early years. It discusses current issues and debates that are relevant to the pre-service teacher drawn from research and understanding of current curriculum documents. It also covers knowledge of key areas of science and detailed explanations of how to guide children's learning in different environments with case studies and practical examples.

Fleer, M. (2015) Science for Children. Port Melbourne: Cambridge University Press.

This textbook introduces the reader to the pedagogy of early childhood and primary science education. Its extensive coverage of various approaches to teaching and learning science provide depth that will allow for informed choices in practice. It also unpacks how knowledge construction takes place across and within communities and cultures.

REFERENCES

ABC (2017) 'T-rex "not strong enough" for running locomotion, researchers say', ABC News, 19 July. www.abc.net.au/news/2017–07–19/t-rex-not-strong-enough-for-running-locomotion-researchers/8722432

Aitken, J., Hunt, J., Roy, E. & Sajfar, B. (2012) *A Sense of Wonder: Science in Early Childhood Education.* Albert Park: Teaching Solutions.

Australian Curriculum Assessment and Reporting Authority (ACARA) (2015a) Australian Curriculum. www.australiancurriculum.edu.au/

Australian Curriculum Assessment and Reporting Authority (ACARA) (2015b) Australian Curriculum Science Foundation—10. www.australiancurriculum.edu.au/f-10-curriculum/science/?strand=Science+Understanding&strand=Science+as+a+Human+Endeavour&strand=Science+Inquiry+Skills&capability=ignore&priority=ignore&elaborations=true

Australian Curriculum Assessment and Reporting Authority (ACARA) (2015c) Australian Curriculum Science Key Ideas. www.australiancurriculum.edu.au/f-10-curriculum/science/key-ideas/

Beeley, K. (2012) *Science in the Early Years: Understanding the World through Play-based Learning.* London: Featherstone Education, Bloomsbury Publishing plc.

Blake, E. & Howitt, C. (2012) *Science in Early Learning Centres: Satisfying Curiosity, Guided Play or Lost Opportunities?* in K.C.D. Tan & M. Kim (eds). *Issues and Challenges in Science Education Research: Moving Forward* (pp. 281–298). Dordrecht: Springer, pp. 281–98.

Brooks, J. G. (2011) *Big Science for Growing Minds: Constructivist Classroom for Young Thinkers.* New York: Teachers College Press.

Campbell, C. & Chealuck, K. (2015) 'Approaches to Enhance Science Learning', in C. Campbell, W. Jobling, & C. Howitt (eds), *Science in Early Childhood* (2nd edn). Port Melbourne: Cambridge University Press.

Campbell, C. & Jobling, W. (2010) A Snapshot of Science Education in Kindergarten Settings. *International Research in Early Childhood Education*, 1(1): 3–20.

Campbell, C., Jobling, W. & Howitt, C. (eds) (2015) *Science in Early Childhood* (2nd edn). Port Melbourne: Cambridge University Press.

Charlesworth, R. & Lind, K. (2013) *Maths and Science for Young Children.* Belmont: Wadsworth, Cengage Learning.

Department of Education, Employment and Workplace Relations (DEEWR) (2009) *Belonging, Being & Becoming: The Early Years Learning Framework for Australia.* ACT, Australia: Commonwealth of Australia.

Dockrell, J.E., Braisby, N. & Best, R.M. (2007) 'Children's Acquisition of Science Terms: Simple Exposure Is Insufficient', *Learning and Instruction*, 17(6): 577–94.

Edwards, K. & Loveridge, J. (2011) 'The Inside Story: Looking Into Early Childhood Teachers' Support Of Children's Scientific Learning', *Australasian Journal of Early Childhood*, 36(2): 28–35.

Fleer, M. (2015) *Science for Children.* Port Melbourne: Cambridge University Press.

Fleer, M., Gomes, J. & March, S. (2014) 'Science Learning Affordances in Preschool Environments', *Australasian Journal of Early Childhood*, 39(1): 38–48.

Hacking, M. (2014) 'Challenges and Opportunities for Australian Science Education', *Professional Educator*, 13(5): 4–7.

Harlan, J. D. & Rivkin, M.S. (2008) *Science Experiences for the Early Childhood Years: An Integrated Affective Approach* (9th edn). New Jersey: Pearson Education, Inc.

Kelly, L. (2015) 'Is Science Important in the Early Years?' in D. Stead & L. Kelly (eds), *Inspiring Science in the Early Years: Exploring Good Practice.* Maidenhead: McGraw-Hill Education, Open University Press.

SCIENCE

GINETTE PESTANA

National Curriculum Board (2009) Shape of the Australian Curriculum: Science. https://acaraweb.blob.core.windows.net/resources/Australian_Curriculum_-_Science.pdf

Nolan, A. (2015) 'Science in the National Early Years Learning Framework', in C. Campbell, W. Jobling & C. Howitt (eds), *Science in Early Childhood* (2nd edn). Port Melbourne: Cambridge University Press.

Petriwskyj, A. (2013) 'Science', in D. Pendergast & S. Garvis (eds), *Teaching Early Years: Curriculum, Pedagogy and Assessment.* Crows Nest: Allen & Unwin, pp.107–24.

Rennie, L.J. (2005) 'Science Awareness and Scientific Literacy', *Teaching Science, 51*(1): 10–14.

Robson, S. (2012) *Developing Thinking and Understanding in Young Children: An Introduction for Students* (2nd edn). Oxon, UK: Routledge.

Russell, T. & McGuigan, L. (2016) *Exploring Science with Young Children*, London: SAGE Publishings Ltd.

Sharp, J., Peacock, G., Johnsey, R., Simon, S., Smith, R., Cross, A. & Harris, D. (2014) *Primary Science: Teaching Theory and Practice* (7th edn). London: Sage Publications.

Smith, K. & Fitzgerald, A. (2013) 'Making Sense of Primary Science', in A. Fitzgerald (ed.), *Learning and Teaching Primary Science.* New York: Cambridge University Press, pp. 1–16.

Touhill, L. (2012) 'Inquiry-based Learning', *NQS PLP e-Newsletter, 42*, 1–4. www.earlychildhoodaustralia.org.au/nqsplp/wp-content/uploads/2012/10/NQS_PLP_E-Newsletter_No45.pdf

Tu, T. (2006) 'Preschool Science Environment: What Is Available in a Preschool Classroom?' *Early Childhood Education Journal, 33*(4), 245–51.

Vygotsky, L.S. (1987) 'Thinking and Speech', in R.W. Rieber & A.S. Carton (eds), *The Collected Works of L.S. Vygotsky* (vol. 1: 'Problems of General Psychology'). New York: Plenum Press.

Worth, K. & Grollman, S. (2003) *Worms, Shadows and Whirlpools: Science in the Early Childhood Classroom.* Portsmouth, NH: Heinemann.

PART THREE
PROFESSIONAL PRACTICE

Part 3 focuses on the underpinning principles and practices of early childhood teaching: the 'how' and 'why' of teacher practice. It is concerned with the application of theory to practice and begins with an introduction to professional practice that invites you to join this 'community of practice'.

Observation, planning, assessment and evaluation are key aspects of the early teacher's professional role and responsibilities: these are the focus of Chapters 11 and 12.

Chapters 13, 14 and 15 give attention to relationships and, in particular, the importance of understanding children as individuals and knowing and working with families in partnership relationships. The emphasis given to relationships is confirmed in the key national document that guides early childhood education: the Early Years Learning Framework.

> Children learn about themselves and construct their own identity within the context of their families and communities. This includes their relationships with people, places and things and the actions and responses of others … Relationships are the foundations for the construction of identity—'who I am', 'how I belong' and 'what is my influence?'

(DEEWR, 2009, p.20)

Chapter 16 focuses on teaching practice issues in contemporary society. The chapter provides provocations and points for discussion as you prepare to enter the teaching profession. We have chosen issues that are important to us as teacher educators committed to quality teaching and teachers in a contemporary society. Chapter 16 also serves as a conclusion to this book and draws out key messages from the previous chapters related to contemporary teaching practice.

Introduction to Professional Practice

Ann Hooper

Chapter objectives

In this chapter, we will:

- reflect on personal perceptions of who teachers are and their roles and responsibilities
- discuss the image you have of yourself as a teacher and describe your emerging philosophy as a teacher
- critically examine where this image of yourself as a teacher comes from in terms of socio-historical images and educational philosophy perspectives
- discuss planning documents in current use in early childhood or junior school settings
- discuss the professional, legal and ethical responsibilities of early childhood professional teachers
- examine the importance of critical thinking, reflective practice and research, including the researcher, in the context of 'evidence-based practice' and 'best practice'.

Key terms

codes of conduct and ethics	ethical behaviour	research
duty of care	mandatory reporting	

> As a teacher, it's your role to grow and develop the minds in your classroom.
>
> Every child must succeed in an education worth having.
>
> (AITSL, 2017)

Congratulations on your decision to become an early childhood teacher. In making this decision you join a very special group of people who share a commitment to the youngest and often most vulnerable members of our society. This binds us in our belief that providing young children with the best start in life increases their opportunities to grow, thrive and develop to their full potential. We see our role as a privilege, but the weight of this responsibility is also heavy. The consequences of our work are profound and longlasting as we work with young people in their vital, formative years.

One of the most important aspects of the pre-service teacher's role is to be inducted into the *profession* of teaching; this will assist and support you on your journey to become the very best teacher you can be. Our children deserve no less.

Professionalism involves commitment to codes of practice and professional standards. We have deliberately used the term *commitment* here to avoid any possibility of assuming professionalism is simply demonstrated through *compliance* with the codes and standards. Commitment is about actions that go beyond compliance; it is about attitudes and a determination to do one's best. Professionalism is not something that happens when you graduate and formally join the teaching profession; it is developed, practised and demonstrated in your attitude to your studies; and your relationships with your fellow students, lecturers and other professionals, children and their families, while on practicum placements. A commitment to learning and improving is the foundation of this developing professionalism.

Over your years of study, you will spend time in a variety of settings as you engage in practicum experiences. This is like a master–apprentice model, where you have the opportunity to watch, learn and practise your own developing skills, theories and understandings about young children and teaching and learning under the watchful, supportive eye of an experienced teacher. These experiences are crucial to your progress, so how you approach these opportunities and the relationships you form in the varied settings you work in is most important.

The success of all these experiences in your Initial Teacher Education studies will largely depend on you, your attitudes and your willingness to engage with the teaching profession.

Introduction

It is not uncommon for Initial Teacher Education students to commence their journey with ideas of grandeur, believing that they will be the ones to make the positive difference in the lives of the children they teach. Often, if your personal experiences of schooling have not been so positive, you might be determined that you will do things differently, or if your encounters were generally positive, you will draw on those experiences to ensure 'your' children are similarly encouraged. Either way, most new and pre-service teachers see themselves as 'champions' of young children and believe that, under their care, children will thrive and flourish. And this is admirable. We all want the best outcomes for children, and high-quality teaching and learning experiences are key to this. There are limits, though, to this glorification of your role. Many beginning teachers see themselves as 'owners' of the children in their care from February to December, at which time, usually, they are passed on to the next teacher, all the better for having been with you for twelve months.

This view is similar to seeing education as a 'one-man show'—as having your own 'business', if you like—where you, and only you, know what is best for this group of children, and, if left alone to do the 'job' for which you are well equipped, all will be well. This is not an uncommon scenario in education, where many teachers work alone, 'behind closed doors', and for many teachers, it is their preferred way of being.

This is, however, a very narrow view of the role of a teacher and certainly not one that is in the best interests of children. You may have heard the phrase 'it takes a village to raise a child'—this applies so aptly to our work in early childhood education. To be a professional requires you to be part of a group that shares common beliefs and ways of being and acting that uphold the values of that group. To think that we alone can provide the very best for young children is short sighted at best, and arrogant at worst. In the school or centre in which we work, we must see the children as 'our' children, and believe that by working in collaboration with all the stakeholders who have an interest in these children, their needs will be better served. Chapter 13 emphasises the importance of building and maintaining relationships with other professionals and families; these partnerships are fundamental to the professional role of the teacher.

Many educational settings now value and advocate for an environment where teachers are provided with the time and tools to collaborate and become lifelong learners, in the knowledge that they collectively are ultimately able to increase achievement for children's learning far beyond what any of them could achieve alone. I recall my first whole-school staff meeting at my new school, where it struck me like a bolt of lightning that I was part of something bigger here—that although throughout my years of training to be a teacher, where all I could dream about was the day I would have 'my' class of children and what a difference I would make to their lives, I realised that, in isolation, my impact would be minimal, but with a team of 'like-minded' professionals working collaboratively together for the wellbeing of all the children in our care, anything was possible. We would be the village.

This chapter provides the foundation upon which pre-service teachers develop their beginning understanding of themselves as future teachers in prior-to-school and primary school settings. The concept of teacher as pedagogue is examined through an overview of early childhood teaching, and teaching techniques undertaken in the context of describing their emerging philosophy as a teacher. This discussion draws on historical and contemporary contexts underpinned by theory and research. Attention is drawn to institutional, community and political expectations; and institutions, associations and legal responsibilities designed to support teachers in their role. The chapter discusses advocacy and issues associated with professional accountability, the Code of Ethics and the United Nations Convention on the Rights of the Child.

The initial focus is on the planning process, interpreting current frameworks and curriculum documentation and linking these to practice and children's learning. The chapter introduces the reality of the changing role of the teacher in contemporary Australian education. This calls on an analysis of the importance of critical thinking and reflective practice across a broad area of care, teaching and learning.

What is a professional?

The terms 'profession' or 'professional' are used widely and often loosely. The word can mean somebody who does something for a living: a professional baker, a professional golfer.

It can mean anyone who does an especially good job: 'You're a real pro'.

More formally, it means a member of an occupation with recognised professional status that is attained through an educational program. In general, professionals embrace the corporate identity and values of their profession, and model these for the clients—in our case, the children we teach, and their families.

Professionalism underpins all aspects of early childhood education practice and emphasises a constant awareness and application of codes and guidelines for professional conduct, self-reflection and continual improvement. Gaining a professional qualification is not the end of your learning or commitment to professional development and improvement. A commitment to ongoing professional learning, reflecting your continuing interest in research and developments in the profession (teaching), is an important part of this professionalism.

Teachers are professionals who belong to a 'community of practice', where knowledge is used by people to achieve particular outcomes (Edwards, 2009).

As people enter a new profession, they need to learn the language and knowledge of that professional group in order to participate and contribute to that community. It can be understood as a type of induction into a 'culture' that, like all cultures, has a shared history,

ANN HOOPER

traditions, practices, tools, language and values. The professional culture of education holds specific understandings about children, learning and knowledge. These understandings change over time in response to new research, so it is important to keep abreast of changes. Education and the teaching profession have a particular language for talking about observing, programming and planning, and 'newcomers' must learn how to participate in this dialogue in order to contribute to the profession (Edwards, 2009).

> A profession is a disciplined group of individuals who adhere to ethical standards and who hold themselves out as, and are accepted by the public as possessing special knowledge and skills in a widely recognised body of learning derived from research, education and training at a high level, and who are prepared to apply this knowledge and exercise these skills in the interest of others. It is inherent in the definition of a profession that a code of ethics governs the activities of each profession. Such codes require behaviour and practice beyond the personal moral obligations of an individual. They define and demand high standards of behaviour in respect to the services provided to the public and in dealing with professional colleagues. Further, these codes are enforced by the profession and are acknowledged and accepted by the community.
>
> (Professions Australia: www.professions.com.au/defineprofession.html)

This is true of the profession of teaching, and throughout this chapter we will examine the codes of behaviour and practice and the role of ethics and moral obligations inherent in this important profession. You will examine deeply and reflect on your own identity as a pre-service teacher, and consider what has shaped this. You will understand that your current perception of the profession of teaching will and should be challenged, reconsidered and continually adjusted. You will begin to understand that your journey extends far beyond your years of study and that, as a professional, you will be committed to continuous self-improvement, deep reflection on your practice and evolving philosophies, and an openness and willingness to work with, and learn from, colleagues in the quest for better outcomes for children.

As a professional you belong to a particular 'community of practice', where knowledge is used by like-minded people to achieve particular outcomes. These groups or communities understand similar types of knowledge and have a language for speaking about this knowledge to others in the profession. New members of the profession need to learn the language and knowledge in order to participate and contribute to the community. Early childhood education represents a community of practice because it holds specific knowledge about children and learning and has specific ways of enacting the craft of teaching as well as a particular language for talking about all aspects of their work (Edwards, 2009).

National goals for the twenty-first century

A number of the significant shifts in policy and practice affecting the field of early childhood education and care that were to mark the 1990s had their beginnings in the late 1980s. In September 1988, the Australian Early Childhood Association (AECA) established a working party to develop the first Code of Ethics for the Australian early childhood profession. In May 1999, the Commonwealth Child Care Advisory Council (CCCAC) was given new terms of reference by the Minister of Family and Community Services (Warwick Smith). Through a process of consultation with the community and the early childhood sector, the advisory council was charged with exploring and reporting 'on the nature of child care in 2001 and beyond' (CCCAC, 2001, p.161). This culminated in a report: *Child Care Beyond 2001*. One of the key recommendations of the committee's report was the development of a national children's agenda. This agenda would 'put the best interests of children as a central focus of Australian society' (CCCAC, 2001, p.6) and contribute to improving the status and standing of children, and those working in the children's services profession. The report also made a number of recommendations concerning improved childcare flexibility and access.

The year 2007 saw the election of a Labor government. One of the first acts of the government was to introduce national early childhood reform, addressing many of the issues of fragmentation and unequal access to early childhood education raised in previous reports.

The reform agenda introduced Australia's first national early childhood curriculum—the Early Years Learning Framework (EYLF). It sought to improve access to early childhood education and care, especially to pre-school in the year prior to school. The CCCAC was replaced by the Australian Children's Education and Care Quality Authority (ACECQA). The ACECQA administers the National Quality Framework (NQF), which establishes baseline and aspirational standards for early childhood program quality.

In December 2008, the Ministerial Council on Education, Employment, Training and Youth Affairs (MCEETYA) endorsed national goals for school education. The preamble declares that:

> Improving educational outcomes for all young Australians is central to the nation's social and economic prosperity and will position young people to live fulfilling, productive and responsible lives. Young Australians are therefore placed at the centre of the Melbourne Declaration on Educational Goals.
>
> (MCEETYA, 2008, p.7)

The specific goals identified are summarised as:

> Goal 1: Australian schooling promotes equity and excellence
>
> Goal 2: All young Australians become:
> * Successful learners
> * Confident and creative individuals
> * Active and informed citizens.
>
> (MCEETYA, 2008, p.3)

The Melbourne Declaration

Goal 2 of the MCEETYA (2008) declaration states that:

> The teachers and leaders who work in Australia's schools and educate young people are of fundamental importance to achieving these educational goals for young Australians. Excellent teachers have the capacity to transform the lives of students and to inspire and nurture their development as learners, individuals and citizens. They provide an additional source of encouragement, advice and support for students outside the home, shaping teaching around the ways different students learn and nurturing the unique talents of every student. (p.11)

Goal 2 also identifies 'Strengthening early childhood education' and recognises that:

> Governments have important roles to play in ensuring that children receive quality early childhood education and care. The period from birth through to eight years, especially the first three years, sets the foundation for every child's social, physical, emotional and cognitive development. Early childhood education

ANN HOOPER

and care provides a basis for life and learning, both within and beyond the home, and is supported by healthy, safe and stimulating environments.

Children who participate in quality early childhood education are more likely to make a successful transition to school, stay longer in school, continue on to further education and fully participate in employment and community life as adults (p.11).

The 2009 National Early Childhood Development Strategy *Investing in the Early Years* states that early childhood education and care are vital for young children to have the best start in life (COAG, 2009a). As in the early years of education provision for the Australian colonies, education is regarded as a social investment. The difference now is that this 'social investment' is recognised as delivering the best human, social, educational and economic returns when it is applied specifically to early childhood education, including the pre-school years.

The National Early Childhood Development Strategy promotes:

- parents as the most influential educators in their child's early life
- addressing disadvantage and vulnerability
- promoting early learning and successful transition to school
- building human capital and economic prosperity.

These important objectives have developed significantly from earlier views on the purpose of early education and learning, and are informed by significant research and evidence showing that early growth and development of children provide the foundations for future learning and success (COAG, 2009a).

Image of a teacher

In Chapter 1 you were invited to articulate and reflect on your image of the child, and your concept of childhood. Here you are invited to engage in the same critical reflection, this time focusing on your *image of the teacher* and the image you have in your mind of the sort of teacher you aspire to becoming.

As with all images and perceptions, there is wide variation in people's views of what a teacher is and what they 'should' be like. Each of you will bring to this 'image' many experiences (good and bad): influences of significant people, including your parents, teachers and friends; influences from popular media, news items, commentary, films and literature (what images of teachers do films such as *Dead Poet's Society*, and *Kindergarten Cop* promote?); and, of course, ideas and research you are introduced to in your current studies.

Some of you will have recently completed twelve or thirteen years of education, or you may have spent some years in the workforce; some of you may have children of your own. These experiences will form your 'default' position—your current philosophy. All your thoughts and actions will be shaped by your philosophy, even if it is not yet a coherent and consciously articulated philosophy or theory. Your personal view of the world, how you make sense of what you see, including your view on learning and how children learn best, is your personal philosophy. Your philosophy should continue to be shaped and influenced by new knowledge and the experiences you gather over the course of your studies, and, as you continue to engage in reflective practice, during your years as a teacher. To become an effective teacher it is vital that you frequently question and critique your own views and are aware of what shapes them. If your actions and thinking are only shaped by your own views and ways of seeing the world, how likely are you to be able to accommodate or understand the views of others? It is important, and part of your professional responsibility, to always be prepared to reflect and be open to the possibility of change (McArdle et al., 2015).

STOP AND REFLECT

Explore your own assumptions and preconceptions, including:

- Has a particular teacher positively or negatively influenced your idea of what a good teacher is and should be?
- What makes a good teacher?
- List the characteristics of a good classroom.
- What makes a good student?
- Consider where your perspectives come from.

Developing a critical perspective

Over the course of four years you will (I hope!) have your preconceived notions:

- challenged
- criticised
- confirmed.

Therefore, it is important to know what you think and what it is that has shaped this thinking and understand that this will influence your practice. In Chapter 1, Malaguzzi was quoted as observing that your image of the child is 'where your teaching begins'. Your ideas or image of the teacher also directly contribute to your attitudes towards your studies and your teaching practice.

You are encouraged to be prepared to articulate and reflect on your ideas and engage in respectful discussions with your peers, to open your mind to new and diverse points of view. As you cultivate your professional persona, it is vital to develop a questioning and critical perspective: Why do I act the way I do? Who is affected by my actions? How could I act differently/do this differently?

Reflective practice and critical perspectives are important tools that you should have in your professional 'tool kit'. Reflective practice includes being able to question and hypothesise reasons why things work well, and why they don't. Taking a critical perspective is a core element of the work of the contemporary professional teacher (McArdle et al., 2015). Critically reflecting on your work involves questioning and reconsidering beliefs and practices that can be taken for granted and re-examining them in the light of new knowledge, contexts or the specific needs of particular children. 'Teacher as researcher' is a critical aspect of your developing skills as a professional, and should be built into your practice: ensure you make time and take the opportunity to think about what you are doing, why you are doing it, who it influences positively and who might not be well served by your habits of practice.

ANN HOOPER

Working and learning in teams with colleagues can support new ideas and provide opportunities for viewing learning through the perspective of others (remember the idea of the village needed to raise a child).

> A crucially reflective teacher understands that there are options for acting differently that may produce better outcomes for more children.
>
> (Churchill et al., 2011, p.69)

It can be difficult to challenge the ideas that the community values because new ideas have to measure up against traditional ideas that have long been important to that community. This becomes an issue of our 'habits of minds'—we continue to do things because 'that's the way we do things here'.

It is important to find opportunities to work and learn with colleagues and other professionals to share ideas and to have existing ideas challenged. This will assist to support new learning and is critical in developing a professional approach to teaching (Edwards, 2009).

Understanding our beliefs

The beliefs and values teachers hold about education shape how they interpret teaching and learning and what is seen as 'good' or appropriate practice for children. As we all hold different beliefs, it is not always possible to have agreement on what constitutes appropriate education for all children. It is important to appreciate that parents and children also have beliefs and must be acknowledged in our decision making. Being aware of your values is a means of ensuring you are sensitive to beliefs and values held by parents and children. This can enhance your ability to respond in the best interests of children (Edwards, 2009).

STOP AND THINK

- List ten things you consider to be important elements of being a professional teacher.
- Prioritise this list from most important to least important.
- Briefly explain how and why you have chosen these ten elements, and the rationale for your prioritisation.

How we work: duty of care

We have agreed that our work with children is important and carries significant responsibilities. How, then, are teachers guided in their work to ensure they uphold the values of the profession and always work in the best interests of the child?

There are a number of professional documents and guiding principles that have been developed for the profession to support and guide us in our everyday work.

Here are some key points about your **duty of care**.

duty of care a legal and ethical obligation and duty that you have as a professional to take care of and keep children safe.

- All teachers must understand their legal obligations as they undertake their work with children.
- You cannot train or be prepared for every potential issue.
- Understanding your duty of care is mandatory (i.e. it is a requirement, not a choice).

A fundamental obligation that you have as a professional is to keep children safe.

The idea that you are legally responsible for the children in your care can be daunting. 'Duty of care' is a legal term, but essentially it is about your professional judgment, and reasonable and ethical behaviour (McArdle, et al., 2015). As a professional it is incumbent on you to have an accurate understanding of your duty of care responsibilities, and their limits, when working with all children. All teachers have a responsibility to take reasonable steps to protect children from risks of injury, including psychological distress, as well as risks within the centre or school and in the online learning environment. This duty also requires protection from potential risks that a teacher should reasonably have foreseen, and against which preventative measures could be taken. The concept of duty of care is more than children's physical welfare and can include matters both on and off the school grounds/centre and matters in and out of school/centre hours of operation. Duty of care extends beyond a child's physical safety and wellbeing to include moral, intellectual and social wellbeing. It also extends to other members of the learning community.

Basic standards of care required by schools and centres may include:

- provision of suitable and safe premises
- provision of an adequate system of supervision
- implementation of strategies to prevent bullying
- ensuring that medical assistance is provided to a sick or injured student.

The nature of the duty of care will vary according to the situation—for example, the standard of care required when taking a group of pre-school children for swimming lessons will differ from that of teaching a group of Year 6 students in a classroom.

Child protection

At all times, teachers must be acting in the best interests of the children in their care. This includes:

- reporting to Child Protection all allegations or disclosures of physical abuse, sexual abuse, emotional abuse and neglect
- reporting to Child Protection when a belief is formed that a child has been harmed or is at risk of being harmed
- making children's ongoing safety and wellbeing the primary focus of decision making
- sharing appropriate information, expertise and resources with other service providers supporting children
- protecting and promoting the cultural and spiritual identity of children and maintaining their connection to their family and/or community of origin
- enabling children and their families to access appropriate services in order to reduce the long-term effects of abuse and neglect.

The *National Framework for Protecting Australia's Children 2009–2020* (COAG, 2009b) includes a description of 'the problem': what needs to change, a national approach and a discussion of the framework. The National Framework contains six supporting outcomes:

1 children live in safe and supportive families and communities
2 children and families access adequate support to promote safety and intervene early
3 risk factors for child abuse and neglect are addressed

ANN HOOPER

4 children who have been abused or neglected receive the support and care they need for their safety and wellbeing
5 Indigenous children are supported and safe in their families and communities
6 child sexual abuse and exploitation is prevented and survivors receive adequate support (COAG, 2009b).

Each state has its own requirements and reforms around child protection based on this National Framework. These can be found in Appendix A: Current Initiatives and Reforms of the National Framework (COAG, 2009b).

Mandatory reporting

mandatory reporting
the legislative requirement for selected groups of people to report suspected cases of child abuse and neglect to government authorities.

Mandatory reporting is an important legal requirement of teachers. All schools and centres have policies and procedures around how to manage such incidents, and it is highly unlikely that you will have to manage such a situation without the support of management. It is important, however, that you begin to understand what the requirements are for you in relation to your duty of care to young children.

It is mandated that staff members must make a report to Child Protection as soon as practicable after forming a belief on reasonable grounds that a child is in need of protection.

There may be reasonable grounds for forming a belief if:

- a child states that they have been physically or sexually abused
- a child states that they know someone who has been physically or sexually abused
- someone who knows a child states that the child has been abused
- a staff member observes signs of abuse, including non-accidental or unexplained injury, persistent neglect, and poor care or lack of appropriate supervision (DEECD and DHS, 2010).

Confidentiality is provided for reporters, unless a court requires the reporter to attend court (Marbina et al., 2010).

Policies and procedures

It is incumbent on you, and part of your professional responsibility, to ensure you are aware of and well informed about the various school-based documents and procedures designed to ensure the protection and wellbeing of the children in your care. When on practicum, you need to be informed of the range of policies and practices peculiar to the setting in which you are working. Your supervising teacher will support you in this matter.

Given our role in working closely with young children, it is not surprising that teachers are expected to demonstrate a higher level of 'care' than others. However, so long as you take all reasonable care and carefully follow policies and procedures, you are undertaking your duty of care.

Some practical examples of this are:

- be where you are supposed to be (including 'yard duty')
- do not leave children unsupervised
- think ahead to anticipate potential risks
- evaluate the likelihood of the risk and potential severity of harm

- take risk-management actions in advance (schools have risk-management pro-forms and strict procedures to be followed)
- know and follow school/centre policies and protocols.

Record keeping

Documentation is an important part of your daily accountability and record keeping is imperative in your accountability. Records to be kept may include:

- attendance records
- accident/incident reports
- assessment records.

As a rule of thumb, you are encouraged to keep all records—careless disposal can be seen as unprofessional. Consider carefully how and what you record—notes are not for your eyes only and can be required by governance legal bodies. Keep notes factual—document what happened, not what you think could have occurred—and avoid commenting based on opinion or emotion. Increasingly, Australian schools have become more defined and regulated by official accreditation frameworks, including teacher registration and professional standards that identify the key elements of a teacher's work. There is an expectation that teachers will behave ethically and comply with all requirements. In short, teachers are expected to predict, recognise and manage all forms of risk related to their work with children. A good motto is 'being there and taking care' (Churchill et al., 2011).

Ethics in teaching

Teachers are expected to behave ethically at all times. Our young children are the most vulnerable people in our communities and those who care for them are awarded an enormous privilege and at the same time a significant responsibility for their protection and safety. It is incumbent on you as you enter this profession to know your responsibilities and become familiar with the relevant regulatory and governance bodies you are answerable to. As a profession, we are expected to abide by and implement guidelines set down by our profession for the actions and decisions we take.

Ethical behaviour involves making informed, responsible decisions and acting with discretion, respect and consideration of the rights of others. When you first go out on practicum, and as a beginning teacher, you will have access to significant amounts of privileged information about children, their families and staff at the centre/school. You will be expected to understand that these relationships are built on trust and respect and that you need to honour these and at all times uphold your professional responsibility (McArdle et al., 2015).

ethical behaviour making informed, responsible decisions and acting with discretion, respect and consideration of the rights of others.

Teaching as a moral craft

Teachers make moral decisions every day in the course of their work. They decide when and to whom they give attention, which learning and teaching strategies to employ, who to work with and who to leave to work alone, how much time is given to an individual child, how each child is engaged with, the way they are spoken to, the body language used in response to each child, and much more. Teachers continually make trade-offs among competing demands, and all their actions are guided by their values (Clarke & Pittaway, 2014).

STOP AND REFLECT

What do you value most in your relationships with children? Consider …

- *fairness:* treating children even-handedly
- *power or control in limited situations:* not overextending your authority, seeing children as belonging and having a voice in their learning
- *truthfulness:* truly valuing honest communication
- *rights:* respecting everyone's entitlements and being aware of potential violations of rights
- *duties/obligations:* following through with your actions.

Teachers need to let *all* children know that they are respected and acknowledged as unique individuals. It is important to remember that *you* set the moral and ethical climate in your classroom. This is a huge responsibility and can have significant implications for the well-being of all children in the room. If you choose to ignore moral issues, such as pretending not to overhear children racially slurring another child because it is too uncomfortable to deal with, you are giving permission for this behaviour to continue. If, on the other hand, you make it clear through your words and actions that all children in your class will treat each other with respect, you are providing a powerful role model and setting up a culture in your room where all children will be accepted and feel a sense of belonging.

> You have the power and the responsibility to set the learning 'climate' in your room.
>
> (Clarke & Pittaway, 2014)

STOP AND REFLECT

Consider:

- Should schools be accountable for the social and emotional development of children as well as academic performance?
- What are the implications of this in early years environments?

Supporting early childhood professionals

In most professional organisations, documents and policies are developed and enacted to support those who work in the profession to adhere to the high standards and expectations set by the body. Such documents can be found in the field of education and they support us to undertake our work in a consistent and professional manner. All members of the profession are expected to be guided by these documents.

The Code of Ethics

Professionals who adhere to the Code of Ethics act in the best interests of all children and work collectively to ensure that every child is thriving and learning. The first Code of Ethics for the Australian early childhood profession was developed in 1988; it was widely cited and used for 19 years. The first review of the Code of Ethics began in 2003, with the second version launched in 2007. The second review of the Code of Ethics began in 2014 with the third (current) version approved by the Early Childhood Australia National Board in February 2016. The core principles in this Code of Ethics are based on the fundamental and prized values of the profession. They act to guide decision making in relation to ethical responsibilities.

Being ethical involves thinking about everyday actions and decision making, either individually or collectively, and responding with respect to all concerned. Early Childhood Australia's Code of Ethics recognises that early childhood professionals are in a unique position of trust and influence in their relationships with children, families, colleagues and the community, therefore professional accountability is vital. The code is not intended to, and could not possibly, provide easy answers, formulae or prescriptive solutions for the complex issues early childhood professionals face in their work. As an aspirational document, it does provide a basis for critical reflection, a guide for professional behaviour and principles to inform individual and collective decision making. These core principles—which require a commitment to respect and maintain the rights and dignity of children, families, colleagues and communities—are:

- Each child has unique interests and strengths and the capacity to contribute to their communities
- Children are citizens from birth with civil, cultural, linguistic, social and economic rights
- Effective learning and teaching is characterised by professional decisions that draw on specialised knowledge and multiple perspectives
- Partnerships with families and communities support shared responsibility for children's learning, development and wellbeing
- Democratic, fair and inclusive practices promote equity and a strong sense of belonging
- Respectful, responsive and reciprocal relationships are central to children's education and care
- Play and leisure are essential for children's learning, development and wellbeing
- Research, inquiry and practice-based evidence inform quality education and care.

(Early Childhood Australia, 2016)

In addition, the Code specifies that:

Early Childhood Australia recognises that Aboriginal and Torres Strait Islander people have been nurturing and teaching children on this land for thousands of years. The Code of Ethics acknowledges Aboriginal and Torres Strait Islander traditional ways of being and caring for children.

(Early Childhood Australia, 2016)

STOP AND THINK

We encourage you to access Early Childhood Australia's Code of Ethics at www. earlychildhoodaustralia.org.au/our-publications/eca-code-ethics/ and to discuss practical, real ways of implementing the principles it discusses. Compare the new document with earlier additions and note the changes. How do they reflect the changing values and culture of our modern society?

ANN HOOPER

The importance of the Code of Ethics

Early Childhood Australia's Code of Ethics is an inspirational (and aspirational) document that symbolises professional commitments and ethical responsibilities, the profession's history and current obligations.

- It is a way of looking (a lens) that enables early childhood professionals to recognise the rights, entitlements and strengths of children, families and communities.
- It is a strong tool for advocacy, based on the United Nations Convention on the Rights of the Child (1989).
- It is a way of uniting the sector, providing us with a common language and shared values.
- It is a framework for reflection, promoting a team approach to solving ethical issues and collectively reflecting on the profession's values.
- It is a guide for decision making and provides ethical signposts.
- It is a call to action: protection for young children in unethical situations, reflecting the strong history of early childhood professionals advocating on behalf of children and families.

Each principle or commitment in the code reflects or is based on a value position. Values are deeply held beliefs that commit people to action, or underpin their responses to issues. Acting on value commitments requires personal qualities such as courage, honesty and perseverance. Adopting the code means honouring these values, qualities and processes. It is a professional responsibility. These principles are based on fundamental and prized values of the profession (Early Childhood Australia, 2016).

STOP AND REFLECT

- How are your values formed?
- What values do you hold as important for your work with and on behalf of children and families?
- Do you think your values change over time or with further experience? If so, why?

Other guiding documents

A number of documents have also been developed by regulatory bodies such as the Victorian Institute of Teaching (VIT) and the NSW Institute of Teachers—part of the NSW Education Standards Authority (NESA)—that provide standards for the behaviour and professional practice of all teachers registered to practice. Like the documents developed by Early Childhood Australia, they are prized principles that guide our work. The Victorian Institute of Teaching is an independent statutory authority for the teaching profession, whose primary function is to regulate members of the teaching profession. Similarly, the NSW Institute of Teachers

> ... oversees a system of accreditation and recognition of a teacher's professional capacity against Professional Teaching Standards. These Standards aim to provide a common reference point to articulate and support the complex and varied nature of teachers' work. They describe what teachers need to know, understand and be able to do as well as providing direction and structure to enhance the preparation, support and development of teachers.
>
> (NESA website)

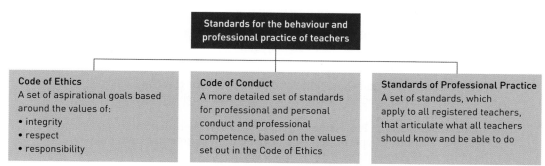

Source: www.vit.vic.edu.au/conduct/victorian-teaching-profession-code-of-conduct/
Pages/faqs-about-the-code.aspx#related.

It is a requirement for all early childhood teachers (ECTs) working in approved centre-based early childhood services to be accredited.

A very useful guide for assisting in finding evidence that is particularly applicable to early childhood is a publication by the Board of Studies Teaching & Educational Standards NSW (BOSTES) titled *Proficient Teacher Evidence Guide: Early Childhood Teachers* (2013).

Figure 10.1 is an example from the BOSTES guide showing a standard, the focus and specific evidence that can be obtained from an early childhood context.

Also useful is the New South Wales Government's 'Great Teaching, Inspired Learning: Blueprint for Action' (NESA, 2013), which includes 47 actions for improving teacher quality

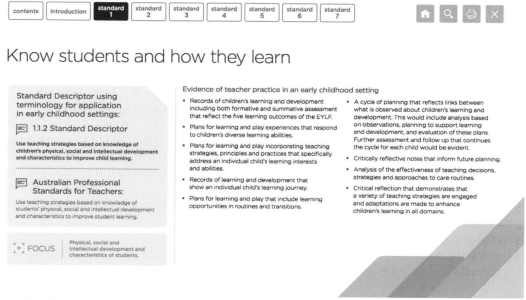

Figure 10.1 Know students and how they learn

Source: BOSTES, 2013, p.13.

ANN HOOPER

and student learning outcomes in New South Wales schools. This blueprint was developed in response to research and feedback from extensive consultation with the community about teacher quality.

The plan includes actions to:

- better understand and share what makes an excellent teacher
- ensure beginning teachers are well suited and thoroughly prepared for the classroom
- make the Australian Professional Standards for Teachers central to delivering fair and accountable performance and accreditation processes and high quality professional development for all teachers
- ensure career pathways and improved support for school leaders.

(NESA, 2013)

References in this section of the chapter are predominantly based on our experiences in Victoria and New South Wales. However, all states have accreditation systems and regulatory bodies with similar codes of ethics and conduct and are informed by the National Standard of Professional Practice.

Putting the codes into practice

The codes are not intended to be used as a rigid set of rules; they are designed to help teachers navigate and resolve difficult professional and ethical dilemmas. While there may be no single correct solution to ethical issues that present themselves in the course of your work, you should be able to account for your actions by referring to the codes. Use the codes, along with any other codes and/or policies developed by your employer or school, to guide your professional practice (VIT, 2015).

The codes should be treated as an educational tool to help the profession define and redefine its values, assist individual teachers to be vigilant about ethical tensions and develop principled ways to resolve issues (VIT, 2015).

The Victorian Teaching Profession Code of Conduct

The Victorian Teaching Profession Code of Conduct is an example of a set of principles or standards for the behaviour and conduct of all Victorian teachers. It does not cover every specific situation but provides guidelines for ethical behaviour. The Code of Conduct is based on the core values articulated by the profession in the Code of Ethics, which was published in 2005. The Code of Conduct identifies five key areas that are important for guiding teachers in their practice, including:

1 relationships with students
2 relationships with parents
3 relationships with colleagues
4 personal conduct
5 professional competence. (VIT, 2015)

The Victorian Teaching Profession Code of Ethics

The Victorian Teaching Profession Code of Ethics draws on the VIT Standards of Professional Practice and codes of conduct for teachers developed by schools and other registration authorities. Its purpose is to make transparent the ideals to which we, as a profession, aspire. The values include:

- *integrity*: acting in the best interest of students; maintaining a professional relationship with students, parents, colleagues and the community; and behaving in ways that respect and advance the profession
- *respect*: acting with care and compassion, treating students fairly and impartially, holding our colleagues in high regard and acknowledging parents as partners in the education of their children
- *responsibility*: providing quality teaching, maintaining and developing our professional practice and working cooperatively with colleagues in the best interest of our students (VIT, 2015).

The Code of Ethics promotes the values that guide our practice and conduct and enables us as a profession to affirm our public accountability. It assists to promote public confidence in our profession.

You are strongly encouraged to spend time with your peers examining these documents and to consider what they mean to you at this early stage of your career. You should also reflect on them frequently as you become active in the profession.

Once again all states and territories have their own versions. The information and values expressed by New South Wales are very similar to those from Victoria:

> Our *code of conduct* is based on the principles of *fairness, respect, integrity and responsibility*. The department is committed to improving the social and economic wellbeing of the people of NSW through the provision of high quality education and training.
>
> (NESA 2015)

Standards of professional practice

In 2013, the Australian Professional Standards for Teachers (APST) were implemented. The standards are designed to clarify the knowledge, practice and professional engagement required for teachers—they also provide a common language for teachers, teacher organisations, professional associations and the public. A summary of the standards is provided in Table 10.1. You are encouraged to investigate the Australian Institute for Teaching and School Leadership (AITSL) website for a full explanation of the standards.

Over the course of your studies, you will have an opportunity to become familiar with these documents and to understand how they impact on the important work that we do.

Table 10.1 Australian Professional Standards for Teachers

DOMAINS	PROFESSIONAL KNOWLEDGE		PROFESSIONAL PRACTICE			PROFESSIONAL ENGAGEMENT	
Standards	1 Know learners and how they learn	2 Know the content and how to teach it	3 Plan for and implement effective teaching and learning	4 Create and maintain supportive and safe learning environments	5 Assess, provide feedback and report on learning	6 Engage in professional learning	7 Engage professionally with colleagues, parents/ carers and the community

Source: AITSL, 2011, p.3.

Regulations and standards

As in any organisation, regulations and standards defining minimum compliance for early childhood education and care exist across both Commonwealth and state jurisdictions. Regulations cover such areas as record keeping, physical space, staff qualifications, staff–child ratios, health and safety, with compliance linked to the licence of the service to operate. State and territory governments have now jointly developed and agreed upon National Standards for long day care, family day care and outside school hours care. As noted in the introduction, being a professional involves more than meeting minimum compliance standards. The standards must be met and complied with, but professionalism requires a higher standard than meeting the 'minimum' and doing just what is required.

Early childhood services

Registered early childhood services must comply with children's services regulations, which identify areas where duty of care is a consideration, including:

- delivering and collecting children from the service
- supervision
- behaviour management
- equipment safety
- injuries to children
- medical treatment
- food allergies
- understanding your legal responsibilities
- maintaining relevant records.

As a result, there are some implications for early childhood education environments. In general, it can be said that a teacher's duty involves taking reasonable care to:

- adequately supervise children
- protect children from dangerous situations and activities
- maintain safe premises and equipment
- protect children from bullying and violence.

STOP AND THINK

- How do you think the points above may impact on the rights of children in early learning environments?
- Consider situations where children's rights may be diminished in light of the points above. How could you respond and advocate for the children?

Privacy and confidentiality

Information privacy is imperative as it protects people's ability to choose with whom to share information about themselves. Privacy generates and nurtures trust between families and teachers and promotes openness as well as confidentiality.

In recent years the use of digital tools in education has grown, and it is common for teachers to use these tools to gather evidence of student learning and to make learning more visible to parents and carers. The use of images of children in context are a powerful way for teachers to reflect on children's learning and their own teaching practice. However, we need to ensure that these images are used *only* for this purpose and we must be vigilant in knowing who has access to the images. It is essential to ensure that parents have consented to such images being used in this way. Careful storage and distribution of images and information we have of children is a significant duty of care. Under no circumstances should images be posted on public spaces.

Teacher standards, and **codes of conduct and ethics** can often initially appear overwhelming, and many of my students, when first confronted with all this information, feel nervous and apprehensive that they may not be able to meet such high expectations and 'rules' governing their work. It can be useful to see these as guidelines or signposts rather than 'thou-shalt' statements, as well as using them as tools for reflection of your practice and 'conversation starters' with other professionals. Many of the standards are woven into your practicum expectations, and as such can be seen in practical ways in light of the work you do rather than as abstract notions that may seem daunting. It is important to remember that the codes of conduct and ethics and other similar frameworks are there to guide you in your work, important decision making and personal reflections in ways that are in keeping with the profession you now belong to.

codes of conduct and ethics documents that provide guidance and direction for practice and decision making relating to contemporary values and ethical behaviour in teaching situations.

The professional teacher's work

This is an exciting time for early childhood education, with what is now a wide recognition within community and government of the importance of quality care, education and relationship building during the early years and the impact this has for the future of education, health and wellbeing outcomes for children, *and* social and economic futures for families and communities. An understanding of significant research undertaken in recent times into early childhood highlights:

- the importance of the early years in a child's life
- the crucial role of the family, the community and the environment
- the importance of building strong relationships and partnerships with families.

ANN HOOPER

This has resulted in new initiatives and reforms across both state and Commonwealth governments. In 2006, the Council of Australian Governments (COAG) met in Canberra to discuss a number of issues of national importance. This was an historic meeting with significant outcomes, with all governments agreeing to work together to deliver a substantial new National Reform Agenda. COAG agreed to concrete, practical initiatives, including a commitment to early childhood. In short, COAG acknowledged:

> The importance of all children having a good start to life and that opportunities to improve children's life chances, especially for children born into disadvantaged families, exist well before children begin school, and even before birth;
>
> That high quality and integrated early childhood education and care services, encompassing the period from prenatal up to and including the transition to the first years of school, are critical to increasing the proportion of children entering school with the basic skills for life and learning; and
>
> A commitment to giving priority to improving early childhood development outcomes, as a part of a collaborative national approach.

(COAG, 2009a)

Blueprint for Early Childhood Development and School Reform:
An Overview

A Victorian Government initiative

In 2008, as part of the Victorian Government's vision to integrate education and care and focus on improved outcomes for children, young people and families, the Department of Education and Early Childhood Development (DEECD) was created, bringing together early childhood services and schools. The DEECD had responsibility for early childhood education, and school-aged services under this new governance arrangement. The DEECD links early childhood services with other services that support families with young children, including maternal and child health services, child protection, mental health, Aboriginal services, health and disability.

In response to this coming together of early childhood and schools into one government department, a new policy direction was announced and outlined in the Blueprint for Education and Early Childhood Development and School Reform in 2008. The government's mission was to 'ensure a high-quality and coherent birth-to-adulthood learning and development system to build the capability of every young Victorian' (p.11).

National Curriculum frameworks

In December 2009, the COAG agreed to establish a new National Quality Agenda for early childhood education and care through the implementation of a National Quality Framework (NQF). The NQF is the result of an agreement between all Australian governments to work together to provide better educational and developmental outcomes for children using education and care services. The NQF introduces a new quality standard to improve education and care across long day care, family day care, preschool/kindergarten and outside-school hours care.

Quality education and care shapes every child's future and lays the foundation for development and learning. The early years are critical for establishing self-esteem, resilience, healthy growth and a capacity to learn. Research strongly suggests that high-quality education and care early in life leads to better health, education and employment outcomes later in life. Young children need quality care and attention that meets their individual needs. Two identified influences on the quality of care are caregiver qualifications and lower staff to child ratios. These factors are particularly beneficial for very young children and those from disadvantaged backgrounds.

Substantial research shows that higher qualified educators improve outcomes for children. The higher their qualifications, the greater their understanding of child development, health and safety issues and of the importance of relationships. These educators are better equipped to lead activities that inspire children and help them learn and develop.

A central focus of the NQF is on outcomes for children. This is why all education and care services must provide a program that is based on an approved learning framework, which considers the developmental needs, interests and experiences of children and takes into account their individual differences.

Source: http://acecqa.gov.au/national-quality-framework/introducing-the-national-quality-framework#sthash.xJfxknPl.dpuf.

Early Years Learning Framework (EYLF)

The EYLF is the first national framework for Australia developed to 'enrich children's learning experiences through purposeful actions by educators in collaboration with children and families' (Goodfellow, 2009, p.2).

The EYLF applies to services for children from birth to five years, including kindergarten (pre-schools), long day care, family day care, home-based care, occasional care, playgroups, mobile services and Multifunctional Aboriginal Children's Services (MACS).

The EYLF is a significant document for all educators of young children. It is a nationally endorsed curriculum framework for early childhood educators that outlines the key concepts that underpin and support their practices and is:

- a resource to support children's learning
- a tool for curriculum decision making
- a document that can be shared with families and others when explaining the nature of the early childhood educator's work
- a statement of principles and practices that highlights the role of early childhood education within a national view of children and families.

The concept of 'Belonging, Being and Becoming' is an underlying theme of this document, which recognises that children 'live within' and are 'influenced by' the context of their 'family, community, culture and place' (Goodfellow, 2009, p.10):

BELONGING, BEING & BECOMING

The Early Years Learning Framework for Australia

- *belonging* recognises that children are connected and have meaningful relationships with others
- *being* recognises the present and how the child experiences this
- *becoming* recognises change and children's growing understanding, ability and learning.

ANN HOOPER

The EYLF and all other state frameworks, including the Victorian Early Years Learning and Development Framework (VEYLDF), emphasise:

- play-based learning (exploring, investigating, active, open-ended)
- professionals talking to each other (integrated service delivery)
- recognising that all children learn in different ways and at different rates and times (recognising diversity and promoting flexible delivery)
- families as their child's first teacher. Families understand their children better than anyone else (support for building parent/professional relationships and collaborative practices).

Curriculum documents for schools

Curriculum documents mapping learning for children and young people are enclosed in the Australian Curriculum. The National Curriculum F–10 sets out what every student should learn during their first eleven years of schooling. The curriculum is the common set of knowledge and skills required by students for lifelong learning, social development and active and informed citizenship.

The three dimensions of the Australian Curriculum are illustrated in Figure 10.2. Three cross-curriculum priorities are woven through eight learning areas (English, Mathematics,

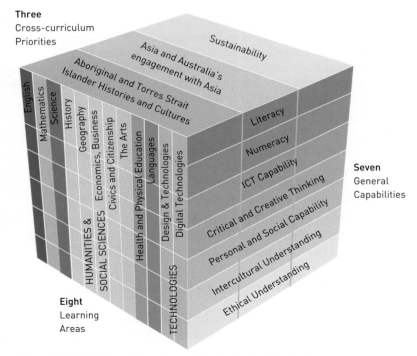

Figure 10.2 The three dimensions of the Australian Curriculum

Source: Australian Curriculum, 2017.

Science, Humanities and Social Sciences, The Arts, Health and Physical Education, Languages, and Technologies) and seven general capabilities (Literacy, Numeracy, ICT Capability, Critical and Creative Thinking, Personal and Social Capability, Intercultural Understanding, and Ethical Understanding).

Over the years of your course, you will become very familiar with these documents as you learn to plan, design and implement rich, effective learning experiences for young children, both in the prior-to-school years and primary school levels.

The many roles of teachers

The EYLF suggests that the educator's role is 'complex and multi-faceted' (DEEWR, 2009). In order to support children's learning, teachers engage in the following roles:

- reflecting on practice
- planning learning environments
- interacting to support and extend learning
- documenting children's learning.

Assessment of children's learning is another role that is gaining greater prominence in early childhood education. This topic is addressed in Chapter 12.

Teaching: a complex task

Teaching requires professionals to respond to children's needs through verbal and non-verbal cues, to develop goals (in consultation with families and colleagues), and to understand child development and current theories on how children learn. Teachers need to know when to intervene with a comment, question or suggestion during play and to understand principles and practices in relation to equity, diversity, disability and indigenous and multicultural communities. They must consistently demonstrate a sense of what is fair, respectful and ethical (MacNaughton & Williams, 2009).

Learning and teaching through play

Planning and teaching for learning through play has long been considered a key feature of early childhood education. It is a feature that distinguishes it from other sectors of education and is deeply grounded in our history. The EYLF has a specific emphasis on play-based learning and teaching. It acknowledges that children have a right to play under the principles of the United Nations Convention on the Rights of the Child (UNICEF, 1989).

The play of young children is associated with many realms of learning and development, including intellectual outcomes (skills and understandings), cognitive outcomes including curiosity and persistence, memory and thinking skills, language and literacy skills, creativity of thought and imagination, strategies for problem solving, and thinking ability. Similarly, play fosters vital social and emotional development including emotional skills and understanding, the capacity to begin to understand others' feelings and the development of empathy. It also encourages independence and promotes opportunities for children to begin to regulate their own behaviour. Active play is related to the development of physical skills and good health through increased metabolism and energy expenditure. In addition, active

ANN HOOPER

play is strongly related to the development of physical skills and good health (adapted from Barblett & Kennedy, 2008, pp.5–6).

Play and play-based learning are discussed in detail in Chapter 4. Here the point being emphasised is that play has so much to contribute to the development of young children, and this is why early childhood professionals rigorously protect and advocate for play to be an integral part of any learning program for children. Teachers play a vital role in the nature of children's play as the relationships between children and adults are central to learning and teaching through play.

We have only touched on the various roles and responsibilities of the early years teacher. There is much to learn here. Bringing learning to life for young children and engaging children in rich and relevant learning experiences is the core of our work.

Reflective practice

In our profession, new ideas backed by new research around young children and learning are emerging all the time. It is not sufficient to expect to learn all there is to know about our field by simply completing a university degree: 'life-long learning' is imperative and part of our professionalism. We must forever be on a search, like hunters and gatherers, for continuously improving our knowledge and practice. Reflective practice and critical inquiry are important tools that teachers, new and experienced, should frequently engage in.

Within the documents that guide our practice, specific reference is given to ongoing reflective practice. Reflective practice helps teachers to generate questions and think deeply about what is working well, and what is not, and why. Teachers who reflect on and critique their work purposefully collect data and evidence and analyse these to develop a deeper awareness or insight into what might be happening.

Reflective practice is an ongoing, dynamic process of thinking honestly, deeply and critically about all aspects of professional practice with children and families. It occurs spontaneously as well as in essential planned reflection time. Most importantly, reflective practice leads to action.

> Reflection is more than thinking and discussing—it is also about deconstructing, unpacking or pulling things apart to gain better understanding, seeing connections and appreciating different perspectives. Reflection can help you to recognise and continue good practices, to change and improve what is not working well, to challenge practices that are taken for granted, to monitor all aspects of practice on an ongoing basis and know when you need to find more information or support from others.
>
> (DEECD, 2009)

Critical reflection does not mean being critical or criticising. In education it entails rethinking some way of acting or thinking that has been taken for granted, then re-examining it in light of what we now know about how children learn and develop. It is important for you in these early days of developing your professionalism, to critically reflect on what you think and believe about children, your image of children, and how that image might impact on how best to support them to thrive and flourish. As discussed earlier, your position will have been strongly influenced from your experiences, but now in the light of your studies, discussions with peers and teachers, readings and research you may need to realign these ideas.

Seven characteristics of reflective practice

According to Pollard (2002, cited in Marbina et al., 2010, p.8), there are seven characteristics of reflective practice:

1 an active focus on goals, how these might be addressed and their potential consequences
2 a commitment to a continuous cycle of monitoring practice, evaluating it and re-visiting it
3 a focus on informed judgments about practice, based on evidence
4 open-minded, responsive and inclusive attitudes
5 the capacity to re-frame one's own practice in light of evidence-based reflections and insights based on research
6 dialogue with other colleagues, in-house and with external networks
7 the capacity to mediate and adapt from externally developed frameworks, making informed judgments and defending or challenging existing practice.

STOP AND REFLECT

Here are some questions that might assist you to reflect critically:

- What do I believe about young children and how will this affect my practice?
- How will I negotiate differences of opinions and ethical dilemmas?
- Do I plan learning based on the belief that each child is unique, or do I plan the experiences that are easiest for me to implement and manage? (McArdle et al., 2015)

You might like to try the following reflective practice strategies.

Reflective practice strategies

- *Keep a journal or diary*: This may contain stories, drawings, articles, symbols or photos. It may include prompts for further reflection or reminders for thinking or discussing. Wikis or blogs set up for sharing with colleagues can also be powerful.
- *Meetings*: Leaders or colleagues may set up meetings specifically designed for reflection. They should be purposeful and provide critical questions to stimulate deep thinking.
- *A mentor*: A more experienced person can guide you, question you or offer a different perspective for you to contemplate.
- *Professional learning*: Visit other settings, join a network, read literature, research papers and attend conferences.
- *Action research*: Action research is an approach to professional practice involving a cycle of reflection and investigation on a topic of interest, a concern or a question about practice within a setting. The process is systematic, ethical, participatory and collaborative. The term 'research' in this context is about finding evidence about the topic or concern through strategies such as observations, collecting information or interviews. This evidence is compared with or linked to professional literature on the topic or focus. Actions are taken in response to the findings of the literature and the practice evidence. The actions are monitored and evaluated, and revised if necessary and the cycle begins again. The value of this type of research is that it is

ANN HOOPER

situation specific, is aimed to improve practice for a specific group of children, and is owned and implemented by teachers themselves around issues that are important to them and their children (DEECD, 2012).

Who can we reflect with?

- *Ourselves:* These are personal ideas that you are contemplating in your own mind, as you reflect on your own practice.
- *Colleagues:* Learning together with colleagues draws upon the diverse knowledge, experiences, views and attitudes of individuals in the group.
- *Families:* Children learn in the context of their families, and families are the primary influence on children's learning and development. Shared reflective practice with families can support partnership building.
- *Children:* Helping children to reflect supports and promotes learning in different ways. Reflective questioning or 'wondering aloud' helps children to think more deeply about their responses. Reflective questions are open, requiring answers other than 'yes' or 'no' (DEECD, 2012).

Research

research finding evidence about the topic or concern through strategies such as observations, collecting information or interviews.

Good teachers are researchers. They learn how to ask 'why' questions. It is important to not just read or consume research, but to reflect, consider and weigh up opinions of others and discover any light they may shine on their practice. Good teachers use evidence from appropriate research to make informed decisions about their work. Research is a tool that helps us answer important questions about early childhood—questions that otherwise may remain unanswered were it not for the willingness of academics, practitioners and participants (children and adults) to engage with the research process (MacNaughton et al., 2010, p.3).

Reviewing and validating practices

Reading and reviewing research literature requires pre-service teachers, teachers and early childhood professionals to reflect on and critically appraise the information and research. Investigative reading increases our knowledge and understanding of theory, opinion and practice to improve learning environments for children and our support and relationships with their families. Reviewing current, credible and peer-reviewed journals enables teachers to keep informed of current research and issues in relation to best practice and innovation. You will be provided with many opportunities during your studies to engage with such articles and you are encouraged to not just read them, but to analyse, reflect and make connections to what they mean for you as you work to develop the knowledge, skills and dispositions to make a difference to the lives of the young children you will teach.

Actively debate the issues with your peers and aim to be able to articulate your thinking. By doing this you will continue to enrich your personal philosophy and be in a better position to advocate for children and your profession.

SUMMARY

- Look inwards honestly and deeply to understand your own views and any biases you bring to your image of the teacher at this early stage of your journey, and understand that this image requires frequent revisiting and possible realignment and repositioning throughout your career.
- View your role as a teacher as a collaborative one, and resist the idea that you can work in isolation and that you alone can be all things to all children. Use the imagery of a village, and how in a village all significant members collectively work to contribute to the wellbeing of its young and vulnerable.
- Teachers engage in many and varied roles through their work, including facilitating play, which is important in maintaining a well-balanced early childhood learning program.
- Early childhood practices have been shaped by the particular social and political contexts in which they were developed. They are reflective of particular historical periods and the views of the time regarding the nature of childhood and how children learn and develop. The beliefs and values educators hold about education influence how they interpret learning and teaching, which in turn defines what is seen as 'good' or appropriate practice for children. Being aware of your own values is a means of ensuring you are sensitive to the beliefs and values held by parents and children and can enhance your ability to respond.
- There are many documents, policies and procedures to assist all members of our profession to work in coherent and consistent ways that reflect the values of the profession and that have the very best interests of all children at their core.
- Our children are among the most vulnerable and powerless people in our communities. As an aspiring early childhood professional, you have a special responsibility to always act within the highest moral and ethical framework.
- There are many documents and policies that support all teachers to strive to provide consistent, high-quality learning for all children in Australia.
- Contemporary teachers engage in reflective practice to ensure they remain informed and their practice continues to develop in the best interest of the children and families they serve.
- Teachers are on a journey of lifelong learning where involvement with colleagues and authentic research assists them to frequently re-evaluate their views and practices in light of new evidence. They need to possess a habit of mind that is open to critiquing the status quo, always with the purpose of better serving the young children they are privileged to guide and teach: their 'village'.

FURTHER REFLECTION

- Why have you decided to join the teaching profession? What do you hope to achieve on a personal level as you embark on this career?
- Consider positive and negative experiences you have had as a student. How do they impact on or influence the type of teacher you aspire to be?
- Can you nominate an outstanding teacher you know? What qualities do they have that stand out for you?
- How do you currently view the role of the teacher in an early learning setting? How would you describe your philosophy around how children learn best? What about the role of parents and families in children's learning?

ANN HOOPER

- What strategies do you have in your 'tool box' for developing positive relationships with others in your new role? How do you manage challenging relationships?
- What are the key values that inform your work with children and families? Would your values and beliefs be similar to or different from those of other colleagues and professionals? What approaches can you use to negotiate shared understandings when others hold different values or beliefs?

GROUP DISCUSSION

In groups, discuss the ethical practice scenarios below: explain why they might be referred to as *moral dilemmas.* Prepare a response to each issue and share this with the other groups.

1 At a staff meeting in a childcare centre, a staff member makes the comment, 'It would be much easier for us if we worked with the children and didn't have to think about their parents'. Several other staff members laugh at this comment and say they agree with him. No one challenges this opinion.

2 Dee, a family day carer, is at her scheme's network meeting. While they are waiting for the guest speaker to arrive, several of the carers start to talk negatively about another carer who is not present. Dee listens for a few minutes and then questions the appropriateness of making these types of comments publicly. Dee suggests that if they have a real concern the carers should raise this matter in private with the scheme's coordinator.

3 Bobbie and Sasha are playing a board game at their after-school program. Jai, who has been playing near them, starts talking to the girls and asks if he can join the game. Bobbie shakes her head and says, 'No way, we don't like boys'. Jai stares at Bobbie and after a few moments, he walks away to find something else to do. A staff member overhears this exchange but says nothing. (Source: NCAC, 2009).

CLASS ACTIVITIES

1 Begin to construct a portfolio in which you gather and compile evidence of your developing skills, reflect on your experiences and emerging ideas and store links to interesting or confronting research papers or articles. Be prepared to share interesting articles with your fellow students and reflect on the various viewpoints held by members of your group.

2 Obtain copies of the ECA *Code of Ethics* and, in small groups, allocate a section of the document to each person in the group. Each person becomes an 'expert' on their section, and reports back to the whole group. At the conclusion, all members are informed of the main elements of the document.

FURTHER READING

Council of Australian Governments (COAG) (2009) Protecting Children Is Everyone's Business: National Framework for Protecting Australia's Children 2009–2020, Commonwealth of Australia.

The six supporting outcomes of the National Framework are comprehensively discussed in this document, including strategies for different three-to-five-year periods.

REFERENCES

Australian Institute for Teaching and School Leadership (AITSL) (2011) *Australian Professional Standards for Teachers.* Carlton, Vic: Educational Services Australia, February.

Australian Institute for Teaching and School Leadership (AITSL) (2017) Understand the Teacher Standards. www.aitsl. edu.au/teach/understand-the-teacher-standards

Barblett L, Hydon C. & Kennedy A. (2008) *The Code of Ethics: A Guide for Everyday Practice.* Research in Practice Series, vol. 15, no. 1. Watson, ACT: Early Childhood Australia.

Board of Studies Teaching & Educational Standards NSW (BOSTES) (2013) *Proficient Teacher Evidence Guide: Early Childhood Teachers.* NSW: BOSTES. https://educationstandards.nsw.edu.au/wps/wcm/connect/ 5b21b98c-116b-4f2e-a386-56e77c48f5a8/bostes-proficient-teacher-evidence-guide--early-childhood-teachers .pdf?MOD=AJPERES&CVID=

Churchill, R., Ferguson, P., Godinho, S., Johnson, N., Keddie, A., Letts, W., Mackay, J., McGill, M., Moss, J., Nagel, M., Nicholson, P. & Vick, M. (2011) *Teaching: Making a Difference.* Milton, Qld: John Wiley & Sons.

Clarke M. & Pittaway, S. (2014) *Marsh's Becoming a Teacher.* NSW: Pearson.

Commonwealth Child Care Advisory Council (CCCAC) (2001) *Child Care: Beyond 2001.* Australia: Department of Family and Community Services

Council of Australian Governments (COAG) (2009a) *Investing in the Early Years: A National Early Childhood Development Strategy.* Commonwealth of Australia.

Council of Australian Governments (COAG) (2009b) *Protecting Children Is Everyone's Business: National Framework for Protecting Australia's Children 2009–2020.* Commonwealth of Australia.

Department of Education and Early Childhood Development (DEECD) (2008) *Blueprint for Education and Early Childhood Development.* Melbourne: Victorian Government.

Department of Education and Early Childhood Development (DEECD) (2009) *Victorian Early Years Learning and Development Framework for All Children from Birth to Eight Years.* Early Childhood Strategy Division, Melbourne: Victorian Government.

Department of Education and Early Childhood Development and Department of Human Services (DEECD and DHS). (2010) *Protecting the Safety and Wellbeing of Children and Young People.* Melbourne: Victorian Government.

Department of Education and Early Childhood Development (DEECD) (2012) *Victorian Early Years Learning and Development Framework, Practice Principle Guide: 8 Reflective Practice.* Melbourne: Victorian Government.

Department of Education, Employment and Workplace Relations (DEEWR) (2009) *Belonging, Being & Becoming: The Early Years Learning Framework for Australia.* ACT, Australia: Commonwealth of Australia.

Early Childhood Australia (2016) *Code of Ethics.* Watson, ACT: Early Childhood Australia Inc. www. earlychildhoodaustralia.org.au/our-publications/eca-code-ethics/

Edwards, S. (2009) *Early Childhood Education and Care: A Sociocultural Approach.* Castle Hill, NSW: Pademelon Press.

Goodfellow J. (2009) *The Early Years Learning Framework: Getting Started.* ACT: Early Childhood Australia, *16*(4).

Kennedy, A. (2001) 'The Nature of Values in Early Childhood Education: An Analysis of the AECA Code of Ethics', *Australian Journal of Early Childhood, 26*(4): 18–25.

MacNaughton, G. & Williams, G. (2009) *Techniques for Teaching Young Children: Choices for Theory and Practice* (3rd edn). Australia: Pearson.

MacNaughton, G., Rolfe, S. & Siraj-Blatchford, I. (2010) *Doing Early Childhood Research.* NSW: Allen & Unwin.

Marbina, L., Church A. & Tayler, C. (2010) *Victorian Early Years Learning and Development Framework: Evidence Paper, Practice Principle 8: Reflective Practice.* Victoria: Department of Education and Early Childhood Development (DEECD).

McArdle F., Gibson M. & Zollo L. (2015) *Being an Early Childhood Educator.* Crows Nest, NSW: Allen & Unwin.

Ministerial Council on Education, Employment, Training and Youth Affairs (MCEETYA) (2008), *Melbourne Declaration on Educational Goals for Young Australians.*

National Childcare Accreditation Council (NCAC) (2009) *Putting Children First, 29*: 9–11, March. http://ncac.acecqa.gov.au/educator-resources/pcf-articles/Ethics_a_part%20_of_everyday_practice_Mar09.pdf

NSW Education Standards Authority (NESA) (2013) 'Great Teaching, Inspired Learning—Blueprint for Action'. http://educationstandards.nsw.edu.au/wps/portal/nesa/about/initiatives/great-teaching-inspired-learning

NSW Education Standards Authority (NESA). http://educationstandards.nsw.edu.au/wps/portal/nesa/home

State of Victoria (2007) *The National Reform Agenda: Victoria's Plan to Improve Outcomes for Early Childhood.* Melbourne: Department of Premier and Cabinet.

United Nations Convention on the Rights of the Child (1989). www.unicef.org.au/Upload/UNICEF/Media/Our%20work/childfriendlycrc.pdf

Victorian Institute of Teaching (VIT) (2015) 'Code of Conduct and Ethics'. https://www.vit.vic.edu.au/professional-responsibilities/conduct-and-ethics.

Observation-based Planning

Melissa Colville

Chapter objectives

In this chapter, we will:

- examine historical and contemporary theories that underpin child observation, namely developmental theory and sociocultural theory
- consider how to observe children using a variety of observation methods
- introduce the planning cycle (observe, question, plan, act, reflect, evaluate)
- consider the ethical implications and difficulties related to child observation and assessment
- discuss these key concepts:
  - the place of observation and assessment in early years curricula
  - the relationship between theory and observation methods
  - the theories that underpin different observation methods
  - the place of observation within the planning cycle
  - the role of privacy and confidentiality
  - how an anti-discrimination approach can combat observer bias.

Key terms

anecdotal record	event samples	story dictation
checklist	running record	time sample
developmental theory	sociocultural theory	work sample

> ### Observation inspires good teaching.
>
> (Curtis & Carter, 2012, p.1)

When I think about child observation and how it inspires good teaching, a personal and powerful teaching experience immediately comes to mind. Early in my teaching career, I ran a pre-kinder room with my own small group of children. One of these children, Dylan, could be quite physically aggressive towards the other children; he often hit them.

I attended a workshop entitled 'Challenging Behaviours' with the purpose of finding strategies to manage Dylan's behaviour. Can you see my biased view in this statement? I viewed the challenge to be Dylan's behaviour. This is probably because my informal observations of the issue at this point were of Dylan hitting a child and/or this child's negative reaction to being hit, and to complicate the issue there was never a clear explanation given by either child of what had unfolded.

The workshop taught me about an observation technique called 'event samples' and, in particular, how this could uncover the possible reasons for children's challenging behaviour. When I returned to work the next day, I began taking event samples of Dylan. An event sample requires the observer to record the antecedent—that is, what happens *before* the behaviour (e.g. prior to the hitting). This was an important element I had not previously observed. I carefully observed

Dylan's play and, across several event samples, I discovered a pattern. Dylan would be happily playing on his own, usually with the train set (this was one of his favourite learning experiences). Another child would enter the play in a way that would disturb Dylan's play—for example, the child would pick up a train, place it on the track and noisily push it into Dylan's train. Dylan would then become frustrated and hit the child. Discovering this pattern changed my thinking dramatically.

Now I could see why Dylan was so upset! I no longer viewed the issue as simply 'Dylan's aggressive behaviour', but began to view the wider context. I reflected on the relationships and interactions of *everyone* in the room—specifically, the way all the children entered each other's play, the way they responded to a child disturbing their play (I no longer only focused on only Dylan in this regard), and the way I responded to the children. I also reflected on the physical environment, in particular the way the train-set area was set up. All of these factors became a focus in my planning. I made the train area bigger and added more materials, and I worked on how I communicated with the children, and the children's communication with each other. I saw positive change! Change, most importantly, in the relationships I had with the children, and the relationships they had with one other. We became more collaborative and cooperative as a group and Dylan no longer hit other children when he became frustrated. Looking back, perhaps one of the most rewarding things to come from this was my relationship with Dylan. I was so happy to see him arrive in the morning and enjoyed our day together with the other children. I no longer viewed him or his behaviour as an issue in our otherwise wonderful group. Observations, in this case event samples, did indeed inspire good teaching!

Introduction

This chapter is about child observation and assessment. Observing and assessing children is an important part of the teacher's role. Observations are a vital tool for early childhood teachers to build an understanding of children's interests, abilities, play, learning, development and wellbeing. When you observe children, you will develop your understanding of both the individual child and children as a group. Another benefit of observing children is that you develop a greater appreciation of each unique and individual child. We use our observations of children to question and assess each child's learning and development and, from this, we plan learning experiences to further support their learning. This is one of the main purposes of child observation and assessment. Children grow and develop in various ways, and as this chapter will show, there are numerous methods that can be used to observe, document and assess children, each with their own strategies and techniques. There are a number of theories that underpin child observation. These theories fall within developmental theory or sociocultural theory, and will influence the way we view and assess our observations of children. What you will learn in your early childhood teaching course will challenge you to reflect on the way you view children and their behaviour, and your views will likely change over time. Your views and beliefs will also play a role in how you observe and assess children. Identifying your views and beliefs about children and about children in relation to observation and assessment is an important first step in the observation and planning cycle. Once your views and beliefs have been identified, you can begin observing children. A variety of thoughtfully written child observations, documented in collaboration with others, provide the strong foundation needed to carry out the planning cycle. The planning cycle (observe, question, plan, act, reflect and evaluate) will be carefully reviewed, and throughout this discussion the specific example of a child, Zoe, will be referred to. The ethical implications of child observation and assessment, including privacy and confidentiality, will also be carefully considered. This chapter will conclude with a discussion on the difficulties related to child observation and assessment, in particular observer bias.

STOP AND REFLECT

- What experience have you had observing children?
- Has this experience included writing formal child observations?
- What have you learnt from your observations of children?
- How have these experiences contributed to how you view children and child observation and assessment?
- Why do you think observation might be the best way to assess a child's play, development and learning?

Historical and contemporary theories

From an early time, scientists have been interested in understanding children's development, including the process by which children grow and the influences on their development. Observations of children by early psychologists and educators such as Froebel, Freud, Montessori, Skinner and Piaget have provided the foundation for what is understood about child development. As a pre-service teacher, you will learn about the theory of 'normal' child development and growth. 'Normal development' is what is considered to be the usual developmental progress for a specified age group (also known as milestones). This traditional developmental approach (**developmental theory**) is based on the view that children's development is related to distinct stages—that children develop in stages according to their age (often referred to as 'ages and stages').

These stages are characterised by qualitative differences in children's behaviour; they are believed, by those subscribing to the developmental approach, to be predetermined and universal (across all cultures), and determined by the child's genetics and environment. Developmental milestones are the behaviours or skills we usually see in young children as they grow and develop; examples include crawling, walking and talking. Developmental milestone charts or **checklists** suggest a 'typical' range of development within the development domains: social, emotional, physical and cognitive. For example, in terms of the child's physical development, at the age of eighteen months, children are walking 'well with feet only slightly apart' (Sheridan et al., 2014).

Teachers using a developmental perspective would use developmental milestone charts or checklists to help them determine whether children are showing a) typical development for their age (a predictable course of development), b) atypical development (behaviours outside the 'normal or expected' range of development, e.g. learning and social disabilities), c) delayed development (when a child has not reached milestones by the

> **developmental theory** child development is viewed in a series of distinct stages of development according to the age of the child (ages and stages); typical behaviour and skills (developmental milestones).

> **checklist** a list of specific traits or behaviours an observer is looking for.

MELISSA COLVILLE

expected time) or d) advanced for their age (advanced when compared to children of their own age). Determining children's level of development is particularly important when early intervention is needed, i.e. for a child with a disability. However, all children are individual and unique. Children develop in their own ways, at their own rates, and there is great variation in what age different children achieve the same skill. In some cases, children may miss out on some developmental experiences, e.g. crawling. Developmental milestone charts should therefore be viewed as a guide only. Individual differences in children can make it quite difficult to distinguish delays in maturation (developmental delays) versus normal variations in development. Therefore, it is essential to be conscious of and alert to how culture contributes to shaping children's development.

More recently there has been an increasing interest in how child development occurs within historical, social and cultural contexts. Child development and learning has changed over time as the context of children's communities change. Lev Vygotsky, one of the founders of **sociocultural theory**, emphasised the influence of children's social–cultural context, in particular the central role that families and cultural groups play in children's development and learning. For example, Western culture often values and encourages children's independence rather than children's interdependence.

sociocultural theory how knowledge and understanding are constructed and embedded in social and cultural contexts.

Sociocultural theory emphasises the power of learning with others. Sociocultural theorists believe learning is best supported through interaction with others, specifically a more capable and skilled adult or peer. This More Knowledgeable Other (MKO) scaffolds children's learning within their Zone of Proximal Development (ZPD). The ZPD (as mentioned in previous chapters) is the distance between what children are capable of on their own (the child's actual level of development) and what they are capable of with the guidance of a MKO (their potential level of development). Scaffolding (a term used by Bruner and taken from the building industry) is the support the MKO provides, such as demonstrating a task or beginning to solve a problem, which is then gradually withdrawn as children learn to complete the task and/or solve the problem on their own. Teachers applying sociocultural theory view children's development in relation to their social relationships and cultural background and aim to scaffold children's learning within their ZPD. They also collect information from families as a valuable contributor to the observation planning cycle.

Traditional methods of observation that use a developmental approach such as running records and checklists tend to focus on individual children's development in separate developmental domains (physical, cognitive, social and emotional). Planned experiences for children are often based on individual developmental objectives using developmentally appropriate learning experiences. An objective might be for children to count five objects using one-to-one correspondence (each number matches an object). Some have argued that these methods can limit our thinking into focusing on children's 'needs' and 'weaknesses' rather than 'strengths' or 'interests'. Contemporary observation and assessment approaches, which often use a sociocultural perspective, focus on children's strengths—for example, learning stories. The teacher's role is to build and extend upon what children currently know and do. A strengths-based approach supports children's existing strengths and capabilities as opposed to focusing on a problem or concern (a deficit approach). Sociocultural approaches view children as agentic, strong and capable. When we view children as 'agentic' and having 'agency', we acknowledge their ability to make choices and decisions that influence and impact the world around them (DEEWR, 2009). Children are seen as directors of their own learning, and therefore their voice and ideas are included in the observation planning cycle. Current observation and planning approaches also focus on the child within a *group*, rather than the child developing as an *individual*; so observations focus on children's interactions. Shifting the view of children as *individuals* to *part of a group* was an important shift I made in my event sample observations of Dylan.

STOP AND REFLECT

- How do you view the development of children?
- Would you use a developmental chart or checklist to observe a child? Why? Why not?
- Do you think developmental milestones are relevant for all children? Why? Why not?
- Do you think developmental milestones are relevant across all early childhood contexts? Why? Why not?
- How might considering children's sociocultural context be helpful when assessing their development?

Theories help us explore different perspectives on how children learn and develop. Theories that underpin child observation have changed over time: from historical theories, such as developmental theory, to contemporary theories, such as sociocultural theory. Approaches to observation and planning have changed in conjunction with these changes in theory. The traditional developmental approach to education has long shaped teachers' approach to observation, planning and curriculum.

Similarly, sociocultural theory has had an impact on teaching and learning practices and produced new curricula and ways of thinking about early childhood education. Sociocultural theory can be identified in a range of curricula, including Reggio Emilia and the New Zealand curriculum Te Whāriki, each with their own documentation methods.

Within Australia, teachers' observation and planning is supported by the Early Years Learning Framework (EYLF). The EYLF (DEEWR, 2009) recommends teachers draw on a range of theories and perspectives, including developmental and sociocultural theories, to support their understanding of children, and to challenge traditional ways of seeing children, learning and teaching. This is essential to better understand children and, in turn, support their learning, development and wellbeing.

States across Australia may use their own framework as well as the EYLF. These additional frameworks are aligned and complementary to the EYLF and the national agenda. For example, teachers within Victoria use the Victorian Early Years Learning and Development Framework (VEYLDF). These two documents are approved under the National Quality Framework (NQF) and share five learning outcomes for children:

1 Identity
2 Community
3 Wellbeing
4 Learning
5 Communication.

Teachers within early childhood settings use their frameworks to guide their decisions in interpreting and assessing children's learning and development.

MELISSA COLVILLE

The EYLF Planning Cycle

The EYLF Early Years Planning Cycle describes the process early childhood teachers use to collect and interpret observations, and to plan for and reflect on children's learning and development. The planning cycle consists of the following steps:

- observing
- questioning
- planning
- acting
- reflecting and evaluating.

We will now look at each of these steps in detail.

Observing children

Observing children involves gathering information about them in a variety of settings: within their family, the community they live in and the early childhood setting. There are many reasons why we observe children: to monitor and recognise changes in their play and behaviour; to monitor their learning progress; to learn about their relationships, their interests, ideas and opinions; to recognise illness; to have documentation for legal purposes; and to provide a program and environment that supports and enhances their learning, development and wellbeing. Observing children enables teachers to further develop their professional knowledge and evaluate and reflect on their professional practice, including how they plan for and implement effective teaching and learning (AITSL, 2011). Teacher reflection should take place throughout the planning cycle.

There are many ways to document children's learning and development, and while there are no mandated templates on how a teacher should do this, our documentation needs to be meaningful, relevant and helpful in making children's learning visible. The focus of our documentation should always be on the quality of observation rather than the quantity (although quantity is also important). Teachers need to observe children in meaningful ways on a regular basis, building a portfolio of observations and assessments that lead to an understanding of children's learning and development as well as their needs. Multiple assessments over time will help provide a more accurate and complete picture of children.

We will now explore a range of traditional and contemporary documentation approaches used to assess children's learning and development.

Note: I have used the terms 'observation', 'question' and 'plan' in my observation examples to align with the EYLF; however, other terms are used and are interchangeable. For example, 'observation' may be written as 'description of the event'; 'question' may be written as 'interpretation', 'analysis' or 'assessment'; and 'plan' may be written as 'implications', 'planning' or 'extension of learning'. You may also come across other terms not mentioned here.

Running records

running record a detailed description of everything that happens in the order that it happens.

A common and traditional method for observing children in the early learning setting is a **running record**. Running records are a detailed description of everything that happens in the order that it happens. The observer documents in sequence exactly what the child says and does, including their language, behaviours, actions and interactions, usually over a short period of time (i.e. several minutes). In my experience running records tend to be more accurate than observations that are written later from memory, and this is one of the benefits of this method. The observer is a non-participant; this means you are positioned away from the child and fully focused on writing the observation rather than interacting with the child. As a participant observer, you might be reading a book with a small group of children. As running records are written as the situation unfolds, they are in present tense; 'Shona *runs* around the yard' (rather than *ran*). The observer is required to write quickly so it is useful to use an abbreviation or shorthand. Running records can give a rich, detailed insight into children's interactions, behaviour, development and interests, which can be used to inform your planning.

RUNNING RECORD			
Child's name: Archie	**Age:** 2.8 years	**Time:** 9.40 am	**Date:** 9.9.16

Context/Setting: Inside at the large Lego table in a long day care centre. **Observer:** Lucy

Observation: Archie is sitting at the Lego table and Julian is standing next to him. They are both looking at their own Lego creations in their hands. Julian flies his creation around, saying 'Ahhh gzzz'. Archie stands and lifts his creation into the air, responding 'Ahh!' as he lowers his creation to the floor. A small piece of his Lego breaks off and he picks it up and joins it back. He looks to Julian and smiles. Archie says 'I fly. I fly' and Julian says 'I fly' with Archie. Julian is flying his creation and says 'doot–doot'. Archie then pulls a few parts off his creation and places it on the table, and wanders off leaving Julian playing.

Question: Archie appears to like Julian's company and is enjoying creative and imaginary play with his Lego creation (Identity, Learning). Archie is communicating with Julian both verbally and non-verbally (Communication). Archie fixes his creation with ease when a piece falls off.

Plan: The Lego is popular with Archie and the other children, so this learning experience should be continued (Learning, Wellbeing, Community). Involve Archie and a small group of children in washing/cleaning the Lego at the end of the week in the sink with water and dish soap and then laying them out on a towel to dry (Community).

Anecdotal records

Anecdotal records are brief narrative accounts of a specific incident or an interesting event and are traditionally focused on a single child or area of development (e.g. physical, cognitive). Although this is a traditional observation method, if the focus of an anecdote is on children engaged in social interaction, the observation would support sociocultural theory. Anecdotal records are useful for recording children's strengths, interests and development. Anecdotes can record how children communicate, both verbally and non-verbally; what they do; physical gestures and movements; and their interactions with people and materials. Essentially, an anecdote records a story of what the observer has seen. One of the benefits of an anecdotal record is that the observer may be interacting with the child (a participant). However, they may also be positioned away from the child (non-participant). Anecdotal records are usually written after the event when the observer has more time and is therefore written in past tense. As this observation method relies on memory it can be difficult to remember specific detail, such as the language the child uses. However, anecdotes are easy to use and quick to write so they are a popular observation method in early learning settings, as well as school. Anecdotal records can help teachers plan learning experiences and interventions for children.

anecdotal record
a brief narrative account of a specific incident or an interesting event traditionally focused on a single child or area of development (e.g. physical, cognitive).

MELISSA COLVILLE

Note: The term 'kindergarten' in this chapter refers to the year prior to school (this is known as pre-school in some other states of Australia).

ANECDOTAL RECORD			
Child's name: Child A	**Age:** 3.5 years	**Time:** 10.30 am	**Date:** 12.8.16

Context/Setting: Child A has just come inside after outdoor play. Pre-kindergarten room **Observer:** Sally

Observation: Child A said to Sally 'Help my shoes off?' Sally responded, 'You do as much as you can and then I'll help you from there'. Child A then attempted to undo the buckle of her right sandal using first 3 fingers from both hands; after not being successful the first time, she re-attempted. Then after being unable again, said 'I can't'. Sally suggested to 'have another try'; she said 'no more, I can't'.

Question: Child A is reaching out and communicating her need for assistance (Identity). Her confidence in coping with new experiences is developing. Her resilience in persisting with challenges is also developing (Identity).

Plan: I would like to encourage a positive attitude towards putting sandals on independently. Child A will be encouraged to practise this task as it comes up each day and more positive language will be modelled such as 'I think it's hard but I'll try' rather than 'I can't'. As she develops confidence and notices her improvements this will foster the feeling of accomplishment (Identity, Wellbeing).

Checklists

A checklist is a list of specific traits or behaviours an observer is looking for. Checklists vary in length and complexity and may be designed for any developmental domain, such as physical, cognitive, emotional and social development. Checklists are a traditional observation type and have a strong link to developmental theory. A typical checklist provides an outline of skills children are expected to master at a particular age (developmental milestones). The observer ticks each item on the list to indicate its presence or absence, or in some cases the *strength* of the behaviour. This is a relatively quick and easy way to record information. There may also be a 'comments' section where the observer can record additional details if needed. Checklists are usually completed over a period of time: a week or two. Information from other observation methods such as running records can be used to complete checklists. By completing checklists at different times throughout the year, teachers can identify specific skills or behaviours children have mastered as the result of maturation or experience. In conjunction with other observational methods, checklists may be useful when writing developmental summaries on children. Two different templates are shown below. Observation templates will vary so it is important to try different templates and see which work best for you.

DEVELOPMENTAL CHECKLIST	
Child's name: Millie	**Age:** 10 months

Context/Setting: Indoors and outdoors. Babies group in a long day care centre.

Observer: Sarah

Observation: Physical development: *Codes:* **D** demonstrated **DD** demonstrated with difficultly **DA** demonstrated with assistance **X** not able—not observed

Cont.

DEVELOPMENTAL CHECKLIST

AGE	OBSERVE	CODE	DATE/ OBSERVATION
8–12 months	Sits without support	D	5.10.16
	Crawls	D	5.10.16 Millie has been crawling for 2 months
	Stands by pulling themselves up using furniture	D	5.10.16 Millie often pulls herself up using the table
	May stand alone	DA	5.10.16 Millie stands holding an educator's hands
	Uses hands to self-feed	D	5.10.16 Millie uses both hands to feed herself
	Moves objects from hand to hand	D	12.10.16
	Picks up and throws small objects	D	12.10.16

Question: Millie demonstrates age appropriate physical development in both her gross and fine motor skills (Learning).

Plan: To encourage Millie's physical development, in particular her ability to stand by providing sturdy pieces of furniture for her to pull herself up, and to stand Millie in front of an educator, holding hands, so she can bounce up and down and build her leg muscles (Learning).

DEVELOPMENTAL CHECKLIST

Child's name: Elise   **Age:** 7.5 months

Context/Setting: Observer: Brooke

Observation: Social and Emotional Development:

AGE	OBSERVE	YES	NO	DATE	COMMENTS
4–8 months	Responds to own name	X		9.10.16	Elise either turns her head and smiles, or smiles and moves her chest forward at the sound of her name.
	Shows more comfort around familiar people	X		9.10.16	
	Plays games like Peek-a-boo	X		12.10.16	Elise will lift a small blanket up in front of her face and pull it down when the educator says 'Peek a boo!'
	Laughs, especially in social interactions	X		5.10.16	Elise laughs often.
	May cry when parent leaves the room	X		13.10.16	Elise has recently begun to cry when her parent leaves the room.
	Displays happiness when seeing faces they know	X			Elise turns and smiles when a familiar educator walks into the room.

Question: Elise displays age-appropriate social and emotional development (Identity, Wellbeing, Community). She demonstrates a clear-cut attachment to her parents by crying when they leave the room (Communication).

Plan: To provide Elise with comfort when her parent/s leave and to help her develop a secure attachment with her educators by providing sensitive, responsive and consistent care (Identity, Wellbeing).

MELISSA COLVILLE

Time samples

time sample observing children for specified periods of time during the day (e.g. every 30 minutes) to see what they are doing or what behaviour they are displaying, and perhaps at what time of day the behaviour is more common.

Time samples are typically used in early learning settings and involve children being observed for specified periods of time during the day; for example, every 30 minutes. The frequency of time can be as often as is appropriate to the child and situation; the observer will determine this. Time samples can be used to see what a child is doing or what behaviour they are displaying, and perhaps at what time of day the behaviour is more common. This method is also useful to identify children's overall participation within the learning environment. Observers can identify how the children use equipment, what play areas are being used and how they are being used, and the types of social or language interactions between children. It is preferable that the observer does several time samples in the same week to compare and find possible patterns between the time samples. The information gained from time samples can then be used to make changes in the program appropriate to the children's needs.

OBSERVATION RECORD			
Focus child: Zoe	**Age:** 2 years	**Time:** Every 30 minutes	**Date:** 10.6.15
Context/Setting: Indoors in the toddler room.			

OBSERVATION TYPE	TIME SAMPLE	EARLY YEARS LEARNING FRAMEWORK
Observation: 9.00 am: Zoe began to sing 'Twinkle, Twinkle Little Star' along with the educator. When she didn't know the words she kept up with the tune with a humming noise. 9.30 am: Zoe holds her arms up towards the teacher after falling over. 10.00 am: Zoe was building a tower of small blocks (seven so far) and singing 'Baa Baa Black Sheep', keeping up with the tune correctly and pronouncing many of the words correctly. 10.30 am: An educator is reading a book to Zoe. Zoe reaches out and turns some of the pages and pulls all of the tabs. Zoe repeats some words and phrases such as 'hat' and 'cat' and 'round and round'.	**Question:** *Please note: You will be asked to 'question' this observation in a later section.* **Plan:** *Please note: You will be asked to 'plan' for this observation in a later section.*	**Identity** – Children have a strong sense of identity **Community** – Children are connected with & contribute to their world **Wellbeing** – Children have a strong sense of wellbeing **Learning** – Children are confident and involved learners **Communication** – Children are effective communicators

Event samples

event samples brief narratives written preceding and following a specified behaviour; useful for identifying the causes and possible consequences for certain behaviours and interactions.

Event samples are brief narratives written preceding and following a specified behaviour, and are useful for identifying the causes and possible consequences for certain behaviours and interactions; as in my story about Dylan. This observation method is often used for challenging behaviours such as physical aggression (e.g. hitting). Event samples can also be useful for children who are unsettled and display behaviours such as clinging to adults or frequent crying. Event sampling is usually recorded using the ABC technique (Antecedent/Behaviour/Consequence):

- *Antecedent*: what is happening immediately *before* the behaviour that may have triggered the behaviour (specific times of day, setting, people and learning experience). The observer can reflect on: What happened? When did it happen? Where did it happen? Whom did it happen with?

- *Behaviour:* define the behaviour in terms of what it looks like (e.g. hitting, shouting).
- *Consequence:* What happened after the behaviour, or as a result of the behaviour (e.g. the behaviour was ignored, the child was counselled).

The ABC technique is used to identify patterns of behaviours and the context in which they occur (identifying the context was an important discovery in my observation of Dylan). It is important for the observer to consider the possible function of, or reason for, the child's behaviour—for example, getting or obtaining attention from peers or others, or expressing frustration. The knowledge gained from this observation method can be used to identify possible triggers of the behaviour. Possible triggers can then be limited or eliminated, and/or changes made in interactions and/or the program.

EVENT SAMPLE: ABC (ANTECEDENT/BEHAVIOUR/CONSEQUENCE)				
Child's name: Dylan		**Age:** 4.2 years		
Setting: Kindergarten				
Observer: Melissa				
Behaviour: Physical aggression—hitting				
DATE/TIME	LEARNING EXPERIENCE	ANTECEDENT	BEHAVIOUR	CONSEQUENCE
When the behaviour occurred	What learning experience was going on when the behaviour occurred	What happened right before the behaviour that may have triggered the behaviour	What the behaviour looked like	What happened after the behaviour/as a result of the behaviour
28.3.16 10.15 am	Train set	Child A came over to the train set, picked up a train, placed it on the track and noisily pushed it into Dylan's train.	Dylan made a grunting sound and hit Child A.	Child A sat back and started to cry and Dylan continued playing with his train.
29.3.16 2.40 pm	Train set	Child A and Child B came over and sat in front of the train set. Child B took a piece of train that was in front of Dylan.	Dylan yelled 'No!' and threw his hands up into the air. 'No!' and hit Child C on the arm.	Child C hit Dylan.
30.3.16 10.30 am	Train set	Dylan was playing with the train set on his own. I did not observe Child C entering the play.	Dylan hit Child C.	Child C started to cry and said 'He hit me', and Dylan hung his head.

Question: Dylan often enjoys playing on his own (solitary play), particularly with the trains (identified as one of his favourite learning experiences). Dylan shows frustration when his play is disrupted by another child. He will hit the child involved rather than verbalise his feelings.

Plan: I will read relevant stories and have discussions with the group about appropriate ways to enter other children's play, helping the group to understand things from someone else's point of view, and appropriate ways to respond when we feel angry or frustrated. I will actively involve Dylan in this discussion by asking open-ended questions such as 'Rather than hitting someone, what could we do?' The train area will be made bigger with more materials for children to share. I will reflect on how I communicate with and view the children to strengthen our relationship and promote positive peer relationships. I could also add games that involve sharing and turn taking into the program.

MELISSA COLVILLE

Work samples

work sample
a sample of a
child's work
usually collected
and collated with
different samples
of the same
child's work.

Work samples include samples of children's work, photos and/or photocopies of their work. Work samples are common in both early learning and school settings. Samples could include children's drawings, paintings, pastings, cuttings or writing. Further information is provided when we document the context and the processes involved, so we should include written comments about the work; the learning experience can be briefly described by the teacher as well as children's comments such as what they did or said at the time. If questioning children about their work, it is important to use open-ended questions. The open-ended question, 'Tell me about your drawing?' provides an opportunity for the child to explain their work. Commenting on a child's drawing, for example 'Oh, you've drawn a farm with farm animals', when their drawing is of something else can be very disappointing to a child, so open-ended questions are best. Additional comments provide further insight into children's learning and development as well as further thought for reflection on the program. Samples of children's work over time can provide evidence of children's ongoing progress as well as their strengths and interests. They also provide an opportunity for children, families and teachers to share and appreciate children's learning. I recommend that children, in collaboration with the teacher, choose samples of their work to include in their portfolio, thus giving them a sense of agency.

WORK SAMPLE		
Child's name: Jet	**Age:** 15 months	**Date:** 7.3.16
Setting: Multi-age long day care setting; 6 months–2.5 years.		
Observer: Ellie		
Observation: Jet held the crayon in his fist and dragged it around the paper, making lines and scribbles on the page. He moved his head from side to side and made sounds as he drew, such as 'da da', and 'doh'.		
Question: Jet's scribbles appear random and he is exploring the materials in a playful way, which is developmentally appropriate (Learning). This learning experience is helping to develop Jet's hand–eye coordination and fine motor skills (Learning). Jet is using sounds to communicate (Communication).		
Plan: Promote Jet's creativity by providing a range of art materials, such as a chalkboard and finger painting (Learning). It is important to encourage Jet's language, so the educators should talk with Jet frequently (Communication).		

Learning stories

Learning stories evolved from New Zealand's Te Whāriki curriculum and are a popular observation method used in Australian early childhood settings. A learning story tells a story about the child, the setting, the child's interactions and their process of learning, and is written in an interesting and engaging way. Depending on the specific format used—and these can differ—a learning story combines what is observed, how the child interacts with the environment and how this is interpreted by the adult; teacher reflection is used to interpret and make meaning of what they have observed. Learning stories are less clinical than other observation methods, and in my opinion, more enjoyable to read. Because they are so engaging, learning stories can prompt interesting conversations with parents and families. Children and parents are encouraged to contribute to learning stories. They can be involved in writing learning stories, often in response to the teacher's observation and reflection. Learning stories are a contemporary observation approach that sees the child as developing within their social and cultural context and therefore uses a sociocultural perspective. Learning stories focus on children's strengths and interests, attending to what they *can* do, rather than what they *can't*, which is a contemporary teaching practice. In essence, learning stories *describe* children's learning, *review* their learning and decide *what's next* to further support children's learning.

LEARNING STORY		
Child's name: Brendan	**Age**: 2 years	**Date**: 23/8/16
Setting: Toddler room		

Title: 'Hit that wind chime!' **Written by:** Mang

Observation: The learning story (describe the learning experiences that unfold):
Brendan spotted Marissa from the other end of the yard and, looking at her, yelled, 'Riss! Where are you?' 'I'm here Brendan. Where are you?' Marissa replied, making eye contact with Brendan. 'I'm here!' Brendan said with a smile on his face and ran over to where Marissa sat. As he ran, the wind chime suspended by a string above Brendan lightly grazed his head and made a soft chime. Looking up at the wind chime, Brendan laughed and with one arm, swiped to hit it. The wind chime swung wildly and loudly sending him into hysterical laughter. He maintained his gaze at the wind chime and continued to try to hit it. Marissa sat close by and encouraged Brendan, saying 'That's it Bren. There it goes! Listen to the sound it makes'. Brendan would look up at Marissa every so often to laugh and receive warm smiles. So much fun!

Question: Analysis of learning (What did the child/group do and understand during this experience?)
Brendan initiated conversation with Marissa, an adult, playfully pretending he could not see her. He realised how hitting the wind chime with his hand would make it move and make a sound (Learning). He used his hand–eye coordination to make contact with the wind chime and his gross motor strength to make it move. He was delighted by this action, enough for him to keep doing it (Wellbeing). Brendan checked back in with Marissa to share in his joy. Marissa happily reciprocated.

Plan: Extension of learning (What opportunities will you provide to extend on this experience?)
An extension of Brendan's gross motor skills might be to suspend objects that are more difficult for Brendan to hit, or add objects that require a different muscle movement, such as pulling (Learning).

Links to the Early Years Learning Framework (Identity, community, wellbeing, learning, communication):
Outcome 1: Brendan feels safe, secure and supported as he receives a positive response from his teacher.
Outcome 3: Brendan is demonstrating a strong sense of wellbeing as he interacts and communicates with his teacher and actively engages in his environment.

Family input:
It is wonderful to see Brendan having so much fun at childcare.

MELISSA COLVILLE

Story dictation

story dictation
when an observer
listens to a child
telling a story or
describing an
event and writes
down word for
word what the
child says.

Story dictation involves the observer listening when a child tells a story or describes an event and writing down word for word what the child says. The observer is an active listener and a scribe. Stories can be very short (one or two phrases) or lengthier (multiple sentences or paragraphs). The observer may need to remind children to speak slowly or repeat what they have said so they can keep up with what they are saying and/or use abbreviations. If a child loses track of what they are saying, the observer should read what has been written up to that point. By repeating the child's words, both the observer and the child can understand what has been said. When the child says the story is over, it can be read back to them. The observer can then ask the child if they want to change or add anything. Any changes the child suggests should then be made and the revised story read to the child. Stories usually take place during free play time and can be written or typed. Children's stories and accompanying pictures can be placed together and made into a booklet. Through story dictation we can document and assess, in particular, children's language development and their early literacy skills. Over time, the most common subjects of children's stories can be identified. One of the benefits of story dictation is that it helps children develop a lifelong love of stories and books. Dictating a story also gives a child the teacher's full attention, helping to build a secure and trusting relationship.

STORY DICTATION		
Child's name: Mabel	**Age:** 5 years	**Date:** 15.7.16
Setting: Sessional kindergarten		
Observer: Ben		

Observation: Child's story: Okay. Josie, Makayla and Holly (Mabel counts on her fingers one at a time as she says each name). Makayla was wearing pink. Josie (Mabel laughs) was wearing green and Holly was wearing blue. They all went to the ball, and suddenly, then (Mabel pauses for several seconds), they saw a dragon. They were scared. They screamed (Mabel screams). Then the dragon blew fire and flew away into the sky (Mabel waves her hands around). Whew! They danced around and (Mabel says singing) *they sang the song*. It's a nice place they went to. The people were so happy. They loved each other. So everybody, bye!

Question: Mabel tells a story about three of her friends (Identity). We have recently been discussing fairytales, and these themes appear to be reflected in Mabel's story (going to the ball, the dragon). Mabel's receptive language and audition (listening skills) has meant that she has understood the teacher's instructions for telling a story (Communication). Mabel is using spoken language to explore feelings and is able to tell a series of events (Communication). Mabel can form words and sounds correctly: correct speech, and her speech is dramatic (Communication).

Plan: To read Mabel her story and ask her if she would like to draw a picture to go with her story. To read Mabel's story to her again later in the week and ask her if she would like to continue her story. If so, this should be recorded as a story dictation.

Photographs

Photographs have become a popular observational method in early learning settings and schools. Photographs can be taken of a child's interest or engagement in a learning experience, or their demonstration of a particular skill or attempts at a new task. Photographs can also document children's learning and development as a group: their social interactions, relationships, learning processes and group dynamics. Photographs can be particularly useful in documenting children's social interactions in a group project. It is important for observers to think carefully about what is worth capturing in a photo and how the photo can contribute to an understanding of children's learning. A series of photos showing a developing skill or idea is often more useful than a single photograph. On their own, photographs are not useful assessments. They should also be accompanied by some form of written documentation that adds to the story of the photo. This documentation can be in the form of an anecdote and places the photo in context—for example, an explanation of the group project the children are working on. You can also ask children open-ended questions to gain further information. Children should also be encouraged to take photographs of their own experiences and/or interests. Photographs should be shared with families: parents love to see photos of their own children learning and having fun. Photographs may also be combined with other observation methods, such as learning stories.

PHOTOGRAPH/S		
Child's name: Setia	**Age:** 5.2 years	**Date:** 17.3.16
Setting: Sessional kindergarten		
Observer: Madeline		

Photograph/s:

Observation: While working on a puzzle Setia said to the teacher 'this is pretty easy 'coz if you get stuck you can just look here' and she pointed to the picture of the puzzle on the puzzle box. When Setia completed the puzzle she called to the teacher 'I'm finished! Come look!' Setia had a huge smile on her face.

Question: Setia is learning pattern recognition, problem solving and how to source support for herself (Learning). The accomplishment of finishing the puzzle enhances Setia's self-esteem and confidence (Identity, Wellbeing).

Plan: Include other more challenging puzzles that also have picture clues (Learning). It would be important to scaffold these trickier puzzles so Setia persists when she is challenged.

MELISSA COLVILLE

Portfolios

Portfolios are an individual systematic collection of documents that reflect what children do in the early childhood setting. Portfolio documents emphasise both the *process* of learning and the *product*. They are popular in early learning and school  settings. Portfolios are a contemporary approach that involves children and their families, and thus uses a sociocultural approach. Appropriate portfolio items include a variety of products such as teacher records, photographs, children's artwork, writing, checklists and communications from parents. Student portfolios (primary school) often include children's essays, journals, summaries, research notes, self-assessments and teacher comments. Portfolio products can be chosen to represent different areas of child development—for example, cognitive, physical, social and emotional development. They can also relate to the learning outcomes of parents and teachers, and/or EYLF or Australian Curriculum learning outcomes. It is important that the contents of a child's portfolio is individualised to show their uniqueness and children should help choose which items they would like in their portfolio. The material in a portfolio should be organised in chronological order and should demonstrate children's ongoing development over time. Although time consuming, both children and their families love portfolios; children love to show off their portfolio and families love having their child's portfolio as a precious keepsake.

Choosing an observation method

The choice of observation method will depend on the type of behaviour you want to assess and the amount and type of detail you need. Another important consideration is whether the information needs to be collected for one child or for the entire group. You will be given a focus child (or focus children) to observe while on practicum. You will plan learning experiences for your focus child, along with other children in the group based on your observations. The amount of focused attention required by the observer also needs to be considered. The EYLF (DEEWR, 2009) recommends that teachers use a variety of strategies to collect, document, organise and interpret what children know, can do and understand.

When my early childhood teaching pre-service teachers attend practicum, they are required to use a variety of observation methods and professional templates. Observations must be written on each child in a range of learning experiences and routines to learn their true value. My pre-service teachers tend to show a preference for particular observation methods. From early childhood teaching pre-service teachers' accounts, early childhood settings also seem to do this—for example, learning stories are particularly popular. The possibility of error is reduced when *multiple* and *varying assessments* are gathered and analysed, so this practice is a must.

Individual observations of children in everyday experiences are called 'formative' assessments. A 'summative' assessment is obtained by reviewing the observations gathered over time and writing a summary of what children have learnt. Summative assessments are often done at the end of the school year and are useful for discussing children's progress with parents.

STOP AND REFLECT

- If you have documented observations previously, what methods have you used?
- How have you chosen which recording method to use?
- Have the observation methods you chose been useful, or would another observation method have been more appropriate?
- Which observation methods do you feel most comfortable using?

Observing children is not an easy task. It requires skill and expertise and is developed over time with practice. When observing children, it is recommended that you keep a pen and a small notepad with you to record your observations. As a non-participant observer, you will need to blend into the background so the outcome of the observation is not affected. You can do this by sitting back unobtrusively, where you can easily see children and the learning experience you are going to observe. You should also be able to hear what children are saying.

This is a more formal type of observation where the observer is away from children's play or instruction (e.g. running record); however an observer can also be a participant observer. This means the observer is involved with the child or children and records the observation later from memory (e.g. anecdotal record). If a child asks you what you are doing when you are writing an observation, a simple explanation can be given—for example, that you are doing some writing about the children's play. There are many things to look for when you are observing a child, e.g. which toys or learning experiences does the child choose? Does the child play on their own or with others? How does the child interact and communicate with others? Is the child actively engaged and interested in their environment? You can also observe specific areas of the child's development—for example, their language skills.

When writing an observation, it is important to use descriptive language, rather than interpretive language. Descriptive language provides facts or information ('Jamie threw a block down *with force*'), while interpretive language explains the meaning of something ('Jamie threw the block down *angrily*'). It is important to only record what you see and not to interpret while you observe. It is the child's observable actions that should be described. The exception to this rule is learning stories, where the observer's interpretation and reflection is included within the observation itself. When you have finished your observation, read over what you have written to ensure it is descriptive, that it makes sense and that you have all of the information you need.

Who are we observing?

Babies

We learn more in our first year than at any other time in life. Careful observation of babies will uncover unique children who are very responsive to people and their environment. We can observe babies during everyday routines, focusing on their learning and interactions in relation to the EYLF learning outcomes and developmental milestones. This will enable us to observe babies holistically (through all developmental domains) and determine their level of development (i.e. whether they are

Cont.

MELISSA COLVILLE

meeting age-appropriate milestones). Babies have many ways of communicating, both verbal and non-verbal. Therefore, we can observe babies' expressive language (vocal communication), such as cooing and babbling, and their receptive language (what the baby understands), such as listening and responding to instructions—for example, by pointing to something. It is important for babies to engage with adults. With a *responsive* adult they can develop a sense of security and trust, the foundation for a secure attachment. Observing a baby development is a wonderful process!

Toddlers

Toddlers are excited to explore and discover the world. They are learning to master many new skills, such as walking and talking, enabling them to communicate and move around in new and exciting ways. Toddlers can experience strong feelings and are learning how to manage them. We should be extra sensitive when we document toddlers' frustrations (e.g. when they can't accomplish something) and when they test our limits (e.g. constantly saying 'no'). Toddlers often observe the play of other children or play next to them. Relationships with peers can be challenging at times, as toddlers are often unable to share and compete for toys with other children. Although toddlers are developing their sense of separateness from others and their independence, their need for, and attachment to, primary caregivers is still very strong.

Pre-schoolers

Pre-schoolers are gaining more confidence in their abilities. They are more capable and independent than toddlers—for example, they can run and jump, use language more proficiently (improved grammar), and dress and undress themselves. Pre-schoolers' imaginations are growing. They love to role play and pretend—for example, dressing up as Mum or Dad and cooking in the home corner. We can observe pre-schoolers' creative and problem-solving skills as they play more complex games and complete more difficult tasks. Friendships are more important at this age. However, children will vary in how they relate to and connect with others, so we should observe how they get along with each other and resolve conflicts. This is an important stage of development, as pre-schoolers progress in their ability to understand the perspective of others, empathise and collaborate.

School children

School-aged children are furthering their ability to follow the teacher's instructions, to read, write, spell, problem solve and use numbers. The Australian Curriculum sets out what students are expected to learn in all schools. Teachers link students' learning with the Australian Curriculum achievement standards to identify their *point of learning progression* (a learning progression is the pathway of learning as students progress towards the mastery of knowledge and skills). Play is still important for this age group (see Chapter 4 for information on children's play). Teachers track children's learning against The Victorian Early Years Learning and Developmental Framework's five learning outcomes: identity, community, wellbeing, learning and communication. One important factor that will impact students' progression towards the achievement standards and the learning outcomes is peer acceptance. Research has shown a link between peer popularity and academic achievement: students who develop positive peer relationships/friendships achieve more academically. Therefore, students' peer relationships need to be thoughtfully observed and considered.

Questioning observations

The next stage of the EYLF Early Years Planning cycle requires teachers to 'question'—that is, to question and analyse what has been observed. The EYLF defines assessment as '… the process of gathering and analysing information as evidence of what children know, can do and understand' (DEEWR, 2009, p.17). This is part of the ongoing planning cycle. Analysing an observation means to methodically and in detail (typically in order) explain and interpret the data. Essentially, an interpretation gives meaning to our observations. For example, an interpretation might identify the cause of or reason for children's behaviour. Assessing children's learning and development can be a difficult part of the planning process as it requires objectivity and careful consideration of all the details. Some questions to consider when analysing observations include:

- What developmental skills can be identified?
- What role has the sociocultural context played in the child's play, development and learning?
- Who else's perspectives and interpretations can I include?
- How can this analysis be used to plan experiences for children?

Good analysis takes knowledge and skill and it develops over time. Guided by the EYLF (DEEWR, 2009) observers take a *holistic approach* by reflecting on *all* domains of children's development, including their cognitive, physical, social and emotional development. This enables teachers to support all areas of children's development. Cognitive development involves children's thought processes, such as remembering, problem solving, and decision making, as well as how they understand and use language. Physical development is how children move and have physical control over their bodies and includes their gross motor skills (large muscles, used for running) and fine motor skills (small muscles, used for writing and drawing). Social and emotional development is largely related to children's relationships with others and includes aspects such as their emotional expression and understanding, and how they interact with others, including their ability to share and cooperate. While often categorised as separate domains, these developmental domains interrelate because what happens in one developmental domain influences what happens in another—for example, the state of our relationships (our social development), influences our emotional development.

Children's learning from birth to five years should also be assessed in relation to the EYLF's five learning and developmental outcomes: identity, community, wellbeing, learning and communication. Links to one or more of these learning outcomes should be made within each observation. Children's *stage of learning* should also be assessed—for example, in the school setting the progression of their writing skills, from *beginning* (minimal skill and understanding) through to *mastery* (a deep understanding where the child is ready for new challenges). The *content descriptions* in the Australian Curriculum (ACARA, 2017) are used to assess children's learning progress. To provide further clarity for teachers, there are *elaborations* that expand on the content descriptions, as well as an overview of the *achievement standard*. This assessment information is organised under different learning areas (e.g. English, Mathematics) from Foundation to Level 2 (five to eight years).

Children's social interactions and relationships are another important feature of child observations that require our analysis. Research has shown that children's relationships shape the way they see themselves, others and their world. Children's relationships affect *all* areas of their development. Analysis of children's interactions and relationships can uncover how they relate to others, including whether they experience positive interactions with peers and teachers, understand the rules and responsibilities that facilitate successful relationships, can resolve conflict in appropriate ways, and are included in or excluded from children's play.

Current approaches, particularly in birth-to-five settings, also analyse children's learning interests and strengths; this can include the materials or experiences that are of interest to them. Children's interests and strengths motivate them to acquire new skills, and importantly, the teacher can use their interests and strengths to support and enhance their learning environment. Children's interests and strengths are often observed when they are engaged in free play, so this is a good time to analyse what they are interested in and good at. Their strengths and interests should be discussed with their parents/family as early as possible. Conversations focusing on their interests and strengths help us build positive relationships with families, and then if, and when, challenging issues arise, challenging conversations can be easier to have.

My early childhood teaching pre-service teachers have commented that understanding children's learning and development through observation becomes clearer when they write their first child summary. This child summary (or child profile) is based on their collection of child observations, usually documented over the first week. By questioning a variety of child observations, students begin to see a pattern in what children enjoy, what they are learning and how they are developing.

STOP AND THINK

Consider how you might analyse and assess the following time sample.

- What do you notice about Zoe's developmental skills?
- Can you see evidence of her language skills? Her social development? Her physical development?
- Can you make connections to any of the five learning and developmental outcomes?
- What do you perceive to be Zoe's strengths and interests?

OBSERVATION RECORD			
Focus Child: Zoe	**Age:** 2 years	**Time:** every 30 minutes	**Date:** 10.6.15
Setting: Indoors			

OBSERVATION TYPE	TIME SAMPLE	EARLY YEARS LEARNING FRAMEWORK
Observation: 9.00 am: Zoe began to sing 'Twinkle. Twinkle Little Star' along with the educator. When she didn't know the words, she kept up with the tune with a humming noise. 9.30 am: Zoe holds her arms up towards the teacher after falling over. 10.00 am: Zoe was building a tower of small blocks (seven so far) and singing 'Baa Baa Black Sheep', keeping up with the tune correctly and pronouncing many of the words correctly. 10.30 am: An educator is reading a book to Zoe. Zoe reaches out and turns some of the pages and pulls all of the tabs. Zoe repeats some words and phrases such as 'hat' and 'cat' and 'round and round'.	**Question:** **Plan:**	**Identity** – Children have a strong sense of identity **Community** – Children are connected with & contribute to their world **Wellbeing** – Children have a strong sense of wellbeing **Learning** – Children are confident and involved learners **Communication** – Children are effective communicators

Below is my own interpretation and assessment of Zoe's play, development and learning. I observed Zoe and wrote this observation record.

OBSERVATION RECORD			
Focus Child: Zoe	**Age:** 2 years	**Time:** every 30 minutes	**Date:** 10.6.15
Setting: Indoors			

OBSERVATION TYPE	TIME SAMPLE	EARLY YEARS LEARNING FRAMEWORK
Observation: 9.00 am: Zoe began to sing 'Twinkle, Twinkle Little Star' along with the educator. When she didn't know the words she kept up with the tune with a humming noise. 9.30 am: Zoe holds her arms up towards the teacher after falling over. 10.00 am: Zoe was building a tower of small blocks (seven so far) and singing 'Baa Baa Black Sheep', keeping up with the tune correctly and pronouncing many of the words correctly. 10.30 am: An educator is reading a book to Zoe. Zoe reaches out and turns some of the pages and pulls all of the tabs. Zoe repeats some words and phrases such as 'hat' and 'cat' and 'round and round'.	**Question:** Zoe joins in nursery rhymes and is aware of the tune to the song and some of the words (Learning, Communication). Zoe communicates her need for comfort (Identity). Zoe appears to enjoy singing (strength and interest) and uses recognisable words (Learning, Communication). Zoe's understanding of the way books work is developing as she turns pages singly and pulls the tabs (Learning). Zoe is repeating words from interactions with the teacher (Learning, Communication). **Plan:**	**Identity** – Children have a strong sense of identity **Community** – Children are connected with & contribute to their world **Wellbeing** – Children have a strong sense of wellbeing **Learning** – Children are confident and involved learners **Communication** – Children are effective communicators

STOP AND REFLECT

- Are there any similarities between your own interpretation of Zoe and mine?
- How does my interpretation differ from your own?
- What is the significance of these differences?
- How might collaborative approaches help us to understand Zoe's learning and development?

The importance of collaboration in analysis

Children are complex individuals and it is important to accurately assess their learning and development. One way of doing this is to work collaboratively with families. As part of a partnership it is important to utilise families' perspectives, knowledge, experiences and expectations. Parents have a unique knowledge of their child; they know their child's strengths and interests, and can often help explain their child's behaviour. In turn, teachers provide families with information about their children's play, learning and development in the context of the early childhood or school setting. Shared parent and teacher knowledge provides a perfect combination of rich information to help us in our work with children.

MELISSA COLVILLE

Parents' ongoing contribution to the assessment process is vital. For teachers and parents to engage in regular two-way conversations about children's learning, observations and planning, teachers need to develop confidence and strong communication skills. They also need to create time and space to regularly share information. As part of our everyday practice, we can communicate with parents at drop-off and pick-up times, through phone conversations, email, in parent meetings, and by sending information home to be read, responded to and returned (Beaty, 2014). When teachers and parents combine their understandings of the child, new and shared understandings and reflections can emerge and parents can be assured the teacher knows, understands and values their child.

Talking with other teachers about your observations of children can also contribute to a more accurate understanding and assessment of children. My pre-service teachers have found these discussions highly effective in understanding their focus children. Teachers can share not only their early childhood professional knowledge and experience, but also their knowledge of the individual child. These discussions are valuable in building communication and strengthening the student–teacher relationship.

Diverse perspectives can assist in how we make meaning from observing children. When sharing our perspectives, we need to be open to feedback and different viewpoints. An important question to reflect on when sharing our different perspectives is what might explain *why* that person holds that perspective? Staff in early childhood differ in their qualifications and experience. Working together allows *all* of those involved to develop their knowledge, skills and understanding of both individual children and children 'as a group'. This communication between staff can also strengthen our relationships and understandings of each other.

Teachers can actively involve children in assessing their learning and development. For example, children from three to four years of age onwards can be asked to explain how they learnt something or who helped them to learn. Teachers honour children's agency by including their views of their own learning and gaining further insight on them. Multiple sources of information—from children, parents and colleagues—provide us with a range of perspectives on each child and help us to form a more rounded and less biased view of children's learning and development.

Using professional knowledge to assess children

Professional knowledge is one of the three professional standards for Australian teachers (AITSL, 2011). Professional knowledge includes knowing children and how they learn. We assess children by making judgments based on our professional knowledge, including our knowledge of the frameworks and a range of theories on children's play, learning and development. A sound understanding of developmental milestones, along with sociocultural theories, will support you to effectively assess children's play, development and learning. For example, sociocultural theories and post-structural theories (which promote equity and social justice (MacNaughton, 2003) may help you be aware of making judgments on race, disability or gender stereotypes. While these factors may be relevant (e.g. disability can explain a child's physical skills), we must be careful not to express bias. It is recommended that you consult a variety of books on child development and theories for a more rounded view of the child.

It is important to know and understand children deeply. Careful analyses help teachers (in partnership with children, families and other professionals) to determine how children are progressing towards the learning outcomes and if not, what might be impeding their progress. Accurate interpretations can be made through repeated, detailed objective observations that consider children's environments, experiences and developmental levels (Bentzen, 2009, p.59). Children who may need additional support can be identified, and support and assistance for families in accessing specialist help can be provided. All settings are required to keep assessment records of children in their care, so I recommend that you try and view as many examples as you can while on practicum to learn about different approaches to observation and assessment. Observations come in many forms and it is from the analysis of these diverse records that teachers plan learning environments to support children's learning.

Planning children's learning

Planning and documenting children's play, development, learning and wellbeing will be an important part of your professional teaching role. To plan environments and experiences that build on and extend children's learning you should start with your analyses of child observations and consider what other learning is possible.

When you are on practicum, your planning ideas should always be discussed with your supervising teacher. They can provide you with important feedback, based on their knowledge of children and their families, the context and environment, and their professional knowledge of early childhood in general. These discussions build your own knowledge and help you form a professional working relationship.

Look again at Zoe's observation record earlier in the chapter and consider the implications of our interpretation/assessment and what we might plan.

STOP AND THINK
• What other learning is possible for Zoe?   • What might you plan for Zoe?   • Why have you chosen this plan for Zoe?

Planning should not be based on a *single* observation of a child, but rather a *range* of observations. These observations are compared to determine a pattern, often focusing on the child's strengths and interests. An appropriate focus for children's learning can then be chosen. Based on my analyses of Zoe's learning in this and other observations, and through discussion with colleagues and Zoe's mother, I chose a learning experience to foster Zoe's literacy learning. My discussion with a colleague uncovered a favourite nursery rhyme book she read to her daughter, 'My very first Mother Goose'. Zoe's mother confirmed that Zoe loves to read stories at home, although she does not own a nursery rhyme book. There are a multitude of learning experiences that could be offered to Zoe to extend her literacy learning. These include singing, puppet play, finger plays, a wide variety of books and/ or writing materials, and Zoe can read and be read to. As part of the planning process the environment, routines, materials and resources, the teacher's role and teaching practices and documentation methods should be considered. We must also meet the relevant legal requirements that apply to the particular service—for example, the frameworks, the Australian Curriculum, Children's Services Regulations, centre/school philosophy and policies.

MELISSA COLVILLE

Below is my own plan for Zoe. This is only *one* plan in the curriculum. I have considered the learning opportunities for Zoe, and how they might be evident when implementing this plan—how I would recognise Zoe is achieving the learning outcomes and objectives/specific purposes. I recommended that you use a variety of templates to see what works best for you in your setting. You will implement a number of plans on practicum, both indoor and outdoor, to make up the curriculum program. These plans usually accumulate over your practicums, leading to full control of the program.

Learning experience	
Nursery rhymes	**Date:** 17.6.15

Indoor or outdoor experience: Indoor

Age group and number of children (children involved in the learning experience): 2–3-year-olds, 3–4 children

Rationale (Why you are doing this learning experience, e.g. observation of children's interests, learning opportunities):
Over the past two weeks Zoe has shown an interest in reading books and singing. Discussion with Zoe's mother has uncovered that Zoe loves reading books at home, although she does not have any nursery rhyme books.
This experience will offer Zoe several learning opportunities: to listen to the rhymes and hear new words and rhythm patterns; practise and develop her language skills by joining in verbally; appreciate literature in a fun experience, and interact with the professional as she scaffolds Zoe's learning.

Links to learning outcomes (frameworks—focus on those most likely to be achieved and give examples of how they will be achieved through your learning experience):
Zoe is an effective communicator (Communication); she will practise and develop her language skills by saying the words of the rhymes aloud.
Zoe is a confident and involved learner (Learning); she will develop her understanding of the relationships between the text and illustrations by pointing to particular illustrations when asked.
Zoe is connected to and contributes to her world (community); she will develop a further appreciation of nursery rhymes by being positively involved in the experience.

Objectives/specific purposes (include 2 or 3 specific, observable objectives):
For Zoe to practise and develop her language skills by saying the words of the rhymes aloud (Communication).
For Zoe to further develop her understanding of the relationships between the text and illustrations by pointing to particular illustrations when asked (Learning).
For Zoe to further develop an appreciation of nursery rhymes by being positively involved in the experience (community).

Equipment/resources (used in the learning experience):
'My very first Mother Goose' book.

Learning experience process (What will happen/how the learning experience will unfold—include teaching strategies):
During play time (non-routine) read chosen rhymes ('Baa Baa Black Sheep', 'Humpty Dumpty', 'Down by the Station') to Zoe in the book corner. Other children may also want to join the learning experience.
Begin by inviting Zoe to listen/read the book. Get Zoe's attention by commenting on and pointing to the pictures. Model enthusiastic singing of the rhymes. Ask labelling questions (e.g. What's that?). Wait for an answer and respond positively, or if necessary provide the answer (e.g. Yes, it is a sheep). Provide feedback to Zoe's responses (e.g. It's like a cow, but it's a sheep). Read further rhymes if Zoe shows an interest.

Evaluation (What happened / How the child/children responded: evaluate the whole experience—objectives/specific purposes, equipment/resources, general suitability of the learning experience):

Family input (parents' comments and/or suggestions):

Modifications and strategies for future learning (changes to the current experience):

Reflective practice

Planning and evaluation should be based on sound professional knowledge and evidence-based practice. The EYLF principles and practices reflect contemporary theories and research on children's learning, and underpin practice that supports all children's progress towards the learning outcomes. This means we consider the frameworks principles and practices when making planning decisions. To do this, we begin by understanding our own pedagogy: *our* principles and practices, which have been influenced by *our* knowledge, beliefs, values, attitudes and perceptions. Then we work to make our principles and practices consistent with the framework. You should, for example, consider your theoretical perspectives. If you use a developmental approach, your planning would be based on children's individual development, and experiences would be planned to achieve developmental goals and milestones. Conversely, if you used a sociocultural approach, experiences would be connected to children's social and cultural contexts. It is important to note that these theories do not have to be exclusive. I have combined both theories in my planning and I encourage you to do the same.

STOP AND THINK

- Does this plan reflect developmental theory or sociocultural theory? How? What does this mean for Zoe's learning and development?
- Which theories influence your practice when you plan for children? Why?

There is no specific format to use in our planning documentation, so each teacher will have their own understandings and ideas on how to use the EYLF principles, practices and learning outcomes within their documentation. The learning experience for Zoe has been planned against the learning outcomes as a way to support her learning and links to the principles and practices. For example, this plan aims to build *secure, respectful and reciprocal relationships* (EYLF principle), and to be *responsive* to Zoe's strengths, abilities and interests (EYLF practice), using *intentional teaching* (EYLF practice).

Acting: putting plans into action

The next stage of the planning cycle is putting the plans into action. It is important to observe the implementation of the planned learning experience to be able to effectively evaluate and reflect. We may discover when implementing a plan that they do not always unfold as we expect; there may be unanticipated outcomes, including how children respond. I recall being disappointed when this happened to me as a pre-service teacher on practicum. However, as pointed out by one of my supervising teachers, these unexpected outcomes are all part of the learning process.

When I discuss this with my pre-service teachers, I hear wonderful stories about their own unexpected responses from children. Most often, students' stories focus on the children's unexpected capabilities, particularly the babies'! One student once commented that her planned learning experiences 'never went as planned'. When children respond in ways that are different from what we expect, we learn more about them and also about ourselves—and then we can gain further awareness, skills and knowledge.

MELISSA COLVILLE

It is critical that we support children's learning by being *responsive* to children when implementing a learning experience; we need to follow their lead. You will see from the evaluation of Zoe's learning experience that she did not want to read the book the first time she was asked; therefore the plan was implemented at a later time. We need to learn to respond to children *in the moment*. Therefore, our written plans may vary when we implement them in response to the child/ren's needs and interests. We can reflect on our ability to be responsive to children both during and after we implement our plans. Putting our plans into action, particularly when we are actively involved in the learning experience, is one of the most enjoyable parts of the observation–planning cycle.

Reflecting and evaluating

The final part of the planning cycle is to evaluate and reflect on the effectiveness of the learning experience/curriculum and how it could be improved using the EYLF practices, principles and learning outcomes. It is particularly important to evaluate the children's experience. How have they benefited from this learning experience? What have they learnt? We should also reflect on our interactions and teaching strategies (our practices). Were they successful? How could they be improved? Child and family involvement is equally important. How were children and families involved in our planning? How could they could be further involved? When we evaluate and reflect on our planning we review the learning opportunities for children, the environment and experiences we have offered, and the approaches that were taken to promote children's learning, development and wellbeing. We also reflect on pedagogy that will suit the context and the children. Observations and assessment of children's learning is used to inform our future curriculum plans. Children need opportunities to practise, consolidate and extend their knowledge, skills and understandings, so we build on our previous plans.

My plan below includes the evaluation, family input, modifications and strategies for future learning, with links to the EYLF practices, principles and learning outcomes.

Learning experience
Nursery rhymes Date: 17.6.15
Indoor or outdoor experience
Indoor
Age group and number of children (*Children involved in the learning experience*)
2–3 year olds, 3–4 children
Rationale (*Why you are doing this learning experience?—e.g. observation of children's interests, learning opportunities*)
Zoe has shown an interest in reading books and singing. This experience will offer Zoe a number of learning opportunities: to listen to the rhymes and hear new words and rhythm patterns; to practise and develop her language skills by joining in verbally; to appreciate literature in a fun experience; and to interact with the professional who scaffolds Zoe's learning.
Links to learning outcomes (*frameworks—focus on those most likely to be achieved and give examples of how they will be achieved through your learning experience*)

Cont.

Zoe is an effective communicator (Communication); she will practise and develop her language skills by saying the words of the rhymes aloud.

Zoe is a confident and involved learner (Learning); she will develop her understanding of the relationships between the text and illustrations by pointing to particular illustrations when asked.

Zoe is connected to and contributes to her world (Community); Zoe will develop a further appreciation of nursery rhymes by being positively involved in the experience.

Objectives/specific purposes (*include 2 or 3 specific, observable objectives*)

For Zoe to practise and develop her language skills by saying the words of the rhymes aloud (Communication)

For Zoe to further develop her understanding of the relationships between the text and illustrations by pointing to particular illustrations when asked (Learning)

For Zoe to further develop an appreciation of nursery rhymes by being positively involved in the experience (Community)

Equipment/resources (*used in the learning experience*)

'My very first Mother Goose' book.

Learning experience process (*what will happen / how the learning experience will unfold—include teaching strategies*)

During play time (non-routine) read the chosen rhymes ('Baa Baa Black Sheep', 'Humpty Dumpty', 'Down by the Station') to Zoe in the book corner. Other children may also want to join the learning experience.

Begin by inviting Zoe to listen to/read the book. Get Zoe's attention by commenting on and pointing to the pictures. Model enthusiastic singing of the rhymes. Ask labelling questions (e.g. What's that?). Wait for an answer and respond positively, or if necessary provide the answer (e.g. Yes, it is a sheep). Provide feedback to Zoe's responses (e.g. It's like a cow, but it's a sheep).

Evaluation (*What happened?—how the child/children responded; evaluate the whole experience—objectives/specific purposes, equipment/resources, general suitability of the experience*)

Two other children joined in this experience: Aurora and Toby. The book was a suitable resource as the children were actively engaged and responsive: pointing to the pictures, making animal noises and at times, singing along (Communication; Community).

Unanticipated outcomes: Zoe was not interested in the book when first asked so I asked again later. She had her fingers in her mouth on the first reading, which prevented her from speaking. Once the three rhymes were sung, Toby joined Harrison at the puzzle table, however Zoe and Aurora were interested in looking through the rest of the book.

Objectives: Zoe said some of the words to all of the rhymes, and was involved in looking at the text and illustrations, pointing to particular features when asked. Zoe responded positively to the experience, smiling and being responsive. Zoe responded when I pointed to and commented on the pictures and when I asked questions. This maintained her interest. Waiting for an answer and responding positively assisted in a positive reaction from Zoe: eye contact, smiling and talking (Learning, Communication, Community). (Secure, respectful and reciprocal relationships; Intentional teaching)

Discussing this learning experience with Zoe's mother before implementing this plan has been valuable, and her input (see below) has strengthened our home–centre link.

Family input (*Parent comments and/or suggestions*)

It is wonderful to see Zoe so engaged. I will buy a nursery rhyme book and look forward to singing nursery rhymes with Zoe (*Zoe's mother*). (Partnerships; Continuity of learning and transitions)

Modifications and strategies for future learning (*Changes to the current experience*)

To continue singing nursery rhymes to Zoe and the children throughout the day

To continue reading/singing the nursery rhymes to Zoe and the children from the book

To provide Zoe and the children with other nursery rhyme books, with different rhymes and illustrations

To provide Zoe and the children with a wide variety of literature

To continue to observe Zoe's responses to these learning experiences

To continue to communicate with Zoe's parents about Zoe's learning and planned learning experiences (Intentional teaching; Responsiveness to children; Partnerships)

MELISSA COLVILLE

Planning with families

We need to make sure the planning process is visible to, and shared with, children and families. This can be done in a variety of ways including a wall plan, journal, folder, diary and/or visual displays. We should ask ourselves, 'Who is this for?' and adapt our documentation accordingly. Families have different preferences, so our planning should be communicated in a variety of ways. This includes communicating with families in their first language. To demonstrate how children learn through play, we not only communicate what the child is *doing*, but focus on what the child is *learning*. For example, a two-year-old playing with blocks (what they are *doing*) is *learning* about concepts such as size and balance, and cause and effect (one event—the cause—makes another event happen—the effect, e.g. educational pop-up toys). We need to continually reflect on what families need and want; so, input from families should be continually sought. While documenting our planning for children and families we need to remember that nothing can replace the value of face-to-face communication. We therefore need to make the most of any opportunity to communicate with families in person. Reflective practice is used to generate new knowledge and ideas. When evaluating and reflecting on our planning, we need to ask, What is working and what could we improve?

The ongoing planning cycle

Children are ongoing learners, and teachers use the planning cycle to support children's continual learning. The frameworks principles, practices and learning outcomes are used as a guide throughout the observation–planning cycle, and children and families' ongoing input is sought. The planning cycle begins with formative assessments (observations) of children to determine their current learning and development. These observations are then analysed and assessed in relation to children's interests and strengths. This assessment allows the teacher to plan experiences to extend children's learning. Teachers implement both planned and spontaneous learning experiences to promote children's positive interactions with others and their positive learning dispositions. Children's responses and learning are monitored, documented and reflected upon. Once the planning cycle is complete, it begins again with child observation.

Ethical implications and considerations

Observation and assessments of children are legal and professional requirements that need to be undertaken in an ethical manner. Ethics shape what we do; they determine our morals, values and rules of behaviour. There are many important ethical implications for observing young children; and importantly, this includes obtaining informed written consent from families and for confidentiality to be assured. Our Code of Ethics (Early Childhood Australia, 2016) states that we 'respect families' right to privacy and maintain confidentiality'. As a pre-service teacher, with the support of your practicum supervising teacher, you will ask the child's parent to give their written permission to observe their child. *You also need to assure the parent that all personal information will remain strictly private and confidential.* This means that you will not reveal the child's identity within your documentation; for example, you might refer to the child as 'Child A' or use a pseudonym (a false name—for example, using the name Chelsea for Eve). All information on the child is to be kept private and should not be made public, shared with family and friends, or be available to anyone without the parents' consent. The parent should be provided with a copy of their written permission form and you should also keep a copy. Although parents should have access to the information documented on their child, it may be more appropriate for you to provide general, verbal feedback on the observations you have made. The child's progress is best discussed between the parent and the (professional) teacher.

As well as providing consent, parents should be involved in the observation and planning process. Parents have access to the information collected, particularly portfolios and learning stories, which are designed to be shared with families. We need to encourage parents to contribute their observations and understandings of their child to gain a more complete picture. Parents are a wonderful source of information, and can offer observations of their child in a variety of settings (e.g. the home and the community). Teachers and parents can also form a strong home–centre link, where teachers plan together with parents to offer children consistency at home and in the early childhood program. Teachers and parents should work together to monitor children's progress and use this information to inform the educational program and establish shared goals. This collaboration should be ongoing and continuous. If, at any time, sensitive information needs to be discussed with parents, this should occur in a private space.

Confidential information (personal, sensitive information) about children and their families should only be shared with people who 'need to know' to better meet the needs of the child and family. Those who 'need to know' include our co-workers. When teachers share information, this contributes to our collective knowledge about a child or group of children. Teachers may also share child observations with other early childhood professionals, such as early intervention specialists who may also be working with the child. Teachers only reveal confidential matters when appropriate; information should not be passed on unless it is in the best interests of the child. There are circumstances where confidentiality can be breached, such as a child requiring protection. As a teacher, you may discover that a child is being abused or neglected. It is now mandated that early childhood teachers report cases of child abuse and neglect. In the case of child protection, information can be shared with professional agencies, such as the Department of Human Services and Child First (in Victoria). Under the 'Code of Conduct and Ethics' (VIT, 2015) school teachers can breach confidentiality to prevent or lessen a serious threat to life, health, safety or welfare of a person (including the student), as part of an investigation into unlawful activity, if the disclosure is required or mandated by law, and/or to prevent a crime or enforce the law.

Teachers are advised to be cautious about storing and displaying observational records. Under the 'National Quality Standard, Quality area 7: Leadership and service management', Australian Children's Education and Care Quality Authority (ACECQA, 2011) requires evidence that records are stored appropriately to protect confidentiality. Documentation may be stored in a computer, folder or portfolio and should be labelled and dated. For information stored in a computer, 'Read only' protection and/or passwords can be used to control access, or information can be kept on an encrypted memory stick. Our Code of Ethics (ECA, 2016) requires that we 'safeguard the security of information and documentation about children, particularly when shared on digital platforms'. Folders containing child information can be kept in the office or staff room, in a locked cabinet. Portfolios are usually

MELISSA COLVILLE

accessible within the classroom; however, they can be clearly labelled with the child's name. Displaying and sharing children's information can present a challenge for teachers. For example, parents may exercise their right to exclude their child from shared photos. Separating children's observations, or in this case photos, can be difficult as we often gather information and photographs that include more than one child. Martin (2014) aptly points out that it is much easier to have a policy that covers the whole group or class and is understood and signed by the parents.

Maintaining children's and families' privacy and confidentiality in these, and other ways upholds the rights of children and families. Settings will have their own policies and practices determining who has access to information and how information is displayed and stored. These policies are best written in conjunction with families. The settings policies as well as our legal requirements and expectations, must be followed at all times, and if you are ever unsure, you must seek clarity. The ethical implications of observation and assessment can be complex and we should expect that more ethical issues will arise, particularly with changes in technology. Keeping up to date on this topic will be paramount. Current recommended texts include Hobart, Frankel & Walker (2014), Bentzen (2009) and Martin (2014).

STOP AND THINK

- What are the ethical implications of child observation and record keeping?
- Are all ethical implications of child observation also a legal issue?
- Who has access to the information you are collecting?
- When can confidentiality be breached?
- How and where should you store the information you have gathered?
- What are the potential issues you might face when sharing children's information and documentation on digital platforms?
- Is it appropriate to display children's information such as babies' feeding, sleeping and elimination patterns on a chart or whiteboard for everyone to view? Why might this be an issue for some families?

Challenges of observation

There are many difficulties and challenges associated with child observation, and therefore not all can be included in this chapter. One difficulty relates to the detail provided: the less detailed an observation is the more open to interpretation (and error) the analysis or interpretation can have.

STOP AND THINK

Consider the following observation of three-year-old Michael: *Michael picked up a jug of milk. He moved the jug toward his glass. He hit the glass and tipped it over. The milk spilled.*
   Consider the detail, or lack of detail, provided in this observation.

- What important details do you think are missing from this observation?
- What questions do you have?
- How might the lack of detail jeopardise the interpretation of this observation?

Our questions may include: How big is the jug? How full is the jug? Did Michael hold the jug with one or two hands? How did Michael react when the milk spilled?

Another difficulty or challenge with observation is no two people will interpret an observation in the exact same way. Two open and honest teachers can observe the same child at the same time and what they see and interpret will depend on what they look for and their own perspectives. Teachers' personal feelings, values and attitudes can influence the interpretation of a child's behaviour. The theoretical perspective used as a basis to interpret an observation will also shape the analysis and assessment of the child. For example, if you took a developmental view of the observation of Michael, you might consider Michael's age: children around three years of age can pour without spilling (Sheridan et al., 2014). If you took a sociocultural view you might consider Michael's sociocultural context, more specifically his independence: does he pour his own drinks? There are several ways a teacher might interpret the observation of Michael: Michael was careless; Michael was inexperienced in handling a jug; Michael wasn't paying attention to what he was doing; Michael lacked the strength needed to lift the jug; Michael lacked the hand–eye coordination necessary to pour from the jug.

So, which interpretation is most accurate? Rich detail in an observation provides the foundation for a more accurate interpretation. Observing Michael with a jug on several occasions over time will also produce a more accurate analysis. Furthermore, team and collaborative approaches (including family partnerships and collaboration with colleagues) will contribute to the quality of child observation and planning. When we work with others we uncover a diverse range of perspectives and when we incorporate these perspectives we have a less biased view of the child. Sharing information provides teachers with a range of insights on each child that then help to form a more rounded, balanced picture of the child.

Observations and assessment should be carried out with *sensitivity, objectivity* and an awareness of *anti-discrimination practice*. We are sensitive when we consider the many different factors that can affect children's behaviours, including hot weather, fatigue, illness and discomfort, or a change in routines or staff. There are also many factors that affect *our* observation, including our sensitivity and awareness, the influence of our personality and controlling our bias (Bentzen, 2009, pp.70–1). Being sensitive means carefully considering the language we use when we write observations. Consider the sensitivity of these two statements: Child A has no friends; Child A is spoilt. One of the best ways to ensure the language we use is sensitive is to imagine that you are the child's parent: how would you feel reading this observation if it was about your child? How would you feel reading that your child has no friends, or is spoilt? I have used this technique with pre-service teachers, and always with success. If in doubt, you can also check with your supervising teacher.

So how can we be objective and avoid bias? Being objective means you are not influenced by personal feelings or opinion; what you write is based on 'fact'. Hobart and Frankel (2004, p.8) state that observers need to be 'entirely objective and unbiased', and recommend that observations are written in a 'detached and impartial manner being sure that you are not influenced by prior knowledge of the child or the family, your personal feelings towards the child and your expectation of her behaviour and development'. Do you think this is possible? Can we be entirely objective and unbiased? MacNaughton (2003, p.150), among others, argues that 'observation is always skewed by the observer's biases'. One of the best ways to

MELISSA COLVILLE

avoid bias is to describe only *observable actions*; without making judgments or conclusions. Judgments or conclusions are made in your interpretation, in collaboration with others, for a less biased view.

Anti-discrimination practice challenges prejudice in regards to issues such as race and gender. Children may be brought up in a culture different from our own and this may cause us to have cultural bias. There is concern that assessment of children from diverse backgrounds can be biased. Van Hoorn and colleagues (2015, p.143) state that too often assessments lead to over-identification and misdiagnosis of children from diverse cultures, languages and backgrounds as having language or other developmental delays. It is vital that we respect, understand and include children's culture within our program. Children's identity is formed through their culture, and the development of a strong cultural identity is essential to children's healthy sense of who they are and where they belong (DEEWR, 2010, p.21).

Using a sociocultural approach will assist us when we observe and interpret children's play, learning and development. When we consider different circumstances and cultural traditions we expect variations in children's behaviour. Cultures, and families within these cultures, differ in terms of infant care and attachment, discipline, cooperation, gender roles, moral development, children's responsibilities, family roles and intellectual priorities (Rogoff, 2003). The greater understanding and knowledge we have of other cultures and families' backgrounds, the less likely we are to make judgments based on our own upbringing and background. In the Australian context, this includes valuing Aboriginal and Torres Strait Islander cultures. Reciprocal and mutually valued partnerships of teachers and families are therefore needed (Van Hoorn et al., 2015, p.143). Ongoing learning and reflective practice (DEEWR, 2009, Principle 5) on cultures other than our own is essential.

Finally, there may be a case where you record something worrying: a problem, concern or issue. Cause for concern can include health issues, developmental issues, behavioural challenges, abuse or neglect, emergencies, and reactions to trauma (Martin, 2014, p.329). Therefore, further observation and investigation may be needed. Many causes of concern are minor; however, some may be more serious. If this is the case, you should seek help from professionals. Either way, as a pre-service teacher you should discuss any concerns with your supervising teacher, practicum assessor or practicum coordinator.

Conclusion

There is no one way of observing that is 'true' or objective, as every individual observes through the lens of their values, beliefs, experiences and perceptions. Because observation is never a neutral process, it is essential to critically examine the influences that shape our ways of seeing and recognise the filters that limit what we see and how we interpret (QCAA, 2014). We need to create new possibilities for how we see, interpret and understand children's learning (QCAA, 2014). Collaboration with others and wide professional reading are two important ways of seeing and understanding more. Through deep reflection and critical thinking, we can improve the ways we see, interpret, understand and work with children and families during the observation-planning cycle.

SUMMARY

- Curtis and Carter (2012, p.1) state that 'observation inspires good teaching'. Relationships are the keystone of early childhood education and good teaching. They are strengthened through positive and thoughtful engagement in the observation-planning cycle—as seen in the example of Dylan at the beginning of the chapter—and collaboration is essential. We need to develop strong partnerships with children, families and our colleagues. There are benefits for all involved when we work in partnership together.
- Thoughtful observation encourages us to observe children using a variety of methods. It is underpinned by our understanding and by critically reflecting on historical and contemporary theories.
- Developmental theory provides us with guidance on how children learn and develop, while sociocultural theory supports our understanding of children's learning and development within a sociocultural context.
- The frameworks inspire us to think deeply about the planning cycle: how to best observe children, question their learning, plan for their learning, act on what we have planned and reflect on what we have planned. Knowing, understanding and engaging with the frameworks will assist us in improving our approaches to documentation and planning, as well as guide our teaching practice.
- The ethical implications and difficulties related to child observation and assessment require us to be respectful of, and sensitive to, children and families, and to thoughtfully reflect on the consequences of our actions for everyone involved. When reflecting on child observation and assessment and making important observation and planning decisions, we must always come back to what is best for the individual child. We must also possess high expectations for children and, perhaps more importantly, for ourselves.

FURTHER REFLECTION

- Are your observations and planning consistent with the EYLF frameworks? How do these frameworks influence your relationships and teaching?
- What do you need to learn about children's strengths, culture, learning and development to interpret your observations more accurately?
- What aspects of your observation and planning knowledge and practice need to be further developed?

GROUP DISCUSSION

1 What biases about children, families and/or culture might you hold? How could you address these biases in your work with children and families?
2 How can we work in partnership with families throughout the observation and planning cycle?
3 What conversations can you have with children, families, colleagues and other professionals to improve your observation and planning knowledge and skills?
4 What contemporary theories that underpin child observation are *not* detailed in this chapter?
5 What other observation methods (*not* mentioned in this chapter) can be used to observe children?
6 What questions do you need to ask to effectively reflect on and evaluate your observation and planning?
7 What ethical implications and/or difficulties related to child observation and assessment have you experienced on practicum or in an early childhood education setting? How have these experiences been handled?

MELISSA COLVILLE

CLASS EXERCISE

1 In small groups:
   – Watch a video clip of a young child playing with other pre-service teachers. Note what you observed. How clear is your observation? Have you clearly identified the learning that has taken place? Have you included all of the details needed for your particular observation method (e.g. name, age, date and other specific details; the antecedent, behaviour and consequence for an event sample)?
   – Compare your observations with those of the other pre-service teachers. What were the similarities? What were the differences? Why do think this was? Would you change what you have written in your observation? Why?
2 Examine theories *not* detailed in this chapter that underpin child observation (e.g. post-structural theory).
3 Examine observation methods *not* detailed in this chapter.

FURTHER READING

Australian Curriculum, Assessment and Reporting Authority (ACARA) (2017) Australian Curriculum. https://www.acara.edu.au/
   Recommended reading for more information on school-aged children.

Australian Government, Early Years Learning Framework Practice-based Resources— Developmental Milestones. http://files.acecqa.gov.au/files/QualityInformationSheets/QualityArea1/ DevelopmentalMilestonesEYLFandNQS.pdf
   Recommended reading for more information on children from birth to five years. Developmental milestones are divided into sections—physical, social, emotional, cognitive and language—for various age groups (e.g. birth–four months).

Beaty, J.J. (2014) Observing the Development of the Young Child (8th edn). New Jersey, U.S.: Prentice Hall.
   This highly recommended book discusses how to observe, record and interpret the development of children from three to five years. Beaty includes a range of observation methods and advice on how to support children with hands-on learning experiences. This is a practical, easy-to-read book covering different areas of children's development: cognitive development, physical development, emotional competence and social competence and more. Beaty also highlights the important role families play in child observation and assessment.

Bentzen, W.R. (2009) Seeing Young Children: A Guide to Observing and Recording Behaviour (6th edn). Belmont, CA: Delmar Cengage Learning.
   This book addresses the theoretical and practical aspects of child observation and assessment. Bentzen goes into detail on how to observe, record and interpret children's behaviour from birth to eight years. Guidelines for children's growth and development are also provided.

Bradford, H. (2012) Planning and Observation with Children under Three. New York: Routledge.
   The learning experiences for the birth to three-year-old age group need to be holistic, relevant and challenging. This text draws on recent research and explains the links between observation, planning and assessment. Practical case studies and activities are provided with reflective practice encouraged. This is a useful, easy-to-read text for those working with babies and toddlers.

Clark, A. & Moss, P. (2011) Listening to Young Children: The Mosaic Approach (2nd edn). London, England: National Children's Bureau.
   This book offers teachers a range of ways to listen to, and understand, young children's perspectives. The Mosaic approach combines traditional ways of observing children with participatory tools—for example, children use cameras to document what is important to them. Clark and Moss include case studies of the Mosaic approach in action and offer guidance on how teachers can adapt the framework in different settings. This approach values children's competency and their contribution.

Curtis, D. & Carter, M. (2012) The Art of Awareness (2nd edn). St. Paul, MN: Redleaf Press.

This book offers an insight into our practical work—what we notice and see when we observe children—through a number of 'study sessions'. The authors offer new ideas and strategies, emphasise cultural awareness and encourage their readers to consider different points of view.

Department of Education, Employment and Workplace Relations (DEEWR) (2009) Belonging, Being & Becoming: The Early Years Learning Framework for Australia. ACT, Australia: Commonwealth of Australia.

Our Australian framework guiding our principles, practices and outcomes, 'Assessment for learning' (pp.17–18), is essential reading for guiding our observation and assessment of children's learning and development.

Fleer, M. & Richardson, C. (2004) Observing & Planning in Early Childhood Settings: Using a Sociocultural Approach. ACT: Early Childhood Australia.

This rare and important Australian text draws from Barbara Rogoff's work and uses a sociocultural perspective rather than the more popular, traditional focus on developmental domains. Fleer and Richardson include numerous practical examples of observing children using a sociocultural approach, which recognises the impact of society and culture on children's learning and development. A must-read for all pre-service teachers.

Hobart, C. Frankel, J. & Walker, M. (2014) A Practical Guide to Child Observation and Assessment (4th edn). Cheltenham, England: Oxford.

This highly recommended book provides a great foundation for pre-service teachers in understanding child observation and assessment. The authors discuss how and why we observe children, and provide descriptions of a variety of observation methods along with examples. This book focuses on children aged birth through to primary school and discusses a number of aspects of child observation covered in this chapter.

Martin, S. (2014) Take a Look: Observation and Portfolio Assessment in Early Childhood. (6th edn). Toronto, Canada: Pearson.

Another highly recommended book focusing on the assessment of children in early childhood and the early years of school, Martin presents a detailed and practical discussion of a variety of observation methods. Insightful discussions also include the observers' 'lenses and filters' and ways to evaluate children's environments. This is a valuable foundation text for pre-service teachers wanting to learn about child observation and assessment.

Mindes, G. (2011) Assessing Young Children (4th edn). New Jersey, U.S.: Delmar.

This book focuses on young children from birth to eight years, and is a worthwhile text for highlighting the inclusion of all children, in particular those in early childhood special education. It includes discussion of numerous observation techniques, as well as issues associated with observations, such as their limitations and avoiding bias. Numerous child examples are also included (see 'Building a child study' examples).

Palaiologou, I. (2012) Child Observation for the Early Years (2nd edn). London, England: SAGE/Learning Matters.

This book focuses on children from birth to five years of age and includes an overview of the theoretical background to child observation, and discussion on the role of observation including its link to curriculum. Recording and analysing the curriculum is covered in detail, along with the ethical implications of observation and key issues such as objectivity, and parent, staff and child involvement.

REFERENCES

Australian Children's Education and Care Quality Authority (2011) *Quality Area & Leadership and Service Management*. www.acecqa.gov.au/leadership-and-service-management

Australian Curriculum, Assessment and Reporting Authority (ACARA) (2017) Australian Curriculum. http://www.acara.edu.au/curriculum

Australian Institute for Teaching and School Leadership (AITSL) (2011) 'Australian Professional Standards for Teachers: Professional Practice', Education Services Australia, p.12.

Beaty, J.J. (2014) *Observing the Development of the Young Child* (8th edn). New Jersey, U.S.: Prentice Hall.

MELISSA COLVILLE

Bentzen, W.R. (2009) *Seeing Young Children: A Guide to Observing and Recording Behaviour* (6th edn). Belmont, CA: Delmar Cengage Learning.

Curtis, D. & Carter, M. (2012) *The Art of Awareness* (2nd edn). St. Paul, MN: Redleaf Press.

Department of Education, Employment and Workplace Relations (DEEWR) (2009) *Belonging, Being & Becoming: The Early Years Learning Framework for Australia.* ACT, Australia: Commonwealth of Australia.

Department of Education, Employment and Workplace Relations (DEEWR) (2010) *The Educators' Guide to the Early Years Learning Framework for Australia.* ACT, Australia: Commonwealth of Australia.

Early Childhood Australia (2016) *Code of Ethics.* Watson, ACT: Early Childhood Australia Inc. www.earlychildhoodaustralia.org.au/our-publications/eca-code-ethics/

Hobart, C. & Frankel, J. (2004) *A Practical Guide to Child Observation and Assessment* (3rd edn). Cheltenham, England: Nelson Thornes.

Hobart, C., Frankel, J. & Walker, M. (2014) *A Practical Guide to Child Observation and Assessment* (4th edn). Cheltenham, England: Oxford.

MacNaughton, G. (2003) *Shaping Early Childhood: Learners Curriculum.* Maidenhead, England: McGraw-Hill Education.

Martin, S. (2014) *Take a Look: Observation and Portfolio Assessment in Early Childhood* (6th edn). Toronto, Canada: Pearson.

Queensland Curriculum and Assessment Authority (QCAA) (2014) *Meaningful Observations: Examples of Documented Observations.* www.qcaa.qld.edu.au/downloads/p_10/qklg_pd_mod4_exp2_doc_observ.pdf

Rogoff, B. (2003) *The Cultural Nature of Human Development.* New York: Oxford University Press.

Sheridan, M., Sharma, A. & Cockerill, H. (2014) *From Birth to Five Years: Children's Developmental Progress* (4th edn). London, England: Taylor & Francis.

Van Hoorn, J., Nourat, P.M., Scales, B. & Alward, K.R. (2015) *Play at the Center of Curriculum* (6th edn). New Jersey, U.S.: Prentice Hall.

Victorian Institute of Teaching (VIT) (2015) 'Code of Conduct and Ethics'. https://www.vit.vic.edu.au/professional-responsibilities/conduct-and-ethics.

Assessment and Evaluation

Sue Lancaster with Frances Burton

Chapter objectives

In this chapter we will:

- develop an understanding of the characteristics and practices of assessment and evaluation and help you feel confident in discussing specific pedagogical issues relating to assessment and evaluation within early years environments
- examine what is meant by assessment and evaluation and their interrelationship in both early years and school environments
- discuss the multiple roles, benefits and purposes of assessment and evaluation in ensuring effective evidence-based practices and programs in early childhood
- review the planning cycle/unit of work of which assessment and evaluation are components with reference to the subtle differences in focus in early years and school environments
- discuss and illustrate the different types of assessment within the broad categories of formative and summative assessment (*for*, *as* and *of* learning)
- explore examples of different strategies and formats for 'gathering and analysing information about what children know, can do and understand' (DEEWR, 2009)
- consider teaching practices and program content including self-assessment, self-evaluation, peer assessment and peer evaluation
- highlight ways of ensuring the value and appropriateness of evaluation and assessment approaches through interrogating such issues as validity, reliability and consistency for student skills and knowledge development.

Key terms

assessment
evaluation

moderation
partnership approach

transition statement

Many Australian children have grown up knowing AA Milne's charming verse that begins 'When I was one ...' If you are familiar with this verse, you will recall that it offered the perspective of a six-year-old child (Christopher Robin) as he looked back on his own ages and stages of growth, learning and development from the 'beginning' age of one. Its enduring charm is at least partly derived from Christopher Robin's confidence in his own completeness and 'maturity'. The verse also highlights the difference this child's perspective offers to the more formalised and strandardised adult perspective that is generally linked to assessment of the child. Christopher Robin's account of where he is and what he has become by the age of six is playful and imaginative, but it is also the voice of a child with a strong sense of self and identity. Looking back with the confidence of a six-year-old, he is exactly where he wants to be with confidence in his mastery of learning and development. He now feels so clever that he wants to stay six for ever.

This verse, the words of an adult in the mid twentieth century, may capture the understandings of many of you about children of the time (here, of Christopher Robin). Together with the many accompanying pieces of verse in this volume, the playfulness in the young child's observations, imagination and self-thought—including Christopher Robin's self-assessment of 'where he is now', and 'where he has come from'—is captured in daily routines and experiences. Some of you may be familiar with these verses and may be reminiscing; others may be thinking about children's development and learning from birth to school entry and beyond, and reflecting on *why* and *how* assessment and evaluation have become important in children's early formative years and thinking—isn't this a time for play and exploration?

STOP AND THINK

- What comes to your mind when you hear the terms 'assessment' and 'evaluation' in the early years prior to school; for babies, toddlers and three–five-year-old children in childcare, four–five-year-old children attending community kindergarten/pre-school programs, and young children attending family day care or in the care of a nanny?
- Do you think that a six-year-old child should have a voice in their own assessment of their learning?

STOP AND REFLECT

- Recall your own experiences of early childhood education prior to school and think about what you enjoyed in this early stage of your learning.
- Return to your own prior-to-school experiences and think about assessment and evaluation in those years.
  - What form did it take?
  - How did you feel about assessment?
  - What was assessed and measured?
  - What was assessment used for?
  - Were you involved?
  - Did your family participate in the program, and if so, how?

---

assessment
observing, measuring and using evidence for the purpose of identifying effectiveness and possibilities for improvement.

evaluation
observing, measuring and using evidence for the purpose of judging and ascertaining value.

Introduction

Multiple assessment and evaluation strategies and practices used in both prior-to-school environments (birth to school entry) and the more formal years of schooling (the foundation/reception stage, through to the end of the primary years) will be explored in this chapter, with a particular focus on the birth-to-eight-year-old child. We will consider **assessment** and **evaluation** for each of these stages of children's learning, development and wellbeing.

This holistic perspective invites you to reflect on and 'wonder' about 'what' and 'why' there are similarities and differences within these two teaching and learning environments underpinning the focus of assessment and evaluation. The chapter begins by exploring assessment and evaluation strategies and practice in early childhood environments prior to school, followed by discussion relating to transition—the processes that link the two learning environments—and finally the exploration of assessment and evaluation strategies and practices in the primary school years.

Examples in the form of provocations and tasks are provided for reflection and discussion throughout the chapter. Further information in the form of annotated resources for exploration and discovery are included to support your ongoing learning as you move through the degree to becoming a graduate teacher in an early childhood or school environment.

The previous two chapters introduced you to subject matter in relation to professional practice and planning, including the Early Years Planning Cycle (EYLF), so you will be familiar with the language of the early years documentation (gather information; question/analyse; plan; act/do; reflect/evaluate) used in the birth-to-school entry environments (DEEWR, 2009). As you read through this chapter you will become familiar with other descriptors and acquainted with the language of the school system as unfamiliar terminology is introduced to describe familiar processes. For example, the early childhood planning cycle may be referred to as a unit of work in a school environment. You will also further your knowledge about the rationale and importance of assessment and evaluation from early development to adulthood.

Assessment and evaluation of young children

In 2008, the National Academy of Sciences in the Unites States released a comprehensive book, *Early Childhood Assessment: Why, What and How* (Snow & Van Hemel, 2008), that provoked thinking about the reasons why 'assessment of young children's development and learning has recently taken on a new importance'.

It can provide joy and a sense of reward when a child masters a particular milestone, shares an idea or supports peers in their play. However, there is much more to this, and current ways of practice and understanding include the need for *purposeful* and *systematic* assessment and evaluation as key components of program planning, using multiple tools and processes.

As we return to explore assessment and evaluation and their role in early childhood environments in detail you may find yourself reflecting on the picture of childhood reflected on at the beginning of the chapter in the verse 'Now I Am Six' as you come to a viewpoint of what assessment and evaluation mean for you in your teaching capacity working with young children birth to eight and beyond.

The current National Legislative Framework for Early Childhood Education and Care services prior to school, implemented in stages across states and territories in Australia from 2009, is outlined in Table 12.1.

These are important documents that you will need to refer to in your teaching role. You may already be familiar with some of these documents; if so, it is important that you revisit them

Table 12.1 Education and Care Services National Law 2010

The National Law underpins regulations and standards for early education and care services within Australia (www.acecqa.gov.au/national-law).

Education and Care Services National Regulations 2012 (amendments in 2013)
The National Regulations support the National Law by providing detail on a range of operational requirements for education and care services within Australia. This includes practice standards, operational requirements and processes, rating, and assessment and monitoring (www.acecqa.gov.au/national-regulations).

***Belonging, Being & Becoming: The Early Years Learning Framework for Australia* (EYLF) (DEEWR, 2009)**
The EYLF provides a broad direction for practice in early childhood services for educators, teachers and other professionals, volunteers, students, and family and community who work within or attend these services (https://www.dss.gov.au/sites/default/files/documents/05_2015/belonging_being_and_becoming_the_early_years_learning_framework_for_australia.pdf).

***My Time, Our Place* (MTOP) Framework for School-Age Care in Australia, 2011**
The MTOP framework supports the ongoing development of children in school-age care services. It ensures that they have opportunities to participate in leisure and play-based activities that are responsive to their needs, interests, and choices (www.education.gov.au/my-time-our-place-framework-school-age-care-australia).

National Quality Framework (NQF) 2012
The standards are a key to improvement in education and care services for long day care, family day care, pre-school/kindergarten, and outside school hours care for Australia (www.acecqa.gov.au/national-quality-framework/explaining-the-national-quality-framework#sthash.1ytZNT5d.dpuf).

and reflect on how they connect with and incorporate assessment and evaluation in early childhood education and care environments. In this next section, it is also important to keep in mind the different expectations, documentation and guidelines relating to various services, such as maternal and child health, childcare, kindergarten/pre-school, family day care and outside school hours care. Different rules and organisational structures exist in different states and territories, such as the age at which a child must commence and/or attend school, incorporation of kindergarten within the school structure, and community-managed or private early education and care. Similarly, there are different terms used for programs in the year prior to compulsory schooling—for example kindergarten, pre-school or 'pre-prep'.

In some states and territories of Australia, frameworks and guidelines that respond to particular aspects within these jurisdictions have been developed alongside and in addition to the national documentation. These documents are widely used within the states and territories. However, these documents incorporate and complement those developed at a national level and all recognise the national agenda for education and care. While examples from or references to state and territory documents may be made in this chapter, a national approach is presented in most instances.

In conjunction with the law, regulations, frameworks and standards for early childhood education and care, there are other services that provide key support for children, their families, teachers, educators and carers during the early years:

- Services such as maternal and child health provide regular assessment for general developmental progress as well as specific assessment and referral for children with signs of developmental delay or health issues.

- Early childhood intervention professionals support children with disabilities or developmental delay in education and care environments as well as in the home or clinic prior-to-school entry.
- Children, youth and family practitioners support families in need of help in parenting and caring for children, and may also become guardians if children are unable to be cared for in the family home for short or extended periods of time.

Professionals working in these services provide specific assessment and evaluation of children's development, health and wellbeing and should become part of your professional conversations, both for sharing professional practices and information when required and approved by the family, and adding to your knowledge and understanding of children's and families' needs. This enables the provision of an integrated and holistic approach for children and their families that further facilitates quality outcomes for children's learning. All of these services also operate under specific legislation, frameworks and standards relevant to their profession. For information about these services contact the relevant government department in your state or territory.

Note: You will be aware of the elements of the EYLF and the principles, practice and learning that are linked to and support specified learning outcomes. At this point you may consider searching for the relevant state or territory guidelines and other documentation that relates to assessment and evaluation in your area.

While the importance of ongoing and authentic assessment and evaluation are now accepted more generally, in some environments these processes remain an unresolved contemporary issue in early childhood literature and debate, with uncertainties about how, when and what tools should be used, what form they can take, who should undertake these processes, how often and in what circumstances, and for what purpose. There are also queries about how assessment and evaluation fit with play theory, emergent curriculum, enquiry learning and children's role in assessment and evaluation or the engagement of parents (see Chapter 14 for details) in these processes.

Until recently, assessment and evaluation have not received the visibility that other components of the planning cycle for early childhood have received. When it is discussed, it is often in isolation to meet a specific purpose (e.g. collecting data for transition to school or for a referral for specialist support for the child and family). However, discussion about the importance of assessment and evaluation for planning is becoming more visible at a deeper level than only looking at what children are doing in isolation—it is now exploring and reflecting in depth children's engagement, communication and relationships (see Chapter 13) during their learning experiences. More resources are now available, providing support for teacher/educator practices and understanding of the importance of assessment and evaluation, and their roles in these processes for quality learning and development outcomes for young children. For example, the Australian Children's Education and Care Quality Authority (ACECQA, 2017) and Early Childhood Australia (ECA) have provided fact sheets, articles and journal items (ECA, 2017) and state governments have undertaken research and projects to support best practice for their particular state or territory.

In addition you will find many resources to support your practice and pedagogy available online or from textbooks, webinars, journals, through government and organisational support programs and services, practice guides, newsletters, professional development

Figure 12.1

Source: www.vcaa.vic.edu.au.

seminars and a growing number of self-initiated professional practice networks. All types of assessment strategies contribute to assessment for learning and development, but their intended purposes need to be considered (e.g. are they formative or summative?).

The EYLF is a key process used in early childhood services and is discussed in other chapters of this book. Figure 12.1 focuses on the cyclical process, and its key points for planning and implementing learning experiences. It will help you consider where assessment and evaluation fit.

The data collected (assessment) using observations of children's engagement in relationships with teachers/educators and peers in their 'active learning environments' provides information for respectful and authentic reflection (evaluation) using specific criteria for quality learning outcomes for individual and groups of children (DEECD, 2009).

However, assessment and evaluation do not end at the point where the teacher 'collects information'; these reflective processes are ongoing throughout the cycle and are repeated.

Assessment and evaluation are used for many purposes and have multiple forms. Data and reflection can inform and authenticate planning for professional development; a new project that builds on children's voice and interests; discussion with parents or specialist practitioners; school **transition statements**; reports for funding bodies or committees of management to inform submissions for funding; and accreditation. It is important to consider how you set up your environment; how you interact, engage and communicate with others in the education and care environment; and how you support children's wellbeing and provide an inclusive environment for all children as part of your everyday pedagogy. Benchmarking against relevant legislation and policy, standards, ethics and codes of conduct should also be considered when assessing and evaluating data, including observations (Pugh & Duffy, 2014).

transition statement
a statement recording a child's strengths, interests and ways of learning to support transitions from prior-to-school to school settings.

What is assessment and evaluation?

As indicated above, assessment and evaluation are not static events, but rather parts of an overarching process used throughout pedagogical practices where teachers develop and implement active teaching and learning environments for children's learning, development and wellbeing, and engage family and community in effective and purposeful relationships (DEEWR, 2009).

The National Government notes that:

> Assessment for children's learning refers to the process of gathering data and analysing information as evidence about what children know, can do and understand.
>
> (DEEWR, 2009)

This example from the Victorian Early Years Learning and Development Framework (VEYLDF) extends our understanding:

Early childhood professionals assess children's learning in ways that:
- inform ongoing practice
- measure progress in learning
- identify where intervention, focused support or referral may be required.

(DEECD, 2009)

Assessment *for* (formative assessment), *as* (processes/through) and *of* learning (summative assessment) are common terms used in the school environment to describe the three key forms of assessment from foundation/reception, through to the end of secondary education. In early childhood environments educators and teachers will be more familiar with terms such as *review*, *reflect*, *implications* and *interpretation* or the VEYLDF's *inform, measure, identify*. However, these terms—assessment *for*, *as* and *of*—are becoming more frequently used in early childhood education due to the growing connection between these two areas of children's learning and development. While it is important to make these connections across sectors when assessing and evaluating children's skills and needs in the early years prior to school, it is equally important to keep in mind the children's developmental capacity, sociocultural understandings and the importance of play as a tool for learning. The quality of the relationship between the child, their family and the teacher is also important in the quality of the assessment and how feedback is delivered on any assessments.

Pugh & Duffy note that formative assessment (assessment for learning):

… requires practitioners to get to know children really well, over time and using observation to build a clearer picture of the child, including their needs, interests and learning styles.

(Pugh & Duffy, 2014)

The role of play in assessment and evaluation and the connections to the three processes above is discussed in Fleer (2013). Fleer's discussion explicitly focuses on assessment of children's engagement in play as the catalyst [context] for learning in early childhood environments where assessment *for* play refers to what teachers provide and how they support children in their play; assessment *through* [or *as*] play is related to concepts, language and actions used by children during play and assessment *of* play refers to changes in outcomes (learning).

The emphasis on the importance of play for children's learning in their prior-to-school years is now more widely recognised as a powerful form of engagement for children's learning by those working not only within but also outside early childhood environments. This greater understanding of the importance of play in children's learning is a result of the collaborations of multi-professional experts and neuroscience research of the twentieth century documented by Shonkoff and Phillips (2000). This understanding is also documented in a paper jointly authored by ECA and the Australian Curriculum and Reporting Authority (ACARA, 2017) to inform teachers, family and community about the varied settings for learning in Australia from early childhood to end of school, and how these settings complement and link with each stage of the child's education. This includes acknowledging the importance of play and other early childhood practices for the development of early learning and for the dispositions for future learning, including 'problem solving, experimentation, hypothesising, researching and investigating', to support more advanced

SUE LANCASTER WITH FRANCES BURTON

learning as the child transitions from prior-to-school environments to primary and then to secondary school and beyond (ECA, 2017) stating:

> The Early Learning Framework (EYLF) respects children as competent and resourceful learners from birth and aims to extend that learning in a variety of early learning settings in partnership with children and families.
>
> (DEEWR, 2009)

In support of the above is the powerful statement from the Australian Government acknowledging the importance of the early years as the foundation for learning:

> The Shape of the Australian Curriculum (p.10) recognises the EYLF establishes the foundation for effective learning in school and through life and aims to build on those foundations as learners move through schooling.
>
> (ECA, 2017)

STOP AND REFLECT

- What are your expectations or experience of documentation in relation to assessment and evaluation? This could be from your own childcare, kindergarten/pre-school or school experience, your work experience, previous practicums or how you imagine you could document children's work for assessment and evaluation.
- What was the main form of documentation and how was it used as a tool for assessment and evaluation?
- Do you think this was a fair and effective way of assessing and evaluating teaching and children's learning?
- What other forms of assessment and evaluation could be used?

So far, discussion has related more specifically to assessment and evaluation *for* learning. Now we will move on and consider assessment and evaluation *as* or 'through' children's engagement in learning activities and environments.

Assessment and evaluation *as* learning occurs when teachers involve children actively in assessing their learning and development. By monitoring and thinking about what and how they learnt with adults and peers, children see themselves as learners and can use this information to learn more effectively and take more control over their learning.

Assessment and evaluation *as* learning recognises that children are competent and capable learners from birth. When teachers ask children to explain how they learnt something or who helped them to learn, they are using assessment as a tool to support learning.

This is also the time when your engagement with children is intense and where you are often making spontaneous pedagogical decisions and responses—for example, do you enter into the play at this point or not? Do you suggest and provide additional resources to enrich the play at this point or do you wait for more signals from the children or to be asked? Is this the time to ask a question or to comment on the play or might this disrupt the rhythm of the play and should you stand back and absorb the engagement *as* learning and document for further reflection or not?

Being able to make these decisions is a key role of the early childhood teacher. However, there will always be times when you reflect on your engagement as children are playing and engaging with peers, adults or resources and your choice of action may not be the most useful one for that situation. This is a time when you need to remember that, just as children learn through their choices (whether useful or not), so do adults—and if, on reflection of your action, your choice was not the most appropriate one, you should see this as a learning opportunity and consider alternative strategies for future practice. Remember also that these decisions, while they may be challenging for a pre-service teacher, will become more spontaneous and valid as you gain experience.

The scenario 'Evie's day' is an example of assessment and evaluation as learning. Take some time to read and reflect on the responses and engagement of the pre-service teacher in the scenario. Then put yourself in the role of teacher and document this observation as a learning story for the child's journal. Remember that everyone will see things both differently and similarly.

Evie's day

Evie (four years of age, attending kindergarten) chose to start her day with the stickle bricks.

She put two pieces together that had cow motifs on them and said, 'Look at the doggies'.

The pre-service teacher replied, 'Are you sure they are doggies?'

'Yes,' Evie said in a confident manner.

Evie then moved them around in the air.

The pre-service teacher asked, 'Are your doggies flying?'

Evie just laughed and continued to fly them around in the air.

She then put them down and started pushing other pieces together.

When she finished Evie said, 'I made a rocket'. Evie paused, 'Why does it have a pointy nose?'

The pre-service teacher responded, 'I'm not sure, Evie'.

Evie continued the dialogue: 'Five, four, three, two, one, Blast Off!' and continued to fly her rocket around in the air and then crashed it to the ground.

STOP AND REFLECT

To authenticate your responses to 'Evie's day', ask yourself:

- Is this the outcome that I expected?
- What more could I have planned for?
- I was surprised with the way the experience wandered from the intent.
  Was this because I had misread my understanding of the play and did not see what was behind the actions in my observations?
- Did I focus too much on what the child was 'doing', with insufficient attention given to what might have been the purpose behind the observation, which may have provided a different account of what I observed?
- Did I consider the child's recent development clearly by giving her time to consolidate her new learning? Did I provide sufficient scaffolding based on my knowledge of Vygotsky's theory of ways children learn, to support the new learning?
- Were my expectations too high or too low and, based on my ideas, did they not take into consideration the child's interests, strengths, emotions, preferences and learning styles?

SUE LANCASTER WITH FRANCES BURTON

The professional practice example below, prepared by a final year pre-service student during practicum, demonstrates documentation that responds to some of the questions above in a four–five-year-old kindergarten program. This pre-service student used an art folio to document her observations of children's interests, extensions and further ideas, and asked herself, Why am I doing this? These questions were part of the program planning process used by the supervising teacher at the kindergarten.

The focus for planning during this practicum relates to sustainability, and the creatures in the surrounding environment included frogs, which stimulated broader exploration for learning about other animals and insects.

Professional practice

Day 1: Children's interests

Reading

Throughout the day children listen intently to stories being read to them as small groups in the book area or as a larger group at 'mat time'. They demonstrate strong concentration and listening skills as they sit quietly and show engagement through appropriate facial expressions in responding to the story. They are able to confidently answer questions and contribute to discussions about the story.

Extensions/further ideas:

- Stories about frogs
- Children are invited to engage in small groups or as individuals to compose a whole-class 'frog story' with scaffolding from the teacher.
- Suggest illustrations based on the children's story (this may appeal to children who were not interested in the literacy story component).

Why am I doing this?

- To further children's learning about frogs (life cycle, habitat, food, varieties)
- To further develop literacy, communication and team skills and fine motor skills

Singing

Children have shown interest and enjoyment in learning new songs relating to animals—they listen for the words, sing the songs, ask to do it again and suggest actions.

Extensions/further ideas:

- Introduce dramatic play based on the children's interest in frogs as the focus to start the experience using the frog song.
- Introduce other songs and movement experiences.

Why am I doing this?

- To maintain and extend their interest in frogs
- To promote dramatic play to encourage communication between children and to promote gross motor skills

Repeat for Day 2.

Day 3: Children's interests and modifications

Children have been particularly interested in the life cycle of the frog and have learnt the meaning of the word *metamorphosis*, which they repeat in a playful manner. One of the children asks, 'What other animals 'metamorphosis'?' This is an inquiry question I can further explore with the children.

Extension/further ideas:

- Read *The Very Hungry Caterpillar.*
- Discuss the life cycle of the butterfly.

Why am I doing this?

- To maintain their interest in reading
- To extend children's knowledge about other animals that undergo metamorphosis
- To further research the inquiry question, encouraging children to use the computer in pairs (this will also support their communication and shared learning)
- To encourage group discussion and further knowledge
- To encourage focus and concentration for some children

Assessment *of* learning and development summarises what children know, understand and can do at a particular point in time. Assessment of learning and development includes large-scale population assessment strategies such as the National Assessment Program—Literacy and Numeracy (NAPLAN) and the Australian Early Development Census (AEDC).

Bruce (2011) describes *summative* assessment as a process that is about 'taking stock, pausing and bringing together everything known about the child's progress'.

Transition statements such as the Victorian 'Transition Learning and Development Statement', or the New South Wales 'Transition to School Statement' are examples of assessment *of* learning used to transfer consistent information about children's knowledge at the point of transition from their early childhood prior-to-school environment to the school environment. This assessment can be particularly useful for planning supports and strategies in advance of children commencing school when concerns about children's learning and development are shared across these two environments. In Victoria, the transition statement is shared with the family after it has been completed. In New South Wales, the transition statement is completed by children's early childhood educators/teachers in cooperation with the family.

This statement may also include areas where children will need support and where there may be behavioural concerns, a diagnosed or potential disability, a medical condition or adjustment issues, all of which should be identified and discussed using open, honest and respectful language with parent engagement, input and consent to share this information.

Pre-service teachers may be surprised to hear that parents, rather than professionals or other people in their professional network, are often the first to identify their child as having a learning issue or an irregularity in their development. This means that teachers and pre-service teachers should listen carefully and consider parental concerns, and speak openly and respectfully about anything they share relating to the child. Parents are usually relieved to hear that their child's teacher may have similar concerns and from this point, action and shared responsibility can be discussed and supports put in place. Denying or downplaying the issue or problem with comments such as 'the parent is not ready to hear this' are not

SUE LANCASTER WITH FRANCES BURTON

helpful for the child's ongoing learning and development, or the family's wellbeing. This can sometimes be a difficult discussion. Parents are mainly seeking the best for their children and will, in most cases, discuss and accept referral and interventions to support their child. In some instances the family may seek further opinions, which the teacher needs to accept and support, as this can be important for the family's further understanding and acceptance of a possible developmental delay or disability leading to referral and support at a level that reflects the family situation and current acceptance.

We will now introduce 'Liam's story' (prepared by a pre-service teacher with modifications and references added, where appropriate) as an example of the processes behind assessment and evaluation in the form of a hypothetical team meeting to evaluate existing learning and development relating to a four-year-old boy, Liam, attending a community kindergarten. The scenario highlights the concepts of inclusion, team work, continuity of learning outcomes, family engagement and building broad networks to support Liam's additional needs. You will be challenged by Liam's story at two points in this chapter and again in Chapter 15.

Liam's story

Preamble

At the age of three, Liam began attending an early childhood intervention service where he received support to help his communication, motor skills and self-help skills. A diagnosis of Liam's developmental profile is yet to be fully investigated. When Liam commenced kindergarten at the beginning of the year, the early intervention professional suggested the kindergarten program focus on Liam's social and self-help skills. It is now approaching Term 2 and the team involved—director Helen, teacher Rachael, educator Jill and additional support educator Tara—have gathered to discuss Liam's progress and evaluate any assessments for planning to further support Liam's learning and development at kindergarten, leading to transition to school in the coming year. After Helen welcomes the team and confirms the purpose of the meeting, Jill commences the conversation.

Team meeting

Jill: It is not much progress for an entire term. I just don't think there has been enough improvement when you also factor in the issues that have coincidently developed.

Tara: I don't agree with that statement. You can't compare Liam's progress to other children. Although there have been challenging moments, we need to remember that not only does Liam have additional needs but that this is only his first term in an early childhood educational setting.

Helen: Putting the subsequent issues aside for a moment, Jill, can you elaborate on how you view Liam's progress?

Jill: I have not observed any development of his cognitive skills, he doesn't initiate communication with any educator …

Tara: In order for any child to achieve, those around them must meet their basic needs first, with support, guidance and care. Liam is still becoming comfortable in this environment and in order to achieve certain goals, he first needs to build confidence and trust.

Rachael: I do believe Liam is becoming more comfortable in this environment, and perhaps it took a little longer than it should have. Our expectations and goals for his learning were quite overwhelming for not only Liam but all of us. I recently attended a meeting with his ECIS worker and she elaborated that an inclusive early childhood setting should not be 'regarded as an extension of the intervention service but as a new environment in which the child needs to function' (Foreman & Arthur-Kelly, 2014). Social skills and problem-solving skills are specific to our setting and that is what she would like us to focus on.

Helen: That is great feedback, Rachael. I think it is important for us all to remember that this is a team effort. 'Early childhood practitioners are not expected to know every possible health condition or disability' (Lindon, 2012), thus amplifying the importance of early childhood services to acknowledge, connect with, and provide networking services to the local and wider community. I hope you plan to maintain this comprehensive communication with Liam's ECIS worker.

Rachael: We have created a group email between his early intervention teacher, occupational therapist, speech pathologist and physiotherapist that shares communication about current strategies and the ongoing progress of Liam's development. This enables us to stay consistent with our approaches but to not double up on areas of intense focus. I also plan to visit Liam at his group program once a month to gain further insight and knowledge from the early intervention professionals that Liam works with.

Jill: Does this mean we don't need to work on specific goals with Liam, such as his toilet training and physical development?

Rachael: Like with every child, we support, assist and educate them in every way we can. Liam's 'communication, motor and self-help skills that have been targeted in the intervention service can be practiced' (Foreman & Arthur-Kelly, 2014) in our environment. However, in regards to our program planning, she would like us to focus on Liam's social skills and problem-solving abilities.

Jill: Will we also be kept up to date with what is happening with Liam, to ensure consistent practices?

Rachael: Of course, providing clear, open and ongoing communication through the role of genuine partnerships empowers all members to be an active voice in the child's development, wellbeing and education. This not only provides consistency for all involved but also stronger foundations for the child to thrive. However, confidentiality must be adhered to.

In addition to establishing an ongoing line of communication, Liam's ECIS worker and I have created an individualised developmental plan for Liam. Through this plan we can see that the various professionals he works with are addressing all areas of his development. In our section, we focus on his social skills and problem-solving abilities. Ongoing documentation is not only promoted for all children but is especially beneficial for children with a disability (Forster, 2014). Liam 'will need to have the opportunity to develop or practice specific skills and those opportunities will not occur without deliberate strategies being put in place' (Forster, 2014).

Helen: This plan will be helpful in transitioning to Term 2 and beyond. It is so much simpler. We were on the right track with our activity plan for Liam in regards to his social development and enhancing his problem-solving skills but I can see that it may have been overwhelming for him. We just need to transfer the same intention and learning into something more realistic for him.

Rachael: Exactly. Our goals need to be more simple and refined, and that is clearly portrayed on the new individual plan.

Cont.

SUE LANCASTER WITH FRANCES BURTON

Jill: I still think we need to do something about his toilet training though.

Tara: I have been reflecting about the success of the visual aids that we have incorporated into Liam's daily experiences. I researched further into how we could support Liam to communicate using visual supports and perhaps we could use photographs of the toileting routine for visual cues and prompts.

Helen: It appears Liam does respond well to visual aids. This provides insight into Liam's cognitive capabilities as he has been using these visual supports effectively, which suggests that he is able to interpret the meaning, transfer the knowledge to its concrete meaning and have the 'desire to communicate with others'.

Rachael: Exactly, Helen. This strategy may not only meet Liam's individual needs but also provides an opportunity for Liam to flourish to the best of his abilities and his social inclusion.

Helen: We just need to ensure that this strategy is consistent with Liam's home life and at his group program.

STOP AND THINK

Many challenges emerge from this scenario and now is a useful opportunity for you to stop and think on it before we leave Liam's story for a while. You may find the provocations in the questions below useful for informing your views.

- Jill commences the conversation. How do you feel about Jill's statement about Liam's presence in the kindergarten program? Whose needs was Jill expressing?
- Tara responds to this comment providing a different viewpoint. How might you have responded here (remembering Jill is the permanent support educator and Tara is the additional support educator)? How did this affect the following dialogue between Jill and Tara? Whose needs was Tara's response addressing?
- When teacher Rachael enters the conversation, does this alter the discussion and if so, what strategies does Rachael use? What role and whose needs was Rachael portraying in her views about Liam's progress? What strategies did Rachael employ?
- How do you see Helen's role in this discussion? What were the strategies she used and why?
- Did the tone of the meeting change and if so, at what point, and what strategies were used? Were they effective and why?
- How do you feel about Liam's presence in the kindergarten?

Considerations for the early years

Based on the discussion above, assessment and evaluation *for, as* and *of* children's learning require careful consideration by educators, teachers and other professionals. Current literature and research by Kennedy & Stonehouse (VEYLDF, 2012) has identified a number of ways of making these considerations.

Here is an adapted version of some of these from the VEYLDF (2012).

All assessment should:

- inform practitioner planning and practice, based on the curriculum or program
- include children's views of their own learning; through comment, questioning, documenting and sharing learning outcomes with children they are more likely to become aware of their learning and progress and to develop an understanding of the relationship between effort and success.
- be authentic and responsive to how children demonstrate their learning and development 'fit for purpose' and consider the age of the child
- draw on families' perspectives, knowledge, experiences and expectations
- consider children in the context of their families, and provide provision for support for families when necessary
- value the culturally specific knowledge embedded within communities about children's learning and development
- be transparent and objective, and provide families with information about their children's learning and development, and about what they can do to further support their children's learning and development
- gather and analyse information using resources that are familiar and of interest for children using a wide range of situations (individual/group, indoor/outdoor, routines/child directed play/challenging moments), and sources (other staff/specialist staff, families, peers)
- use everyday environments where children feel comfortable, ensuring the language is familiar to the children and considering the time of day for the assessment (if it is a formal testing situation) so that children are not tired or hungry
- be unbiased and non-judgmental
- provide the best possible advice and guidance to children and their families.

STOP AND REFLECT

Reflect on the points above and think about *how you* might embed these considerations in the preliminary task of planning for assessment and evaluation. It is also an appropriate time to study the 'Early Childhood Code of Ethics' (2016), developed to support decisions in early childhood educational spaces engaging families, childhood professionals, communities, colleagues and students (ECA, 2016), and to consider how you would use the information in this document to support your practices, specifically in relation to assessment of children in early childhood spaces. The preamble to this document reflects some of the discussion above:

> Being ethical involves thinking about everyday actions and decision making, either individually or collectively, and responding with respect to all concerned. The Code of Ethics recognises that childhood professionals are in a unique position of trust and influence in their relationships with children, families, colleagues and the community, therefore professional accountability is vital.
>
> (ECA, 2017)

This means that any assessment must be purposeful, authentic, non-intrusive and results should be shared with those who not only need to know for planning purposes, but who have a right to know. This includes the child, the family and any other professional involved in the child's education and care, with the proviso that permission for release of any information has the parent's permission, and where possible, the permission of the child or young person.

The role of documentation

Finding out about children's learning also involves thinking about *how* learning will be captured, made visible and documented. As a pre-service teacher you will be familiar with these terms from your lectures, practicum and reading previous chapters in this book as well as other resources. Those of you working in the sector will have developed and/or used various forms of documentation, including project work and a variety of observational formats; running records, time-based records, anecdotal records, learning stories; and use of information technology, such as photographs, video and iPad footage. These are all valuable tools for documentation, but their appropriateness needs to be considered in terms of what the intended purpose of the assessment is.

A recent form of documentation used for planning that has excited and engaged pre-service teachers is art folios (sometimes called floor books). These have been used in different ways including as a tool for the pre-service teacher to document all facets of the planning process for their own purposes. Others have used this format for sharing with families at the end of the session, including photographs and narrative about children's experiences and learning. They have also been used by the pre-service teacher for reflection and evaluation to inform the next steps in planning for individuals and groups of children. These visible forms of documentation can also be a catalyst for engaging families in conversations and sharing new insights about their child, providing valuable information for consideration in assessment and evaluation for future planning.

Computer images and video footage are also a popular way of sharing children's engagement and learning in play situations and for later reflection for authentic planning using forms of reflection, assessment and evaluation.

Journals are a familiar way of documenting children's progress by collecting items of work drawings, paintings, narratives, photographs, and other items chosen by children or staff and sometimes by families for inclusion. These journals are generally visible in children's space for access by parents, staff and children. In some environments these journals are relatively 'dormant'. However, with teacher intent, they can become a living document when two or more children seek their journals out and begin looking through them, which at some point stimulates conversation between the children about the content: who they have painted, what they collected and preserved from the playground, remembering when and how they did the work, and comparing their work within the conversation. These provide a vivid and authentic conversation for assessment and evaluation of children's learning, and validate journal documentation as a genuine assessment and evaluation tool.

Assessment and evaluation across professions

Following birth, and throughout the prior-to-school years, children will attend a variety of services where children's development and learning is monitored and assessed. Professionals commonly engaged with young children and their families may include a maternal and child health nurse, a specialist early childhood teacher, an allied health practitioner, early childhood intervention professionals or medical practitioners within a hospital or community setting. Each of these professionals will assess children for different purposes and evaluate the outcome and plan for action dependent on their role and their profession, using different forms of assessment according to child and family needs and circumstances.

For example, maternal and child health nurses use specific checklists at specified periods to document any early detection of developmental delay or health issues; and early childhood intervention practitioners such as specialist educators, psychologists, physiotherapists, occupational therapists, speech pathologists and social workers support children with a disability or developmental delay and their families.

All early childhood intervention professionals will seek to identify children's functional capacity for everyday living, evaluating their strengths and interests through play observations and/or checklists discussed with the family as part of assessment for planning, and providing advice for families and educators/teachers in mainstream services such as childcare and preschool/kindergarten. These practitioners may also provide therapy, support and activities in the home, in small group sessions at the service or individual therapy, which usually includes both the child and the parent. This type of support, which recognises that the parent knows their child best, and that it is the family environment where the child spends most of their time, is referred to as a **partnership approach**, where the professional and family work together in collaboration to support the child.

A recent development is the Abilities Based Learning and Education Support (ABLES) assessment resource available to better support teaching and learning for children with developmental delay or disability for Victoria. This resource, with specified criteria linked to prior-to-school and school outcomes and standards, assesses children's abilities and disposition for learning and informs learning goals and individual learning plans, which are linked to effective research-based teaching and learning strategies. Outcomes can be monitored at various intervals using a suite of purposeful data reports. Though it was developed in Victoria, ABLES is relevant to other states and territories.

partnership approach where the professional and family work together in collaboration to support the child.

Transition to school

Thinking about the transition to school should commence around the middle of the year prior to the first school year. Teachers and educators in most states and territories of Australia use specific assessment tools to support this important transition from early years to a more formal school environment. In some states this takes the form of a transition statement for all children with additional information for children requiring additional support. These statements are usually completed by both parent and teacher and provide information and supporting conversation with teachers and family across the services. The statement may include children's strengths, abilities and interests, learning styles and needs. It may also include examples of learning by the child such as a drawing of themselves/ their family and for some children written captions or stories dictated to and scribed by the teacher or parent.

SUE LANCASTER WITH FRANCES BURTON

Liam's story (cont.)

Helen: Rachael, have you talked to Dianna (Liam's mother) about the possibility of introducing a keyworker?

Rachael: It is on my list of things to do.

Helen: I am wary of you overloading yourself and I think introducing a keyworker would be of great benefit to all stakeholders involved. I have printed out a fact sheet for you to show Dianna.

Tara: What is a keyworker?

Rachael: The keyworker's role is to build a closer relationship with the child and their family and ultimately be the link between all of the professionals involved in the child's care. Beneficial to any transitions the child or their family may be making, the keyworker will ultimately know and understand the child and their family's needs well and be able to provide informed advice, suggestions or communication to other professionals (Bigby & Clement, 2008).

Tara: Oh, that would be so beneficial. And I believe that Dianna would appreciate one so much.

Helen: Tara, I would like you to elaborate on that topic in a moment. I appreciate how much progress we are making, but as time is a factor we must press on. I hear Liam's parents have expressed concerns about his future school placement.

Rachael: Brad and Dianna are apprehensive about his progress in transitioning to school and have expressed concern about his future educational options and needs.

Jill: Do you think he will be ready for school by the end of the year?

Rachael: It is too early to tell. With our collaborative relationship with Liam's Early Childhood Intervention Service (ECIS) professionals now established, Liam will be well supported over the remainder of the year. Liam's cognitive score on the Wechsler Intelligence Scale for Children (WISC-IV) does concern me though.

Tara: 'Including young children with disabilities and additional needs in mainstream services is widely recognised as best practice' (Webster & Forster, 2012, p.9).

Helen: I agree with you, Tara, 'students with additional needs have the same right to enrol as others [do]' (Foreman & Arthur-Kelly, 2014). However, we need to provide a variety of options and information for Dianna and Brad so they can make an informed decision about what is best for Liam.

Tara: A best decision is an informed one. I was recently on the Raising Children's website and there is a services pathfinder section to aid in transitions of children who are diagnosed with autism. I printed out the section specific to kindergarten-to-primary schooling transitions.

Helen: This is a way that 'families can learn about school options and about how to be a good advocate for their child' (raisingchildren.net.au).

Jill: Perhaps we could introduce Dianna to other families who have already made this transition to school.

Helen: All great ideas. I would like you to share this information with Dianna and I also would like to set up a meeting with Dianna, Brad, Jill and myself to talk through their concerns and share some future options. I would also like to update them on what we have implemented today and hear any input they may have. It is important for them to know they are not alone.

Rachael: I believe that this is an area we could improve on, our relationship with Liam's family I mean.

Tara: I agree. I have great concerns for Liam's mother, Dianna, becoming overwhelmed, and his sister Briana.

Helen: You touched on this before Tara, please go on.

Tara: I have been having many discussions with Dianna as she picks Liam up in the afternoons and I feel she has really been opening up about some struggles she has been having at home. I have been documenting concerns or issues she has mentioned. I have printed a copy for you to look at.

Helen: That is very thorough of you! I commend your initiative.

STOP AND THINK

There are many changes in this part of the scenario compared to the discussion at the beginning of the team meeting. Reflect on the scenario so far and consider the following questions.

1 What differences have you recognised as the scenario developed? Who were the main facilitators for a shared viewpoint? What processes did the team members go through, and what strategies did they use?
2 Why were changes necessary and what were the outcomes?
3 Who benefited from the changes, how and why?
4 What have you learnt from the scenario so far?

The team meeting scenario continues in Chapter 15, with a focus on inclusion and diversity.

Connecting early childhood development and the school environment

As in the early years, schools use many different assessment and evaluation resources, tools and strategies according to children's development and learning, year levels, task and purpose, which will be discussed later in this chapter. However, one assessment tool relevant to both areas is the Early Education Developmental Census (AEDC)—formerly known as the Australian Early Developmental Index (AEDI). The AEDC is an Australia-wide assessment that is undertaken by teachers in children's first year of full-time school and it measures children's development in relation to five domains: physical health and wellbeing; social competence; emotional maturity; language and cognitive skills; and communication skills and general knowledge. The results of these assessments are not applied to individual children, but provide a population-wide picture of children's development that is used by school and community to inform decisions about priorities and resourcing, and to support planning for better education and school outcomes and for children's adult health into the future (www.aedc.gov.au/).

SUE LANCASTER WITH FRANCES BURTON

Recapitulation

The quotation 'know children really well'—Pugh & Duffy (2014)—that we discussed in relation to *for* learning is equally important in assessing and evaluating ongoing play and children's responses within their learning environment for *as* and *of* learning.

This means that assessment and evaluation are ongoing, where teachers seek information in a variety of situations and time frames, seeking others' opinions (parent, other staff members, children and their peers). Reflecting on children's ongoing developmental growth and capacity across multiple domains and the variance of this growth and change also remains an important consideration. Just as a seesaw goes up and down, so to some extent does children's development as they explore, experiment, wonder, reject, accept and practise new skills, knowledge, values and purposes—returning to the known before embedding the new as part of their being.

This playful learning is reflected upon in the beginning of this chapter where the six-year-old child in the verse asserts a confident sense of his own 'belonging' (about self and identity), of 'being' (acceptance of self and acknowledging others) and of 'becoming' a part of community with a developed sense of self; an identity formed.

We are also reminded that the quality of learning opportunities, good health and wellbeing, and meaningful engagement, acknowledging young children's capacity and agency in the relationships they experience with their family and other important adults in the community, is most important during the child's early years for future learning, development and a successful life as an adult.

While this verse was not written as an academic statement, nonetheless it is a useful synergy with contemporary research that informs us that learning is ongoing and that the quality of learning opportunities, health and wellbeing, meaningful engagement and the relationships children experience with their family and other important adults is extremely important during the early childhood years for future learning, development and a successful life as an adult. It also reminds us that children's self-assessments are an important part of this ongoing process.

The following discussion will provide you with further skills and knowledge relating to assessment and evaluation in primary schools and specific outcomes for children's further learning and development. As you connect these two areas of education it will be useful to consider the differences and similarities of expectations and strategies and what and why there are differences and similarities in these processes.

Assessment in primary schools

Let us begin this section with an overview of the purposes of assessment within the primary school. In a nutshell, assessment is used to assist students' learning. It does this by assisting teachers and students to make judgments about what students currently know so that teachers and/or students can plan for future learning. At a broader level, all assessment is reported within the school community to teachers and through the bi-annual reports. Students' learning progress is monitored through assessment and this is reported to families. Children's and schools' achievement levels are reported to government through such tests as NAPLAN.

We include students within the assessing process because assessment may be organised by the teacher, but it is equally important for developing students' ability to self-assess their own learning progress. The relevance of these types of assessment within primary school assessment practices will be further explained under the headings of Assessment *for* learning', 'Assessment *as* learning' and 'Assessment *of* learning'. These forms of assessment have already been discussed in the prior-to-school section of this chapter.

As we look at how these assessment processes are applied within the primary school context, please consider how they are the same across these educational sectors and how they differ. The similarities will relate to analysis of child, student and teacher learning and the cycle of plan, implement, assess and review. You might find differences relate to the level of detail and the formality of school processes.

The assessment process consists of several steps, including a form of judgment and feedback process.

1 The first step in all assessment—such as diagnostic tests, portfolio samples, annotated observations or pre- and post-test documentation—is the *collection of information as assessment evidence.*

2 The second step is to *analyse* the assessment evidence for the information it contains about students' learning.

3 The third step is to make a *judgment* about this information. Does it indicate to you, the teacher, that the student has a beginning, moderate or deep understanding of the content or process? How do you make this judgment? You make the judgment by reference to the curriculum standards, on your own or as part of a school team **moderation** process involving other teachers. We will look at moderation in more depth later in this chapter.

4 The fourth step is *your response* as a teacher. This will include your use of the information to inform your future planning to meet the learning needs of your students. It will also include giving feedback to students. It should also be used for your own professional evaluation as a professional reflection on your teaching.

We will exemplify the steps of this process through a review of the beginning assessment process as prior-to-school children transition to the primary school.

Primary school teachers require information about their students so they can best plan students' future learning. Teachers begin the school year with formal and informal assessment of students. This may include a transition report from students' previous prior-to-school experiences (DEECD, 2009), which gives teachers some information about the previous physical, social, emotional and cognitive development of students. This transition assessment process has already been discussed in detail in the prior-to-school section of this chapter. In this section, the focus is on the primary teacher's use of assessment to establish their own benchmarks so they can teach within the school curriculum guidelines. Teachers need to collect their own information to enable them to make judgments in relation to the curriculum they have to deliver as central to their professional responsibility and accountability. This formal assessment is of students' levels of cognitive ability and may include formal mandated assessment (DET, 2016; State of Victoria, 2017) as well as school-based assessments (QCAA, 2014, p.3) and teachers' own personal assessments. From these processes teachers begin to collect and analyse information about their students to inform their planning across the curriculum. Teachers may rely on the transition assessment from the prior-to-school setting and their own judgment to assess students' social and emotional skill levels.

moderation
the process of comparing and sharing work with a view to improving consistency of assessment.

SUE LANCASTER WITH FRANCES BURTON

Diagnostic testing

Diagnostic testing takes place in the early days of the school year as all new students complete one-on-one tests in Literacy and Numeracy (DET, 2016; State of Victoria, 2017) or alternatively the assessment may be based on portfolio samples (NSW, 2016).

The literacy tests include reading, writing, speaking and listening tests that give teachers an overview of children's levels of skills that they can use to individualise their planning so they are meeting the needs of each individual student as well as the needs of students as a group. As a teacher you will need to preview the tests, organise the resources and read further information about the testing process.

As an example (see Table 12.2), the *English Online Interview Guide* (DET, 2016) gives a comprehensive overview of the process and the range of tests involved. It also outlines the range of skills and understandings that children are assessed on.

As a teacher, you will hold a semi-structured conversation with children and note their particular responses. You will then be able to identify their skills (e.g. their ability to contribute to a conversation; include nouns and verbs in sentences; retell a story; and how much detail they will include in this retell). As you identify children's level of skill, you will also become more aware of the range of skills held by the children in your school-entry (foundation) class. This information allows you to plan your teaching more effectively to assist children's learning.

You should be familiar with the 'observe, plan, implement, evaluate, plan' cycle already discussed in this chapter in terms of prior-to-school assessment. The same model is used within the primary school context. In this setting, planning and assessment occurs at the whole-school level, the sub-school level, and the year level, and for you as a beginning teacher your focus will be at your grade level. Your planning and assessment for each term is generally organised through year level teams. You will be well supported in what you will be teaching and assessing by both the broader school policies and your team level guidelines. You will be given time and support from your more experienced teaching colleagues, one of whom will become your mentor and assist you with the initial diagnostic testing as well as analysing and reporting your results.

If you have the opportunity to visit school-entry (foundation/reception) classes of a primary school, please make an opportunity to discuss both the literacy and numeracy initial testing program with the relevant teacher.

Table 12.2 Oral language and listening comprehension

CONVERSATION TASK	VOCABULARY AND STORYTELLING TASKS	RETELLING TASK (E.G. *CLEVER MAX*)
• Contribution to a conversation • Quality of ideas and vocabulary • Clarity of speech	• Nouns • Verbs • Synonyms • Narrative skill • Quality of ideas • Grammar • Linking	• Including the context, complication, resolution and story end in the retell • Number of logically sequenced events included in the retell • Vocabulary and sentence structure used

Source: DET, 2016, p.12.

Beginning mathematics assessment

Research that has been influential in the Australian context on the assessment of early numeracy focused on three main areas of mathematics: number, measurement and space (or spatial relationships). It resulted in the development of a series of 'growth points' (State of Victoria, 2017). These may be looked at as 'stepping-stones' in children's growth of mathematical knowledge.

These growth point 'stepping stones' are not tied to specific ages, and not all children will move through all the steps, but they are suggestive of the developmental progress children will make.

Here, for example, is a list of the 'counting growth' points.

Counting growth points

1. Not apparent
2. *Not yet able to state the sequence of number names to 20*
3. Rote counting (reciting number names, in some form of order)
4. *Rote counts the number sequence to at least 20, but is not yet able to reliably count a collection of that size*
5. Counting collections
6. *Confidently counts a collection of around 20 objects.*
7. Counting by 1s (forward/backward, including variable starting points; before/after)
8. *Counts forwards and backwards from various starting points between 1 and 100; knows numbers before and after a given number.*
9. Counting from 0 by 2s, 5s and 10s
10. *Can count from 0 by 2s, 5s and 10s to a given target*
11. Counting from x (where x >0) by 2s, 5s and 10s
12. *Given a non-zero starting point, can count by 2s, 5s and 10s to a given target*
13. Extending and applying counting skills
14. *Can count from a non-zero starting point by any single digit number, and can apply counting skills in practical task* (State of Victoria 2017a).

STOP AND REFLECT

- As you reflect on your understanding of how children learn to count, compare the counting growth points with the counting observation notes in Table 12.3. Outline the links between these two documents.
- Try to create links to your understanding of early counting from your readings in Mathematics (Gelman & Gallistel, 1978).
- Consider how this observation and recording process of assessment is similar to and different from the observations used within the prior-to-school sector.

SUE LANCASTER WITH FRANCES BURTON

Table 12.3 Observation notes, counting

QUESTIONS	OBSERVATIONS
1 Teddy task *Show the child the teddies and get the cup.* *Cup must be able to hold more than 20* Please take a big scoop of teddies … Please put in a few more teddies to fill up the cup (at least 20) **a** Hold them in front of you … Tell me how many teddies you think are in the cup. **b** Please check to find out.	• There must be more than 20 teddies in the cup for the task to be valid • Note if estimation is realistic • Note if students tip the teddies out of the cup or if they remove them one by one • If they tip them out, do they touch and move the teddies so they know which ones they have counted? • Are they organised in their approach to the task? • Do they demonstrate 1:1 correspondence? • Note the first point of difficulty
2 Counting forwards, backwards and breaking the sequence Please count for me by ones without the teddies. Start counting from … I'll tell you when to stop. **a** 1 … 32 **b** 53 … 62 **c** 84 … 113 *(Remember to note first difficulty)* **d** Count backwards from 24. I'll tell you when to stop (24, 23, …15) (*If child hesitates say, 'like, 24, 23 …'*) **e** Count backwards from 10. I'll tell you when to stop. (*If child hesitates, say, 'like 10, 9, …'*)	• Do they understand the phrase 'count for me by ones'? • Sometimes children do not realise that the regular counting sequence is actually counting by ones. For some students, they link the count by phrase to counting by 2s, 5s or 10s. • Note the first point of difficulty, also any points of hesitation. Until students are confident with the number sequence they may hesitate at the decade transitions. • Many students stop at 100 and need to be prompted to continue or have difficulty counting beyond 109. They often say 109, 200. • Listen to the pronouncement of numbers, particularly the teen numbers. • Counting backwards is more difficult than counting forwards – children may begin to count backwards and then start to count forwards. • Note if prompts were needed for counting backwards.

Source: State of Victoria, 2007.

We hope you can see from the diagnostic task detailed and the observation notes that the process you will follow is clearly identified and the prompts will indicate the mathematical skills and knowledge you will be looking for in your assessments.

Once these assessments of your beginning school children have been completed and you have, together with your team of beginning year teachers, established what you will teach for the term, it is time to plan your weekly lessons. In many primary schools in literacy and numeracy, time is set aside for teachers to jointly plan the week's lessons. It is imperative that within each lesson there should be provision for assessment.

The assessment planned within each lesson should contain elements of 'assessment *for* learning', 'assessment *as* learning' and 'assessment *of* learning'. You have already met these concepts in terms of prior-to-school assessment. Here we will explain them in terms of primary school assessment practices.

Assessment *for* learning

This occurs when you as the teacher use inferences about student progress to inform your teaching. In practical terms you may include assessment for learning at the beginning of each planned session using such questions as:

'Tell me about …'

'Do you remember what we learnt about—for example—the number 5?'

'What have we been learning about cycling?'

'What do you already know about birds?'

'Can you retell the story of the three little pigs?'

You may also use this same strategy as you begin a new unit of work. These are sometimes just oral responses, but often it is useful to create some form of record, either pictorial or written (e.g. via a photograph on an iPad). This will give you documentary evidence of your assessment. You may do this as, I have suggested, with your whole class or you may ask children to create their own record.

One approach to this formative assessment is mind or concept mapping. This is where you ask children to brainstorm the ideas that they already have about the new topic. In simple terms, students use words, pictures, combinations of both or more structured formats such as a fishbone (SLSS, 2008, p.21) to express their ideas about a topic. It encourages children to look for links between their ideas and therefore to deepen their understanding of the topic. As a teacher, your observation and analysis of children's concept maps can be used to inform your future planning.

When students create their own concept maps, they can assess their own learning. This is assessment *as* learning and is one form of self-assessment. It is most effective for students when they revisit their concept map at the end of the period of study of a topic, assess what they initially knew, and then add to or alter their concept map. Such an assessment tool is useful because it allows students to be aware of the learning they have made over the course of the subject.

Assessment *as* learning

Assessment as learning may also occur within an individual lesson when students are asked for feedback on their understanding and they are given structured formats to respond to. This may be in a beginning class, identifying their understanding with their choice of traffic light colours. They may choose green to show that they understand the task or concept, red to show that they don't understand the topic and yellow to show that they are not sure of the topic or process. Alternatively, the teacher may suggest other strategies that students may use to share their own responses to the learning, such as symbols or icons—for example, thumbs up or down or sideways.

It is important to encourage students to develop their own self-assessment skills as an empowerment strategy. The example previously given of students' response to their learning within a lesson is one strategy. Another is to work with students to set goals for their learning over a term or over a unit of work and then to encourage them to assess their own progress on these goals.

SUE LANCASTER WITH FRANCES BURTON

Assessment *as* learning is fostered through all school subjects that follow an inquiry or investigative child-centred pedagogy. It is important to remind you of the link between teaching pedagogy and assessment process. Subjects such as Science, the Social Sciences and Technology all support an inquiry approach to learning. These subjects support student self-assessment skill development as well as teacher-led assessments.

Assessment of learning

This is about your responsibility as a teacher to make judgments of children's progress in learning. These judgments are generally made in terms of children's progress in meeting the curriculum standards as identified in state and national documentation such as the Australian Curriculum (ACARA, 2017). These assessments may be school-based (e.g. rich assessment tasks); pre- and post-tests; the use of success criteria; school moderation; or reporting processes. They may also include national assessments such as NAPLAN.

Rich assessment tasks

Rich assessment tasks, sometimes referred to as authentic tasks (Downton et al., 2006) are those where the assessment is set within broader real-life situations. Often more than one skill and/or knowledge of children is being assessed at the one time.

As an example, children may be asked to design, make and evaluate a caddy or toolbox in which they will keep their pencils and associated tools. Through this activity, children working together in small groups need to collaborate on a design, assess suitable materials, problem solve to ensure that it will work and be fit for purpose, then undertake some form of self, group and class evaluation. This will require use of their design skills, literacy and mathematics skills and knowledges, scientific awareness of materials, and technological knowledge of structures as well as information technology to present their task to others. It also requires higher order thinking and social skills. The one task may be used as a summative assessment of a range of skills and knowledge across several curriculum areas.

As an assessment tool, rich or authentic tasks have a number of benefits:

- As they are set in real-life contexts, they are accessible and engaging for all students.
- They allow students to make decisions within the open learning process as they choose their way to solve the problem.
- They give students the opportunity to communicate their ideas to others, as well as to give reasons for the decisions they make.
- As a *process* and *product* such tasks also give children the opportunity to innovate, show their creativity and consider broader real-life issues such as sustainable use of materials and practices.

Pre- and post-tests

Many schools and teachers develop or customise commercial tests to use as their own set of tests that allow them to check students' individual progress against the curriculum standards. They often use these customised tests in a pre- and post-test process to check students' learning and to give them feedback on their skills, knowledge and understandings. Such a process is often a part of the school's overall assessment program in Mathematics and Literacy. The process may take place over weeks and it is used to inform future planning. As an example, students may be given a pre-test on a series of number concepts focused around the addition process. From the results of this initial test, students may have their lessons in targeted sub-groups on particular aspects of addition. At the end of the set period of time, students re-sit the test and the evidence of their improvement in skills, knowledge and understandings is shared with them. It is important to give students feedback on their academic and social progress. Such formal assessment is also recorded as evidence of the progress students are making as a group or class. This is an example of evidence-based assessment.

This form of assessment is most useful where students' skills, knowledge and understandings are able to be clearly identified. The individual tests require time and attention to detail for development and modification. Teachers develop them carefully using the outcomes of the curriculum documents as their guide. Commercial bodies provide tests that schools and teachers may use or may adapt to meet the particular requirements of their community of learners. Individual teachers, teaching teams and schools develop their tests and use and refine them over a number of years. In developing this practice, teachers are looking for consistency of their results as a measure of students' academic progress against the curriculum standards.

Moderation

This is the teacher's individual and the teachers' collective process of making judgments regarding students' learning. Teachers make their judgments based on the assessment evidence. This includes the results of pre- and post-tests but also of individual samples of students' work such as drawings, models, dramatic performances, sporting skills, as well as mathematical and literacy skills. Teachers attend regular meetings where they bring samples of student work and the results of tests. Together they use their professional judgment to assess student samples against the requirements of the curriculum documents. They support and professionally check the evidence as to whether it meets the required standards. In this process they set and maintain consistent judgments about their students' learning.

NAPLAN

No doubt you have heard of and been a participant in NAPLAN testing as a student. Now you need to think about this process as a teacher. NAPLAN (ACARA, 2017) is an example of formal judgments made on student learning through a nationally organised assessment process. Students at Years 3, 5, 7 and 9 sit a series of formal assessments. The results of these tests are collated across the states and then the individual student results are returned to the school and to the parents to give feedback on the achievements of their students against National Curriculum benchmarks. These are predominantly in Literacy and Numeracy, though Science assessment is also included.

The intent of the assessment is to review individual student learning, school, district, state and national trends in terms of national standards but also to look for trends in areas of success in student learning and areas that require further educational, financial and policy support. The results allow broader education government bodies to look at curriculum and resourcing requirements from local to national levels.

SUE LANCASTER WITH FRANCES BURTON

Both school-based assessment and national assessments such as NAPLAN give feedback to the school and teachers about the learning of their students and the effectiveness of their teaching. As such they exemplify a major role of all assessment—that is, to guide future planning of and for learning.

SUMMARY

- Bronfenbrenner's theory of multiple environments/systems is a philosophy that children live, learn and experience life.
- Changing influences affect contemporary education and lifestyle within Australia, which ultimately impacts on the education of young children through their school years and to adulthood.
- Early childhood practitioners, educators and teachers understand that a holistic approach is the pedagogy of teaching and learning, including assessment and evaluation.
- Pedagogy in this context encompasses everything pertaining to children's needs; current knowledge and strengths; and the influences, values, language and culture of their family and community.
- Assessment and evaluation are influenced by teachers' experiences; cultural and socioeconomic background; views of children (e.g. competent and able, or unable); philosophies; biases; and capabilities of those working in, and managers of, early childhood organisations, as well as the demographics of the educational setting and surrounding community, together with the natural and made environments.
- Globalisation and the advancement in communication and information technologies have implications for government policies and new directions.
- Research recognising the importance of a quality early childhood education based on solid relationships was needed as a shared responsibility across communities. In response, a commitment towards a common Australian national education and care system was developed with a focus on the role of the teacher in assessing and evaluating the information gathered to support children's learning, development and wellbeing, drawing on the learning cycle for early years and the three elements of assessment and evaluation—*for*, *as* and *of* learning—that run through the planning cycle.
- The role of the teacher in the assessment and evaluation process seeks to embed the notion of a pedagogy that is authentic and requires deep reflection regarding practice—one that explores possibilities and suggests provocations for planning the next steps of children's further learning, leading to the transition period to school between the ages of four-to-six years.
- Assessment and evaluation processes are ongoing, take many forms and contribute to the delivery of quality programs for children's learning, development and wellbeing for a successful and healthy childhood, and into the future as an adult.
- The purpose of assessment in the primary school sector includes assessment:
  - as a strategy for teachers to be aware of students' learning
  - as a guide for teachers to evaluate (critically reflect on) the success of their teaching
  - to enable teachers to plan for future learning
  - to enable teachers to give feedback to students about their progress and achievements in learning
  - to enable teachers to professionally review their teaching and use of curriculum materials.

- School assessment entry forms enable a smooth transition from the prior-to-school sector to primary school. These include diagnostic and portfolio assessment tools and their use in the assessment of beginning literacy and numeracy skills, concepts and understandings.
- Other forms of assessment include the use of graphic organisers as both self-assessment and teacher-assessment tools; as well as pre- and post-tests and formal mandated testing such as NAPLAN.
- Significant types of assessment also apply in the primary sector of education, including assessment *of* learning, assessment *for* learning and assessment *as* learning.

FURTHER REFLECTION

- Think about what you know about assessment after reading this chapter. Create a concept map or mind map focused on your current understanding of the assessment process. Then find another way to express your understanding of assessment in the primary school context (e.g. graphic organisers). What do you notice?
- Can you summarise the difference between tests and assessment?
- Reflect on your own experiences with tests. What did you learn from the testing processes at primary or secondary school?
- How do you define assessment?
- What are activities that you see as assessment?

GROUP DISCUSSION

In small groups, review Table 12.3, 'Observations notes, counting'.
- Find some resources such as counters or teddies and practise the script in Table 12.3.
- Discuss what this might tell you about children's knowledge of number.
- As one large group, discuss how you would use this information to plan for student future learning.

CLASS EXERCISES

1 Expanding on the group discussions above, set up an opportunity to video children you work with (perhaps this could be a class action project over a semester).
  – Follow the processes described (ensure you video unscripted play situation).
  – Following reflection and discussion of the scores, conclude the exercise with a recommendation for quality improvement in one variable.
2 Collect examples of assessments completed by students of primary school age. Consider what they tell you about the students' learning.
  – Classify the examples of assessment as open or closed questions.
  – Reflect on how you might change the assessments to include some student self-assessment and create an example.
  – Reflect on how you might plan for students' further learning.
3 Collect some samples of student writing. Compare them with the English learning outcomes. Annotate the samples as evidence of the standards.
4 Collect some samples of NAPLAN tests. Discuss the types of questions asked. Find examples of closed and open questions. Is any self-assessment included?

FURTHER READING

Australian Curriculum, Assessment and Reporting Authority (ACARA) (2017) The Australian National Assessment Program: Literacy and Numeracy (NAPLAN). Canberra. www.nap.edu.au/docs/default-source/ default-document-library/naplan-assessment-framework.pdf?sfvrsn=2

> This document is worth reading in some depth as it will give you a comprehensive understanding of this formal mandated process of assessment. As a teacher you are required to understand both the purpose and the process of such an assessment tool.

Connor, J. (2011) Foundations for Learning and the Connections between the Early Years Learning Framework and the Australian Curriculum. Canberra, ACT: ECA–ACARA.

> This publication as a collaboration between prior-to-school and school domains. As indicated in the title it describes the links between the EYLF and the Australian Curriculum, highlighting current expectations for teaching and learning of a common approach across the varied situations and landscape of Australia. The document is easy to read, based on information currently in practice and provides confirmation of government directions and suggestions for collaborative conversations between the two education and learning environments. The document also highlights the importance of mutual respect and continuity of support for children's learning in the vital early years in all education and learning environments.

Department of Education and Training (DET) (2016) English Online Interview. Melbourne: State of Victoria. www.education.vic.gov.au/Documents/school/teachers/teachingresources/discipline/english/assessment/ Education%20State%20EOI%20Guide%202017%20%28updated%29.pdf

> This is an excellent guide to assessment tools you may use to help you understand the literacy skills, concepts and understandings of young students. It will also give you the language and strategies needed to make decisions about your students' literacy learning.

Hunter Institute of Mental Health (2014) Connections: A Resource for Early Childhood Educators about Children's Wellbeing. Canberra, ACT: Australian Government Department of Education.

> This deals with children birth-to-eight years and provides resources for reflection to inform practice in supporting children's mental health and wellbeing. The rationale for the approach comes from research showing that when children receive support in relation to their mental health and wellbeing in early childhood they are more likely to develop a 'strong foundation for developing the skills, values and behaviours they need to experience positive physical and mental health as an adult'. The resource will be particularly useful in providing concepts to consider for successful practice across a broad and varied client group. Mental health issues commonly known to impact child mental health and wellbeing are discussed as well as practices necessary to support child and family in these circumstances.

Marbina, L., Mashford-Scott, A., Church, A. & Taylor, C. (2015) Assessment of Wellbeing in Early Childhood Education and Care: Literature Review. Melbourne, Vic.: Victorian Curriculum and Assessment Authority.

> This literature review focuses on the wellbeing of children birth-to-five years of age and includes key characteristics of young children's wellbeing and existing tools for assessment for 'sharing knowledge across multidisciplinary settings'. Each tool is described and discussed in easy-to-read language. Practice principles for assessment by early childhood professionals are also included advocating a 'holistic approach' and 'children's own reports' as part of the assessment.

State of Victoria, Department of Education (DoE) (2007) Mathematics Online Interview: Observation Notes, Counting, Section A. www.education.vic.gov.au/studentlearning/teachingresources/maths

> This is a very useful beginning example of the assessment tools available to you as a teacher. It is worthwhile reflecting on and making links to your growing understanding of how children learn mathematically.

REFERENCES

Australian Children's Education and Care Quality Authority (ACECQA, 2017). http://www.acecqa.gov.au/

Australian Curriculum, Assessment and Reporting Authority (ACARA) (2017) *The Australian National Assessment Program: Literacy and Numeracy* (NAPLAN), Canberra, www.nap.edu.au/docs/default-source/default-document-library/naplan-assessment-framework.pdf?sfvrsn=2

Bigby, C. & Clement, T. (2008) *Making Life Good in the Community*. Melbourne: Department of Human Services.

Bruce, T. (2011) *Early Childhood Education* (4th edn). UK: Hodder Education.

Department of Education (DoE) (2007) *Mathematics Online Interview: Observation Notes, Counting, Section A*. www.education.vic.gov.au/studentlearning/teachingresources/maths

Department of Education and Early Childhood Development (DEECD) (2009) *Scaffolding Numeracy in the Middle Years*: 'A useful grid—the story', Melbourne.www.education.vic.gov.au/Documents/school/teachers/.../maths/.../snmyasstopt2.pdf

Department of Education, Employment and Workplace Relations (DEEWR) (2009) *Belonging, Being & Becoming: The Early Years Learning Framework for Australia*. ACT, Australia: Commonwealth of Australia.

Department of Education and Training (DET) (2016) *English Online Interview*. Melbourne: State of Victoria. www.education.vic.gov.au/Documents/school/teachers/teachingresources/discipline/english/assessment/Education%20State%20EOI%20Guide%202017%20%28updated%29.pdf

(Department of Education and Training) (2017) *Mathematics Online Interview: School User Guide*. Melbourne, Author. www.education.vic.gov.au/Documents/school/teachers/teachingresources/discipline/maths/continuum/moiinterviewuserg.pdf

(Department of Education and Training) (2017) Assessment advice. Author, www.education.vic.gov.au/school/teachers/support/Pages/advice.aspx

Downton, A., Knight, R., Clarke, D. & Lewis, G. (2006) *Mathematics Assessment for Learning: Rich Tasks and Work Samples* (3rd edn). Melbourne, Mathematics Teaching and Learning Centre: Australian Catholic University and Catholic Education office.

Early Childhood Australia (ECA) (2017). www.earlychildhoodaustralia.org.au/

Fleer, M. (2013) *Play in the Early Years*. Melbourne: Cambridge University Press.

Foreman, P. & Arthur-Kelly, M. (2014) *Inclusion in Action*. South Melbourne, Vic.: Cengage Learning.

Forster, S. (2014) 'Hanging Out Program: Interaction with People with Profound Intellectual and Multiple Disabilities As a Primary Role, Not an Optional Extra'. Paper presented at the Communicate, Participate, Enjoy! Solutions to Inclusion Conference. Preston, Vic.: Australia.

Gelman, R. & Gallistel, C.R. (1978) 'The Counting Model', in The Child's Understanding of Number. Cambridge Ma: Harvard University Press, pp.73–82.

Lindon, J. (2012) *Understanding Child Development*. UK: Hodder Education.

Milne, A.A. (1959) *The World of Christopher Robin*. London: Methuen.

NSW Education Standards Authority (NESA). (2016) http://educationstandards.nsw.edu.au/wps/portal/nesa/home.

Pugh, G. & Duffy, B. (2014) *Contemporary Issues in the Early Years* (6th edn). London: SAGE Publications Ltd.

Queensland Curriculum and Assessment Authority (QCCA) (2014) *School-based Assessment: The Queensland System*. South Brisbane: State of Queensland. www.qcaa.qld.edu.au/downloads/approach2/school-based_assess_qld_sys.pdf

Second Level Support Service (SLSS) (2007) Using Graphic Organisers in Teaching and Learning. Navan, National Development Plan. http://pdst.ie/sites/default/files/GraphicOrganiserFinal.pdf

Shonkoff, J.P. & Phillips, D.A. (eds) (2000) *From Neurons to Neighborhoods: The Science of Early Childhood Development.* Washington, DC: National Academy Press.

Snow, C.E. & Van Hemel, S.B. (eds) (2008) *Early Childhood Assessment: Why, What, and How.* Washington, DC: National Research Council. The National Academies Press. https://doi.org/10.17226/12446.

State of Victoria (2017) *Summary of the Early Numeracy Research Project Final Report.* Author, Melbourne: State of Victoria. www.eduweb.vic.gov.au/edulibrary/public/teachlearn/student/enrpsummaryreport.pdf

State of Victoria, (2017a) *Framework of mathematical learning.* Author, Melbourne, www.education.vic.gov.au/ Documents/school/teachers/teachingresources/discipline/maths/continuum/moiinterviewuserg.pdf.

Victorian Early Years Learning and Development Framework (VEYLDF). (2012) http://www.vcaa.vic.edu.au/ documents/earlyyears/veyldf_for_children_from_birth_to_8.pdf.

Webster, A. & Forster, J. (2012) *Participating and Belonging: Inclusion in Practice.* Malvern, Vic.: Noah's Ark.

The Importance of Relationships

Carol Carter

Chapter objectives

In this chapter, we will:

- consider the important features and strategies of quality relationships and learning and teaching partnerships
- examine and analyse different relationships including teacher–child; peer socialisation; family–teacher, and learning communities and communities of practice
- identify and discuss potential barriers to relationships and partnerships.

Key terms

co-construction of meaning   inter-subjectivity   pro-social skills

community of practice   primary socialisation   sustained shared thinking

> Young children experience the world as an environment of relationships, and these relationships affect virtually all aspects of their development—intellectual, social, emotional, physical, behavioural, and moral.
>
> (Center on the Developing Child, 2004, p.1)

From the above quotation, you can see how important relationships are and how vital it is for children to form strong, nurturing relationships, particularly as they view their world through these relationships. How young children form, forge and maintain relationships is critical in the light of the influence it will have on *all* developmental aspects and the lifelong impact that early experiences of relationships have on future relationship building. The nature and effectiveness of children's relationships, be they with adults or other children, in a learning and teaching environment are also important.

Take a moment to think about the teachers who have taught you. What is it that you remember the most about them? Is it *what* they taught you, or the *type of relationship* that you had with them, or both, that you remember most clearly? I think that, for most of us, aspects of our relationship with those who have taught us will form our most vivid memories. Research (such as in Hattie & Yates, 2014; and McDonald, 2010) identifies that classroom relationships are the single most significant factor in determining student engagement, motivation and subsequent success. Children who develop warm, positive relationships within early experiences or education, for example with their pre-school teachers, are more excited about learning, more positive about coming to school, more self-confident, and achieve more in the classroom (Center on the Developing Child, 2004, p.1).

I have learnt a great deal about relationships from the children I have taught over the years. Here are just a few stories to share with you as a starting point for our discussion about relationships. Throughout the chapter I will refer back to these and other stories, as a chapter on relationships needs to be filled with voices that get to the heart of relationship building. I have used pseudonyms to protect the identities of the various people spoken about in this chapter.

Michelle: Finding the positive

From the moment I knew who the children were I was going to be teaching in Year 1 I was 'warned' about Michelle. I was told terrible tales of her behaviour by her previous teachers and even by her parents. Being conscious of the dangers of a self-fulfilling prophecy and allowing others to cloud my judgment, I made a deliberate decision to consistently focus on the positive in my relationship with Michelle. This was not easy, given our experiences on that first day of school, which will forever be indelibly imprinted in my memory. As the children were leading into the classroom, Michelle, having placed herself at the back of the line with a broad, smug smile on her face and Texta in hand, drew a line along the classroom wall as she walked. On entering the classroom, she then proceeded to lick the face of a child sitting next to her with remarkable dedication and gusto! Without condoning her behaviour, positive I was and positive I continued to be throughout the months that followed, despite frequently finding it difficult to stay positive. At first, the positive way in which I engaged with Michelle was somewhat contrived and not always genuine. As the months passed it became easier and easier, and gradually Michelle's behaviour changed, based, in part, on my attitude and relationship towards her and, in part, on a growing emotional maturity leading to a less consistent need for attention. At the end of the year, my relationship with her was such that she was the child I found the most difficult to let go and see leaving my classroom. Thirty-three years later I am still occasionally in touch with her via email.

Amy: Really, really listening

Although this happened many years ago, in my first year of teaching, I still wake up in a cold sweat some nights after dreaming once again about the damage I may have caused so many years ago. Amy was the kind of child who loved to talk—and talk she did! Whenever it was her turn to tell us her news, or for show and tell, or on any other occasion, she would go on and on and on. As a newly graduated teacher I did not possess any strategies to cope with this incessant talking. So, my solution was simply to let her talk. I had got into a dreadful habit of switching off and appearing to listen at the same time. On this occasion, she was doing her usual talking and I was thinking about the class plans for the day while half listening to her talking. As the phrase 'that's nice' came out of my mouth, I realised that she had been talking about a death in the family. I will never forget the look on her face and even though I did try, there was nothing I could do. Amy taught me the importance of genuinely and carefully listening in a learning and teaching situation.

Nicholas: Laughter and Sharing

Four years ago, one of my ex-students contacted me via Facebook. Today Nicholas is a school teacher and has his own family. He reminded me of the day that I was a little unhappy with the class and told them it was time that they 'pulled up their socks'. An entire class of Prep children, literally and solemnly, tried to pull up the socks that they were wearing. I burst out laughing and the entire class, most of whom did not fully understand what was so funny, laughed with me. Nicholas said that this laughter and the many other occasions that we laughed together was what he remembered the most about our classroom relationships. He also remembered the stories I told them where I wove all the class members into the story. He explained that it was only when he began telling his class and his own son stories that he realised how well I knew each and every child in my class because of how the stories reflected the class and their interests. The other thing he remembered is how I would share little things about myself and that I was always honest with them. He remembered how the principal had to put the transparency on the overhead projector (that's what we used before PowerPoint and interactive whiteboards) for me because I was shaking so badly and that when, weeks later, one of the other members of his class asked why I was shaking at the open day, I told them honestly that it was because I was very scared and nervous of speaking to such a large group of parents and children who were going to be in my and other classes. Nicholas taught me that aspects of my teaching that I had not considered important, including laughter and sharing qualities of ourselves, impacts on the quality of relationships.

Introduction

In this chapter, we will examine the building and maintaining of relationships, based on essential techniques and strategies for effective learning and teaching partnerships. I have emphasised different types of relationships, from a micro to a macro level, beginning with the child as an active agent within teaching and learning partnerships and the inter-subjective relationships that constitute effective partnerships. Different relationships that are discussed and analysed include teacher–child; peer socialisation; family–teacher; learning communities and communities of practice; practicum relationships and professional partnerships. Although they are discussed separately, the nature and qualities of relationships are such that they do overlap and are not meant to be seen as entirely separate from each other.

The chapter outlines theories of socialisation and community engagement linked to teaching and learning partnerships between families, schools, and early childhood and childcare services. Sociocultural theories, including critical theories, underpin the critical reflection on different types of teaching and learning relationships.

Relationships involve connections and interconnections. Human relationships consist of connections between people who interact with one another. Socialisation is a dynamic, interactive process that provides people with ways of participating effectively in society. It is this process of socialisation that enables us to form relationships with others and to become members of different communities and groups. Having relationships, ranging from close connections to distant acquaintances, is a part of being human. Fostering positive relationships in early childhood is not only essential for their healthy development, but is an important predictor of effective relationship and partnership building in later life. It is crucial, for this and a range of other reasons, that we pay rigorous attention to the relationship and partnership aspects of our learning and teaching practices.

CAROL CARTER

It is as important—if not more important—to reflect critically and plan carefully for socialisation and relationship building as it is to consider such aspects as content and learning intentions. How to build and sustain effective relationships should be an integral part of our learning and teaching. **Primary socialisation** is the process of gaining basic skills to build relationships and function in society and usually occurs in the family. Secondary socialisation—such as in schools and in interaction with peers—occurs outside the family.

Relationships involving teachers, children and their families are particularly important for children's identity formation as well as their feelings of belonging and emotional and social wellbeing. 'Relationships are the foundations for the construction of identity—"who I am", "how I belong" and "what is my influence?"' (DEEWR, 2009, p.20).

Relationships become *partnerships* when people recognise that they have a working relationship and are committed to working together towards shared responsibility and common objectives and purposes. In early childhood teaching, partnerships are formed and forged from a commitment towards the wellbeing of the child. Sound partnerships are based on strong, positive relationships of reciprocal trust and respect that involve ongoing shared commitment and negotiation. The transition from relationships to partnerships requires time, effort, commitment and ongoing communication and work. Continuous reflection on the quality of our learning and teaching relationships and how various educational partnerships are formed, maintained and improved, is extremely important.

> **primary socialisation** is the process of gaining basic skills to build relationships and function in society and usually occurs in the family.

STOP AND REFLECT

- What do you consider to be your own strengths and weaknesses in forming relationships?
- Reflect back on your own education: how do you think teaching and learning partnerships have changed over time?
- Consider school and early learning settings and how the notion of childhood has changed. Your reading of earlier chapters in this book will be of use in your thinking about partnerships.
- What is the connection between socialisation, relationships and partnerships in learning and teaching?

Relationship building

When I ask Initial Teacher Education students—on completion of a semester-long subject concerning relationships in teaching and learning partnerships—what they have learnt, these students generally focus on the importance of positive communication. That is because positive, purposeful, quality communication is central to any relationship and particularly in relationships within an educational environment. Communication that is respectful, ongoing and open and that takes place within non-judgmental and non-threatening environments, is crucial for any meaningful relationship building where there is mutual trust and collaboration.

Let's go back for a moment to the story about Michelle, who taught me about positive relationships. Studies (for example in Roorda et al., 2011) have shown that the quality of relationships has a greater impact for children identified as 'at risk', such as Michelle, and as such it is even more important to promote positive relationships in non-threatening environments. Although acknowledging the importance for children such as Michelle, all relationships are strengthened by building positive relationships. Here are some ways of positively fostering relationships that I found worked with Michelle and that I have subsequently used in all my relationship building.

It is crucial to communicate confidence in people's ability and to recognise and acknowledge achievement, no matter how small it may seem. We need to seek out opportunities to reinforce verbally and non-verbally what children are doing well. We need to pay active attention to what could be considered the 'small things' so that we notice when people are 'down', when they are trying, when they have improved, when they need encouragement and support, and so on. Here is an example from my own experience. In the days when 'gold stars' were popular and used extensively and when I still believed in them as a way to extrinsically motivate children, I had just handed out my Grade 2 workbooks when Sally literally started racing around the classroom, excitedly dancing, singing and shouting. Once I had got her to settle down I discovered that the cause of her excitement was that in 'all her time at school' (Prep to Grade 2) she had watched all her friends get stars but she had never got one herself. Now Sally had an enormous challenge with coordination and her writing was poor. However, I had noticed that she was trying hard and that, if one did not become too fixated with the technical part of her writing, what she wrote was generally quality work. Noticing the strengths of Sally's work, and that she was trying, not only strengthened our relationship, but also led to Sally's greater sense of confidence and self- worth. Not surprisingly, over time, Sally's work improved.

Clear, unambiguous, open, authentic communication is an essential ingredient in any supportive, enabling relationship. Unlike the way I responded to Amy in the story above, speaking to one another and active listening are very important. Rather than thinking about what we want to say next, or being distracted by our own thoughts, we need to really, really listen to each other if we are to build sound relationships. There are a great many 'rules' involved in active listening, such as leaning towards the person who is speaking, signalling that you are listening, verbally reflecting on what is being said and having a way of sitting that shows you are open to the communication. While these are helpful techniques, I believe if we follow a recipe-type format the listening can become contrived and, for me, feeling and being genuine and authentic is the most desired form of communication in relationships.

STOP AND REFLECT

- Can you remember an experience when you were in an educational setting and you were not treated with respect?
- What was that experience? Was it that you were not listened to, or was it something else? How did you feel?
- How did this experience influence your learning? For example, were you inspired to learn more or try harder? Or were you discouraged and 'turned off' learning?
- What does this experience teach you about your relationships in future educational settings?
- How do you feel and respond when someone notices and tells you that you are doing something well?

CAROL CARTER

We need to focus on strength-based approaches to learning and teaching relationships and the unique contribution that each member of an educational environment brings to the learning and teaching process. A strength-based approach embraces the sharing of our own strengths and the empowering of others in the relationship to use their different or complementary strengths.

Supportive and enabling relationships flourish best in an environment where excessive rivalry and competition are avoided and collaboration and ownership are fostered. Relationships require compromise; the encouragement of diverse perspectives; the honouring of diversity; and the negotiation of roles, responsibilities, tasks and activities, based on the strengths that are brought to the relationship. While relationships are not static and do require flexible, responsive action, these roles, as well as expectations, need to be clearly defined (Stonehouse & Gonzalez-Mena, 2004, 2008; Reed & Sansoyer, 2012).

As you read the learning story 'Let's play basketball', think about what aspects of a strength-based approach, clear communications and acknowledgement are evident in the story.

Let's play basketball

Luke is a little hesitant about leaving his mum this morning. The kindergarten teacher knows that Luke likes playing with balls. 'What if we play with the balls outside?' she suggests. Luke leaves his mum and joins the teacher, asking, 'Can I play with the balls now?' The teacher takes four large balls out of the storeroom and gives them to Luke and his friend Emma. Excitedly, Luke begins to kick a ball and then throws it to his friend Emma. 'Can I play basketball?' Luke asks the teacher. The teacher gets two baskets from the storeroom. 'We don't have a basketball ring at Kinder but what if we use a basket?' she asks Luke.

Luke nods his head. Emma is there and watching. Luke lines the two baskets next to each other. He picks the grey basket and says, 'This is my basket'. He points to the blue basket and says to his friend Emma, 'This is yours'. Luke stands a few steps away from the basket and tries to throw the ball into the basket, but misses. 'You can do it,' says the teacher. The second time, Luke gets the ball into the basket. 'Good job!' says the teacher. 'Yay,' shouts Emma.

STOP AND THINK

- How are a strength-based approach, clear communication and acknowledgment made use of in the learning story 'Let's play basketball'?
- What else do you notice about relationships from this observation?
- What do you see as important aspects of creating and maintaining positive relationships in educational settings?
- How will this impact on your learning and teaching?

We need to foster spaces where there is respectful dialogue between the people in the relationship and where genuinely reflective conversation takes place. An educational environment where we move away from the firing of questions and statements and uni-directional answers (e.g. one child to teacher) and towards an environment where conversations, communal exploration, 'sustained shared thinking', decision making (Siraj-Blatchford & Manni, 2008) and sharing who we are provides such a dialogical space.

In learning and teaching relationships, we should also be mindful of maintaining clear, professional boundaries. So, when I talk about sharing who we are, I am talking about sharing appropriate information about ourselves and about getting to know the people in the relationships, as I described in the story of Nicholas and the class. I am not talking about inappropriate sharing of highly personal information, such as when a former colleague of mine continually told her pre-school children stories about the 'ups and downs', break-ups and getting back together of her relationships.

Sustained shared thinking and **inter-subjectivity** contribute to quality relationships in early childhood educational settings. Sustained shared thinking refers to 'an effective learning and teaching interaction, where two or more individuals work (often playfully) together in an intellectual way to solve a problem, clarify a concept, evaluate activities, or extend a narrative' (Siraj-Blatchford & Manni, 2008). Sustained shared thinking involves people working together to reflect on and solve problems or challenges over an extended period of time. Inter-subjectivity involves interpersonal, reciprocal responses and sharing of experiences, understandings and feelings via a link, or bridge, between yourself and others. Inter-subjectivity provides a common communication platform of **co-construction of meaning** as each person in the relationship adapts and modifies their perspectives in close collaboration with the other person in the relationship (Berk 1994, cited in MacNaughton & Williams 2008, p.374). Collaboration can provide a 'collective energy' that increases productivity (Percy-Smith & Thomas, 2006).

Here is a very brief example of sustained shared thinking.

> **sustained shared thinking** people working together to reflect on and solve problems or challenges over an extended period of time. It refers to 'an effective learning and teaching interaction, where two or more individuals work (often playfully) together in an intellectual way to solve a problem, clarify a concept, evaluate activities, or extend a narrative' (Siraj-Blatchford & Manni, 2008).

> **inter-subjectivity** interpersonal, reciprocal responses and sharing of experiences, understandings and feelings via a link, or bridge, between yourself and others.

> **co-construction of meaning** collaborating to make shared meaning.

The volcano

Anna is sitting outside with a student teacher. A group of children are working together on an experiment. 'We did a volcano before but it didn't work,' says Anna. 'Yes, it didn't work,' Prakesh confirms. 'I wonder why it didn't work the last time?' muses the student teacher. The children use each other's ideas to have a sustained conversation around why they feel the experiment had not worked the last time. Anna, Jade, Sam and Prakesh and the student teacher make the volcano together, using sand and mud. 'We need trees here,' says Prakesh. He reaches up to a tree and picks a few twigs. Some of the children collect some mulch and scatter it around the base of the volcano. They keep co-constructing until the whole group is happy with their volcano.

The Initial Teacher Education student reads out the instructions for the experiment. The children talk about what they are going to do. With the help of the teacher they negotiate the different tasks and take turns to add various ingredients (such as red food colouring, bicarb soda and vinegar). Anna is pouring vinegar into the mixture. '*Wow*, this is awesome!' she shouts. This is working and it's so cool,' says Jade. 'Look! Look how the lava is coming out of the volcano,' says Sam. The children are talking, watching and explaining to other children as the bubbly, red vinegar flows down the volcano.

CAROL CARTER

Working together to share information and the ability to honour diversity and articulate different understandings, perspectives and values in the co-construction of meaning are invaluable components of all quality relationships. The greater the balance of power in relationships, and where partners are seen to be interacting equally, the greater is the area of shared meaning, connection and understanding, as illustrated by Jordan (2009) in Figure 13.1.

Relational power is the ability to influence or control with a probable outcome of the people perceived as having the most power being able to carry out their own will despite any resistance. The statuses of people within relationships are frequently hierarchical, with people on top having more power than those at the bottom. Inequality strongly affects the nature and quality of relationships. Both positive and negative forms of power impact on relationships and relationship building. If we take the opposite spectra of power relations, namely domination and cooperation, we will begin to see some of the impact of power on relationships. In relationships where the levels of inequality are high and dominance prevails, there are frequently feelings of fear, and mistrust and the efficiency and strength of these relationships is of a low quality. In relationships where power is more or less equal and where cooperation prevails, there are frequently feelings of trust and respect and the efficiency and strength of these relationships is of a high quality.

Power relationships are not necessarily as straightforward as this discussion suggests. As discussed in Chapter 3, from a Foucauldian (1988) perspective, individuals and organisations develop various dialogues and practices to conform with, circumvent or contest existing power–knowledge relationships. Kemmis (2009, p.466) claims that the ways in which humans relate to each other within educational environments are always 'shaped by previously established patterns of social relationships and power'.

From a sociocultural constructivist perspective, pre-existing cultural imagery and cultural practices surround children as they begin to construct and make sense of their world.

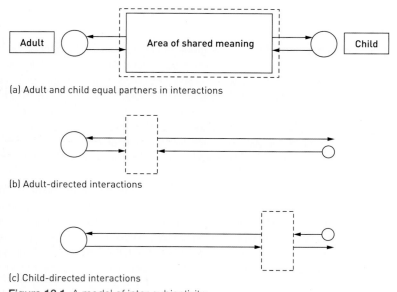

(a) Adult and child equal partners in interactions

(b) Adult-directed interactions

(c) Child-directed interactions

Figure 13.1 A model of inter-subjectivity

Source: Jordan, 2009, p.46.

Cultural meanings regulate the way children view the world and children come to see certain cultural practices and meanings as 'normal' and desirable ways of operating. The power of these cultural images and meanings impact on children's agency and their chances of constructing their own meanings. In the same way, social structures as well as expected and established relationships and positions of power between teachers and children may 'distort, privilege and silence' meaning-making. We need to find ways to establish relationships that move away from patterns of power and privilege that hinder children's senses of agency (Anning et al., 2009, pp.57–62).

I will return to this concept of power when we examine the different relationships in this chapter.

STOP AND REFLECT

- What are some examples in your life of strong quality relationships?
- What makes them quality relationships?
- How do you think power relationships impact on educational settings?
- How could the sustained shared thinking in 'The Volcano' be extended and developed?

The child as an active agent

As discussed in Chapter 1, agency is the ability to act independently, to make your own free choices and decisions, and to impose these choices on the world. Children are active partners in their own learning and building of relationships. Children are not just passively socialised into the cultures and norms of their societies. Rather, socialisation and relationship building takes place through interaction (Giddens & Sutton, 2013), during which children are active agents engaging as participants and interpreters who gradually develop the capacities required for relationship building. This active engagement may result in children accepting, opposing, rejecting or reinterpreting aspects of the information, norms and values that are seen to be a part of their culture.

> Children are always learning about the impact of their personal beliefs and values. Children's agency, as well as guidance, care and teaching by families and educators shape children's experiences of becoming.
>
> (DEEWR, 2009, p.20)

Sociocultural approaches acknowledge the child as an active agent capable of directing their own learning and value the role of the teacher in building on, enriching and extending what children are coming to know and do (Connor, 2011, p.1). This is evident from some sociocultural theorists and theories, such as Bronfenbrenner, Vygotsky and Bruner, discussed previously in this book. The processes of building and extending what children are able to do is a part of the Zone of Proximal Development (Vygotsky) and Scaffolding (Bruner) discussed in earlier chapters.

Social Relations Theory (SRT), developed by Kuczynski and others (Kuczynski & Parkin, 2007) assumes that all humans, from childhood, are intentional, proactive, self-regulating active agents who directly contribute to their life circumstance. SRT proposes three resources of power and agency: 'individual resources', which includes physical strength and control over information; 'relational resources', which involves access to personal relationships as a support for their exercise of agency; and 'cultural resources', which refers to the rights, entitlements and constraints conveyed to individuals. These are the laws, customs and practices of a culture. For instance, the recognition and endorsement of children's rights within a culture provides an important source of legitimacy and power to children's agency.

Relationships with babies and toddlers

Infants: birth to 12 months

Infants communicate and interact with their coos, gurgles and grunts, facial expressions, cries, body movements (such as cuddling or back arching), eye moments (such as looking towards and looking away), and arm and leg movements.

Inter-subjectivity through connection, focus and facial expressions and the 'I' (Mead, 1967) or spontaneous, subjective, impulsive part of the not yet fully socialised self is present from birth. Children develop as social humans by imitating and mirroring the actions of those around them. At around two months, face-to-face exchanges are constantly seen and highly intentional communication takes place at around nine months.

Toddlers: 12 to 36 months

Toddlers communicate and interact with a combination of gestures and sounds, one-word or two-word sentences, positive and negative emotional expressions and body movements.

Infants begin to, and toddlers continue, develop the ability to form relationships that involve mutual recognition, exchanges and reciprocal relationships through primary socialisation usually with a significant other. Significant others are people who play important roles in the early socialisation of children. At around twenty months infants connect in shared representations. Toddlers continue to imitate and mirror behaviour.

Pre-schoolers: 3 to 6 years

Pre-schoolers begin to talk and interact using full sentences. They begin to recognise the connection between spoken and written communication. Pre-schoolers often talk to themselves when playing and working on tasks such as puzzles and art activities.

Pre-schoolers begin to display explicit understanding and intentional connections with others. Children's play progresses from simple imitation to acting out an adult role or 'taking the role of the other'. This is when children acquire a sense of self, or the social component of the self, the 'me' (Mead, 1967). Children begin to become self-aware and understand themselves as separate agents—as a 'me'—by seeing themselves through the eyes of others.

School children: 6 to 12 years

School children reflect more deeply on the nature of relationships and connections, and seek more justifications for the way things are. They can understand and talk about the perspective of another person and are beginning to recognise the influence their behaviour can have on others. At this age children spend more time talking and playing with friends.

- What are the most effective ways to communicate with children?
- How can teachers encourage children's communication and relationship-building at different stages of their development?
- How can teachers make sure that children have agency and that their voices are heard?

Child–teacher relationships

Teaching is about guiding, enabling and supporting knowledge, skills and values acquisition and extending personal vistas, possibilities and perspectives. It is about encouraging and engaging someone to learn or understand something by way of example or experience. Teaching and learning are intertwined and inseparable concepts. To teach is to make informed decisions about what and how children learn. 'To teach well implies learning about students' learning' (Ramsden, 1992, p.8). Learning about how individual children learn requires a caring, democratic, dynamic relationship between the child, the teacher and the knowledge that is being taught. In this kind of relationship children develop what has been termed 'autonomous ethics' (Kohn, 1996) where they operate out of a sense of what is ethical, responsible and 'right', as opposed to an autocratic power dynamic and relationship, where children are forced to comply with the teacher's will. It is the kind of relationship that is evident, particularly in Michelle's story. You might find it interesting to refer back to Chapter 1 and consider the educational philosophies of John Locke and John Wesley, and the relevance of these to this discussion.

Child–teacher relationships are crucial to the learning and teaching that takes place. This is whether the teaching takes place informally or through a formal process where certain types of skills and knowledge are conveyed, usually though a pre-designed curriculum document in specialised settings such as kindergartens/pre-schools and schools. In informal teaching, relationships are mediated through personal knowledge, the context and the immediate requirements of the moment or place. Relationships are mediated through curriculum frameworks in prior-to-school settings and national and state curricula documents in school settings. Within this mediation we need to ensure that our focus is not too strongly on task-based relationships as opposed to people-based relationships.

Learning and teaching partnerships

Learning and teaching is a partnership in which the partners involved bring their own expertise, skills and experiences in order to extend, enrich and authenticate the process. Teachers are partners who bring to the process a number of skills: expertise and experiences; and a formulated, constructed understanding of disciplines (e.g. literacy or mathematics). That is not to say that this knowledge and understanding is exhaustive or 'complete' or that this knowledge remains static during learning and teaching processes.

Teachers contribute knowledge from their own experiences to enrich, challenge and extend children's learning. The responsibility for structuring and initiating the learning process is in the hands of the teacher, even where the curriculum is negotiated with the learners, or an emergent or inquiry-based approach (discussed in Chapter 5) to learning and teaching is followed. Teachers are responsible for strategies and mechanisms, informed by theory, for guiding and scaffolding the learning process and enabling learners. Learners are partners who bring to the process their prior learning as well as new perspectives, opinions and fresh ideas. Irrespective of whether they are children or (like you) adults, learners bring to the partnership the ability and need to construct their own understanding; the responsibility for their own learning; and different ways of participating in and processing learning.

CAROL CARTER

Whether joining in children's play, working with children to solve a problem or chatting with children about their experiences, teachers or educators relate to children as partners, seeking out children's signals, cues and intentions and collaborating with them to carry out and expand upon their intended activity (Hohmann & Weikart, 1995, p.35). We need to actively 'join in' children's play, 'tune in' and respond to children's views and ideas, model thinking and problem solving and appropriately 'challenge' children's existing ideas about how things work (e.g. by asking such questions as 'I'm wondering why the water keeps disappearing into the sand').

Diverse socialisation and cultural background impacts on teacher–child relationships and requires recognition that each child comes from a unique background. As discussed in detail in Chapter 6, teachers need to consider each child's individual characteristics and own immediate and wider contexts. Quality relationships and quality classrooms lead to children's engagement, motivation, sense of confidence and self-belief and ultimately, successful outcomes and achievement.

Engagement and belonging

Engagement refers to the physical, intellectual, behavioural and emotional participation and connection that participants bring to their own learning and teaching. Children's engagement in learning environments has two components. The first component is the degree of attention, curiosity, effort, investment and persistence the children show. The second one is that of involving children in decision making and giving them a voice in the learning and teaching environment. Caring, empathetic and effective teachers are at the heart of children's engagement in the learning process. It is teachers' actions and their creation of a safe, supportive and engaging environment that encourages participation and meaningful learning.

Teachers establish quality learning environments that give children a strong sense of belonging when they foster positive relationships, connect with children and provide children with a sense of safety and purposefulness. The EYLF refers to the need for 'children [to] feel safe, secure and supported'. It is believed that:

> this is evident, for example when children: build secure attachments with one and then more familiar educators; ... sense and respond to a feeling of belonging ... [and] establish and maintain respectful, trusting relationships with other children and educators.

(DEEWR, 2009, p.21)

Safety not only refers to being safe in the physical sense, but also the feelings of safety that are developed through a sense of belonging and trust. Trust needs to be earned; it comes from how we behave to tell children we are trustworthy. Our use of tone, facial expression and gestures infer our trustworthiness and children are excellent at detecting fake behaviour and emotions. Knowing your students, initially by name and then more about each one, is an obvious but important step in creating a trustful and supportive environment.

McDonald (2010, pp.248–51) talks about a number of practical strategies that we can use to connect with students. Some of these are:

- by smiling, acknowledging students and making them feel like they belong
- by welcoming and greeting students, making time to have one-on-one conversations and encouraging a general atmosphere of friendliness

- by noticing absences and recognising when students return to the classroom—that is, appreciating the presence of students
- by finding a way of saying 'Thank you' or 'I appreciate the way you ... (verbally or in a special note)
- by responding to students' needs and interests and working collaboratively.

Particularly when children are vulnerable, trust and caring will help them to care about the educational environment and create emotional bonds and a sense of belonging and wellbeing. Identification and how strongly children identify with the learning spaces and learning practices will contribute to this sense of belonging.

Inclusion and equity

As contemporary Australia has a rich cultural diversity, teacher–child relationships need to carefully consider inclusive processes by which diverse groups or individuals are supported, respected, and valued through creating affirming and welcoming spaces and climates that elicit a sense of belonging.

In relation to diversity, for example, according to the Australian Bureau of Statistics (30 June 2016), 28.5 per cent of Australia's estimated resident population (6.9 million people) was born overseas from about 200 countries with more than 300 different ancestries and languages spoken. People born overseas, or who had at least one parent born overseas, made up almost half (49 per cent) of the Australian population. The census also shows that Australia has a higher proportion of overseas-born people (26 per cent) than the United Kingdom (13 per cent), the United States (14 per cent), Canada (22 per cent) and New Zealand (23 per cent).

In 2011 there were:

- 5.3 million first generation Australians (27% of the population)
- 4.1 million second generation Australians (20% of the population)
- 10.6 million third-plus generation Australians (53% of the population).

Perth, Sydney and Melbourne had the highest proportion of overseas-born people, with more than one-third each.

(ABS, 2011)

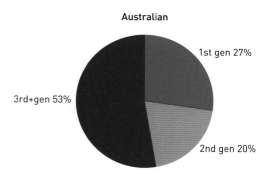

This did not include the diversity of people who are not Australian citizens living and working in Australia.

The first and second generation Australians hail from a wide variety of countries with the eight countries (from largest to smallest) representing the largest number of Australians originally from another country. These countries were the United Kingdom, New Zealand, China, India, Italy, Vietnam, the Philippines and South Africa (2011).

Of the 548,370 people identified as being of Aboriginal and/or Torres Strait Islander origin in the same statistics from 2011, 90 per cent were of Aboriginal origin, 6 per cent were of Torres Strait Islander origin and 4 per cent identified as both. In the Northern Territory, just under 27 per cent identified themselves as of Aboriginal and/or Torres Strait Islander origin. In all other jurisdictions, 4 per cent or less of the population identified themselves in this way. Victoria had the lowest proportion at 0.7 per cent of the state total.

CAROL CARTER

You are likely to need to form relationships and facilitate engaging learning environments that include a variety of perspectives based on such factors as gender, culture, spirituality, race, ethnicity, socio-economic circumstances, learning needs and language. Having children from diverse backgrounds in your educational settings is a rich resource for learning and teaching, and intercultural understanding. Chapter 15 focuses on inclusive practice for diversity and provides details on how teachers respond to the challenges of diversity.

Here is a combination of what various pre-service teachers have talked about observing in relation to inclusive relationships while they were on practicum.

Practicum experiences

I observed educators engaging in discussions with children about the similarities and differences among people and connecting children to everyday experiences. For instance, explaining how we are all people and have traits that make us similar such as emotions, eating and sleeping. Yet discussing the different ways in which we behave according to the cultures of our families where possible, educators encouraged children to notice differences and learn about different cultures. For example, 'Hussein's mother wears a special head scarf called a hijab. That is different from Leo's mother, who does not wear anything on her head'.

Adding simple cultural dress-ups in the home corner, playing cultural music at meal times, singing songs in different languages children may know or reading stories from different cultures are simple ways that teachers can use to encourage young children's cultural awareness and enhance teacher–child relationships.

Here are some examples of groups who were frequently excluded from or marginalised within education (UNESCO, 2009, p.7):

- Abused children
- Child labourers
- Refugees or displaced children
- Religious minorities
- Migrants
- Poverty-stricken children
- Child domestic workers
- Girls
- Ethnic minorities
- Linguistic minorities
- Children in conflict zones
- Street children
- Indigenous people
- Children with disabilities
- Women
- Rural populations
- Nomadic children
- HIV/AIDS orphans.

Equity is also a key to inclusion and learning and teaching relationships with children from diverse backgrounds. Equity is not the same as equality where all children are treated the same. Equity is about the qualities of fairness, justice and impartiality. Equity means giving as much opportunity to one child as another. If you look at the picture of the three children looking over the fence, you will see that each child is given a different level of support in order to see over the fence, but they have all been given a fair chance to look over the fence.

Bourdieu's (1986) concept of different capitals (including cultural and social capital) as discussed in Chapters 3 and 14, is significant for education and educational relationships. Cultural capital is the knowledge and skills gained through family background and education. It is our cultural knowledge that serves as the currency to help us navigate a culture and alters our experiences and the opportunities available to us. Social capital is the social networks and memberships, knowledge and connections that enable people to accompany their goals and extend their influences.

A similar concept is 'funds of knowledge', which, as discussed in Chapter 3, are culturally specific skills and knowledges required for the effective operating of individuals, families and communities (Moll et al., 1992, p.133). Integrating funds of knowledge into classroom activities creates a richer and more highly scaffolded learning experience for students.

People have different amounts and kinds of capital that they bring to the 'game of life', but their criteria for success and classroom relationships should not be capital dependent. Children with different capitals and funds of knowledge should be empowered to use

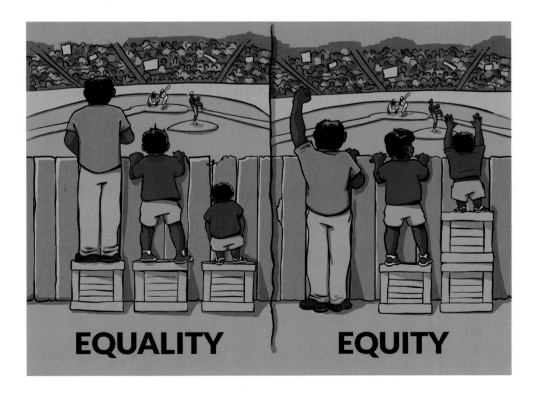

EQUALITY   **EQUITY**

CAROL CARTER

these resources as insiders and not made to feel like outsiders where their cultural and social capital is different from the dominant cultural and social capital in the learning environment (Gee, 2008). Children should be empowered to use their own funds of knowledge and develop these further through the classroom relationships that are embraced. Where relationships of mutual respect and trust are established; where there is joint ownership of space and reciprocal decision making; where children's ideas, opinions and capitals count; and where teacher–learner interaction is bi-directional, there will be teacher–children relationships of inclusion and equity.

When teachers move away from their role as expert, they can come to know their students and the families of their students in new and distinct ways. We begin to see that the students have rich cultural and cognitive resources from their home backgrounds and that these resources can and should be used in their classroom in order to provide culturally responsive and meaningful lessons that tap into students' prior knowledge. Intentional teaching and active learning are reciprocal components of successful adult–child interactions. Particularly within early childhood contexts, we need to plan carefully for when and how to intervene so that we are not overly intrusive or domineering. Intervention, not interference and control, can be used in teacher–child relationships. An alert and sensitive adult is a participant–observer who knows when to become involved in the learning process and when to leave children to shape their own learning. This also means becoming skilled at identifying the intention behind signals sent by children.

This example from Thompson (2005, p.6) is, in my view, a fine example of how the teacher waits intentionally, observes carefully and selects the exact right moment to intervene through questions, with quality, creative sharing taking place.

Professional practice

A four-year-old slowly pushes both hands through a wide smear of blue paint on the large painting before her. Swirling her fingers around and around, she is so engrossed that she does not notice her teacher sit quietly beside her. Finally, the child pauses.

Leaning back from her creation, she notices her teacher smiling at her. 'I see you're working very hard,' the teacher says. 'Can you tell me about your painting?' Looking up with a shy smile, the girl says in a soft but animated voice: 'The wind came and blew ALL around!'

Family → Teacher

The child as active agent

The child, as active agent, is at the centre of the learning and teaching relationship, with the quality of the teacher–child relationship in the early years impacting significantly on engagement in learning and socialisation in later life.

STOP AND REFLECT

- What do you think are the most important aspects of teacher–child relationships?
- What other words can you think of that are part of the teacher–child relationship?
- How would you provide children with a sense of belonging in an educational setting?

Teacher–family relationships

Learning outcomes are most likely to be achieved when early child educators work in partnership with families.

(DEEWR, 2009, p.12)

As the next chapter is focused on working with families, this section in chapter 13 will simply highlight some of the key issues around teacher–family relationships. Working with families and communities will be extended and developed further in the next chapter. The importance of partnerships with families is continually emphasised within documentation, particularly related to early childhood, as in the 2009 quotation above. Indeed, so important are partnerships and the need to ensure that the focus is on relationships and partnerships, that within the revised Victorian Early Years Learning and Development Framework (VEYLDF, 2016), 'Family-Centred Practice' has been renamed 'Partnerships with families'. The significance of families in children's lives is recognised throughout the EYLF as well.

As a teacher in the future in an early childhood setting you will need to interact with parents, or primary carers, every day. Different people may act as the children's primary caregivers, including birth parents, adoptive parents, grandparents and foster parents. Young children seeing parents (or caregivers) welcomed and comfortable in the early childhood setting will themselves feel secure in the environment.

There is no one blueprint for parent partnerships because of the complex nature of working with different human beings. We need to provide multiple ways for families to choose how to be partners. However, it is crucial for teachers to be constantly linking, networking and communicating with parents and to be assisting parents to move beyond mere involvement in their children's education to partnerships where they work together with the teacher. Strong adult–adult partnerships underpin and facilitate all other learning and teaching relationships. Teachers are often the first contact when parents experience difficulty. Providing welcoming environments, communicating and negotiating are the first key steps to effective parent–teacher partnerships.

Outcomes that are most likely to be achieved with strong teacher–parent partnerships include valuing each other's knowledge of each child; valuing each other's contribution to and roles in each child's life; trusting each other and communicating freely and respectfully with each other; sharing insights and perspectives about each child; engaging in shared decision making; and modelling and practice inclusiveness.

Children whose parents are involved in their learning are more likely to have an easier transition from kindergarten/pre-school to school, higher levels of confidence, more positive attitudes to learning and better learning outcomes. The evidence suggests successful family partnerships are achieved when:

- early childhood services and schools engage with all families
- families have a say in and can directly contribute to programs such as extra-curricular activities
- there is a shared understanding of the importance of academic and personal development between families, early childhood services and schools.

Successful family partnerships significantly impact across all stages of children's lives, including:

- better learning and development outcomes in the early years and in school
- increased engagement in learning and development

CAROL CARTER

- smoother transition to and from school
- higher retention rates of children in education
- increased confidence, social skills, emotional resilience, communication skills, and general wellbeing
- a reduction in the effects of disadvantage among children from low socio-economic backgrounds.

Family partnerships

There are seven dimensions of family partnerships that teachers need to take into account.

1 *Communicating:* Engaging families and staff in regular, meaningful two-way communication about children and young people's learning needs
2 *Connecting learning at home:* Involving families in their child's learning activities at home, including learning activities that involve the families' culture, history and language
3 *Building community and identity:* Ensuring early childhood services and school practices, policies and programs reflect and value the diversity of families in their community
4 *Recognising the role of the family:* Recognising families as the first and primary educators of their children. Acknowledging the lasting influence families have on their children's attitudes and achievements
5 *Consultative decision making:* Facilitating family participation in consultation and decision-making as participants in governance and advocacy through parent associations, committees and other forums
6 *Collaborating:* Developing relationships with the not-for-profit sector, community groups and business to assist families' abilities to improve learning and development outcomes for children and young people
7 *Participating:* Including families in day-to-day aspects as well as in philosophies, goal-setting and so on.

Each person involved in the parent–teacher partnership may experience different aspects of the partnerships that are valuable. Teachers may experience an increased knowledge of each child, may benefit when their efforts are valued through feedback and may have additional parental resources for enriched learning experiences that link directly to the capital and funds of knowledge of the children. Parents may experience feelings of support for the ways in which they are engaging with their children; they may benefit from the knowledge and skills of the teachers, who are professionals and experts in their field and they may develop an enhanced sense of self-esteem through participating as partners and having their ideas and concerns taken seriously. Children may experience a sense of security and self-worth in a new and changing environment that their parents are welcomed in and are an important part of. Through parent–teacher collaboration and communication, children may experience knowledgeable and consistent responses (Gestwicki, 2010, pp.173–6).

Barriers to effective partnerships

A lack of communication and understanding, and ignoring differences and diverse needs and values, leads to barriers to effective partnerships. There are a number of other barriers and challenges to effective partnerships (Gestwicki, 2010). Some are specific to teachers, some are specific to parents and some impact on both teachers and parents. Time constraints, 'busy-ness' and stress (including from parents and teachers working long hours with little flexibility) are factors that can impact negatively on parent–teacher partnerships. Issues of trust and power (e.g. leading to negative judgments about family or teacher capabilities), as discussed earlier in the chapter; ideas of parent involvement that are no longer useful (e.g. offering traditional forms and times that no longer suit busy parents); overly close relationships with parents (friendships that cause biases, the exclusion of others and skew relationships with other parents); or too distant relationships (parties find it difficult to communicate with each other or teachers sets themselves up as 'experts' who have no need or time to share with parents).

Differences in backgrounds, values, experiences, views on roles, and in viewing children's needs as well as personal factors (e.g. introverted temperaments) can have an impact on teacher–parent relationships. A parent's own experiences in educational settings (positive or negative) set up some expectations for their interactions with teachers for their own child. Prior experiences with families may influence teachers' expectations. Teachers or families may find it challenging to identify and communicate key experiences, ideas or issues. Families or teachers may be uncomfortable about communicating their needs, or do not have enough fluency in the language of learning and teaching.

Challenges

Challenges should be viewed as opportunities for early childhood services, schools and families to find new ways of working together.

Challenges that families may face include:

- transport difficulties
- their own experiences of education
- language and cultural differences
- parents' health and wellbeing
- financial circumstances
- confidence about their skills and abilities.

Early childhood services and schools also face challenges. Such challenges might include:

- complex working environments
- lack of knowledge on the research and importance of family partnerships
- limited understanding of the contribution families can make to children's outcomes
- little understanding of how to effectively engage with parents and minimal preparation for this role
- language and cultural differences
- power imbalances.

Forming effective relationships

Following are some points to consider when negotiating parent–teacher relationships.

- Every person is worth valuing, honouring and respecting.
- All parents want their child to be and feel safe and for their child to do the best they can.
- All parents want to feel valued and respected and to have some influence over what happens to their child.

CAROL CARTER

Effective teacher–parent relationships include active participation and involvement, with each person involved contributing and being kept informed; ensuring that, no matter who has the final responsibility, each person in the relationship has a chance to have their say; and that each person is involved in deciding what will be done and how. Honesty is crucial and neither person should try to hide anything from the other. Each person should have confidence in the other and know that they value working with them. The teacher should find out what people know and can contribute to the learning environment and the collective interest of teachers, parents and children should be considered. Teachers should create a fair environment where they do not give preferential treatment to any individual. They are there to, primarily, meet the needs of children and parents not their own needs. The teacher's first responsibility is to act ethically and professionally and not be hampered by considerations of personal friendships and biases (Hood, 2012).

Some steps in relationship building, particularly in first encounters with parents, that could be considered are:

- approach parents gently—initially some 'small talk' for uncertain parents can be helpful
- find out how people like to be addressed—perhaps begin by offering that staff are called by first names
- give choices to nurture relationships—choices should be neutral and without bias
- focus and concentrate attention on the person being addressed—if timing seems to be inappropriate, suggest another time to meet
- each person should use clear language to share information and ideas and avoid possibilities of misunderstanding. Use of professional jargon may lead to misunderstandings and create barriers
- active listening is essential—being acutely receptive to what the parent is saying; showing through your body language and telling them that you are listening; making eye contact (if culturally appropriate); avoiding looking around and looking interested
- respond empathetically and attempt to reflect what you think parents are saying and feeling
- prompt, extend and explore by using such questions as, Can you tell me more about …? and reflecting back accurately (e.g. You say …)
- use appropriate, often open, questions that allow parents to express themselves freely (e.g. what did you do then?)
- be comfortable with pauses and pausing
- use summarising statements that pull together what the teacher and parent have been saying
- to negotiate successfully, we need to believe that the other person has a right to have a view, even if we cannot agree with it
- separate the person from the problem
- listen and show them that you intend to work with them because you value, respect and acknowledge them
- focus on interests, not positions
- look for underlying issues and wishes on both sides
- generate a variety of possibilities before making a decision (e.g. Let's brainstorm some ideas and work out what will work for …)
- define objective standards as the criteria for making the decision (e.g. How will we know if it has worked? What will we see happening?)

With children as the central focus of socialisation and learning, families (as primary agents) and teachers (as secondary agents) work collaboratively to create the best possible outcomes and supportive learning communities for children.

STOP AND REFLECT

- When have you felt welcome, or unwelcome, in an educational environment?
- What do you think contributed to your feeling welcome or what could people in that environment have done to make you feel more welcome?

Family

Other, such as Media

The Child as active agent

Teacher

Peers

Peer socialisation

Peer groups are significant to human development, learning and wellbeing because they satisfy certain basic needs: the need to belong to a group and the need to develop a sense of self (Berns, 2013). Through socialisation and relationship-building with peers and others, children develop a sense of belonging to groups and communities (DEEWR, 2009).

Young children spend a majority of their time at home, making these settings their primary environments (Bronfenbrenner & Morris, 1998). Even though the time spent at home may have changed significantly for many children, it is still considered to be their primary environment. When they are in secondary environments, such as an educational setting, positive peer relationships provide emotional support and can help to foster moral understanding. The feelings of satisfaction and security that most children gain from interacting and forming relationships with peers outweigh any friendship challenges children may have. The social skills learnt within peer relationships help children create a strong foundation in the classroom. A positive outlook on future relationships can increase school engagement and equips children with pro-social skills that will be important throughout their lives (Stuhlman & Pianta, 2009). **Pro-social skills** refers to a set of skills linked to cooperation, helping others and sharing, which develops across all ages but begins in infancy. Pro-social skills include self-regulation, empathy, turn taking, compromise and respectfulness.

Peer relationships provide opportunities for interaction with 'equals' and spaces for the acquisition of skills including collaborative, pro-social, cognitive, psychological and physical skills (Berns, 2013, pp.259–61). You will have read about the theories of attachment of Bowlby

pro-social skills a set of skills linked to cooperation, helping others and sharing, which develops across all ages but begins in infancy. Pro-social skills include self-regulation, empathy, turn taking, compromise and respectfulness.

CAROL CARTER

and others in Chapter 3. Children with attachment issues tend to have difficulty forging peer relationships (Berns, 2013). Especially vital are the skills needed to initiate and maintain social relationships and to resolve social conflicts, including communication, compromise and negotiation (Asher et al., 1996). Children who lack ongoing peer involvement may also miss opportunities to build a sense of social self-confidence.

Socialisation is a lifelong process where we learn about social expectations and how to interact with others. Peer groups allow children to form relationships and learn without the direction of adults. Friendships are formed from a very early age. Young children (from about two to four years old) increasingly want more peer and less caregiver attention. Most infants and toddlers meet peers on a regular basis, and many are able to experience long-lasting relationships with particular peers that start at birth. By around six months of age, infants can communicate with other infants by smiling, touching and babbling. By the time they are around two years of age, they show both pro-social and aggressive behaviour with peers, with some toddlers clearly being more aggressive than others.

Children's friendships and friendship groups can also be in a constant state of flux. While some friendships may persist for lengthy periods of time, it is not uncommon for children to move in and out of friendships and make such statements as, 'You're not my friend' and 'I'm not playing with you' when there may have been a strong connection with the child to whom this remark is addressed even moments before the remark is made. The same can be said of statements such as 'they won't let me play' or 'she won't give me the ball', which are constant refrains in pre-school settings. Some level of conflict is a natural occurrence in children's lives, and frequently among adults as well. Children who are able to manage conflict are happier, have deeper, more long-lasting friendships and are more successful in learning environments. Sometimes children resolve these issues quickly for themselves; or skilled teachers can support children to cooperate and play with each other again, sometimes in a matter of seconds. However, the most useful and beneficial course of action is to work with children and help them to acquire the skills they need to solve relationship challenges and resolve conflicts. Educators need to scaffold children to develop the capacity to listen to each other and to see each other's points of view.

For some children, however, peer relationships continue to be more complex and persistently challenging, with issues such as exclusion, bullying and antisocial behaviour. Some children are actively rejected by peers. Others are simply ignored, or neglected. Children who are rejected by peers display low rates of prosocial behaviour, high rates of aggressive, disruptive, inattentive, immature or impulsive behaviour and social anxiety (Berns, 2013, p.278). Some children (shy, fearful or anxious children) withdraw from peer interactions and, in this way, their ability to gain acceptance and make friends is limited. Children's prosocial behaviours, temperaments and abilities to regulate their emotions, physical responses and behaviours lead to social acceptance. The extent to which children are seen to be similar to their peers also fosters social acceptance. On the other hand, children tend to encounter social rejection when they are perceived to be dissimilar from their peers. This may occur, for example, when children are of a different ethnic group or sex, are seen to be physically unattractive or are newcomers to their current educational setting. Family issues can have damaging effects on children's peer relations. For example, children of divorcing parents may act out feelings of anger at school, eliciting rejection from peers in the process. Children with family problems such as parental alcoholism may be reluctant to bring friends home, avoiding close friendships as a result.

It is sometimes believed that, while peer relationships are crucial during adolescence, peer relationships are less important in early childhood when strong bonds with family members are more influential. However, this is not the case, as early experiences of not being accepted by peers and having difficulties creating relationships with peers, have negative consequences for children's subsequent social and emotional development.

We need to teach children valuable skills to help them get along with their peers. For example, we can show them how to play and communicate well with others, control feelings of aggression and solve problems that may arise in social situations. We can help children to develop social skills through such avenues as stories, pictures or working with puppets, and we can encourage the practice of these skills (e.g. through role plays and games). We can also deliberately and intentionally teach children how to deal with various social situations such as sharing a toy, taking turns and apologising. We can provide opportunities for play that reinforce positive interactions. We can show children how to initiate play through approaching other children, asking questions and supporting their peers. Large groups can be threatening to children who lack self-confidence. Shy children may therefore benefit from opportunities to interact with peers in small groups.

Learning communities

Learning communities are made up of people who share a common purpose. They collaborate to draw on individual strengths, respect a variety of perspectives, and actively promote learning opportunities. The outcomes are the creation of a vibrant, synergistic environment, enhanced potential for all members, and the possibility that new knowledge will be created.

(Kilpatrick, Barrett & Jones, 2012, p.11)

If we examine the above comprehensive definition of learning communities, the first important aspect is the idea of a learning community consisting of people who have a cooperative, collective shared relationship without which the learning community would not be able to function effectively. We need to recognise that the group of people who make up a learning community may have different cultural identities, backgrounds, belief systems, values and perspectives. What binds the group together is the sharing of common interests and purposes that lead to interaction and communication and a sense of identifying with and belonging to the group. Cooperation and combining of ideas and thoughts within a learning community has the effect of producing something greater than the ideas and thoughts of one individual. It is an extension of the idea that 'two heads are better than one'. To become a member of a particular community, and engage with community members, we need to learn the rules, conventions and cultural dimensions of the particular learning community. As a 'vibrant' environment the culture of the community is not static and is continually invented and re-invented by individuals and groups within the learning community.

Two types of societal relationships (Tönnies & Hart, 2001) have been referred to as *Gemeinschaft* (close community or communal society) and *Gesellschaft* (distant community or associational society). The enabling aspects of a small *Gemeinschaft* community are that it consists of a close-knit culture with a small number of people located in a self-contained, small geographic area. The people in this type of community know each other well and have

CAROL CARTER

face-to-face contact with each other. There is a strong sense of belonging and identity within a mutually supportive community committed to the needs and interests of the group. The disenabling, negative aspects of such a small, tightly connected community are that there may be a focus on conformity to the group and therefore little scope for individuality or respecting diversity. 'In groups/out groups' may exist within dominant power relations and structures. The *Gesellschaft* communities are large scale with distant relationships based on exchange of information. A sense of identity is not connected to a particular place or location. It is a culture based on 'me'—what I want, what I can get—on individualism and the freedom to use the associational society how I wish and to choose to connect or not connect to the distant community as I wish. This means it may be more impersonal, selfish, de-humanising and fragmented.

What does all this mean to early childhood relationships and settings?

As teachers and future teachers, we need to build and foster learning communities in early childhood settings that embrace and include children, staff, family and wider community members. These learning communities need to utilise the enabling aspects of small local communities as well as accessing the broad knowledge base and resources of large-scale associations and connections. Creating supportive learning communities as well as interacting and building relationships with local communities and community members are important interrelated aspects of community engagement.

Creating effective learning communities and community engagement is an essential part of what we do as early childhood teachers. These communities provide members with a sense of ownership and instil a sense of community by forging quality relationships and strong connections and bonds. It is central to the themes contained in the EYLF—for example, within the statement 'Children learn about themselves and construct their own identity within the context of their families and communities' (DEEWR, 2009, p.20).

For some children and families, early childhood settings may provide their first contact with a wider community beyond the home. As Bronfenbrenner's (2005) bio-ecological system states, spheres of connection become less personalised as they expand outwards. Teachers in early childhood settings can help develop supportive community relationships as well as play a part in connecting families to services in their local community. Community engagement can provide teachers with a wealth of rich resources and information. Community knowledge and expertise may also provide teachers with additional perspectives for understanding and connecting with children and families within their particular learning communities and can link learning to real-life experiences. Community engagement will differ from context to context and will depend on such aspects as who the people are in the educational setting; what their and the local communities' needs are; and their commitment to regular, genuine, ongoing engagement. Early childhood settings can be engaged with communities at different levels ranging from extensive communal projects, such as a sustainability project, to inviting a family member to share their expertise. In a learning community, leaders and participants work together to help everyone learn. All those involved respect the diversity of interests, beliefs and knowledge that exist among the community members.

Here is a combination of what various Initial Teacher Education students have talked about in relation to family participation in learning communities they observed while on practicum.

Professional practice

Families should have options and multiple entry points for how they choose to participate. On practicums, I have seen a mother, who was a dentist, come and visit the day care centre to teach the children about hygiene and I saw a grandfather who was a gardener come in to plant trees with the children. At the kindergarten, opportunities existed for parents to engage in consultative decision making via involvement in the parent committee and contributing to the centre's philosophy, goals, policies and programs. The parent foyer room stood out for me while I was on my practicum placement. This room was filled with information relating to families, beliefs and practices, community groups and events in the area, effective transitions to school and a range of information relevant to the lives of children and families in the centre.

Professional relationships and communities of practice

In educational settings, to ensure quality education, professionals from a variety of backgrounds need to work together in a cohesive, systematic and inclusive manner to achieve the most desired outcomes for children and families (Lumsden, 2005; Bruder, 2010). This is best achieved by the professionals in educational settings seeing themselves as part of a learning community, or a **community of practice**, and forming collaborative relationships with the people, or groups, who are a part of that community.

A community of practice is a group of people who come together informally or formally and share expertise, commitment to a particular field of practice, such as early childhood education, or are involved in a joint enterprise, such as running a day care centre. They learn how to improve their practice as they interact regularly with others. These groups of people share common concerns, 'experiences and knowledge in free-flowing creative ways that foster new approaches to solving problems' (Wenger & Snyder, 2000, p.140).

When we work with others to plan, teach and learn in an educational environment, it is helpful to our professional relationships as well as the quality of learning and teaching, if we share and acquire expertise from within our own community of practice, as well as broader communities of practice (such as educational associations and organisations, other centres, kindergartens or schools in our local area). Relationships and sharing information across communities of practice and settings can be vital. For example, an understanding of school children's existing knowledge and experiences, including those gained in prior-to-school settings, will contribute to smooth transitions as well as have an impact on how well the schools can cater for individual needs.

It is important to build a community of practice that does not promote only the views of those who are most dominant. Instead, there should be sharing of the gained experience and different specialist knowledge of the community members. Professional relationships that are genuinely committed to ensuring quality education and care and to achieving important outcomes for children will function and flourish in an environment that enables constructive discussion, decision making and positive criticism. Strong early childhood

community of practice a group of people who come together informally or formally and share expertise, commitment to a particular field of practice, such as early childhood education, or are involved in a joint enterprise, such as running a day care centre.

CAROL CARTER

professional relationships in communities of practice enable professionals to understand and appreciate each other's skills and ways of viewing the world; communally problem solve and plan effective, consistent approaches to children and families; and develop authentic, holistic learning pathways.

As with the other types of relationships discussed in this chapter, communication, trust, mutual respect, shared goals and a sense of connectedness are vital ingredients for successful professional partnerships. Open communication is essential and needs to happen in such a way that individual needs and differences are openly acknowledged. Effective communication needs to be supported by the structures and routines that are set up in educational settings. This includes creating time and opportunities to communicate, share and plan collaboratively and cooperatively.

Cardini (2006, p.412) argues that although collaboration is theorised about and desired, cooperation in professional partnerships (including between pre-service teachers and their host teachers) is very hard to achieve; in practice partnerships tend to show unbalanced relationships between different people depending on positions of power. Challenges may arise from competitive relationships where partners may have different explicit and implicit interests.

I am reminded of my first year of teaching in a foundation class with two other colleagues who formed my community of practice. We would plan a frame together and then adapt it to our own needs. If teacher A and I made or collected resources and activities, we would share them. If teacher B found or made anything she would keep them to herself. In addition, teacher B would extend and improve on the activities we had shared with her but would not let us see or use any of these improvements. The explicit reason she gave, when asked by teacher A, was that she was 'not good at sharing', though implicitly, I believe she wanted to be seen to be a 'better teacher' and ultimately to achieve a leadership position. Perhaps she didn't believe that a leader could also be a collaborator who cooperatively developed and shared 'expertise'.

Challenges to communication and negotiation of meaning may also stem from people in the professional relationships having different backgrounds, philosophies, expertise or expectation. Professionals with different backgrounds may, for example, have different ways of viewing, describing and sharing the complexities of early childhood learning and development (Wesley & Buysse, 2001; Lumsden, 2005; Weiner & Murawski, 2005).

While there are undoubtedly challenges in working with early childhood professionals, there are also enormous benefits of working in partnership with other professionals who have rich, different backgrounds, experience and expertise, which make it essential to pursue these working relationships no matter how challenging they may be. It encourages us to reflect more deeply on our own practices, provides us with a wide repertoire of skills, strengths and expertise and exposes us to other ways of being and viewing the world of early childhood. It seems to me that we need to move away from notions of constant and complete agreement that tend to drive actions and decisions in the workplace. We do need to recognise power dynamics and issues of dominance and establish working relationships in which disagreement, struggle and dissenting voices are encouraged in discussion. This, of course, needs to take place in a spirit of respectful dialogue and sensitivity.

Here is a combination of what various Initial Teacher Education students have talked about experiencing on practicum in relation to professional relationships in a community of practice.

Professional practice

The partnership I most enjoyed observing was the partnership between educators in an early learning centre. The rooms looked very different from one another, the dynamics between teachers and assisting teachers were very different and the ways in which they went about programming and documenting appeared completely different. Yet the commitment they all had to understanding the children in their care was incredible. I had the privilege of sitting in on a meeting with the kindergarten teachers and though it was quite obvious that there were things they disagreed about, their shared goal of seeking to understand how children were experiencing their teaching and learning was maintained as the priority and their critical feedback of each other's work was shared and valued as a way to grow and further develop their programs.

There is so much going on in these centres before the children even arrive. The staff are setting new and different experiences so their environment is inviting and different every day. I had the opportunity to see the networking and collaboration that occurred between staff members. They constantly worked as a team, covering each other for breaks, sharing information about observations of the children and working together to create appealing experiences for the children. Observing how the staff all work together had helped me to see that much more can be achieved when people work together as a community.

Our own community of practice is generally situated within a specific context and culture—for example, a pre-school that has a particular culture of learning and teaching. The idea of professional experience, or practicum, is located in 'situated learning' where, in a community of practice, knowledge is presented and acquired in real, authentic contexts, within settings and situations that require and involve that knowledge. Social interaction and collaboration are essential components of situated learning. During practicum, you become part of a specific community of practice where you need to learn the practice of teaching but also the rules, routines and beliefs that function within that specific community. A pre-service teacher, or a beginning graduate teacher, may engage initially in what Lave and Wenger (1991) term 'legitimate peripheral participation'.

As the beginner or novice moves from the periphery (or edges) of a community to the centre, they become more trusted, active and engaged within the community and are viewed as a knowledgeable 'expert' who fully belongs to the particular community of practice (Lave & Wenger, 1991). It is the beginning stages of this process that need to be carefully negotiated as, for example, practicum relationships rely on close collaboration between the different people involved (Turner & Sharp, 2006)—different perspectives, expectations and levels of perceived expertise. Different people within these relationships may have different biases and interests, and relationships sometimes become competitive and defensive, rather than collaborative and proactive. Once again, effective communication and the achievement of common understanding are crucial, as well as the re-framing of these relationships as cooperative partnerships rather than a hierarchical teacher and learner model.

CAROL CARTER

SUMMARY

- Classroom relationships are significant for engaging and motivating children. By examining different types of relationships, recurring themes emerge—for example, maintaining open, effective, ongoing communication; actively, genuinely and positively listening and participating; committing to working together; building reciprocal trust and respect; sharing appropriate aspects of ourselves; displaying empathy and care alongside efficiency; building on a sense of community and belonging; and moving away from established patterns of communication, power and privilege.
- All relationships take time to grow and need to be nurtured within reflective conversational spaces that honour diversity and do not exclude people based on cultural and social capital, or funds of knowledge. Relationships also need to be maintained, and their maintenance requires critical reflection on how, why and what makes these relationships work. We need to focus on ways of empowering others in the relationship and sharing our strengths and experiences.
- Connections where we can share parts of ourselves and where, as in the story of Nicholas and myself, we can laugh together and feel a sense of belonging and community, will have a profound effect on learning and teaching and our capacities to build genuine, strong relationships.

FURTHER REFLECTIONS

Why are relationships so important?

These questions might help you answer this reflection question:

- Why do you think people want to form bonds and connections?
- When are relationships most needed or valued?
- What do you think would happen to a child who did not form any relationships within a classroom community?

GROUP DISCUSSION QUESTIONS

Here are some discussion questions that can be used to reflect on relationships in early childhood. In reflecting on these questions for yourself or contributing to class and group discussions you need to use your own opinions and experiences as well as what you have learnt from reading and engaging with this chapter.

1 In what ways do you think relationships contribute to quality early childhood education?
2 If you were asked to provide advice to a teacher who was experiencing challenges in building relationships, what would you say to help them improve their relationships with:
   - children?
   - families?
   - communities?
   - work colleagues and other professionals?

CLASS EXERCISE

Focusing on the role of the teacher, describe and reflect on the characteristics of effective partnerships between the teacher and two or more of the following: family, community, other teachers, and individual or groups of children. In the piece of writing, reflect on the benefits of forming these partnerships and discuss the challenges faced and strategies used when developing and maintaining these partnerships, informed by current and emerging theory. Try also to reflect on essential skills and qualities required by the teacher that enhance these partnerships and inform effective teaching and learning outcomes for all children.

FURTHER READING

Chapter 14 links to this chapter. As such, much of the suggested reading to be found in Chapter 14 also applies to this chapter.

REFERENCES

Anning, A., Cullen, J. & Fleer, M. (2009) *Early Childhood Education: Society and Culture,* (2nd edn), London: Sage Publications.

Asher, S., Parker, J. & Walker, D. (1996) 'Distinguishing Friendship from Acceptance: Implications for Intervention and Assessment', in W. Bukowski, A. Newcomb & W. Hartup (eds) *The Company They Keep: Friendships in Childhood and Adolescence. Cambridge Studies in Social and Emotional Development*, Cambridge, UK: Cambridge Univ. Press, pp. 336–405.

Australian Bureau of Statistics (2011), www.abs.gov.au/AUSSTATS/abs@nfs/mf/3417.055.

Australian Bureau of Statistics (2016), www.abs.gov.au/Population

Berns, R. (2013) *Child, Family, School, Community; Socialization and Support,* (9th edn), Belmont, USA: Wadsworth Cengage Learning.

Bourdieu, P. (1986) The Forms of Capital, in J. Richardson (ed.) *Handbook of Theory and Research for the Sociology of Education*, New York: Greenwood.

Bronfenbrenner, U. (2005) *Making Human Beings Human: Bio-ecological Perspectives on Human Development*, Thousand Oaks: Sage Publications.

Bronfenbrenner, U. & Morris, P. (1998) The Ecology of Developmental Processes, in R.M. Lerner (ed.) *Theoretical Models of Human Development, 1*(5), New York: Wiley.

Bruder, M. (2010) 'Early Childhood Intervention: a Promise to Children and Families for Their Future', *Exceptional Children, 76*(3): 339–55.

Cardini, A. (2006) 'An Analysis of the Rhetoric and Practice of Educational Partnerships in the UK: an Arena of Complexities, Tensions and Power', *Journal of Education Policy, 21*(4), 393–415.

Center on the Developing Child (2004) 'Young Children Develop in an Environment of Relationships', Working paper 1, National Scientific Council on the Developing Child, Harvard: Harvard University.

Connor, J. (2011) *EYLF Professional Learning Program: Intentional Teaching*, Australia: Early Childhood Australia.

Department of Education, Employment and Workplace Relations (DEEWR) (2009) *Belonging, Being & Becoming: the Early Years Learning Framework for Australia.* ACT, Australia: Commonwealth of Australia.

Department of Education and Training (Victoria) (DET)/Victorian Curriculum and Assessment Authority (VCCA) (2016) *Victorian Early Years Learning and Development Framework: For all children from birth to eight years*. State of Victoria, Australia: Department of Education and Training.

Early Child Australia. (2012). *National Quality Standard Professional Learning Programme: Sustained, shared thinking* www.earlychildhoodaustralia.org.au/nqsplp/wpcontent/uploads/2012/09/NQS_PLP_E-Newsletter_No43.pdf

Foucault, M. (1988) *The Final Foucault,* Cambridge, MA: MIT Press.

Gee, J. (2008) *Social Linguistics and Literacies: Ideology in Discourses,* (4th edn), London: Routledge.

Gestwicki, C. (2010) Developmentally Appropriate Practice, (4th edn), South Melbourne: Cengage Learning.

Giddens, A. & Sutton, P. (2013) *Sociology,* (7th edn), Cambridge: Polity Press.

Hattie, J. & Yates, G. (2014) *Visible Learning and the Science of How We Learn*, UK: Routledge.

Hohmann, M. & Weikart, D. (1995) *Educating Young Children: Active Learning Practices for Preschool and Child Care Programs*, Washington DC: High/Scope Press.

CAROL CARTER

Hood, M. (2012) 'Partnerships: Working Together in Early Childhood Settings', *Research in Practice Series*, *19*(1). Deakin West, ACT: Early Childhood Australia.

Jordan, B. (2009) in A. Anning, J. Cullen & M. Fleer, (eds), *Early Childhood Education: Society and Culture,* (2nd edn), London: Sage Publications.

Kemmis, S. (2009) Action Research as a Practice-based Practice, *Educational Action Research*, *17*(3), pp.463–74.

Kilpatrick, S., Barrett, M. & Jones, T. (2012) 'Defining Learning Communities', Discussion Paper, Tasmania: University of Tasmania.

Kohn, A. (1996) *Beyond Discipline: from Compliance to Community*, Alexandria, VA: ASCD (Association for Supervision and Curriculum Development).

Kuczynski L. & Parkin C. (2007) 'Agency and Bidirectionality in Socialization: Interactions, Transactions, and Relational Dialectics', in J. Grusec & P. Hastings (eds) *Handbook of Socialization Research,* New York, NY: Guildford, pp.259–83.

Lave, J. & Wenger, E. (1991) *Situated Learning: Legitimate Peripheral Participation*, Cambridge: Cambridge University Press.

Lumsden, E. (2005) 'Joined Up Thinking in Practice: an Exploration of Professional Collaboration', In T. Waller (ed.) *An Introduction to Early Childhood: a Multidisciplinary Approach,* London: Paul Chapman Publishing, pp.39–54.

MacNaughton, G. & Williams G. (2008) *Teaching Young Children: Choices in Theory and Practice,* UK: McGraw-Hill Publication.

McDonald, T. (2010) *Classroom Management: Engaging Students in Learning*, Melbourne: Oxford University Press.

Mead, G H. (1967) *Mind, Self, and Society from the Standpoint of a Social Behaviorist*, Chicago: The University of Chicago Press.

Moll, L. Amanti, C. Neff, D. & Gonzales, N. (1992) *Funds of Knowledge for Teaching: Using Aa Qualitative Approach to Connect Homes and Classrooms, Theory into Practice*, http://uwyosocialliteracies.pbworks.com/f/MollFunds.pdf

Percy-Smith, B. & Thomas, N. (2006) *A Handbook of Children and Young People's Participation: Perspectives from Theory and Practice*, London: Routledge.

Ramsden, P. (1992) *Learning to Teach in Higher Education*, London: Routledge.

Reed, M. & Sansoyer, P. (2012), 'Quality Improvement: Integrated Working', in M. Reed & N. Canning (eds) *Implementing Quality Improvement and Change in the Early Years*, UK: SAGE, Chapter 3.

Roorda, D.L., Koomen, H.M.Y., Spilt, Jantine L. & Oort, F.J. (2011) 'The Influence of Affective Teacher–Student Relationships on Students' School Engagement and Achievement: A Meta-Analytic Approach', *Review of Educational Research, 81*(4): 493–529.

Siraj-Blatchford, I. & Manni, L. (2008) '"Would You Like to Tidy Up Now?" An analysis of adult questioning in the English Foundation Stage', *Early Years: An International Journal of Research and Development*, *28*(1): 5–22.

Stonehouse, H. & Gonzales-Mena, J. (2004) *Making Links: a Collaborative Approach to Planning and Practice in Early Childhood Services*, Castle Hill, NSW: Pademelon Press.

Stonehouse, H. & Gonzales-Mena, J. (2008) 'Making Links Parents Partner: a Guide for Parents about What Matters in Early Childhood Services', Castle Hill, NSW: Pademelon Press.

Stuhlman, M. & Pianta, R. (2009) 'Profiles of Educational Quality in 1st grade', *Elementary School Journal*, 109, 323–42.

Sylva, K., Melhuish, E., Sammons, P., Siraj-Blatchford, I. & Taggart, B. (2004) The Effective Provision of Pre-School Education (EPPE) Project: Findings from Pre-school to end of Key Stage 1. http://eppe.ioe.ac.uk/eppe/eppefindings. htm.

Thompson, S. (2005) *Children as Illustrators: Making Meaning through Art and Language*, Washington DC: SAGE.

Tönnies, F. & Harris, J. (ed.) (2001) *Community and Civil Society*, Cambridge: Cambridge University Press.

Ttofi, M.M. & Farrington, D.P. (2011) Effectiveness of school-based programs to reduce bullying: a systematic and meta-analytic review. *J Exp Criminol, 7*, 27–56.

Turner, W. & Sharp, S. (2006) 'Evaluating the Effective Relationships and Participation in Teacher Education Partnerships', in J. Gray (ed.) *Proceedings of the 2006 Australian Teacher Education Association Conference,* Fremantle, WA: Australian Teacher Education Association, pp.286–8.

UNESCO (2009) Policy Guidelines on Inclusion in Education unesdoc.unesco.org/images/0017/001778/177849e.pdf

van Uden, J.M., Ritzen, H. & Pieters, J.M. (2014) Engaging students: The role of teacher beliefs and interpersonal teacher behavior in fostering student engagement in vocational education. *Teaching and Teacher Education, 37*, 21–32.

Weiner, I. & Murawski, W.W. (2005) 'Schools Attuned: a Model for Collaborative Intervention', *Intervention in School & Clinic, 40*(5), 284–90.

Wenger, E. (2000) Communities of Practice and Social Learning Systems. *Organization Articles*, 7(2): 225–246

Wenger, E. & Snyder, W. (2000) *Communities of Practice: the Organizational Frontier*, Harvard Business Review.

Wesley, P.W. & Buysse, V. (2001) 'Communities of Practice: Expanding Professional Roles to Promote Reflection and Shared Inquiry', *Topics in Early Childhood Special Education, 21*(2): 114–23.

CAROL CARTER

Working with Families and Communities

Estelle Irving and Sue Lancaster

Chapter objectives

In this chapter, we will:
- discuss the importance of families in children's lives
- consider the diversity of families
- look at the links between family circumstances and educational outcomes
- examine the challenges and rewards of working in partnerships with families.

Key terms

chronosystem

cultural capital

exosystem

macrosystem

mesosystem

microsystem

> There is no such thing as a baby … if you set out to describe
> a baby, you will find you are describing a <u>baby and someone</u>.
> A baby cannot exist alone but is essentially part of a relationship.
>
> (Winnicott, 1960)

Winnicott is making a point that is central to this chapter: each child you will be teaching experiences their life through and with their relationships with others. Winnicott's particular interest was in the mental health of babies; he recognised that babies and very young children are dependent on their relationships with others to provide for their basic survival needs of food, protection, love and meaningful interaction with others. These necessities are provided in the context of relationships. All development and learning is mediated through relationships and, as Bronfenbrenner's model highlights, a baby's first and most influential relationships are in their family.

It is important to recognise that early childhood teachers work both directly and indirectly with families. They work directly though establishing and maintaining recognised and intentional, mutually beneficial partnerships, with the shared goal of the best outcomes for the child. They also work indirectly in that children bring with them internalised beliefs, routines, attitudes, cultural practices and values that all derive from their family. How teachers understand, value and respond to these will affect children's experiences of early childhood education—including whether they feel they belong in that setting, and how they learn.

Introduction

This chapter is about families and their importance, not just in the everyday lives of children, but in their education and educational outcomes. In Bronfenbrenner's (1979) ecological systems model, families are positioned in the microsystem and recognised as the first and most important influence on children's learning and development. The importance of family context and the enduring impact on how and what children learn is reflected in the common claim that the family is the child's 'first teacher'.

The importance of families to children's lives and the interlinking of family and education are given expression in key documents and policies that form the foundation on which early childhood teaching is built. These include the Early Years Learning Framework (EYLF) (DEEWR, 2009), but reach further back into the twentieth century to the United Nations Convention on the Rights of the Child (UNCRC, 1989). The preamble to the UNCRC proclaims that:

> … the family, as the fundamental group of society and the natural environment for the growth and wellbeing of all its members and particularly children, should be afforded the necessary protection and assistance so that it can fully assume its responsibilities within the community,
> … the child, for the full and harmonious development of his or her personality, should grow up in a family environment, in an atmosphere of happiness, love and understanding.

This chapter is also about the importance of early childhood teachers working with families and the powerful results that this collaboration can bring. Working with families is complex and requires an ongoing commitment: it brings challenges along with rewards. To work effectively with families, early childhood teachers need to know individual families, and understand the importance of families in their children's lives and their impact on how children learn and develop. The chapter explores the diversity of families and it provides an overview of the changes that are affecting Australian families and communities. The impact of these changes on children and childhood is also discussed.

Understanding families and the challenges they face is an important part of understanding children in the context of their lives. Vygotsky, whom you met in earlier chapters, helps us to understand learning as a social experience and therefore the importance of understanding this context that Vygotsky referred to as the 'social situation of development' (Vygotsky, cited in Anning et al., 2009, p.6).

The 'social situation of development', and the contexts and circumstances in which children are being reared and in which they experience their childhoods, have changed profoundly. The pace of change is continuing to accelerate. Early childhood teachers have an important role to play in supporting children and their families to manage these changes.

In the previous chapter, the focus was on relationships as *partnerships*. This chapter extends this discussion to focus specifically on the family and the family context of children's learning, development and wellbeing. Our focus on families is because the relationship that is most important in a child's life is the family. We learn our first language here, and our family's values and cultural practices shape our first experiences of life. Families are recognised as children's first teacher because of the primacy of this learning.

ESTELLE IRVING AND SUE LANCASTER

A discussion of the family as a social institution and its impact on children sets the scene for the main focus of the chapter, 'Working with families and communities'. The chapter reflects on the challenges and rewards of working with families from diverse backgrounds and family circumstances. An examination of work practices and processes, professional responsibilities and boundaries, duty of care, confidentiality and privacy that support the protection of children form part of this content.

The importance of families

> Families and kinship members have primary influence on their children's learning and development. They provide children with the relationships, opportunities and experiences that shape each child's sense of belonging, being and becoming.
>
> (DET, 2016, p.5)

> It is perhaps stating the obvious that family is central to the lives of children.
>
> (Baxter, 2016, p.2)

Families are at the heart of how we situate and define ourselves and our identity: 'My family comes from …'; 'In our family, we …'; and 'I am a daughter, sister, auntie, mother of …' One of the first things a child learns is who their family is. Imagine for a moment how you might feel if you were not able to answer the question of 'Who is my family?'

A baby's first experience of relationships is almost always within the family. Other relationships—with health professionals or carers, for example—are mediated through the family. As discussed in relation to Bowlby and attachment theory in Chapter 3, this relationship is foundational to our sense of who we are, who we can become, and where and with whom we belong. It is also important to our sense of our value to others and it forms the foundation for other relationships through our lives. You will recognise the links between these fundamental questions that lie at the heart of our sense of self and our sense of identity and the themes of the Early Years Learning Frameworks (EYLF): *Belonging, Being* and *Becoming*.

STOP AND REFLECT

Here is a very simple exercise: If your home was on fire (and assuming that no one's life was in danger), and you could only save one or two things, what would they be?

It probably won't surprise you to learn that most people choose to save family mementos—most commonly family photos. These are regarded as precious and irreplaceable, linking our sense of who we are and who we belong to, to our family stories and history.

Objects that may have much greater financial value do not have the enduring 'priceless' value of family photos. Stripped down to such a simple choice, the value of family is highlighted.

---

microsystem
the first and most directly influential system in Bronfenbrenner's model, it emphasises the importance of the family for a child's overall development.

Bronfenbrenner's ecological systems model also helps us to understand that babies and children can only be understood in the context of their family. The first 'system' or layer of influence in the whole environment described by Bronfenbrenner is the **microsystem**. Face-to-face relationships with families, friends and known caregivers characterise this system in which the child is at the centre. The microsystem is the most direct and influential of the systems because it has the closest relationship to the child. Bronfenbrenner's model describes the environmental interconnectedness of the systems, including the interactions and relationships between families and services that include early childhood education. The **mesosystem** consists of interactions between a person's microsystems: these include the relationships that families have with, for example, early childhood teachers. Just as we need to understand the family context of each individual child, when we look at the interconnected 'systems' described by Bronfenbrenner, we can see that the next step is to recognise that families need to be understood in the context of their communities and the wider society—that is, in the context of the interconnected, wider 'systems'. Family circumstances, including family resources (cultural and material), the neighbourhood in which the family lives and the interactions and relationships between family and other people (and organisations) will all affect how a child develops—including how and what the child learns.

....

mesosystem interactions between a person's microsystems to the immediate community such as childcare, pre-school and school.

Families and culture

Culture refers to socially learnt and enacted values, beliefs, symbols, traditions and practices that collectively become a shared way of life. Culture is not an exotic detail or 'add-on' factor in our lives: it is not like a piece of clothing that we can put on or off at will. Culture is at the heart of the EYLF's 'being' and 'belonging', and it is in the context of their families that children learn their culture. The most obvious markers of culture are in the visible representations of clothing, food and language—but culture is much deeper than this. It provides the basis for our way of life and our identity.

A family's cultural practices that have a direct impact on a baby's early experiences include, for example, whether or not a boy is circumcised; what, how and when the baby is fed; where a baby sleeps (e.g. in a separate room or co-sharing with the parents); how the baby is handled and dressed; and how the baby's social, emotional and physical needs are met. However, cultures are not monolithic or uniform and we cannot assume, for example, that all families who originate from the same country will have exactly the same values, traditions and practices. Instead, cultures are adapted within class and ethnic groups, and by individual families, even where there may be overarching similarities. In some instances, within the same country, deep divisions and hostilities—even civil war—divide different ethnic and religious groups, so that any assumption that there are ties and commonalities based on country of origin should be avoided.

Families also have individual histories, and these include their own variations or adaptations of cultural practices, rituals and traditions. For example, an immigrant family may modify the food they consume on festive occasions and many Australians who identify as Christians may negotiate how they will celebrate Christmas with different relatives.

Learning about learning

A key point to keep in mind is that babies and children are also *learning about learning*. Families provide resources for their children's learning that vary significantly from one family to another. Some families provide books and music lessons for their children, for example; others may participate in sporting activities. Through what is provided, and in their interactions with children, families also convey attitudes about learning and about

ESTELLE IRVING AND SUE LANCASTER

cultural capital
the knowledge and skills gained through family background and education.

education. In Chapter 13, these resources are referred to as **cultural capital**—they are a type of social or cultural resource, described as:

> … a bank of knowledge and understanding about communication, culture and power in the society in which they [children] live, and how to be successful.
> One way of ascertaining the level of cultural capital in a child's life is to measure the following:
>
> - Whether they are taken to museums
> - Whether they are taken to concerts
> - The number of books in the home
> - Whether the child reads for enjoyment
> - Whether the child has extracurricula activities
> - Whether the child is encouraged to have hobbies.
>
> (Jaeger, cited in Holmes et al., 2015, p.143)

Children who have been regularly read to, and whose families introduce them to songs, nursery rhymes and counting games, for example, are better prepared for school than children who may not have had these experiences. These are also among the experiences that are provided for children in high quality early childhood education, where they contribute cultural capital along with enhanced educational outcomes. For children who don't have these experiences in their families, the value of 'cultural capital' experiences provided in early childhood education is particularly important.

Bronfenbrenner's model adds another dimension to our understanding of how and what children learn about learning: it highlights that the individual characteristics of each child mean that children do not necessarily share the same experiences as their siblings. The child's gender, temperament, health and age are all factors that contribute to these individual experiences. In Bronfenbrenner's model, these characteristics are recognised as unique for each child, but they do not occur in a vacuum. Instead, social and cultural patterns surround these characteristics and provide a lens for how individual children are perceived.

Families and gender

One of the differences that relates to the distribution of family resources—including access to education—is the gender of the child.

Gender is about beliefs, values and practices: it is learnt and experienced in the context of culture—the culture of the family, and the wider society and its institutions, including educational institutions.

Families enact gendered roles and practices in everyday life. These provide visible models for children, and they link to opportunities and resources available to them. A baby's gendered learning begins from birth—or even, arguably, before birth in the anticipatory planning ('What colour clothes should I buy for the baby'?) and dreaming ('We'll go shopping together if the baby is a girl') that accompanies pregnancy.

If you have a sibling of a different gender from you, it is very likely that your parents do not treat you all in exactly the same way—perhaps, for example, boys in your family are allowed more freedom, or girls are expected to read more and care more about their appearance. Possibly, it may be assumed that an older daughter will take on care responsibilities for younger siblings, while an older son may be expected to help his father with outdoor home maintenance chores. These are examples of how children learn gender roles within their families and they may also link to the distribution of many resources within the family, including parental attention and investment in education.

Educational opportunities and outcomes related to educational success and progression, versus failure and incomplete education, have wide-ranging ramifications that include but go well beyond employment rates (and type of employment), income and lifelong earning capacity. Housing, relationships—even health status and life expectancy—link to educational opportunities and outcomes. In all these outcomes, gender is a potent predictive factor. Despite practices that include anti-bias education in early childhood education and active encouragement of girls and boys to choose subjects that are not gender-stereotyped, these patterns persist. Your fellow students, studying for a career in early childhood education, for example, are highly likely to be female. You might like to reflect on why you have made your decision to pursue this area of study, and whether your family supported your decision.

Family background and educational outcomes

Gender is not the only predictive factor associated with unequal educational outcomes. The significance of a child's family is deeper than this. Beginning in the 1970s, sociological research into educational outcomes found that, contrary to what had been assumed, educational outcomes were *not* strongly predicted by, or associated with, a child's intelligence or how hard they worked. Instead, a child's family background and circumstances (plus the child's gender) were identified as key predictors of educational and (later) employment outcomes. The relative advantage or disadvantage for children was linked to their parents' occupational levels (reflecting their own education and therefore their income) and where the family lived. In other words, class and socio-economic status were more consistent predictors of educational success than children's abilities. In Australia, this pattern is confirmed in census data (Holmes et al., 2015, p.143) and the use of postcodes as a proxy for determining who is disadvantaged. Put simply, where you live as a child *matters*, and not just in terms of what it is like to live in a particular location. Of course, choice of where a family lives is limited by income, and income relates to educational opportunities and resources—so there is a circular link between these. But, as discussed briefly in Chapter 13, it is not a simple equation of more money equals better educational outcomes for children. Money on its own does not buy 'cultural capital'.

To give an example of how cultural capital is not necessarily correlated with material wealth: an immigrant (or asylum-seeking) family may come to Australia with few material possessions and no wealth to draw on, but with a high regard for education. This family may participate in cultural events, read to their children from books borrowed from the local library and take their children to community events, such as church. In all these everyday family practices and experiences, parents are building a foundation for their children's education and demonstrating a positive regard for education and an implied understanding that education can lead to better life outcomes. Such attitudes and the ways in which they are demonstrated in everyday life can be regarded as a type of inheritance of cultural capital or advantage, rather than an inheritance of money or material items, for their children. Weighing against these positive aspects of cultural capital, however, may be negative stereotyped views about these families: these may affect the relationships in the mesosystem, which may exclude or marginalise the family.

ESTELLE IRVING AND SUE LANCASTER

These findings, which link family cultural capital to educational success rather than the intelligence of the child or how hard they work, raise questions about the value of education, and challenge the belief that education will always be a pathway to greater opportunities and upward social mobility. The picture they revealed was that education was essentially reproducing the existing social structure with all its prevailing inequalities based on class, race, gender, religion and status. Providing high quality early education, working with families, supporting them in their parenting role, assisting with access to services, and sharing your knowledge of education with their knowledge of their child, are strategies that help all children to reach their full potential, regardless of gender, class or socio-economic status.

Though material and financial disadvantage is the most powerful obstacle to full access to opportunities, without intentional and genuine practices that include families who lack cultural capital, it is unlikely that these children will achieve their full potential.

Why not?

The earlier discussion referred to cultural capital being not just a 'bank of knowledge' but also involving an 'understanding about communication, culture and power'. Valuing education, reading to children and taking them to museums (for example) are specific examples of the 'bank of knowledge' aspects of cultural capital, but knowing how to communicate with teachers and schools (and other early childhood and family services) is also important. Communication is a two-way interaction that is about being heard, understood, respected and valued; it is about knowing the 'right' words, channels and processes that underpin effective communication. Parents who may have had negative experiences of education may be reluctant to approach, or not know how to communicate effectively with, teachers. They may fear being ridiculed or patronised. Their children may 'inherit' this cultural trait unless teachers actively engage with and facilitate open and respectful communication with the family.

A child who cannot see their own culture and family practices reflected in the educational setting is unlikely to feel engaged, respected and valued. Using professional jargon that families do not understand, assuming that all families are basically the same (that is, like our own family), providing information forms that only allow a single definition of family or use terms that relate to a specific culture or religion—for example, asking for a child's Christian name, or displaying images of children and families that do not reflect those of families using the service—are examples of practices that shut families out of effective communication and the development of meaningful relationships. All of these examples convey the message that only certain children and families are really welcome. They display at best a lack of consideration; at worst, they indicate a lack of respect. Respect for children's cultural identity is specifically prescribed in Article 29 of the UN Convention of the Rights of the Child (1989), which refers to:

> The development of respect for the child's parents, his or her own cultural identity, language and values, for the national values of the country in which the child is living, the country from which he or she may originate, and for civilizations different from his or her own …

Education should be concerned with providing opportunities for children to reach their potential and to succeed in life, and to become active participants and contributors to society. However, if children and their families do not feel they belong in that setting or service or that it is alien to them and disconnected to their life, then children are unlikely to flourish.

STOP AND REFLECT

- In an educational or work environment, have you as an adult or as a child experienced a sense that you and your family of origin were not valued or welcomed?
- What created that sense?
- What were the consequences of this?
- Did you flourish and achieve your full potential there? Why or why not?

If we imagine 'the child' as some sort of context-less and uniform 'object' ('*the* child' instead of '*this* child'), we overlook the reality that the children you will teach don't come to you as a 'blank slate', ready to absorb all the knowledge you provide. They do come to pre-school and school to learn, but children are not passive sponges who simply soak up information and learning: they question, wonder, respond, resist, negotiate, make sense of what they experience and—as Bronfenbrenner's model illustrates—they do so in specific time and place, family and community contexts. When children arrive at early childhood education and care services, they come from families that are unique and real. At the end of each day, children return to their families. What happens in those families and how teachers work with families has a lasting impact on what and how children learn and how they develop.

Defining the family

Chapter 1 discussed the variety of ways in which children have been seen and understood, and made the point that there is no consensus in Australian society about children and childhood. We can make the same point about the family: there is great variety in how people define family, and there is no agreed-upon definition of family. Rather than consensus, definitions are contested, with groups lobbying for recognition of their definition.

One *type* of family that has been clearly defined is the nuclear family. This family type includes a married man and woman, and their biologically related (or adopted) children: it is referred to as 'nuclear' because this core family group constitutes a 'unit' and that unit has been regarded as the foundation block of society. In the mid twentieth century, the period in which the nuclear family was the norm, it was viewed as a microcosm of wider society; as such it fulfilled many of the core functions of society, including socialisation of children (especially into gender roles) and the care of young children. This small, intact family unit was believed to be particularly suited to modern, mobile, industrial society.

Family life in Australia through most of the twentieth century centred on communities formed in specific locations—rural and suburban—often at the localised level of streets and immediate neighbourhoods. In mid-century, post-Second World War Australia, the connection between family life and the suburbs intensified and it reflected a strongly held belief that the suburbs were the best place to rear children. In that era, the norm was for mothers to stay at home as home-makers (housewives), to tend the house, shop, cook, clean and provide the day-to-day care of their children. Divorce was rare, and the stability of the family was reinforced by the relatively low mobility of the population. Home ownership, often referred to as 'the great Australian dream' (and certainly the normal Australian family aspiration), was achievable for most families.

Children grew up in known, familiar communities. High (male) employment contributed to that stability. A shared consensus about how the family was defined extended to a shared consensus about the roles and responsibilities of parents. The dark side of this strong consensus and the norm of the highly gendered nuclear family was that families that did not conform to the accepted way of life were liable to be excluded or marginalised. There was, for example, a taken-for-granted assumption that young adults would marry, and strong pressure on women who became pregnant outside of marriage to give their child up for adoption. Indigenous families with their extended kinship ties and lineages that did not conform to the prevailing ideal of a single unit, were not recognised as legitimate families. Immigrant families from non-English-speaking backgrounds were regarded with suspicion and few services were available for their support.

Most people married, and did so with the expectation that this was a taken-for-granted precursor to having children. Within nuclear families, parents, for the most part, stayed together, and they stayed in the same neighbourhood—often in the same house for the duration of their children's childhood or even beyond then.

It is easy to romanticise that suburban way of life and these families and assume that high marriage and low divorce rates meant there were no tensions and difficulties. That is not the case, of course, and some parents endured unhappy marriages, but for children at least, family life was stable in a way that can hardly be imagined in Australia in the twenty-first century.

In the 1960s the dominance of the nuclear family was challenged by many social and political forces including the 'women's liberation' movement. Women's growing access to higher education raised aspirations for employment and greater financial and social independence.

In the twenty-first century, the nuclear family is still the single largest family type in Australia, but it is no longer the majority family type. There is currently no single dominant norm for families: instead, there is growing diversity (Baxter, 2016).

Governments struggle with this diversity in terms of establishing a workable definition that can be applied, for example, for welfare benefits. The national Census, conducted in Australia every five years through the Australian Bureau of Statistics (ABS), provides data that is essential for government planning of services and infrastructure, including, for example, where early childhood and family services are needed, and where new schools should be built. The definition adopted by the ABS attaches to households:

> A family is defined by the ABS as two or more persons, one of whom is at least 15 years of age, who are related by blood, marriage (registered or de facto), adoption, step or fostering, and who are usually resident in the same household.
>
> Each separately identified couple relationship, lone parent–child relationship or other blood relationship forms the basis of a family. Some households contain more than one family.
>
> Non-related persons living in the same household are not counted as family members (unless under 15 years of age).
>
> (Qu & Weston, 2013)

The example above illustrates the difficulties associated with establishing a definition that captures the diversity of experiences in Australian society in a way that is meaningful and resonates with individuals' own experiences, values and beliefs. While it is understandable that the ABS is primarily focused on *households* rather than considering the locational spread of an increasing number of families, it overlooks the reality that families are fluid, mobile and increasingly unstable: they are far more than 'households'.

Our families are so fundamental to our lives and identity that there is a risk we assume that our own experiences and definition of family are shared by everyone. 'Both lack of awareness and ethnocentrism—the tendency to believe that one's own group is superior to others—tend to cloud our views of families other than our own' (Hartley, 1995, p.5).

The diversity of families

In Chapter 2, you were introduced to the idea that childhood is socially constructed and experienced. Our understanding of children and childhood is shaped in particular time and place contexts, and reflects our culture and the structure of society. Culture and social structure are also keys to understanding the family as a social institution: as in childhood, we experience families individually and personally, but our families and our individual choices (for example, 'Will I marry and if so, at what age will I marry?') are also part of wider social and cultural patterns. Families are both intensely personal and social—they are 'located across the so-called 'private' and 'public' realms of life' (Hartley, 1995, p.5). Individual circumstances of families differ, of course, and every family is also subject

to change (sometimes quite dramatically) and our perspectives on and experiences of family will also change with our age and life cycle. However, there are wider social patterns and norms relating to the family as a social institution that we can identify. For example, living together prior to marriage is now common, marriage rates have declined, age at first marriage has increased, so too has the age at which women have children (if they have children at all). Our ethnicity and religion may also help shape our expectations of family and what we regard as normal or deviant.

The privileging of nuclear families (e.g. in law and access to government welfare benefits, or the right to adoption of children) has been evident since the mid twentieth century, but its privileged status is now challenged, including the achievement of 'marriage equality' (legal recognition of same-sex relationships).

Families are not static. Individual families change, and the family as a social institution also changes. As the brief discussion of the nuclear family above revealed, families have changed significantly since the norm of the nuclear family in mid twentieth century Australia. This change has accelerated over the past two or three decades—families are now more varied in their structure and more diverse culturally and ethnically.

ESTELLE IRVING AND SUE LANCASTER

STOP AND REFLECT

Think about your own family (however you define it):

- How do your current family circumstances (structure, expectations, practices, roles, norms) differ from those of your parents' or your grandparents' generation?
- What changes have occurred in the period since you were a child?
- Are these changes exclusive to your family or are they part of wider patterns of change?
- Have your friends experienced similar changes?
- What do you think drives these changes?

Your responses to the reflection questions above are likely to mirror many of the changes that are currently occurring in Australian families.

These changes relate to:

- family structures
- family roles and responsibilities
- education, including early childhood education and care provisions and settings
- material conditions of families
- work and leisure patterns
- greater mobility of families and increasing housing insecurity.

Bronfenbrenner's ecological systems model provides a framework for thinking about these factors and it allows us to see their interconnectedness. One of the significant changes to work, for example, is the increased participation of women (and particularly mothers of young children) in paid employment. Women are returning to work sooner after giving birth, driving an increased need for early childhood education and care services. Family roles and responsibilities are likely to be re-negotiated when both parents are working, and especially so if the mother is the primary (or only) 'breadwinner'.

Family structures

> ... a growing number of children are raised by cohabiting rather than married parents, by single parents, by step parents and by same sex parents, with many children moving in and out of these different family structures as they grow up.
>
> (Golombok, 2015, pp.1–2)

> ... it is now possible for a child to have up to five 'parents' instead of the usual two. These may include an egg donor, a sperm donor, a surrogate mother (who hosts the pregnancy) and the social parents who are known to the child as mum and dad.
>
> (Golombok, 2015, p.1)

It is important to recognise that though the nuclear family was the norm in the past, there has never been just a single family type, and the representation of the nuclear family (married, heterosexual couple, living together with their biological children) as the type of family structure that everyone experienced in the past is a myth. However, the diversity of families in Australian society now is unprecedented. This diversity extends beyond structures or types of families to beliefs, expectations, roles and responsibilities and what are referred to as 'lifestyle choices'. We noted earlier that there is no societal consensus about how family is defined: there is also no shared understanding of what responsibilities a family should independently fulfil (if any) and what should be the role and responsibilities of the state. Continuing debates around the role and responsibilities of teachers—for example, is it the teacher's role to provide education around sexuality—are highlighted in this context of diverse beliefs and family expectations.

Below is a 'snapshot', summarising some of the most significant changes in family structures:

- Marriage is now seen as a choice, not a social expectation/obligation (with some exceptions, usually related to religion).
- Marriage rates have declined.
- There is little if any stigma attached to being single.
- Cohabitation or 'de-facto' relationships rates have increased.
- High divorce rates are fairly stable (with a trend of a slight increase), in contrast to the initial dramatic spike that followed the 1975 Family Law Act and 'no fault' divorce.
- Social shame and stigma of divorce has decreased significantly.
- Serial marriages/relationships are now normalised and socially accepted.
- There has been an increase in single-parent families, the majority of which are headed by mothers.
- There are new pathways to single-parent families (including preconception and deliberate choice). In the past, the most common pathway to becoming a single parent was following the death of the co-parent and re-marriage was highly likely.
- Provision for welfare support of single parents means reduced financial pressure to give children up for adoption, and reduced imperative to re-marry.
- The nuclear family is still common, but there is an increase in 'blended' families—and these are now more complex.
- Increasingly families are unstable and complex, with complex needs.
- There are more shared-care/custody arrangements for children.
- There are fewer extended or multi-generational family households (but more young adults still living in the parental home).
- Same-sex couple families and their recognition as legitimate families have increased.

At this point, you may be thinking about and/or rethinking your views of early childhood education for young children attending prior-to-school and school environments, and the focus given to family, community and partnership.

STOP AND THINK

Take some time to study the list above and write a brief response to each point, including:

- what this may mean for your learning and practice as a pre-service teacher
- what this may mean for your role as a graduate teacher in your first year of practice in prior-to-school and school environments.

Your responses to these points will most likely vary from being very similar to, through to very different from your colleagues' or co-students'. This is a consequence of both the time and the changes in contemporary society and lifestyle discussed in the first part of this chapter, and required practice change. You may also have considered experiences that influenced your own education, your current daily life, or observations in a work environment and your understanding of 'the child'.

ESTELLE IRVING AND SUE LANCASTER

Changing communities

Just as families have changed to become more diverse and less stable, communities have also changed. Families are increasingly mobile, and less rooted in long-term locations. The mid twentieth century ideal of mother at home while the breadwinner father worked to support the family and pay the mortgage has long been replaced by households where the single parent works, or both parents work (or, in some cases, no parent works).

Most families still live in the suburbs, but they move more frequently than in the past, and living in close proximity to extended family (including grandparents) is increasingly uncommon. As families struggle to pay mortgages or rents, many suburbs are empty during working hours—vacated by commuting workers. These suburbs are referred to as 'dormitory' suburbs: they are places where families come home to sleep, rather than sites of vibrant communities.

Reinforcing this disconnection from a neighbourhood, many children are driven to and from their early childhood education setting or school, which may or may not be local. Neighbours may provide occasional emergency care, but this is more likely to be formalised through early childhood education services by qualified educators and teachers.

Impacts on children and childhood

In Australia, census data shows that most children are born into a family where both their biological parents live together, at least initially (Baxter, 2016, p.3). Until relatively recently, people married with the expectation that this was a precursor to having children. Now though, marriage is no longer tied strongly to parenthood. Some people marry with no intention of having children, and it is now common (and socially acceptable) for parents to be living in a 'de-facto' relationship, with or without an intention of marrying in the future. One of the real benefits to children of the acceptance of unmarried parents is that children born into these families are no longer stigmatised as 'bastards' and labelled as 'illegitimate', as occurred in the past.

This picture of biological parents living together with their children changes as the child grows and the likelihood that their parents will no longer share the household increases with the child's age (Baxter, 2016, p.3). Until the passing of family law reforms in the 1970s, divorce was very difficult and involved social shame because one partner needed to be named as being 'at fault'—infidelity (which had to be proven to the court) being the main reason. The introduction of 'no-fault' divorce in 1975 simplified the process of obtaining a divorce and removed the associated shame. Though separation and divorce of their parents is challenging for children, the lack of shame and shaming of children whose parents are divorced has been another gain for children as they no longer have to carry that stigma.

It is widely acknowledged that families are becoming more complex, but less attention is given to how this is affecting children's lives. One source of information about Australian children's lives comes from 'Growing Up in Australia: the Longitudinal Study of Australian Children' (DSS/AIFS/ABS, 2017). Data from this long-term, large-scale research shows that children's family lives and living arrangements are becoming correspondingly more complex, particularly where their parents separate and re-partner (sometimes multiple times) and other children join the family. Extended family members may disconnect (voluntarily or involuntarily) from the newly formed family and this can disrupt children's own relationships with these family members, especially where there is hostility between the parents and 'old' family members, such as a grandparent.

As noted earlier in the chapter, science and medical interventions now make it possible for a child to have multiple 'parents'. These parents may come and go at various stages of the children's lives—and may themselves form new families. While the stigma and negative stereotyping of family variations may have diminished, children have to negotiate their place in increasingly complex families and households.

The increased mobility of families, noted earlier, is also experienced by children, and may disrupt the development of friendships, connection with family members and continuity of their education. Communities are less likely to be formed around neighbourhood or location than they were in the past. The concept of a family 'home' as a base for children (and other family members) is challenged by increasing housing instability, lack of affordable housing, family mobility and family instability. In mother-headed, single-parent households, moving is often an outcome of financial difficulties, and a contributor to other stresses, particularly if the move is away from established support networks. These families are at increased risk of poverty, poor standard housing (in poor locations) and unstable housing.

First time mothers (and fathers) are generally older now. Older parents have more life experience and may be more financially secure, and therefore be in a stronger position to support their children—though this is not always the case. One outcome of delayed parenthood that is gaining recognition is that grandparents are correspondingly older and may not be in a position to provide as much support as relatively younger grandparents can. Some of these older grandparents are themselves in need of family care and support, putting pressure on families at a time when parents need support for their own children.

Among the positive changes for children in Australian families is the increased and growing recognition of the importance of the early years of childhood. This recognition has led to the provision of higher quality early care and education and support services for children and their families. Raising children is now regarded as a shared responsibility; early childhood teachers work in partnerships with families and recognise and value the family context of child learning, development and wellbeing. Children's educational outcomes are increased through these partnerships, and their everyday, lived experiences of childhood are enhanced. These are significant gains for children and their families.

Working with family and community

The narrative that follows will consider the characteristics and implications of working with family and community underpinned by a professional partnership approach. You will be exposed to ideas, strategies and provocations to support your teaching for learning and development of whole-of-life skills for children, with a focus on professional partnerships.

These partnerships will be examined from a micro to a macro level, beginning with the child (micro level) as an active agent within teaching and learning partnerships and the inter-subjective relationships (macro level) that constitute an effective partnership. Different partnerships that are discussed and analysed will include:

- teacher–child
- teacher–family
- teacher–community.

ESTELLE IRVING AND SUE LANCASTER

At the macro level, you are encouraged to become familiar with current state and federal policies relevant to education, and how these are interpreted in documentation and practices by early childhood education and care services and within primary schools.

Strategies discussed to enable the establishment of effective partnerships and the exchange of information with children, family members and fellow professionals across a broad range of professional practice contexts include:

- strength-based (asset-based) practices
- additional support needs for vulnerable families and children at risk of harm
- advocacy
- embedding the rights, interests and safety of children within the context of their family, early childhood and school environments and other social constructs.

From an educational perspective, this approach to the concepts of family and community (professionals partnerships) challenges the teacher to go beyond teaching what children/students are expected to understand (where the teacher is the holder of all knowledge) to a teaching approach that embraces the context of the child, or student, and family and community—sharing knowledge, information and understandings. This is the beginning of building a professional partnership that requires the teacher to reflect on the child's experience, and parent and community expectations and needs for the child as 'learner'. This involves consideration of what the child's culture and prior knowledge may bring to their being, learning and development. When a teacher is engaged in this shared learning model, it is expected that learning and teaching goals are more likely to be achieved.

Theoretical basis for practice change

Early childhood education has been influenced considerably by the sociocultural theory of Bronfenbrenner, based on a systems approach to learning and development. This chapter has previously applied this theory to discuss the importance of family and community for children's development (microsystem) and beyond the family to the immediate community such as childcare, pre-school and school (mesosystem).

In this section, the perspective widens to organisations where children are not direct participants, such as local councils and support networks (**exosystem**) and the broad society, culture and nation (**macrosystem**) with the concept of *time* that surrounds the entire model at any given period (**chronosystem**). If you reflect on the many comments in relation to changes in family life discussed previously in this chapter, you will notice that various stages of change can be seen within specific time frames or periods.

This theoretical approach requires teachers to consider all of the various environments, relationships, values, cultures, ethnicities, communities and organisations, stretching from children's immediate families to community, through to national and international influences and connections that may have played a part in each individual child's growth and understandings across time frames.

As a pre-service teacher, you are ethically bound to recognise that families have rights, as well as expectations, in relation to their children's education and care, and should be engaged at all levels in the learning process that builds on each family's strengths, ability and capacity to participate in education and care decisions in relation to their child, and for the wellbeing of the community (ECA, 2016).

exosystem includes people and places that children may not interact with often themselves but that still have a large effect on them, such as parents' workplaces, local councils, extended family members, support networks, the neighbourhood.

macrosystem the largest and most remote system; still has an influence on the child (e.g. broader societies cultures and nations).

chronosystem the concept of time that surrounds the entire model at any given period.

Teachers also engage in partnerships with children, recognising that children have agency over their actions with peers and teachers, and the broader care and education community. Community networks are important too; when teachers participate in community networks they learn from these relationships by exploring community service options and possibilities for supporting the needs of young children and their families within their communities.

As a pre-service teacher, you will also begin to develop an understanding of cultural difference through your reflection on engagement with community cultural events and through the arts. This is demonstrated in the following narrative, provided with the permission of pre-service teachers in my class, following their visit to the Melbourne Museum's Bunjilaka Aboriginal Cultural Centre:

> The visit made me feel the pain of the past and made me want to be more culturally sensitive … I was really moved by the smallpox epidemic and the grieving of the women.
>
> Reading the quotes made my understanding real … understanding how important the Elders were in teaching … so much of their culture is tied to the land … place and culture is inseparable whereas Anglo-Saxon people separate place and culture.
>
> I noted the importance of the possum skin cloaks and seeing and understanding this has transformed the way I will now view these cloaks.

These shared narratives demonstrate the powerfulness of authentic community-based experiences in addressing some of the uncertainties encountered by early childhood teachers in engaging with diversity and complex family situations. By watching and seeing, listening and hearing, reading and doing, pre-service teachers may become more comfortable to embrace an authentic engagement and understanding of difference across all cultures that will support the development of healthy family, community and professional relationships. This may then lead to active partnerships to support quality education and care for all young children, resulting in better outcomes for their future.

STOP AND REFLECT

- What do you already know about working with families, community and professional partnerships?
- What do you need to know about how to build strong professional partnerships with families and community?
- Why is it important that you understand these concepts?

Government policy informing practice

Government policy that informs practice includes government legislation and policy, national and state frameworks, and curriculum documentation and standards. Working together with families and other professionals is now recognised as a 'core professional activity' of the early childhood educator and teacher (Hood, 2012). This is also an expectation for teachers in school settings underpinned by the Australian Professional Standards for Teachers (AITSL, 2011) and the Quality Standards for Early Childhood (ACECQA).

ESTELLE IRVING AND SUE LANCASTER

STOP AND THINK

Take time to read and reflect on the two practice standards listed below in relation to professional partnerships with colleagues, families and communities using the resources and tools available on the websites for prior-to-school and school environments.

1 The National Quality Standard (NQS Standard 6): *Collaborative Partnerships with Families and Communities* (http://acecqa.gov.au/nqf-changes)
2 The Australian Professional Standards for Teachers (AITSL Standard 7): *Engage professionally with colleagues, parents/carers and the community* (www.aitsl.edu.au/australian-professional-standards-for-teachers/standards/list).

Think about how you would show your commitment to these specific practice standards in relation to professional partnerships within the early years prior to school and the school environments.

- Are there differences in philosophy and expectations between these environments? What are they and why do you think this is?
- Are there similarities in philosophy and expectations between these environments? What are they and why do you think this is?

The importance of working together as a sector and forming professional partnerships in supporting best outcomes for children's learning, development and wellbeing is now widely accepted and embedded within policies and programs acknowledging that:

- a coordinated family-centred system is needed to support families effectively
- children's development is altered by interventions that change the balance between risk and protective factors, thereby shifting the odds in favour of more adaptive outcomes (Shonkoff & Phillips, 2000)
- family involvement helps children get ready for school, promotes school success and prepares youth for further education
- quality relationships and experiences in children's early years are important for early social and emotional development, determining whether a 'sturdy or fragile foundation' is established, upon which future cognitive development builds (Shonkoff, 2006).

With this development comes the expectation that these policies will also be embedded in practice. However, questions still arise about what 'working together' and 'working with families' mean in practice, and why these are important. The following vignette captures this uncertainty.

Collaboration challenges

A teacher was overheard talking with a colleague about the changes taking place in the centre in which she worked, and the challenges that had been raised at a recent staff meeting.

At her centre, she said, 'We are currently spending most of our team meetings talking about meeting the requirements for accreditation: what remains to be done, who will do it and what resources are needed.'

The usual issues were raised in relation to time, workload and meeting regulatory requirements while staff met and worked on the accreditation task. The teacher went on to explain that, as in previous meetings, the question of working in partnership with families and communities remained an area of confusion as opinions varied on questions of *why, how, what* and *when*.

The teacher suggested starting by asking the simple questions that had been on the minds of all staff: Why do we need to involve families, how do we do this, and what can we do to encourage family and community involvement?

With a sigh, the closing comment from this staff member was:

'I suppose the same comments will be made at our next staff meeting. Even though we are working on accreditation there is little commitment or enthusiasm from most of the staff and when someone asks for clarity it is dismissed with a shrug and told it just needs to be done.'

STOP AND THINK

- How would you rate the situation at this service, given the importance of partnerships and a capacity to work effectively?
- Now reflect on the situation and think about:
  - the issues for the organisation, management and staff
  - as morale appears low, what could be put in place to support staff and improve the current situation?

The answers are not just about the National Quality Standards for early childhood or the Australian National Curriculum for schools: this provocation is about how it *feels* to work in an environment where the qualities we value in our interactions with children are carried through into our interactions and relationships with families, co-workers and other professionals. This is about a culture of respect, cooperation and valuing the knowledge and strengths of others, and acknowledging that this complements our own professional knowledge and expertise and enhances our capacity to work effectively. When teachers acknowledge these principles and practices, families and community will also *feel* welcomed, respected and accepted.

Australian research about parent views in early childhood education and care settings confirms the importance of professional partnerships with family and community, finding that:

> parent perceptions of social support in their childcare setting were the best predictors of parental satisfaction with care ... When parent–professional communications are direct, personal and two-way, outcomes are improved ... trusting parent–professional relationships are built through regular personal communication ... mothers benefit from close relationships with professionals.
>
> (Rolfe & Armstrong, 2010)

Provision of quality opportunities for children's learning, and experiences that reflect children's needs and understandings, is an expectation of the majority of families whose children attend early childhood services. However, the research above adds a further dimension to family expectation: that the service embraces families in a manner that promotes engagement, two-way communication and understanding; creating an atmosphere of belonging and authentic partnerships; highlighting the importance of how parents *feel*; and the *nature* of the relationship. For example, the family who has been late in collecting their child on several occasions over the past few weeks is treated with respect the educator notes this and asks, 'Is there anything we can do to help?' rather than pre-judging (e.g. as 'lazy') and criticising the parent in relation to their lateness.

Teacher–family professional partnership

Parent partnerships can sometimes be confused with parent *involvement* (e.g. attending excursions as an additional adult). A *partnership* is an ongoing relationship with specific responsibilities that are negotiated.

Partnerships require engagement that is mutually agreed, including:

- mutual respect and trust
- sensitivity to the perspective of others (empathy)
- ongoing open 'both ways' communication
- recognition and valuing of the unique contribution and strengths of each partner in the partnership
- a common goal that is clear and agreed on, namely the children's wellbeing
- teamwork and the absence of rivalry or competition
- shared decision making (Stonehouse, 2001).

These interpersonal relationships support the family in their parenting role, while at the same time recognising the parents' role as primary caregiver and holder of multiple understandings of their children's development, idiosyncrasies and functional capacities.

Other factors that you, as the teacher, should consider include:

- your personal beliefs about the value of children and childhood (explored in Chapter 1)
- the value of professional knowledge relating to planning for children
- principles of inclusiveness and equity of access to services (see Chapter 15 for further reading)
- acknowledging parents as their children's first teacher, providing support and encouraging them in raising their child
- keeping the best interests of children uppermost at all times
- understanding that a parent–professional partnership is not the same as a friendship.

Stonehouse (2001) also discusses the benefits of engaging families in and enabling them to contribute to the organisation, its philosophy and program. This can be facilitated when teachers:

- engage with families in determining priorities and goals for children while at the service
- recognise and acknowledge family strengths, and potential vulnerability when seeking assistance from families, such as participating in fundraising events or seeking their presence in the program
- acknowledge that the majority of families are able to identify and mobilise social support networks and community resources. This means you have a monitoring role

The different perspectives of parent and teacher roles

PARENTS	TEACHERS
Parents are the most influential people in the child's early and formative years	Teachers are highly significant people, especially when the family is small.
Parents know far more about their child than any teacher will ever know.	Teachers have a professional body of knowledge about how children grow, develop and learn.
Parents make an emotional commitment to their child.	Teachers can be objective because they see a range of children, and their teaching role is necessarily different.
Parents' commitment and contact is long-term.	Teachers are mobile and may teach a child for a year or less.
Parents are usually not 'prepared' for parenting in a formal way.	Teachers are usually trained professionals, but in the early childhood field qualifications vary enormously

Source: Ebbeck & Waniganayake, 2005, p.91.

in most cases, but for some families support to access services will be required. This may take the form of making the phone call for an appointment on the family's behalf, providing information about community supports such as those provided by local government, or referring to outside support services such as a specialist paediatric professional

- share information and engage families in discussion regarding transitions within the service, or when children are getting ready to transition to school, discussing the myths and expectations.

If conflicts arise, working ethically to respect and protect the rights of children and families when making decisions about providing care and learning is a must.

Advocacy: empowering vulnerable families

Advocacy is described as:

> a way to raise issues and ask for change to make a difference for children's lives.
>
> (Smale, 2010)

> about speaking out, acting and writing to promote and defend the rights, needs and interests of people who are in some way disadvantaged.
>
> (Gibbs, 2003)

> protecting people who are vulnerable or discriminated against, or are difficult to provide services to ... empowering people who need a stronger voice to express their own needs and ultimately their own decisions.
>
> (Gibbs, 2003)

In the past, families experiencing social and economic disadvantage were often labelled 'hard to reach'. However, there is a growing consensus that:

> There is a growing concensus that, rather than thinking about certain families as being hard to reach, it is more useful to think of them as being difficult to engage and retain.
>
> (Slee, 2006 cited in CCCH. Policy Brief (18) 2010)

ESTELLE IRVING AND SUE LANCASTER

Advocacy for under-threes

Because of the importance of attachment in the early years of a young child's life for effective outcomes later in life, the under-three years age group has been chosen as an example of advocacy for young children in an education environment. The discussion is also an example of the child–teacher partnership. Many of you already have a good grasp of the needs of toddlers and the complexities of their lives, but for others this will be a relatively new experience and at times your understandings, expectations and perceptions of children and childhood will be challenged.

Toddlers are:

> adapting to their rapid growth and development in their bodies, minds and emotions, and to their new found 'independence'... simultaneously and continuously using these new attributes in their exploration and learning about themselves, other people and the world.
>
> (Young, 2015)

Young (2015) uses the term 'tuning in to toddlers', noting toddlers' capacity for exploration and learning, including their hypothesising and testing of their current and new skills. 'Tuning in' to their attempts at social encounters and responding to their expressions of emotions as they learn to self-regulate their behaviours, with realistic expectations of each individual toddler and in-depth reflection, 'enable us to see each toddler as a complex individual' (Young, 2015) and enables us to make informed and appropriate decisions.

Remember, each baby or toddler will be different, emerging from their experiences of culture, language, capacity, ability to learn, health and wellbeing. At times, toddlers and young children can challenge our own capacity in different ways and contexts. This means we will be required to use all our senses, our knowledge and understandings of children, child development, teaching and learning theory and practice, and knowing ourselves and our community. The extent of the effectiveness of your capacity to understand children's meanings will depend on the strength of the relationship (the professional partnership) you have built with the young children.

Remember too that the depth of the professional relationship the parent has with their child's teacher will be seen by, and be reassuring for, the young child and therefore:

> Supporting parents and educators in good communication and relationship building should be a high priority.
>
> (Young, 2015)

Examples for a successful relationship and being an advocate for young children include:

- greeting the parent and their child, learning and correctly using their names each time you see them;
- being genuinely interested in what parents say to you and what the child does or says;

- working as a team with a 'key worker' allocated to the child, aiming for stability, consistency and continuity;
- considering routine times as 'connection times', where you can engage in joyful activities [such as] Peek-a-boo, singing, rocking and talking;
- meaningful and two-way communication and conversations resulting in 'sustained shared thinking' for learning;
- programming that is flexible and free-flowing, free from adult imposed interruptions unless absolutely necessary for the children's health and wellbeing;
- small groups where toddlers are able to lead their own play through the setting up of activities and environments based on information, observations and reflections, child characteristics and awareness of any mood changes.
- keeping in mind that the teacher's role is not to 'entertain' but to be 'with' the toddler.

(Young, 2015, p.914)

As toddlers grow and develop, their engagement in the early childhood partnerships takes on a more overt nature, for now as young children they have developed a more sophisticated communication system; learning and cognition has evolved considerably; and social interaction and emotional development are more attuned to 'others' than as toddlers, leading to more engagement in and control over their individual and group learning opportunities.

Kennedy talks about this sharing of ideas, working together as partners and forming relationships as a learning community, which involves:

- working collaboratively for a common purpose or vision;
- sharing skills and understanding to achieve improved outcomes;
- forming partnerships with others (staff/families) to build new knowledge about children as individuals and as members of the community to facilitate progress toward an identified goal;
- showing respect for diversity and difference; and
- establishing a climate of trust and demonstrating a willingness to try new things to achieve improved outcomes for children.

(Kennedy, 2014)

Advocacy and working in partnership requires enabling environments where:

1 Children are *listened to*
2 Children are *supported to express their views*;
3 Children's *views are taken into account*;
4 Children are *involved in the decision-making* processes;
5 Children *share power.*

(Shier (2001), cited in Kennedy, 2014)

The principle of children being heard is expressed in Article 12 of the UN Convention on the Rights of the Child (UNCRC, 1989):

States Parties shall assure to the child who is capable of forming his or her own views the right to express those views freely in all matters affecting the child, the views of the child being given due weight in accordance with the age and maturity of the child.

STOP AND REFLECT

Thinking about your experiences, what have you seen that demonstrates these practices?

For some of you this will not be difficult as you may be working in this area, have children of your own, or babysit for friends.

For those of you who have little knowledge of young children or babies you could access the Early Childhood Australia website and the e-learning videos at Connecting with Practice (EYLF and NQS) (http://www.ecrh.edu.au).

- Take brief observations of the child–teacher interactions.
- Give a score of Low/Medium/High.
- Write a short paragraph explaining what you observed relating to the five (5) points above and the rationale for your score.

Acknowledging that children and students come to their care and/or education setting with a set of values, learnings from, and understandings of, their previous experiences, they have much to contribute towards their learning. Even the youngest children in most cases bring knowledge that when they smile a response is likely to result from a caring adult, demonstrating children's ability to gain a response and possibly further purposeful engagement and learning. This ability to be active in their own learning does not, however, mean children have overall control of when, how and what learning takes place in the formal education environment. As a young children's advocate for learning, the teacher's role is to monitor children's progress and provide opportunities for further learning and growth, thereby supporting children's agency.

Practicum placements and partnerships

Practicum experiences in early childhood and primary school environments provide new learning experiences where pre-service teachers test their emerging teaching and learning philosophy and practice. This will take place as you negotiate options for children's care and learning and as you test their understanding of behaviour guidance and children's moral development, together with planning curriculum-based lessons and strategies for children's learning and teaching, in consultation with your supervising teacher.

Pre-service teachers may be engaged in developing and refining their *listening* and *reflective* skills, and in assessment tasks developing folios and resources that require consideration of family and community needs.

This includes discussing issues and challenges for practice such as:

- What does the service do to engage and support the family? What do I need to know and provide, or do I need to change my views?
- Where there are specific needs such as those relating to disability, socio-economic, or cultural considerations, asking, 'What is it at this point in time that the family want/ need to change, to support child and family functioning'? This situation may be where a referral to a specific service is required and where community networks are called upon that will form part of the decision making.

Working with community

This letter was written by a pre-service teacher completing her final practicum placement in a kindergarten (pre-school) environment for the committee of management's monthly meeting, at the request of her supervising teacher.

Dear Committee Members

During the past three weeks I have been taking on the role of room leader for both the red and blue group at your children's kindergarten. The kindergarten has been very supportive and my mentor Anthea has helped and guided me along the way. I feel as though I have learnt and grown as a teacher being at this kindergarten. I have really enjoyed getting to know all the children and families.

I have been working with the children and focusing on their interests, through taking observations and talking to the other teachers. I have found out what the children are interested in and have planned my experiences around what the children like. My main focus for the children has been numbers, letters, spring time and insects.

Some of the experiences I have set up inside this week are playdough with natural materials, playdough with numbers, matching letters, construction with trucks, rocks and sand, drawing, painting, a nature table, and craft—where children have been making butterflies and drawing and making insects.

The children have also been engaged in dramatic play through playing in the café which has been set up, as well as a hairdresser's. These experiences have been teaching children to explore different identities through play, using their imagination and exploring the environment.

I have also been focusing on science with the children, through letting them explore magnets and physics, by looking at what rolls down the ramp. Together as a group and individually, children were able to explore different objects to see what will roll or slide and how having the ramp at different levels can impact on the speed of an object going down the ramp. These experiments have allowed children to think and consider why things happen, to investigate and express their thoughts and ideas by encouraging them to think creatively.

At group time I have been focusing on music and movement and playing musical games with the children such as the game of 'Doggy doggy, who's got the bone', 'Musical dots' and 'Who is missing?'

This week is also Grandparents' and Special Friends' day. The children have been working on a performance as well as making bookmarks and invitations to send out to their grandparents and special friends for the day. I have used the group time to teach the children about letter writing and what information needs to be in a letter. I helped and assisted the children to write a letter for their grandparents and special friends which the children decorated. This has led to the children making a letter box and writing letters to each other.

During my time here I have built relationships with the children, educators, teachers and families. This is my last week with the children and I am going to miss everyone at this kindergarten.

Yours sincerely
Lucinda

STOP AND THINK

This letter is an example of engaging family and community using a partnership approach. You might ask the following questions:

- What purpose/s does this letter meet in terms of professional partnerships for the pre-service teacher, other teachers and the committee of management?
- If you were a member of the committee of management, what might your response be to the letter and its content?
- What opportunities does this open for discussion at the meeting?
- What have you learnt as a pre-service teacher about the teacher's role on practicum placements from this letter?
- What does this letter tell you about the philosophy, values and practices of this kindergarten in relation to family, community and professional partnerships?

SUMMARY

- There are a number of family and community provocations, changes and challenges for building professional partnerships, sociocultural and socio-ecological theory, best-practice, government legislation, guidelines, curriculum and standards, and advocacy for children through an equitable, ethical and social justice lens.
- Understanding effective ways of working with families and communities through forming professional partnerships is an important learning outcome for Initial Teacher Education, the quality of which will impact on the quality of child and student learning and strong relationships between teacher and children/students in your centre or school.
- Clear messages about working with families and communities that are relevant to all early childhood teachers include:
  - it is important to understand that others may not share your view of what a family is or does
  - knowing about children's families is important
  - working with the children's families requires genuine communication
  - young children need to be able to recognise their families and their culture in the early childhood education setting
  - research on early childhood education shows that high quality education makes a difference to outcomes, particularly when the family is genuinely involved and the relationship between the family and the teacher is a partnership.
- This chapter draws on the psychodynamic approach that:

  > … emphasises the emotional content and meaning of all experiences and creates links between the dynamics of individual development and that of family and community life.
  >
  > (Neven, 1996)

- Although this approach is more usually applied in the social science field, it is also reflected in key theoretical approaches underpinning educational practice based on the sociocultural models of Vygotsky and the socio-ecological systems model of Bronfenbrenner.

FURTHER REFLECTION

- Reflect on changes to families and their lifestyles over the past century and consider how this may have influenced the move towards more visible and purposeful professional partnerships with children, families and community today.
- How will you build or further develop professional partnerships with children, families and communities in prior-to-school or school environments?
- What are the key components of these partnerships?

GROUP DISCUSSION

Looking deeper into what lies behind what you see and hear:

1 How do you manage reconciling differences?
2 Think about a challenge you have faced that was easy to resolve.
   - Why was it easy?
   - What skills, knowledge and persuasion did you use?
   - Were there any power issues involved in the issue?
   - Was there a 'winner' and a 'loser' in this scenario?
   - How did you feel after the discussion?
   - Think of a 'What if' question that may have changed the outcome.

CLASS ACTIVITIES

Thinking about the changes to the NQS, read through the information provided in Standard 6 and discuss how you would respond to the eight descriptors identified in this standard. In your discussion think about the key characteristics of partnerships and how these are embedded within practice through advocacy, strength-based practice and empowerment. The questions are adapted from the descriptors for the NQS relating to collaborative partnerships with families and communities.

1 How would you develop and maintain respectful relationships with families and support their parenting role?
2 From the time of enrolment, how would you involve families in the service and support their contribution to service decisions?
3 How would you acknowledge and respect the expertise, culture, values and beliefs of families and share decision making about their children's learning and wellbeing?
4 How would you make available information about the service and relevant community services and resources to support parenting and family wellbeing?
5 Why are collaborative partnerships that enhance inclusion, learning and development important?

FURTHER READING

CHILDREN AND THEIR FAMILIES

Department of Social Services (DSS), Australian Institute of Family Studies (AIFS) Australian Bureau of Statistics (ABS) (2017), Growing Up in Australia: The Longitudinal Study of Australian Children (LSAC). www.growingupinaustralia.gov.au/
   This is a major study following the development of 10 000 children and families from all parts of Australia. The study commenced in 2004 with two cohorts—families with 4–5-year-old children and families with 0–1-year-old

infants. Growing Up in Australia is investigating the contribution of children's social, economic and cultural environments to their adjustment and wellbeing. A major aim is to identify policy opportunities for improving support for children and their families and for early intervention and prevention strategies.

FAMILY PARTNERSHIP MODEL

If you are interested in learning more about a research-based model, with specific techniques and practices designed for professionals working in partnership with vulnerable families or those where children have additional needs, the following references are highly recommended.

Davis, H., Day, C. & Bidmead, C. (2002) Working in Partnership with Parents: The Parent Adviser Model. London: Harcourt Assessment.

This is the original text for the Family Partnership Model. It includes many examples of working in partnerships with families, and is particularly useful for critical reflection.

Hood, M. (2012) 'Partnerships: Working Together in Early Childhood Settings', Research in Practice Series, 19(1). Deakin West, ACT: Early Childhood Australia.

Hood's focus is building partnerships with families and the skills in developing these, including *active listening*, *attending*, *empathetic responding* (acknowledging the issue as real), *prompting and exploring*, *reflecting back accurately*, *questioning* (using open questions), *pausing*, *summarising, enthusing* and *encouraging*, and *negotiating*.

FAMILIES AND COMMUNITIES

Bowes, J., Grace, R. & Hodge, K. (2016) Children, Families and Communities: Contexts and Consequences (5th edn). Australia and New Zealand: Oxford Press.

A comprehensive approach describing how children, families and communities influence each other through the relationships and experiences they are exposed to. Children's development is discussed, with an emphasis on the context of their everyday experiences and the consequences of these contexts. Varying characteristics of children such as developmental disability, giftedness and ethnicity, and the consequences of these characteristics for their development, are discussed. The book includes the influences of family, education and care services; media and technology; the changing contexts of play in contemporary society; relationships with peers; bullying; isolation of families, child protection and out-of-home care; and for Australian Indigenous families the realities and consequences of the 'Stolen Generation'. In the final chapters, government policy is addressed and related to influences and consequences for children living in traumatic circumstances.

Holmes, D., Hughes, K. & Julian, R. (2015) Australian Sociology: A Changing Society (4th edn). Melbourne, Vic.: Pearson Australia.

This sociological account of families in Australia draws on multiple issues and consequences for modern Australia including social media, inequalities, Aboriginality and racism, gender and the rise of diversity for partnering. Also examined are issues of immigration, climate change and global warming, globalisation, religion, political power, diversity, deviant behaviour and the decline of the 'nuclear family' as a consequence of these transformations.

DIVERSITY

Diversity has many forms and differences. This means that it is important that you acknowledge the many differences that families and their children bring to the service and the classroom. The following further readings are included to support your reflections about all families and children's participation in the program, asking: Am I providing access, inclusion and active participation in the program for all families and children?

Derman-Sparks, L. & Edwards, J. (2012) Anti-Bias Education for Young Children and Ourselves. Washington, DC: National Association for the Education of Young Children.

Anti-bias education from the perspective of these authors is the 'provision of multiracial, multilingual, and multicultural' programs for children to 'support their development … and to give them the tools they need to stand up to prejudice, stereotyping and bias'. This reference provides ideas and strategies for working with children from multiple backgrounds, languages and cultures. The chapters include easy-to-read accounts of the key concepts, with questions, scenarios and examples. There is also a section titled 'Voices from the Field', which provides authentic accounts of perceptions and practice.

Giugni, M. & Mundine, K. (2010) Talkin' Up and Speakin' Out: Aboriginal and Multicultural Voices in Early Childhood. Castle Hill, NSW, Australia: Pademelon Press.

An Australian publication based on an anti-bias education model addressing a variety of challenges for educators and teachers across Australia with several chapters discussed in terms of dichotomies such as Aboriginality/ Whiteness, Gender/Sexuality, Ethnicity/Language, Spirituality/Religions and further challenges regarding abilities ('letting the other be the other'), refugee inclusions and exclusions, activism and politics.

REFERENCES

Anning, A., Cullen, J. & Fleer, M. (2009) *Early Childhood Education: Society and Culture* (2nd edn). London: Sage Publications.

Australian Institute of Family Studies (DSS/AIFS/ABS). (2017) *Growing Up in Australia: The Longitudinal Study of Australian Children*. http://data.growingupinaustralia.gov.au/index.html.

Australian Institute for Teaching and School Leadership (AITSL). (2011) *Australian Professional Standards for Teachers*. https://www.aitsl.edu.au/teach/standard.

Baxter, J. (2016) 'The Modern Australian Family'. Australian Institute of Family Studies.

Department of Education and Training (DET) (2016) *Victorian Early Years Learning and Development Framework*. Melbourne: State of Victoria.

Department of Education, Employment and Workplace Relations (DEEWR) (2009) *Educators' Guide to the Early Years Learning Framework for Australia*. ACT: Commonwealth of Australia.

Early Childhood Australia (ECA) (2016) *Code of Ethics*. Watson, ACT: Early Childhood Australia Inc. www.earlychildhoodaustralia.org.au/our-publications/eca-code-ethics/

Ebbeck M. & Waniganayake M. (2005) *Early Childhood Professionals Leading Today for Tomorrow*. Australia: Elsevier.

Gibbs, L. (2003) *Action, Advocacy & Activism: Standing Up for Children*. Marrickville, NSW: Community Child Care Co-operative Ltd (NSW).

Golombok, S. (2015) *Modern Families: Parents and Children in New Family Forms*. Cambridge, UK: Cambridge University Press.

Hartley, R. (1995) *Families, Values and Change: Setting the Scene in Families and Cultural Diversity in Australia*. Melbourne: Australian Institute of Family Studies.

Hood, M. (2012) 'Partnerships: Working Together in Early Childhood Settings', *Research in Practice Series, 19*(1). ACT: Early Childhood Australia.

Holmes, D., Hughes K. & Julian, R. (2015) *Australian Sociology: A Changing Society* (4th edn). Melbourne, Vic: Pearson Australia.

Kennedy, A. (2014) 'Intentional Teaching: Acting Thoughtfully, Deliberately and Purposefully', *Research in Practice Series, 21*(4). ACT: Early Childhood Australia.

Neven, R. (1996) *Emotional Milestones from Birth to Adulthood: A Psychodynamic Approach*. Australia: ACER.

Qu, L. & Weston, R. (2013) 'Australian Households and Families', *Australian Family Trends,* no. 4. Melbourne: Australian Institute of Family Studies.

Rolfe, S. & Armstrong, K. (2010) 'Early Childhood Professionals as a Source of Support: The Role of Parent–Professional Communication', *Australian Journal of Early Childhood, 35*(3). Melbourne: Deakin.

Shonkoff, J. (2006) 'The Science of Early Childhood Development: Closing the Gap Between What We Know and What We Do'. Victoria: Department of Human Services.

Shonkoff, J. & Phillips, D.A. (eds) (2000) 'Board on Children, Youth and Families', *From Neurons to Neighbourhoods: The Science of Early Childhood Development.*

Slee, P. (2006) Families at Risk: Their Strengths, Resources, Access to Services and Barriers. Adelaide, South Australia: Shannon Research Press. http://ehlt.flinders.edu.au/education/FamilyNeeds/families%20at%20risk%20online.pdf.

Smale, S. (2010) 'Advocacy to Promote Children's Wellbeing and Rights', *Every Child, 16*(3): 20–1.

Stonehouse, A. (2001) 'Lessons from the "Roadshow"', *Partnerships for Children—Parents and Community Together.* Melbourne: Centre for Community Child Health.

UNCRC (1989) https://downloads.unicef.org.uk/wp-content/uploads/2010/05/UNCRC_united_nations_convention_on_the_rights_of_the_child.pdf?_ga=2.33418108.376425593.1513479208-698925879.1513479208

Winnicott, D.W. (1960) 'The Theory of the Parent–Infant Relationship', *International Journal of Psycho-Analysis*, *41*: 585–95.

Young, M. (2015) 'Tuning in to Toddlers', *Research in Practice Series*, *22*(3). Early Childhood Australia: Canberra.

Inclusive Practice for Diverse Learners: Gifted Children

Ann Hooper with Sue Lancaster

Chapter objectives

In this chapter, we will:

- discuss strategies for working inclusively as a teacher in partnership with families to enhance the learning and development of all children including those who demonstrate exceptional abilities
- examine your own beliefs and attitudes around gifted children and understand how these have been influenced
- analyse the concepts of 'gifted' and 'talented' according to a range of models and theoretical approaches and articulate a clear philosophy and rationale for meeting the needs of exceptional children in early childhood and primary educational programs
- discuss indicators used in the identification of giftedness and exceptional abilities of young children
- explore the social and emotional issues facing some gifted children in relation to other diverse learners
- explain the pedagogical implications and approaches for working with children identified as gifted and talented
- relate the role of play experiences, already discussed in Chapter 4 for all children, specifically for children who show exceptional talent and giftedness
- describe the range of potential policy issues related to the inclusion of children with exceptional abilities/talents and the educational rights of gifted children and their families
- analyse the impact of exceptional abilities for children, the family and the educational service.

Key terms

acceleration	inclusion	self-esteem
differentiated curriculum	norm-reference	sociocultural capital

In relation to children, I will:

- ensure that children are not discriminated against on the basis of gender, sexuality, age, ability, economic status, family structure, lifestyle, ethnicity, religion, language, culture, or national origin
- respect children as capable learners by including their perspectives in teaching, learning and assessment.

(ECA, 2016)

These are among the principles that guide ethical practice for early childhood professionals in Australia: the two reproduced above are directly relevant to the principles and practice of inclusion for diverse learners in early childhood education.

Introduction

This chapter will briefly outline the concept of inclusion and inclusive practice and identify the diversity of learners attending the environments where you will find yourself teaching in the future. The chapter will set the parameters for inclusive practices for *all children* both in early childhood and school environments, and discuss the intended outcomes and strategies for achieving these expectations.

Following a general introduction to the overarching principles of inclusive practice, the content will specifically focus on an in-depth account of working with children who are gifted learners with giftedness demonstrated by extraordinary talent in their academic learning or other areas of talent such as music, the arts or physical prowess. Focusing on 'inclusive practice' for gifted children is relatively controversial and giftedness is often overlooked in the early years and in the primary school classroom and referred to as not requiring the additional support that would enable these children to optimise their exceptional potential. By contrast, it is expected that children with a diagnosed disability, a health condition, whose first language is other than English, from a low socio-economic background and struggling to meet class expectations, or with emotional and social issues that are affecting their wellbeing should and will receive additional support for their learning and wellbeing for a successful future. While it is unquestionable that children with the sorts of additional needs listed above should receive this support, this principle of children's right to support that allows them to achieve to the best of their abilities and without discrimination does not extend to the gifted and talented child at a commensurate level.

What is inclusive practice?

Inclusive practice has been described as:

> taking into account all children's social cultural and linguistic diversity (including learning styles, abilities, disabilities, gender, family circumstances and geographic location learning), in curriculum decision-making processes. The intent is to ensure that all children's experiences are recognised and valued. The intent is also to ensure that all children have equitable access to resources and participation, and opportunities to demonstrate their learning and to value differences.
>
> (DEEWR, 2009)

The Early Childhood Australia (ECA) *Code of Ethics* (2016) referred to at the very start of this chapter advocates for 'democratic, fair and inclusive practices [that] promote equity and a strong sense of belonging'. The *Code of Ethics* promotes 'act[ing] in the best interests of all children and work[ing] collectively to ensure that every child is thriving and learning'.

This view is reinforced in the Early Years Learning Framework (EYLF) where the key words used to describe the learning outcomes—*identity, connected, wellbeing, confident* and *involved learners* and *effective communicators*—are also words that describe inclusive practice.

STOP AND REFLECT

Reflect on your understanding of inclusive practice and complete the sentences below, demonstrating your understanding of inclusion in an educational setting.

- I know my identity is being respected when …
- I feel connected when …
- I know when my wellbeing is being supported when …
- I feel confident and involved in my learning when …
- I know I am an effective communicator when …

These outcomes are supported by principles that indicate the concept of inclusion in all aspects of children's learning and development. These principles also reflect the way you think about the experiences prepared for children in early childhood environments that support quality inclusive practice and *how* you deliver these experiences so that they incorporate:

- secure, respectful and reciprocal relationships
- partnerships
- high expectations and equity
- respect for diversity
- ongoing learning and reflective practice.

In Chapter 12 you were introduced to Liam's story as an example of assessment for planning and learning. Liam's story is also a model of inclusive practice demonstrating the thoughts of various staff members as they reflect, evaluate and discuss Liam's progress for future planning. Below is the final extract of Liam's story. We have added references (where relevant) that link the discussion to the research-based literature, though these were not part of the actual conversation as it was recorded. You may recall that Liam has additional needs related to autism spectrum disorder, but as you read his story, you should also keep in mind that the inclusive practice approach that is recorded here could also apply to children who have exceptional abilities.

Liam's story (cont.)

Helen: I remind you that 'early childhood practitioners are not expected to know every possible health condition or disability' [Lindon, 2012, p.75], or children exhibiting learning difficulty or those who demonstrate exceptional learning above that expected of a child their age. This means that we need to further our connections with the many support services and funding options available to support Liam and his family. We cannot do this alone or by just listening to their concerns, hardship or achievements, though I know you are doing more than this. Perhaps you could pass on some of these concerns to Liam's Early Childhood Intervention Services [ECIS] worker, Rachael.

Rachael: Definitely. I might also brainstorm further with Tara on some possible strategies for Dianna and her family.

Helen: Before our time runs out today, I would like you to share what actions you have taken about the biting incident. Additionally, we also need to work out how we are going to respond to the recent complaints from various stakeholders who have expressed concern in regards to Liam's placement at this kindergarten.

Rachael: On reviewing the Behavioural Assessment Sheet, I can see clearly what triggered the incident. Liam is quite obsessed with the toy trains and due to his under-developed social skills there are social disputes and conflicts that occur when he is playing with them. I have also printed an article on biting and displayed it in our daily communications journal for the families to read.

Jill: This is what I was saying at the beginning of the meeting. It is unsafe for the other children.

Rachael: There has only been one case of a biting incident, Jill. We need to assist Liam by drawing upon a range of communication strategies during social disputes and transitions.

Tara: Perhaps we could ensure that there is always an educator present when Liam is playing with trains. This seems to be when he becomes the most aggravated.

Rachael: We also need to further develop all of the children's pro-social skills, which we have already been doing. But I do admit, we need to work on greater behavioural strategies for Liam, especially in large group moments.

Jill: What about the many parents who agree that it is a risk having Liam at the kindergarten?

Tara: Are you saying that Liam does not have a right to be here? All children should be recognised as children first, regardless of their differences. The United Nations Convention on the Rights of the Child [1989] key principles identify and support this practice.

Jill: I am not saying that he doesn't have a right to an education, but suggesting that there may be better options suited to his needs.

Rachael: Regardless Jill, our Inclusion policy states to 'promote inclusive practices and ensure the successful participation of all children at our pre-school. By encouraging the development of meaningful relationships between children with and without disabilities, or any other diverse learning needs requiring additional support during the early years, a foundation of constructing an inclusive community throughout the lifespan is established' [Guralnick, cited in Webster & Forster, 2012]. This is the type of world we aim to build, and nurturing inclusive attributes for children and families is how it begins.

Rachael: We need to educate our families, as well as educating and caring for their children.

Jill: How are we going to do that?

Helen: Perhaps both you and Tara could work on a piece for next week's newsletter, detailing the importance of positive inclusive behaviours. I would like you to refer to our Inclusion and Equity policy, highlighting our commitment to all adults and children being treated equitably regardless of level of ability or additional needs. I also would like you to utilise the Convention on the Rights of the Child and you also should include reference to our governing frameworks.

Tara: Yes. We can use our planning time on Friday, Jill.

Jill: Sure.

Helen: After all families have had a chance to read the informative piece, I will provide a questionnaire for them to fill out to see if it has made an impact, or to pinpoint any ongoing issues.

Rachael: While we are talking along the lines of professional development, I would like to propose that I undertake a free online learning course that supports early childhood professionals to develop a greater understanding of young children who exhibit behaviours of autism spectrum disorder, provided by the state government.

Tara: Would I be able to do it also?

Helen: I think that is a great idea and Jill you could attend too so the whole team have access to the information for future discussion and planning for all the children in your care. With many diverse needs to cater for it is of high importance that all services and their teachers and educators have a well-developed knowledge base and resources for various diversities to best support their families and children [McNaughton & Williams, 2008, p.77].

I admire your enthusiasm and commitment to Liam and his family. As we conclude this meeting I'd like to thank you for all of your hard work and remind you of the difference you are making in Liam's life and that of his family. Ensure you follow through with all that we have discussed, maintain communication and we shall reconvene in a month.

Rachael: I will follow up immediately with time options for our meeting with Dianna and Brad.

Helen: Thank you, Rachael.

STOP AND THINK

Reflect on this transcript from the early childhood teachers' meeting and identify *where* and *how* the conversation meets the characteristics for inclusion: secure, respectful and reciprocal relationships, partnerships, high expectations and equity, respect for diversity, ongoing learning and reflective practice.

- Are there any areas you would have addressed differently and why?
- Are all staff members treated with respect in this scenario? Give examples.
- What is the outcome you would hope to see following this meeting and what needs to be put in place to achieve this?
- How has this scenario helped you towards a better understanding of the concept of inclusion in practice?
- While this scenario is focused around a child who has additional learning and development needs, the concepts and principles discussed in this team meeting are relevant to any child and family requiring adjustments of any kind, to support their child's further learning and development. Remember too that the need for additional support and options, such as the 'seesaw effect' discussed in Chapter 12, will go up and down with additional support required at different times, for different reasons and in varying intensity.

Strength-based practice

A strength-based focus for children within the education context in Australia reflects the principles and practices of the late twentieth century underpinning interventionist programs that supported children with a disability. The research of early interventionists such as Turnbull and colleagues (2000) advocated for a change in practice, from a model that viewed disability and other vulnerabilities as a problem requiring a 'treatment' or a deficit model of practice focused on what children could not do, to a focus that recognises the value of identifying children's strengths and capacity. This strength-based model embraces the concept of empowerment and capacities, rather than seeing the child and family in the context of needing ongoing help due to their weaknesses and deficits (Turnbull et al., 2000).

McCashen (2000) identifies five 'foundational' characteristics that underpin the strength-based approach to service delivery and teaching:

1 respect
2 sharing
3 collaboration
4 social justice
5 transparency.

In this model the partners' 'intrinsic worth, rights, capacities and uniqueness' are considered in the teaching situation, and 'information and existing skills and knowledge is shared' as children and students engage in exploration, imagining, creating and 'doing' and for older children, questioning and discussing validity and opinion (McCashen, 2000).

A strength-based approach is a core element of inclusive practice and is relevant to all learning and teaching environments. Regardless of differences, each student brings a unique capacity (**sociocultural capital**) for learning to the learning and teaching environment. This means there is a responsibility for the teacher to probe, discover and nurture the *strengths* of each child and student (Carter & Lancaster, 2014).

This is the essence of a strength-based approach that empowers both students and teachers with a focus that sees and prioritises:

- opportunities *versus* problems
- solutions *versus* 'fixing'
- abilities *versus* liabilities
- doing 'with' *versus* doing 'to'.

In the past, the term **inclusion** has mostly been used when talking about families who have children with a disability. This very limited view is now challenged, and inclusion is understood to be much broader than this, reaching out to many diversities and differences in our society, both in early childhood programs and in school environments. The principles and practices of inclusive practice, based on a strength-based approach, apply to the needs and rights of *all* children.

This chapter will now move to probe the importance of inclusive practice for children who are gifted and talented and practices to support their families. At the outset, we invite you to explore your own perceptions of the concept of 'giftedness' in children and how this has been influenced. For many Initial Teacher Education students, this chapter may challenge many deeply held convictions and open up new ways of thinking about the role of the teacher in supporting these children. Many common mythologies that still abound around gifted children will be exposed and challenged. Understanding the characteristics of the gifted child, how teachers can identify such children in their classrooms, and most importantly, how they can provide rich and engaging learning environments, will be explored.

Who is the gifted child?

You may not have thought deeply about your own image of children who are gifted, but you will have an image, and this will have been developed based most likely on your past experiences and the views and values of those around you who have influenced your

sociocultural capital the unique capacity for learning that every student brings to the learning and teaching environment.

inclusion an honouring of the multiple differences and diversities in our society and creating learning environments that are inclusive of all.

thinking—this will be your 'default' position. As in Chapter 1 of this book, where you were invited to explore your own 'image' of the child so as to begin to understand what has shaped and informed your views, here you are encouraged to consider your image of the gifted and talented or exceptional child. Fundamental to developing professional responsibilities is the capacity for you to explore deeply your own belief and philosophies on gifted children and to understand how your 'mental model' has been developed and influenced. This becomes your 'default position' and will consciously and subconsciously impact on your attitudes and behaviours towards gifted children and their families.

Aren't all children gifted?

When we think of the word 'gift' many will argue that all children are precious, special gifts. I recall a mentor once explaining to me that at the beginning of each new academic year, she viewed each of her new little charges as 'gifts'—each one wrapped in their own unique way, some with vibrant colourful layers, easy to unwrap, others come plain packaged and require time and patience to slowly unravel and reveal the gift inside. It is an image that has stayed with me, and one I treasure. In this context all children are gifts. However, when we refer to children being 'gifted' or 'talented', we are suggesting a very different notion. At times, some people find the terms 'gifts' and 'talents' when referring to a select group of children a little disturbing. If we talk about 'gifted' children, does this mean some children aren't gifted? Perhaps this suggests that some children are of less value than others?

Let us look closer at the issues. Identifying children as gifted does not mean they have greater worth than other children, just as identifying children as developmentally or physically disabled doesn't mean they are of less worth. Identifying children as having learning characteristics that are significantly different from those of most of their classmates is not an issue of the children's *worth* at all; instead, it is an issue of *need*, and of *social justice*. Gifted children and developmentally disabled children have different learning needs from most of their classmates and as teachers we have to respond positively and constructively to these needs.

Doesn't everyone have a gift?

Those who claim this may be confusing gifts with personal strengths. Everyone has a personal strength, something we do better than we do other things. Similarly, most of us also have a personal weakness. We need to differentiate between the two, and not confuse our personal weaknesses with disabilities. Equally, we shouldn't confuse our personal strengths with gifts. In essence, giftedness is advanced development. Children who are gifted have the potential to perform at levels considerably beyond what might be expected for their age. So, there are children who demonstrate high performance, or who have the potential to do so, and we have a responsibility to provide optimal educational experiences to fully develop talents in as many children as possible, for the benefit of the children and society.

Throughout this section, then, we are using the term 'gift' to define an ability or aptitude significantly beyond the average and we describe children who possesses that ability as 'gifted'. We are using the word in a temporal sense to express a temporal concept (Gross, 2004)—that is, giftedness relates to 'time' and the ability of these children measured against other children of a similar age.

ANN HOOPER WITH SUE LANCASTER

Reflective Practice

gifted - exceptional - talented - highly able

What are your personal responses to these terms? If possible, consider any personal experiences you may have had in the past that have shaped your thinking and identify these.

Porter (2005) suggests that gifted children in early childhood contexts have often been overlooked. In addition, some teachers may hold traditional misconceptions of giftedness—for example, that gifted children will succeed regardless. As a result, many teachers may be limited in the support they are willing or able to give to gifted children. Consequently, a teacher's personal understanding and philosophy about giftedness will influence the learning experiences they provide for the children in their care. Thus, responsibility for catering for gifted children is influenced by what early childhood teachers think and understand about giftedness (Cohen, 2011).

Over the course of this chapter you will learn further about the rights and needs of gifted children, and the implications for you as their teacher. Knowing your current understanding and potential biases is essential, as is opening your mind to challenging your views so as to increase your capacity to advocate for, and meet, the learning needs of gifted, and indeed, all children. As discussed in Chapter 1, reflective practice involves ongoing, active thinking about one's own beliefs, values, assumptions, prejudices and the ways in which these can shape the actions we might take.

I have found in class with Bachelor of Early Childhood Teaching students, that they were quite surprised at their own deeply held views around this concept. Many publicly acknowledged that they did not have positive views, and many could remember working with 'gifted' students who they found difficult to associate with and basically 'un-cool'. A number of students acknowledged that these views were common, and often based on ignorance or the way in which others in their social group, including parents and teachers, responded to and treated gifted students. I commend them for their willingness to confront their biases and their preparedness to open their minds to a contrary view.

Defining giftedness

Defining the term gifted has been no easy task as numerous definitions have been suggested over time, but no single definition of giftedness is accepted by everyone. This can lead to some confusion as to what it means to be gifted. Parents and educators can find it difficult to communicate because of different definitions and understandings of what we mean by the term. Some definitions do not consider a child or adult gifted unless they can demonstrate that giftedness, which usually means excelling in school or in a particular field, while others see giftedness as the potential to excel whether that potential is reached or not. The lack of consensus on the meaning of giftedness fuels argument that there is no such thing. It suggests to others that giftedness is a social construct that does not yet have a firm set of beliefs attached to it. To help eliminate the confusion, it is useful to understand where the term comes from and the different perspectives that led to the various definitions that exist today.

The term 'gifted children' was first used in 1869 by Francis Galton. He referred to adults who demonstrated exceptional talent in some area as gifted—for example, a gifted chemist. Children could also inherit the potential to become a gifted adult, and Galton referred to these children as gifted children.

Lewis Terman extended Galton's interpretation of gifted children to include high IQ (IQ—or Intelligent Quotient—describes a person's intelligence level compared to other individuals in the population). In the early twentieth century he began a long-term study of gifted children, whom he defined as children with IQs of 140 or more. (A score of 100 on an IQ test indicates a performance at exactly the normal level for that age group; thus 140 is well above what would be expected for a child compared to their peers of the same age.) His study found that IQ alone could not predict success in adulthood. Terman's view led to definitions of gifted that not only included high IQ, but also the notion that giftedness should be a predictor of adult achievement.

Leta Hollingworth, too, believed that the potential to be gifted was inherited. However, she felt that providing a nurturing home and school environment were also important in the development of that potential. In 1926, she published her book, *Gifted Children, Their Nature and Nurture,* which led to definitions of gifted as childhood potential that must be nurtured in order for it to be developed in adulthood.

Renzulli (1978) proposed that there were three basic traits that interacted and characterised successful, outstanding individuals: above average general ability, high level of task commitment or intrinsic motion, and creativity. This became known as the Three Ring Model.

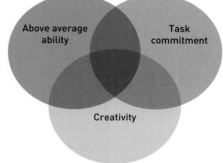

Where the three rings overlap is said to be where the gifted and talented students are found

Tannenbaum (1983) defined giftedness in young children as an extraordinary promise for productivity or performance in the areas of work that are *publicly prized*. This is an interesting idea and one we will look at in more depth shortly.

Prior to 1985, definitions used in Australia were predominantly based around a person's performance—that is, usually highly successful and highly motivated. This promoted a fairly stereotypical view of the concept of giftedness. It did, however, ignore the notion of the 'hidden gifted'—those gifted children who, for various reasons, were not translating high abilities or potential into achievements.

Definitions that view giftedness as a *potential* to be developed make a distinction between what a child *is capable of achieving* and what the child *will achieve*. That children may have exceptional potential is part of what makes them gifted. Children's environments determine whether potential leads to achievement, and as such, the importance of providing an appropriate environment is highlighted. This has significant implications for teachers.

François Gagné's (2002) Differentiated Model of Giftedness and Talent (DMGT) proposes a clear distinction between these two most basic concepts in the field of gifted education.

The main elements are:

- giftedness and talents are *not* synonymous
- giftedness is seen as the possession of natural abilities/aptitudes at levels beyond what is expected for the age of the child
- talents are the high achievements that the child may demonstrate (significant beyond what might be expected at a given age)
- a child may transfer from giftedness (potential) to talent (achievement) dependent on many factors, which Gagné refers to as *catalysts*.

ANN HOOPER WITH SUE LANCASTER

CATALYSTS

INTRAPERSONAL (IC)

Physical: characteristics, handicaps, health, etc.

Motivation: needs, interests, values, etc.

Volition: will-power, effort, persistence.

Self-management: concentration, work habits, initiative, scheduling, etc.

Personality: temperament, traits, wellbeing, self-awareness & esteem, adaptability, etc.

GIFTEDNESS = TOP 10%

NATURAL ABILITIES (NAT) DOMAINS

Intellectual (IG)
Fluid reasoning (induct./deduct.), cristallized verbal, spatial, memory, sense of observation, judgment, metacognition.

Creative (CG)
Inventiveness (problem-solving), imagination, originality (arts), retrieval fluency.

Socioaffective (SG)
Intelligence (perceptiveness), communication (empathy, tact), influence (leadership, persuasion).

SensoriMotor (MG)
S: visual, auditory, olfactive, etc.
M: strength, endurance, reflexes, coordination, etc.

Positive/ negative impacts

DEVELOPMENTAL PROCESS
Informal/formal learning & practicing (LP)

Positive/ negative impacts

TALENT = 10 %

SYSTEMATICALLY DEVELOPED SKILLS (SYSDEV)

FIELDS
(relevant to school-age youths)

Academics: language, science, humanities, etc.

Arts: visual, drama, music, etc.

Business: sales, entrepreneurship, management, etc.

Leisure: chess, video games, puzzles, etc.

Social action: media, public office, etc.

Sports: individual & team.

Technology: trades & crafts, electronics, computers, etc.

CHANCE (CH)

ENVIRONMENTAL (EC)

Milieu: physical, cultural, social, familial, etc.

Persons: parents, teachers, peers, mentors, etc.

Provisions: programs, activities, services, etc.

Events: encounters, awards, accidents, etc.

Source: https://www.google.com.au/url?sa=i&rct=j&q=&esrc=s&source=images&cd=&cad=rja&uact=8&ved=0ahUKEwjM6tSg1t3XAhVl2LwKHdyoA1UQjRwIBw&url=https%3A%2F%2Fgiftedstudentliteracy.weebly.com%2Fgagnes-differentiated-model-of-giftedness-and-talent.html&psig=AOvVaw3ob48NsPDWa6PVe5p-oXlY&ust=1511834962034586.

This theory has had significant impact on how educators view gifted children and is now widely accepted by educators and policy makers. It has also influenced contemporary approaches to educating the gifted. The Victorian Department of Education (DET, 2012) refers to Gagné's model in its policies related to meeting the needs of these children. Implications for teachers of this model include recognition that children's potential for

Source: Gross, 2004.

high achievement relies on the input from the environment, including the quality of the education they receive.

We pride ourselves on being a nation rich in cultural diversity. In our society, different abilities and achievements are valued by different cultures. It may be that in some cultures, creative gifts are more valued than academic gifts, while other cultures value sporting ability very highly. You will recall in the definitions above that Tannenbaum referred to areas of giftedness related to those things that 'publicly prized'.

STOP AND THINK

Look at the cartoon above.

- What are the messages we can take from this?
- What abilities are valued by the communities you interact with?
- What abilities are less valued?
- Is it 'cool' to be talented in some subjects but less so in others? If so, why?

Mythologies and misunderstandings

Many people have strongly held beliefs about the concept of giftedness and the rights of gifted children. Listed here are views held by many people in schools and the community.

- All children are gifted in some way.
- Identifying and catering for the potentially gifted is elitist. It is inequitable to provide extension for some.
- Even if they are very bright, children should stay with their chronological age peers.
- When so-called 'gifted children' level out—usually three years into 'formal' schooling— it will become evident that strategies such as acceleration impair their development, particularly their social and emotional development.

ANN HOOPER WITH SUE LANCASTER

- All basic low-level tasks must be executed perfectly before extension can be considered and extension activities should be undertaken out of class.
- Children experiencing learning difficulties could not be gifted.
- Gifted children grouped together will become arrogant and snobbish.
- Other more needy students are more deserving or in need of special attention.
- Parents 'hothouse' their children. Once the child is away from their influence they will revert to 'normal' developmental expectations.
- All parents think their children are gifted.

STOP AND REFLECT

- Are any of these statements similar to your own thoughts?
- Which statements do you think would reflect community views?
- Are there any statements that you feel very strongly about or would defend?

It would be interesting for you to come back to this list at the conclusion of your studies on this topic to see if you can provide reasons as to why they are referred to as myths.

Characteristics of gifted children

How can we identify gifted children in our classrooms?

Despite popular belief that gifted children are mainly from upper, middle class or professional families, the truth is they occur in the same numbers in all socio-economic, indigenous and cultural groups. The challenge for early childhood teachers is to be aware of and know how to identify children who are gifted if they are to effectively meet their needs. Every early childhood professional will be working with gifted children. It is estimated that 10–15 per cent of children are gifted, which means a typical early childhood group or school class will contain at least two gifted children. Many will have more, so it is imperative that professionals reflect on their practice and seek professional learning opportunities to increase their understanding and knowledge of giftedness and talent in young children. It is imperative if we are to meet the needs of gifted children in our classrooms that we are well placed to understand some generalised characteristics that may assist in their identification.

A word of caution though: some people in the field are most reluctant to formally identify young children for fear of labelling and pigeonholing them. It is important to understand from the outset that, like all children, gifted children are individuals with their own unique qualities and dispositions and they will have diverse strengths, interests and learning needs.

STOP AND REFLECT

Connecting with your prior knowledge
- Consider your own dealings or interactions with children/students who you thought were gifted.
- List the observable characteristics that you believe they may have had in common which identified them as potentially being gifted.

Academics and researchers have compiled lists that contain many of the shared characteristics that these children may have in common, which can be most helpful in supporting teachers to better understand and ultimately provide richer learning experiences for them. So what are some of the factors we should consider when identifying a potentially gifted child? There are many underlying biases that can interfere with a teacher's ability to identify high potential in young children. For example, children from different and diverse cultural backgrounds may not fit our narrow or pre-determined ideas about what it means to be gifted. It is important to examine our own biases and stereotypical thinking to guard against this trap.

Individual assessments and observations are 'snapshots' only, and provide information about what the child can do at a particular time. To authentically identify a young gifted and/or talented child requires a collection of evidence over time—that is, a 'photo album' rather than a single photo. Quite often, and for a variety of reasons, children may not perform 'on demand', and thus not demonstrate their full potential on one particular task. Young gifted and talented children's development is often uneven, with peaks and troughs that can be unpredictable. Therefore, multiple assessments and observations over time are necessary to identify advanced development or learning.

Many young gifted children in early childhood settings are not presented with an opportunity or support to demonstrate their gifted potential, or to develop this potential into talent, and thus may go unnoticed. (Remember the implications of Gagné's 'catalysts' for developing gifts to talents.)

There are a number of characteristics that can signal to a parent or teacher that a young child might be gifted. Certain behaviours can be observed that may indicate when a child's thinking or learning is advanced. Let us look more closely at some of the common characteristics many young children display that may indicate they are potentially gifted.

- They reach developmental milestones—particularly language development and walking— earlier than children of the same age.
- They master new toys quickly—they have a low threshold for boredom.
- They demonstrate complex play ideas that can baffle their peers.
- They enjoy the company of older children and display emotional sensitivity and empathy.
- They recall past events in detail, and have an impressive memory and an extended concentration span.
- They create stories, rhymes and jokes at an early age.
- Their vocabulary is well advanced, and they can read before school age, often with little intervention.
- Early incessant questioning is common, and they seek out adults to provide stimulation and have an intense curiosity.
- They show interest, are creative, and learn and understand material quickly.
- They demonstrate frustration and lack of common play interests with peers.
- They can display an intense interest in social justice.

STOP AND THINK

- Return to the list you compiled earlier. What are the similarities/differences between your prior knowledge and the knowledge you now have of the varied characteristics of potentially gifted children?
- Which characteristics do you think might be more easily observed in young children?

ANN HOOPER WITH SUE LANCASTER

Being gifted at an early age

Being gifted is not always easy for the child and catering for individual children can also be challenging. We know that between the ages of four to seven years is a rapid period of cognitive growth. Gifted children learn faster than others, and when this is neither identified nor catered for children can easily become bored and disengage. Not all the characteristics of gifted and talented students are seen as positive.

Davis and Rimm (1998) identified negative characteristics that gifted students may display, such as stubbornness, uncooperativeness, cynicism, sloppiness and disorganisation, a tendency to question authority, emotional frustration and absentmindedness. These are often exhibited by gifted underachievers and students with a learning disability, which we will learn more about later in the chapter

> The challenge for teachers is to identify the *reasons* for the underlying behaviour, rather than labelling a child with behavioural issues and consequently discounting the possibility of giftedness.
>
> (Merrick & Targett, 2004)

Identification methods

Research strongly argues that it is imperative for the long-term wellbeing of gifted children that they are identified *as early as possible*. Unfortunately there may be many issues that prevent teachers from identifying or recognising gifted children in their classrooms, particularly in the early years. These include:

> Teachers overlook giftedness—this may be due to personal bias or lack of knowledge or training
>
> Gifted children may hide their abilities—often they have internalised very early on that it is not 'cool' to be seen as gifted
>
> Experience in the learning environment is not challenging—so there is no opportunity to display potential
>
> Fine motor skills impede ability—the brain is operating at a higher level than skill development
>
> May be creatively or emotionally but not academically gifted—and often this is not valued as highly
>
> Individual learning style is not catered for—so again, there is limited opportunity to demonstrate potential.
>
> (Merrick & Targett, 2004)

What, then, are some of the options or *tools* teachers can use to assist in the identification of a potentially gifted child in the classroom?

There are a number of procedures that can be most valuable in identification; however, guidelines need to be followed to achieve a holistic view of the child. Procedures for identification should be multifaceted, holistic, dynamic and ongoing and involve parents or caregivers, children, teachers and other professionals (Merrick & Targett, 2004).

It is essential that the identification methods selected match the sociocultural context of the children and that teachers are aware of limitations of some tools for certain groups (e.g. indigenous, lower socioeconomic or minority cultural groups). For example, when assessing children's literacy comprehension skills, ensure the content of the book reflects children's experiences in relation to family and local community nuances. Essentially, a wide range of strategies that are responsive to age, need, location, background and school/centre resources should be utilised.

Generally speaking, identification tools can be divided into two categories: *subjective* (*qualitative*) and *objective* (*quantitative*). A closer look at some of these identification tools can assist in choosing the most effective ones for the context.

Subjective identification

Subjective observation involves people close to children being aware of any of the characteristics discussed above.

- *Educators:* teachers can gather evidence of children's progress, strengths, interests and areas of need through the systematic gathering of their work, records of discussions and observations of their interactions with peers and teachers.
- *Parents/caregivers:* carers closest to children see them across time and situations. They are well equipped as informants. Research indicates that parents are statistically more successful in identifying gifted characteristics than teachers (and debunk the myth that all parents view their children as gifted, and that parents 'hothouse' their children).
- *Peer nomination:* classmates can perceive their peers' abilities with some clarity, often recognising characteristics of other gifted children. They see children in a range of settings and can make valuable observations. The design of peer nomination forms must be relevant and useful to the purpose (e.g. 'Who is the best problem solver? Who is the best artist?').

  There are some limitations to using peer nomination as an indicator, however, as peers may not like or respect the gifted child, and often children may want to include their best friends. Also, peers may not be aware of other children's abilities; this makes this tool less reliable for younger children. Children identified through this method should undergo further subjective/objective means.
- *Self-nomination:* children can be asked to opt in for programs and nominate themselves for inclusion. Many children, even at a very young age, are capable of seeing where their talents lie and are keen to share if given the opportunity. Interviewing young children can be particularly effective. Some limitations of using this approach are that children may not want to be seen as different (that is, they have already learnt that to be different is not valued), and of most importance is the relationship between the adult and the child: a child will be reluctant to disclose if there is a lack of warmth and respect (Merrick &Targett, 2004).

Objective identification

It is not always necessary to have a formal identification of giftedness, such as through an IQ test, if a child is being catered for appropriately, is achieving well and is thriving. There are times though, when formal identification is required. Parents may wish to have their child's giftedness confirmed, or a formal assessment may be required for early school entry or for participation in special programs. The results of formal assessments, such as IQ tests, need to be interpreted carefully, as some children, particularly from culturally diverse or disadvantaged backgrounds, do not perform as might be expected as the tasks on such tests may favour certain demographics (e.g. children from Anglo-Saxon middle-class families). IQ tests can help to identify children with some learning difficulties, or when the children's teacher has not been able to identify their advanced potential, or seeks to ignore or deny it. If the results of an IQ test do not match your own observations of a young child, continue to document evidence and ensure you continue to plan appropriately for their learning needs.

Underachievers

Gifted children are among our greatest academic underachievers, but are often unrecognised as being either gifted or underachieving. This idea is surprising to many, as I found with pre-service students. Most of them expect that a gifted child will in fact be successful, regardless of whether they are specifically catered for or not. This fuels the mythology that gifted children will succeed and do not need special attention or consideration.

Who, then, are the academically gifted underachievers? Generally speaking, underachievement is widely recognised as a discrepancy between potential and performance.

Gagné's model and underachievement

Earlier in this section we learnt about Gagné's model of giftedness and talent. This model is very useful in that it clearly conceptualises underachievement, as it differentiates between 'gifted' and 'talented'.

Consider Emily, for example, who possesses high academic potential (gift) in the area of maths (having been assessed in the 99th percentile on a standard IQ test), but at school her performance (talent) sees her working at mid-class level in all areas, including maths. Her teacher was surprised when shown the IQ test results. Emily is a gifted academic underachiever.

What are some factors that can lead to children such as Emily not learning to their capacity? To answer this, let us explore the notions of *self-esteem* and *self-efficacy*, both of which can impact on a child's attitude and disposition to learning.

Self-esteem is a concept that refers to people's overall evaluation of themselves. It is an appraisal of one's own worth. You can usually tell whether a person has a high self-esteem or low self-esteem by their behaviour and reactions to the environments. Self-esteem is the opinion people have about themselves. Children internalise very early on their sense of worth, based on experiences and relationships with key people in their lives.

Self-efficacy differs slightly in that it is a self-assessment by someone about their ability to perform a given task or face a situation. This is the feeling that builds up as you go on learning and mastering different abilities in life. In fact, self-efficacy is a strong belief in your own ability to succeed against all odds. For instance, a child may not know how to play football and may have a low self-efficacy for ball games, but that doesn't result in a low self-esteem if they don't think of ball games as being important in their life. Therefore, children can have an overall high level of self-esteem, and still experience low self-efficacy for a

self-esteem your overall evaluation of yourself.

certain skill. Children's levels of self-efficacy will determine whether coping behaviours will be initiated (e.g. task avoidance or behavioural problems to mask feelings of inadequacy), how much effort they will put into a task and how long it will be sustained in the face of difficulty or challenge. Many people have a separate self-efficacy for most activities they engage in. Consider the child who loves books and flourishes in their reading development, but approaches mathematical tasks with disdain.

Source: Chaffey, 2004.

Put simply, self-efficacy is your self-belief that you can approach and successfully complete a task. A child with low academic self-efficacy may choose not to try, or to put in minimal effort, for fear of failing, or for some gifted children, for fear of not living up to others' high expectations of them. Such children give up quickly when difficulties arise, and are likely not to be identified as gifted.

Other underachievement factors

We touched briefly on other factors that can mask underachievement. Let us now look at some of these in more detail.

- *Forced-choice dilemma:* the forced-choice dilemma (Gross, 1989) can be a significant contributing factor to underachievement for many gifted children. Essentially, this is when children feel they must choose between acceptance, either by the group, a peer or a teacher, and demonstrating their capabilities.
- *Twice exceptional or double-labelled children:* some gifted children may also have disabilities such as visual or hearing impairment, cerebral palsy, behavioural problems, attention deficit hyperactive disorder or autism spectrum disorder. Often it can be the disability that is the focus and this can mask the child's giftedness.
- *Perfectionism:* gifted children can make high demands on themselves, and sometimes feel they need to do things perfectly. This can be a positive driver as it can motivate children to work hard to do things well. However, in its more negative form, it can lead gifted children to avoid taking the risk of trying new things if they feel they may not succeed or reach their own high standards.
- *Boredom:* gifted children who are presented with learning experiences that are below their knowledge or skill levels, or at too slow a pace, will quickly become bored. Children who are unrecognised as being gifted are especially vulnerable as behaviours arising from boredom can often be interpreted as behavioural or immaturity problems rather than those of a gifted, bored child.
- *Aboriginal or Torres Strait Islander populations:* gifted children from these populations are underrepresented in virtually all types of educational provisions. It is important to realise they do exist in our schools in the same proportions as other community groups. Often their gifts and talents are heavily masked. These children are likely to experience two underachievement factors more strongly: the forced-choice dilemma and low academic self-efficacy.
- *High expectations:* the need for teachers to have high expectations for all children is strongly advocated in the EYLF documents. It is crucial for all children, but particularly for gifted children. Research strongly supports the view that high teacher expectations can have a positive influence on all children in our schools. This is particularly so

ANN HOOPER WITH SUE LANCASTER

for underachieving children. Of course, it also follows that teachers who have low expectations for children or teachers who have 'given up' negatively impact on all children significantly (Chaffey, 2004). It is important to note, however, that our expectations for children need to be realistic, recognising that every child can learn, but that some children require quite different opportunities and supports to do so.

STOP AND THINK

Tom is in Year 2. He simply refuses to participate in most literacy activities. He frequently tunes out and no amount of encouragement changes his attitude. When pushed, he can display negative behaviours and even aggression. Mrs Long, his teacher, has given up trying to motivate him.

- How might you interpret this behaviour?
- Is it possible that Tom's potential in literacy is heavily masked due to his disengagement?
- Could this be a strong indicator of low self-efficacy?
- Might he be an 'invisible' gifted child? What could you do in this situation?

Emotional and social development

It is important to view children's learning and development from a holistic view. It is not possible to separate learning from emotions. Understanding, identifying and responding to the emotional and social development of all children will, in turn, support academic learning.

In this section we will explore and begin to understand the social and emotional characteristics of gifted children. Like all children, for some gifted children issues related to social and emotional development can present as they develop their ability to understand and relate to the world around them and their relationships with others. Research suggests (Tomlinson et al., 2003) that gifted children are socially, emotionally and intellectually as robust as other children so long as their environments are adjusted to meet their social, emotional and intellectual development. But others, particularly highly gifted children or children with a-synchronised development, need additional support.

A-synchronised development in gifted children is when the development of intellectual, emotional and physical traits are divergent.

> Parents often describe these children as being many ages at once. A five year old, for example, might read third-grade books, lack the small motor coordination necessary for kindergarten art projects, have lengthy conversations with adults, and struggle to communicate effectively with age peers—all at the same time.
>
> (Rivero, 2012)

The higher a child's intellectual ability, the more a-synchronised development is likely to be. At times, advanced intellectual development can lead teachers and parents to expect more advanced behaviour from children: it is important to remember that advanced intellectual ability does not enable the gifted child to manage their emotions better than any other child.

Gifted children who may be thinking at a higher level than their peers can feel 'different' or isolated from their peers. We sometimes see this when they become frustrated that other children cannot understand their more sophisticated play ideas. Because they can think at a more abstract level, they can become upset when other children don't play by the rules. It is important to remember that the gifted child is just that—a child—and like all children they can, at times, become overwhelmed by their feelings. They will sometimes need adult help or support in coping with their emotions, just like other children will.

As for most children, gifted children seek out friends with whom they can share their thoughts, ideas and feelings. They are often searching for 'like-minded' peers or 'true peers'. This can be difficult in an early childhood setting as there may not be an opportunity to find such a soul mate. Young children rely heavily on adults to support them in social situations. Young gifted children may seek out adult interactions for stimulation and to share their ideas with. Often we can be tempted to 'send' the child back to play with the other children. To spend some time interacting with a gifted child may be one of the most important things you can do for them (Morrissey, 2012).

Children in early learning environments quickly learn the importance of peer relations and have a strong need to feel a sense of belonging and acceptance. We know that every child needs to feel they *belong* and it is as much the teacher's responsibly to facilitate children's friendships and belonging to the group as it is to teach them colours and numbers. Children who face social issues at these critical formative years can experience issues long term.

Emotional characteristics

Young children may demonstrate some common affective traits or characteristics including the following: strong sense of what is just and appears fair (seen in questioning those who do not rigorously follow the 'rules'); heightened empathy and morality (deep caring or passionate about causes such as animal welfare); intense emotion (upset about what is seen to be trivial); sophisticated types of play and preferring the company of older children (referred to as 'true peers'); asynchronous development (for example, emotional development may be different from intellectual development or may cause frustration when technical writing skills and control are not as developed as their ability to produce creative, extensive ideas for writing); and having a more mature sense of humour and feeling different to their classmates (Morrissey 2012).

Issues can arise for children when their needs are not being addressed and these can manifest in a number of ways. Young children can pick up very early on if their 'differences' are not recognised and validated. They may, in fact, learn to hide their abilities to 'fit in' with the dominant group or to receive teacher approval if they do not feel valued. Some coping strategies that children can develop when emotional issues arise may include:

- *hiding or denying their giftedness*: young children can learn to hide talents such as reading earlier than their peers as they learn early that to display abilities and opinions that are different from those of others can lead to ostracism (forced-choice dilemma).
- *conforming to peer expectations*: young children can learn to 'dumb' down their abilities in order to gain peer acceptance.

Children learn early that they can be penalised for knowing too much, particularly if they are in an environment where their abilities are not valued by the teachers, and consequently, by other children, and they can 'turn off'. These young children need to feel that they are accepted by important adults and other children. If their abilities are not validated they can feel unaccepted. Gifted children can greatly benefit from interaction

norm-reference
comparing children
against each
other so that they
are seen as, for
example, average
or above average.

with others of equal ability—this can assist them to develop successful social skills and a positive self-concept.

- *norm referencing*: as humans we develop a sense of self from our interactions with those around us. Young children begin to 'compare' themselves with their peers from about the age of seven. Many gifted children reach this stage much earlier. This can have implications. Consider, for example, a five-year-old child beginning school already reading at an advanced level. They may **norm-reference** themselves against others in their class who are only beginning to learn the alphabet. If the child is struggling with their own self-concept they may choose to mask their reading abilities to 'fit in' with the other children.

STOP AND THINK

At home, Sally, aged five, was reading more like an eight-year-old, but when she entered school her teacher placed her in a pre-reading group because she showed no signs, in class, of being able to read. The teacher and Sally's mother later found that she was pretending, at school, to be a non-reader because her best friend was in this group. Sally's mother found that she was confusing being liked with being 'like'. She had been convinced that if she did not behave 'like' the other children, they would not like her. She realised she was different in her reading abilities, the games she liked playing and the way she felt about many things, and she quickly camouflaged the most obvious of these differences.

- How might you support Sally to manage this situation so she feels comfortable to work at her intellectual capacity and does not feel she has to choose between this and her friendships?

The importance of developing friendships

> When gifted children are asked what they most desire, the answer is often 'a friend'. The children's experience of school is completely coloured by the presence or absence of relationships with peers.
>
> (Silverman, 1993)

It is important to understand that children form friendships not primarily on the basis of chronological age, but on the basis of similarities in developmental stages. Many gifted children develop the capacity to make social comparisons earlier than the average child and their play interests can differ from those of their age-peers. Social issues facing gifted young children can include:

- *lack of same ability peer group*: this can lead either to loneliness or compromise between their interests and the need to maintain relationships. This is often a dilemma in early childhood settings where access to older, 'like-minded' peers is limited
- *unrealistic demands of others*: this can come about when others assume that the child's higher level of cognitive reasoning matches their stage of emotional development
- *misunderstandings of other children*: their higher levels of thinking and emotional development, including high levels of moral understandings, can have them at odds with their peers, and they can often be labelled as 'bossy' or uncooperative
- *a need to learn tact*: young gifted children can benefit from explicit teaching of social skills and strategies to use to assist them to play more effectively with others.

For gifted children, the need for friendship and peer acceptance is just as important as it is for all children. Responses from other children that affirm their sense of self are paramount. Typically this includes peer acceptance of the children's intellectual ability, even if their behaviour differs from that of their age-peers.

Supporting parents and carers

The most frequent concerns for parents and carers of young gifted children include:

- lack of resources or information
- the ignorance and misinformation that still exists about gifted learners
- the curriculum generally is lock-step where every child is expected to learn the same material at approximately the same age
- educational systems increasingly focus on basic minimal levels of competence and achievement
- socialisation is viewed as more important than academic achievement
- parents feel isolated and stigmatised because of attitudes towards gifted children, particularly from other parents, and sadly from some educators.

STOP AND THINK

- How are these issues facing parents linked to the mythologies we referred to earlier?
- As an informed professional, how could you support parents in your community in their role of carers of young gifted children?

Issues facing schools/centres

Resourcing and allocation of limited funds has been, and still remains, a significant issue for schools. Decisions need to be made on where the allocation of resources is directed. Some schools may feel that gifted children will succeed regardless and this mythology may lead to resources being limited or not allocated at all to meeting the needs of gifted children.

Some leaders and teachers in schools have not had access to current research or department policy on the rights of every child to access a learning environment that caters to their needs; they may not have the skills to identify and cater for such children or they may hold strong biases that influence the actions they do, or do not, take. Gifted children have rights and need strong advocacy to ensure all educational facilities recognise and cater for their needs. It is our moral obligation.

In our communities and societies some people hold egalitarian philosophies (i.e. believing in the principle that all people are equal and deserve equal rights and opportunities) and do not believe in providing more support or extra opportunities for gifted children.

They believe this is unfair and is giving such children an advantage over 'normal' children. They believe that all children should have the same opportunities and treatment.

Such thinking greatly restricts some children's rights, and confuses equality with sameness. *True equality* is providing all children access to a rich and engaging learning environment that allows each to reach their true potential, and that will require different things for different children. It is, in fact, a social justice issue.

It is also not uncommon for parents of gifted children to be ostracised from other parents as, again due to misunderstanding and biases, parents can see gifted children as having greater opportunities than their own children and this can lead to criticism and exclusion. (My BECT students were shocked to hear that some parents sometimes wish their child was not gifted. Such are the battles and difficulties still confronting them, particularly around finding a supportive learning environment where they are accepted by peers and teachers, and provided with a rich and engaging curriculum that meets their specific needs. Does this surprise you?)

Encouragingly, there are also many exciting alternatives to this model happening in many excellent schools today—where cross age, vertical grouping, acceleration and individualised learning programs are commonplace. Such environments have much more potential to see children as unique individuals and to offer learning experiences based on philosophies that reflect inclusivity and diversity. However, some schools and education institutions operate in a more rigid, formal curriculum and pedagogy where there is little opportunity or incentive to address the individual needs of children

Learning environments

In this section we will explore some teaching and learning strategies and approaches that can support learning for gifted children, including grouping children for learning, the role of acceleration, a discussion on the concept of developmentally appropriate learning, advantages of play and the role of differentiated curriculum and pedagogical approaches.

There are established views in the literature that suggest children's later learning achievements are related to their early school experiences (Grant, 2013). This places significant responsibility on early childhood teachers to ensure they provide a rich and appropriate learning environment for all children. Grant (2013) suggests three main areas of focus:

1 experiences of the learning environment
2 experiences of the relationships
3 communication between learning environments, including the home.

Supportive environments

Hannah, aged four, became so interested in numbers that she constantly sought ways to increase her knowledge and skills. Her parents became actively involved in her interests, working closely with her and ensuring that the aspects she was interested in were taught accurately. Hannah thrived in this environment.

Hannah started at a local pre-school with a different philosophical approach to what she had experienced at home—a wide range of materials were provided, children were mostly free to move from activity to activity and a developmental approach to interpreting children's needs with mostly non-interventionist teaching strategies was employed. Predominantly, child-initiated play was the focus. Hannah did not settle well. She cried when she was left, and frequently throughout the day. Her teacher explained to her parents that, in her view, Hannah was demonstrating emotional immaturity, and that with further opportunity to 'play' with and interact with other children she would mature.

Hannah loved learning at home. She had developed a well-established 'cognitive learner identity'. At pre-school her advanced intellectual ability had not been identified or acknowledged, and her issues were identified as social immaturity, and as such, Hannah did not connect pre-school with 'learning'.

STOP AND THINK

Research suggests that for a gifted child, and in fact all children, to thrive, supportive child–educator relationships combined with emotional security and high levels of intellectual stimulation are paramount (Grant, 2013).

- Consider Hannah's situation. Which of the components suggested for a positive, productive learning environment are present? Which are lacking?

In an early childhood setting, teachers are well placed to focus on individual children, with some freedom to plan children's learning around their interests and strengths, rather than being constrained by a set curriculum. One important element to consider when working with gifted children is to keep an open mind, and not place a ceiling on what you think children of a particular age are capable of. Although in this section we are discussing strategies and action that may be beneficial for gifted children, it is important to see that the philosophical underpinnings of these approaches can also be applied to all children in your class, true to inclusive practice.

Typically, many gifted children present as eager to learn and very curious. Programs developed to follow their interests can focus and engage them. Some examples of practices and approaches that can support gifted children to thrive in the classroom include:

- *high expectations*: one of the key practice principles of the Early Childhood Framework (ECF) is that teachers must have 'high expectations' for every child. In the context of the gifted child, our expectations must be based on children's individual capabilities, even where this means going well beyond what we might expect for a child of that age
- *a focus on individual strengths and interests*: opportunities for long-term projects of the child's choice where they are able, as much as possible, to self-direct. These could include research projects, artistic creations or construction projects. Scaffolding and support through the planning and implementation stages should be given as required. Often, such projects can become springboards for other children to become involved, which can support positive interactions between children
- *community connections*: access and utilise community resources and expertise to build on children's interest. For example, if a child has a significant interest in dinosaurs, accessing a member of the community with a background in palaeontology to work with the child would be beneficial. While working individually with the gifted child, this expert could also present items of interest to the whole group, providing opportunities for all the children

- *self-directed learning:* provide opportunities for children to choose and access materials for their own creations. We can limit children's opportunities when we 'set up' the room with little opportunity for children to self-select, so arrange storage areas that children are free to choose from. Engage children in the design and layout of the learning areas—both internally and externally. Allow children to have input into the design of the learning program itself
- *partnerships:* become a co-learner with the child. We know children can move from the unknown to the known when working with a more knowledgeable person. Assist children to find out about their areas of interest: assist them in selecting resources that will develop their understandings, including the use of information technology; read information that is relevant as children may not be able to read the information but they may still be able to understand the advanced concepts if we provide the support needed to access it
- *language:* characteristically, many gifted children have advanced vocabulary skills and the capacity to build on these beyond what might be expected for their age. Provide rich language environments and introduce new vocabulary, including the use of technical terms in their areas of interests. For example, if a child is interested in dinosaurs, introducing terms such as 'extinct' might expand the child's thinking to include current animals that are at risk of becoming extinct.

It is important to support the gifted child, as we do all children, in all areas of their development. Often teachers feel they need to focus more on the areas that are not so well developed, and for gifted children this can be seen as social issues (recall Hannah's situation). It remains important to continue to challenge them in their areas of strength as well as supporting areas that are more age-typical. As with Hannah, if a gifted child is under-challenged, they will be unhappy and unlikely to thrive on any level (Morrissey, 2012).

The role of play

Throughout this book, we have emphasised that play is fundamental to learning and development for all children. You will now understand that play contributes to children's cognitive development, social skills and emotional wellbeing. Furthermore, as stated by Post (2014),

> It is the foundation for children's earliest social relationships, enhances the parent–child bond, and lights the spark of creativity and passion. Children discover, what brings them joy and intrigue, and what is meaningful. …
> Sometimes it is assumed that gifted children need less play than others. Their intensity, introversion, and focused interests can be misinterpreted as evidence that they don't need time for play … Yet, gifted children need the same unstructured play as other children. Arguably, even more so. Here's why:
> - Gifted children thrive when they can be creative, inventive, and use their minds productively.
> - Play can incite their love for learning and discovery.
> - Gifted children benefit from learning to cooperate with peers. They grow from learning to adapt with friends who are not gifted, and by meeting the challenge when with gifted peers.

- They learn important lessons about social skills, managing anxiety, coping with competitive feelings, and what types of social interactions feel comfortable for them.
- Gifted children develop a sense of mastery when they accomplish something challenging, and a demanding play situation may require more from them than an academic environment.

Differentiation

Differentiated instruction is a philosophy of teaching and learning that recognises and responds to student differences in readiness, interests and learner profile. Teachers who implement differentiated instruction successfully understand that in their classrooms there will always be developmental differences among children. A **differentiated curriculum** is necessary for gifted children whose potential is unlikely to develop without modification to the age-typical curriculum. Meeting children at their own level requires teachers to understand *what* to teach, how to *modify* instruction in ways that are likely to promote excitement for learning, and how to implement and use *assessment* strategies effectively. Let's look more closely at these strategies.

differentiated curriculum curriculum that strives to cater for the individual needs of all children in the educational setting.

What to teach

Teachers must have a solid understanding of the learning goals and developmental progression of important skills and knowledge. When teachers know clearly where to take children instructionally, it becomes apparent which children will need support to reach the goals and which children have already mastered them, and so require modification. Children learn and develop at varying rates. Acknowledging this means teachers will be willing and able to modify their instruction so that *all* children benefit.

Differentiation begins with a high quality curriculum that addresses key concepts, ideas and skills that all children are to learn. It promotes active learning, incorporates real-life experiences and connects to children's interests (Tomlinson et al., 2003).

Differentiation is also inextricably linked to effective assessment, particularly pre-assessment. Pre-assessment enables teachers to uncover what children know, understand and can do *before* they begin the learning experience. Ongoing formative assessment enables teachers to monitor learning *during* the teaching process. It is important for all students, but particularly gifted students, as nothing diminishes children's enthusiasm for learning more quickly than having to spend time learning concepts or skills they have already mastered.

Curriculum provisions for young learners should also include opportunities for enrichment, extension and acceleration within and, at times, beyond the classroom. What do we mean by enrichment, extension and acceleration, and how do they differ from each other?

- *Extension*: strategies that go beyond standard year level work, but do not result in advanced placement is referred to as extension (e.g. a child in a Year 2 class who is advanced in maths works towards Year 3 level maths).
- *Enrichment*: strategies that provide for a broader exposure to year-level curriculum is referred to as enrichment (e.g. a child, again advanced in maths, may be provided with

more challenging problem-solving tasks related to the topic the regular class is working towards).

- *Acceleration:* any strategy that results in advanced placement for a child is referred to as **acceleration**: this is usually seen when a child skips a year level, begins school earlier than same-age peers or, as is seen in more progressive environments, when children work in vertical class grouping situations—for example, a child gifted in Year 2 maths attends maths classes with the Year 3 class and then returns to their Year 2 home class for other lessons (Davis et al., 2011).

acceleration
any strategy that results in advanced placement for a child.

The notion of a child skipping a class or being granted early admission to pre-school or school has been hotly debated. For many gifted children, this is an authentic and valuable option. Research suggests that early school entry or grade acceleration can be most successful when the following conditions are met.

- The child is achieving at well above average in one or more academic areas.
- The child, the parents and the receiving grade teacher are happy about it.
- The child has the self-help, social and emotional skills to cope, or is provided with additional support in these areas as required (Gadzikowski, 2013).

Appropriate developmental programming

Many settings design learning environments based on 'developmentally appropriate' guidelines. Such programming is determined by the age of the children, set milestones based on knowledge about normal child development and predictable sequences of growth and change, all of which provide a framework within which teachers prepare learning. However, let us explore this in the context of our discussions so far. Can/should developmentally appropriate learning apply to *all* children?

Consider children with disabilities, delayed development, cultural difference, and developmentally a-typical children, and what is developmentally appropriate for children whose rates of social and physical development is a-synchronised with cognitive potential. How do we construct a model for creating truly developmentally appropriate programs for young children? We should consider the following.

- Address children's individual differences—this has been the cornerstone of all our discussions to date and is appropriate for all children.
- Gifted children tend to develop the ability to deal with abstract material earlier than is seen in other children. It may be appropriate to offer a child access to material and methods of learning that are far in advance of the rest of the group. Consider Hannah again: her levels of mathematical concept development might mean she can work at more abstract levels of mathematical reasoning than other children. Simply working on counting to ten, which may be seen as developmentally appropriate for a four-year-old, would be inappropriate for her.
- Gifted children often seek out structured activities for intellectual stimulation, and if denied these they can feel demoralised. This may cause tension in a learning environment that only promotes a fixed model for learning, as was the case for Hannah. To declare knowledge and mastery inappropriate unless children are of the proper age is potentially stifling to young minds. Developmentally appropriate learning approaches must be appropriate for each individual child.

Grouping children

Teachers can be intentional about the way children learn from each other. They can intentionally place children in close proximity to each other so children with similar interests or ability can work together. Children can be organised in how they share tasks and can be assigned specific roles within a group. Group sizes can vary from small to large to whole group. It is important that decisions about grouping should be made to balance the needs of the particular group of children, and ensure safe supervision, classroom management and the individual needs of each child. There are significant benefits to providing opportunities for mixed-age groups. The diversity of ability and knowledge in mixed-age groups creates a rich and complex learning environment that goes beyond modelling and imitation. All children can benefit from working with children of varying abilities; the crucial element in setting up groups for effective learning is flexibility. Ideally, group assignments should be temporary and children should be continually assessed and reassigned to groups as their abilities and interests change and develop. Grouping children according to a range of factors, including shared interest, learning styles or similar personalities, can support children's sense of belonging and acceptance within the group (Gadzikowski, 2013).

Conclusion

Every early childhood educator will work with gifted children. Teachers can only effectively support young, gifted children when they acknowledge the rights of all children to access a learning environment that respects them, provides warm, accepting relationships for them and keeps an open mind about what they are capable of achieving. One thing that this discussion is attempting to highlight is that giftedness can have many facets and hence gifted children will present with many different needs—an idea that is still difficult for many educators to acknowledge. If early childhood teachers are to address the diverse needs of gifted children, they will need to provide a variety of different learning experiences every day. This discussion also highlights the importance for *all* children's individual needs to be understood and accommodated regardless of their strengths and differences, reflecting 'Inclusive practice for Diverse Learners'.

SUMMARY

- Gifted children can be found in most classrooms.
- The definition of 'gifted' and 'talented' are dynamic and still evolving.
- Identifying gifted children in the learning environment is vital if we are to provide them with learning opportunities that meet their needs.
- All children, including gifted children, are unique. However, gifted children may demonstrate similar characteristics that can assist teachers in identifying them as being potentially gifted, and thus provide learning experiences that meet their needs.
- Using varied observation tools over a period of time assists in more reliable identification.
- Identification tools can assist in the systematic identification of gifted children: they need to be varied, with evidence gathered over time (photo album) and inclusive of all cultures and socio-economic levels.

ANN HOOPER WITH SUE LANCASTER

- There are many factors that contribute to children not achieving their potential. It is important for teachers to understand these and to be vigilant in observing behaviours that might flag such a situation.
- The costs of inaction by educators can result in serious disadvantage for these children, which can have implications for their future learning and the development of a positive self-image.
- Gifted children may have special social and emotional needs.
- Catering for the gifted child in a classroom is a key responsibility of an early childhood teacher.
- There are a variety of pedagogical approaches and teaching strategies that can successfully support gifted children, including differentiated curriculum and varied grouping strategies.
- Play-based learning has a significant role to play in enriching the lives of gifted children.
- There are still a number of deeply held negative mythologies in our communities.
- Importantly, teachers need to reflect on their practice and ask, Am I including all children in my class and am I attending to their needs, strengths and interests effectively?
- For gifted children, inclusive practice requires that they are identified early, feel socially that they belong, and have their learning needs carefully catered for, as is the practice for other children. They also need informed, passionate professionals to advocate for their needs, and this is a wonderful opportunity for you as you embark on your teaching career to truly make a difference in the lives of all young children.
- Our professional obligations dictate that we endeavour to know, understand and meet children's learning needs, in all their forms.

FURTHER REFLECTION

- How have your views/knowledge on your responsibility as a professional teacher to cater for the needs of every child in your care developed?
- How would you advocate for the rights of gifted children to a colleague with different views?
- How are rights of gifted children the same as or different from the rights of all children?

GROUP DISCUSSIONS

1 Consider, and discuss with others, which forms of grouping may best help gifted students cope positively with the forced-choice dilemma.
2 Work together to construct a school policy outlining a detailed plan for deciding how to determine if a potentially gifted child should be accelerated.
3 Explain how various grouping practices (including acceleration) address the characteristics and needs of gifted students.
4 What do you understand by the term 'invisible' underachiever? What might you look for in deciding whether a child in your class might be an invisible underachiever? Why can it be difficult to 'spot' an underachiever?
5 Gagné's Differentiated Model of Giftedness and Talent provides an excellent mechanism for understanding underachievement. Create a poster for your school that explains this for staff.
6 Why do young, gifted children and their families need educators and other professionals to advocate for them? What role can you play in breaking down misunderstandings and mythologies still held by many people today?

CLASS EXERCISES

1 What is the government's stand on catering for gifted children in schools today? Investigate various Education Department policy papers to determine their position on inclusion of gifted children. How can you utilise these documents to support your position when supporting the rights of gifted children?

2 There are a number of services available to support children, families and educators catering for gifted children. Research two of these services and identify who they support and what provisions they offer. Discuss with your classmates how you could utilise these services as a teacher of a gifted child (e.g. direct parents to support services, increase professional learning for colleagues, discover learning resources to assist you to develop appropriate learning experiences).

FURTHER READING

Davis G., Rimm S. & Siegle D. (2011) Education of the Gifted and Talented (6th edn). Australia: Pearson Education.

This text provides comprehensive information on all aspects of the gifted learner, including matching instruction with need, the role of creativity and gifted children with disabilities,

Gadzikowski, A. (2013) Challenging Exceptionally Bright Children in Early Childhood Classrooms. St Paul, MN: Redleaf Press.

This very practical book provides excellent information on identification; differentiation; how to conduct conversations with young, gifted children by asking questions and providing authentic feedback; connections; helping children learn from each other; classroom strategies for the early reader, advanced mathematician and young scientist; strategies for supporting social–emotional development; and how to work with parents and families of exceptionally bright children.

Gross M. (2004) Gifted and Talented Education. Professional Development Package for Teachers (Modules 1 & 3). Sydney: University of NSW, GERRIC Gifted Education Research Resource and Information Centre.

This comprehensive publication, developed as a set of modules for professional development of teachers, provides both theory and practical applications for teachers to both understand and cater for gifted children.

Morrissey A. (2012) Young Gifted Children: A Practical Guide to Understanding and Supporting Their Needs. Albert Park, Melbourne: Teaching Solutions.

A very practical guide covering the key elements of definition, mythologies, identification, planning for learning and transition to school. Includes a range of practical strategies and suggestions for working with young gifted children in early childhood settings.

Porter L. (2005) Gifted Young Children: A Guide for Teachers and Parents. Sydney: Allen & Unwin.

A practical guide to identifying and supporting young children who may be gifted or talented. A good resource for teachers and parents to use to gain a common understanding of the issues related to educating and supporting gifted children.

Sousa D. (2009) How the Gifted Brain Works. Australia: Hawker Brownlow Education.

This text provides in-depth information on the characteristics and profiles of gifted learners in primary and secondary levels. This reader-friendly guide gives teachers the help they need not only to recognise and challenge their gifted learners, but also to support gifted students who underachieve.

Sutherland, M. (2012) Gifted and Talented in the Early Years (2nd edn). Moorabbin, Vic.: Hawker Brownlow.

This book focuses on gifted and talented children in the early years and includes topics such as: identification, physical movement/motor development, music, literacy and language, mathematics, and making sure learning is fun and for all.

REFERENCES

Carter, C. & Lancaster, S. (2014) 'Exploring Strategies and Techniques to Support Learning and Teaching in Diverse Higher Education Contexts', *The International Journal of Diversity in Education, 13*(3). Illinois, USA: Common Ground Publishing.

Chaffey, G. (2004) *Gifted and Talented Education.* Professional Development Package for Teachers (Module 4). Sydney: University of NSW, GERRIC Gifted Education Research Resource and Information Centre.

ANN HOOPER WITH SUE LANCASTER

Cohen, L. (2011) *Simplicity in Complex Times: Six Principles for Teaching the Gifted.* Revista de Psicologia. 29(1). 131–151. http://www.scielo.org.pe/pdf/psico/v29n1/a05v29n1.

Davis, G. & Rimm, S. (1998) *Education of the Gifted and Talented* (4th ed). Boston: Allyn & Bacon.

Davis, G., Rimm, S. & Siegle, D. (2011) Education of the Gifted and Talented (6th edn). Australia: Pearson Education.

Department of Education, Employment and Workplace Relations (DEEWR) (2009) Educators: Belonging, Being & Becoming: Educators' Guide to the Early Years Learning Framework for Australia. Canberra: DEEWR.

Department of Training (DET) (2012) Inquiry into the Education of Gifted and Talented Students 2010–2012. Parliament of Victoria. www.parliament.vic.edu

Early Childhood Australia (ECA) (2016) *Code of Ethics.* Watson, ACT: Early Childhood Australia Inc. http://www.earlychildhoodaustralia.org.au/our-publications/eca-code-ethics/

Gadzikowski, A. (2013) *Challenging Exceptionally Bright Children in Early Childhood Classrooms.* St Paul, MN: Redleaf Press.

Gagné, F. (2002) 'Transforming Gifts into Talents: The DMGT as a Developmental Theory', in N. Colangelo & G.A. Davis, *Handbook of Gifted Education* (3rd edn). Boston: Allyn & Bacon, pp. 60–73.

Grant, A. (2013) 'Young Gifted Children's Transitioning into Pre-school and School: What Matters?' *Australian Journal of Early Childhood, 28*(2).

Gross, M. (2004) *Gifted and Talented Education.* Professional Development Package for Teachers (Modules 1 & 3). Sydney: University of NSW, GERRIC Gifted Education Research Resource and Information Centre.

Lindon, J. (2012) *Equality and Inclusion in Early Childhood* (2nd edn). London: Hodder Education.

McCashen (2000) *The Strengths-Based Approach: A Strengths-Based Resource for Sharing Power and Creating Change.* Bendigo, Vic.: St Lukes Innovative Resources.

McNaughton, G. & Williams, G. (2008) *Techniques for Teaching Young Children: Choices for Theory and Practice* (3rd edn). Frenchs Forest, NSW: Pearson Education.

Merrick, C & Targett, R. (2004) *Gifted and Talented Education.* Professional Development Package for Teachers (Module 2). Sydney: University of NSW, GERRIC Gifted Education Research Resource and Information Centre.

Morrissey, A.M. (2012) *Young Gifted Children: A Practical Guide to Understanding and Supporting Their Needs.* Albert Park: Teaching Solutions.

Porter, L. (2005) Gifted Young Children: A Guide for Teachers and Parents. Sydney: Allen & Unwin.

Post, G. (2014) 'Different Than the Rest: Social Challenges of Gifted Adolescents'. Gifted Challenges blog. https://giftedchallenges.blogspot.com.au/2013/02/different-than-rest-social-challenges.html

Renzulli, J.S. (1978) 'What Makes Giftedness? Re-examining a Definition', *Phi Delta Kappan 60*: 180–4.

Silverman, L. (1993) *Counseling the Gifted and Talented*. Denver: Love.

Rivero, L. (2012) 'Many Ages at Once: The Science Behind the Asynchronous Development of Gifted Children', *Psychology Today*, 24 January. www.psychologytoday.com/blog/creative-synthesis/201201/many-ages-once

Tannebaum, A. (1983) *Gifted Children: Psychological and Educational Perspectives*. New York: Macmillan.

Tomlinson, C.A., Brighton, C., Hertberg, H., Callahan, C.M., Moon, T.R., Brimijoin, K., Conover, L.A. & Reynolds, T. (2003) 'Differentiating Instruction in Response to Student Readiness, Interests & Learner Profiles', *Journal for the Education of Gifted Child*. Australia: SAGE, *27*: 119–45.

Turnbull, A., Turbiville, V. & Turnbull, H. (2000) 'Evolution of Family-Professional Partnerships Models: Collective Empowerment as the Models for the Early 21st Century', in S. Shankoff & L. Meisels (ed.), *The Handbook of Early Childhood Intervention*. UK: Cambridge University Press.

United Nations Convention on the Rights of the Child (1989). www.unicef.org.au/Upload/UNICEF/Media/Our%20work/childfriendlycrc.pdf

Webster, A. & Forster, J. (2012) *Participating and Belonging: Inclusion in Practice: Inclusion Resources for Early Childhood Educators and Consultants.* Malvern, Vic.: Noah's Ark.

Teaching Practice Issues in Contemporary Society

Carol Carter with Melissa Colville and Mary Hughes

Chapter objectives

In this chapter, we will:

- reflect on your understanding of effective, quality teaching practice
- examine teaching practice issues and challenges in contemporary society
- recognise the tensions that exist between teacher autonomy and curriculum packages
- consider particular aspects related to teaching practice, such as leadership, outdoor education and culturally responsive pedagogies
- understand some links between topics in other chapters and teaching practice.

I *really*, *really* struggled, as a novice teacher, in my first six months of teaching five- and six-year-old children. My struggle occurred despite enjoying and doing well in my practicums, or practical experiences, despite leaving university with good grades and feeling confident in my ability to teach, despite being taught by university lecturers who had, themselves, taught for many years and shared sound practical experiences and advice with me, and despite my commitment to quality teaching. My colleague (an experienced teacher and my self-appointed mentor) kept telling me on a daily basis, 'Teaching isn't easy'. What an understatement! Teaching practice is, in fact, highly complex, made even more so by the diverse needs of different, unique groups of children.

I was fortunate in having supportive colleagues and a principal who listened endlessly to my tales of woe, offered carefully considered advice from her invaluable treasure chest of experiences and expertise and gave me the space and encouragement to grow as a teacher.

There were funny moments, too, like the day I told the children in my class, who were purposefully falling off their chairs, that the next person who fell off a chair would need to go and sit in the cubby house in the play corner—and then I sat down and fell off my chair, so I had to go and sit in the cubby house. There were silly moments, like when I told a child I did not like her behaviour, she started to cry and I promptly burst into tears at the thought of upsetting her. There were also moments of extreme panic when I felt that the entire classroom was in a state of chaos and I felt helpless …

As the years passed, I became what I consider to be a good teacher but still, on occasion, having disastrous teaching moments (always learning through critical reflection though); experiencing tensions between my beliefs and what I felt were expectations (for example, allowing the children in my care to make a productive noise and then insisting that they work in silence when other teachers came past); and being unable to explain my teaching philosophy of enabling creativity when other teachers judged my classroom as messy because there were projects waiting to be completed on the classroom floor (e.g. clay puppet heads in bottles)).

When I became involved in pre-service teacher education, I saw Initial Teacher Education students who believed implicitly in enabling and constructivist approaches to teaching, but when confronted with new challenges, unconsciously resorted to the authoritarian, rigid teaching styles that they had experienced as children.

Introduction

If you were to ask practising teachers you know about their first experiences as a teacher, I'm sure that many of them would have similar stories to mine. My story, and the stories you may hear from other teachers, while acknowledging the complexity and challenges that have always existed in teacher practice, is not designed to put you off teaching. Rather, I have shared my story with you to illustrate the importance of constantly reflecting on teaching practice, continually working on understanding, improving and learning about effective practice; and the need to contextualise issues related to teaching practice within contemporary societies.

As explained previously in this book, the Australian Institute for Teaching and School Leadership (AITSL, 2011) has developed Australian Professional Standards for Teachers. The aim is an admirable one of strengthening the skills and development of *all teachers*. The qualities embedded in these professional standards are what quality teachers require, but what is even more desirable is the ability to continually learn and grow through our professional teaching practice. It has been argued that in Australia we need to shift from arguing for quality teachers, and what that entails, to fostering quality teaching by focusing on our continual learning as teachers. In my story, it is not *where* I started out that made the difference but rather *the lessons I learnt* and how I *applied* what I learnt to my future teaching that increased my effectiveness as a teacher.

STOP AND REFLECT

- What do teachers you know say about their earliest and current experiences of teaching practice?
- How is this similar to or different from the experiences talked about at the beginning of this chapter?
- What have you learnt from different teachers' views about the experiences of teachers in different stages of their teaching career?

The authors in this book are committed to the notion of quality early childhood teaching practice that is informed by seminal ideas and thinking and that addresses the challenges, changes and particular needs of learners and teachers in contemporary society. As such, contemporary teaching practice has been considered within previous chapters of this book. Teaching practice issues have been integrated into the text and discussed in relation to particular learning areas and key topics. However, what is happening in the 'real world' of teaching in contemporary society and the related issues concerning teaching practice have not been specifically considered.

This final chapter focuses on teacher practice issues. This focus serves two purposes: firstly, we provide the beginnings of a discussion of some teaching practise issues that we consider to be important for Initial Teacher Education students and for those who are about to embark on their journey as graduate teachers. Secondly, as the final chapter in this book, it will look back on the various chapters of the book and draw out key messages and conclusions, specifically in relation to contemporary teaching practice.

Issues that will be discussed include the impact of global educational reform movements (GERMS) on teaching practice; practical experiences of Initial Teacher Education (ITE) students and novice teachers; culturally responsive teaching practice; the role of the education leader in early childhood; and children's lifestyles and the importance of quality outdoor play. The beginning discussions around various issues are not meant to be decisive and conclusive. Rather, they are meant as provocations, to provide challenges and reflections as you prepare to enter the 'noble' profession of teaching.

Global education reform movements

Globalisation and the global education reform movements (sometimes referred to as GERMS) have resulted in both opportunities and challenges for teaching practice in early childhood education. Contemporary access to international research evidence, and policy and engagement with early childhood education initiatives and practices across the world provide a rich backdrop for determining policy and quality teaching practice. In addition, the contemporary economic, market-driven focus on education globally provides strong motivation for the provision of early childhood education as an important, cost-effective investment for the future.

One of the challenges we face in contemporary society is ensuring that our teaching practice continues to be focused on issues that are broader than economic and global ideas and imperatives. To do this we need to balance global and local considerations in our teaching practice. Throughout this book we have been talking about the importance of context. We need, therefore, to balance GERMS with contextual understanding of requirements for education (CURE).

The focus on national and international tests and standardisation may impact on early childhood teaching practice. The first annual National Assessment Program—Literacy and Numeracy (NAPLAN) tests take place at Level 3 of formal schooling in Australia, and international benchmarks such as Programme for International Student Assessment (PISA) are based on older children (e.g. fifteen-year-olds). However, the pressure for children to perform can lead to a push to more formalised curriculum and increased focus on 'academic' content in the early years. We believe our teaching practice needs to resist this type of thinking and doing and keep alive our commitment to early childhood education as distinct and needing to focus on children's intrinsic motivation to learn and be curious about their worlds. Recognising and honouring the importance of *relationships* is another priority for early childhood education, as we have emphasised in many chapters in the book.

The worldwide emphasis on numeracy and literacy, while extremely important, has also resulted in the narrowing of curriculum, notions of literacies and implementation of more formal teaching strategies in primary schools, including the early years of schooling. Our teaching practice also needs to resist what we know to be inappropriate for learning and teaching within early childhood environments. Our teaching practice needs to embrace the notion of holistic learning. Children need to be presented with challenging tasks that promote exploration and interaction within environments that are appropriately challenging and supportive. We need to ensure that the focus on working to increase literacy and numeracy results does not result in less time for teaching children in creative, active ways and for, example, neglecting such areas as the Arts, which are instrumental in, particularly, children's literacy learning.

As professionals, we have a responsibility to reflect critically, take into account our own principles, values and beliefs and act according to them. Studies conducted recently and reported in an article in the *Asia–Pacific Journal of Teacher Education* (Ell et al., 2017) pointed to 'personal beliefs and values' as the most crucial element that they 'think influence learning to teach …' (p.336). Autonomy appears as a factor in studies examining teacher motivation, job satisfaction, teacher burnout, retention, professionalism and empowerment in teaching. Autonomy does not mean doing whatever you like, but it does allow creativity, critical reflection and responding in a principled manner to individual situations and contexts. Global educational reforms involving accountability have led to tensions between teacher autonomy and specific children's needs on the one hand, and strict regulation, global, prescriptive teaching packages and standardisation on the other.

A teacher's sense of lack of empowerment and authority may stem from curriculum constraints and teaching packages that teachers are encouraged to simply implement without any further consideration. The curriculum frameworks are, in my view, broad enough to allow for consideration of children's needs and interests and provide teachers with a certain amount of autonomy to plan for learning and teaching that resonates with their own philosophies and beliefs and are responsive to the characteristics, needs and interests of the children they are teaching. However, within certain educational contexts and with misreading of curriculum framework requirements, there is the real potential of feelings of disempowerment and a lack of autonomy impacting on teacher practice. Where education 'is so intensely focused upon standards, metrics, and a production line that it neglects to allow people to lead personally meaningful lives, to trust and value them for who they are, and celebrate what they bring to the classroom … individuals pay a heavy motivational and emotional price' (Carr, 2015).

I have also heard graduate teachers in their first year of teaching criticising the institutions where they have studied for espousing different beliefs and practices from those they see in 'real life'. Despite the positive move towards making teacher education more practical, 'hands-on' and relevant, this is likely to still occur as it is also a function of teacher education institutions to inspire pre-service and graduate teachers to aspire to the ideal, even though it may not necessarily be reflected in the everyday worlds of the classroom. Also, there is variation in the quality of practice (and resources) in different early childhood education services and primary schools. Reflecting on these variations and regarding them as learning experiences are more productive responses than simply criticising Initial Teacher Education courses for the discrepancy that sometimes is visible between what is taught and what is seen and experienced. Contrary to some global reforms that offer ideas across contexts, while theories, tips and strategies are available, as a human endeavour, there are no recipes for learning and teaching. The same teaching strategies will not necessarily work for the same teacher with different children, different classes or on different days, let alone across different contexts.

Classroom ready

Being 'classroom ready' is something that has received a great deal of attention since the Teacher Education Ministerial Advisory Group's report (TEMAG, 2014). This is both highly desirable and extremely complex, as my story—as well as the fact that most teachers vividly remember their first teaching experiences—shows. One of the ways that this readiness is seen to be possible is the provision of extensive and quality practical experiences within Initial Teacher Education programs. However, this experience is not a guarantee of classroom readiness, and there also needs to be an ability and willingness to learn from the experience and strengthen skills. As a pre-service teacher and then as a graduate teacher, you also need to actively pursue experiences that may be outside your 'comfort zone' and to take productive risks.

It is also important to remember that the effectiveness and quality of a teacher cannot be judged simply from meeting the professional standards of teaching:

> Who teachers are and how they behave is one of the most underrated competencies of learning to teach. Caring, flexibility, resilience, respecting diversity, overcoming inequities, advocating for children, leadership and positively communicating with colleagues and parents are all as vital as content knowledge and pedagogical prowess.
>
> (Fischetti, 2016)

Collaboration, support systems and partnerships grounded in reciprocal respect are also essential ingredients for becoming classroom ready. Just as the support of a colleague and principal helped me through my first year of teaching, so the nature of your relationships with mentors and colleagues will impact on your confidence and readiness to teach. Strong partnership agreements between education environments and teacher education institutions have been encouraged and built in recent times. Positive aspects of these partnerships are the communities of practice that have been developed and the reciprocal nature of the partnerships. Potential negatives are that Initial Teacher Education students may not see a wide variety of teaching practices because their teacher education institution may be locked into particular partnerships.

Mentor relationships that are ongoing and where the teacher understands what mentorship entails and is willing to spend the time required to provide quality mentoring, are most helpful. The most effective relationships are not authoritarian and hierarchical in nature, but are where the mentor and mentee are engaged in learning and teaching. It seems that mentoring is effective when new teachers 'fit well' into their educational environment. The challenge appears to lie where new teachers espouse educational values and principles of professionalism that are at odds with the educational environment. While it is always preferable to communicate and work with teachers in the same context, strategies have been used by novice teachers, such as seeking support provided by teacher collaboration, mentoring, and professional networks and communities of practice beyond their immediate environment.

CAROL CARTER WITH MELISSA COLVILLE AND MARY HUGHES

When you face teaching practice challenges, it is important that you don't personalise them. You need to understand that the challenges you face are shared by others in your early childhood teaching environment and systems of early childhood (Adoniou, 2016).

Culturally responsive teaching practice

Ensuring culturally responsive teaching practice is a significant issue given that Australia is one of the most culturally diverse countries in the world and that inclusion and equity are two of the most fundamental principles within contemporary education. Culturally responsive teaching practice honours diversity and empowers participants from diverse cultures and backgrounds in the class, viewing them as rich resources for teaching and learning and for expanding our understanding of diverse worldviews.

Teaching practice that is culturally responsive engages learners in relevant sharing and interpretation of various knowledges and ways of producing and processing knowledge. Within any learning and teaching environment there is a need to provide 'culturally responsive curriculum' (Veblen et al., 2005) and resources that 'reflect the dynamic cultural landscapes in which young people live' (Nicholson, 2005, p.160). As Joseph (2009, p.150) states, '… demographic changes in our classroom' require us to build up valuable pedagogies that ensure that we are 'catering for and taking advantage of individual and cultural differences in learning'.

Within the 'Melbourne Declaration on Education Goals for Young People' (2008) is the broad goal (Goal 1) that: 'Australian Schooling promotes equity and excellence' (2008, p.7). One of the ways in which this goal is seen to being achieved is to 'ensure that schooling contributes to a socially cohesive society that respects and appreciates cultural, social and religious diversity'.

Culturally responsive teaching practice includes diverse stories and voices. As Brooks states:

> … the more stories we have available to us the richer are our resources … the more voices and narratives we listen to, the more abundantly we experience our lives … for both their differences and their similarities, we can hardly afford to let some voices remain marginal and silenced and other voices dominate.
>
> (Brooks, 2000, p.169)

The 'iceberg model' of culture (Hall, 1976) is one I find useful when identifying authentic culturally responsive curriculum for my teaching practice. The smallest part, or the 'tip of the iceberg' that is above the surface of the water consists of those parts that are most visible and also the most superficial aspects of culture, such as dress, food and greetings. The main part of the cultural iceberg is below the water; it is invisible and involves deeper aspects of culture, such as beliefs, norms and concepts, so we have to metaphorically dive below the surface to see and appreciate its impact and value.

I have had many conversations with pre-service teacher students about their fear of being seen as tokenistic in—and therefore avoiding—any teaching practice or content relating to different cultures. My position on this issue is that we need to start somewhere and that it is, for instance, acceptable to start at a relatively superficial level as in a cultural 'show and tell' day or what McMahon (2003) refers to as 'stomp, chomp and dress-up activities'. It is important to recognise this as the *starting point* and not the *end point*, as it then leads to deeper, more culturally authentic and responsive teaching practice.

STOP AND REFLECT

- What do you think are the strengths you could bring to the teaching profession?
- What are you looking forward to most in your future teaching practice?
- What do you think are the challenges you will face in your teaching practice and in becoming 'classroom ready'?
- How do you think you could overcome these challenges so that you are classroom ready?
- How will you ensure you teach in a culturally responsive manner?

The educational leader: context, culture and complexities

Mary Hughes

The early years in children's lives have been acknowledged as crucial in forming the foundations for lifelong learning and social participation. Having access to high quality early learning and care has been recognised as a key factor in determining the long-term benefits and outcomes for young children. In response to this, successive Australian governments have placed early childhood education and care at the forefront of national and state legislation in an effort to address quality standards in the sector.

In 2012, all Australian states and territories agreed to the establishment of The National Quality Framework (NQF) to 'raise quality and drive continuous improvement, ensuring that Australian children in a range of early childhood settings receive the best possible start in life' (ACECQA, 2013, p.85). These settings include kindergartens, pre-schools, long day care centres, early learning centres within schools and mobile kindergartens in rural and isolated areas. The framework stipulates a requirement for the appointment of an educational leader in each setting: someone who will support, guide and build the capacity of educators. The legislation is quite brief in its description of the position, which allows providers to make their own decisions. Consequently, the role of the educational leader varies from setting to setting according to the context, needs and requirements of each. There is flexibility with regard to qualifications of the educational leader—the person appointed may hold a diploma or a degree—but there is an expectation that they have the ability to lead curriculum and sustain an early childhood pedagogical approach aimed at improving learning outcomes for young children. This role may well be one that you take on if you work in early childhood education settings. The regulations also state that service providers must appoint a leader to '... guide other educators in their planning and reflection, and mentor colleagues in their implementation practices' (ACECQA, 2013, p.85).

The guidelines for appointing an educational leader and a clear role description have been left intentionally broad. This means that settings and services can interpret and implement the role according to their current needs, and tailor it to fit with their own vision. How the educational leader carries out their duties will look different in a country sessional kindergarten with a small enrolment and two staff, from how it will look in a large suburban long day care setting with twenty staff members. Very often, the director of a centre will take on the administrative and management role, while the educational leader guides and

CAROL CARTER WITH MELISSA COLVILLE AND MARY HUGHES

supports the team in developing curriculum and pedagogy. It is important that they work together, as well as collaborate with the team, to create a vision for children's learning and development.

> 'Management' was, and in some contexts, still is, how leadership is understood in early childhood education and care. Managers focus on the smooth running of day-to-day work; they plan, organise, direct, co-ordinate, monitor and control. Management activities can be undertaken without enacting leadership. On the other hand, *leaders* focus on the future, building and communicating a shared vision and engaging, enabling and empowering people.
>
> (Rodd, 2006)

Good leadership and a strong vision, especially for pedagogy and curriculum, impacts greatly on improved outcomes for children, according to the findings of the EPPE project, a major longitudinal study undertaken in the UK (Sylva et al., 2004). Other recent studies investigating enactment and implementation of pedagogical leadership in Finland (Heikka et al., 2012) also support the view that 'pedagogical leadership is connected with not only children's learning, but also the capacity building of the early childhood profession' (Heikka et al., 2012). Findings from these studies indicate that pedagogical leadership is understood as a contextual and cultural phenomenon.

'Distributed', 'participative', 'facilitative' or 'collaborative' models of leadership call for a shift away from the traditional vision of leader as one key individual towards a more collective vision, one where the responsibility for leadership rests within various formal and informal leaders (Siraj-Blatchford & Manni, 2007, p.20). These approaches to leadership are favoured in the early childhood sector where they are perceived as being more relational.

There are a number of important skills that an effective educational leader requires, according to Hirsh-Pasek (2014). These essential twenty-first-century skills consist of 'collaboration, communication, content, critical thinking and confidence'. This list can be expanded by adding 'creative problem-solving' skills, essential in transferring theory into practice (Wagner, 2014). Being a good communicator and fostering positive relationships with others is essential. Being proactive in the role also helps—offering suggestions and supporting others to implement changes in a non-threatening way is far more effective than waiting for them to ask.

An educational leader who is informed about current research and shares it in small, 'bite-sized' chunks can assist and motivate educators to improve the quality of teaching and learning in the centre. Working alongside others in the children's rooms (if possible) and collaborating at planning time to support, guide, mentor and coach colleagues can inspire others to improve their practice. The biggest challenge facing educational leaders is to effect long-lasting and valuable change in early childhood education and care, which will improve educational outcomes for young children.

Quality outdoor play in natural environments

Melissa Colville

Connecting theory with practice has been a long-time love of mine. This comes, in part, from the many years I spent working with children before I undertook my early childhood teaching degree. Once I began my studies, I always tried to relate what I was learning in my course to my practice; and I hope you will do the same. The link between theory and practice informs my teaching as a lecturer in an early childhood Initial Teacher Education program. Students in this program learn about theory and research, but more importantly, they need to be able to apply what they learn to real-life situations and issues in early childhood education. Pre-service teachers always enjoy it when theory and research is linked with real-life stories. One of the issues for pre-service students, however, can be the difficulty of applying theory in practice: 'It sounds good in theory, but it's not so easy in practice'. This is no doubt an issue that you will face at one time or another. One of the current issues that my pre-service teacher students face—sometimes in their workplace, but more often on practicum placement—is the quality of outdoor environments. Sometimes, the issue is not even of quality, it is simply that there is little or no real opportunity for young children to experience an outdoor environment, even though this is a requirement for early childhood education and care services (NQS Quality Area 3: Physical environment) (ACECQA, 2011).

Experiencing and playing in the outdoors

Our EYLF (DEEWR, 2009) describes children's outdoor play environments as including plants, trees, edible gardens, sand, rocks, mud, water and other elements from nature. Children, especially babies, learn through all five senses and this kind of natural environment is just the stimulation they need. Natural spaces of this kind invite open-ended interactions between children, spontaneity, risk-taking, exploration, discovery and connection with nature (DEEWR, 2009). Natural outdoor spaces foster children's appreciation of the natural environment and develop their awareness of the environment, therefore providing the foundation for ongoing environmental education (DEEWR, 2009). Quality outdoor environments also offer children opportunities to be active, messy, noisy and to play on a large scale (ACECQA, 2013). Quality outdoor environments support children's wellbeing, their learning, their communication, their identity and their sense of community: all five of the EYLF's learning outcomes.

In her presentation at an early childhood education conference, Jeavons (2017) described two critical factors when it comes to the quality of young children's outdoor play: the amount of space per child, and the organisation and quality of space. In the outdoor environment where children like to run and play, space per child needs to be more than 'the bare minimum'. Quality outdoor environments need to be organised so they can function properly. For example, similar learning experiences (e.g. physical activities such as climbing, swinging, running, jumping and ball games) are placed close to each other. Children's physical activity is incorporated into the space design: tree trunks placed as a divider between a concrete path and tanbark area can be used by children to walk on. Environments need to promote children's physical development and skills, exercise and

CAROL CARTER WITH MELISSA COLVILLE AND MARY HUGHES

movement, balance, fitness and strength, judgment and risk-taking. A range of surfaces are included (including natural surfaces such as grass), with separate areas or small spaces indicating the purpose of the space. A variety of learning experiences are offered: sand play, water play, mud/dirt play, swings, bikes, space to run, challenging climbing equipment, construction play, art experiences, dramatic play areas, private/secret places such as cubbies and vegie gardens. In quality outdoor environments, children are given time to play, and the outdoor area is set up and changed on a daily basis (just like the indoor environment!) (Jeavons, 2017).

Children in today's society are less likely to have access to outdoor play spaces in natural environments and are spending long periods of time in sedentary activities. Therefore, the quality of the outdoor environments that we provide plays an important role in fostering children's learning, development, and wellbeing. However, too often we are seeing outdoor environments that lack the sensory qualities of nature, as described in our EYLF. Instead, we see 'simulated' outdoor environments with fake grass and plastic features. These artificially created environments may be visually representative of nature, but they lack the very qualities that make the natural environment of the outdoors so important. Plants don't grow, there are no scents from flowers, leaves don't change with the seasons, insects don't inhabit these sterile environments and there is none of the joy of experiencing mud or finding a bird's nest in a tree. Children, particularly babies and toddlers who are learning through their senses, need the real experiences of nature that the outdoors provides, and they need an environment rich in sensory experiences.

We are also seeing outdoor spaces that only meet the bare minimum requirements for size. This is sometimes a design issue: the larger outdoor space has been divided into a number of much smaller sections for very specific age groups. What do the designers and manufacturers of these environments know about the benefits of being outdoors, and of multi-age learning for both younger and older children? We're seeing more outdoor spaces with undifferentiated surfaces: one span of synthetic grass or rubber. Toddlers, in particular, need to learn to walk on different textured surfaces for balance and muscle control. We see environments where there is a lack of spatial separation and organisation, and this is often in conjunction with just one surface cover.

When physical activities are organised, and separated from more sedentary activities, conflicts between quiet play and busy movement are less likely. My pre-service teacher students have often discussed outdoor areas that are not set up and changed on a regular basis—areas where there are very few learning experiences offered for children (e.g. with limited, fixed features that can't be manipulated by children). In some cases, children have been denied access to a particular learning area or experience. My Initial Teacher Education students (some of whom work in early childhood) have talked about the pressures parents place on educators and teachers, particularly around safety and messy play. One pre-service student commented that a mother from her early childhood service did not want her child playing in the sandpit as it was 'messy play', and so the educators followed this mother's request.

Stories have also been shared of educators who supervise but do not interact with children, or educators who spend outdoor time talking with each other rather than supervising or interacting with children. These are some of the examples of outdoor environments that both my pre-service students and I have seen. There is clearly a tension between these kinds of outdoor environments and those described as best practice in early childhood theory and research.

One particularly concerning issue for me is *time*: children need time to engage in rich play outdoors. However, there are groups of children who do not even go outdoors. Children are being denied access to the outdoor environment, either on a regular basis, or in some cases, they have no access at all. Can you guess which age group I am talking about? If you guessed (or already knew) that babies are this group, you are correct.

I still remember one of my first practicums as an early childhood teaching student. I was placed in a toddlers' room in a long day care setting, with another student placed in the babies' room next to mine. She commented that the babies in her group never went outside and asked me if this was normal. I had at least five years' experience at this time, in services that took babies outdoors every morning and afternoon, with few exceptions. I told her that babies need, and have the right to, outdoor play! I have also seen similar practices in my work in early childhood education and care services. In particular, I recall a babies' room I worked in as a casual childcare worker that had a bathroom between ours and the next babies' room. Neither my group of babies, nor theirs, were taken outside during the entire two weeks I worked at this centre, and I suspect they were not taken outside at all. The outdoor environment was on the rooftop of the centre, and I was told it was 'too difficult to get the babies up there'. 'Too difficult' due to the children's individual routines and the physical effort involved for the educators, as the babies needed to be placed in a cot and wheeled up the ramp. I was a casual staff member employed through an agency, so I felt I was not in a position to challenge this practice.

CAROL CARTER WITH MELISSA COLVILLE AND MARY HUGHES

STOP AND THINK

- What do you think you might do in this situation?
- What if you worked with staff who did not take the children outdoors?
- Would it make a difference what age group the children were?

Beginning in their second placement, the Initial Teacher Education students I teach are required to implement both indoor and outdoor plans, on a daily basis. Every year, there are always a number of our students who contact me (their practicum coordinator) because the babies rarely or never go outside on a daily basis. So, the students are concerned about how to implement their outdoor plans. They are also concerned that the babies are missing out on important experiences. Students are encouraged to discuss the 'requirement' of outdoor planning for their 'assessment' with their supervising teacher; however, in most cases this has not made a difference. Students relay the following main reasons for not going outdoors: the educator says the weather is too cold, the educator says we'll go out 'soon' (but this does not happen), or the educator reports that parents do not want their children to go outside because either they are sick or they don't want their children to become sick. Practices such as these contradict our NQS (ACECQA, 2011, Quality Area 3), which states that facilities are designed or adapted to ensure *access and participation by every child in the service* and to allow *flexible use, and interaction between the indoor and outdoor space*.

ACECQA (2012) aptly states that our philosophy informs our practice. Therefore, it is important to question our understanding of children's learning. ACECQA (2012) encourages us to reflect on some important questions.

- Do we believe children learn as much outside as inside?
- How does our learning environment demonstrate our knowledge of how young children learn and develop?
- Do we equally value both the outdoor and indoor learning environments as places that support children's learning, creativity, social engagement and sense of belonging?
- Do we see outside play as merely a place for children to 'let off steam' and give them opportunities to take physical risks?
- Should teachers be active participants in children's learning, both indoors *and* outdoors?
- Do we currently plan for learning inside and outside differently? Why? In what way is our planning different?
- Do children have the choice to move freely between indoor and outdoor environments?

- Who is in charge of the decision making? Who makes the decisions about how access to inside and outside areas is determined? Who decides if it's too cold to play outside?

The answers to these questions and the choices we make have a direct impact on the quality of learning opportunities available to children. In Chapter 4, I posed the question, 'What are your beliefs and values about the importance of outdoor play in the natural environment?' This is an important question that I invite you again to consider, this time with the added questions:

- How are you going to ensure that your beliefs and values about the outdoor environment are practised?
- How will you ensure that children are deeply engaged in their outdoor play?

Teaching practice

This section refers to each chapter of this book in relation to issues of contemporary teaching practice, drawing out key messages and conclusions that focus attention on what you have learnt about teaching practice in each of the chapters.

In *Chapter 1* you learnt how our image of the child informs our interactions with children. How you view children will directly impact on your teaching practice as you work with young children in your care. Contemporary views of children as agents of their own learning is a view that will directly impact on your teaching practice. The concept of reflective practice that you were introduced to is crucial for learning about, and improving, your teaching practice.

In *Chapter 2* you examined the social construction of childhood and began to recognise (a key consideration for your teaching practice) that teachers can and do have an impact, not just on individual children's lives, but on how childhood is perceived, experienced and valued. You have agency in this and you can be an agent of change.

In *Chapter 3* you were encouraged to consider your personal perspectives and implications for early childhood learning and teaching in relation to the different theories and theoretical perspectives that were written about. Taking an eclectic view (which takes into account diverse perspectives) and making use of the valuable and worthwhile aspects of different theorists' work and perspectives will form a solid theoretical basis for the contemporary teaching practices that you engage in.

In *Chapter 4* you were introduced to the benefits of play. The pressure to reduce time for play-based learning that was spoken about is a serious contemporary issue in teaching practice due to the impact of wanting children to engage in formal learning at an earlier age. Using the contents of this chapter you will be able to articulate the compelling benefits of a play-based curriculum for children's learning and development.

In *Chapter 5* you were encouraged to think critically and carefully about the beliefs, values, ideologies and agendas embedded in the ideas on, and applications of, curriculum and pedagogy. Even though you may not have much influence on broad curriculum choices, at this stage, the practice of teaching constantly requires you to make pedagogical and curriculum choices and these must be informed choices made through critical reflection.

In *Chapter 6* you were introduced to practical and theoretical considerations and information concerning the learning and teaching of mathematics in early childhood. An important aspect to remember for your teaching practice is that mathematical learning for young children needs to be a part of, and relevant to, their everyday lives. It needs to be visible to them and they should have the confidence to persist in and enjoy their mathematical learning. You, too, as their teacher need to learn to recognise the mathematical learning of the babies, toddlers and pre-schoolers and how best you can add to their experiences and to their language.

In *Chapter 7* you were introduced to the theory and practice underpinning the teaching of language, literacy and children's literature. You were reminded of the central role of play in young children's learning and the need to consider play-based approaches as well as direct, intentional teaching in your teaching practice. The role of teachers who inspire and effectively teach both the skills and concepts of language and literacy and a love of language was discussed.

In *Chapter 8* you explored the integrated nature of the Arts within early childhood education as well as each Arts discipline, focusing on particular features, purposes and practical examples that will be useful for your teaching practice. You were introduced to broad concepts that apply across the practice of teaching the Arts and using the Arts as a method of teaching and learning, such as aesthetic understanding and holistic education, as well as terms specific to particular forms, such as process drama.

In *Chapter 9* you explored how children learn science through forming conceptual understandings of phenomena in the world that surrounds them. You learnt that this not only happens alone but through a social process and that experts and cultural environments have a big role to play in the development of science learning, and understanding and helping children become more science literate. Directly relating to effective teaching practice, you were urged to carefully select and use appropriate teaching strategies such as interactive talking, supporting discussions and effective questioning to ensure success in implementing science activities with young children.

In *Chapter 10* you were provided with a sense of what it is to belong to a profession. You were invited to view your role as a teacher as a collaborative role. You were introduced to the many documents, policies and procedures that assist all members of our profession to work in coherent and consistent ways that reflect the values of the profession. You examined how contemporary teachers engage in reflective practice to ensure they remain informed and to ensure their practice continues to develop in the best interest of the children and families they serve. You were introduced to some of the many and varied roles teachers engage in through their work and looked at the role of the teacher as being on a journey of lifelong learning, where involvement with colleagues and authentic research assists you to frequently re-evaluate views and practices.

In *Chapter 11* you were introduced to the notions of observation 'inspiring' quality teaching and being essential for effective planning. Relationships, as the keystone of early childhood education and good teaching, were seen as being strengthened through positive and thoughtful engagement in the observation planning cycle, and collaboration was viewed as essential. Thoughtful observation, informed by historical and contemporary theories, will encourage you to observe children using a variety of observation methods.

In the first section of *Chapter 12* you were introduced to the processes and teacher roles and responsibilities for children's learning in early years' prior-to-school entry environments with a focus on assessment and evaluation. The role of the teacher in assessing and evaluating the information gathered to support children's learning, development and wellbeing discussed in this section—drawing on the learning cycle for early years and the three elements of assessment and evaluation that run through the planning cycle reflecting *for*, *as* and *of* learning—is essential information for teaching practice in contemporary society.

In the second section of the chapter you considered the purposes of assessment in the primary school sector of education and the steps you need to follow within the assessment process in your teaching practice were outlined. Diagnostic and portfolio assessment tools; the use of graphic organisers as both self-assessment and teacher assessment tools; the use of pre- and post-tests and formal mandated testing such as NAPLAN and other forms of assessment used and considered within contemporary primary school teaching practices were considered. There was a review of the types of assessment that occurs within the primary school and an illustration of the teacher's significant professional role in this process.

In *Chapter 13* different types of learning and teaching relationships and the information that is important in maintaining enabling and supportive partnerships were shared with you. Ways of fostering classroom relationships to engage and motivate children included in this chapter are directly linked to teaching practice. Some of these are the importance of maintaining, open, effective, ongoing communication; actively, genuinely and positively listening and participating; commitment to working together; building reciprocal trust and respect; sharing appropriate aspects of ourselves; empathy and care alongside efficiency; building on a sense of community and belonging; and moving away from established patterns of communication, power and privilege. All relationships take time to grow and need to be nurtured within reflective conversational spaces that honour diversity and do not exclude people based on cultural and social capital, or funds of knowledge. Relationships also need to be maintained, and their maintenance requires critical reflection on how, why and what makes these relationships work within teaching practice in contemporary society.

In *Chapter 14* you were left with the message that understanding effective ways of working with families and communities through forming professional partnerships is an important learning outcome for Initial Teacher Education and contemporary teaching practice. The quality of professional partnerships will impact on the quality of learning and teaching and strong relationships between teacher and children/students in your centre or school.

In *Chapter 15* you were provided with a broad understanding of the diverse and varied needs of all children in our early learning settings and a working knowledge of inclusive practice from a strength-based perspective. Our professional obligations dictate that we endeavour to know, understand and meet our children's learning needs, in all their forms. The rationale for the focus on the gifted and talented child as an example of inclusion was a deliberate decision, to highlight the fact that inclusion is for *all* children and is vital for a just and civil society that values all children and their families equally, regardless of ability, disability, race or culture. This means that children's individual needs will be understood and accommodated regardless of their strengths or weaknesses.

Conclusion

We hope that, as you have engaged with the theories, philosophies, ideas, resources, information, interests and passions in the different chapters of this book, you have gained insight into the complexities, as well as the joys and privileges, of working in the field of

CAROL CARTER WITH MELISSA COLVILLE AND MARY HUGHES

early childhood teaching. Teaching in early childhood requires continual critical reflection, attention to praxis and current research, lifelong learning, commitment and hard work.

The inspiration for, and the title of this book, *The Child in Focus*, is not just an empty, meaningless sentiment or simply a useful catchphrase to encapsulate our ideas for this book. It is a crucial part of our thinking and *being* as teachers and initial teacher educators. Whatever else we see as necessary for quality teaching practice, keeping the child in focus and understanding and supporting children's needs and interests is paramount. We trust that through the remainder of your studies and your future teaching journey you will remember and sustain the notion of the importance of keeping 'the child in focus'.

REFERENCES

Adoniou, M. (2016) 'What's So Hard about Teaching? Words of Advice for New Teachers', *The Conversation*, March. https://theconversation.com/whats-so-hard-about-teaching-words-of-advice-for-new-teachers-56884

Australian Children's Education and Care Quality Authority (ACECQA) (2011) *The National Quality Standard.* Sydney, http://acecqa.gov.au/national-quality-framework/the-national-quality-standard.

Australian Children's Education and Care Quality Authority ACECQA (2012) *An Environment for Learning*, e-newsletter no. 30. http://files.acecqa.gov.au/files/NEL/NQS_PLP_E-Newsletter_No30.pdf

Australian Children's Education and Care Quality Authority (ACECQA) (2013) *The Indoor and Outdoor Environment*, http://files.acecqa.gov.au/files/NEL/indoor-and-outdoor-environment.pdf

Australian Government (2008) *The Melbourne Declaration on Educational Goals for Young Children*. http://www.curriculum.edu.au/verve/_resources/National_Declaration_on_the_Education_Goals_for_Young_Australians.pdf.

Australian Institute for Teaching and School Leadership (AITSL) (2011) *Australian Professional Standards*. https://www.aitsl.edu.au/teach/standards.

Brooks, A. (2000) 'Cultures of Transformation', in A. Wilson & E. Hayes (eds), *Handbook of Adult and Continuing Education*. San Francisco: Jossey-Bass.

Carr, S. (2015) 'Are Teachers Suffering from a Crisis of Motivation?' *The Conversation,* 7 October. https://theconversation.com/are-teachers-suffering-from-a-crisis-of-motivation-48637

Department of Education, Employment and Workplace Relations (DEEWR) (2009) *Educators: Belonging, Being & Becoming: Educators' Guide to the Early Years Learning Framework for Australia.* Canberra: DEEWR.

Ell, F., Haigh, M., Cochran-Smith M., Grudnuff, L., Ladlow, L. & Hill, M. (2017) 'Mapping a Complex System: What Influences Teacher Learning During Initial Teacher Education?' *Asia Pacific Journal of Teacher Education*, 45(4): 327–45.

Fischetti, J. (2016) 'Five New Frameworks That Can Drive Teacher Education Reform', *The Conversation*, 5 April. https://theconversation.com/five-new-frameworks-that-can-drive-teacher-education-reform-56812

Hall, E. (1976) *Beyond Culture*. Oxford, UK: Anchor.

Heikka, J. (2014) *Distributed Pedagogical Leadership in Early Childhood Education in Finland.* Macquarie University, Sydney, Australia, and University of Tampere, Finland.

Heikka, J., Waniganayake, M. & Hujala, E. (2012) Contextualizing Distributed Leadership Within Early Childhood Education: Current Understandings, Research Evidence and Future Challenges, EMAL 41(1): 30–44, http://ecadmin.wdfiles.com/local--files/leadership-administration/Distributed%20Leadership%20within%20EC.pdf

Hirsh-Pasek, K. (2014) 'Inspiring Great Ideas. A Conversation with Mitch Resnick', *Redefining Play. Reimagining Learning, The Idea Conference. The LEGO Foundation.* Billund, Denmark, 8–10 April.

Jeavons, M. (2017). *Against the synthetic grass tide–planning quality outdoor environments for young children.* Early Childhood Education Conference, Melbourne: May 26 - May 27th, 2017.

Joseph, D. (2009) *Cross- and Intercultural Engagement.* In P. Burnard and S. Hennesey (Eds.), Reflective Practices in Arts Education. Dordrecht: Springer.

McMahon, B. (2003) 'Putting the Elephant in the Refrigerator: Student Engagement, Critical Pedagogy and Anti-Racist Education', *McGill Journal of Education*, 38(2): 75–91.

Nicholson, H. (2005) *Applied Drama: The Gift of Theatre.* New York: Macmillan.

Rodd, J. (2006) *Leadership in Early Childhood* (3rd edn). Australia: Allen & Unwin.

Siraj-Blatchford, I. & Manni, L. (2007) *Effective Leadership in the Early Years Sector: The ELEYS Study.* Institute of Education: London.

Sylva, K., Melhuish, E., Sammons, P., Siraj-Blatchford, I. & Taggart, B. (2004) *The Effective Provision of Pre-School Education (EPPE) Project: Final Report: A Longitudinal Study Funded by the DfES 1997–2004.* [Report]

Teacher Education Ministerial Advisory Group (2014) *Action Now: Classroom Ready.* Canberra: Department of Education.

Veblen, K., Beynon, C. & Odom, S. (2005) 'Drawing on Diversity in the Arts Education Classroom: Educating Our New Teachers', *International Journal of Education & the Arts*, 6(14): 1–17.

Wagner, T. (2014) *From Play to Purpose: An Interactive Keynote.* Billund, Denmark.

Glossary

acceleration
Any strategy that results in advanced placement for a child.

accommodation
The process of alteration when an existing schema does not work.

aesthetic understanding
People's perceptions and affective understanding of what they may consider to be beautiful or pleasing to the senses.

agency
The ability to act independently, to make own free choices and decisions, and to impose these choices on the world.

agentic
A child with agency.

alphabetic principle
An understanding of the systematic and predictable relationships between written letters and spoken sounds.

anecdotal record
A brief narrative account of a specific incident or an interesting event traditionally focused on a single child or area of development (e.g. physical, cognitive).

arts integration
When the Arts are combined, blended and taught together to fuse skills and knowledge, as opposed to teaching each Arts discipline as a discrete and separate form.

arts-based curriculum model
Uses the creative, visual and performing arts as a context to structure and teach other subjects.

assessment
Observing, measuring and using evidence for the purpose of identifying effectiveness and possibilities for improvement.

assimilation
The process of gathering new information from the environment and fitting it into our existing structures or schema.

attachment
The emotional bonds that babies develop with their parents and other key caregivers.

attributes
Characteristics that define an object or element so that it can be sorted or classified.

belonging
Feeling accepted, developing attachments and trusting those who care for you.

blending
Joining sounds or phonemes together to form words.

Cartesian concept of number
Linked to geometry and algebra and involves points on a grid. The most simple form (one dimensional) is a number line.

checklist
A list of specific traits or behaviours an observer is looking for.

chronosystem
The concept of time that surrounds the entire model at any given period.

co-construction of meaning
Collaborating to make shared meaning.

codes of conduct and ethics
Documents that provide guidance and direction for practice and decision making relating to contemporary values and ethical behaviour in teaching situations.

community of practice
A group of people who come together informally or formally and share expertise, commitment to a particular field of practice, such as early childhood education, or are involved in a joint enterprise, such as running a day care centre.

conceptual subitising
Makes use of different strategies for identifying the number of items without counting them one by one. For example, breaking six dots into two groups of three.

concrete
Something tangible and physical; the opposite of abstract.

constructivism
A theory of knowledge that argues that people construct bodies of meaning and knowledge out of experience.

content or syllabus
A view of curriculum where curriculum is seen as what is studied as the subject matter or an object.

cultural capital
The knowledge and skills gained through family background and education.

demonstration
A practical exhibition and explanation of how scientific phenomena or experiments work or are performed.

developmental theory
Child development is viewed in a series of distinct stages of development according to the age of the child (ages and stages); typical behaviour and skills (developmental milestones).

developmentalism
Various developmental theories that all involve clear stages linked to maturation.

Developmentally Appropriate Practice (DAP)
A term used by the NAEYC to describe programs grounded in child development theory and research designed to meet the developmental needs of children.

differentiated curriculum
Curriculum that strives to cater for the individual needs of all children in the educational setting.

discourse
The ideas and frameworks (or paradigms) that dominate social thinking and discussion and, in so doing, 'silence' or marginalise alternative voices or views.

diverse learners
Includes learners from racially, ethnically, culturally and linguistically diverse families, learners with diverse abilities and needs and learners of different socioeconomic status.

duty of care
A legal and ethical obligation and duty that you have as a professional to take care of and keep children safe.

Early Years Learning Framework (EYLF)
A national framework that provides broad direction for practice in early childhood services for educators, teachers and other professionals, volunteers, students and for family and community who work within or attend these services. 'Belonging, Being & Becoming' are the themes of the EYLF.

effective questioning
When a range of responses are accepted, anticipated and built on. Effective questioning engages children and leads them on a journey of discovery and information.

emergent curriculum
An emergent curriculum model is open-ended, flexible and includes children's interests as a primary focus.

equilibrium
The balance that is attained between assimilation and accommodation as we adapt to new experiences.

ethical behaviour
Making informed, responsible decisions and acting with discretion, respect and consideration of the rights of others.

ethology
Emphasises that behaviour is strongly influenced by biology and is linked to evolution.

etymological knowledge
The origins of language and words, or where they have come from.

evaluation
Observing, measuring and using evidence for the purpose of judging and ascertaining value.

event samples
Brief narratives written preceding and following a specified behaviour; useful for identifying the causes and possible consequences for certain behaviours and interactions.

exchange process
Exchanging money for goods or items of equal value.

exosystem
Includes people and places that children may not interact with often themselves but that still have a large effect on them, such as parents' workplaces, local councils, extended family members, support networks, the neighbourhood.

exploration
Active, hands-on searching and discovering of information, resources or spaces.

expressive vocabulary
Being able to use vocabulary to put thoughts into words and sentences (speaking and writing).

funds of knowledge
Sociocultural resources and sources of constructed knowledge and skills that develop through time and are specific to communities, families or individuals.

games with rules
Games such as board games, card games and sport, or playground games such as hopscotch and tag, involving two or more players.

guided investigation
The action of children systematically inquiring and investigating through a process of teacher scaffolding.

holistic education
Where all aspects of learning are considered and developed, including social, emotional, physical, cognitive and creative domains.

identity
The concept of the self and how one is formed from background and life experiences, some aspects of which there is no choice, such as birthplace, and other aspects where there is choice, such as philosophy.

ideology
A collection of conscious and unconscious ideas and attitudes that form a belief system which characterises the thinking, goals and expectations of a group of people.

inclusion
An honouring of the multiple differences and diversities in our society and creating learning environments that are inclusive of all.

inclusivity
The act of including children who might otherwise be excluded or marginalised.

integrated curriculum
An integrated curriculum links ideas, skills, content or knowledge across different learning areas.

inquiry-based curriculum
An inquiry-based curriculum is a process where students are guided to identify questions, gather information, think critically and solve real life problems.

intentional teaching
When teachers are explicitly, actively and deliberately engaged in children's learning. Their decisions and teaching strategies are purposefully and thoughtfully considered.

interactive talk
A collaborative exchange and dynamic flow of ideas where participants are active, build on each other's ideas and can have an effect on one another.

internal working model
A cognitive framework for how children understand and think about themselves, others and the world.

inter-subjectivity
Interpersonal, reciprocal responses and sharing of experiences, understandings and feelings via a link, or bridge, between yourself and others.

kindergarten
'Children's garden'.

learning story
A story about what a child has been observed doing in an early childhood program.

macrosystem
The large and most remote system; still has an influence on the child (e.g. broader societies cultures and nations).

mandatory reporting
The legislative requirement for selected groups of people to report suspected cases of child abuse and neglect to government authorities.

maturation
Moving towards optimal physical, emotional, social and cognitive function through achieving specific developmental milestones.

media arts
Relies on technological aspects and digital materials to creatively communicate stories and explore concepts. Identifying media and technology for a variety of purposes and audiences are important considerations.

mesosystem
Interactions between a person's microsystems to the immediate community such as childcare, pre-school and school.

microsystem
The importance of family and community for a child's development.

mime
Using gestures and body movements to portray actions and ideas without the use of speech.

moderation
The process of comparing and sharing work with a view to improving consistency of assessment.

modernity/modern era
The period of the rise of science and associated technological advancement.

morphemic knowledge
The structures of words and small chunks or parts that help to make a word meaningful.

nature
What is in us—what we are born with.

negative reinforcement
Strengthening behaviour by removing an unpleasant reinforcer.

norm-reference
Comparing children against each other so that they are seen as, for example, average or above average.

number sense
Being able to understand and work with numbers to perform mental maths operations and use numbers in real-world contexts.

nurture
The whole physical, social and cultural environment in which a child is reared.

object permanence
When a child can identify that an object exists even when it is out of sight.

onset and rime
A form of segmentation of sounds in syllables. A syllable can usually be divided into two parts: the onset, which consists of the initial consonant or consonant blend, and the rime, which consists of the vowel and any final consonants.

operations
Ways of doing something—or procedures, or actions—that are carried out in a particular order or manner.

partnership approach
Where the professional and family work together in collaboration to support the child.

perceptual subitising
The instantaneous recognition (usually small numbers under 5).

phonemes
The smallest parts used to make up whole words.

phonemic awareness
The ability to discriminate between different sounds.

phonological knowledge
The understanding of the relationship between sounds and letters, and the manipulation of these.

play-based curriculum
A planned intervention by a skilled educator who is concerned with promoting educational goals that are aimed at realising a child's potential.

play-based learning
'A context for learning through which children organise and make sense of their social worlds, as they engage actively with people, objects and representations'. (DEEWR, 2009)

positive reinforcement
Reinforcement through reward; used to strengthen behaviour.

practice play
Where children repeat an action over and over, such as putting objects inside a container, tipping them out and putting them in the container again.

primary caregiving
Enables each child to have a special person to go to and each parent to have a primary contact.

process drama
A participatory activity where the participants explore a problem, fictional situation, theme, text or idea, often based on a social, moral and ethical dilemma, by working in and out of role.

pro-social skills
A set of skills linked to cooperation, helping others and sharing, which develops across all ages but begins in infancy. Pro-social skills include self- regulation, empathy, turn taking, compromise and respectfulness.

receptive vocabulary
The collection of words children can understand and respond to, though they may not be able to say (or write) these words (listening and reading).

running record
A detailed description of everything that happens in the order that it happens.

scaffold
The ongoing support provided to a learner by an expert.

scaffolding
Concerned with what is erected while a building is being constructed or restored. The scaffold that the adult puts up allows the child to take carefully structured and supported steps in learning and constructing meaning and, once the child manages without help, the scaffold is removed, just as when a building has been completed.

schema/schemata
Mental image/s used to organise our experiences to make sense of the world.

science literacy
An awareness of currently accepted scientific understanding and how it is presented, as well as questioning and seeking evidence of how and why it shapes our lives.

segmenting
The process of breaking words down into segments or discrete units of sound such as vowels or consonants.

self-efficacy
The beliefs and expectations we develop about our own abilities and characteristics resulting in our producing specific performance accomplishments and confidence in our ability to exert self-control.

self-regulation
Involves personal organisation and the attainment of goals through a process of motivating oneself and guiding one's thoughts, behaviours and attitudes.

social category
Childhood is differentiated as a life stage, separate from other age-based social categories in the lifespan, including the socially recognised category of the adolescent or teenager and adulthood.

socially constructed
Created in society and changing just as society itself changes.

sociocultural capital
The unique capacity for learning that every student brings to the learning and teaching environment.

sociocultural theory
How knowledge and understanding are constructed and embedded in social and cultural contexts.

spiral curriculum
Beginning with basic ideas and then repeatedly revisiting and building upon them at certain intervals until the student has grasped subject or skill areas at a more sophisticated level each time.

story dictation
When an observer listens to a child telling a story or describing an event and writes down word for word what the child says.

structure of patterns
Learning about the ways in which elements are organised and structured to form patterns. The understanding of predictable and integrated elements leads to the ability to generalise.

subitising
The ability to recognise a number of objects without counting.

sustained shared thinking
People working together to reflect on and solve problems or challenges over an extended period of time. It refers to 'an effective learning and teaching interaction, where two or more individuals work (often playfully) together in an intellectual way to solve a problem, clarify a concept, evaluate activities, or extend a narrative' (Siraj-Blatchford & Manni, 2008).

symbolic play
Where children are able to imagine something that is not present.

symbols
Characters used to represent functions and processes, for example +(plus).

tabula rasa
The theory that at birth the (human) mind is a blank slate.

theories of play
Theories that uncover perceptions of how and why children play.

time sample
Observing children for specified periods of time during the day (e.g. every 30 minutes) to see what they are doing or what behaviour they are displaying, and perhaps at what time of day the behaviour is more common.

transition statement
A statement recording a child's strengths, interests and ways of learning to support transitions from prior-to-school to school settings.

transmission approach
A teacher-centred approach whereby teaching is the act of transmitting (or feeding) knowledge from the teacher's mouth to the students' heads.

United Nations Convention on the Rights of the Child (UNCRC)
The key document that actively promotes an image of the child as a holder of specific rights in their own right.

visual art
Art forms that are viewed and created for visual perception.

visual level of knowledge
How words look; concepts about print, letter–sound relationships and spelling patterns in words.

vocabulary
The words children must know in order to communicate effectively. In educational terms, it can be described as 'oral vocabulary' or 'reading vocabulary'.

work sample
A sample of a child's work usually collected and collated with different samples of the same child's work.

Zone of Proximal Development (ZPD)
The distance between what children can do on their own and what they can do with assistance or guidance.

Index